Fodor's

ITALY

FODOR'S TRAVEL PUBLICATIONS

NEW YORK • TORONTO
LONDON • SYDNEY • AUCKLAND

WWW.FODORS.COM

CONTENTS

KEY TO SYMBOLS

- Map reference
- Address
- Telephone number
- Opening times
- Admission prices
- Underground station
- Bus number
- Train station
- Ferry/boat
- Driving directions
- Tourist office
- Tours
- Guidebook
- Restaurant
- Café
- Bar
- Shop
- Number of rooms
- Air conditioning
- Swimming pool
- Gym
- Other useful information
- ▷ Cross reference
- ★ Walk/drive start point

90

168

282

394

UNDERSTANDING ITALY

UNDERSTANDING ITALY

Understanding Italy is an introduction to the country, its geography, economy, history and its people, giving a real insight into the nation. Living Italy gets under the skin of Italy today, while The Story of Italy takes you through the country's past.

UNDERSTANDING ITALY

From well-kept beaches, small picturesque villages and dramatic mountain scenery to historic cities with a wealth of art and architecture, Italy offers something for all visitors. Since Turin hosted the Winter Olympics in 2006, this northern city has been the focal point of winter sports in Italy, and the growth of European budget airline routes has opened up other regions of the country not previously considered as main holiday destinations. Just as Rome wasn't built in a day, so Italy cannot be explored in a single visit. The country is truly a year-round holiday destination, with a vibrant arts and music scene, world-class sporting events, colourful festivals, unforgettable food and some of the best shopping in Europe.

LANDSCAPE

Italy is a mountainous Mediterranean country extending south from the Alps, with two major offshore islands, Sicily and Sardinia, and several groups of smaller islands. It covers an area of about 300,000sq km (116,000sq miles) and has a coastline running for 7,600km (4,723 miles). It is over 1,500km (930 miles) long, a contrast to the width, which you can drive across in 3 to 4 hours.

The chain of the Apennine Mountains runs down the country from Genoa in the north to Reggio di Calabria in the south, covered in huge tracts of forest. Northeast of Genoa lie the flat plains of the Po Valley, immensely fertile and so intensively farmed. These mist-laden plains are backed by the Alps, stretching eastward from the French border at Ventimiglia through to Slovenia, with the most scenic ranges, the Ortles and Dolomites, in the east. The stereotypical classic Italian rolling hill landscape dotted with vines and lined with cypress trees is confined to central Italy, and is seen at its best in Tuscany and Umbria.

ECONOMY

Italy is a modern industrialized nation. Business and commerce revolve around Milan in the north, but the deep south remains one of Europe's most economically depressed areas.

Apart from natural gas, the country has few natural resources, with no substantial deposits of oil, iron or coal. Furthermore, much of the land is unsuited to agriculture and Italy is a net food importer. The country's economic strength lies instead in the processing and manufacturing of goods, primarily in family-owned firms. The major industries are car manufacture (the Fiat company was founded in Turin), textiles, clothing and footwear, ceramics, precision machinery and chemical production, and food processing. Sixty-two per cent of the population is employed in either tourism or the service industries. Major trading partners include the US and other countries within the European Union, with the car and fashion industries in particular exporting worldwide.

POLITICS

The Republic of Italy was created in 1948; since then there have been well over 60 governments. The head of state is the president, chosen by an electoral college drawn from the houses of parliament and regional representatives. Decision-making lies with the lower house, the Chamber of Deputies, which is directly elected. The upper house, the Senate, is made up of six representatives from each region, plus a number of senators-for-life. The complicated proportional representation electoral system has been responsible for a series of coalition governments, many of which have been suspected of corruption at the highest level. The *Mani Pulite* (Clean Hands) investigation in the 1990s extinguished the *tangentopoli* (bribetown) climate, leading to the downfall of some of the old-established parties. Scandals continue and governments come and go, but there is a genuine feeling that Italy is moving forward.

THE BEST COASTAL AREAS

The Amalfi Coast (▷ 370–371) A stretch of coast south of Naples, with towering cliffs, steep, green mountains and fabulous views over the azure sea.
Cinque Terre (▷ 122, 136–137) 'The Five Lands'—a string of higgledy-piggledy fishing and holiday villages, where cliffs, covered in terraced vineyards, lead down to hidden beaches.
Costa Smeralda (▷ 404) Sardinia's Emerald Coast, where natural beauty and clear waters combine with chic resorts.
Gargano Peninsula (▷ 374–375) The spur of the 'boot'—a limestone peninsula fringed with turquoise waters, relaxed fishing villages and small resorts.
Riviera di Levante (▷ 133) A beautiful area south of Genoa, renowned for its up-market resorts and dramatic cliffs.

Above *Ferraris are manufactured in Italy*
Left *A Fiat Bambino in Pallanza, Lago Maggiore*
Opposite *A Roberto Cavalli shop in Florence*

THE BEST ART CITIES

Florence (▷ 228–265) Buildings and art collections that provide an insight into the revolutionary Renaissance.
Naples (▷ 354–357) A variety of architecture, from Gothic to baroque, and some of the finest classical art collections in the country.
Ravenna (▷ 210) Glorious Byzantine mosaics, among the world's finest.
Rome (▷ 64–117) Artistic delights spanning 2,000 years, encompassing architecture, sculpture, painting and mosaics.
Siena (▷ 286–288) A perfectly preserved medieval city with an artistic heritage and cityscape focused on the Italian Gothic.
Venice (▷ 158–199) A city built on water, crammed with treasures covering over 1,000 years of art history.

ITALY'S REGIONS

ROME

Italy's compelling capital has a staggering wealth of monuments, museums, galleries and architecture spanning almost 3,000 years. Above all, Rome is a vibrant modern capital, where life continues to buzz through the patchwork of its ancient, medieval and modern streets.

THE NORTHWEST

Lombardy is heavily industrialized, but it also has beautiful valleys and Alpine foothills and some splendid historic towns. Among these are Cremona, Mantua and Bergamo. To the north lie the lakes—Orta, Iseo, Garda and Como, popular destinations for Italians and visitors alike. **Piedmont**, at the foot of the Alps, borders France and is renowned for winter skiing and summer walking, found at their best in the Parco Nazionale del Gran Paradiso. For culture there's Alba, a lovely mix of narrow streets and medieval, Renaissance and baroque buildings. This region is known for its stuffed pastas, and connoisseurs will enjoy the famous red wine, Barolo, and the white truffles. **Liguria** is Italy's Riviera, a tiny region between the Alps and the Mediterranean, tucked around the Gulf of Genoa and curving northwest towards France. The rugged coast, scattered with chic, glitzy resorts famous for their seafood, contrasts with the unspoiled and largely unknown interior.

VENICE

Venice is the main draw of the Veneto, with its artistic treasures and melting pot of cultures.

THE NORTHEAST AND EMILIA-ROMAGNA

The Veneto is a rich and developed region spreading from the flatlands and lagoon northward into the Dolomites. Its cities include thriving Padua, with its medieval core, centuries-old university and tempting shopping; the Palladian delights of Vicenza, Europe's textile capital; and rich, historic Verona. **Friuli-Venezia Giulia** has mountain ranges in the north, spiritual retreats in the east and Adriatic lagoon land to the south. The ancient past is preserved in towns like Aquileia and Cividale del Friuli. Trieste is the regional capital, its grandiose architecture balanced by the airiness of Udine. **Trentino-Alto Adige** is a German-Italian region in the far northeast, created in 1919. The Alto Adige is German, while Trentino is distinctly Italian, a contrast of cultures evident in the region's main towns. Bolzano (Bozen), Bressanone (Brixen) and Merano (Meran) are markedly German in character, while Trento is undoubtedly Italian. **Emilia-Romagna** is famous for its artistic towns and for its cuisine. Prosperous Bologna, with its venerable university, is the capital, and culture-lovers will find plenty to admire—the Byzantine mosaics of Ravenna and Parma's Lombard-Romanesque duomo and baptistery. Lower-key delights lie in Piacenza and the late Luciano Pavarotti's home town of Modena.

FLORENCE

Florence, renowned as the cradle of the Renaissance, has long been on the tourist map.

TUSCANY AND UMBRIA

Tuscany has an abundance of picturesque towns, attracting huge numbers of visitors each year, but leave time for the rural pleasures in the wooded hills of Chianti, famous for its wine, and the rolling honey-hued landscape, dotted with cypress trees. Topping the list of bigger towns is Siena, with its shell-shaped Campo and medieval architecture, closely followed by Pisa, with its famous Leaning Tower. **Umbria,** whose capital is Perugia, is Italy's only landlocked region. Orvieto, with its striking cathedral, far in the west, is the other main town. Between these is a clutch of smaller towns: medieval Gubbio, Assisi, St. Francis's birthplace, laid-back Spello, and Montefalco. Umbria also has blue waters at Lago Trasimeno, dramatic gorges in the Valnerina and the towering mountains of the Sibillini.

LAZIO AND THE MARCHE

Lazio is a quiet and low-key region with a gentle landscape. Rome is close to many of the key sights—the stunning baroque gardens at Tivoli, the towns of the Alban Hills known as the Castelli Romani, and the ancient Roman port of Ostia. The Etruscan settlements of Cerveteri and Tarquinia are older still, and medieval Viterbo is culturally fascinating. **The Marche** is tucked away inconspicuously in the east on the calf of Italy, across the Apennines. This is an unspoiled region with historic towns, long stretches of coastline and a green, hilly interior. The main attraction is Urbino, a classic Renaissance ducal town, but don't miss compact Ascoli Piceno in the eastern valley and the tiny fortress town of San Leo. There are plenty of family resorts to choose from—Pesaro is the most notable, with its old town and well-groomed, sandy beaches.

THE SOUTH

Campania has the vibrant city of Naples as its capital, a coastline dotted with picturesque villages between Sorrento and Amalfi, the jewel-like islands of Ischia and Capri, and a wealth of archaeological sites: Pompei, Herculaneum and Paestum. **Molise** is remote and undiscovered; nearby, the **Abruzzo** is better known, chiefly for its superb Parco Nazionale d'Abruzzo, Italy's third-largest park. The Gran Sasso massif is a magnet for outdoor enthusiasts and wilderness-lovers. L'Aquila is the region's bustling and prosperous capital. **Basilicata** has superb mountain scenery, seen at its best in the Parco Nazionale del Pollino. Enjoy the coastline on both the Mar Tirenno and Golfo di Taranto, delve back in time in Matera to the east, an ancient settlement peppered with cave houses, or travel south for archaeology at Metaponto. **Calabria,** Italy's toe, is an undeveloped region with a long coastline and mountains inland. The Sila range, with

its rolling plateaux and dense woodlands, shouldn't be overlooked. **Puglia,** the heel of Italy, is more prosperous than other regions in the south. Highlights include the port of Bari, with its labyrinthine old town and Norman cathedral and exuberant Lecce, one of Italy's finest baroque towns. More relaxing is the Gargano Peninsula, the spur of the boot, a limestone promontory dotted with fishing villages.

SICILY AND SARDINIA

Sicily, to the southwest of the toe of Italy, has enough to keep you busy for weeks. Palermo is the capital, its vitality rivalled only by the lava city Catania and the ancient Greek settlement of Siracusa. There's more of archaeological interest at Greek Agrigento, Selinunte and Segesta. On the east coast is Mount Etna, one of the world's largest active volcanoes, and the town of Taormina, famous for its classical theatre. Quieter, but equally attractive, are Noto, a superb baroque town, the inland town of Enna and the north-coast fishing port of Cefalù, with its beaches and Norman cathedral. **Sardinia,** 200km (124 miles) to the west of the mainland, is renowned for its idyllic coastline, clear waters, classy resorts and wild interior. Walled Cagliari is the capital, and Nora is the island's premier archaeological site with Phoenician, Carthaginian and Roman remains. There is an abundance of coastal resorts too—the Costa Smeralda in the northeast, the Riviera di Corallo in the northwest, and Cala Gonone in the east.

ROME

The Basilica di San Pietro (▷ 74–75) Marvel at the overwhelming opulence of the Roman Catholic landmark.
The Musei Vaticani (▷ 82–87) Don't miss one of the world's greatest museums, home to Michelangelo's Sistine Chapel.
The Colosseo (▷ 76–77) See this ancient arena lit up at night.
The Piazza di Spagna (▷ 89) Stroll through the piazza before climbing the Spanish Steps for great views across the city.
The Galleria Borghese (▷ 81) Spend a morning or afternoon viewing this wonderful art collection, in verdant surroundings.
Antonio al Pantheon (▷ 111) Mix with the local clientele and sample authentic Roman cuisine.
Piazza Campo dei Fiori (▷ 89) Enjoy a taste of everyday Roman life at the morning market.
San Giovanni in Laterano (▷ 94) Admire the baroque splendour of Rome's cathedral.
The Pantheon (▷ 90) Step inside this impressive example of the grandeur of ancient Rome.
Lancelot (▷ 116) Retreat to the cool space and warm welcome of the Lancelot hotel at the end of a day's sightseeing.

THE NORTHWEST

The Parco Nazionale del Gran Paradiso (▷ 132) Some excellent walking in majestic mountain scenery.
Milan (▷ 126–129) Explore the art and architecture and indulge in some of the world's best retail therapy.
La Barrique, Turin (▷ 153) Sit back and enjoy fresh seasonal, regional produce at this family-run restaurant.

Bellagio (▷ 123) Tour around Lake Como by car or ferry from here.
Hotel Florence, Bellagio (▷ 155) Stay at this beautiful lakeside hotel on Lake Como.
Isole Barromee (▷ 124) Take a boat trip to the idyllic Borromean Islands in Lago Maggiore.
Mantova (Mantua, ▷ 131) Survey some of the 500 rooms of the vast complex of the Palazzo Ducale, once the home of the Gonzagas.

VENICE

The Canal Grande (▷ 168–169) Take *vaporetto* No. 1 down this famous waterway for a panoramic presentation of elegant architecture.
The Basilica di San Marco (▷ 166–167) Appreciate this mind-blowing overview of Venetian art and history.
The Accademia Bridge (▷ 169) Admire the view along the Canal Grande towards the wonderful church of La Salute.
Antiche Carampane (▷ 196) Seek out this off-the-beaten-track restaurant, for the best fish in the city.
Burano, Murano and Torcello (▷ 165, 174, 185) Spend a day exploring the lagoon islands.
The Scuola Grande di San Rocco (▷ 186–187) Take in Tintoretto's great cycle of paintings.
Rialto (▷ 180) Make a morning visit to the Rialto food markets and admire the fruit and vegetables piled high and the shiny fresh fish and seafood.
Pensione Accademia (▷ 199) Stay in the Pensione Accademia in Dorsoduro, the perfect Venetian base—but be sure to book ahead.
Shopping (▷ 192–193) Browse among the shops for handmade carnival masks and Murano glass.
Ca' Rezzonico (▷ 165) Visit this palace for a glimpse of the ostentation and grandiose style that characterized 18th-century Venetian life.

THE NORTHEAST AND EMILIA-ROMAGNA

Bologna (▷ 204–205) Spend time strolling through the arcaded streets—don't miss the Strada Maggiore.
Verona (▷ 212–214) Admire the Roman Arena before exploring the area around the Piazza delle Erbe.
The Grande Strada delle Dolomiti (▷ 216–217) Drive along this route past mountain views, high passes and picturesque villages.
Villa Madruzzo, Trento (▷ 227) Drink in the mountain air while staying in country-house comfort at this 18th-century villa.
Parma (▷ 209) Shop for *prosciutto di Parma* (Parma ham) and *Parmigiano Reggiano* (Parmesan cheese) before taking in the city's artistic treasures.
Ferrara (▷ 206) Take a tour of this historical town, once the Este powerbase—don't miss the Castello Estense.

FLORENCE

The Duomo, Campanile and Battistero (▷ 236–239) Appreciate this harmonious trio of Renaissance church buildings.
The Galleria degli Uffizi (▷ 240–241) Trace the development of Italian painting and admire the treasures.
The Piazza della Signoria (▷ 250) Sit at a café table and people-watch in the heart of historic Florence, while you admire some of the city's most compelling statuary.
Il Latini (▷ 262) Enjoy a meal at this restaurant, famous for its traditional Florentine cooking.
The Galleria Palatina, Palazzo Pitti (▷ 246–248) Admire the superb Renaissance pictures and then relax with a picnic in the Giardino di Boboli.
Shopping (▷ 256–257) Track down Florentine products such as ceramics, leather and marbled paper.
San Lorenzo (▷ 253) Visit the Medici family church and the Biblioteca Laurenziana next door, before moving on to the Cappelle Medicee.
Soggiorno Antica Torre (▷ 265) Stay in the heart of the city in this quintessentially Florentine hotel.

TUSCANY AND UMBRIA

Siena (▷ 286–288) Wander around one of Italy's most perfect medieval cities.
Fiesole (▷ 274) Take an evening trip here for a quiet dinner and great views of Florence lit up at night.
Granaro del Monte (▷ 314) Enjoy the very best of Umbrian cooking in the heart of the Sibillini Mountains.
Montalcino and Montepulciano (▷ 276, 277) Sample the great red wines of Montalcino and Montepulciano in their place of origin.
Assisi (▷ 270–271) Follow the pilgrim trail to this lovely Umbrian town, the birthplace of St. Francis.
Norcia (▷ 278) Drive up the Valnerina to Norcia to eat some of Italy's finest pork products and pasta dishes rich in truffles.
Orvieto (▷ 279) Admire the fine façade of Orvieto's duomo before shopping for ceramics.
Grand Hotel Continental, Siena (▷ 319) Stay the night in opulent surroundings a couple of minutes' walk from Siena's glorious Campo.

LAZIO AND THE MARCHE

Tivoli (▷ 330–331) Take time out surrounded by the shade and rushing water of the Villa d'Este gardens.
Ascoli Piceno (▷ 324) Drive down the Tronto Valley to this relatively undiscovered jewel with its beguiling piazza.
La Vecchia Urbino (▷ 341) Eat the very best of the Marche's regional dishes in Urbino's top restaurant.
Sirene (▷ 343) Spend a night in magical Tivoli at the Hotel Sirene and be first at the Villa d'Este in the morning.

THE SOUTH

Naples (▷ 354–357) Explore the treasures and streets of this vibrant and theatrical city.
Pompei (▷ 360–363) Step back in time into a Roman town preserved by the eruption of Vesuvius in AD79.
The Amalfi Coast (▷ 370–371) Drive along the corniche road south of Naples, punctuated by pretty villages.
La Caravella, Amalfi (▷ 382) Discover the secrets of modern southern Italian cooking.
Costantinopoli 104, Naples (▷ 388) Use this stylish hotel, with garden and swimming pool, as a base for exploring the Amalfi Coast.

SICILY AND SARDINIA

Monreale (▷ 398) Visit the Norman cathedral famed for its Greco-Byzantine and Sicilian mosaics.
Osteria dei Vespri, Palermo (▷ 415) Intimate restaurant with fine regional cuisine.
Stromboli (▷ 394) Climb the slopes on the Aeolian island and get close to an active volcano.
Agrigento (▷ 392–393) Watch the night draw in around the magnificent Greek temples.
Cala Gonone (▷ 402) Be immersed in the beauty of this spectacular coastline where beaches are pearly-white and the sea swimming-pool blue.
Nora (▷ 405) Journey back to Carthaginian times at Sardinia's most evocative site, perched on a promontory overlooking the sea.

Above *Bellagio, on Lake Como*
Left *Florence's duomo seen from the Campanile*

TOP EXPERIENCES

Visit Rome for artistic delights spanning 2,000 years, encompassing architecture, sculpture, painting and mosaics.

Stroll out in the early evening anywhere in Italy and join the locals for the *passeggiata*.

Head for Venice, crammed with palaces, churches, museums and galleries built on the water; a unique visual experience.

Sample some of the local dishes—Italian cooking is regional, seasonal and fresh, and there is always something local on the menu.

Visit Florence, a city whose buildings and art collections are a product of the Renaissance at its most revolutionary.

Head for a bar and enjoy an excellent cup of coffee.

Shop for the best of Italian style or seek out sumptuous textiles, sophisticated stationery and a wide range of handmade gifts.

Take a walk in the country—from north to south there are beautiful areas waiting to be explored.

Browse in a food market, a feast of colour and aromas, and an inspiration for all cooks and food-lovers.

Swim in warm, clear sea off sandy beaches or rocky coasts.

See Europe's most dramatic volcano on Vesuvius, and its most active at Etna, on Sicily.

Look in on a gladiator school—just to watch, if not to enrol.

Explore the Shakespeare connection in Rome *(Julius Caesar),* Verona *(Romeo and Juliet),* Venice *(Merchant of Venice)* or Sicily *(Much Ado about Nothing)*,among others.

See Naples at Christmas,when the churches light up with nativity displays that outshine anywhere else.

Explore Ostia Antica, the one-time port that put Rome on the map.

Head south to discover the quaint beehive-domed *trulli* houses in Alberobello.

Going for a song? Milan's La Scala opera house is the place to catch an aria, or walk in the footsteps of the world's greatest composers and divas in the museum.

Sample a glass of wine in Italy's beautiful wine areas.

Below *Looking out over the Grand Canal in Venice from the loggia of the Ca' d'Oro*

LIVING ITALY

Italy covers an area of about 300,000sq km (116,000sq miles) and is surprisingly mountainous, with the Alps forming a natural northern barrier and the Apennines running from the French border down the middle of the country to Sicily. South of the Alps is the Po Valley, the country's largest flat, fertile area, intensively farmed and irrigated. The central regions of Tuscany, Umbria and Lazio are hilly rather than mountainous, ideal for grape and olive cultivation. Farther south and on the islands of Sicily and Sardinia the climate is drier and harsher and the soil generally poorer. Although 1.4 million people are employed in farming, only 28 per cent of Italy is arable and most farms are small. Visitors to the major cities quickly become familiar with the problems of air pollution and over-aggressive housebuilding, yet there are signs that Italy is becoming eco-friendlier. The country has a sprinkling of green Members of Parliament and senators, and the national parks are working hard to educate people about the importance of the countryside and endangered habitats.

Clockwise from above *The serene beauty of Lake Garda; a European grey wolf (*Canis lupus*); Stromboli erupting in 1998*

OLIVE BRANCH

You can see olive groves along the length of Italy, from the shores of Lake Garda through Tuscany to Sicily, and the production of olive oil is as varied and complex as wine. Half of Italy's output is from Puglia and Calabria in the south. Italian olive trees have become a victim of their own beauty—they are frequently stolen and sold on to private 'collectors' to decorate their gardens, both abroad and in the north of Italy, despite legislation to protect them. Unfortunately many of the replanted trees die within 12 months. The practice of uprooting ancient olive trees is particularly prevalent in the south, where thieves and farmers use mechanical diggers to prise up the precious specimens.

BLACK RUNS

Italians love their volcanoes, so much so that they live and farm on their fertile slopes (asparagus is particularly popular) and even holiday on them. Plucky skiers can whiz down Etna, Europe's tallest and most active volcano and the focus for some well-managed ski resorts. The most popular among locals is Piano Provenzana, as the slopes on the northern side of Etna receive more snow. The other main ski town is Linguaglossa, which means 'big tongue of lava'. Of course the resorts face unique problems—the last eruption destroyed ski lifts and cable cars—but passes are cheap and you get the added bonus of some great views of the sea, with a literal whiff of danger thrown in.

ALPINE ASSISTANCE

To get close to the great Italian outdoors, head for a *via ferrata*. *Vie ferrate* are metal ladders, pegs, bridges and ropes cemented onto the mountainsides to help walkers reach otherwise inaccessible areas of the Dolomites without specialist climbing equipment. They are not for the faint-hearted though—some sections are vertical and you will need a good head for heights. Climbing aids were first introduced around 100 years ago, used by soldiers during the two world wars, but only became popular with climbers from the 1930s onwards when the Bochette Way was opened. Today there are dozens of routes, maintained mostly by the Club Alpino Italiano—the Italian Alpine Club (www.cai.it).

UNDER THE SEAS

There's more to the Italian coastline than its golden sands and rugged cliffs. Beneath the waters are some unique marine environments, home to fish and sea creatures and a huge range of vegetation. Prompted by fears that these delicate areas were under threat, and acting in many cases in conjunction with the WWF, the Italian national parks service has succeeded in creating underwater reserves in many coastal areas. The Parco Arcipelago Toscano is the Mediterranean's largest marine reserve, covering all seven islands, and their surrounding waters, off the Tuscan coast, an area of 74,653ha (186,632 acres). Both shoreline and underwater habitats are extremely varied, making the range of species internationally important. Spreads of rare red coral, fan corals and sea grasses are home to a colony of *Hippocampus guttulatus*, an increasingly rare seahorse.

CRYING WOLF

Once hated and killed by villagers and shepherds alike, the Apennine wolf has been nursed back from its state of near extinction in the 1970s. There are now around 400 European wolves living in Italy and numbers are still growing by about 7 per cent a year. If they continue to thrive, environmentalists believe that they could spread throughout the Alps and cross over into nearby countries. Success is most evident in the Parco Nazionale d'Abruzzo, where Operation St. Francis has educated locals about the wolf population, enticing them away from hunting and leading to the establishment of a wolf museum in the park village of Civitella Alfedena (▷ 358). This has also increased visitor numbers to the area and transformed the economy of a once-decaying village—a striking and encouraging example of the powers of ecotourism.

SOCIETY AND POLITICS

Italy has some of the most densely populated areas in Europe, as Italians gravitate towards the cities for economic reasons, leaving their native regions behind. Women's roles are evolving, particularly in the north, with many continuing with their careers after marriage. Over the last 20 years the birth rate has fallen alarmingly, while the divorce rate has rocketed, affecting traditional patterns. Despite this, family and community ties remain strong. The tradition of the family gathering to eat together regularly is still a very real one (51 per cent of Italians live within 15 minutes of their mother's home). The concept of family underpins all Italian relationships, whether it's between actual blood relations or simply in the construction of a familiar world of personal ties. Despite past political turmoil, the Italian way of life remains enviable—southern Italians in particular work fewer hours, have more holidays and enjoy a lower cost of living than their frenetic northern European counterparts.

Clockwise from above *Emanuele Filiberto, his father Prince Vittorio Emanuele and his mother Princess Marina Doria attending Mass in May 2003 in the Pantheon in Rome; an Italian family; Prime Minister Silvio Berlusconi*

ROYALTY

If you thought the British Royal Family was having a rough time, pity the former Italian sovereigns. Exiled 50 years ago to Genoa after rather too fulsome support for Mussolini, the royals have long argued for their right to return home. Following a change of heart by the Italian parliament, they have made something of a comeback. Vittorio Emanuele, the son of Italy's last king, Umberto II, and just nine years old when he left, returned to Italy (albeit briefly) in December 2002 to talk with Pope John Paul II and swear allegiance to the Republic. Though the family has denied any possibility of wearing a crown again, this hasn't stopped Vittorio's son Emanuele Filiberto from appearing in a television commercial for olives that make you 'feel like a king'.

MAMMA'S CHILDREN

These days, the stereotypical image of a prosperous, pasta-serving *mamma* surrounded by a house full of kids is way off the mark. In 2010, Italy had one of the lowest birth rates in the world, at 8 per 1,000 inhabitants, and one of the lowest fertility rates, with 1.2 children born per adult woman (compared with 1.7 in the UK and 2.0 in the US, for example). The national figures disguise dramatic regional contrasts. In the industrial north the birth rate figures are even lower, while those for the country areas and south of Italy are much higher. Parents do continue to play a key role in their children's lives, however. At the last count, some 56 per cent of 25- to 29-year-olds still lived with their parents and, with the cost of living high, the number is increasing. According to the Italian statistical institute Eurispes, the large number of adults living at home is connected to the low birth rate figures: 'Young people are getting married less, and until they do marry they prefer to live at home'.

THE BERLUSCONI FACTOR

Silvio Berlusconi, Italy's richest man, has been surrounded by controversy throughout his business and political career. He owns a media empire that includes three television channels, newspapers, an advertising agency and one of Italy's top soccer teams, AC Milan. Milanese born, he made his first serious money in the city's property boom of the 1960s, before turning his attention to the media with the de-regularization of state-controlled television. Moving seamlessly into politics, he was twice Prime Minister, losing to Romano Prodi in 2006. In 2008 Italians once more flocked to the polls, disillusioned with their stagnant economy, soaring inflation and the constant political infighting. Berlusconi stormed back into power, heading Italy's 62nd post-war government and sweeping away the scores of splinter parties. However, controversy dogged him again in 2009 during an acrimonious divorce, which gave rise to colourful allegations concerning his private life.

NEW MEN

The role of husbands is beginning to change—as shown by the establishment of the Italian Association of Househusbands in the town of Pietrasanta in Tuscany. While working opportunities for women in Italy have improved, females still tend to do the majority of the household tasks, working or not. This is where the association comes in, teaching men how to do housework, cook, clean, and even enjoy it. At the moment it has 2,000 members—mainly those who have chosen to leave the workplace or whose wives are the main breadwinners—and there is growing interest from around the country. Best of all, like Italian housewives, they can also claim pension benefits relating to their work at home.

NEW WOMEN

Most Italian businesses are family affairs and increasingly it is women who are taking up places in management and in boardrooms, not to mention political parties and the civil service. Perhaps a by-product of women raising their career expectations is that the traditional role of women running the home while the men go out to work is being replaced by either the need for two incomes or a drive by university-educated young women to assert their independence and develop a career of their own. Ten per cent of Italian MPs are women, and, though their ranks have undoubtedly been swelled by the Prime Minister's influence, they are by no means all 'Berlusconi Babes'.

There is a long-established Italian tradition of craftsmanship and luxurious living, dating back to the Roman era and continuing after the glittering Renaissance courts. With this background, the native sense of style and the cult of the *bella figura*, it's not surprising that fashion and design are booming. Italians seem to infuse everything with elegance, whether it's gorgeous clothes or cars, interior or exterior building design, washing machines or typewriters. The sense of style spills over into the media and the creative arts, too, evident in the cutting-edge sharpness of Italian magazines and the distinctive and unmistakable films of Italian-born Federico Fellini and Michelangelo Antonioni. Enterprising and creative Milan is one of the world's genuine style capitals, a hotbed for must-have fashion items and accessories—Gucci, Armani, Prada, Missoni, Versace—as well as affordable, zappy wardrobes from Max Mara and the super-giant Benetton. Italian style is famous worldwide: the rich and stylish cruise the roads in Italian cars by Ferrari, Lamborghini and Maserati, and deck their houses with functional and sleek furniture, fabrics and gadgets.

Clockwise from above *A line-up of vintage Lancias parked on the waterfront in Portofino; a couple shopping for jewellery in Rome; zipping around the streets of Milan on a scooter*

LITTLE STINGER

The Vespa scooter was built and named by Enrico Piaggio—'*Sembra una vespa*' ('It looks like a wasp')—to meet post-war needs for an affordable means of getting around for the general public, both men and women, that kept their clothes clean (Piaggio now produces a range of clothing and accessories, too). The scooter owes its revolutionary construction to the aeronautic background of its designer, Corradino d'Ascanio. From humble beginnings it became a cult icon, its elegantly simple look coming to symbolize a sense of freedom and independence for each new generation, thanks to careful image adjustments. Consequently it has been a scene stealer in films from Fellini's *La Dolce Vita* to Austin Powers' *Goldmember*.

BENETTON—A SUCCESS STORY

Luciano Benetton is said to have sold his accordion to buy his sister a knitting machine, setting the ball rolling for the development of one of the retailing world's great success stories. Today, there are over 7,000 Benetton stores in more than 120 countries, selling affordable and stylish knitwear and much more besides. The company owns huge tracts of Argentina, where some of its 280,000 sheep are raised, and the wool from these animals only provides about 10 per cent of the company's annual requirements. On a global scale, Benetton has had far more impact than big Italian fashion names such as Armani, Missoni, Pucci, Gucci, et al. Lines differ from country to country—and the Italian stores definitely have the cutting edge.

LA BELLA FIGURA

The concept of *bella figura* means many things—keeping up a good front, not making a fool of yourself, and above all, looking good. It's a little bit presence, and a little bit self-respect, and a little bit being careful not to let the side down. The opposite is *brutta figura*, as in the expression *fare una brutta figura*, to show oneself up. Around 60 per cent of Italian women buy a new wardrobe twice a year, their choice dictated by the latest shades and styles. When the seasons change, it is common for women to take a day off work just to rearrange their wardrobe. Italians spend up to 50 per cent of their disposable income on clothes and fashion, and designer wear is considered an option for all. It's not what you've got, but what you project that's important.

ALL THAT GLITTERS

Italians love glitter—gold-threaded and sequined clothes, chains round their wrists and necks, precious stones glinting on fingers and hanging from ears. Even small, rural towns have expert jewellers. It's no coincidence that Europe's biggest mass-market jewellery production town is Arezzo in Tuscany, home to the world's largest gold manufacturing plant. Italians change their jewellery like their wardrobes, with the seasons, and jewellery 'must-haves' are pushed as hard as fashion. Italy's longest established high-end jeweller is Bulgari, which has been creating fabulous pieces since 1905. Watch the stars arriving for the Oscars and the odds are that up to half of them will be wearing Bulgari jewels.

PININFARINA

The Pininfarina company was founded in 1930 by Battista Pininfarina, who was inspired by a meeting with Henry Ford and the entrepreneurial culture of America. His cars came to embody the idea of democracy in car design—an international approach, extremely unusual in Italy at that time, which marked him out as a unique designer. The company's down-to-earth approach means that it has been happy to work on 'normal' cars such as the Peugeot 205 and the Austin-Morris 1100 (its 1952 Ambassador also revolutionized the design of small cars in the US), as well as the more exciting and sporty names such as Ferrari and the sports car Enjoy, winner at the Geneva Motor Show 2003.

The role Italy's history plays in the 21st century is particularly apparent in the continued lively celebration of ancient annual festivals around the country. Physically, it's simply impossible to avoid the artistic remains and treasures of the country's many previous cultures. With 44 UNESCO World Heritage Sites, Italy stands at the top of the international list for cultural importance. The artistic heritage spans over 4,000 years, comprising archaeological sites, monuments, churches and works of art. In the last 50 years Italy has made outstanding achievements in the field of restoration, preserving important treasures nationwide and rising superbly to challenges such as the aftermath of the 1997 earthquake in Umbria. However, the ongoing process of decay is still frightening. Many regions contain nearly abandoned towns and villages, churches have been looted and stand empty, and often the scaffolding around historic buildings remains in place for years. There's no easy answer in a country with so many treasures, but it's generally agreed there could be a better balance between the money poured into the major attractions and the neglect of a broad conservation infrastructure.

Clockwise from above *Basilica di San Francesco, Assisi; Venice's Palazzo Ducale during a flood; the ruins at Selinunte in Sicily; detail of a mosaic in Villa Imperiale, Sicily*

CAN YOU SPOT A FAKE?

If you fancy a masterpiece but don't have millions to spare, you can commission a genuine fake from artist-to-the-stars Daniele Donde, whose client list included the late Diana, Princess of Wales. Donde is the latest in a long line of fine Italian copyists, including Alceo Dossena (1878–1937). A sculptor and stonemason, Dossena was so good that unscrupulous dealers started to sell his work as the real thing, and experts and museums simply couldn't tell the difference. When the artist found out what was going on, he blew the whistle on the charade and took his dealer to court, claiming that he had been cheated out of thousands of lire. It is believed that many of his pieces are still collected and exhibited unwittingly as genuine originals today.

GOING UNDERGROUND

Underneath modern Rome is a buried city encountered by building developers who constantly unearth new remains whenever they start to dig. St. Peter's Basilica sits on top of a massive Roman necropolis, but to get a closer look at Rome's history head for the 12th-century Basilica of San Clemente near the Colosseum, below which you can see the original fourth-century and even earlier first-century buildings, including a temple dedicated to Mithras. So extensive are the city's remains that guided visits are now offered by several tour operators. These include Roma Sotteranea (www.sotteranea.it), an association devoted to the underbelly of the capital. New excavation has also enabled experts to reconstruct digitally the badly preserved ruins of one of Rome's earliest and greatest edifices, the Temple of Apollo, rebuilt under Emperor Augustus in the first century BC.

TRAVELLING WITH HISTORY

In October 2007 the first rails for a new €715 million tram system in Florence, aimed at relieving city-centre congestion, were laid. Three routes were planned, one of which was to run past the duomo, with its 15th-century Brunelleschi dome, Giotto's bell tower and the baptistery with its superb bronze doors. Conservationists were up in arms, claiming the supertrams would ruin the city centre, both aesthetically and, by the vibrations they would cause, physically. In February 2008, thousands of protestors marched in Florence in advance of a local referendum, supported by Prime Minister Silvio Berlusconi. Two Florentine art professors, Antonio Paolucci and Giorgio Bonsanti, begged to differ, claiming trams would save, rather then destroy, the city centre, though both agreed the route was unfortunate, and that pedestrianizing the entire city centre was the only real solution.

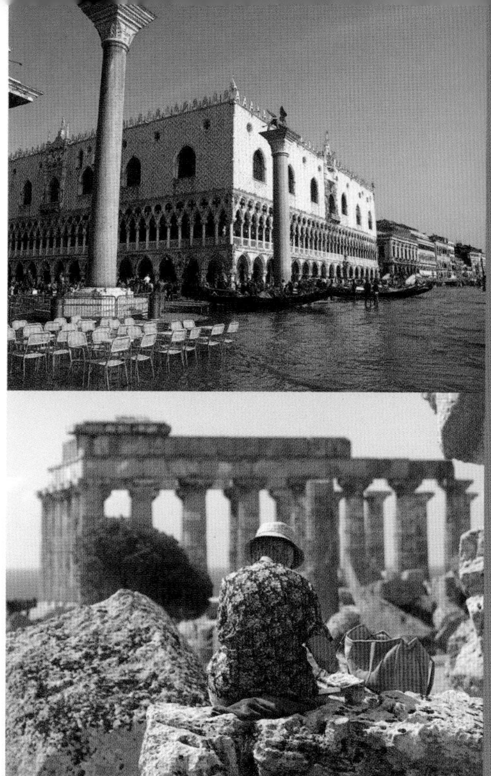

FRAGILE FRESCOES

In terms of restoration, frescoes are in many ways the most pressing concern of experts and conservationists piecing together the past. Buildings and stonework also require urgent restoration, but, with frescoes, time is of the essence. Fresco technique involves applying pigment to wet plaster, the drying process causing a chemical reaction that fixes the image permanently into the plaster. The condition of centuries-old frescoes deteriorates for a number of reasons; some problems go as far back as the artist's original application of the pigments, while others arise through dampness and pollution. New techniques are being developed all the time, ensuring that, with proper attention, frescoes will survive indefinitely.

ACQUA ALTA

Venice has been battling against water for 1,500 years—it has sunk more than 123cm (48in) over the last 100 years—and scientists now estimate that, unless dramatic action is taken, the city will be destroyed by the end of this century. Dedicated groups such as Venice in Peril (www.veniceinperil.org) and Save Venice (www.savevenice.org) raise awareness and international support, and the latest move by the Italian government is to install huge flood-control barriers, a series of 78 mobile gates that can be used during high tides. The Moses Project, as it is known, is not without its critics: environmentalists claim it will cause irreparable damage to the area's ecosystem.

Although Church and State are theoretically separate in Italy, the Catholic Church is so well established that its position of strength seems to be unassailable. Around 85 per cent of native-born Italians are still nominally Roman Catholic but fewer than 10 per cent attend Mass regularly and many young Italians take divorce, birth control and abortion for granted. Many churches, not only in Rome but also in remote villages, are treasure houses of art from past ages of religious devotion and some are thus becoming monuments, museums and art galleries more than places of active worship. The 21st century will bring further challenges. Not least of these is growing immigration from Africa, Asia and the Middle East, resulting in increased numbers of practising Buddhists and Muslims in the country. This is causing political and social conflict, as seen in the divisive comments of Prime Minister Silvio Berlusconi about Islam following the terrorist attacks against the US on 11 September 2001. But the Church thinks in centuries, not decades, and continues to view modern-day apathy with equanimity.

Clockwise from above *Pope Benedict XVI meets his cardinals; a Swiss Guard wearing the distinctive uniform designed by Michelangelo; a mosaic crucifix in the church of San Clemente, Rome*

VATICAN CITY STATE

Technically, the Vatican is not part of Italy, though it lies within the heart of Rome. It is an independent sovereign state which negotiates with governments around the world and is represented at the United Nations and in other political bodies. Vatican City is the smallest city state in the world, one-third the size of Monaco, and has fewer than 1,000 permanent residents, mainly church officials and a security force, the Swiss Guard. It issues passports and produces its own euro coins and bank notes and its own stamps. The independence of Vatican City is guaranteed by the Lateran Treaty of 1929, amended in 1984, when the main change was that the Catholic Church would no longer be the official state religion of Italy. Nonetheless, its values and traditions are deeply ingrained in Italian culture and everyday living.

A NEW POPE

On 2 April 2005 Pope John Paul II died after serving 26 years as head of the world's 1.1 billion Roman Catholics. Millions of pilgrims flocked to the Vatican to attend the emotional open-air service which accompanied his funeral in St. Peter's Basilica. The election of his successor then gripped the media for several weeks. The new pope is elected in strict secrecy by a conclave of cardinals, who hold successive ballots until a cardinal has garnered the two-thirds of the vote he needs to be elected. After each ballot, the ballot papers are burned; if a victor has emerged, the papers are burned with a special chemical that produces white smoke—a visible signal to the faithful waiting outside that a pope has been chosen. The process can take weeks, but on the second day of voting, after just four ballots, Cardinal Joseph Ratzinger emerged as Pope Benedict XVI on 19 April 2005. He was installed as the new pontiff in a Mass in Piazza San Pietro.

THE SAINTS

By the time he died in 2005, Pope John Paul II had declared 476 new saints and had beatified 1,320 people, setting them on the way to sainthood. This virtually doubled the number of saints recognized by the Catholic Church. Until John Paul's papacy, saints were only declared after a lengthy legal process, during which the candidates were posthumously put on trial while their sanctity was proved. John Paul speeded up the process by basing the qualification on the prospective saint's life, and making local bishops, rather than Roman lawyers, responsible for gathering the information. He believed that everyone who lived a Christian life was eligible for sainthood. The result was not only a vast number of new saints, but the emergence of a new type of saint: ordinary people rather than primarily those who had followed a specifically religious life. John Paul II was himself beatified in 2011.

PAPAL AUDIENCE

General audiences with the Pope are usually held on Wednesdays at 11am in St. Peter's Basilica, or in the Aula Paolo VI, the hall of papal audiences, and are open to the public. In the summer they are held in St. Peter's Square or at the Pope's summer residence south of Rome, Castel Gandolfo. To participate in a general audience, you must apply for a ticket to the office of the Prefetto della Casa Pontificia, 00120 Città del Vaticano (tel 06 6988 3114) at least two weeks in advance. A few tickets are usually available the day before at the Bronze Door of St. Peter's Basilica. If you are a Catholic, you will be asked to bring a letter of introduction from your parish priest and you will need to show a passport or ID card to the Swiss Guard at the entrance.

SANTA CASA

Italy has many pilgrimage sites, most holding saints' relics. But pilgrims to the town of Loreto come to see the Virgin Mary's house (▷ 325). According to pious legend, this humble cottage—scene of the Annunciation and Jesus's family home—was miraculously transported by angels from Nazareth to Loreto in the late 13th century. Recent investigations indicate that, after the Crusades, a noble Byzantine family called Angeli did actually ship the stones of the Holy House to Italy, where it was rebuilt. It has only three walls; the fourth side was formed by a grotto dug out of the rock in Nazareth, a common arrangement for houses of that time. Technical comparisons have shown the Loreto house and the Nazareth grotto to be contiguous.

Sport is part of daily life in Italy, a country that has its own daily newspapers devoted entirely to the subject—*La Gazzetta dello Sport* (pink in colour) and the *Corriere dello Sport*. The Italian Olympic Committee's president, Gianni Petrucci, has stressed the importance of promoting all sports within the country, but football (soccer) is the undisputed king by some distance (though when it comes to actually taking part, bicycling probably has the edge). Italy also has a passion for skiing, skating and other winter sports, which fully justified the selection of Turin as the venue for the 2006 Winter Olympics, and northern Italy now has some of the finest and most up-to-date winter sports facilities anywhere in Europe. But football continues to dominate the headlines, whether it's pay-TV negotiations delaying the start of the season, or the progress in European competitions of Italy's leading sides, AC Milan, Juventus and Inter Milan. There is interest in other sports, notably bicycling and motor racing. The Italians' obvious ability in ball games extends to basketball, handball, volleyball and tennis, not to mention rugby (the national side is now firmly established in the prestigious Six Nations tournament) and, perhaps more surprisingly, cricket.

Clockwise from above *The fast-paced bareback horseracing of the Palio in Siena; football (soccer) shirts for sale; men playing cards in Palermo, Sicily; paragliding in Spello, Umbria*

GLADIATOR SCHOOL

For the last 10 years the fun-loving Gruppo Storico Romano, based at the appropriately historical address of Via Appia Antica in Rome, has been running regular gladiator training classes with frighteningly authentic swordplay and in full gladiatorial regalia. The range of courses corresponds to your level of interest, from introductory training, two months of twice-weekly sessions (after which you can specialize in various weapons and styles), to total-immersion courses that last three days. At the end of a course, 'survivors' are given a medal and declared *tiro* (beginner gladiator). Rather like the craze for replacing a trip to the gym with toned-down fighting techniques, the idea of keeping fit and relieving stress is as strong among Gruppo members as their proud interest in Roman history.

WORLD BEATERS

In spite of the national team's ignominious exit from the 2010 FIFA World Cup, Italy remains Europe's most successful football nation. Italian clubs have won 27 major European trophies, and their national team has won more World Cups than any other nation in Europe. In fact Italy is the second most successful national team in the entire history of the World Cup, having won a total of four titles—in 1934, 1938, 1982 and 2006. Football arrived in Italy in the last quarter of the 19th century, though its beginnings are somewhat obscure: some records say it was imported by an Englishman in Genoa, others that it was brought to Turin by an Italian merchant who saw the game while working with an English textile firm.

A RIDE AROUND ITALY

Italians view their equivalent of the Tour de France with passion. The Giro d'Italia, for professional bicyclists, is one of the three European Grand Tours—Spain is home to the third—and has been held each May since 1909, lasting approximately three weeks. The 3,480km (2,180-mile) route runs north from Sicily to Milan, taking in every type of terrain, with the emphasis on mountain roads. In 2007, Danilo di Luca wore the coveted *maglia rosa* (pink jersey, inspired by the pink pages of *La Gazzetta dello Sport*) for the final stages, cruising in to become the winner. There's glory attached to the *maglia verde* (green jersey), too, worn by the rider with the best time and speed records in the mountain sections.

DRIVING SKILLS

Italy has a passion for motor racing. It has bred some top Formula 1 drivers, including current stars Giancarlo Fisichella and Jarno Trulli, and the Ferrari race team is the pride of Italy. If you are a motorsport fan, Italy offers several classic race weekends. The Grand Prix circuit at Monza, near Milan, is on the Formula 1 calendar usually in early September. You can also see the stars of Formula 1 in action on the San Marino Grand Prix circuit at Imola, usually in April, at the start of the European motor-racing season. If you prefer two wheels, Lonigo, near Vicenza, hosts motorcycle races from the Speedway World Championship.

PACKS OF CARDS

Bridge players will know that the Italians are keen on their cards, but if you observe a card game in Italy, the deck and game may look strange. In place of clubs, hearts, spades and diamonds many areas also have coins, cups, swords and clubs. Packs—which have a marvellous medieval design and no queen—also vary regionally in their shape (Trento's are long, Naples' are small) and number (most games use 40, some use 52). While some games, like Scopa—a complicated capture game—are nationally popular, there are regional playoffs such as *madrasso* (similar to bridge) in Venice and *coteccio*, a trick-taking game, in Trieste.

For centuries, visitors to Italy have found something invigorating about the country, whether it be the cultural aspects beloved of the Grand Tourists, or the personal growth described in E. M. Forster's *A Room with a View*. Family life, sociability, food and drink, civic pride and cultural interests all play their part in shaping the concept of *la dolce vita*—the sweet life—as does the obsession with style and design. *La dolce vita* is a double-edged attitude, though, as outlined in Fellini's famous film, which did much to internationalize the philosophy: Fellini shows a post-war Italy enjoying a period of relative stability and wallowing in a haze of decadence. But elements of the sweet lifestyle are on the wane, with increasing European homogenization threatening the survival of the traditional siesta and the *passeggiata*, the early evening stroll. And there is some doubt whether the Italians are entirely devoted to their *dolce vita* anyway: a recent poll by Censis shows that more than a quarter of them are not.

Above left to right *The poster for Fellini's film; the famous Volpetti delicatessen in Rome*

THE PERFECT ESPRESSO

Whether it's made in a one-cup pot at home—the iconic Moka Express—or comes from a gleaming chrome machine in a bar, all Italian coffee is made by the espresso method. In bars, freshly ground coffee is put into a filter, compressed, and attached to the espresso machine. Hot, but not boiling, water is forced through, producing an intense, aromatic brew with its distinctive *crema* (cream) on top. Milk is frothed with steam from a separate nozzle and added to make the perfect cappuccino (which in Italy is only drunk before noon). The roast varies from region to region, becoming increasingly potent the farther south you go, but Romans claim to make the best coffee because their water is so good.

SLOW FOOD

The essence of Italian cooking is good ingredients, but no less important is the way meals are prepared, eaten and appreciated. To this end, the Slow Food movement was born in Italy in 1986, now an international lobby, promoting the enjoyment of eating. It also campaigns to preserve ingredients threatened by environmental degradation, industrial standardization and strict hygiene legislation. Members regard themselves as 'eco-gastronomes' whose main priority is to counter what they see as shabby eating habits, particularly junk food. Slow Food promotes its ideals through events and festivals, and publishes *The Ark of Taste,* a catalogue of products and dishes close to extinction (www.slowfood.com).

THE STORY OF ITALY

GREEKS, PHOENICIANS, ETRUSCANS

Surrounded by water and cut off from the European landmass by a mountain barrier, the boot-shaped peninsula of modern Italy was destined to develop into an exceptionally individual country. Its shores were easily reached by eastern and southern invaders, the great early civilizations of the Phoenicians and Greeks. From their colonies in present-day Sicily and Sardinia, the Phoenicians established trade routes with Carthage, while the Greeks set up a new and magnificent empire in the south, totally assimilating the native people. Farther north, the enigmatic Etruscans, whose history and language have barely been penetrated, were the dominant civilization and they established a confederation of 12 sophisticated city states. As their power grew, they edged out the other northern indigenous peoples, the Ladini, the Ligurians and the Sabines. With the emergence of Rome, their civilization waned and their culture and influence were eclipsed by the growing empire.

Clockwise from above *The farewell of Admetos and Alketis, a scene on an Etruscan vase found in Vulci; the sixth-century bronze of Romulus and Remus in the Musei Capitolini in Rome; the Hellenistic Greek theatre at Taormina, rebuilt by the Romans; an illustration of a Phoenician sarcophagus*

PREHISTORIC BUILDINGS AND BRONZES

Little is known about the first Sardinians or where they came from. The prehistoric tribes that dominated the island between 1500 and 500BC are known as the Nuraghi, the same name given to their temples and necropolises, which are scattered all over the island. For years Sardinian peasants believed that they were the tombs of a race of giants from whom they were descended. Enigmatic structures, they are mainly round, with a vaulted interior, connected to an upper terrace by stairs and corridors. Equally mysterious are the hundreds of eighth-century BC bronze statuettes that have also been found on the island depicting gods, people and animals.

MAGNA GRAECIA

In the eighth century BC, the Greeks colonized southern Italy and Sicily, establishing hugely prosperous colonies collectively known as Magna Graecia. The cities of Syracuse, Sybaris, Metapontum and Tarentum became richer than many cities in Greece. By 400BC, however, the Romans had moved in and sacked the most important, but some superb archaeological sites remain, often in beautiful settings in little-visited parts of the country: Paestum, south of Salerno; Metapontum, with its archaeological museum; and on Sicily the theatres in Taormina (▷ 401) and Siracusa (▷ 399), and the temples at Segesta, Selinunte (▷ 400) and Agrigento (▷ 392–393).

THE ETRUSCANS

Much of what we know about the Etruscans comes from discoveries made in their necropolises, huge stone cities of the dead found at the sites of their main settlements in central Italy. Their cities of wood are long gone, but the stone cemeteries remain. The tombs were lavish; some, as at Cerveteri and Orvieto, take the form of miniature houses lining paved streets, while others, like Tarquinia, are beautifully decorated underground chambers. Elsewhere there are apartments full of funerary niches, known as *colombari*. These tombs for the afterlife were often filled with statues, jewellery and vases, and decorated with religious scenes of people hunting, fishing, playing games and dancing.

THE PHOENICIANS

The Phoenicians came from modern-day Lebanon, emerging in the 12th century BC as what was to become the greatest trading nation of the ancient world. The Greeks called them Phoenicians after the valuable purple dye derived from molluscs that they exported all over the ancient world. They were middlemen as much as anything, buying in and selling on goods from all over the Mediterranean. The early Italian civilizations were good customers, and the Phoenicians, from their western power base of Carthage, established trading settlements in Sicily and southern Italy. To the north, the Etruscans were eager for luxury goods, particularly purple-dyed fabrics and Greek pottery, which were traded for Etruscan items such as jewellery and mirrors.

THE LADINI

The far northern valleys of the Dolomites, where the regions of Trentino-Alto Adige and the Veneto meet, are still home to one of Italy's oldest peoples. The Ladini, a distinct ethnic group with their own language and culture, have lived here since 4000BC. Their epics portray a history of battles, triumphs, disasters and treachery. Threatened by Germanic tribes from the north and marauders from the south, the Ladini were constantly at war, invoking their primitive divinities for help. When Christianity arrived, they blended the new religion with the old, investing Christian saints with their gods' powers. Ladino is still spoken in the area around the Sella Mountains, and the people preserve much of their ancient culture and customs today.

ROMAN EMPIRE

The Roman Empire prospered at the expense of the Etruscans, who were absorbed into Roman culture and finally displaced. After conquering Italy they spread out over the rest of the Mediterranean. Their ideas and inventions formed the bedrock for much that is familiar in today's society. Fundamental concepts of law and order, justice, democracy, literature and philosophy were adopted and developed by the Romans. They also gave those they conquered a taste for good plumbing, warm houses, paved roads and luxurious living. The Roman era lasted almost 1,000 years, evolving from a high-minded republic to a hedonistic empire. Periods of expansion and prosperity were tempered by civil unrest, and from AD300 the empire was divided into separate eastern and western territories. By AD400, the emperors were reliant on the support of disenchanted mercenaries in their conquered territories, and the frontiers collapsed. The barbarians moved in and a dark veil descended over Italy.

Clockwise from above *Hubert Robert's painting* The Fire of Rome, 18 July AD64; *the Atrium Vestae in the Foro Romano, where the Vestal Virgins lived; Julius Caesar (102–44BC)*

ROME IN FLAMES

According to legend, Emperor Nero played the fiddle and watched while Rome burned in AD64, having set fire to the city to get an idea of how Troy had looked in flames. It's a notorious tale, but fails to stand up to scrutiny, as violins were not invented for another 1,500 years. Two-thirds of the city did burn that year, though: Nero considered much of the city ugly and wanted to rebuild on a grand scale, so rumours were rife that the fires had been started on his orders. To see the results, head for the ruins of Nero's Golden House, near the Colosseum, one of the largest and most ostentatious palaces in the world in its heyday.

JULIUS CAESAR

Soldier, orator, first consul of Rome and financier, Julius Caesar looked fate in the eye in 49BC, when he left the battlefields of Gaul to challenge his rival Pompey for control of the empire. He took his troops with him, and as he approached the River Rubicon, the boundary between Gaul and Italy, he was faced with a major decision. It was a heinous crime to enter Roman territory with an army without informing the Senate. He vacillated, unable to decide whether or not to risk all. Then came his famous words, 'Let the die be cast' and he crossed the river to march on Rome. By 44BC he had been appointed ruler for life; a few months later he was dead, assassinated on the Ides of March.

HANNIBAL AND THE ELEPHANTS

Even before the great Carthaginian general Hannibal arrived at the foothills of the Alps to invade Rome, his battle elephants had had an adventurous trip from their starting point in Spain. They had to cross the River Rhône, deep and fast, and evade the Roman sentries. The river was too deep for the elephants to wade through, so Hannibal had water wings made for them from inflated bladders, and floated them across. Thirty-seven elephants made it to the Alps and the crossing took 19 days, trudging through late snow and struggling on the slopes. The descent into Italy was too steep for many of the elephants, and most perished, while only a few of the remainder made it through the following winter.

C. JULIUS CÆSAR.

EX:NUM:MUS:GUL:HUNTERI.

WHAT THE ROMANS DID FOR US

Superbly practical, the Romans' inventions made life easier and more comfortable. Good road networks were essential to travel their huge empire. Some still exist, others are the foundation for today's highways. Aqueducts efficiently brought fresh water over long distances to prosperous cities. Bathing was now a feasible option and people benefited from hot and cold running water, steam baths and clean toilets. The latter were often communal—a great place to catch up on the gossip. Cold winters were made bearable by central heating, with hot air being circulated under the floors by a flue system. The Romans also invented dozens of small gadgets—reliable water clocks, cooking utensils, brushes, combs, mirrors, and comfortable chairs and beds.

VESTAL VIRGINS

The Vestal Virgins were the custodians of the sacred fire, a perpetual flame of great religious significance. This cult involved the safety of the state, and the smoke emerging from the circular marble Temple of Vesta, goddess of the hearth, was a sign that all was well. There were six Vestals, girls of unblemished character recruited from irreproachable families. They served the goddess for 30 years: 10 learning their duties, 10 performing them, and 10 passing on their knowledge. Sacred to Vesta, they enjoyed incredible privileges, but led circumscribed lives, constantly watched by the chief priest and his spies. If a Vestal slipped, the punishments were severe. Breaking the vow of chastity was seen as betraying the faith of Rome and the offender was buried alive.

For the next 500 years chaos whirled through Italy. Visigoths, Ostrogoths, Vandals and the ferocious Huns moved south, as the remnants of the Roman Empire were bitterly contested. The Ostrogoths emerged triumphant in the west, while the Byzantines held the east. The Ostrogoths continued moving west and established a presence in southern Italy and Sardinia that was to last 500 years. To the north, the Lombards moved south into Italy, gradually extending their power. The Franks eased east from Gaul and allied themselves with the papacy, which led to the Frankish ruler Charlemagne being crowned Emperor of the Holy Roman Empire. No dynasty or ruler was stable, nothing endured. Charlemagne's empire collapsed, and by the year 1000 Italy had no official ruler. Into the void swept the Normans, synthesizing their culture with the half-Arab, half-Byzantine south. The power of the papacy grew, the Holy Roman Empire rose again, and time was ripe for the start of two centuries of conflict on the issue of papal versus imperial supremacy. The Guelphs supported the pope, the Ghibellines the emperor, and Italy was torn between the two.

Clockwise from above *A Byzantine mosaic of Empress Theodora with her court, in the Basilica of San Vitale, Ravenna; the death of Alaric after the sack of Rome; oranges are an Arab import*

THE CORONATION OF CHARLEMAGNE

Charlemagne (747–814), King of the Franks and de facto ruler of Western Europe, came south in the winter of 800 to help Pope Leo III deal with the Lombards. On Christmas Day he attended Mass in Rome, and while he was kneeling in prayer the Pope picked up a crown and set it on Charlemagne's head, declaring him Emperor of Western Europe, apparently to Charlemagne's surprise. The story is probably apocryphal, and it's more likely that the Pope and would-be Emperor cooked up the plan between them beforehand. The coronation was a boost to them both; it enhanced Charlemagne's reputation, while stressing the power of the papacy to make kings, increasing their temporal and spiritual clout.

THE SACK OF ROME

By AD410 the writing was on the wall for the tottering Western Empire. The Visigothic chief, Alaric, had blockaded Rome for two years, hoping for loot and prestige. The Western Roman Emperor, Honorius, now based in Ravenna, refused his demands, and Alaric, his patience finally snapping, let his troops loose on the already dying city, and for three days, the Visigoths plundered, killed, raped and looted.. Less than 50 years later the Vandals re-enacted the sack of Rome even more spectacularly, incidentally making their name a byword for mindless destruction. The great Roman cities and civic buildings gradually decayed, but they were still used, and Latin continued to be widely spoken. The might of Rome collapsed, not with a bang but a whimper.

CULTURAL U-TURN

The Lombards, a Germanic barbarian tribe, moved south into Italy in the sixth century AD. They arrived with barbaric customs, such as drinking out of their enemies' skulls, and set up their capital in Cividale del Friuli in the far northeast. Within a century they had moved farther south under the ruthless King Aistulf, taking Ravenna, and embraced Christianity and its culture. They left some of the most beautiful and serene artworks of the Dark Ages, gently smiling saints and charming reliefs, while their excavated tombs have yielded fabulous gold jewellery, crosses, swords and shield-holds. The designs are sinuous and intricate, the workmanship sophisticated. The Lombards were defeated by the Franks in 774, leaving a fascinating artistic legacy behind.

LARGER-THAN-LIFE LADIES

Roman and Byzantine Ravenna produced two remarkable women, both captured in the city's stunning mosaics. Galla Placidia was half-sister to the fifth-century Roman Emperor Honorius, and was kidnapped by the Goths, creating a major scandal when she married one of her abductors and fought beside him in battle. The other leading lady was Theodora, wife of Emperor Justinian, who lived in the sixth century. Her previous professions as circus entertainer, sex-show performer and prostitute made tongues wag. Aristocratic Romans were horrified when the sagacious Justinian married her and she embarked on a consortship of bad conduct, marked by acquisitiveness, corruption and venality.

RED HAIR AND FOOD FOR THE GODS

Sweeping into southern Italy and Sicily in the 11th century, the Normans created one of the Mediterranean's most vibrant cultures. They intermarried with the dark-skinned southerners, leaving a genetic legacy that is still alive and well in Sicily. Reddish-orange hair, straight Norman noses and startlingly blue eyes are found in even remote villages, and some Sicilian dialects still contain substantial numbers of French words and phrases. The Arab inheritance appeals to the tastebuds. Rice and oranges, extra-sweet desserts and pastries stuffed with nuts and candied fruit, and fish served with couscous are all Arab imports. Street food vendors sell dishes that wouldn't seem out of place in a souk.

Confusion continued into the 13th century, with the south and Sicily hotly contested by the French and the Aragonese, the papacy fleeing to Avignon, and the political power of the major rulers under pressure all over the country. But times were changing, and no more so than in central and northern Italy. By 1300, some 300 virtually independent city states had emerged, with a concept of citizenship radically different from that of the traditional lord-and-vassal relationship. Growing wealth from commerce and trade provided a good breeding ground for the birth of a ruling class in many of these cities, but one where the ruling class constantly feuded among itself for supremacy. Fed up with the bloodshed and perpetual vendettas, by the 15th century many cities had opted for rule by a single overlord strong enough to maintain order, so that by the second half of the 15th century most city states were under princely, rather than republican, rule. The day of the *signore* had arrived. Italy was well on the way to taking the political shape it was to maintain up until unification in the 19th century.

Clockwise from above *Marco Polo travelling by caravan, from a 14th-century Catalan atlas; the Cappella Colleoni in Bergamo; a marble statue of Dante in Florence's Piazza Santa Croce; frescoes by Ghirlandaio depicting the life of St. Francis of Assisi in Santa Trinità, Florence*

ST. FRANCIS OF ASSISI

St. Francis was born to wealthy parents in 1182, and spent his youth drinking and womanizing. He continued in this way until a spell in prison turned him to God. In 1209 he decided to dedicate his life to preaching. His message was simple—do away with material goods, love God in poverty, chastity and obedience, and see the Lord's hand in the beauty of the world. He loved nature, and is famous for blessing birds and animals—beautifully depicted by Giotto in a fresco in Assisi (▷ 271). He attracted 12 followers and obtained papal permission to found a religious order, the Franciscans. In 1224, he received the wounds of Christ on his hands and feet and in his side, and died two years later. He was canonized in 1228.

THE BLACK DEATH OF 1348

The Black Death, which wiped out between 25 and 50 per cent of Europe's population over four years, arrived in Italy from China via a Genoese ship returning from the Black Sea in spring 1348. Most people who fell ill contracted the bubonic strain of the disease, transmitted by infected fleas carried by rats. The first symptom was the appearance of the dreaded buboes, pus-filled swellings around the neck, armpits or groin. Death usually followed within a week. With no defence and no understanding of the cause of the plague, people started to panic, and law and order broke down. It was at this time that the Florentine writer Giovanni Boccaccio wrote his great work *The Decameron,* documenting individual accounts of suffering.

THE LANGUAGE OF LITERATURE

After the fall of Rome, Latin was still widely spoken throughout Italy, but a Latin that was constantly evolving as the waves of invaders introduced new words from their own languages. During the more prosperous times of the 13th and 14th centuries, scholarship and literature once more found a place, and the earliest of the new writers all spoke the Tuscan dialect, rich in Latin roots. Dante, Boccaccio and Petrarch wrote in Tuscan, which became established as Italy's literary language and later became the country's official language. The other dialects clung on; many are still spoken today, though mass communication is eroding them fast, and there are now few Italians who cannot speak 'pure' Italian as well as their own local dialect.

CONDOTTIERE—MEDIEVAL MERCENARIES

The city states were constantly battling it out for territorial, commercial and political advantage. Their populations were small, and their citizens too busy for campaigns and sieges. The solution was the *condottiere*, a mercenary leader who offered himself, and his men, to the highest bidder. Attracted to the richer contracts, they amassed huge wealth and prestige, and their deeds and deaths were celebrated. Bartolomeo Colleoni, popularly known as 'The Invincible', was born in 1400. He fought for the Venetians and became their captain general, leaving behind the beautiful Colleoni Chapel in Bergamo and donating his wealth to the city of Venice, where he is commemorated by Verocchio's great equestrian statue.

MARCO POLO

In 1295 Marco Polo returned to Venice after 25 years in China. He had learned many Eastern languages on his travels, but returned to find himself a stranger and a little rusty in his native tongue. He came to fame when he was captured in 1298 during the Battle of Curzola and imprisoned in Genoa, where he shared a cell with the writer Rustichello da Pisa. Enthralled by Marco's tales of the court of Kublai Khan, Rustichello turned them into a book, *Divisament dou Monde* (Description of the World). A bestseller, it was translated from French into dozens of languages, and revealed the wonderful wealth of the Orient. The book soon became known as *Il Milione* (the Million), while Marco earned the nickname of Messer Marco Milione, for the huge number of tall tales he told.

Booming economies and relatively stable governments were fertile ground for the flowering of the Renaissance—the 're-birth' of scholarship, architecture and the visual arts. The dynastic families and autocratic rulers of the most important states—Florence, the Papal States, Milan, Venice and Naples—were in competition to establish glittering courts, finance building schemes and patronize the finest minds and artistic talents of the day. Smaller centres were hot on their tails, resulting in an explosion of creativity all over the country. The Renaissance is a relatively modern concept. It wasn't a 'movement' of its time but, in retrospect, the evolution of dramatically new artistic concepts dating back beyond the 14th century, which, with the rediscovery of classical manuscripts and texts, later gave rise to the philosophical movement known as Neoplatonism. This influenced new architecture, new styles of painting and a new approach to sculpture. The restrictions that earlier thinking had imposed disappeared, leaving the way open for huge strides in every field—science and medicine in particular. Astronomers and cartographers re-examined existing theories of the universe and made more accurate maps. This provided the impetus for a wave of exploration and discovery.

Clockwise from above The Creation of Adam *on the ceiling in the Sistine Chapel, Vatican City; Leonardo da Vinci (1452–1519), Galileo Galilei (1564–1642), Niccolò Machiavelli (1469–1527), Christopher Columbus (1451–1506); detail from* Madonna and Child with Angels *by Filippo Lippi in the Galleria degli Uffizi*; *Botticelli's* The Birth of Venus *in the Galleria degli Uffizi, Florence*

MICHELANGELO AND THE SISTINE CEILING

In 1508 Pope Julius II commissioned Michelangelo to decorate the ceiling of the Sistine Chapel in the Vatican. It was a huge task; the incentive was the sum of 3,000 ducats. The surface area is over 500sq m (5,500sq ft), all of which is painted with stories from the Book of Genesis, prophets and sibylls, and enclosed within a *trompe l'oeil* architectural framework. Executed in all temperatures as the artist lay or crouched on a scaffold some 20m (65ft) above the floor, it was physically gruelling work that took him four years to complete. He hated the task, which took him away from his sculpture, writing, 'I am attending to work as much as I can...I don't have a penny...I am unhappy and not in too good health...'.

PATRONS AND ARTISTS

The Renaissance artist certainly didn't see himself as an inspired genius seeking to express himself. His patrons paid him to do a job. Summoned to the great man's presence, artists would be confronted with a complete brief for the proposed commission, down to the last angel in the top right-hand corner. If the painting was secular, every figure in the complicated composition had an iconographic meaning, carefully configured by the philosophers—a mere artist was not deemed capable of working out the deeper significance of a piece. Pigments were expensive, so exact amounts of different tones were specified. Blue, derived from lapis lazuli, was the most expensive of them all; lots of blue means lots of money.

GALILEO GALILEI

Galileo, astronomer and mathematician, made huge contributions to our understanding of the solar system. Born in Pisa in 1564, he pioneered 'experimental scientific method' and was the first to use a refracting telescope to make important discoveries. He supported Copernicus's theory that the Earth and planets moved around the sun, rejecting Aristotle's Earthcentric model. Galileo's Inquisition opponents prevailed over his supporters, and he was told to suppress his opinions—which he did not. At the age of 69, he again faced the authorities, who made him kneel and deny the Copernician theory. He spent his last years in Florence under house arrest, and wrote his greatest work. His dying words supposedly were: 'But it does move.'

ITALIAN EXPLORERS AND FOREIGN FINANCIERS

Christopher Columbus was born in 1451, and lived in Genoa until his seafaring career took him to Portugal and Spain, whose monarchs financed his discoveries. During his four voyages to the Caribbean (1492–1504) he unintentionally discovered the New World while searching for a sea route to Cathay (China). He died in 1506, convinced he had found the 'Indies'. The Florentine Amerigo Vespucci (1454–1512) was better equipped. He studied navigation, which allowed him to calculate the geographical location of Columbus's Indies more accurately, and on a Spanish expedition west in 1499 he observed that the land masses of North and South America were actually separate from Asia.

NICCOLÒ MACHIAVELLI

Machiavelli was born in Florence in 1469. A true patriot, he dreamed of a career in politics and began work as a diplomatic secretary for the Florentine republic, meeting important contemporary political figures. Once the Medici returned to power in 1512, he was out of a job, and turned to writing in the hope of attracting patronage. In 1513 he wrote *Il Principe (The Prince)*, an intensely practical guide to the exercise of raw political power over a Renaissance principality. It cut no ice with the Medici, and the book's reputation continued to haunt him after they fell from power; he never again held public office. He died in 1527, his theories by then so twisted by public opinion that his name has become synonymous with political corruption.

The Italian states did not stay rich and independent for long. As early as 1494 the Duke of Milan made the fatal mistake of asking for French help, and the other European superpowers soon had considerably more than a foot in the door. Spain controlled Naples, Sardinia, Sicily, Milan and parts of Tuscany, the French were on the move in the north, and only the Papal States and Venice remained independent. Great chunks of Italy were bartered between the French and Spanish as alliances changed. Spain hung on to her Italian possessions for nearly 200 years, only to be replaced by Austrian domination as a result of the War of the Spanish Succession. The Austrians were perhaps the most progressive occupiers, preparing the way in the north for early industrialization. With Napoleon's arrival on the scene it was all change once more, and by 1810 he was in command of the whole peninsula. Napoleon introduced political reforms, such as representative assemblies, which were to have far-reaching consequences for the emerging middle class. After Napoleon's defeat at Waterloo, the Congress of Vienna attempted to re-establish the old order, but protest against oppression and occupation grew in the first half of the 19th century.

Clockwise from above *The duomo in Milan; a regatta in Venice from Giacomo Franco's* Habiti d'Houmeni et Donne Venetiane *(c1610); the reclining Paolina Borghese by Canova in the Galleria Borghese, Rome; a baroque facade in Noto, Sicily, rebuilt after the 1693 earthquake*

THE GRAND TOUR

Backpackers of the 21st century exploring the sights and delights of Italy are not the first visitors to fall for Italian pleasures. In the 18th century it was fashionable for young English gentlemen to go on the Grand Tour of Europe, including an Italian jaunt to enrich the mind. In practice it was a glorious excuse for profligate living. The days were spent sightseeing with the tutors, while the nights were given over to drinking, gambling and whoring. Shopping was a serious pursuit, and many of the statues, prints and paintings found in Britain's large country houses were brought home from the Tour. Artists were kept busy churning out portraits of the young gentry. With Joshua Reynolds charging over £150 in London, Roman portraits were a steal at £25.

EARTHQUAKE IN SICILY
In January 1693, the southeastern corner of Sicily was devastated by a series of earthquakes. The shocks continued for three days, accompanied by a blood-red moon, fissures in the land and catastrophic tidal waves. More than 60,000 people perished and churches, civic buildings and houses were destroyed. The quake's epicentre was the Val di Noto to the south of Catania and Siracusa, which were extensively damaged. Of the 45 towns affected, Catania suffered worst, losing two thirds of its entire population. In the years that followed, many towns in the area were rebuilt, almost entirely in the baroque style. Today, they are considered to be the final flowering of the baroque in Europe—an innovative approach to town planning, UNESCO World Heritage town Noto being the finest example.

THE AUSTRIAN LEGACY
The Austrians were big players in northern Italy throughout the 18th century and well into the 19th century, their grip only loosening in 1859 following the war engineered by Count Camillo Cavour and Napoleon III. They hung on longer in the far northern South Tyrol region, which only became part of Italy in 1919, when Mussolini renamed it the Alto Adige. Even today it is still almost completely Austrian in character. German is the first language, the towns and villages are sprinkled with onion-domed churches and traversed by arcaded streets, and all the street signs are in German. The food, in particular, is heavily Teutonic in character, with sauerkraut, *knödel* (dumplings) and strudel all on the menu, and scarcely even a whiff of pasta to be found.

NAPOLEON AND THE POPES
The conqueror of Europe kept the papacy well under control during his years of power. In 1798, French troops invaded Rome, demanding the abdication of the 82-year-old Pius VI; he refused, and was promptly deported to France. Five years later, Napoleon summoned Pius VII to Paris to officiate at his coronation. In 1809, Napoleon proclaimed the Papal States part of the French Empire and the Pope merely the Bishop of Rome. Pius promptly excommunicated Napoleon, who duly retaliated by sending his troops to seize the pontiff and hustle him away to exile. He and his Cardinal of State left in such a hurry that the Pope forgot his spectacles and the two venerable churchmen had less than 5 scudos (€2) between them.

PAOLINA BORGHESE
Napoleon's sister, Pauline, was married to Prince Borghese in 1803, when she was 23, and became Princess Paolina. Beautiful, selfish and spoiled, she was famed in Roman society for her looks, lovers and style. Her wedding present to her husband was a near-nude statue of herself posing as Venus, sculpted by Canova. Rome buzzed with Paolina stories—her clothes and jewels, the huge servant who carried her to her bath, and the use of ladies-in-waiting as footstools. Her lovers were numerous, and ranged from artists, actors and musicians to handsome young army officers. Generally disliked, she had one redeeming feature: her love for her brother. She shared his exile on Elba and gave him her jewels to help fund his final campaign that ended at Waterloo.

FROM UNIFICATION TO WORLD WAR II

Between 1848 and 1860 the movement to oust the occupiers and reform and unite the country grew. It was known as the Risorgimento, the 'resurgence' or 'new arising', and its key players were Giuseppe Mazzini, Giuseppe Garibaldi and Count Emilio Cavour. In 1861, the Kingdom of Italy was proclaimed, albeit without Rome and Venice. It was not until 1871 that the Unification of Italy was complete. The 1880s saw the start of the new nation's colonial expansion into North Africa, which brought Abyssinia (present-day Ethiopia), Eritrea and Libya under Italian control. World War I was seen as a chance to get even with Austria for past wrongs, gaining Trieste and Trentino-Alto Adige at vast cost. Disillusioned with these events, the middle classes turned to the Fascists and their leader, Benito Mussolini, who became dictator in 1925. Allied with Nazi Germany, Italy entered World War II in 1940. As Nazi dominance began to falter in Europe, Italy signed an armistice with the Allies in 1943 and Mussolini was finally captured from the Germans and executed in 1945.

Clockwise from above *Hitler and Mussolini with Hermann Goering (left) and Count Gian Galeazzo Ciano (right) at the Four-Power Conference in Munich, 30 September 1938; the Fiat Factory in Turin, 1917; Giuseppe Garibaldi; a poster showing Hitler and Mussolini combining forces to build a monument dedicated to peace, civilization and work*

GARIBALDI AND THE ONE THOUSAND

A merchant marine captain, guerrilla fighter and man of the people, Giuseppe Garibaldi (1807–82) was a key player in the Unification of Italy. After spending many years in exile, notably in South America, for his part in various uprisings, he came to live in Sardinia in 1854. When the Second Italian War of Independence broke out five years later, he landed in Sicily with 1,000 soldiers (known as the Redshirts), and proclaimed himself dictator in the name of Vittorio Emanuele II of Piedmont. He defeated the Neapolitan troops of the Bourbon King Francis II and captured Palermo. Crossing to the mainland, he then took Naples, handing both Sicily and Naples over to Vittorio Emanuele.

AUSTRIAN ITALY

Before Unification, a big chunk of northeastern Italy, much of it German-speaking, belonged to the Austrian Empire. Some areas, such as the Veneto and Friuli, were soon acquired by Italy, but the South Tirol in particular, proud of its Austrian links and traditions, continued to look firmly towards Vienna, and was loath to change. Politicians in Rome, determined on a fully united Italy, felt differently, and put the reacquisition of the Austrian areas of the country at the top of its list of World War I objectives. At the cost of a huge war debt, 650,000 dead, and a million casualties, the politicians got their way in 1919 when the frontier was moved north to the Brenner Pass, and the South Tirol and Trentino became part of Italy.

MUSSOLINI'S END

By April 1945, the Allies were uncomfortably close to Mussolini's puppet Republic of Salò on Lake Garda, and the ex-Duce, together with his mistress, Claretta Petacci, tried to flee to Switzerland. They were caught at Lake Como by partisans and shot on 28 April. The next day the bodies were taken to the Piazzale Loreto in Milan and strung by their feet from the girders of a gas station, to be kicked, shot at and spat upon by a furious crowd. After a year's interment in Milan's municipal cemetery, Mussolini's body was stolen by surviving Fascists. It was finally returned to his widow in 1957 and buried at his birthplace, Predappio in Emilia, which became a magnet for Fascists.

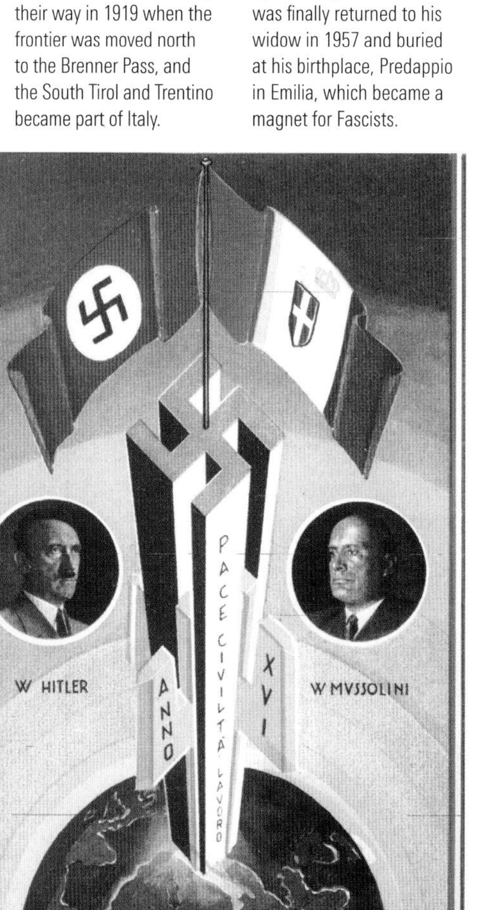

THE PRISONER OF THE VATICAN

Right up to the Unification of Italy, the Papal States sprawled across central Italy, successive popes hanging on to their temporal power. As elsewhere, the people were restless and the Pope needed outside help to retain control. Garibaldi invaded twice during the Risorgimento, but Pope Pius IX somehow hung on to Rome itself. Finally, in 1870, King Vittorio Emanuele seized the city and Rome became the capital of a united Italy. Furious, Pius refused to accept the loss of his holdings and retreated into the Vatican, declaring himself a prisoner. Later popes followed his example, never setting foot outside from election until death. The question was only settled by Mussolini's Lateran Treaty of 1929, which established Vatican City as the world's smallest independent state.

RESISTANCE

Southern Tuscany was one of Italy's strongest partisan regions during World War II, with anti-Fascist and anti-Nazi feeling running high. In 1943, as the Allies moved north from Monte Cassino, Resistance groups in the Val d'Orcia harried the Nazis incessantly, destroying whatever they could. The penalty was death, as it was for sheltering or feeding Allied soldiers on the run. In one infamous episode (dramatized in Spike Lee's 2008 film *The Miracle at St. Anna*), the retreating Nazis massacred 560 civilians in Sant'Anna di Stazzema, on the coast near Viareggio. In Florence, the Resistance was protected by the anti-Nazi German consul, but many farmers and peasants risked their lives and were imprisoned, transported or executed. Memorials can be found in many of the region's hilltop towns.

POST-WORLD WAR II

The years since 1945 have seen successive governments come and go, accompanied by political scandal on a large scale, corruption in high places and terrorism. Despite this, Italy has boomed economically, firmly establishing itself as a front-rank industrialized nation and a key player in influencing style across Europe. Nonetheless, the gulf between north and south remains as wide as ever.

MODERN INDUSTRY
Since World War II, Italy has become a major industrialized nation with a diversified economy. Heavy industry—particularly car production—drives the wealth of the north. The south is not so prosperous and survives on small-scale agriculture, wine production, fruit-growing and olive oil exports. The tourism boom has also become a significant part of regional economies and has helped to attract funding to improve roads and investment in hotels. But Italy's adoption of the euro is blamed by many traders for raising costs everywhere, just as cheaper Eastern European countries are opening up their resorts and attracting visitors in competition with Italy.

TERRORIST THREATS
In addition to the threat of violence from the Mafia, Italy, like many countries, faces the threat of terrorism from Islamic extremists. Italians were shocked when a suspect in the investigation into the 2005 London Underground bombings turned up in Rome and was sent back to Britain to face trial. Coming after the attacks in Madrid and London, this alerted Italians to the possibility that Rome could also be a target for terrorism by Islamic extremists. The abduction of an Italian aid worker in Iraq and the death of a security official escorting her to freedom also added fuel to campaigns calling on Silvio Berlusconi to disengage Italy from the military operation in Iraq.

THROUGH THE BACK DOOR
For the hopeful poor of Africa, Italy offers the best chance of entering Europe, and illegal immigration is an ongoing headache for successive governments. Italy's southernmost territory, the tiny island of Lampedusa (population 6,000), lies 205km (127 miles) south of Sicily and just 113km (70 miles) from Tunisia. Since 2000 it has emerged as a prime transit site for asylum-seekers hoping to enter Europe, with as many as 1,000 people arriving daily. Many are immediately deported, but Africans continue to pay people-smugglers for a transit to the island, knowing that once transferred to mainland detention centres, they will eventually be released. Summer conditions in the island's transit camps are bad, with overcrowding and the constant threat of disease, while every year boats making the crossing sink. Despite the perils, the number of people making this difficult journey is rising every year.

Above left to right *Silvio Berlusconi giving a speech; bottles of Annunziata Barcio in the wine cellar attached to the former Abbey of Annunziata*

ON THE MOVE

On the Move gives you detailed advice and information about the various options for travelling to Italy before explaining the best ways to get around the country once you are there. Handy tips help you with everything from buying tickets to renting a car.

ARRIVING BY AIR

Many visitors to Italy arrive by air, their numbers increasing with the growth of low-cost airline routes from other European destinations and the increasing popularity of short breaks throughout the year. If you're flying direct from another continent you will arrive at Rome Fiumicino, the capital's main airport, or Milan Malpensa, serving Italy's economic capital and the Lakes. Rome and Milan each have a second airport: Rome Ciampino and Milan Linate.

Turin Caselle has doubled in size as a result of the world's attention on Turin as the venue for the 2006 Winter Olympic Games and now rivals Milan as the gateway to the north of Italy. Venice Marco Polo is the main arrival point for northeastern Italy, and most visitors heading for Florence arrive at Pisa, an hour's journey by road or train from the city. Naples is the south's busiest international airport.

Rome Fiumicino (FCO) is 32km (20 miles) west of central Rome and has three terminals: A for domestic flights, B for domestic and some international, and C, with boarding gates connected to the terminal by monorail, for international flights only. All three terminals are big, so allow plenty of time for onward connections. There are interactive information points in arrival and departure areas.

Rome Ciampino (CIA) is 15km (9 miles) southeast of Rome, a short distance from the city ring-road which feeds into the motorway (expressway) network. This is the airport used by budget airlines as their gateway to Rome, though some also use Fiumicino. The departure area is rather small for the volume of traffic generated by budget airlines and the airport can get very crowded at peak times in July and August.

Torino Caselle (TRN) is 16km (10 miles) north of Turin city centre. The airport was expanded and modernized as a result of investment when the city hosted the 2006 Winter Olympic Games. The arrivals and departure areas have doubled in size with additional boarding gates, and the baggage-handling facilities are the most modern in Europe. The airport bus station is linked to the train station in an interchange facility that includes a remote check-in area to ease congestion in the main terminal at peak times. There is a 24-hour medical centre in the arrivals hall, and the new airport was designed with the needs of people with disabilities in mind, with mobility-adapted toilets and special vehicles that can raise a wheelchair from the ground to the door of a

GETTING INTO CITIES FROM THE AIRPORT

Airport (code)	ROME FIUMICINO (FCO)	ROME CIAMPINO (CIA)
Distance to city	32km (20 miles)	15km (9 miles)
Taxi	Price: from €45 Time: 30–45 min	Price: from €35 Time: 30–45 min
Trains/Boats	Fiumicino to Termini Frequency: Every 30 min 6.37am–11.37pm Price: €10.20 Journey time: 35 min Fiumicino to Trastevere Frequency: Every 15 min 6.27am–9.27pm Price: €6 Journey time: 30–45 min	Bus to Ciampino town station, from where trains run to Termini Frequency: Every 15 min 6.30am–11pm Price: €2.40 Journey time: 20 min Anagnina Metro (Line A) to Termini Frequency: Buses run from the airport to Anagnina every 60 min Price: €1.10 Journey time: 20 min
Bus	Night COTRAL bus to Termini and Tiburtina Frequency: At 1.15am, 2.15am, 3.30am and 5am Price: €5 Journey time: 45 min	Bus to Termini: SIT Bus Shuttle Frequency: Every 45 min 8.30am–midnight Price: €6 Journey time: 45 min
Car	Take Fiumicino–Rome motorway and travel eastwards	Take the Via Appia Nuova northwest into the heart of the city

Right *Inside the terminal building at Venice Marco Polo Airport, which serves the northeast of Italy*

plane to ease boarding. The main international car rental companies and several local ones are represented in the arrivals hall, and the airport has direct access to the motorway (highway) network linking the most important places in Piedmont, in northern Italy; southern France; and well-known Alpine holiday and ski resorts in Italy, France and Switzerland.

PISA (FLORENCE) (PSA)	MILAN MALPENSA (MXP)	TURIN (TRN)	VENICE MARCO POLO (VCE)
91km (57 miles) to Florence; 2km (1 mile) to Pisa	50km (31 miles)	16km (10 miles)	By water 7km (4 miles); overland 12km (7.5 miles)
Price: €120–150 to Florence; €6–8 to Pisa Time: 60–80 min to Florence; 10–20 min to Pisa	Price: €65–75 Time: 35–60 min	Price: €26–42 Time: 20–30 min	Land taxi price: €15–18 Time: 15–25 min Water taxi price: €80–110 Time: 20–35 min
Pisa Aeroporto–Firenze Santa Maria Novella Frequency: Every 60 min to Florence, stopping at Pisa Centrale Price: €5.40 Journey time: 75 min For Siena change at Empoli	Malpensa to Milano Nord Frequency: Every 30 min 6.30am–1.30am Price: €11 (discounted tickets for Alitalia passengers) Journey time: 40 min	Casalle airport station to Turin Dora Frequency: Every 30 min 6.50am–9.20pm Price: €8 Journey time: 19 min	Boat Alilaguna service From the airport to the city via Murano and the Lido Frequency: Every 60 min Price: €12 Journey time: 30 min to Murano, 55 min to the Lido, 1 hour 10 min to the city
CPT No. 3 from Pisa Airport to Pisa Frequency: Every 15 min Price: 50c Journey time: 10–15 min	Malpensa to Stazione Centrale Frequency: Every 20 min 5.20am–1am Price: €7 Journey time: 45–60 min	Bus to Porta Nuova Frequency: Every 30 min 5.15am–8.15am and 4.30pm–9pm; every 45 min 8.15am–4.30pm and 9pm–10.30pm Price: €5.50 Journey time: 40 min Bus tickets are available at news-stands, tourist information offices and ticket machines in the arrivals area. 50c extra charge when paying on the bus.	Airport bus (ATVO) to Piazzale Roma, ACTV bus No. 5 to Piazzale Roma Frequency: Airport bus (ATVO) every 30 min, ACTV bus No. 5 every 20 min Price: ATVO €5, ACTV €1 Journey time: ATVO 20 min, ACTV 20 min
From the airport follow the motorway Pisa–Firenze east to Florence	Take the link motorway southeast to the A8 (E62) and follow signs to the city centre	Driving into the city centre takes about 20 minutes (30 minutes in peak time). Turin Airport has direct access to the highway linking the most important places in Piedmont, north Italy; the south of France; and Alpine ski resorts.	N/A

Pisa Galileo Galilei (PSA) is Florence's main entry point for most overseas visitors, 91km (57 miles) west of Florence. It has good road and train connections and handles internal and European flights. The spacious terminal has information desks, a train ticket office and adjoining railway station.

Milano Malpensa (MXP), Italy's main international gateway in the north, is 50km (31 miles) northwest of the city. It has two terminals: Terminal 1 handles domestic and international flights; Terminal 2 is mainly for short- to medium-haul flights and charters. Both terminals have information, hotel reservation and car rental desks.

Milano Linate (LIN), 7km (4 miles) from Milan city centre, handles domestic and European flights. It has a full range of airport services.

Napoli Capodichino (NAP) lies 8km (5 miles) northeast of Naples city centre. This airport handles domestic and European scheduled and charter flights. An airport bus (every 30 min) runs to Piazza Garibaldi and Piazza Municipio; bus Nos 14 and 15 (every 15 min) run to Piazza Garibaldi.

Venezia Marco Polo (VCE) is on the northern edge of the lagoon, 7km (4 miles) from Venice by water and 12km (7.5 miles) by road. Serving the northeast of Italy, it handles mainly domestic and European flights. Its terminal is on three levels (ground floor for arrivals, first floor for check-in and departures, second floor for VIP lounges). Frequent and efficient water-taxi and ferry services carry passengers to Venice.

Some charter and budget airlines use **Treviso San Angelo (TSF),** a small airport 30km (18.5 miles) north of the city.

CAR RENTAL

The major car rental companies have offices at airports, train stations and major cities. You will usually get a better deal if you shop around and reserve from your own country. Local companies will often have airport pickup points, but you may be unable to reserve them from home. If you reserve with a tour operator, it will be able to arrange car rental in advance.

Before you leave, check your insurance and see if you will need additional cover. You will need to show your credit card when you pick up the car and to pay for additional charges.

Drivers of rental cars must be over 21 or 25 (depending on the company) and have a valid driver's licence. Any additional drivers may also have to sign the rental agreement. If you intend to go off public roads, check that the insurance covers this. You will be offered the choice of returning the car filled with fuel; it is cheaper to fill it up yourself just before you return it. Be sure to check thoroughly both inside and outside the vehicle for any damage. If you find any, report it at once and get a company representative to make a note.

CAR RENTAL COMPANIES

Book your rental car before you leave home, by phone or online. These are major international rental groups.

Alamo
tel 0870 400 4562 (UK)
tel 800 462 5266 (US)
www.alamo.com

Avis
tel 0844 581 0147 (UK)
tel 0800 331 1212 (US)
www.avis.com

Budget
tel 0844 581 9998 (UK)
tel 800 527 0700 (US)
www.budget.com

Hertz
tel 0870 844 8844 (UK)
tel 800 654 3001 (US)
www.hertz.com

National
tel 0870 400 4581 (UK)
tel 1-800 CAR RENT (US)
www.nationalcar.com

USEFUL TELEPHONE NUMBERS AND WEBSITES

AIRPORTS

General www.worldairportguide.com

Florence tel 055 306 1300 www.aeroporto.firenze.it

Naples tel 081 789 6111 www.portal.gesac.it

Milan Malpensa & Linate tel 02 748 52200 www.sea-aeroportimilano.it

Pisa tel 050 849300 www.pisa-airport.com

Rome Ciampino tel 06 65951 www.adr.it

Rome Fiumicino tel 06 65951 www.adr.it

Treviso tel 0422 315111 www.trevisoairport.it

Turin tel 011 5676 361 www.aeroportoditorino.it

Venice Marco Polo tel 041 260 9260 www.veniceairport.it

AIRLINES

UK

Alitalia tel 08714 241 424 www.alitalia.co.uk

BMI Baby tel 0871 224 0224 www.bmibaby.com

British Airways tel 0870 850 9850, (UK); 199 712266 (IT) www.ba.com

easyJet tel 0871 244 2366 (UK); 899 678 990 (IT) www.easyjet.com

Flybe tel 0871 700 2000 www.flybe.com

Meridiana tel 00 39 0789 52682 (UK); 89 29 28 (IT) www.meridiana.it

Ryanair www.ryanair.com

Volare Airlines tel 0039 070 4603397 (UK); 0199 414 500 (IT) www.buyvolareweb.com

US

Alitalia tel 800 223 5730 www.alitalia.it

American Airlines tel 800 433 7300 www.aa.com

Continental tel 800 231 0856 www.continental.com

Delta tel 800 221 1212 www.delta-air.com

Northwest Airlines tel 1-800 225 2525 www.nwa.com

United tel 1-800-United-1 www.united.com

US Airways tel 800 428 4322 www.usairways.com

ARRIVING BY FERRY

If you are planning a trip to Sicily or Sardinia, or onwards to Greece, you may want to travel by ferry. With the exception of the short hop across the Straits of Messina to Sicily, it's best to reserve a crossing in advance. You need to arrive at the departure port between 2 and 6 hours before sailing; individual companies will provide details when you reserve. The major ferry ports are clearly marked by road signs with a ship symbol, the name of the destination port and the word *traghetti* (ferries). Overnight ferries have cabins available; these, too, should be reserved in advance.

For faster links to the main islands there is also the hydrofoil, though the frequency of these services tends to be greatly reduced outside the peak summer season. Prices vary considerably, but reserving in advance may get you a good deal. The best way to research Italian ferries is through www.traghettitalia.net, a portal site linking virtually all the major operators, with an online reservations facility. For ferries to Greece, check availability on www.ferries.gr.

ARRIVING BY RAIL

From Britain you can travel by **train to Italy**, via the Channel Tunnel, through either Brussels or Paris. The journey time via Brussels is longer, but if you choose the Paris option you have to change from the Gare du Nord to the Gare de Lyon. Direct trains run to **Rome**, **Florence**, **Milan**, **Turin** and **Venice**.

The choice of routes and fares is highly complex, but it's best to use the **Eurostar** as far as **Paris** or **Brussels** from where trains south are fast and frequent.

Eurostar trains link London with Paris and Brussels in around 2 hours. You must check in 30 minutes before departure and you are allowed two suitcases and one item of hand baggage. You need your passport to clear immigration and customs.

» The total journey time from London to Italian destinations varies from 11 to 15 hours.
» Return ticket prices range from around €250 to around €350.

Both Eurostar and other fast European trains have facilities which include:

» 1st- and 2nd-class seating.
» Bar/restaurant cars.
» Trolley service on day trains.
» Baby-changing facilities.
» Air-conditioning.
» Telephone kiosks.
» Toilets in each carriage, including some that are accessible to wheelchairs.

Smoking is banned inside station buildings and on all trains—even if old window stickers still indicate smoking is permitted.

Sleepers are available from Paris on direct routes to Rome, Milan, Florence and Venice. Accommodation varies from 3-, 4- and 6-berth couchettes to single and double sleepers with integral shower and toilet.

The **Orient Express**, the celebrated luxury train ride to Italy, runs from London to Venice. The journey time is 31 hours, and costs around €1,900 one way.

RAIL PASSES

Prices indicated below are subject to annual revision.

» **InterRail passes** give you complete flexibility. A single-zone pass for standard or second-class travel is valid in Italy but also includes

FERRY INFORMATION AND TICKETS

Frequencies and timings of ferry services vary according to season and demand. A more detailed summary of Italian ferry services is available in the Thomas Cook European Rail Timetable, tables 2515 to 2755.

SICILY

Operator: NGI, tel 090 9284091, 090 679141, freephone 800 250000; www.ngi-spa.it
Departure port: Reggio di Calabria
Arrival port: Messina
Frequency: Every 20–40 min
Duration of crossing: 40 min

Operator: Caronte e Tourist spa, tel freephone 800 627 41; 09037 18510; www.carontetourist.it
Departure port: Villa San Giovanni
Arrival port: Messina
Frequency: Every 10–15 min
Duration of crossing: 25 min

Operators: Tirrenia, tel 081 317 2999; www.tirrenia.it
Snav, tel 081 428 5555; www.snav.it
Departure port: Naples
Arrival port: Palermo
Frequency: 1 daily
Duration of crossing: 11 hours

Operator: Grandi Navi Veloci, tel 899 199 069; www.gnv.it
Departure port: Genoa
Arrival port Palermo
Frequency: 1 daily
Duration of crossing: 20 hours

SARDINIA

Operator: Tirrenia, tel 081 317 2999; www.tirrenia.it
Departure ports: Civitavecchia, Genoa, Livorno
Arrival ports: Cagliari, Olbia, Golfo Aranci
Frequency: From Civitavecchia 1 daily to Cagliari (Fri, Sun via Arbatax), 3 daily to Olbia; from Genoa Jul–Sep 2 weekly to Arbatax, daily to Olbia (Sun 2 sailings); from Naples 2 weekly; from Palermo to Cagliari 1 weekly
Duration of crossing: Civitavecchia to Cagliari 15–17 hours, Civitavecchia to Olbia 9 hours; Genoa to Cagliari 21 hours, Genoa to Olbia 14 hours; Naples to Cagliari 17 hours; Palermo to Cagliari 14 hours

GREECE

Operators: Superfast, Minoan Lines, Blue Star, Hellenic (www.superfast.com, www.minoan.gr, www.bluestarferries.com, www.hellenicferries.com)
Departure ports: Ancona, Bari, Venice (Minoan Lines)
Arrival ports: Patras, Igoumenitsa, Corfu (Blue Star, Minoan Lines)
Frequency: Ancona 3 daily; Bari 1 daily; Venice 2 daily
Duration of crossing: Ancona 19 hours; Bari 16 hours 30 min; Venice 22 hours

TRAIN INFORMATION AND TICKETS

Eurostar St. Pancras, London NW1 2QP, tel 0870 518 6186/020 7843 4250; www.eurostar.com
Rail Europe 1 Regent Street, London SWI, tel 08448 484 064; www.raileurope.co.uk
Trenitalia (Italian State Railways) www.trenitalia.com; www.ferroviedellostato.it
Venice-Simplon-Orient-Express Ltd Sea Containers House, 20, Upper Ground, London SE1 9PF, tel 0845 077 2222; www.orient-express.com

Greece, Turkey and Slovenia and some ferry services across the Adriatic between Italy and Greece. It costs £160 for travellers under 26 and £235 if you're over 26 (child under 12 £115). A two-zone pass is valid for 22 days and also allows you to use trains in France, Belgium, Luxembourg and the Netherlands. It costs £220 for those under 26 and £315 if you're over 26 (child under 12 £162). For the complete freedom of Europe's rail network, an all-zone pass, valid for 1 month, costs £300 for those under 26 and £420 for those over 26 (child under 12 £215).

The InterRail pass gives discounts on cross-Channel services including Eurostar, and is available to European residents.

» **EurRail passes** have similar validity to the InterRail pass for a period of consecutive days' travel and are available for residents of countries outside Europe.

» **Trenitalia** discontinued all travel passes in 2007. Its state-subsidized fares are very low, and the company has introduced the Cartaviaggio system, offering a choice of different types of travel card which enable the holder to obtain some reductions on travel and various other benefits in the form of shopping and hotel discounts. The cards are free, but, unless you're doing an enormous amount of travelling in Italy and planning a lengthy stay, not of great use to foreigners. You can find out more on the Trenitalia website, which has a good English-language version.

Right *A ferry in the harbour at Isola San Pietro, an island off Sardinia*

ARRIVING BY BUS

Italy has few domestic long-distance bus routes, but there are international routes from major cities across Europe.

» **International buses** to Italy from the UK are coordinated by Eurolines (tel 08717 818181, www.nationalexpress.com), a consortium of 30 independent long-distance bus companies. Regular services run from London Victoria Coach Station to 27 cities in Italy, though most journeys involve a change in Paris. The typical adult return fare London to Turin is £125, and London to Rome £160.

» **Destinations:** Ancona, Bologna, Florence, Genoa, Milan, Naples, Padua, Parma, Pisa, Rimini, Rome, San Remo, Siena, Turin, Venice, Verona, with connections to other Italian destinations.

» **Journey time**: London to Milan 22 hours, Florence 28 hours, Rome 30–32 hours, Naples 33–35 hours, all with a stop in Paris of 90 minutes.

» **Tickets** can be reserved online or at National Express travel offices. A Eurolines Pass allows you unlimited coach travel between a choice of 35 cities across Europe, including internal Italian routes between Milan and Siena and Siena and Rome (15 days £160, 30 days £195, 40 days £240).

ARRIVING BY CAR

Driving to Italy, you will need a valid driver's licence, a vehicle registration document, a motor insurance certificate and a passport.

From the UK, you can take the ferry or use the Channel Tunnel. The main routes to Italy run through France, Switzerland and Germany. All cross the Alps; the St. Gotthard tunnel is free, but other passes range from €15–€25. To reach these take the E15 and E17 to Reims, then pick up the motorways. There are toll roads (turnpikes) all along the route (▷ 50). You should allow 11 to 14 hours' driving time to reach the north Italian border.

DRIVING

Italy's road system is comprehensive, with motorways (expressways) covering the entire peninsula from north to south and with trans-Apennine links at regular intervals. In addition, all regions have dual-carriageway (divided highway) and main-road alternatives and rural villages are connected by minor roads. Civil engineering is excellent, with bridges soaring over ravines and well-lit tunnels going through mountains. Given the country's north/south economic divide, the road network is at its best in the north, but even in the south driving is easy and pleasant. However, driving in the cities, particularly in Rome, should be avoided.

Driving is the ideal way to get around if you are concentrating on smaller towns and cities and rural areas. Although it's not for the faint-hearted, you can enjoy panoramic views from the road, famously along the Amalfi Coast (▷ 370–371) and through the Dolomites (▷ 216–217). Italian driving belies its fearsome reputation; once you grasp their rationale, you'll find Italian drivers less erratic and on the whole safer than drivers of many other nationalities.

The best bet is to steer clear of cities. One-way systems, narrow streets, lack of parking, traffic congestion and occasional aggression make city driving stressful. Be prepared for traffic jams in August when all of Italy is on holiday and everyone heads for the roads and motorways, particularly on weekends.

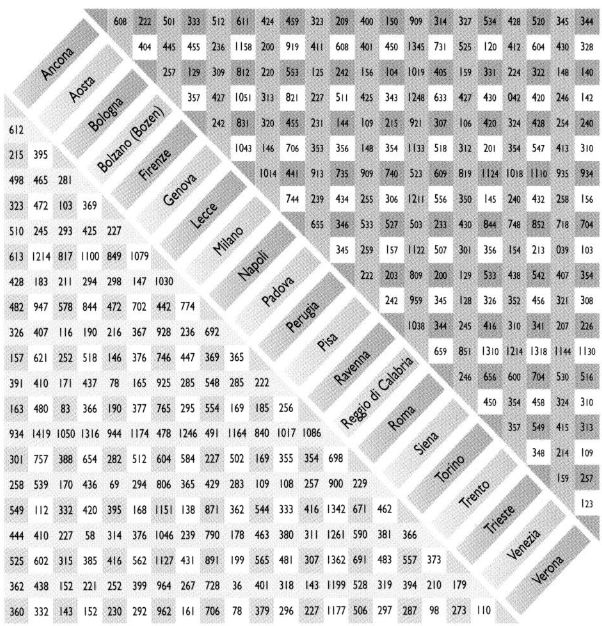

Distance (km)	Ancona	Aosta	Bologna	Bolzano (Bozen)	Firenze	Genova	Lecce	Milano	Napoli	Padova	Perugia	Pisa	Ravenna	Reggio di Calabria	Roma	Siena	Torino	Trento	Trieste	Venezia
Aosta	612																			
Bologna	215	395																		
Bolzano (Bozen)	498	465	281																	
Firenze	323	472	103	369																
Genova	510	245	293	425	227															
Lecce	613	1214	817	1100	849	1079														
Milano	428	183	211	294	298	147	1030													
Napoli	482	947	578	844	472	702	442	774												
Padova	326	407	116	190	216	367	928	236	692											
Perugia	157	621	252	518	146	376	746	447	369	365										
Pisa	391	410	171	437	78	165	925	285	548	285	222									
Ravenna	163	480	83	366	190	377	765	295	554	169	185	256								
Reggio di Calabria	934	1419	1050	1316	944	1174	478	1246	491	1164	840	1017	1086							
Roma	301	757	388	654	282	512	604	584	227	502	169	355	354	698						
Siena	258	539	170	436	69	294	806	365	429	283	109	108	257	900	229					
Torino	549	112	332	420	395	168	1151	138	871	362	544	333	416	1342	671	462				
Trento	444	410	227	58	314	376	1046	239	790	178	463	380	311	1261	590	381	366			
Trieste	525	602	315	385	416	562	1127	431	891	199	565	481	307	1362	691	483	557	373		
Venezia	362	438	152	221	252	399	964	267	728	36	401	318	143	1199	528	319	394	210	179	
Verona	360	332	143	152	230	292	962	161	706	78	379	296	227	1177	506	297	287	98	273	110

Duration	Aosta	Bologna	Bolzano (Bozen)	Firenze	Genova	Lecce	Milano	Napoli	Padova	Perugia	Pisa	Ravenna	Reggio di Calabria	Roma	Siena	Torino	Trento	Trieste	Venezia	Verona
Ancona	608	222	501	333	512	611	424	459	323	209	400	150	909	314	327	534	428	520	345	344
Aosta		404	445	455	236	1158	200	919	411	608	401	450	1345	731	525	120	412	604	430	328
Bologna			257	129	309	812	220	553	125	242	156	104	1019	405	159	331	224	322	148	140
Bolzano (Bozen)				357	427	1051	313	821	227	511	425	343	1248	633	427	430	042	420	246	142
Firenze					242	831	320	455	231	144	109	215	921	307	106	420	324	428	254	240
Genova						1043	146	706	353	356	148	354	1133	518	312	201	354	547	413	310
Lecce							1014	441	913	735	909	740	523	609	819	1124	1018	1110	935	934
Milano								744	239	434	255	306	1211	556	350	145	240	432	258	156
Napoli									655	346	533	527	503	233	430	844	748	852	718	704
Padova										345	259	157	1122	507	301	356	154	213	039	103
Perugia											222	203	809	200	129	533	438	542	407	354
Pisa												242	959	345	128	326	352	456	321	308
Ravenna													1038	344	245	416	310	341	207	226
Reggio di Calabria														659	851	1310	1214	1318	1144	1130
Roma															246	656	600	704	530	516
Siena																450	354	458	324	310
Torino																	357	549	415	313
Trento																		348	214	109
Trieste																			159	257
Venezia																				123

The chart above gives the distances in kilometres (green) and duration in hours and minutes (blue) of a car journey between key towns. The times are based on average driving speeds using the fastest roads. They do not allow for delays or rest breaks.

BRINGING YOUR OWN CAR

Before you leave:

» British drivers should adjust their headlights for driving on the right.
» Contact your motor insurer or broker at least 1 month before you leave.
» Have your car serviced.
» Check the tyres.
» If you don't have a rear-view mirror on the left side, fit one before you go.
» Ensure you have adequate breakdown assistance cover (AA Five Star 0800 444500, www.theAA.com).

You will need:

» A valid driver's licence.
» The original vehicle registration document.
» A motor insurance certificate; at least third-party insurance is compulsory.
» A first aid kit, fire extinguisher and spare bulbs.
» It is compulsory to carry a warning triangle (in case of breakdown) and a fluorescent safety jacket, and to display a nationality sticker (unless you have Euro-plates).
» If you're driving in winter you may need winter tyres or snow chains.

DOCUMENTS

Carry documents with you whenever you are driving; if you are stopped by the *polizia stradale*, *polizia municipale* or *carabinieri* they will want to see them. Both UK and US driver's licences are valid in Italy, but you should also carry a translation. In the UK, the current licences with photographs and the pink, EU-style ones include a translation, but if you hold an older, green licence, you can either update the licence or apply for an International Driving Permit. Holders of US driver's licences should also apply for an International Driving Permit. These permits are not compulsory, but can smooth out problems and act as another form of identification if you need it. Permits can be obtained from the Italian State Tourist Offices or through national motoring organizations such as the AA and AAA.

RULES OF THE ROAD

» Drivers must be at least 18 and hold a full driver's licence.

» Drive on the right and give way to traffic from the right. However, at crossroads (intersections) displaying a precedence, or yield, sign (inverted triangle bearing the words *dare precedenza*) give way to traffic coming from left and right.

» Seat belts must be worn in the front of a vehicle and (where fitted) in the back.

» Children under 4 must have a suitable restraint system. Those aged between 4 and 12 cannot travel in the front of the car without a fitted restraint system.

» Speed limits: built-up areas—50kph (31mph); outside built-up areas—110kph (68mph); motorways *(autostrade)*—130kph (81mph) (if your car is over 1100cc).

» Use dipped (reduced) headlights in non-urban areas during the day and in towns or cities at night. These are compulsory when driving in tunnels, even if they are well lit.

» There are severe penalties for drinking and driving.

» Italy uses international road signs.

MOTORWAYS AND TOLL ROADS (EXPRESSWAYS AND TURNPIKES)

As you approach the *autostrada* take the ticket from the machine on the left-hand side of the car or press the red button to get one. The barrier will lift. Keep your ticket safe, as you will need it to pay when you leave the *autostrada*. Cash payment is normally made to the official in the booth; the amount is displayed on a screen outside the pay window. If you are using a pass or credit card, follow the signs into the Viacard booth.

Slip roads onto and off Italian *autostrade* are short. You may have to stop and wait for traffic to pass before you can join the motorway.

Italians are fast, disciplined drivers on the motorway. Only use the outer lanes for overtaking and be prepared to move continuously between lanes to allow faster drivers behind you to overtake; they often drive up close behind you. Signal before you pull out and while you are overtaking.

Autostrade have regularly spaced service areas *(area di servizio)* with filling stations, bar/restaurant, shops and toilets. There are also occasional rest areas with shady trees and picnic tables, some with toilets.

The Italian *autostrada* network is run by several different companies, which means that both price and frequency of tolls vary greatly. On the whole, northern motorways tend to be more expensive, and you may find a *pedaggio* (toll station) coming up every few kilometres. South of Naples, the A1 *(Autostrada del Sole)* is state-subsidized and free. Motorcycles under 150cc are not allowed on the motorway.

PROBLEMS

If your car breaks down, put on your safety jacket, turn on your hazard warning lights and place the warning triangle 50m (55 yards) behind the vehicle.

If you're driving your own car, obtain assistance from the Automobile Club d'Italia (ACI) by calling 116 and telling the operator where you are, the make of car and the licence plate number. This is not a free service, so it might be better to arrange breakdown coverage with an auto association before you leave home.

If your rental car breaks down, call the rental company on the emergency number included with the car's paperwork. If you have an accident call the police (113), but do not admit liability. Witnesses should remain to make statements and exchange details (name, address, car details, insurance company's name and address).

If you are stopped by the police (*carabinieri*, *polizia stradale* or *polizia municipale*) they will want to see your papers. They may give no reason for stopping you, in which case it is likely to be a random spot check and once they realize you are a non-national they will probably wave you on. The commonest offence is speeding, for which there is a hefty on-the-spot fine. The police must issue fined drivers with a receipt.

SAFETY

For peace of mind, keep car doors locked while you are driving. In large cities, particularly in the south, keep windows shut. Never leave anything visible in the car when you're not using it. Italians usually detach their radios and take them with them.

If you're taking your own car, lower the aerial and tuck in the wing mirrors when you leave the vehicle.

In the countryside watch out for APEs (three-wheeler all-purpose mini-pickups) as their drivers rarely signal their intentions. Be aware of animals, slow-moving agricultural vehicles, soft roadsides and unsurfaced roads, which can be lethal in long spells of drought or heavy rain.

PARKING

Parking in Italy is often difficult, as its ancient and picturesque towns and villages were simply not built to

TRANSLATIONS OF ITALIAN ROAD SIGNS

Accendere Switch on lights	**Parcheggio** Parking
Accendere i fari Switch on headlights	**Parcheggio autorizzato** Parking allowed
Banchina non No hard shoulder	**Passaggio a livello** Level crossing
Caduta massi Falling rocks	**Pericolo** Danger
Crocevia Crossroads (intersection)	**Rallentare** Slow down
Curva pericolosa Dangerous bend	**Senso unico** One way
Discesa pericolosa Dangerous downhill	**Senso vietato** No entry
Divieto di accesso No entry	**Sosta autorizzata** Parking permitted
Divieto di sorpasso No overtaking	**Svolta** Bend
Divieto di sosta No parking	**Uscita** Exit
Entrata Entry	**Vietata ingresso veicoli** No entry for vehicles
Incrocio Crossroads (intersection)	

accommodate vehicles, and parking regulations can be complicated.

» Invest in a parking dial; these are used in permitted parking areas and are displayed in your windscreen to indicate when you arrived. Rental cars are normally already equipped with one; they are also available at tourist offices.

» Many cities have parking zones: blue zones (with blue lines) have a maximum stay of 1–2 hours. Pay the attendant or at the meter. White zones (with white lines) are free and unlimited in some cities, but reserved for residents in others. Yellow zones (with yellow lines) are generally for residents only.

» Pedestrianized historic towns allow cars in to deposit luggage—you may have to obtain a permit first from your hotel.

» Parking areas in the heart of cities are expensive.

» If you arrive at night, check that your chosen parking street does not have a market the following day. If it does, your car will be towed away well before dawn.

» A *zona di rimozione* sign indicates a tow-away zone.

BUYING FUEL

Italian service stations may not be self-service. If there is an attendant, he will fill your tank, check water, oil and tyre pressures and clean the windscreen if requested. Pay him direct; you will have to ask for a receipt *(una ricevuta)*. If they check the tyres it's customary to give a small tip (50c–€1).There are two grades of unleaded petrol or gas *(senza piombo)*, 95 and 98 octane, diesel *(gasolio)* and LPG. Leaded petrol is virtually nonexistent and you will have to buy lead-substitute additive. Fuel prices are generally similar to the UK and considerably higher than the US. Motorway service areas and filling stations in major towns accept credit cards.

If you need **fuel at night**, find a filling station with a 24-hour *(24 ore)* automatic pump. These take €5, €10 and €20 notes. Feed the money into the slot; the fuel will stop automatically when the money runs out. These can be temperamental and often reject old notes.

SCOOTERS

It is tempting to rent a scooter *(motorino)* in the land of the Vespa—ask at a tourist office for details. To rent a scooter you must be over 21 and hold a full driver's licence. You will need to leave your passport and/or a credit card as a deposit. Crash helmets are compulsory.

Scooters are not for the faint-hearted, and if you've never ridden one in a big city Italy is not the place to start. But if you're staying at the seaside or in a quiet rural area, they're economical, fun and easier to park than a car. Italian scooter drivers weave in and out of the traffic. Unless you are experienced, do not be tempted to emulate them.

BICYCLING

Bicycling is popular both as a sport and as a way of getting around, particularly in the northern plains. Tourist offices will be able to give you details of local rental companies and maps of routes in and around towns. If you rent a bicycle you will have to leave your passport or credit card as a deposit. There are few bicycle paths, so you will need to keep your wits about you. Although wearing a helmet is not compulsory, it is recommended that you do so.

ROAD SIGNS

Industrial area or zone

Urban directions to state roads (SS)

(A) Autostrada (motorway/expressway)

(SS) State open road direction signs indicating destination, distance and road number

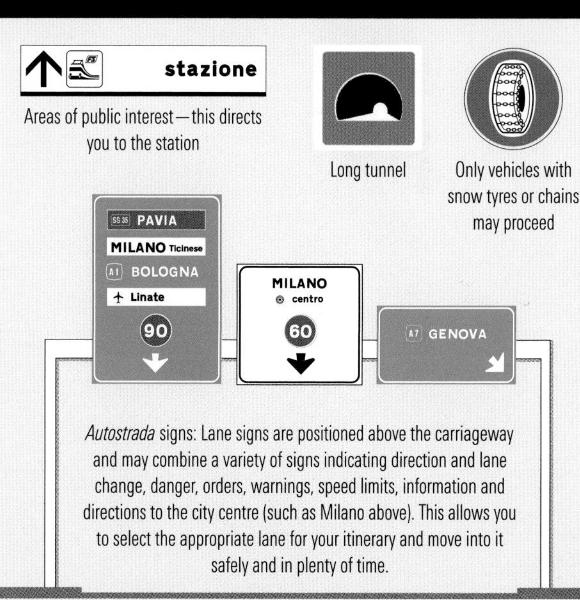

Areas of public interest—this directs you to the station

Long tunnel

Only vehicles with snow tyres or chains may proceed

Autostrada signs: Lane signs are positioned above the carriageway and may combine a variety of signs indicating direction and lane change, danger, orders, warnings, speed limits, information and directions to the city centre (such as Milano above). This allows you to select the appropriate lane for your itinerary and move into it safely and in plenty of time.

BUSES

Italy has no national long-distance bus company. Buses are operated by several different companies, mainly running services within their own region, though there are a few that operate outside their own immediate area. With the low cost of rail travel, longer journeys are more efficient and cheaper by train (▷ 53–55). Smoking is not permitted on public transport.

» If you are planning to use buses to get around a particular region, you can get **timetables and information** from the company office or the tourist information office.

» **Bus stations** are often next to the railway station. In small towns and villages, buses stop in the main piazza. Bus stations in larger towns tend to have toilets, a newsstand, bar and lost-property office.

» **Tickets** must normally be purchased before boarding the bus, and are available from newsstands, shops or *tabacchi* (tobacconists).

RURAL BUSES

Rural buses link outlying small towns and villages with the main regional centres or the larger local towns.

» **Timetables and information** are available from the bus company office (in the region's major towns) or from tourist information offices.

» **Tickets** are available from the bus office, tobacconists, newsstands and sometimes from the driver on board.

» Buses stop at **designated stops**, both at points along the route and in the main piazzas of villages.

» Services are geared to the local population's needs. Many buses operate to suit working and school hours and are drastically reduced on weekends, during school holidays and at night. So if using rural buses you may need to adapt your plans accordingly.

TAXIS

Taxis are available in all towns and cities. Government-regulated vehicles are either white or yellow.

» Always check that the taxi is registered and that the meter is running—avoid taxis without a meter, as they may not be insured.

» It can be difficult to hail a cab, so it is often better to go to a stand or reserve over the phone.

» All charges should be listed on a rate card displayed inside the vehicle.

Left to right *A tram and a taxi outside Milan's Teatro alla Scala; a fast train waiting at the platform in Venice*

» Rates are higher at night and on Sundays and public holidays. Many city taxis have set rates from the airport to the city, but supplements may be added for telephone reservations, luggage and any additional passengers.

» Confirm the price before you begin your journey.

TAXIS

	ROME	MILAN	FLORENCE	VENICE	NAPLES
Colour	Yellow or white	Yellow	White with yellow graphics	A boat with a white cabin	White with yellow Neapolitan emblem
Ranks	Termini, Piazza Venezia, Piazza San Silvestro, Piazza di Spagna, Piazza Sonnino (Trastevere)	Stazione Centrale, Piazza Duomo, Largo Cairoli, Piazza San Babile	Piazza della Repubblica, Santa Maria Novella, Piazza della Stazione, Piazza del Duomo, Piazza San Marco, Piazza Santa Croce, Piazza della Santa Trinità	San Marco, Piazzale Roma, Aeroporto Venezia Marco Polo, Ferrovia (Santa Lucia train station), Rialto	Piazza Garibaldi, Piazza Plebiscito, Piazza Municipio, Piazza della Repubblica, Piazza de Nicola, Piazza Dante
Radio Taxi Telephone Numbers	06 3570 06 4157 06 4994 06 88177 06 5551 06 6645 06 8822	02 6969 02 4040 02 4000 02 8585	055 4390 055 4798 055 4242 055 4386	041 522 2303	081 552 5252 081 551 5151 081 556 4444 081 570 7070
Number of passengers	4	4	4/5	6/8	4
Price	Moderate	Moderate	Expensive	Extremely expensive	Moderate

TRAINS

Italy has an extensive rail system and a variety of train types. Fares are the cheapest in Europe and train travel can be a great way to tour the country and enjoy an ever-changing view of the landscape. Trenitalia, the state railway company, covers the whole country, though there are also some privately operated lines and services. Italian trains have a mixed record of punctuality, which doesn't seem to bother Italians, but can be of critical importance if your journey involves several changes of trains. So be patient and allow plenty of time between arrivals and departures to make your connections.

FARES

Train fares are calculated by distance but vary depending on whether you take a local, regional, InterCity or night train. New Eurostar Italia trains are the most expensive but offer the best service and use modern carriages (cars) of the type used on Eurostar services. Premium fares apply on Eurostar Italia trains and you must pay a €12 supplement if travelling with an InterRail or EurRail freedom pass.

The easiest, and quickest, way to find the price of a train journey is to use the touch-screen ticket machines installed in most stations. They have an English-language option and you can buy tickets and reserve seats.

Return (round-trip) fares are simply double the single ticket price. First-class fares are only a little more than second class, and may be a good option for extra comfort, quiet and reliability of air-conditioning. Local trains are usually second class only.

Point-to-point fares are so cheap that Trenitalia has discontinued its range of travel passes (▷ 48). If you hold a Eurodomino ticket this is still valid, but it's worth considering whether you actually need a train pass at all for Italy. Unless you are spending hours on trains daily, it may be cheaper to buy ordinary tickets to get around, saving your pass for other countries on a tour.

When selecting the train for your destination, bear in mind that while Eurostar Italia trains can reach speeds of 250–300kph (155–185mph), they only reach anything like their top speeds when they run on the new high-speed track between Rome and Florence, Milan and Turin. Where they run on old track their speed is restricted, but journey times are still shorter than InterCity services on the same route because Eurostar trains make fewer intermediate stops.

TICKETS

Ask for either *andata* (one way) or *andata e tornata* (return or round-trip) and tell the ticket clerk which train you want to take, as there may be a supplement to pay. It is cheaper to pay supplements at the time you buy the tickets, as upgrading on board the train involves an additional charge. On long journeys with changes of train at different stations, you may be issued with several tickets, representing the different legs of your journey. Keep them together as onboard inspectors may want to see them all. On the other hand, if two of you are travelling together, you may be issued with only one ticket printed with an indication of two travellers.

Children aged 4–12 travel at half the normal fare; children under 4 not occupying a seat travel free.

VALIDATING TICKETS

Just buying a ticket is not enough for travelling on Italian trains. Whichever train you take you must validate your ticket by punching it in a yellow or red slot machine in the station booking hall before you board the train. This applies even if your ticket is for a reserved seat on a specified train. The ticket inspector may ask you to pay a surcharge of €20 if your ticket does not have the pre-boarding validation mark on it.

TIMETABLES

All stations have timetable posters, one for Arrivals *(Arrivi)* and one for Departures *(Partenze)*. These show every train stopping at the station and all the intermediate stations on the journey. They also show the platform number that the train is

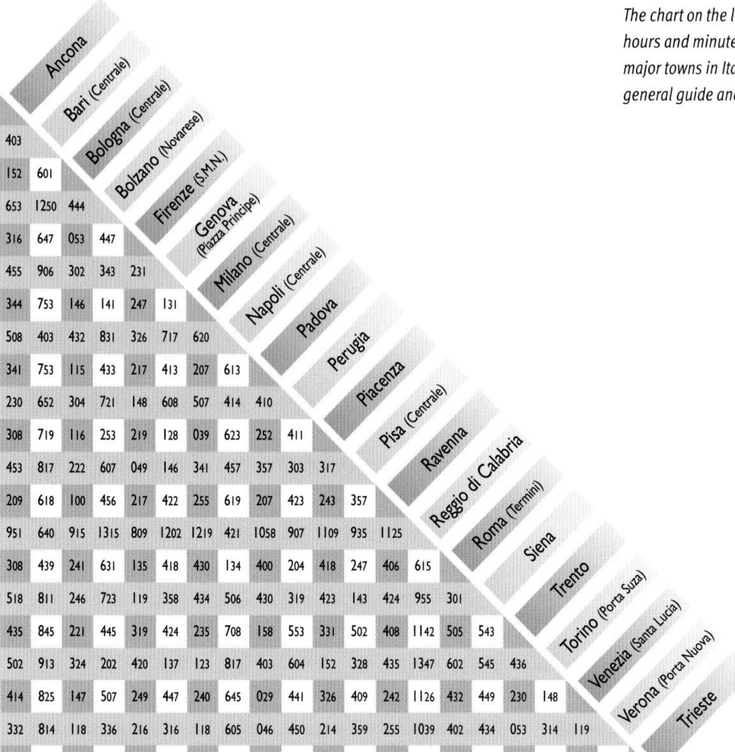

	Ancona	Bari (Centrale)	Bologna (Centrale)	Bolzano (Novarese)	Firenze (S.M.N.)	Genova (Piazza Principe)	Milano (Centrale)	Napoli (Centrale)	Padova	Perugia	Piacenza	Pisa (Centrale)	Ravenna	Reggio di Calabria	Roma (Termini)	Siena	Trento	Torino (Porta Suza)	Venezia (Santa Lucia)	Verona (Porta Nuova)
Bari (Centrale)	403																			
Bologna (Centrale)	152	601																		
Bolzano (Novarese)	653	1250	444																	
Firenze (S.M.N.)	316	647	053	447																
Genova (Piazza Principe)	455	906	302	343	231															
Milano (Centrale)	344	753	146	141	247	131														
Napoli (Centrale)	508	403	432	831	326	717	620													
Padova	341	753	115	433	217	413	207	613												
Perugia	230	652	304	721	148	608	507	414	410											
Piacenza	308	719	116	253	219	128	039	623	252	411										
Pisa (Centrale)	453	817	222	607	049	146	341	457	357	303	317									
Ravenna	209	618	100	456	217	422	255	619	207	423	243	357								
Reggio di Calabria	951	640	915	1315	809	1202	1219	421	1058	907	1109	935	1125							
Roma (Termini)	308	439	241	631	135	418	430	134	400	204	418	247	406	615						
Siena	518	811	246	723	119	358	434	506	430	319	423	143	424	955	301					
Trento	435	845	221	445	319	424	235	708	158	553	331	502	408	1142	505	543				
Torino (Porta Suza)	502	913	324	202	420	137	123	817	403	604	152	328	435	1347	602	545	436			
Venezia (Santa Lucia)	414	825	147	507	249	447	240	645	029	441	326	409	242	1126	432	449	230	148		
Verona (Porta Nuova)	332	814	118	336	216	316	118	605	046	450	214	359	255	1039	402	434	053	314	119	
Trieste	609	1021	337	717	441	646	424	843	230	719	518	606	425	1318	624	648	431	631	203	303

The chart on the left gives the duration in hours and minutes of a train journey between major towns in Italy by the fastest route. It is a general guide and does not allow for delays

expected to use, but confirm this by listening to announcements or asking a member of staff. If you use the self-service touch-screen ticket machines, they will give you details of the timing of your train and offer choices for different parts of the day. If you are touring Italy, it is wise to carry a train timetable such as the latest edition of the Thomas Cook European Rail Timetable, which is updated every month. Trenitalia now offers a searchable train timetable in English on its website (www. trenitalia.com/en/index.html).

GETTING ON BOARD

Station platforms throughout Italy are very low, and passenger carriages (cars) have three steps to negotiate, which can be a nuisance with large suitcases or other heavy baggage. Passengers with a disability should seek help from Trenitalia station staff in advance, to arrange for a lifting machine to help you get on board. Larger stations have a dedicated assistance office for people with disabilities, and it is wise to give 24 hours' notice of your travel arrangements.

Some long-distance InterCity trains, and most international services, are composed of carriages heading to different destinations down the line, so make sure you are in the right section of the train for your journey. Trains to Sicily, for example, are loaded on to a ferry for the short sea crossing between Villa San Giovanni and Messina, and the carriages are reassembled into separate trains heading west for Palermo and south for Taormina, Catania and Siracusa.

NIGHT TRAINS

Night trains are particularly good value for covering long distances, such as to and from Sicily. You have the choice of cabins fitted with beds *(classe)* or couchettes *(comfort)* and advance reservations are strongly recommended as these trains get full, especially in July and August. Reservations can be made through services like Rail Europe, your travel agent, or at main stations in Italy.

AIRPORT TRAIN SERVICES

Most major airports have good train connections to city centres, and trains are a much more economical option than taxis (▷ 44–45). The notable exception is Ancona, where plans to build a rail line to the airport have been delayed by protests from local taxi drivers concerned about losing lucrative business. At Turin Airport a state-of-the-art station was built as part of the modernization leading up to the 2006 Winter Olympic Games.

TRAIN CATERING

InterCity and Eurostar Italia trains usually have a restaurant car serving coffee, cold drinks, and some pre-packed convenience snacks and, at certain times, full meals. Be aware that train catering is very basic and pricey, and not all that it could be, given Italy's resources and tradition for fine food. You may prefer to stock up with your own supplies before your journey.

SECURITY

Train stations are a fertile ground for thieves and hustlers, so take special care over your possessions. Don't leave bags unattended and only accept help from uniformed employees of Trenitalia. Be alert for gangs of children and women who create a commotion to distract attention while attempting to steal from bags or pockets.

LEFT LUGGAGE

Most stations have a left-luggage (deposit) storage facility. Bear in mind that the one at Rome Termini station is often very busy, especially in the early morning when night trains from all over Italy and the rest of Europe pull in. The service is very slow and the staffing arrangements never seem to match these peak periods of demand, so allow plenty of time to deposit your bags before going around the city.

POINTS TO REMEMBER

» Smoking is not permitted inside station buildings or on board any train, even if old window stickers indicate a 'smoking' carriage. Smoking is allowed only in the open air on station platforms.
» For lost property call the station at either your departure or arrival point.
» Except for the smallest, all Italian stations have a ticket office, bookstall, bar, toilets and left luggage facilities.
» Station bars sell food to take away; in larger stations there are also trolleys selling drinks and snacks. Ask for what you want ... *da portare via* (to take away).
» Luggage trolleys (baggage carts) are few and far between. There are porters at Rome, Milan, Venice, Turin, Naples, Genoa and Bologna.
» There are occasional platform changes—check the departure board before boarding. Boards at the end of the platforms show the next train to leave.
» Train doors automatically close 30–60 seconds before departure.
» Intercity, Eurostar and Espressi trains have on-board catering and air-conditioning. Eurostar and Intercity have telephones. All trains have toilets.

DOMESTIC FLIGHTS

The main Italian cities and regional capitals all have their own airports, with daily connecting flights between them and international gateways.

Italy's national carrier, Alitalia, runs regular flights between all the major cities. In addition, there are a number of regional airlines, useful for accessing more out-of-the-way places. Internal flights within Italy make sense if you want to see a lot quickly, and are particularly useful for travelling to Sicily and Sardinia.

» You can use the internet to reserve and purchase tickets on Italy's regional airlines, as well as with Alitalia. If you don't have access to the internet, your travel agent can do this for you.
» Tickets for flights within Italy are relatively expensive (e.g. Naples–Milan costs around €160, Rome–Venice around €135), but advance reservations may secure you one of the limited number of cheap seats available on each flight. Be aware that the popular routes tend to sell out more quickly.
» Check-in times vary from 1 to 2 hours. Security can be very slow, so allow plenty of time for this.
» You will need personal identification; a passport will serve this purpose.
» Most domestic flights have no first- or business-class seats.
» Smoking is not allowed at airports except outside in the open air. There are high fines for smoking inside public buildings, and these can be increased on a scale from €27.50 to €275 if children or pregnant women are present. Smoking is not allowed

INTERNAL AIRLINES

AIRLINE	BASE	WEBSITE	DESTINATIONS
Air Dolomiti	Trieste	www.airdolomiti.it	Alghero, Ancona, Bari, Bologna, Cagliari, Genoa, Milan, Olbia, Naples, Pisa, Rimini, Trieste, Venice, Verona
Air Europe	Milan	www.aireurope.it	Bari , Milan, Naples, Palermo, Rome, Venice, Verona
Air One	Pescara	www.air-one.it	Alghero, Bari, Bologna, Brindisi, Cagliari, Catania, Crotone, Florence, Genoa, Lamezia Terme, Milan, Naples, Olbia, Palermo, Pescara, Pisa, Reggio di Calabria, Rome, Turin, Venice (seasonal: Lampedusa, Pantelleria)
Air Vallee	Aosta	www.airvallee.com	Ancona, Bari, Bologna, Brindisi, Cagliari, Catania, Florence, Genoa
Alitalia	Rome	www.alitalia.it	Lamezia Terme, Milan, Naples, Palermo, Perugia, Pisa, Reggio di Calabria, Rome, Trieste, Turin, Venice, Verona
Alpieagles	Venice	www.alpieagles.com	Cagliari, Catania, Lamezia Terme, Milan, Naples, Olbia, Palermo, Rome, Venice, Verona
Azzurra Air	Bergamo	www.azzurraair.it	Bergamo, Rome
Gandalf	Milan	www.gandalf.it	Brescia, Milan, Pisa, Rome, Verona
Meridiana	Olbia	www.meridiana.it	Bergamo, Bologna, Cagliari, Catania, Florence, Milan, Naples, Olbia, Palermo, Pisa, Rome, Turin, Venice, Verona
Volare	Vicenza	www.volare-airlines.com	Bari, Catania, Milan, Naples, Palermo, Rome, Venice

on the tarmac or on board any aircraft.
» On short trips you are offered a drink; on longer flights a light snack is served.
» Regional airports generally have the usual range of facilities and services, albeit on a small scale.

AIRPORTS NEAR POPULAR AREAS

Below is a list of popular sightseeing and holiday destinations and the airports that best serve them:
Adriatic Riviera—Ancona Raffaello Sanzio (AOI).
Calabria—Lamezia Terme (SUF).
Cinque Terre—Genova Cristoforo Colombo (GOA).
Dolomites—Verona Valerio Catullo (VRN) or Venice Marco Polo (VCE).
Florence—Firenze Amerigo Vespucci (FLR) is 4km (2.5 miles) northwest of the city, and Pisa Galileo Galilei (PSA) is 80km (50 miles) west of the city.
Lake Como—Bergamo Orio al Serio (BGY).
Lake Garda—Verona Valerio Catullo (VRN), Brescia (Verona) (VBS), Milan Linate (LIN), Milan Malpensa (MXP), Milano Orio al Serio (BGY).
Lampedusa island—Lampedusa (LMP).
Milan—Milano Linate (LIN), Milano Malpensa (MXP).
Naples, Sorrento and the Amalfi Coast—Naples Capodichino (NAP) is 6km (3.8 miles) north of the city of Naples.
The Northeast and Emilia-Romagna—Bologna Guglielmo Marconi (BLQ), Venice (VCE).
Pantelleria island—Pantelleria (PNL).
Puglia—Bari Palese (BRI).
Riviera di Levante—Genova Cristoforo Colombo (GOA).
Riviera di Ponente—Genova Cristoforo Colombo (GOA).
Rome—Rome Ciampino (CIA) is 16km (10 miles) southeast of the city, and Rome Leonardo da Vinci Fiumicino (FCO) is 36km (22 miles) southwest of the city.
Sardinia—Cagliari Mario Mameli (CAG) in the south, Alghero Fertilia (AHO) in the northwest and Olbia (OLB) in the northeast.
Sicily—Catania (CTA) in the east, Palermo Punta Raisi (PMO) in the northwest and Trapani (TPS) in the west.
Turin and the Alps—Torino Caselle (TRN) is 16km (10 miles) north of Turin and 48km (30 miles) from the Alps.
Tuscany—Pisa Galileo Galilei (PSA).
Umbria—Perugia International (PEG).
Venice—Venice Marco Polo (VCE) is 13km (8 miles) from the city.

DOMESTIC FERRIES

ISLAND FERRIES

Besides the main islands of Sardinia and Sicily, Italy has a number of smaller islands. Italians have gone

FERRIES TO ITALY'S ISLANDS

	ELBA	GIGLIO	ISOLE PONZIANE	ISCHIA
Mainland port	Piombino	Porto Santo Stefano	Anzio, Formia and others (Terracina, Naples)	Naples, Pozzuoli, Procida
Arrival port	Portoferraio	Giglio Porto	Ponza	Ischia Porto
Journey time	1 hour	1 hour	From Anzio 2 hours, Formia 2 hours 30 min, Terracina 2 hours 30 min	From Naples 1 hour 20 min; from Pozzuoli 1 hour 40 min
Ferry company	**Moby** Nuova Stazione Marittima, Piombino tel 0565 221212 Via Ninci 1, Portoferraio tel 0565 9361 www.mobylines.it **Toremar** Nuova Stazione Marittima, Piombino tel 0565 31100 Calata Italia 23, Portoferraio tel 0565 918080 www.toremar-elba.it	**Maregiglio** Via Umberto 1, Porto, Giglio tel 0564 812 920 www.maregiglio.it **Toremar** Porto Santo Stefano tel 892 123 (Italy): 00 39 081 017 1998 (from abroad) www.toremar.it	**Caremar** Via Ardeatina 114, Anzio Call centre: 892 123 (in Italy); 00 39 081 017 1998 (from abroad) www.caremar.it **Caremar** Banchina Azzurra, Formiatel 0771 22710/0771 23800	**Caremar** Molo Beverello, Napoli tel 081 551 3882 Banchina Redentore e Olimpia, Ischia Call centre: 892 123 (in Italy); 00 39 081 017 1998 (from abroad) www.caremar.it
Advanced reservations	Yes	Yes	Yes	Foot passengers no, cars yes

to these destinations for years, but now foreign visitors are beginning to discover their charms and the pleasures of their laid-back, low-key resorts. All are regularly served by ferries from the mainland, often with a choice of departure ports. Caremar is the main operator providing services to Ischia and Capri, but there are several others, all operating from the Molo Beverello in Naples. It is essential to reserve ferries and accommodation in advance in peak season (July and August). Out-of-season services are drastically reduced, or even, in the case of the more remote islands, nonexistent.
Sicily and Sardinia (▷ 47); www.traghettitalia.net

VENICE

ACTV runs a comprehensive service between the lagoon islands and the city (▷ 61).

LAKE FERRIES

Italy's most beautiful lakes are in the north, and are one of the country's most popular holiday destinations. The big names—Como, Garda and Maggiore—draw crowds throughout the summer, the majority of whom use the lake ferries to enjoy waterborne views. Ferries link the lakeside towns and are as much a useful form of transport as excursion boats. Further south, the two central Italian lakes of Bolsena and Trasimeno have pleasure boats serving their islands.

THE NORTHERN LAKES

Services on Lakes Como, Garda, Maggiore and smaller Iseo are all run by Navigazione Laghi. The service on Lake Como links Cadenabbia, Menaggio, Varenna and Bellagio, a cluster of attractive resort villages in the central part of the lake. Maggiore and Garda have a comprehensive service, with boats making stops at numerous villages on either side of the length of the lakes. The boats on Lake Maggiore cross the border and run into Switzerland. In addition, there are many cruises (including night-time) and excursions to the islands. Tickets are sold in the villages or on board; timetable information is displayed at the landing stages.

Navigazione Laghi
Via L. Ariosto 21, 20145 Milano, tel 800 551801/02 467 6101; www.navigazionelaghi.it

Lago Trasimeno
Excursions run from Castiglione del Lago and Passignano to Isola Maggiore.

Lago di Bolsena
Excursions run from Capodimonte and Bolsena to Isola Bizantina.

CAPRI	ISOLE EOLIE	ISOLE EGADI	PANTELLERIA	ISOLE PELAGIE	ISOLE TREMITI
Naples, Sorrento	Milazzo	Trápani	Trápani	Porto Empédocle	Vieste (Jun–Sep)
Marina Grande	Porto di Levante, Vulcano	Favignana	Pantelleria	Linosa, Lampedusa	San Nicola
From Naples 1 hour 15 min, from Sorrento 50 min	1 hour 30 min	1 hour	5 hours 30 min	To Linosa 5 hours 45 min, to Lampedusa 7 hours 30 min	From Manfredonia 2 hours (hydrofoil); from Vieste 1 hour (hydrofoil)
Caremar Molo Beverello, Napoli tel 081 5513882 Angelina srl, Marina Grande Capri tel 081 8370700 Dott Raniero Morelli, Piazza Marinai d'Italia, Sorrento Call centre: 892 123 (in Italy); 00 39 081 017 1998 (from abroad)	**Siremar** Catalano Viaggi, Via Luigi Rizzo 17, Milazzo tel 0909 284 509 Menaldatours, Via Vittorio Emanuele 235, Lipari tel 0909 880 159 Call centre: 892 123 (in Italy); 00 39 081 017 1998 (from abroad) www.siremar.it	**Siremar** Terminal Aliscafo, Stazione Marittima Molo Dogana, Trápani tel 0923 545455 Catalano Viaggi, Molo S. Leonardo, Favignana tel 0923 921363 Call centre: 892 123 (in Italy); 00 39 081 017 1998 (from abroad) www.siremar.it	**Siremar** Terminal Aliscafo, Stazione Marittima Molo Dogana, Trápani tel 0923 545455 Agenzia Rizzo, Via Borgo Italia 22, Pantelleria tel 0923 911120 Call centre: 892 123 (in Italy); 00 39 081 017 1998 (from abroad) www.siremar.it	**Siremar** Tricoli e Nuara, Via Molo 13 tel 0922 636683 Porto Empédocle Gaetano Cavallaro, Via Principe Umberto tel 0922 972062 Linosa, Sebastiano Strazzera, Longomare L Rizzo, Lampedusa tel 0922 970003 Call centre: 892 123 (in Italy); 00 39 081 017 1998 (from abroad) www.siremar.it	**Tirrenia** Gargano Viaggi, Piazza Roma 7, Vieste tel 0884 708501 Dita Cafiero Emilio, Via degli Abbati 10, Tremiti tel 0882 463008 Call centre: 892 123 (in Italy); 00 39 081 017 1998 (from abroad) www.tirrenia.it
No	Foot passengers no, cars yes	Foot passengers no, cars yes	Yes	Yes	Yes

GETTING AROUND IN ROME

ATAC runs Rome's public transport system, which includes the bus, tram and metro network, all frequent, cheap and reliable. You can navigate the city easily by using just a few lines.

INFORMATION

» The ATAC office is at Piazza dei Cinquecento (tel 06 57 003; Mon–Sat 8–8). Transport details, ticket information and free transport maps are available.
» Online at www.atac.roma.it.

TICKETS

Buy tickets before boarding at *tabacchi* (tobacconists), shops and bars displaying the ATAC logo. Main stops and some metro stations have automatic ticket machines. You can save money by buying an 'integrated' ticket for use on buses, trams and trains.
» *Biglietto integrato a tempo* (BIT) €1.20—valid for 75 minutes for unlimited bus and tram travel plus one metro trip.
» *Biglietto integrato giornaliero* (BIG) €4.50—valid up to midnight on the day of use for unlimited travel on buses, trams, metro, Cotral and FS trains.
» *Carta integrata settimanale* (CIS) €18—valid for a week.
» **Validate your ticket** the first time it's used. The machines are inside buses and trams and just before escalators on the metro. BIT tickets must be validated again if you are using the BIT on the metro. The fine for not validating your ticket is €51 and is strictly enforced.

BUSES

Single-decker buses cover most routes, with the historic centre served by small electric minibuses (routes 116, 117, 119). There are few seats and buses can be very crowded. Be wary of pickpockets.
» **Bus stops** *(fermata)* show the route number, the *capitolinea* (headstop where the service originates) and list the intermediate stops for buses using the stop. The stop where you are is circled.
» Bus drivers do not sell tickets, so buy a ticket before you board.

Night Buses

Services start at midnight and drop off at stops marked with a blue owl logo. Tickets are available on board.

TAXIS

There are taxi stands throughout the city centre, so it is not customary to hail a taxi as it is cruising along the street. Official metered taxis are white or yellow. The meter starts running at €2.60 7am–10pm Mon–Sat and €3.70 Sun and public holidays; €5.10 10pm–7am daily. The meter clicks around in increments of 11c approximately every 20 seconds of the journey. You can phone for a taxi on 06 3570, 06 4944, 06 551, 06 6645, 06 8822 or the central taxi office on 06 671 070 844. Radio taxis charge from the moment they are called so it's normal to find that they already have €5–€6 on the meter. Always ask the operator how long they are likely to be.

METRO (LA METROPOLITANA)

There are **two lines** which intersect at Termini, the main railway station.
» **Trains** run between 5.30am and 11.30pm (12.30am on Saturday).
» **Entrances** are marked with a large white M on a red background.
» **Ticket machines** are below street level; be sure to validate your ticket.
» **Information boards** indicate platforms.
» The metro is always very crowded. Use the route maps displayed in the carriages to find out which side the doors will open at your stop, and start working your way towards the door well before the train stops.

TRAMS

Trams are good for getting to the outskirts. The following routes are great for sightseeing:
3—Villa Borghese, Villa Giulia, modern art museum, zoo and Trastevere.
8—Trastevere.
19—Piazza del Risorgimento for San Pietro. Also serves Villa Borghese, Villa Giulia, the zoo and modern art museum.

DISCOUNTS

» Children under 10 travel free.
» Reductions for students holding ISIC cards.

ATAC have introduced the Roma Pass, a 3-day combined transport ticket and city map which gives reductions and two free entries to museums and attractions. It's on sale at Tourist Information Points; price €25, www.romapass.it

TIPS

» Be aware of pickpockets, who tend to be children or teenagers. The popular, crowded bus 64 (from Termini station to St Peter's Square) is especially notorious for pickpockets.
» Keep shoulder bags and backpacks in front of you on buses and metro trains. Groups of women acting together will sometimes cause obstruction of doors as a distraction while rifling through bags to steal money or valuables.

SIGHTSEEING TOURS OF ROME

ATAC 110 City Tour Every 30 min. Hop on and off (stop 'n' go) ticket €20

ATAC Archeobus From Piazza Venezia hourly. Circuit of archaeological sights including the Via Appia Antica and the catacombs, 2 hours, €15 (€10 with Roma Pass)

Appian Line Piazza Esquilino 6/7, tel 06 4878 6604, fax 06 481 9712

City Sightseeing Rome Red open-top buses with multilingual commentary, running on two lines—line A, departing from Via Marsala (110 mins), and line B, from Santa Maria Maggiore (80 mins); €18; tel 06 228 3957; www.city-sightseeing.com

Green Line Tours Via del Viminale, tel 06 462 0651/06 482 8647/06 4877 2253, fax: 06 4782 3335; www.greenlinetours.com

Stop 'n' Go CSR, Via Barberini 86, ticket €12, tel 06 4782 6379, fax 06 488 3167; www.romecitytours.com

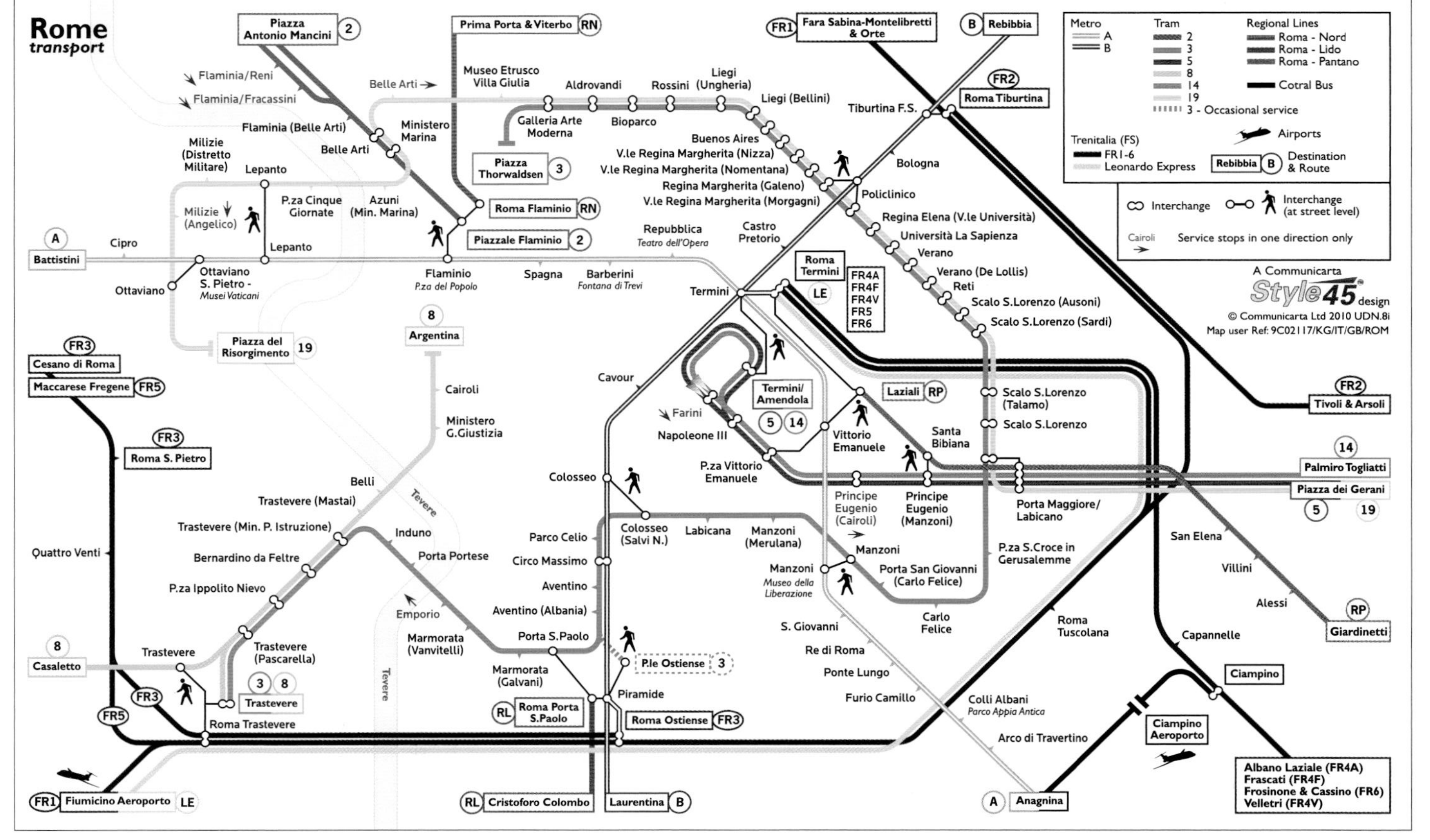
Rome
transport
Metro
A
B
Tram
2
3
5
8
14
19
3 - Occasional service
Regional Lines
Roma - Nord
Roma - Lido
Roma - Pantano
Cotral Bus
Airports
Trenitalia (FS)
FR1-6
Leonardo Express
Rebibbia B Destination & Route
Interchange
Interchange (at street level)
Cairoli
Service stops in one direction only
A Communicarta
Style45 design
© Communicarta Ltd 2010 UDN.8i
Map user Ref: 9C02117/KG/IT/GB/ROM
Piazza Antonio Mancini 2
Prima Porta & Viterbo RN
FR1 Fara Sabina-Montelibretti & Orte
B Rebibbia
FR2 Roma Tiburtina
Flaminia/Reni
Flaminia/Fracassini
Flaminia (Belle Arti)
Belle Arti
Ministero Marina
Museo Etrusco Villa Giulia
Aldrovandi
Rossini
Liegi (Ungheria)
Liegi (Bellini)
Tiburtina F.S.
Galleria Arte Moderna
Bioparco
Piazza Thorwaldsen 3
Buenos Aires
V.le Regina Margherita (Nizza)
V.le Regina Margherita (Nomentana)
Regina Margherita (Galeno)
V.le Regina Margherita (Morgagni)
Bologna
Policlinico
Regina Elena (V.le Università)
Università La Sapienza
Verano
Verano (De Lollis)
Reti
Scalo S.Lorenzo (Ausoni)
Scalo S.Lorenzo (Sardi)
Milizie (Distretto Militare)
Lepanto
P.za Cinque Giornate
Azuni (Min. Marina)
Roma Flaminio RN
Piazzale Flaminio 2
Milizie (Angelico)
A Battistini
Cipro
Ottaviano
Ottaviano S. Pietro - Musei Vaticani
Flaminio
P.za del Popolo
Spagna
Barberini
Fontana di Trevi
Repubblica
Teatro dell'Opera
Castro Pretorio
Termini
Roma Termini
LE
FR4A
FR4F
FR4V
FR5
FR6
8 Argentina
Piazza del Risorgimento 19
FR3 Cesano di Roma
Maccarese Fregene FR5
FR3 Roma S. Pietro
Cairoli
Ministero G.Giustizia
Cavour
Farini
Napoleone III
Termini/ Amendola 5 14
Laziali RP
Vittorio Emanuele
Santa Bibiana
Scalo S.Lorenzo (Talamo)
Scalo S.Lorenzo
FR2 Tivoli & Arsoli
14 Palmiro Togliatti
Piazza dei Gerani 5 19
P.za Vittorio Emanuele
Principe Eugenio (Cairoli)
Principe Eugenio (Manzoni)
Porta Maggiore/ Labicano
Belli
Trastevere (Mastai)
Trastevere (Min. P. Istruzione)
Bernardino da Feltre
P.za Ippolito Nievo
Quattro Venti
Tevere
Induno
Porta Portese
Emporio
Colosseo
Colosseo (Salvi N.)
Labicana
Manzoni (Merulana)
Manzoni
Manzoni
Museo della Liberazione
Porta San Giovanni (Carlo Felice)
P.za S.Croce in Gerusalemme
San Elena
Villini
Alessi
RP Giardinetti
Parco Celio
Circo Massimo
Aventino
Aventino (Albania)
Porta S.Paolo
Marmorata (Vanvitelli)
Marmorata (Galvani)
Pl.e Ostiense 3
Piramide
S. Giovanni
Re di Roma
Ponte Lungo
Furio Camillo
Carlo Felice
Roma Tuscolana
Capannelle
Ciampino
8 Casaletto
Trastevere
Trastevere (Pascarella)
3 8 Trastevere
Roma Trastevere
FR3
FR5
RL Roma Porta S.Paolo
Roma Ostiense FR3
Colli Albani
Parco Appia Antica
Arco di Travertino
Ciampino Aeroporto
FR1 Fiumicino Aeroporto LE
RL Cristoforo Colombo
Laurentina B
A Anagnina
Albano Laziale (FR4A)
Frascati (FR4F)
Frosinone & Cassino (FR6)
Velletri (FR4V)

GETTING AROUND IN FLORENCE

With its compact *centro storico* (historic centre) and pedestrianized streets, Florence is a city made for walking, and you'll be able to reach most of the major sights on foot. For outlying sights you can use the regular and electric buses; the latter run through the heart of Florence and are particularly useful for tourists. Electric trams are planned for the future (▷ 21), and bus routes may be subject to alterations while construction takes place.

INFORMATION

Florence's transport company, ATAF (www.ataf.net), has information desks at Piazza San Marco and Piazza della Stazione; both are open Mon–Fri 8–7, Sat 8–noon, and provide timetables, route maps and tickets. Most bus lines originate from or pass the main terminus next to Santa Maria Novella railway station, and most routes run near the Piazza del Duomo.

TICKETS

» Bus tickets are sold at ATAF offices, *tabacchi* (tobacconists), bars and all newsstands displaying the ATAF logo.
» You can buy tickets on board for an extra 80c.
» All tickets must be validated by punching the ticket in the orange machine behind the driver.

Types of Tickets

» **Single tickets**, purchased before boarding, cost €1.20 and are valid for 70 minutes. They can be purchased on board for €2. The ticket is valid for use on an unlimited number of routes during that 70 minutes and only needs to be validated the first time you board.
» **Combination tickets** are both cheaper and more convenient. A 24-hour ticket costs €5 and a 3-day pass €12; you can also buy a book of four single tickets for €4.50, or invest in a Carta Agile, a swipe card which stores 21 trips, for €20; this can be used by any number of people.
» **Children** travel free if they are less than 1m (3.28ft) tall—check their height against the line marked on the bus validation machine.

BUSES

» The *bussini ecologici* (electric single-decker buses) running through the middle of Florence are the most useful for tourists, passing close to most of the main sights. They are numbered by the letters A, B, C and D. A, B and C run north of the River Arno and D covers the south bank and the Palazzo Pitti.
» Other routes, served by ordinary buses, cover the outer areas and suburbs. Useful routes include:
12, 13—Piazzale Michelangelo.
6, 7—Museo di San Marco.
D, 36, 37—Palazzo Pitti.
12, 13—San Miniato al Monte.
» There are a limited number of night buses.

TAXIS

» Taxis in Florence are white with a yellow design.
» **The meter** is set at €3.20 when the journey starts and there is an additional charge of €1.60 per kilometre within the city limits. If you want to go further agree a price before starting your journey.
» There are various **surcharges** for late-night travel, travel to and from the airport and travel on Sundays and public holidays.
» There are **taxi ranks** at Piazza della Repubblica, Santa Maria Novella, Piazza della Stazione, Piazza del Duomo, Piazza San Marco, Piazza Santa Croce and Piazza Santa Trinità. You can hail taxis on the street when their light is illuminated.
» Your hotel can call you a taxi or contact Radio Taxis on 4390, 4798, or 4242.
» Not all taxis are suitable for people with impaired mobility; call one of the above numbers to ensure you are offered a suitable vehicle.

SIGHTSEEING TOURS

You may want to get your bearings, or simply save your legs, by using a sightseeing bus. City Sightseeing (tel 055 290 451, www.city-sightseeing.it) runs hop-on-and-off buses which cover most of the city. There are two routes; Line A starts at the railway station and Line B at San Frediano, south of the River Arno. Tickets cost €20 for adults, €10 for children aged 5–15, and €60 for a family of two adults and three children. Tickets are valid for both routes. A multilingual commentary is available. The service operates between April and September.

TIPS

» Florence is a small, compact city and you will have little need for public transport except at the start and end of your sightseeing day if you are staying outside the city centre.
» Beware of pickpockets on crowded buses, particularly the Piazzale Michelangelo and Fiesole routes.
» If you're driving through Italy, don't consider driving in Florence; much of the city is closed to cars, there is little parking and an extremely convoluted one-way system.

GETTING AROUND IN VENICE

The best way to move around Venice is on foot; this is how the Venetians themselves get from place to place, combining walking with the judicious use of public transport in the shape of *vaporetti* (water buses) and *traghetti* (cross-Grand Canal ferries). The *vaporetti* (▷ 61) can be a real help in getting round the city for newcomers, though bear in mind that time-wise, they are about the slowest means of transport, often involving complicated routes and changes of boats.

WALKING

Venice is a small city with a few main through routes that link the city's main focus points. These routes are signposted by yellow signs, above head height, indicating the way to five central hubs: San Marco, the Rialto, the Accademia, Ferrovia (the train station), and Piazzale Roma, where the causeway over to the mainland starts.

VAPORETTI (BOATS)

Until you get your city bearings, the public transport boats or water buses, *vaporetti*, run by ACTV, are a lifeline, depositing you, from all over the city and lagoon, back on the familiar territory of the streets surrounding your hotel. Boats run up and down the Grand Canal, round the outskirts of the city and out to the lagoon islands.

Vaporetti run to strict timetables, which are clearly displayed at all stops; you can also get a full timetable from ticket offices at the main departure *imbarcaderi* (landing stages). On the main routes, services start around 5am and run to midnight or just after. Then a regular night service (N), following the route of the number 82, takes over. During the day, the No. 1 and No. 82 run every 10 minutes; the 41, 42, 51, 52, and 62 every 20 minutes; and the DM, LN and T half-hourly. Numbers and final destinations are clearly displayed on a board by the entrance gangway.

TICKETS

For tourists, by far the best ticketing option is to invest in one of ACTV's *biglietti a tempo* (travel cards). These are valid for 24, 48 or 72 hours and cost respectively €16, €26 and €31. They can be purchased at ACTV/VeLa's main office at Piazzale Roma, the ticket booths at main stops and *tabacchi* showing the ACTV logo. If the ticket is not already validated, you must do so by inserting it into the orange punch box at the *imbarcadero*. Validity starts from the moment it is punched. A single ticket for one trip costs €6.50 and must be purchased before boarding.

TRAGHETTI

Traghetti (gondola ferries) ply back and forth from one side of the Grand Canal to the other at seven fixed points. They are the best way of crossing from one side of the Grand Canal to the other if you're a distance from a bridge; they're also a bargain way to experience a gondola ride and a quintessential Venetian experience. The service is run by the gondoliers' cooperative in conjunction with the city council; fares are a flat 50c per crossing.

WATER TAXIS

For moving to and from the airport and getting around the city quickly, water taxis, seating up to eight people, are a solution. They are organized by the Cooperativa San Marco, which operates the services both from stands and via a telephone switchboard; they are inordinately expensive and you can expect to pay between €90–€120 for the trip into Venice from the airport; shorter, city-centre rides will cost almost the same. Taxis charge a night supplement between 10pm and 7am of €8.

Information: tel 041 240 7611
Bookings: tel 041 522 2303; www.motoscafi.com

GONDOLAS

Gondolas today are almost solely used for tourist rides, covering either the Bacino di San Marco and some side canals, or a section of the Grand Canal and some smaller *rii* (Venetian for canals). Fares are set by the Istituzione per la conservazione della gondola e tutela del gondoliere (Gondola Board, tel 041 528 5075; www.gondolavenezia.it). Gondolas can carry up to six passengers; there are no reductions for fewer numbers. Expect to pay €80 8am–8pm for 50 minutes, plus €40 for every 25 minutes thereafter. The price rises to a princely €115 8pm–8am for 50 minutes, plus €50 for every 25 minutes thereafter.

GETTING AROUND IN OTHER MAJOR CITIES

MILAN

www.atm-mi.it

Milan has an efficient integrated transport system comprising trams, buses and a metro. The metro is the easiest and fastest option, though you may have to combine it with a bus or tram.

Metro: There are four lines: red MM1, green MM2, yellow MM3 and blue *passante ferroviario*. These intersect at the hub stations of Stazione Centrale, Duomo, Cadorna and Loreto.

Buses and trams: Routes cover the whole city and the follow the metro routes overground.

Tickets: A single (€1) is valid for 75 minutes from validation and can be used across the entire system for as many bus and tram trips as you want and one metro journey. A book of 10 tickets costs €9.20, and 1- and 2-day travel cards (€3 and €5.50) are also available. Tickets are sold at *tabacchi*, bars, newsstands and metro stations. The network runs from 6am to 12.30am, with night buses continuing until 1.30am.

NAPLES

www.campaniatrasporti.it

Naples is a big, congested city where the best option is generally to walk. You'll have to use the public transport system to reach outlying areas and sights around the Bay of Naples, though. There are several integrated options run by ANM—buses, the Metropolitana, funiculars within the city and three suburban rail systems.

Buses: The best option for short journeys, though they are often crowded and can be very slow in heavy traffic.

The Metropolitana: This is under expansion to cover more of the city.

Funiculars: These run up the hill of the Vomero.

Out-of-town trains: The Circumvesuviana train runs around the bay to Pompei and Sorrento; the Ferrovia Cumana runs west to Pozzuoli and Baia; the Circumflegrea goes to Cuma.

Tickets: Single tickets (€1) are valid for 90 minutes and allow any combination of bus and tram rides plus unlimited travel on two additional forms of transport. Tickets are sold at *tabacchi*, stations and the ANM booth on Piazza Garibaldi, which also has timetables and route maps. A 24-hour pass is available for €2.60.

As in so many countries, the overall picture of facilities for people with disabilities in Italy is mixed. The major problems are often not with transport, accommodation or public buildings, but in the layout and nature of the cities and towns themselves. The historic interest and architectural beauty of many of the main tourist attractions in Italy inevitably make access a challenge. Things are progressing, particularly with regard to public transport and access to museums and galleries, but visitors with disabilities, particularly the wheelchair-bound, will often find that it is not easy getting there in the first place. Italians are generally helpful, but, with some key exceptions, facilities have not yet caught up with those in northern European countries and North America.

» If you have a disability, it is especially important to plan carefully, particularly if you will be travelling on your own. One option is to reserve your holiday with a specialist tour operator.

» Contact your airline in advance of your date of travel. They will let the airports know what assistance you will need.

» Trains sometimes have wheelchair access, and this is indicated on the timetable by a wheelchair symbol. If you need assistance at the station, contact them 24 hours in advance.

» Taxis can take wheelchairs folded and stored in the boot (trunk), but Italian taxis are saloon (sedan)-type cars and getting in and out may be difficult.

» If you are driving, you can use your blue Disabled Person's Parking Badge in Italy.

» Be aware that many streets in historic towns are cobbled and can be very steep.

» Major pedestrian crossings in cities have a sound signal for the visually impaired.

» An increasing number of public places and some museums have information in braille.

» Reserve well in advance and be specific about your requirements when reserving accommodation.

» For a more relaxed trip to Italy, use a car to explore rural areas and the smaller picturesque towns and villages.

VENICE

Venice poses particular problems for wheelchair users, but, with judicious planning, you will be able to see plenty. *Vaporetti* (▷ 61) can take wheelchairs, and some of the major sights are accessible from the *vaporetto* stops without having to negotiate bridges. Facilities inside some museums and galleries are good, and there are hotels and restaurants where you will have no problems.

The tourist office publishes a map with routes suitable for wheelchairs, and four main bridges in the *sestiere* (district) of San Marco have automated ramps; access keys are available from the tourist office. For more information contact Informahandicap (▷ below for contact information).

USEFUL CONTACTS

ATAC DISABLED SERVICES
ATAC manages and provides information on Rome's public transport system.
☎ 800 469540 ⌚ Daily 8–2.30

INFORMAHANDICAP
For excellent information (in Italian but with good maps and useful numbers) for travellers with disabilities in Venice, go to: www.comune.venezia.it or email them via the website

CO.IN SOCIALE (COOPERATIVE INTEGRATE ONLUS)
www.coinsociale.it
CO.IN plans and promotes the building of accessible public spaces in Rome and produces a list of sights that have disabled access.
✉ Via Enrico Giglioli 54, 00185 Roma
☎ 06 232 69231/800 271027 (Italian only)

UNIONE ITALIANA DEI CIECHI (ITALIAN SOCIETY FOR THE BLIND)
www.uiciechi.it (in Italian only)
✉ Unione Italiana dei Ciechi, Via Borgognona 38, 00187 Roma ☎ 06 699881, fax 06 678 6815

SATH (SOCIETY FOR ACCESSIBLE TRAVEL AND HOSPITALITY)
www.sath.org
Lots of useful travel tips for American holiday-makers who are visually impaired or have a disability.

ACCESSIBLE ITALY (REGENCY SAN MARINO SRL)
www.accessibleitaly.com
An Italian travel company that run tours for visitors with disabilities. Local contacts give the company the edge over many foreign operators.
✉ Via C. Manetti 34, 47891 Dogana Borgo-maggiore, Repubblica di San Marino 47031
☎ 0549 941111, fax 0549 907189

REGIONS

This chapter is divided into nine regions of Italy (▷ 8–9). Region names are for the purposes of this book only, and places of interest are listed alphabetically in each region.

Italy's Regions 64–418

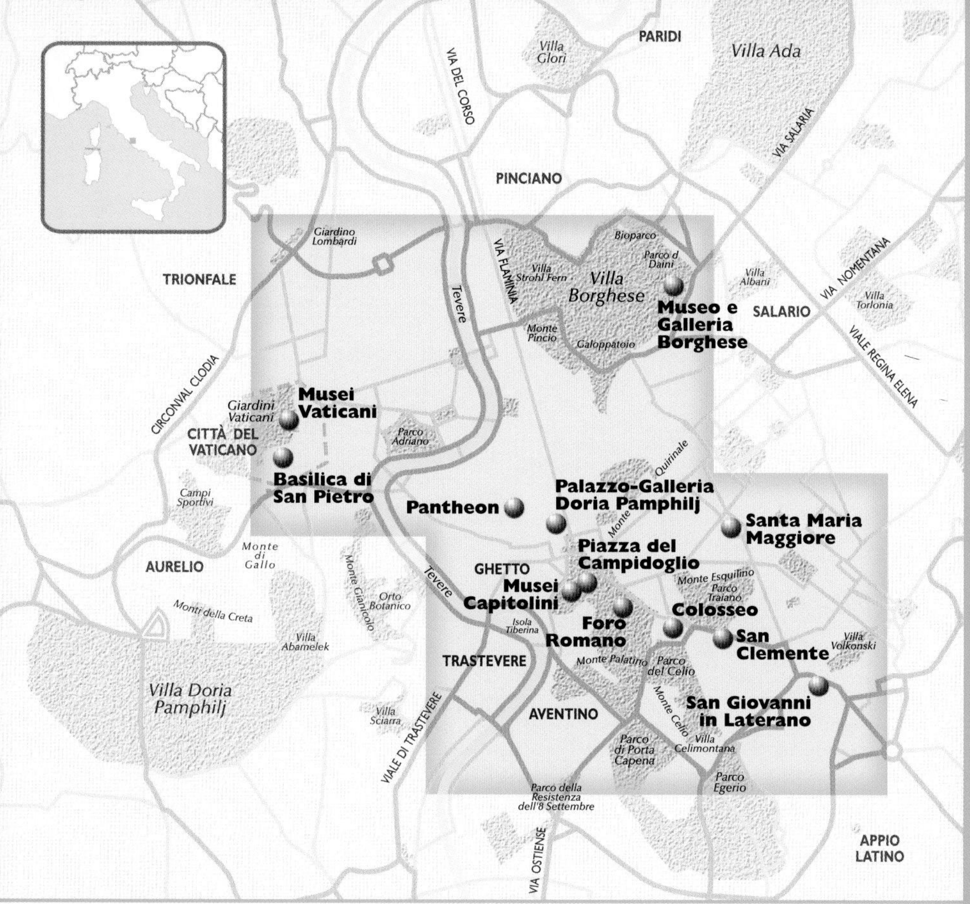

ROME

Rome (Roma), capital of Italy and home to the Vatican, is redolent with 3,000 years of history and packed with monuments, museums, galleries and churches, making it a treasure house of art, architecture and culture. At the same time it's also a thriving city with some of Italy's best shopping, dining and entertainment choices. It's this combination, and Rome's sheer physical beauty, that make it a truly compelling destination.

The city stands on the River Tiber (Tevere) midway between the north and south of the country. Famously built across seven hills, its buildings span the centuries from the days of classical Rome to the 21st century. The area east of the Tiber is roughly bissected by the Via del Corso, which arrows through from the grandiose Piazza del Popolo to the Piazza Venezia, a spacious square dominated by the vast 'wedding cake' of the Victor Emmanuel Monument. South from here is the Forum, the Colosseum, the triumphal arches and the ruins of the ancient buildings that formed the heart of classical Rome. Between the Corso and the river is the *centro storico,* the medieval core, an appealing mix of narrow medieval streets, Renaissance palaces and fine squares and fountains. East of the Corso, there are more historic buildings and some of the city's oldest and most venerable churches, while to the north the beautiful Villa Borghese gardens are a hill-top oasis of green containing some of Rome's best museums. West across the Tiber lies the Vatican, the Pope's separate city state, with its huge St. Peter's Basilica and the fabulous Vatican Museums, and the artisan neighbourhood of Trastevere, now more noted for nightlife and restaurants. There are shopping areas throughout the city, the classiest being clustered around the Piazza di Spagna, a beautiful square backed by the famous Spanish Steps, and Rome is also home to some of the country's best markets.

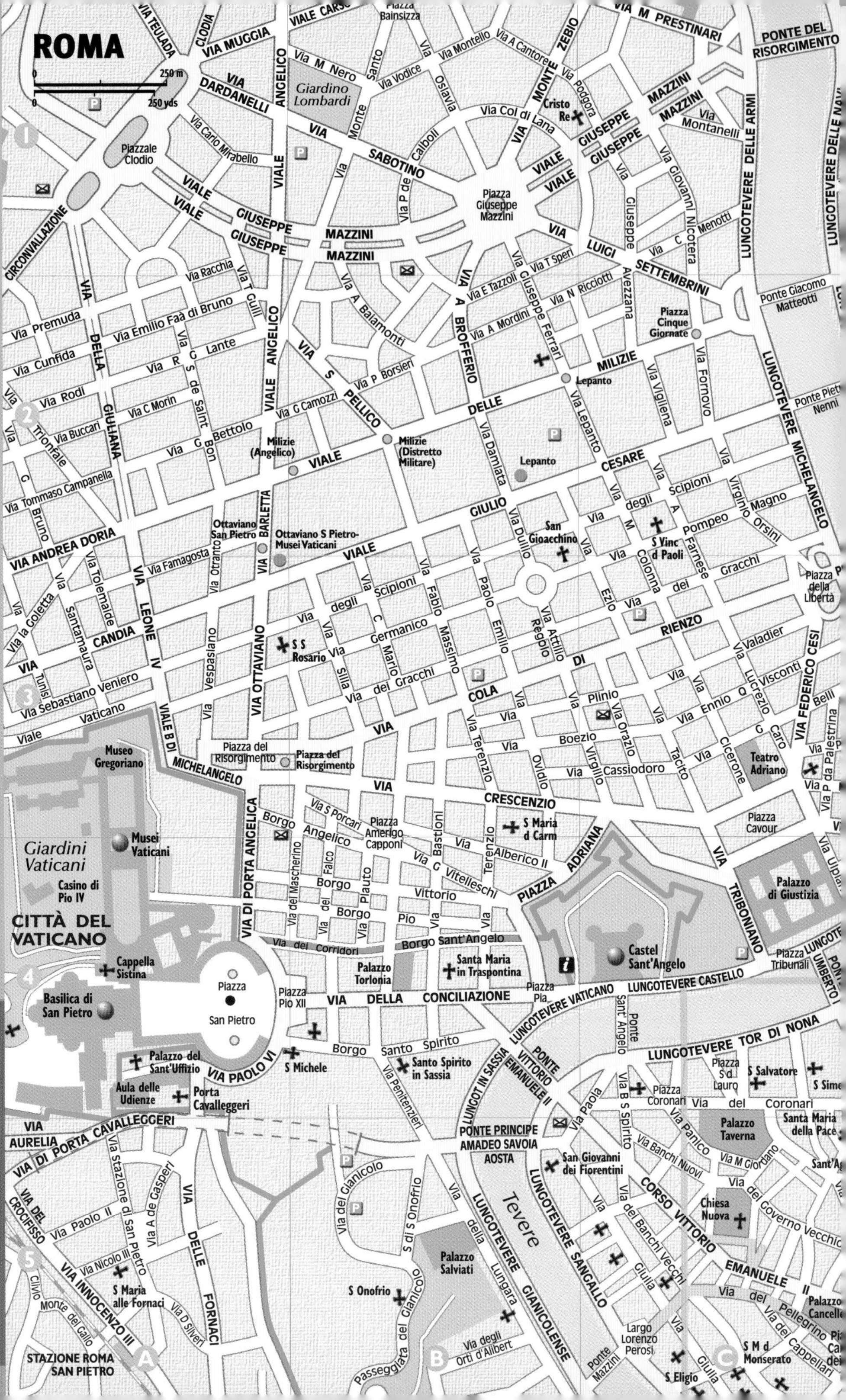
ROMA
0 250 m
0 250 yds
VIA TEULADA
CLODIA
VIA MUGGIA
VIALE CARSO
Piazza Bainsizza
VIA M PRESTINARI
PONTE DEL RISORGIMENTO
VIA DARDANELLI
VIALE ANGELICO
Via M Nero
Giardino Lombardi
Monte Santo
Via Vodice
Oslavia
Via Montello
Via A Cantore
MONTE ZEBIO
Via Podgora
Cristo Re
MAZZINI
GIUSEPPE
Via Montanelli
LUNGOTEVERE DELLE ARMI
LUNGOTEVERE DELLE NAVI
Piazzale Clodio
Via Carlo Mirabello
VIA SABOTINO
Via P de Calboli
Via Col di Lana
Piazza Giuseppe Mazzini
VIA LUIGI SETTEMBRINI
Via Giovanni Nicotera
Via Giuseppe Avezzana
Via C Menotti
CIRCONVALLAZIONE
VIALE GIUSEPPE MAZZINI
Via Racchia
Via T Gulli
VIA DELLA GIULIANA
Via Premuda
Via Emilio Faà di Bruno
Via Cunfida
Via R G Lante
Via Rodi
Via C Morin
Via de Saint Bon
Via Buccari
Via Trionfale
Via G Bettolo
Via G Camozzi
Via A Baiamonti
VIA S PELLICO
Via P Borsieri
VIA A BROFFERIO
Via E Tazzoli
Via Giuseppe Ferrari
Via T Speri
Via N Ricciotti
Via A Mordini
MILIZIE
Lepanto
Piazza Cinque Giornate
Via Fornovo
Via Vigliena
Via Lepanto
LUNGOTEVERE MICHELANGELO
Ponte Giacomo Matteotti
Ponte Pietro Nenni
Milizie (Angelico)
Milizie (Distretto Militare)
VIALE DELLE MILIZIE
Via Damiata
Lepanto
VIALE GIULIO CESARE
Via Tommaso Campanella
Via G Bruno
VIA ANDREA DORIA
Ottaviano San Pietro
VIA BARLETTA
Ottaviano S Pietro-Musei Vaticani
Via Famagosta
Via Otranto
Via Dulio
San Gioacchino
S Vinc d Paoli
Via degli Scipioni
Via M Colonna
Via A Farnese
Pompeo Magno
Via Virginio Orsini
Via dei Gracchi
Piazza della Libertà
Via la Goletta
Via Tolemaide
Via Santamaura
VIA LEONE IV
VIA CANDIA
Via Vespasiano
VIA OTTAVIANO
S S Rosario
Via Silla
Via C Mario
Via Germanico
Via Fabio Massimo
Via Paolo Emilio
Via Attilio Regolo
Via Ezio
VIA COLA DI RIENZO
Via Valadier
Via Lucrezio Caro
Via Q Visconti
VIA FEDERICO CESI
Via Tunisi
Via Sebastiano Veniero
Viale Vaticano
VIALE B DI MICHELANGELO
Via Plinio
Via Orazio
Via Ennio
Via Boezio
Via Terenzio
Via Ovidio
Via Virgilio
Via Cassiodoro
Via Tacito
Via Cicerone
Teatro Adriano
Via Belli
Via Palestrina
Via P da Palestrina
Museo Gregoriano
Piazza del Risorgimento
VIA CRESCENZIO
Piazza Cavour
Giardini Vaticani
Musei Vaticani
VIA DI PORTA ANGELICA
Borgo Angelico
Via S Porcari
Piazza Amerigo Capponi
Via Bastioni
S Maria d Carm
Via Alberico II
PIAZZA ADRIANA
VIA TRIBONIANO
Palazzo di Giustizia
Via Ulpiano
Casino di Pio IV
Via del Mascherino
Via del Falco
Via Plauto
Borgo Vittorio
Via G Vitelleschi
Borgo Pio
CITTÀ DEL VATICANO
Via dei Corridori
Borgo Sant'Angelo
Castel Sant'Angelo
Piazza Tribunali
LUNGOTEVERE
UMBERTO I
Cappella Sistina
Piazza San Pietro
Palazzo Torlonia
Santa Maria in Traspontina
Piazza Pia
LUNGOTEVERE CASTELLO
Basilica di San Pietro
Piazza Pio XII
VIA DELLA CONCILIAZIONE
LUNGOTEVERE VATICANO
Ponte Sant'Angelo
Borgo Santo Spirito
LUNGOTEVERE TOR DI NONA
Palazzo del Sant'Uffizio
VIA PAOLO VI
S Michele
Santo Spirito in Sassia
Via Penitenzieri
PONTE VITTORIO EMANUELE II
LUNGOT IN SASSIA
Piazza S d Lauro
S Salvatore
Piazza Coronari
Via dei Coronari
Aula delle Udienze
Porta Cavalleggeri
Via B S Spirito
Via Paola
Via Panico
Palazzo Taverna
Santa Maria della Pace
VIA AURELIA
VIA DI PORTA CAVALLEGGERI
PONTE PRINCIPE AMADEO SAVOIA AOSTA
San Giovanni dei Fiorentini
Via Banchi Nuovi
Via M Giordano
Sant'Agostino
Via Stazione di San Pietro
Via del Gianicolo
Via di S Onofrio
Via della Lungara
CORSO VITTORIO EMANUELE II
Via del Governo Vecchio
Chiesa Nuova
VIA DEL CROCIFISSO
Via Paolo II
Via A de Gasperi
VIA DELLE FORNACI
Palazzo Salviati
Tevere
LUNGOTEVERE GIANICOLENSE
LUNGOTEVERE SANGALLO
Via dei Banchi Vecchi
Via Giulia
Via Nicolò III
S Maria alle Fornaci
VIA INNOCENZO III
Via Cilvio
Monte del Gallo
Via D Silveri
S Onofrio
Passeggiata del Gianicolo
Via degli Orti d'Alibert
Largo Lorenzo Perosi
Ponte Mazzini
Via del Pellegrino
Via dei Cappellari
Palazzo Cancelleria
S M d Monserato
S Eligio
STAZIONE ROMA SAN PIETRO
1
2
3
4
5
A
B
C

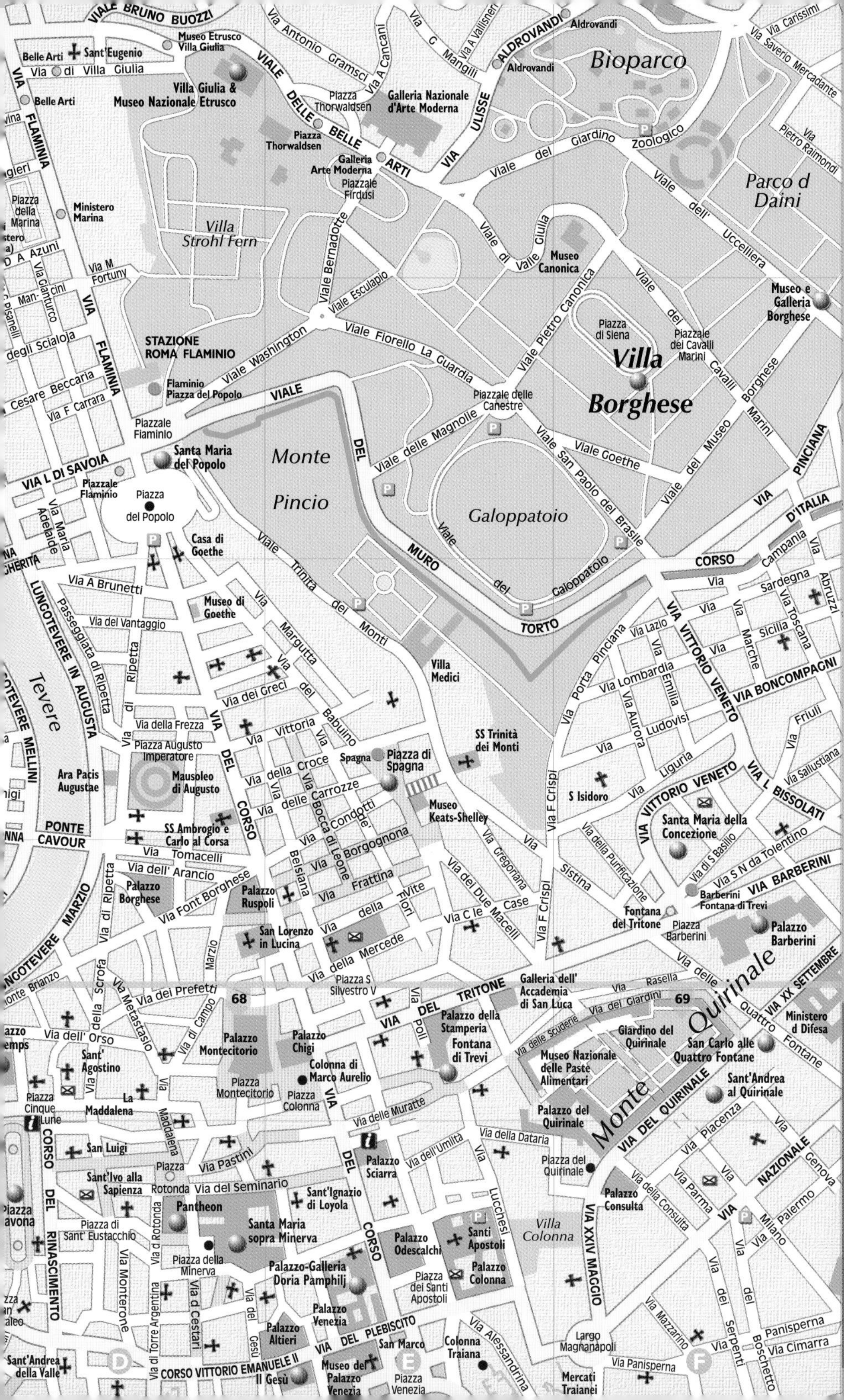

VIALE BRUNO BUOZZI
Museo Etrusco Villa Giulia
Belle Arti
Sant'Eugenio
Via di Villa Giulia
Villa Giulia & Museo Nazionale Etrusco
VIALE DELLE BELLE ARTI
Via Antonio Gramsci
Via A Cancani
Via G Mangili
Via A Vallisneri
VIA ULISSE ALDROVANDI
Aldrovandi
Bioparco
Via Carissimi
Via Saverio Mercadante
Via Pietro Raimondi
Piazza Thorwaldsen
Galleria Nazionale d'Arte Moderna
Galleria Arte Moderna
Piazzale Firdusi
Viale del Giardino Zoologico
Viale dell' Uccelliera
Parco di Daini
VIA FLAMINIA
Piazza della Marina
Ministero Marina
Lungotevere A Azuni
Via M Fortuny
Via Gianturco
Via Mancini
Via Pisanelli
Villa Strohl Fern
Viale Bernadotte
Viale Esculapio
Viale di Valle Giulia
Museo Canonica
Viale Pietro Canonica
Viale dei Cavalli Marini
Museo e Galleria Borghese
Piazza di Siena
Piazzale dei Cavalli Marini
Villa Borghese
Via degli Scialoja
STAZIONE ROMA FLAMINIO
Viale Washington
Viale Fiorello La Guardia
Via Cesare Beccaria
Via F Carrara
Flaminio Piazza del Popolo
Piazzale Fiaminio
Piazzale delle Canestre
Viale delle Magnolie
Viale Goethe
Viale San Paolo del Brasile
Viale del Museo Borghese
Santa Maria del Popolo
VIA L DI SAVOIA
Piazzale Flaminio
Piazza del Popolo
Via Maria Adelaide
Monte Pincio
VIALE DEL MURO TORTO
Galoppatoio
Viale del Galoppatoio
VIA PINCIANA
CORSO D'ITALIA
Via Campania
Via Abruzzi
Casa di Goethe
Viale Trinità dei Monti
Via Sardegna
Via Toscana
Via Sicilia
Via Marche
Via A Brunetti
Lungotevere in Augusta
Passeggiata di Ripetta
Museo di Goethe
Via Margutta
Via Lazio
Via Emilia
VIA VITTORIO VENETO
Via del Vantaggio
Via Porta Pinciana
Via Lombardia
Via Aurora
VIA BONCOMPAGNI
Tevere
Via di Ripetta
Via dei Greci
Via del Babuino
Villa Medici
Via Ludovisi
Via Friuli
Lungotevere Mellini
Via della Frezza
Via Vittoria
SS Trinità dei Monti
Via Sallustiana
Piazza Augusto Imperatore
VIA DEL CORSO
Via della Croce
Spagna
Piazza di Spagna
Via Liguria
VIA L BISSOLATI
Ara Pacis Augustae
Mausoleo di Augusto
Via delle Carrozze
Via Bocca di Leone
Via Condotti
Museo Keats-Shelley
Via F Crispi
S Isidoro
Santa Maria della Concezione
PONTE CAVOUR
SS Ambrogio e Carlo al Corsa
Via Borgognona
Via Sistina
Via della Purificazione
Via di S Basilio
Via S N da Tolentino
Via Tomacelli
Via dell' Arancio
Via Belsiana
Via Frattina
Via Gregoriana
VIA BARBERINI
LUNGOTEVERE MARZIO
Palazzo Borghese
Via Font Borghese
Palazzo Ruspoli
Via della Vite
Via dei Due Macelli
Via Capo le Case
Barberini Fontana di Trevi
Fontana del Tritone
Piazza Barberini
Palazzo Barberini
San Lorenzo in Lucina
Via della Mercede
Via Quattro Fontane
VIA XX SETTEMBRE
Via della Scrofa
Via Metastasio
Via dei Prefetti
Piazza S Silvestro V
VIA DEL TRITONE
Galleria dell' Accademia di San Luca
Via Rasella
Via dei Giardini
Monte Quirinale
68
69
Via dell' Orso
Via di Campo Marzio
Palazzo Montecitorio
Palazzo Chigi
Via Poli
Palazzo della Stamperia
Via delle Scuderie
Giardino del Quirinale
San Carlo alle Quattro Fontane
Ministero d Difesa
Sant' Agostino
Colonna di Marco Aurelio
Fontana di Trevi
Museo Nazionale delle Paste Alimentari
Sant'Andrea al Quirinale
Piazza Cinque Lune
La Maddalena
Piazza Montecitorio
Piazza Colonna
VIA DEL CORSO
Via delle Muratte
Palazzo del Quirinale
VIA DEL QUIRINALE
CORSO DEL RINASCIMENTO
Via Maddalena
Via della Dataria
San Luigi
Via Pastini
Via dell' Umiltà
Via Piacenza
Via Genova
VIA NAZIONALE
Piazza
Palazzo Sciarra
Piazza del Quirinale
Sant'Ivo alla Sapienza
Rotonda
Via del Seminario
Sant'Ignazio di Loyola
Via della Consulta
Via Parma
Palazzo Consulta
Piazza Navona
Pantheon
Santa Maria sopra Minerva
Via Lucchesi
Villa Colonna
VIA XXIV MAGGIO
Via Palermo
Via Milano
Piazza di Sant' Eustacchio
Via d Rotonda
Palazzo Odescalchi
Santi Apostoli
Palazzo Colonna
Piazza della Minerva
Palazzo-Galleria Doria Pamphilj
Piazza dei Santi Apostoli
Via Monterone
Via d Cestari
Via del Gesù
Via dei Serpenti
Via del Boschetto
Via di Torre Argentina
Palazzo Venezia
Palazzo Altieri
VIA DEL PLEBISCITO
Via Alessandrina
Via Mazzarino
Largo Magnanapoli
Via Panisperna
Via Cimarra
Sant'Andrea della Valle
D
CORSO VITTORIO EMANUELE II
Il Gesù
Museo del Palazzo Venezia
San Marco
E
Piazza Venezia
Colonna Traiana
Via Panisperna
Mercati Traianei
F

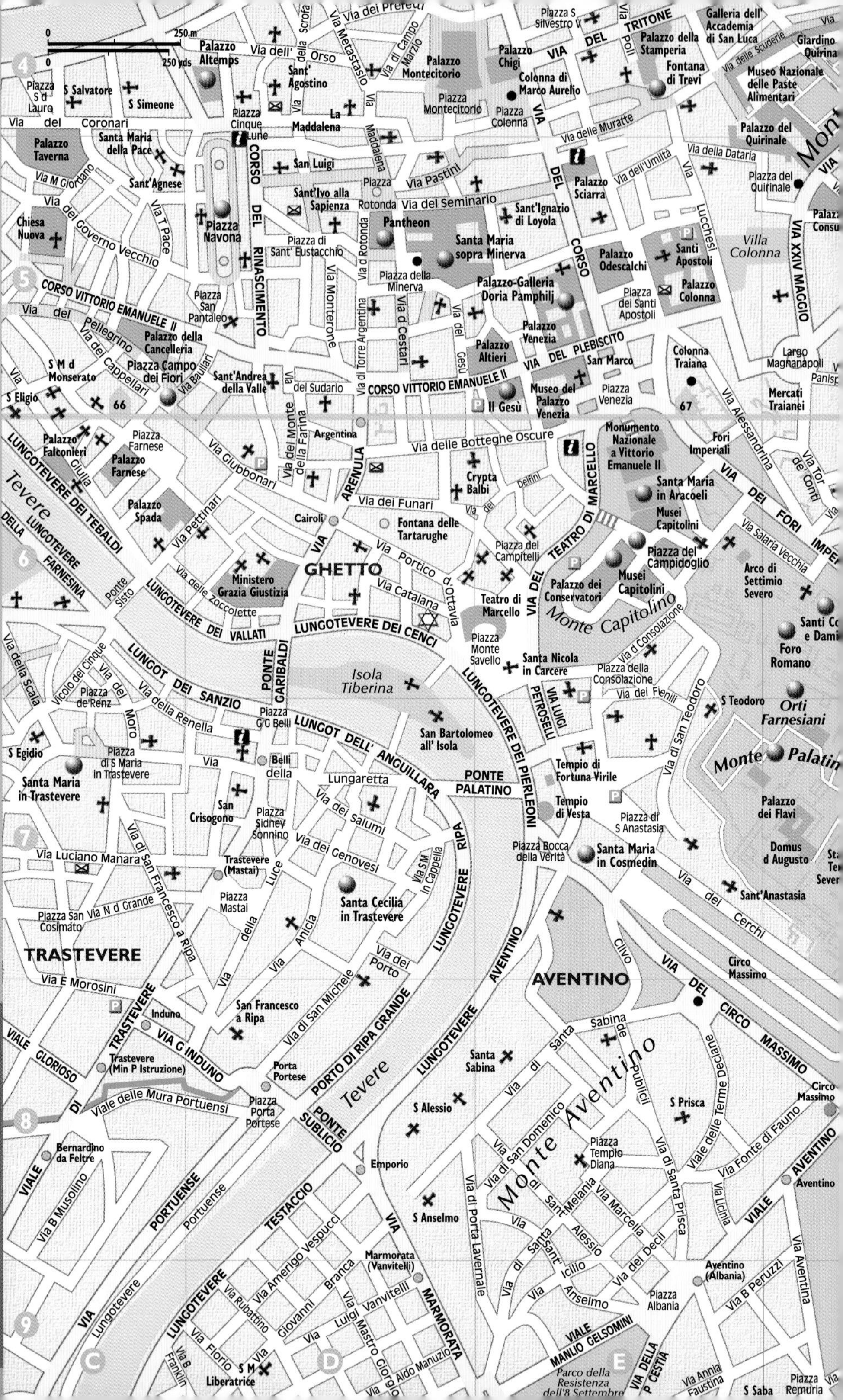

0 250 m
0 250 yds

4
Palazzo Altemps
Via dell' Orso
Via della Scrofa
Via Metastasio
Via dei Prefetti
Via di Campo Marzio
Palazzo Montecitorio
Piazza Montecitorio
Palazzo Chigi
Colonna di Marco Aurelio
Piazza Colonna
Piazza S Silvestro
VIA DEL TRITONE
Via Poli
Palazzo della Stamperia
Fontana di Trevi
Galleria dell' Accademia di San Luca
Via delle Scuderie
Giardino Quirinale
Museo Nazionale delle Paste Alimentari
Palazzo del Quirinale
Piazza del Quirinale
Via della Dataria
Via delle Muratte
VIA DEL CORSO
Piazza S d Lauro
S Salvatore
S Simeone
Sant' Agostino
La Maddalena
Via Maddalena
Piazza Cinque Lune
Via del Coronari
Palazzo Taverna
Santa Maria della Pace
Sant'Agnese
Via M Giordano
CORSO DEL RINASCIMENTO
San Luigi
Sant'Ivo alla Sapienza
Piazza Rotonda
Via Pastini
Via del Seminario
Sant'Ignazio di Loyola
Palazzo Sciarra
Via dell'Umiltà
Via Lucchesi
Mont
Chiesa Nuova
Via del Governo Vecchio
Via T Pace
Piazza Navona
Piazza di Sant' Eustacchio
Via d Rotonda
Pantheon
Santa Maria sopra Minerva
Piazza della Minerva
Palazzo Odescalchi
Santi Apostoli
Villa Colonna
VIA XXIV MAGGIO
Palazzo Consulta
5
CORSO VITTORIO EMANUELE II
Via del Pellegrino
Via dei Cappellari
Piazza San Pantaleo
Via Monterone
Via di Torre Argentina
Via d Cestari
Via del Gesù
Palazzo-Galleria Doria Pamphilj
Piazza dei Santi Apostoli
Palazzo Colonna
Palazzo della Cancelleria
Piazza Campo dei Fiori
Via Baullari
S M d Monserato
Sant'Andrea della Valle
Via del Sudario
Palazzo Altieri
Palazzo Venezia
VIA DEL PLEBISCITO
San Marco
Colonna Traiana
Largo Magnanapoli
Via Panisperna
S Eligio
66
Via del Monte della Farina
Il Gesù
Museo del Palazzo Venezia
Piazza Venezia
67
Mercati Traianei
Via Alessandrina
Palazzo Falconieri
Via Giulia
Piazza Farnese
Palazzo Farnese
Via Giubbonari
Argentina
VIA ARENULA
Via delle Botteghe Oscure
Monumento Nazionale a Vittorio Emanuele II
Fori Imperiali
Via Tor de' Conti
LUNGOTEVERE DEI TEBALDI
Tevere
Palazzo Spada
Crypta Balbi
Via dei Delfini
VIA DEL TEATRO DI MARCELLO
Santa Maria in Aracoeli
Musei Capitolini
VIA DEI FORI IMPERIALI
Via dei Funari
Cairoli
Fontana delle Tartarughe
Via Pettinari
LUNGOTEVERE DELLA FARNESINA
6
Piazza del Campitelli
Piazza del Campidoglio
Via Salaria Vecchia
Via Portico d'Ottavia
GHETTO
Ministero Grazia Giustizia
Via delle Zoccolette
Ponte Sisto
Via Catalana
Arco di Settimio Severo
Teatro di Marcello
Palazzo dei Conservatori
Musei Capitolini
Monte Capitolino
Santi Cosma e Damiano
LUNGOTEVERE DEI VALLATI
LUNGOTEVERE DEI CENCI
Via d Consolazione
Foro Romano
Piazza Monte Savello
Santa Nicola in Carcere
Via della Scala
Vicolo del Cinque
Via del Moro
LUNGOT DEI SANZIO
PONTE GARIBALDI
Isola Tiberina
LUNGOTEVERE DEI PIERLEONI
Piazza della Consolazione
Via dei Fienili
S Teodoro
Orti Farnesiani
Piazza de'Renz
Via della Renella
Piazza G G Belli
LUNGOT DELL' ANGUILLARA
San Bartolomeo all' Isola
VIA LUIGI PETROSELLI
Via di San Teodoro
S Egidio
Piazza di S Maria in Trastevere
Via della Lungaretta
Belli
Tempio di Fortuna Virile
Monte Palatino
Santa Maria in Trastevere
San Crisogono
Via dei Salumi
PONTE PALATINO
Tempio di Vesta
Piazza di S Anastasia
Palazzo dei Flavi
Piazza Sidney Sonnino
Via dei Genovesi
7
Via Luciano Manara
Via di San Francesco a Ripa
Trastevere (Mastai)
Via S M in Cappella
LUNGOTEVERE RIPA
Piazza Bocca della Verità
Santa Maria in Cosmedin
Domus d Augusto
Stadio Terme Severiane
Piazza San Cosimato
Via N d Grande
Piazza Mastai
Via della Luce
Santa Cecilia in Trastevere
Via dei Cerchi
Sant'Anastasia
TRASTEVERE
Via Anicia
Via dei Porto
LUNGOTEVERE AVENTINO
Clivo
Via E Morosini
VIALE TRASTEVERE
San Francesco a Ripa
Via di San Michele
PORTO DI RIPA GRANDE
AVENTINO
VIA DEL CIRCO MASSIMO
Circo Massimo
Induno
VIA G INDUNO
Via di Santa Sabina
Via de Publicii
VIALE GLORIOSO
DI
Trastevere (Min P Istruzione)
Porta Portese
Tevere
LUNGOTEVERE AVENTINO
Santa Sabina
S Prisca
Viale delle Terme Deciane
Circo Massimo
8
Viale delle Mura Portuensi
Piazza Porta Portese
PONTE SUBLICIO
S Alessio
Via di San Domenico
Monte Aventino
Piazza Tempio Diana
Via di Santa Prisca
Via Fonte di Fauno
VIALE AVENTINO
Aventino
Bernardino da Feltre
VIALE
Via B Musolino
PORTUENSE
Portuense
Emporio
TESTACCIO
Via di Porta Lavernale
Via di Sant Melania
Via Marcella
Via Licinia
S Anselmo
Via Amerigo Vespucci
VIA MARMORATA
Marmorata (Vanvitelli)
Via di Sant Alessio
Via dei Decii
Aventino (Albania)
Via B Peruzzi
Via Aventina
Via di Santa Sabina
Via Icilio
Via Anselmo
Piazza Albania
9
VIA Lungotevere
LUNGOTEVERE
Via Rubattino
Via Giovanni Branca
Via Luigi Vanvitelli
Via Mastro Giorgio
Via Fiorio
Via B Franklin
S M Liberatrice
Via Aldo Manuzio
VIALE MANLIO GELSOMINI
Parco della Resistenza dell'8 Settembre
VIA DELLA P CESTIA
Via Annia Faustina
S Saba
Piazza Remuria
C
D
E

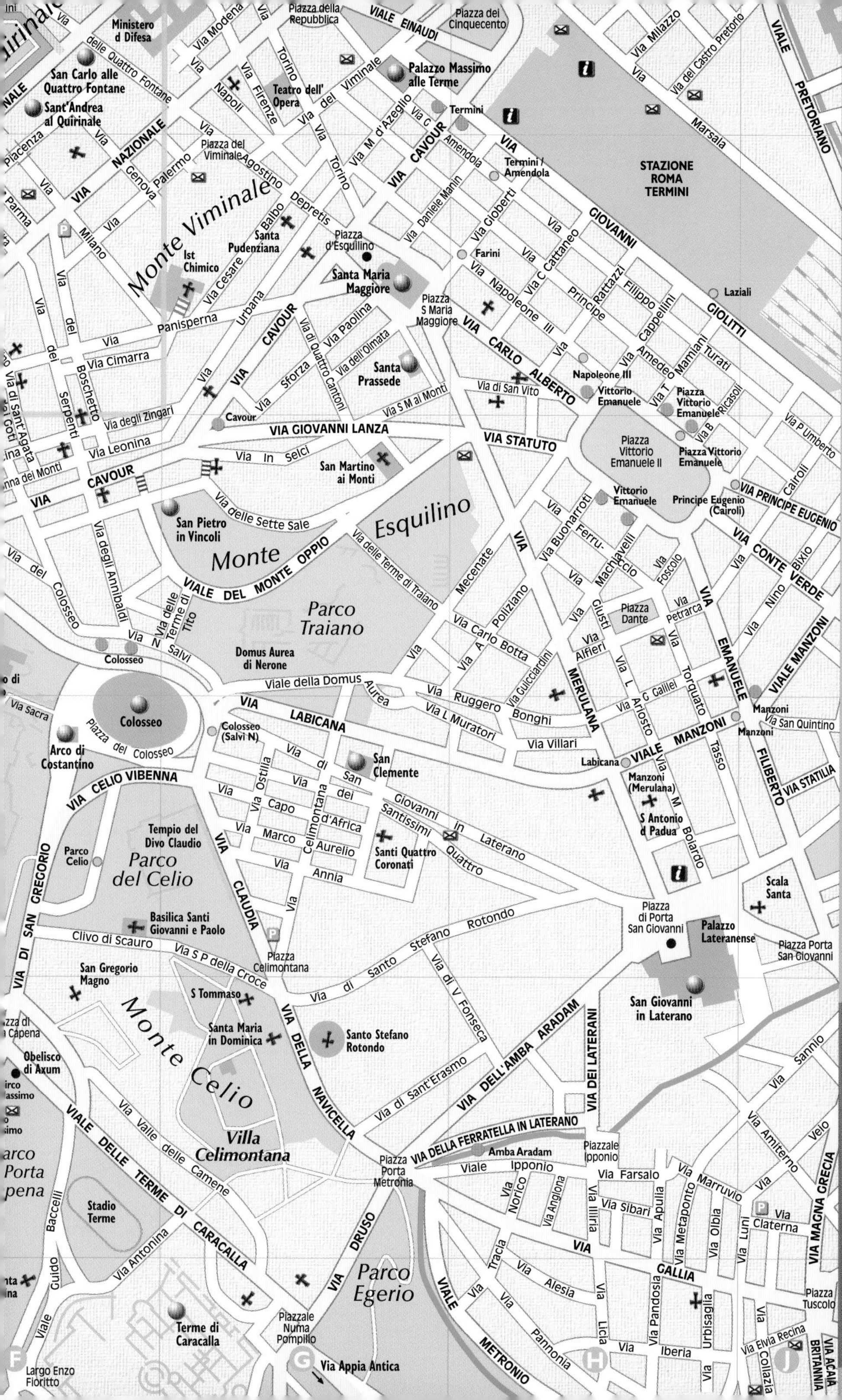

Quirinale
Ministero d Difesa
San Carlo alle Quattro Fontane
Sant'Andrea al Quirinale
Via delle Quattro Fontane
Via Nazionale
Via Modena
Piazza della Repubblica
Viale Einaudi
Piazza dei Cinquecento
Palazzo Massimo alle Terme
Teatro dell' Opera
Via del Viminale
Via Torino
Via Napoli
Via Firenze
Via Genova
Via Palermo
Piazza del Viminale
Via Agostino Depretis
Via Milano
Via Piacenza
Via Parma
Monte Viminale
Ist Chimico
Santa Pudenziana
Via Cesare Balbo
Via Urbana
Via Panisperna
Via Cimarra
Via dei Serpenti
Via del Boschetto
Via degli Zingari
Via Leonina
Via di Sant'Agata dei Goti
Via Madonna dei Monti
Via Cavour
Cavour
Termini
Via C
Via M d'Azeglio
Via Amendola
Termini / Amendola
Via Daniele Manin
Via Gioberti
Piazza d'Esquilino
Santa Maria Maggiore
Piazza S Maria Maggiore
Via Paolina
Via di Quattro Cantoni
Via dell'Olmata
Via Sforza
Santa Prassede
Via S M ai Monti
Via Giovanni Lanza
Via In Selci
San Martino ai Monti
Via di San Vito
Via Carlo Alberto
Via Statuto
Farini
Via Farini
Via Napoleone III
Via C Cattaneo
Via Principe Amedeo
Via Rattazzi
Via Filippo Turati
Via Cappellini
Via Mamiani
Napoleone III
Vittorio Emanuele
Piazza Vittorio Emanuele
Piazza Vittorio Emanuele II
Via Ricasoli
Via B
Via P Umberto
Via Cairoli
Via Principe Eugenio
Principe Eugenio (Cairoli)
Laziali
Via Giovanni Giolitti
Stazione Roma Termini
Via Marsala
Via Milazzo
Via del Castro Pretorio
Viale Pretoriano
San Pietro in Vincoli
Via delle Sette Sale
Monte Oppio
Esquilino
Viale del Monte Oppio
Via delle Terme di Traiano
Parco Traiano
Domus Aurea di Nerone
Viale della Domus Aurea
Via degli Annibaldi
Via del Colosseo
Via delle Terme di Tito
Via N Salvi
Colosseo
Colosseo (Salvi N)
Via Sacra
Piazza del Colosseo
Arco di Costantino
Via Mecenate
Via Buonarroti
Via Ferruccio
Via Machiavelli
Via Foscolo
Via Merulana
Via Poliziano
Via Carlo Botta
Via A
Via Ruggero Bonghi
Via L Muratori
Via Guicciardini
Via Giusti
Piazza Dante
Via Alfieri
Via Petrarca
Via Torquato Tasso
Via G Galilei
Via L Ariosto
Via Emanuele Filiberto
Via Conte Verde
Via Bixio
Via Nino
Viale Manzoni
Manzoni
Via San Quintino
Via Villari
Labicana
Via Labicana
Manzoni (Merulana)
Via M Boiardo
S Antonio d Padua
Via Statilia
Via Celio Vibenna
San Clemente
Via di San Giovanni in Laterano
Via Ostilia
Via Capo d'Africa
Via Celimontana
Via Marco Aurelio
Via Annia
Via dei Santissimi Quattro
Santi Quattro Coronati
Tempio del Divo Claudio
Parco Celio
Parco del Celio
Via Claudia
Basilica Santi Giovanni e Paolo
Clivo di Scauro
Via S P della Croce
Piazza Celimontana
Via di Santo Stefano Rotondo
Via di V Fonseca
Piazza di Porta San Giovanni
Palazzo Lateranense
Scala Santa
Piazza Porta San Giovanni
San Giovanni in Laterano
Via di San Gregorio
San Gregorio Magno
S Tommaso
Santa Maria in Dominica
Monte Celio
Santo Stefano Rotondo
Via della Navicella
Via dell'Amba Aradam
Via dei Laterani
Via di Sant'Erasmo
Piazza di Porta Capena
Obelisco di Axum
Circo Massimo
Parco di Porta Capena
Villa Celimontana
Via Valle delle Camene
Viale delle Terme di Caracalla
Via della Ferratella in Laterano
Amba Aradam
Piazzale Ipponio
Viale Ipponio
Piazza Porta Metronia
Via Sannio
Via Amiterno
Via Veio
Via Marruvio
Via Farsalo
Via Norico
Via Angiona
Via Illiria
Via Sibari
Via Apulia
Via Metaponto
Via Olbia
Via Luni
Via Claterna
Via Magna Grecia
Stadio Terme
Via Baccelli
Via Antonina
Via Druso
Parco Egerio
Viale Metronio
Via Tracia
Via Alesia
Via Gallia
Via Licia
Via Pannonia
Via Pandosia
Via Urbisaglia
Via Iberia
Piazza Tuscolo
Via Elvia Recina
Via Collazia
Via Acaia
Via Britannia
Viale Guido Baccelli
Santa Balbina
Terme di Caracalla
Piazzale Numa Pompilio
Via Appia Antica
Largo Enzo Fioritto
F
G
H
J

ROME STREET INDEX

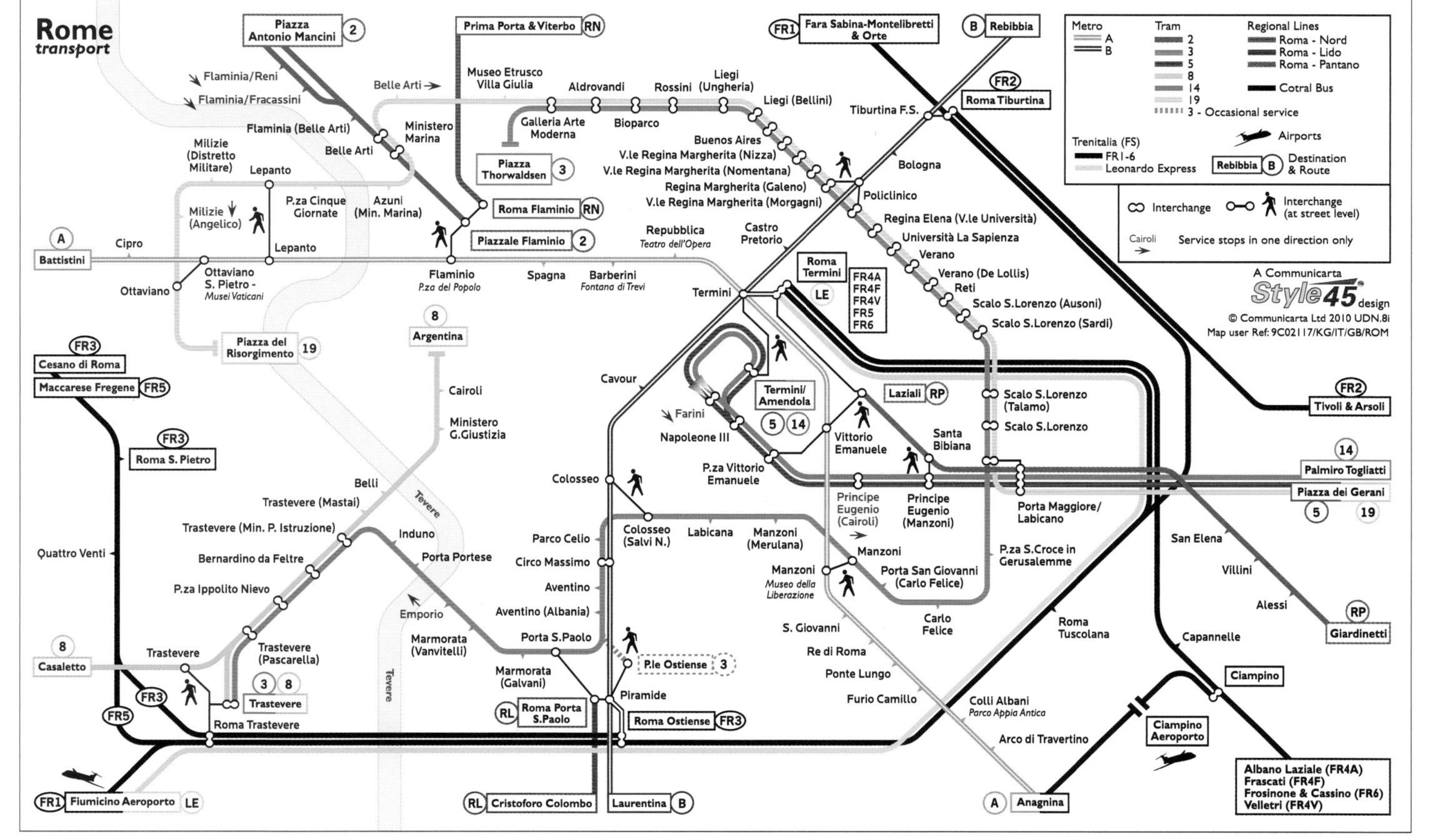
Rome
transport
Metro
A
B
Tram
2
3
5
8
14
19
3 - Occasional service
Regional Lines
Roma - Nord
Roma - Lido
Roma - Pantano
Cotral Bus
Trenitalia (FS)
FR1-6
Leonardo Express
Airports
Rebibbia B Destination & Route
Interchange
Interchange (at street level)
Cairoli
Service stops in one direction only
A Communicarta
Style45 design
© Communicarta Ltd 2010 UDN.8i
Map user Ref: 9C02117/KG/IT/GB/ROM
Piazza Antonio Mancini 2
Prima Porta & Viterbo RN
FR1 Fara Sabina-Montelibretti & Orte
B Rebibbia
FR2 Roma Tiburtina
FR2 Tivoli & Arsoli
14 Palmiro Togliatti
Piazza dei Gerani 5 19
RP Giardinetti
Ciampino
Ciampino Aeroporto
Albano Laziale (FR4A)
Frascati (FR4F)
Frosinone & Cassino (FR6)
Velletri (FR4V)
A Anagnina
Laurentina B
RL Cristoforo Colombo
FR1 Fiumicino Aeroporto LE
8 Casaletto
FR3 Cesano di Roma
Maccarese Fregene FR5
FR3 Roma S. Pietro
A Battistini
Flaminia/Reni
Flaminia/Fracassini
Flaminia (Belle Arti)
Belle Arti
Belle Arti
Ministero Marina
Museo Etrusco Villa Giulia
Aldrovandi
Rossini
Liegi (Ungheria)
Liegi (Bellini)
Galleria Arte Moderna
Bioparco
Piazza Thorwaldsen 3
Buenos Aires
V.le Regina Margherita (Nizza)
V.le Regina Margherita (Nomentana)
Regina Margherita (Galeno)
V.le Regina Margherita (Morgagni)
Tiburtina F.S.
Bologna
Policlinico
Regina Elena (V.le Università)
Università La Sapienza
Verano
Verano (De Lollis)
Reti
Scalo S.Lorenzo (Ausoni)
Scalo S.Lorenzo (Sardi)
Milizie (Distretto Militare)
Lepanto
Milizie (Angelico)
P.za Cinque Giornate
Azuni (Min. Marina)
Roma Flaminio RN
Piazzale Flaminio 2
Cipro
Lepanto
Ottaviano S. Pietro - Musei Vaticani
Ottaviano
Flaminio P.za del Popolo
Spagna
Barberini Fontana di Trevi
Repubblica Teatro dell'Opera
Castro Pretorio
Termini
Roma Termini
LE
FR4A
FR4F
FR4V
FR5
FR6
Piazza del Risorgimento 19
8 Argentina
Cairoli
Ministero G.Giustizia
Cavour
Farini
Napoleone III
Termini/ Amendola 5 14
Laziali RP
Vittorio Emanuele
Santa Bibiana
Scalo S.Lorenzo (Talamo)
Scalo S.Lorenzo
P.za Vittorio Emanuele
Principe Eugenio (Cairoli)
Principe Eugenio (Manzoni)
Porta Maggiore/ Labicano
Colosseo
Colosseo (Salvi N.)
Labicana
Manzoni (Merulana)
Manzoni
Manzoni Museo della Liberazione
Porta San Giovanni (Carlo Felice)
P.za S.Croce in Gerusalemme
San Elena
Villini
Alessi
Capannelle
Roma Tuscolana
Carlo Felice
S. Giovanni
Re di Roma
Ponte Lungo
Furio Camillo
Colli Albani Parco Appia Antica
Arco di Travertino
Belli
Trastevere (Mastai)
Trastevere (Min. P. Istruzione)
Bernardino da Feltre
P.za Ippolito Nievo
Trastevere
Trastevere (Pascarella)
3 8 Trastevere
Roma Trastevere
Quattro Venti
FR3
FR5
Induno
Porta Portese
Tevere
Tevere
Tevere
Emporio
Marmorata (Vanvitelli)
Parco Celio
Circo Massimo
Aventino
Aventino (Albania)
Porta S.Paolo
Marmorata (Galvani)
RL Roma Porta S.Paolo
P.le Ostiense 3
Piramide
Roma Ostiense FR3

IVSSV CLEMENTIS·XIII·PONT·MAX
SOLVTVM

ARCO DI COSTANTINO

The Romans used triumphal arches to commemorate the victories they called 'triumphs', where over 5,000 of the enemy were killed. They went up either at the scene of the victory or in Rome itself, and the Arco di Costantino was the last of these monumental constructions, forming a trio with those of Titus (AD70) and Septimius Severus (AD203), which you'll see in the same area of the Forum. Constantine's arch was built in AD315 to commemorate the battle of Ponte Milvio (AD312). The Christian emperor, fighting under the banner of the new god, defeated his pagan rival Maxentius and was able to declare Christianity the new religion of people and emperor alike. It went up in a hurry, the builders cutting corners by using older sculptural reliefs from monuments around the city as decoration. Look at the reliefs between the statues, and you can see where figures were altered to resemble Constantine rather than earlier emperors. The overall effect however is magnificent, and it's worth remembering that this arch is the direct ancestor of London's Marble Arch and the Arc de Triomphe in Paris.

69 F7 Piazza del Colosseo, Roma Colosseo 60, 75, 85, 87, 175; tram 3, 117

BASILICA DI SAN PIETRO

▷ 74–75.

CASTEL SANT'ANGELO

In AD135 the Emperor Hadrian, builder of Britain's northern Roman boundary wall, commissioned the construction of his mausoleum. It was finished after his death; 200 years later the capital moved to Constantinople and in 410 Rome was sacked by the Goths, the defenders holding out in this vast and fortress-like mausoleum. In 610 the Castel got its present name, when the people of Rome, decimated by plague, saw a vision of the Archangel Michael sheathing his sword on top of the building as, led by Pope Gregory the Great, they processed in prayer for deliverance. Since then, the building has served as prison, fortress and papal residence, undergoing alterations and adaptations for its changing roles. It still retains Hadrian's original ramped spiral entrance, while elsewhere its delights include sumptuous Renaissance frescoed reception rooms, a beautiful chapel in the Cortile d'Onore, designed by Michelangelo, and the *passetto*, a covered walkway which links Castel Sant'Angelo to the Vatican and was designed as a papal escape route. Castel Sant' Angelo houses part of the Museo Nazionale Romano and also stages temporary exhibitions.

66 C4 Lungotevere Castello 50, 00120 Roma 06 681 9111; 06 399 967600 (information) Tue–Sun 9–7. Prison: Sun by guided tour Adult €7, under 18s free Ottaviano–San Pietro

COLOSSEO

▷ 76–77.

FONTANA DI TREVI

Immortalized in Federico Fellini's 1960 film *La Dolce Vita*, this is unquestionably the most photographed fountain in Rome, and has stood here, at the junction of three roads *(tre vie)*, since 1762.

In the middle, Neptune rides a shell-shaped chariot drawn by seahorses steered by giant tritons. Behind is a baroque facade with statues of Plenty, Health and the Four Seasons. In 19BC, General Agrippa built a 19km (12-mile) aqueduct to bring water to the baths near the Pantheon (▷ 90). The story is told in bas-reliefs: on the right a young girl leads Agrippa's soldiers to a spring; on the left he approves plans for the aqueduct. Today the water, called Acqua Virgo, runs underground through one of the few Roman canals still in use.

Toss a coin over your shoulder into the fountain, make a wish and, it is said, you will return to Rome and your wish will come true.

67 E4 Piazza Trevi, 00187 Roma Barberini

FORO ROMANO

▷ 78–79.

IL GESÙ

For fans of the baroque, the highlight of this church, dedicated to the Holy Name of Jesus and completed in 1584, is the chapel of St. Ignatius of Loyola. He lived, died and founded his Jesuit order here, and this chapel is the work of the architect Andrea Pozzo.

68 E5 Piazza del Gesù/Via degli Astalli 16, 00186 Roma 06 697001 Daily 6–12.30, 4–8. Loyola's chapel: Mon–Sat 4–6, Sun 10–12 46, 62, 63, 64, 70, 81, 87; tram 8

Opposite *The illuminated Fontana di Trevi*
Below *Approaching Castel Sant'Angelo across the Ponte Sant'Angelo*

INFORMATION

www.vatican.va

66 A4 Piazza San Pietro, 00120 Roma 06 6988 2019/1662 Basilica: Apr–Sep daily 7–7; Oct–Mar 7–6. Cupola: Apr–Sep daily 8–6; Oct–Mar 8–5 (1 hour before closing, access by elevator only). Museo del Tesoro: Apr–Sep daily 9–6.30; Oct–Mar 9–5.30. Grottoes: Apr–Sep daily 9–5; Oct–Mar 8–5. Necropolis: Mon–Sat 9–3.30. Visits must be requested 2 weeks in advance in writing to Uffizio degli Scavi di San Pietro, tel 06 6988 5318, fax 06 6987 3017. Basilica closed during papal celebrations Basilica: free. Dome: from €8. Museo del Tesoro: €8. Grottoes: free. Necropolis: €12 (includes guide). Free tickets for papal ceremony at main entrance Ottaviano–San Pietro 23, 40Exp, 62, 64 Tours: €5. Groups with reservation. No private tours before 10.30am (tel 06 6988 1662) Via della Conciliazione, Borgo Pio

Above *A view of St. Peter's from across the Piazza San Pietro (a large crowd waits to hear the Pope speak at a free audience on Wednesday mornings)*

INTRODUCTION

Familiar from so many images, the Basilica di San Pietro (St. Peter's Basilica) is grandeur on a monumental scale, the ultimate physical expression of the power and riches of the Catholic Church. It was here, in about AD67, that Emperor Nero had the Apostle Peter crucified, and it was over his tomb, now lying deep beneath the building, that Constantine built the first basilica in AD324. Today's vast building is its successor, and this, the largest Roman Catholic church in the world, is the work of the string of architects employed on its construction from 1547 until 1626. Michelangelo is the most famous; apppointed by Pope Paul III in 1547, he visualized a design based on the Greek cross and topped by a huge dome. His dome still dominates the exterior, but his design was changed to that of a Latin cross. Carlo Maderno was responsible for the interior and portico, while the glorious baroque touches and the encircling colonnade are mainly the work of Bernini.

So perfect are the proportions that, approaching along the Via della Conciliazione, built by Mussolini after the establishment of the independent Vatican State, it is hard to fully appreciate the scale of the complex. The interior is 218m (715ft) long, with the roof above soaring to 137m (450ft). The great feasts of the church see over 60,000 people easily accommodated inside, all dwarfed by the height of the 778 columns, the gilt and marble surrounding the 44 altars, the glitter of the 135 mosaics and the scale of the 395 gesticulating statues. Overwhelming, powerful, opulent and mesmerizing, it's a long way from Christianity's humble beginnings in the hills of Galilee.

WHAT TO SEE

THE PORTICO

The approach to the basilica is impressively grand, through the embrace of Bernini's colonnade (284 columns and 140 statues). The obelisk in the middle of the square was brought here by Caligula from Alexandria in Egypt. As you reach

Bernini's broad staircase, note the central balcony above the portico on your right, the Loggia delle Benedizioni, where the Pope stands to bless the people gathered in the square below. Inside the portico, the last bronze door on the right is the Holy Door, opened only every 25 years, in a Holy Year (the last was 2000). Over the central door is what remains of Giotto's *Navicella* mosaic (1298).

Above *Sun sets over the most famous of churches*

MICHELANGELO'S PIETÀ

The most famous of all the statues in the basilica, now protected by bulletproof glass, is in the first chapel in the south aisle. Michelangelo's *Pietà* was begun in 1498, when he was 24 years old. It is his only signed work; he engraved his name on a band across the Virgin's breast, but later regretted his pride and vowed not to do it again. Look up to see his other contribution to the building, the vast dome, covered in mosaics and gilded stucco.

BERNINI'S SCULPTURES

Directly under Michelangelo's dome is Bernini's *baldacchino*, an amazing bronze canopy 29m (50ft) high. Its twisted columns are decorated with golden olive and laurel branches and bees, the emblem of the Barberini, the family of Pope Urban VIII. It stands over the Altar of the Confession, where only the Pope may celebrate Mass.

Beneath this is St. Peter's tomb, lit by 99 lamps, and to the right sits a statue of St. Peter (attributed to Arnolfo di Cambio from the late 1220s), his right foot worn by the touch of pilgrims. Behind the *baldacchino*, in the end apse, are Bernini's baroque monument to Pope Urban VIII and his extraordinary *cattedra*, which encases a chair that was supposedly used by St. Peter.

At the top of the north aisle, past the Cappella della Colonna—dedicated to St. Leo, who persuaded Attila the Hun to spare Rome—is a chapel containing the monument to Alexander VII, by Bernini, portraying Death as a skeleton. Past many more papal monuments, and almost back at the portico, is the baptistery. The basin is made from an ancient porphyry sarcophagus taken from the tomb of Hadrian.

THE GROTTOES AND THE DOME

Under one of the dome's great supporting pillars is the entrance to the Vatican grottoes, which are lined with tombs of emperors and popes. To climb the dome, take the elevator to the cupola and terrace, then climb the 330 steps for a closer look at the mosaics. The final ascent, via a spiral staircase, takes you to the top of the lantern, from where you can marvel at the panoramic views of Rome.

Below La Pietà, *Michelangelo's sculpture of the Virgin Mary and Christ*

INFORMATION

www.pierreci.it
www.archeorm.arti.beniculturali.it
69 F7 Piazza del Colosseo, 00184 Roma 06 3996 7700 Daily 9am to 1 hour before sunset Adult €9, EU youths (18–24) €4.50, under 18s free. Timed tickets: Palatino and Colosseo valid 24 hours. Roma Archaeologia Card valid 7 days for Colosseo, Palatino, Baths of Caracalla, Palazzo Altemps, Palazzo Massimo, Baths of Diocletian, Crypta Balbi, Tomb of Cecilia Metella and Villa dei Quintili, €20 Colosseo (line B) Tram 3, 8 Tours €5: Apr–Oct daily on the hour 9–5; Nov–Mar on the hour 9–3. Audiotours, €4 Official guide published by the Soprintendenza dei Beni Culturali

Above *The Colosseum is made entirely out of travertine and split into three tiers, each with 80 arches, and an attic*

INTRODUCTION

The ancestor of every modern sports stadium, the Colosseo (Colosseum) stands in the heart of classical Rome, a little to the east of the Forum and encircled by the Caelian, Palatine and Esquiline hills. It was built by the three Flavian emperors, Vespasian, Titus and Domitian, and was initially known as the Flavian Amphitheatre in their honour. Building started in AD72 and progressed fast enough for games to be held in the partially completed arena eight years later. It was the first permanent amphitheatre to be built in Rome, brilliantly combining a design grandiose enough to impress the people with a practicality that could move 70,000 spectators in or out of the building in a matter of minutes.

It got its present name in the eighth century, when the English monk, the Venerable Bede, referred to it as the Colosseum. He probably heard the name from Christian pilgrims returning from Rome, and it derives either from the size of the structure or from the huge statue of Nero that once stood nearby. It was indeed colossal; games were held there right up to the end of the Roman Empire in the sixth century and it was later used as a fortress. The start of the Renaissance in the 15th century saw it take on a new role, as builders used it as an ideal source of ready-prepared building materials for some of the city's finest palazzi. By the late 1700s, the crumbling structure was a romantic and overgrown ruin, dedicated in 1750 as a Christian shrine commemorating the martyrs killed in its arena.

WHAT TO SEE

THE EXTERIOR

The elliptical structure covers about 2.4ha (6 acres), and enough survives of the exterior to give a good idea of its original appearance, though the marble facings, painted stucco and statues have all gone. Externally, the Colosseo measures 188m by 156m (617ft by 512ft) and rises to 48m (159ft), with a facade of three tiers of arches and an attic. The tiers are faced with three-quarter Doric, Ionic and

Corinthian columns, and the attic has square window openings. At the top were 240 brackets and sockets that anchored the *velarium*, a shade and bad-weather canopy that could be pulled across the interior. The holes you see on the walls once held the metal clamps that pinned the massive blocks together; they were pillaged, together with tons of stone, for later building.

THE ARCADES AND SEATING

Inside, arcades run right around the outer edge of the building on each level, linking the stairways that connect the different floors. Passages from the arcades accessed, via 80 doorways, the tiers of marble benches, some still complete. The spectators were arranged by rank, with humble citizens and women at the top, a special box, closest to the action, naturally, for the emperor, and ringside seats for the senators and Vestal Virgins (▷ 31). The tickets, which were wooden plaques, carved with the entrance numbers, are still visible above the exterior arches. The system was very efficient, and the organizers could move up to 70,000 people in or out very quickly.

THE ARENA

The middle of the Colosseo is a jumble of ruins, all that's left of the labyrinthine passages beneath the arena itself. In Roman times, this area had wooden flooring covered with canvas and sand—the word 'arena' comes from the Latin word meaning sand. The four principal entrances were used by the gladiators, stagehands and corpse removers. Far more dramatic entrances were made through trapdoors in the floor—you can still see their outlines. These opened into the passages and lifts from where men and wild animals emerged—tens of thousands of animals, sent to Rome from all over the Empire, were slaughtered at the Colosseo. Other passages were water conduits, and the arena was regularly flooded for water battles.

Gladiatorial games began in the morning with an elaborate procession, the prelude to staged hunts when wild animals were pitted against each other or pursued by *bestiarii*, gladiators specializing in animal slaughter. The lunch break was accompanied by executions, a taster for the day's climax—the individual gladiatorial combats.

Below *Rome's number one landmark is the largest monument of imperial Rome*

INFORMATION

www.capitolium.org
www.pierreci.it
68 F6 Via dei Fori Imperiali, Via Sacra, Via di San Teodoro, Via di San Gregorio (entrance to the Palatino), 00186 Roma 06 3996 7700 Foro and Palatino: daily 9am to 1 hour before sunset Foro: free. Palatino: €9, 18–24 years (EU nationals) €4, under 18s (EU nationals) free. Tickets valid for Palatino and Colosseo. Timed tickets: Palatino and Colosseo valid 24 hours Colosseo Tram 3 Foro: €3.50; daily at 10.30 in English

Above *Tempio di Saturno in the Forum*

INTRODUCTION

It takes a vivid imagination to visualize the Foro Romano (Roman Forum) in its heyday, when this expanse of jumbled ruins and grassy space was the hub of daily life in the capital of the world's largest empire. It still stands in the heart of the city, just behind the looming Victor Emmanuel monument in Piazza Venezia, and below the Capitoline and Palatine hills. Through its heart runs the ancient Via Sacra, the Sacred Way, and it's bounded to the right by the Arco di Settimio Severo and to the left by the Arco di Tito; the chief sights lie between these two.

The Forum's origins as a focal point are ancient; it was important to the pre-Roman Etruscans who drained what was then marshy land to build a temple here to their harvest god in 49BC, and adopted the site as the centre of their social, civic and political life. The Romans, in their rise to power, took it over and expanded it, transforming it physically with temples, triumphal arches and basilicas, and expanding its civic role to encompass the judiciary, commerce, trade and banking of the ever-growing empire. It was here that the tribunes, the men who planned the future of the empire, met, and here too, that the ordinary citizens gathered, the Forum serving their needs much as the piazza in modern Italian towns serves its citizens in the 21st century. By the second century BC space was running out for more building in this cramped area, and in 54BC Julius Caesar built the first of a series of new administrative centres, the Fori Imperiali. With the government and banking moving out, and commerce moving to the new Mercati Traianei round the corner, the Forum's glory days were waning and the area steadily declined. Like the Colosseum, it proved useful to Renaissance stone workers, and its ruins later provided a romantic backdrop to the sketches of Grand Tour travellers.

WHAT TO SEE

VIA SACRA, TEMPIO DI ANTONINO E FAUSTINA, BASILICA AEMILIA

The Via Sacra, which bisects the Forum, linked the Palatine to the Capitoline hills. Holy sanctuaries lined the way, and victorious generals led processions along the route to give thanks to Jupiter in the Temple of Jupiter Capitolinus. Near the main entrance are the remains of the Temple of Antoninus and Faustina, the best-preserved temple in the Forum, chiefly because it was converted into a Christian church in the seventh century. To the right is a large area of broken columns, the Basilica Aemilia, built in the second century AD to house the law courts.

TEMPIO DI VESTA AND TEMPIO DEI CASTORI

Back near the main entrance, by the Via Sacra, is the circular white Temple of Vesta, where the six Vestal Virgins, priestesses to the goddess of fire, kept the sacred fire alight (▷ 31). The women lived in the House of the Vestal Virgins next door (the central courtyard with its three pools survives), dedicating most of their lives to the service of the goddess and receiving social privileges in return.

Nearby are the three Corinthian columns that remain of the Tempio dei Castori (Temple of Castor and Pollux), built to commemorate the Battle of Lacus Regillus, during which the two divine figures helped the Romans defeat the Latins.

BASILICA JULIA, CURIA, ARCO DI SETTIMIO SEVERO

Via Sacra runs westwards beside the steps of the ruined Basilica Julia, built by Julius Caesar after he returned from the Gallic Wars. Across the Forum proper from here is the remarkably intact, red-coloured Curia (senate house), politically the Roman Republic's most important building. It was here that famous orators and statesmen made their speeches.

At the western end of the complex, the white marble triumphal Arch of Septimius Severus was built in AD203 by his sons, Caracalla and Galba, to commemorate the 10th anniversary of the emperor's reign and his victory over the Parthians between AD197 and 202. Statues of Septimius Severus and Caracalla stand on top of the arch. Caracalla had Galba assassinated in 212 and all memorials and images to him destroyed, including removing his image and inscriptions to him from the arch.

BASILICA DI MASSENZIO AND ARCO DI TITO

East of the main entrance to the Foro Romano, the Via Sacra passes the Basilica di Massenzio (Basilica of Maxentius), the largest and most impressive of all the ruins, built by Constantine and Maxentius in the fourth century. Note its arches, constructed of poured cement.

At the far end of the Forum, the Via Sacra is spanned by the Arco di Tito, built on the Palatine after Titus's death in AD70 to commemorate his victory over the Jews and the capture of Jerusalem.

TIPS

» The Forum can be confusing, so before you enter, get an overview of the general layout from Via del Campidoglio, the northern side of Piazza del Campidoglio (▷ 91) or the Orti Farnesiani (▷ 80) gardens.

» Take something to drink, as there are no bars or cafés in the immediate area.

Below left *Detail of the Arco di Settimio Severo*

Below *Tempio di Antonino e Faustina*

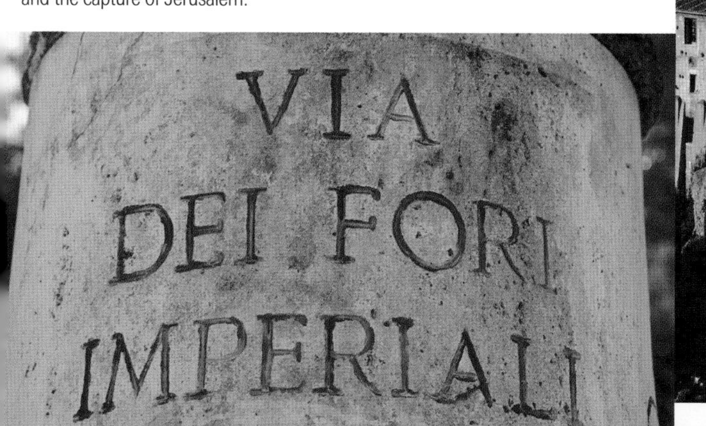

MUSEI CAPITOLINI

www.museicapitolini.org

The Palazzo dei Conservatori and the Palazzo Nuovo make up the Musei Capitolini, home to one of Rome's richest collections of sculptures, mosaics, frescoes and paintings. In 1450 the Palazzo dei Conservatori became the world's first public museum when it began to show bronze statues given to the Romans by Pope Sixtus IV. In the courtyard are fragments of a colossal statue of Constantine. Inside, highlights include the delightful *Spinario,* a first-century Greek bronze of a boy extracting a thorn from his foot, and the famous sixth-century Etruscan bronze of the Capitoline Wolf. The art gallery has a collection of 16th- and 18th-century paintings. The Palazzo Nuovo has more excellent pieces, including energetically carved sarcophagi, the headless *Capitoline Venus* and the bronze equestrian statue of Marcus Aurelius which originally stood in the piazza outside.

68 E6 Piazza del Campidoglio, 00186 Roma 06 6710 2475 Tue–Sun 9–8 Adult €11, EU youths (18–25) €9, under 18s free. Audioguide €5 Colosseo

MUSEI VATICANI

▷ 82–87.

MUSEO E GALLERIA BORGHESE

▷ 81.

ORTI FARNESIANI

A cool retreat, the Orti Farnesiani (Farnese Gardens) are worth climbing the Palatino for. The gardens were laid out in the 16th century by Vignola at the behest of Cardinal Farnese. Shady paths meander through scented orange groves and cypresses.

68 F6 Via dei Fori Imperiali/Via Sacra/Via di San Teodoro/Via di San Gregorio, 00186 Roma 06 3996 7700 Apr–Sep daily 9–7; Oct–Mar 9–3.30 Adult €9; EU youths (18–24) €4.50; under 18s free. Ticket valid for Palatino and Colosseo Colosseo

PALATINO

The Palatino is one of Rome's seven hills, the site of the very first primitive settlement on the Tiber, where the first temples of the city were constructed. Their presence soon made the hill the residential area of choice, pushing business and bureaucracy down the hill into the Forum area. In Republican times the Palatino housed the elite, but later the emperors built their houses here—villas so sumptuous that the hill where they stood gave the English language the word 'palace'. Today, the entire area is covered with the remains of these palaces, the combination of crumbling ruins, mellow brick walls, shady gardens and grassy slopes making the Palatino a truly romantic area. Highlights include the Cryptoporticus, Nero's long semi-subterranean tunnel, the first-century remains of Domitian's palace, where, terrified of assassins, he cowered in rooms faced with black selenite to reflect their arrival, and the well-preserved palace of Septimius Severus. Best of all are the exquisitely frescoed rooms in the ruined house of Augustus, commissioned by Julius Caesar's nephew in 27BC.

68 E–F7 Via di San Gregorio 30, Piazza Santa Maria Nova 53, 00186 Roma 06 3996 7700 Apr–Sep daily 9–7; Oct–Mar 9–3.30 Adult €9, EU youths (18–24) €4.50, under 18s free. Tickets valid for Palatino and Colosseo Colosseo

PALAZZO ALTEMPS

www.pierreci.it

Part of the Museo Nazionale Romano complex and home to a remarkable collection of classical sculpture, the Palazzo Altemps is one of Rome's finest Renaissance buildings. Girolamo Riario, nephew of Pope Sixtus IV, commissioned the palace in 1477 and it was completed by the Altemps family a century later. The Italian State acquired the building in 1982 to accommodate classical masterpieces that had belonged to the Mattei, Altemps and Ludovisi families. The courtyard is the handsomest feature, with marble and frescoes. The highlight is The Room of Moses, which houses one of the most important sculptures in the Ludovisi collection, the *Ludovisi Throne*. The fifth-century bas-relief sculpture depicts Aphrodite rising from the waves.

Above *Excavated remains on the Palatino*

67 D4 Piazza Sant'Apollinare 46, 00186 Roma 06 3996 7700 Tue–Sun 9–7.45 Adult €7, EU youths (18–25) €3.50, under 18s free Audiotours, €4

PALAZZO BARBERINI

www.galleriaborghese.it/barberini

This imposing baroque palace was commissioned in 1623 by Pope Urban VIII, and completed in 1633 by Bernini and Borromini. It houses the national collection of 12th- to 18th-century works once owned by Rome's aristocratic families, but the interior is also a sumptuous expression of high baroque style. In the entrance hall are two remarkable staircases, the wide monumental one on the left by Bernini, and the smaller, spiral one on the right by Borromini. Pietro da Cortona's *The Triumph of Divine Providence*, on the ceiling of the Gran Salone, is considered one of the masterpieces of baroque painting. Other highlights include Titian's *Venus and Adonis*, Raphael's *La Fornarina* and a Holbein portrait of Henry VIII.

67 F4 Via Barberini 18, 00184 Roma 06 482 4184 Gallery: Tue–Sun 8.30–7.30. Apartments: Tue–Sun 9.30–1.15, 2.15–6.45 Gallery: Free. Apartments: Adult €6.30, under 18s €1.30 Barberini

MUSEO E GALLERIA BORGHESE

Cardinal Scipione, Ortensia Borghese's son, was passionate about art and founded this outstanding collection of sculpture and painting. He was also a man without scruples, however. For example, he arranged for Raphael's *Deposition* to be stolen from a church in Perugia and put the painter Domenichino in jail for refusing to give him his *Diana.* In 1620 his collection was moved to the Villa Pinciana. At the end of the 19th century the villa was sold to the Italian State to settle debts, and in 1903 the once-secret gardens were given to the municipality of Rome.

PAOLINA BORGHESE

Room 1 is dominated by the sensuous white marble statue of Paolina Borghese by Antonio Canova (1757–1822). This portrait of Napoleon's beautiful and notorious sister, married off at 23 to the much older Prince Borghese, shows her posing as Venus, reclining semi-naked on a couch, an apple in her hand. She herself commissioned the piece as a present to her husband and it caused immediate scandal—how could she have brought herself to pose virtually naked? 'There was a stove in the studio', she replied. The statue is carved from finest Carrara marble; the sheen is achieved by candle wax.

THE BERNINI SCULPTURES

These rooms display sculptures by Bernini. First is *David,* preparing to fight the giant Goliath. The piece is thought to be a self-portrait. In homage to Bernini's patron, Scipione Borghese, his harp features an eagle's head, a Borghese family emblem. Note how the facial expression changes as you move around the statue. Next is *Apollo and Daphne,* showing Daphne changing into a laurel tree as she escapes Apollo's advances. The energetic statue *The Rape of Proserpina* shows Pluto, god of the underworld, attempting to rape Demeter's daughter.

THE CARAVAGGIO PAINTINGS

The six Caravaggio paintings here are noted for their use of *chiaroscuro,* the balance of light and dark in a single painting. This technique of highlighting figures with a shaft of light from the surrounding darkness, of which Caravaggio was a master, is used beautifully in the *Madonna dei Palafreni.*

RAPHAEL AND TITIAN

There are splendid Umbrian pictures in Room IX, including Raphael's *Deposition* (1507), a picture as much inspired by classical art as religion. It was commissioned in memory of Grifonetto Baglioni, the son of the head of Perugia's leading family. The Venetian artist Titian is represented by four pictures in Room XX, his *Sacred and Profane Love* (1540) standing out for its warm light and soft colours. Painted to celebrate a marriage, it portrays two beautiful women seated on a sarcophagus, one clothed in white, the other semi-naked; its precise iconography remains a mystery.

INFORMATION

www.galleriaborghese.it
67 F2 Piazzale del Museo Borghese 5, 00197 Roma (entrance in Via Pinciana) 06 841 6542 Tue–Sun 9–7 (last entry 5) Adult €8.50, EU youths (18–25) €5.25, under 18s €2. Advance reservations required (06 32810) Spagna or Flaminio 2-hour tour with an art historian in English (9.10, 11.10) and Italian (11.10, 1.10, 5.10), €5. Advance reservations required (through website or tel 06 328 10). Audiotours in Italian, English, Spanish, French and German, €2

TIPS

» Usually 360 people are admitted every 2 hours. Advance booking is essential.
» There is a free guided tour of the Secret Garden on Saturday at 10.30 and Sunday at 9.30 and 10.30. Arrive early, as the tours are limited to 20 people (06 8207 7304).

Left *The reclining statue of Paolina Borghese, sister of Napoleon, by Canova (1804)*

INFORMATION

www.vatican.va
66 A4 Viale Vaticano, 00165 Roma
06 6988 3332 7 Jan–6 Mar, 2 Nov–24 Dec Mon–Sat 10–1.45; 8 Mar–29 Oct, 27 Dec–6 Jan 10–4.45; last Sun of each month 9–1.45. Closed 1, 6, Jan, 11 Feb, 19 Mar, Easter Mon, 1, 20 May, 10, 29 Jun, 15, 16 Aug, 8, 25, 26 Dec Adult €15, child (6–18) €8 Cipro Musei Vaticani, Ottaviano-Vaticano 2-hour guided tour, €4; reserve at information point or tel 06 6988 4676. Audiotours in Italian, English, French, German, Spanish, Japanese, €6 €7.50

Above *A view of the Vatican Museum, dominated by the* Sphere within Sphere *by Arnaldo Pomodoro that stands outside*
Right *Frescoes in the Sistine Chapel*

INTRODUCTION

The vast complex at the Vatican includes the museum, galleries and parts of the papal palace, richly decorated by the world's greatest artists. The galleries, themselves of great architectural interest, have a diverse collection of art, with a particular emphasis on Western art and sculpture.

Pope Innocent III (1179–81) began building a palace near the Basilica San Pietro, and his successors enlarged and embellished it. Major work was carried out under Nicolò V in the mid-15th century, and in the 1470s Sixtus IV added the Cappella Sistina. Both Julius II (1503–13) and Leo X (1513–22) built and decorated further buildings—Julius commissioned Michelangelo to paint the Cappella Sistina and Raphael to decorate his private rooms. In the 18th century the collections were arranged into a museum, with galleries built to display sculpture, paintings, and *objets d'art*—a huge project that continued into the 20th century.

WHAT TO SEE

CAPPELLA SISTINA

The Cappella Sistina (Sistine Chapel) was built by Pope Sixtus IV between 1473 and 1481, both as the pontiff's private chapel and as a venue for the conclave of cardinals that gathers to elect each new pope. It is a huge, cavernous structure, with an intricate cosmatesque mosaic floor and a marble screen by Mino da Fiesole. But, above all, it is the frescoes, entirely covering the walls and ceiling, that attract up to 20,000 visitors a day.

TIPS

» Dress respectfully—shorts and bare upper arms are unacceptable and you will not be admitted.

» To avoid the crowds, arrive as the museum opens, or late in the morning. Wednesday morning can be peaceful as people go to the Piazza di San Pietro for the papal blessing.

» Nearly all sections of the museums are accessible to visitors with disabilities. Wheelchairs are available free of charge and can be booked the day before the visit by calling 06 6988 3860 or at the Special Permits desk in the entrance hall. To collect the wheelchair you must present a valid ID.

» A restaurant with a self-service section, pizzeria and coffee bar is one floor down from the Atrio dei Quattro Cancelli. Go down the stairs near the picture gallery (Pinacoteca), or at the top of the escalators turn right and follow the signs.

Even during the construction of the chapel, Sixtus was planning the interior decoration, settling on scenes from the Old and New Testaments as the subject matter, with an emphasis on the parallels between the lives of Moses and Christ. From Florence, he summoned Sandro Botticelli, together with Domenico Ghirlandaio, Cosimo Rosselli and Perugino. These artists, joined by Pinturicchio, Luca Signorelli and Piero di Cosimo, worked for 11 months, producing a series of glowing works. The two most important scenes are Perugino's *Christ Giving the Keys to Peter* and Botticelli's *The Punishment of Korah,* each showing the Arco di Costantino in the background (▷ 73).

Though undoubtedly masterpieces, they tend to be overshadowed by Michelangelo's frescoes on the ceiling and altar wall, arguably Western art's finest achievement and certainly the largest work ever planned and carried out by one man. Julius II commissioned the ceiling in 1508, and Michelangelo completed it in 1512, an artistic *tour-de-force* combining narrative scenes, architectural *trompe l'oeil* effects and statuesque figures of immense beauty. The central panels illustrate the Creation and tell the story of Noah, surrounded by a decorative scheme dominated by the figures of the Prophets and Sibyls and containing wonderful details, including the famous *ignudi* (nude youths).

Years later, in 1535, Michelangelo was again summoned to the chapel, this time by Paul III, to decorate the altar wall with scenes of the Last Judgement, a task that occupied him until 1541. Even before it was finished, the amount of nudity offended many, not least the Pope's master of ceremonies. Furious, Michelangelo depicted him in the bottom right-hand corner of Hell as Minos, the doorkeeper, complete with ass's ears. Later, Pius IV commissioned Daniele da Volterra to paint over the genitals—an exercise that earned him the name Braghettone, the trouser-maker. This alteration was reversed during the restoration of the chapel frescoes of the 1980s and 1990s, a project said to have cost more than $3 million.

Below *The magnificent spiral staircase in the entrance hall of the Vatican Museums was designed by Giuseppe Momo in 1932*

» A coffee bar with a shop is one floor down from the restaurant.

» Coffee bar Sistina is on the stairs leading to the entrance of the Sistine Chapel (near the toilets).

» In April, May, June, September and October (and also the first two Fridays in July) the museums are open Friday evenings from 7 to 11pm. You must book online and last entry is at 9.30. The itinerary includes the Upper Galleries of the Vatican Museums, the Raphael Rooms and the Sistine Chapel.

STANZE DI RAFFAELLO

In 1508 Julius II embarked on a major project to decorate his private apartments, today known as the Stanze di Raffaello (Raphael Rooms). The Stanza della Segnatura, the Pope's study, is deservedly the most famous room and was Raphael's first major Roman commission, painted between 1508 and 1511.

The four frescoes, compositions imbued with balance and harmony, are allegories representing the humanist ideals of theology, philosophy, poetry and justice. The *School of Athens* emphasizes truth acquired through reason, with all the great Classical thinkers represented and the central figures of Plato—probably a portrait of Leonardo da Vinci—and Aristotle dominating the scene. The figure on the left is said to be Michelangelo, added after Raphael had a sneak preview of his work in the Cappella Sistina. Opposite is the *Disputation of the Holy Sacrament*, while the side walls show *Parnassus*, home to the Muses, and the *Cardinal Virtues.*

Chronologically, the next room to be painted was the Stanza di Eliodoro, with its energy-charged *Expulsion of Heliodorus* and serene *Miracle of Bolsena.* The latter tells the story of the medieval miracle that occurred in that town, when a priest who doubted the doctrine of transubstantiation saw the wafer bleed during Mass. The window wall has a superb night scene, showing the *Deliverance of St. Peter from Prison.*

The Stanza di Costantino depicts the life of Constantine, the first Christian emperor, while the main focus in the Stanza dell'Incendio, commissioned by Leo X, is the miraculous quenching of a *Fire in the Borgo*, which occurred when Leo IV made the sign of the cross.

BRACCIO NUOVO

Famous for its rich collection of classical sculptures culled from excavations and private collections, the Braccio Nuovo (New Wing) is one of the most admired galleries of the Vatican Museums, located towards the end of the Museo

Above *Fresco detail from the Raphael Rooms*

Below *Statue in the Cortile della Pigna*

Above *Monumental head of Emperor Augustus in the Cortile della Pigna (Courtyard of the Pine Cone)*

Chiaramonti. This masterpiece of neoclassical architecture was started at the behest of Pius VII in 1806, inaugurated in 1822 and restored in 2010. The long gallery contains some 150 sculptures, including Roman statues and copies of original Greek statues, as well as floor mosaics, friezes and reliefs from sarcophagi. Among notable works is the famous statue *Augustus of Prima Porta*, excavated at the Villa of Livia in 1863, but perhaps the highlight is the *Colossus of the Nile*. Discovered during excavations in the 16th century under the church of Santa Maria Sopra Minerva, near the Pantheon, the statue of the River Nile dates to the first century AD and is based on a Hellenistic original; the river is shown as a dispenser of blessings, surrounded by little putti, symbolic of fertility. Look, too, for the brace of gilded bronze peacocks that probably came from Hadrian's mausoleum.

PINACOTECA VATICANA

The Pinacoteca, founded in 1816 by Pius VI, occupies a separate building (1932) within the museum complex. It is widely considered to be Rome's best picture gallery, with works from the early and High Renaissance to the 19th century. Among these are some of the most remarkable early paintings in Rome, with Giotto's *Stefaneschi Triptych* stealing the show (Room II). Painted in the early 1300s, it shows the *Martyrdom of St. Peter and St. Paul.* St. Peter is shown being crucified, at his own request, upside down, as he felt unworthy to die the same way as Christ. The next rooms are devoted to 15th-century Italian art; look for Fra Angelico's lovely *Madonna and Child with Saints* in Room III and the serene Umbrian pictures in Room VII, particularly Perugino's luminous *Madonna and Child.* Room VIII is the Pinacoteca's finest, with a collection of Raphael's work, including tapestries, woven in Brussels from his cartoons, that once hung in the Cappella Sistina. Dominating the room, however, is the *Transfiguration*, a sublime work that was hung above the artist's coffin and completed by his pupils later.

The triumphant figure of the ascending Christ pulses with energy amid piercing light and lowering cloud formations, a superb contrast to the artist's first major composition, the *Coronation of the Virgin*, painted when he was only 20. The gentle *Madonna of Foligno* was commissioned in 1512 as a votive offering.

In Room IX is Leonardo da Vinci's unfinished and curiously monochrome *St. Jerome*, one of only a few of Leonardo's works whose authorship has never been disputed. Here, too, is the exquisite *Pietà* by Bellini. Venetian painting is featured heavily in Room X in two canvases by Titian, a glowing *Madonna with Saints* and the subtle *Portrait of Doge Nicolò Marcello.* There are further psychological insights in Caravaggio's despairing *Deposition* in Room XII, all muted tones and intense *chiaroscuro*.

GALLERY GUIDE

LOWER FLOOR

Museo Pio Clementino: The cream of the Classical sculpture collection is in this museum's octagonal courtyard. Two statues here influenced Renaissance sculptors more than any others, the *Laocöon* and the *Apollo Belvedere*. Highlights within include a beautiful Hellenistic *Sleeping Ariadne*, candelabra from the Villa Adriana at Tivoli, and Roman portrait busts, including a splendid Julius Caesar.

Museo Gregoriano Egizio: Founded in the 19th century by Gregory XVI, this museum displays a reconstruction of the Temple of Serapis from the Villa Adriana at Tivoli, mummy cases, mummies and tomb treasures.

Museo Gregoriano Profano: Built in 1963 and opened in 1970, a museum with a collection of antique and Christian art moved here from the Lateran Palace.

Museo Pio Cristiano: A collection of documents and objects illustrating religions of the world.

Museo Storico Vaticano: An unusual collection of modes of papal transportation, including carriages.

Museo Chiaramonti: Another collection of Roman sculpture, in particular portrait busts.

Braccio Nuovo: A beautiful collection in a superb architectural setting.

Biblioteca Vaticana: A huge, brilliantly frescoed hall with letters from Petrarch, Michelangelo and Martin Luther, and King Henry VIII's love letters to Anne Boleyn.

Museo Sacro: Next to the Sistine Chapel, the Museo Sacro was founded by Benedict XIV in 1756. Highlights include the enamel cross given by Pope Paschal (817–824) that contains five pieces of the True Cross, and the ivory Ramboyna Diptych (*c.*900), depicting the legendary Roman she-wolf.

Sala degli Indirizzi: The Room of the Tributes owes its name to the declarations of respect and presentations to the Pope. Restored in 2010, of partiuclar interest is the ceiling decoration, created by applying tempera paint directly to the wall.

Appartamento Borgia: The powerful Borgia family adapted this series of six rooms for the Borgia Pope Alexander VI (1492–1503).

UPPER FLOOR

Museo Gregoriano Etrusco: Founded in 1837, this is a major collection of Etruscan sculpture and funerary art.

Galleria delle Carte Geographiche: This upper-floor gallery links the museums with the papal palace. It was painted in 1580 by Ignazio Danti with maps of Italy, Mediterranean islands, papal possessions in France, the Siege of Malta and Venice.

Galleria dei Candelabri and Galleria degli Arazzi: The Gallery of Candelabra and the adjoining Gallery of Tapestries are impressive for the Roman marble statues, candlesticks and ten vast *arazzi* (tapestries), created by Flemish Pieter van Aelst from Raphael's depictions.

Cappella di Nicolò V: Serene and delicate frescoes (1446–49) by Fra Angelico in the Pope's private chapel.

Below *A map of Sardinia in the Galleria delle Carte Geographiche, painted by Ignazio Danti, a Dominican monk*

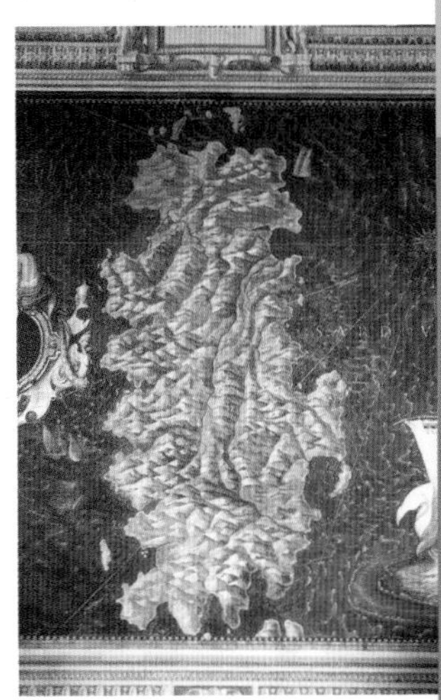

INFORMATION

www.doriapamphilj.it

68 E5 Piazza del Collegio Romano 2, 00186 Roma 06 679 7323 Daily 10–5. Closed 1 Jan, Easter Sunday, 1 May, 15 Aug, 25 Dec Adult €9.50, under 18s €7 (includes audioguide). Reserve concert tickets 10 days in advance Fri–Wed 10–4 and on concert days from 7.30pm (tel 800 907080)

TIPS

» Choose a bright day to visit as most of the paintings are not lit.

» The excellent audioguide, included in the entrance price, will help you fully appreciate what you're seeing.

Above *Painted ceilings and elegant statues in the Palazzo Doria Pamphilj*

PALAZZO-GALLERIA DORIA PAMPHILJ

Overlooking the Via del Corso stands the Palazzo Doria Pamphilj, one of the largest palaces in Rome, still inhabited by the family that originally built it in the 17th century. This continuity of ownership has ensured that the layout and decoration remain very much as they were originally designed, with the art collection displayed as it would have been in the 18th century. Visiting the palazzo provides a window onto a bygone age, and an excellent way to understand the wealth of Rome's princely families.

THE PALAZZO

The palazzo came into the family's possession in the late 16th century, and building work to expand it started at once and continued through to 1731, when Gabriele Valvassori was employed to design a new facade on the Corso and convert the buildings round the inner courtyard into a gallery to display the family's growing art collection. This had been started by Pope Innocent X Pamphilj in 1651, and had grown considerably, with works either being purchased or coming into the family through judicious marriages. Over the following years, the galleries were decorated in the baroque style, and the wonderfully exuberant scheme forms the backdrop for the collection today.

THE COLLECTION

Within the four wings of the gallery the paintings are displayed, as 18th-century fashion dictated, in tiers, rather than singly. There are pictures by just about all the big names in Italian art, as well as masterpieces by the Breughels and other Flemish painters. Pride of place, in a separate room off the first gallery, is given to a remarkable portrait of Pope Innocent X, the Pamphilj pope, by the Spanish artist Velázquez. At its side stands a superb marble bust of Innocent, sculpted in the same year, 1650, by Bernini. Look too, for the collection's superb works by Caravaggio. Other highlights include Filippo Lippi's *Annunciation* and Titian's *Salomè con la Testa del Battista (Salome with the Head of John the Baptist)*.

PALAZZO MASSIMO ALLE TERME

www.pierreci.it

The Palazzo Massimo alle Terme, an imposing building, houses the Museo Nazionale Romano and its extensive collection of sculptures, mosaics, frescoes and coins from the end of the Republican Age (second century BC) to the late Imperial Age (fourth century AD).

The ground floor displays portraits from the Republican period and an interesting collection of coins. In Room V are a statue of Augustus and a marble altar from Ostia showing the wedding of Mars and Venus, along with a sculpture of Apollo and the sleeping Aphrodite from the Villa Adriana in Tivoli. In Room VII is the magnificent statue of Niobe's daughter trying to extract an arrow from her back. Other rooms display portraits, bas-reliefs and sarcophagi, and remarkable mosaic floors and beautiful frescoes discovered in the Villa Farnesina in Trastevere and the Villa Livia on the Palatino. The second floor can be visited only as part of a group or with a guide, so reserve in advance or wait for a group or a guide to come along.

69 G4 Largo di Villa Peretti 1, 00185 Roma 06 3996 7700 Tue–Sun 9–7.45 Adult €7, EU youths (18–24) €3.50, under 18s free Repubblica, Termini X

PANTHEON

▷ 90.

PIAZZA DEL CAMPIDOGLIO

▷ 91.

PIAZZA CAMPO DEI FIORI

Piazza Campo dei Fiori bustles with *trattorie*, bookshops and a famous market. Relax with a drink at one of the *vinerie* (wine bars) and delight in one of the most attractive and lively squares in Rome. In former times it was used as grazing land for cattle—hence the name, which means 'field of flowers'.

It was also the venue for executions. In 1600 the philosopher Giordano Bruno, who advocated the separation of political and religious power, was burned alive on the spot where his statue now stands. The statue, by Ettore Ferrari (1887), along with the Cinema Farnesen, are traditional meeting places for Rome's intellectuals and anti-establishment thinkers.

68 C5 Piazza Campo dei Fiori, 00186 Roma Tram 8

PIAZZA NAVONA

Piazza Navona is a lively, crowded place at the heart of the city, a popular meeting place for both Romans and visitors. You can go to an exhibition at Palazzo Braschi, watch street performers or have your portrait painted. Alternatively, sit and enjoy a drink at one of the outdoor cafés.

The piazza was laid out in the late 15th century on the ruins of a stadium. From 1650 to the late 19th century the square was flooded in summer and used for aquatic games. Brightly painted carriages floated on the water like boats while people freshened up in the temporary 'lake'. Today the real attraction is the famous Fontana dei Quattro Fiumi (Fountain of the Four Rivers), created by Bernini in about 1651, in the middle of the square. It represents the Danube, the Ganges, the Nile and the Rio de la Plata.

At the southern end of the piazza the Fontana del Moro, designed by Giacomo della Porta in 1576, features dragons and dolphins. The central figure of the so-called 'Moor'—actually a marine divinity—was added in the mid-17th century. The Fontana del Nettuno, at the northern end, dates from the 19th century.

68 D5 Piazza Navona, 00186 Roma 23, 30, 62, 64, 70, 81

PIAZZA DI SPAGNA E SCALINATA DI TRINITÀ DEI MONTI

The Scalinata di Trinità dei Monti (Spanish Steps), one of the world's most beautiful staircases, curves its elegant and sinuous way down a steep slope from the church of the same name to the Piazza di Spagna. It's a staircase for posing, relaxing, sitting and meeting friends, and the view from the top is one of Rome's loveliest. The piazza got its name in the 17th century, when the Spanish Ambassador took up residence here, and a century later the French diplomat Etienne Gueffier funded the construction of the steps (1725) to provide a classier approach to the church than the existing muddy slope. In spring huge pots of azaleas adorn the steps and at Christmas a crib is erected halfway up. The English have always been drawn here, and the poet John Keats died of tuberculosis in 1821 in the house at the bottom on the left; today it's a museum. In the piazza is a boat-shaped fountain, the Barcaccia, designed in 1627 by Bernini father and son. It's sunk below ground level to compensate for the low water pressure of the Acqua Vergine that feeds it, often giving the impression of a sinking ship.

67 E3 Piazza di Spagna, 00187 Roma Spagna

Below *Piazza di Spagna with the Barcaccia fountain in the foreground*

INFORMATION

68 D5 Piazza della Rotonda, 00186 Roma 06 6830 0230 Mon–Sat 8.30–7.30, Sun 9–6.30, public holidays 9–1. No visits during celebration of the Sun 10.30am Mass Free Tram 8 to Argentina In the square Audioguide €4 On Piazza della Rotonda

TIPS

» There is not much information to help visitors on site, so have your guidebook handy.
» Have a drink in one of the cafés or sit around the central fountain of the piazza to enjoy the view of the Pantheon.
» The Pantheon is often very crowded, especially at the weekend. To make the most of a visit, go on a weekday or early in the morning.

PANTHEON

The original Pantheon was built by Roman general Agrippa, according to the inscription on the facade. It was erected in 27BC in honour of the heavenly gods and was also dedicated to the Julii family (of which Julius Caesar was a member), who claimed to be direct descendants of gods. Agrippa's building was destroyed in the great fire of AD80 and the Pantheon was rebuilt in the early second century by Emperor Hadrian. In the sixth century, Emperor Phocas gave the Pantheon to Pope Boniface IV, who turned it into a Christian church. The building was then covered in bronze and lead, and despite being pillaged over the years, the covering helped to preserve the dome and other surfaces. Pope Urban VIII had the bronze on the ceiling removed in the 17th century for use on Bernini's *baldacchino* in the Basilica di San Pietro (▷ 74–75), but the bronze doors survive from ancient Rome.

THE DOME

The design is superbly simple: a dome on a circular base attached to a rectangular portico. With a diameter wider than that of San Pietro, this is the largest dome ever built before the introduction of reinforced concrete and is a testimony to the amazing ingenuity of Roman engineers. The height of the dome from the floor is identical to its diameter, 43.3m (142ft). The walls supporting the dome are 7m (23ft) across, and the thickness of the dome itself diminishes from base to apex. The unglazed oculus, the circular hole in the middle of the dome (9m/29.5ft across), is the only source of natural light. A statue of Jove Ultor, the Avenger, who punished the murderers of Caesar, once stood directly under the oculus, and shrines and niches once held statues of the 12 Olympian gods, along with emperors Hadrian and Augustus. The tombs of Italy's first two kings and the artist Raphael are the remaining tombs you can see today.

PIAZZA DELLA ROTONDA

The Pantheon faces Piazza della Rotonda, a pretty square with cafés, a fountain, and a 13th-century BC Egyptian obelisk built by Ramses II, brought to Rome and used in the Temple of Isis and Serapis in Campo Marzio, then moved here by Pope Clement XI. In the evening this is a lively place with people dining or enjoying coffee and ice cream.

Below *The Pantheon and fountain in Piazza della Rotonda*

PIAZZA DEL CAMPIDOGLIO

Michelangelo was called upon to redesign this piazza as part of Pope Paul III's plan to restore the city to its ancient splendour after the Sack of Rome in 1527. The magnificent buildings that stand on three sides of the square—the Palazzo Senatorio, the Palazzo Nuovo and the Palazzo dei Conservatori, built on the site of the great Temple of Jupiter Capitolinus—were part of his scheme.

THE CORDONATA

The new piazza was designed for Emperor Charles V's triumphal entry into Rome in 1536, and the best approach is via the Cordonata, Michelangelo's elegant ramp intended for the emperor. The top of the Cordonata is flanked by two large statues of Castor and Pollux, the mythical sons of Jupiter, standing by their horses. To their left and right is a display of captured enemy arms from the reign of Domitian. The balustrade is embellished with columns from the Via Appia and statues of Constantine the Great and his son Constantine II in full military dress.

THE PIAZZA

The floor of the piazza is inlaid with a star-shaped pattern, in the middle of which Michelangelo placed a plinth for the equestrian statue of Marcus Aurelius. This escaped the fate of the many statues of pagan emperors that were melted down and reused during the Middle Ages. The statue is now safely housed in the Musei Capitolini (▷ 80).

PALAZZO SENATORIO

The Palazzo Senatorio (Senate House) was built during a period when the people of Rome demanded an end to the power of the papacy and re-established a republic. Michelangelo designed a new facade, subsequently built by Giacomo della Porta, and the palazzo became the hub of political activity in the 16th and 17th centuries. A fountain near the steps is flanked by two huge bearded statues representing the Nile, the Sphinx, the Tiber, Romulus and Remus and the she-wolf.

MUSEI CAPITOLINI

Note the twin balconies of the Palazzo dei Conservatori and Palazzo Nuovo, designed by Michelangelo, with statues looking across at each other. These buildings house the Musei Capitolini (▷ 80).

INFORMATION

www.museicapitolini.org

68 E6 Piazza del Campidoglio, 00186 Roma Colosseo All bus services to Piazza Venezia; tram 8 to Argentina In the museum shops (Libreria Capitolina) First floor of Palazzo Caffarelli In the museums

Above *The star-shaped inlay onPiazza del Campidoglio was designed by Michelangelo to emphasize a statue of Marcus Aurelius that stood in the centre of the square until 1981*

SANT'ANDREA AL QUIRINALE

Small but perfectly formed sums up Sant'Andrea al Quirinale, the tiny baroque church designed by Bernini in 1658 as a gift to the Jesuits while he was working full-time as an architect at San Pietro (▷ 74–75). It certainly delighted Pope Alexander VII (1655–67), who came here so frequently that it became a type of papal chapel. It's a dazzling little church, all pale pink marble, gilding and ebullient stucco angels and cherubs. This is sugary baroque at its finest, where the gaiety of the finished product virtually hides the architectural skill needed to create such a sense of grandeur in this tiny space. An elegant flight of steps leads to the entrance portico, and once inside, you'll find yourself in an elliptical space, surrounded by eight deep lavishly decorated side chapels.

67 F4 Via del Quirinale 29, 00184 Roma 06 474 4872 Mon–Fri 8.30–12, 3–7, Sat–Sun 9–12, 3.30–7 Free Barberini

SAN CARLO ALLE QUATTRO FONTANE

www.sancarlino-borromini.it

This extremely small church is said to be no larger than one of the columns supporting the dome of San Pietro (▷ 74–75). Known as San Carlino, it was designed in 1638 by the great baroque artist Francesco Borromini and is opposite his rival Bernini's Sant'Andrea al Quirinale. This was Borromini's first work, but also his last—he committed suicide after adding the facade in 1667. The architecture reflects the tormented and contradictory state of mind of its creator. The interior is simple—an elliptical plan with stuccoed niches—but every concave section is mirrored by its convex opposite, forming strange shapes and visual effects. The intricately designed coffered ceiling, with sunken ornamental panels, exemplifies the bizarre yet elegant effect that Borromini managed to create in such a small space.

67 F4 Via del Quirinale 23, 00184 Roma 06 488 3261 Mon–Fri 10–1, 3–6, Sat 10–1, Sun 12–1 Free Barberini

SAN CLEMENTE

▷ 93.

SANTA CECILIA IN TRASTEVERE

The ancient church of Santa Cecilia lies in the heart of Trastevere. In 303 the site was home to Valerio, an aristocratic Roman, and his wife Cecilia, a converted Christian. Impressed by her piety, Valerio too converted, only to be put to death. Cecilia was arrested as she tried to bury him and condemned to death by suffocation in the steam baths of her house; she survived and was then sentenced to beheading. This too, was a botched job and she lived for several days, singing the praises of Christ, an act which led to her becoming the patron saint of music. She was buried here and a series of churches was built over the spot. The existing church dates from the ninth century; the campanile and lovely portico were added in the 12th century. Walk through the flowery courtyard to enter the church, where your eye is drawn to the main altar. Here, beneath Arnolfo di Cambio's exquisite canopy (1293), is the saint's tomb. She is depicted in a touching and beautiful marble statue by Maderno, lying as she was found, uncorrupted, when her tomb was opened in 1599. The apse is covered with splendid mosaics. Try and time your visit to coincide with access to the superb late 13th-century fresco by Cavallini in the gallery. A fragment of the original, the remains bridge the artistic gap between the hieratic forms of Byzantine art and the naturalistic style of later artists.

68 D7 Piazza di Santa Cecilia 22, 00153 Roma 06 589 9289 Daily 9.30–12.30, 4–6.30. Cavallini fresco: Mon–Sat 10.15–12.15, Sun 11.15–12.15 Church free. Cavallini fresco €2.50. Excavations €2.50 Tram 8; Bus 23, 44

SANTI COSMA E DAMIANO

Consecrated in 526 by Pope Felix IV in honour of twin Arab physicians, this was the first Christian church to reuse a building in the Roman Forum (▷ 78–79). It was formed by joining the library of the Foro della Pace to part of the round temple dedicated to Romulus, the remains of which are still visible inside. In the 16th century, Pope Urban VIII Barberini commissioned the architect Arrigucci to restore the building. The present-day facade of the church and the cloister were built at this time, and the original Roman church was hidden underground in a crypt. The highlight is the sixth-century mosaics in the apse showing the Apostles Peter and Paul presenting the saints Cosmas and Damian to Christ. The baroque high altar partially hides the detail of Christ as the Lamb surrounded by the 12 Apostles. The 17th-century ceiling is decorated with paintings depicting the triumph of the saintly brothers along with the Barberini family emblem, bees.

68 F6 Via dei Fori Imperiali , 00186 Roma 06 699 1540 Daily 9–1, 3–7 Free Colosseo

SAN GIOVANNI IN LATERANO

▷ 94

Left *Stefano Maderno's statue of Santa Cecilia in the church of the same name*

SAN CLEMENTE

The present church was built in the 12th century after its predecessor was damaged in a Norman attack in 1084. The lower church has a similar layout, but was wider, and very little of the original walls of this fourth-century building survive. According to legend, St. Cyril, evangelizer of the Slavs, brought St. Clement's relics to Rome and laid them here in 869. On the lowest level are buildings from imperial Rome, including a well-preserved Mithraic temple.

THE MITHRAIC TEMPLE

Head straight for the underground level by taking the steps in the sacristy down through the first church (second level). Here are two buildings dating from Roman days. One is thought to have been Rome's mint; the second was the house of a rich family, built of brick with an underground courtyard and later converted into a temple to the Persian god, Mithras. Mithraism was a pre-Christian, all-male cult, popular with soldiers, and this is the best-preserved of a dozen Mithraic temples found in the city. The temple was used until the fourth century, when Christians probably destroyed it. From the temple, walk along a narrow passage, at the end of which you can hear the sound of water running in an underground watercourse.

THE LOWER CHURCH—THE FIRST SAN CLEMENTE

Go back up the steps to the lower San Clemente basilica, built in AD375, consisting of a nave and two aisles. Pillars and walls added in the 11th and 12th centuries support the church above. Frescoes date from the 8th to 11th centuries; the one depicting St. Sisinius is remarkable for the inscriptions below, perhaps the oldest in the Italian language.

THE UPPER CHURCH—THE SECOND SAN CLEMENTE

Little altered since it was built, San Clemente is dominated by a choir screen and the golden 12th-century mosaic of the Crucifixion in the apse. Birds and animals are entwined in foliage, the Virgin and St. John stand alongside the cross represented as the Tree of Life, and the four rivers of Paradise spring from the foot of the cross. The cosmatesque inlaid floor is one of the best preserved in Rome.

INFORMATION

www.basilicasanclemente.com
69 G7 Piazza San Clemente/Via San Giovanni in Laterano, 00184 Roma
06 774 0021 2nd and 3rd level: Mon–Sat 9–12.30, 3–6, Sun 10–12.30, 3–6. Upper Basilica: all day 2nd and 3rd level, excavations €5. Upper Basilica, free Colosseo, San Giovanni

TIPS

» Buy a plan before you start, as in the underground and second-level basilicas there is no defined route and you may miss points of interest.
» Start with the underground church.

Above *The Mithraic temple below the church of San Clemente*

SAN GIOVANNI IN LATERANO

The first basilica, named after the family that owned the property on which it was founded, was built by Constantine between AD313 and 318. At the time, it represented the victory of Christianity over paganism. In 314 Pope Sylvester I took up residence in the Lateran buildings and it was the official papal residence until the papacy moved to Avignon in the 14th century, though popes were crowned here until the 19th century. San Giovanni has been rebuilt many times—damaged by Vandals, an earthquake and two fires, it was finally restored by Borromini in the 17th century in the baroque style.

The basilica's 1735 baroque facade by Alessandro Galilei (modelled on San Pietro) is crowned with 15 gigantic statues of Christ, the Apostles and the Church Fathers. The portico has bronze doors taken from the Foro Romano's Curia (senate house), and a huge statue of the first Christian emperor, Constantine. The last door on the right, the Holy Door, is opened only during the Jubilee or Holy Year, every 25 years.

Inside, the central nave is flanked with niches containing statues of the 12 Apostles. The dove from the coat of arms of Innocent X, who commissioned Borromini, is set over each recess, with bas-reliefs depicting stories from the Old and New Testaments. To the right of the entrance a restored fragment of a fresco by Giotto shows Boniface VIII declaring the first Holy Year in 1300. In contrast to the unadorned nave, the transept is a fine example of mannerist ornamentation. A 14th-century tabernacle above the altar contains relics of St. Peter and St. Paul. Several frescoes depict the Good Shepherd, the Crucifixion, the Virgin Mary and various saints. In the apse is a mosaic of the figure of Christ, a 19th-century restoration of a 13th-century copy of a fourth-century original by Jacopo da Camerino and Jacopo Torriti. Notice the small figure of St. Francis on the left, included because da Camerino and Torriti were Franciscan monks.

The most beautiful part of the cathedral is the cloister—a peaceful refuge, with slim columns, and inlaid marble and gold mosaics.

THE BAPTISTERY AND SCALA SANTA

In Piazza San Giovanni, the octagonal baptistery, the first in Christendom, survives from Constantine's era. The Scala Santa (Holy Staircase), a flight of 28 steps with glass sheets covering what is thought to be a trail of Christ's blood, leads to the Sancta Sanctorum, a chapel with frescoes by the great 13th-century painters Cimabue and Pietro Cavallini.

INFORMATION

www.sacred-destinations.com/italy/rome-san-giovanni-laterano
69 H8 Piazza di San Giovanni in Laterano 4, 00184 Roma 06 6988 6433 Basilica: daily 7–6.30. Cloister: daily 9–6. Baptistery: daily 7–12.30, 4–7.30. Scala Santa: daily 9–12, 3–6. Museo Storico del Vaticano: Mon–Sat 9–1 Basilica, Scala Santa, baptistery: free. Cloister: €2. Cappella Sancta Sanctorum: €3.50. Museo Storico del Vaticano: €4 San Giovanni Tours: basilica, cloister, baptistery, Scala Santa (reserve in advance; tel as above, Mon–Fri 9–1, or email), in all languages, €5.50. Guided tour of Museo Storico del Vatticano. Audiotours: basilica and cloister, in all languages, €2. Mater et caput guided tour: tel 06 6988 6392 or email mater.caput@org.va

TIP

» If you go in the morning and have time, walk around Via Sagno, the famous flea market.

Above *Detail of the baroque facade of San Giovanni in Laterano*

SANTA MARIA IN ARACOELI

The church of Santa Maria in Aracoeli stands on the Capitoline Hill at the top of a wide, steep flight of 124 steps. Today's church dates largely from the end of the 13th century, when Franciscan monks took over a Benedictine monastery church. The steps, traditionally climbed by newly married couples, offer a splendid view of the city, and lead to an austere brick frontage lightened only by doors and tiny rose windows. Inside, a gilded ceiling commemorates the Battle of Lepanto in 1571. Other highlights are the marble floor and the pulpit, good examples of cosmatesque inlay work, and Pinturicchio's frescoes in the first chapel on the right, depicting the life and death of St. Bernardino of Siena. The left transept leads to a little chapel dedicated to the Holy Child; its wooden statue is celebrated for its miraculous healing powers.

68 E6 Piazza dell'Aracoeli, 00186 Roma 06 679 8155 Daily 9–12.30, 2.30–6.30 Free Colosseo

SANTA MARIA DELLA CONCEZIONE

www.cappucciniviaveneto.it

Also known as the Church of the Capuchins, this austere Counter-Reformation church is famous for its ghoulish ossuary. It contains the bones of about 4,000 Capuchin monks who lived and died in the once-adjacent convent between 1528 and 1870. The macabre display in the crypt includes chandeliers made from human bones. There are separate chapels for femurs and tibias, pelvises, skulls and skeletons (some still dressed). The floor is scattered with soil from Palestine. The church was built in 1624 by Cardinal Antonio Barberini, a Capuchin monk whose tombstone in front of the main altar is inscribed *Hic jacet pulvis, cinis et nihil* (Here lies dust, ashes, nothing). This brother of Pope Urban VIII clearly did not share the Barberini love of grandeur. Look also for Guido Reni's painting *St. Michael Trampling the Devil.*

67 F4 Via Vittorio Veneto 27, 00187 Roma 06 487 1185 Fri–Wed 9–12, 3–6 Free/contribution to the cemetery Barberini

SANTA MARIA IN COSMEDIN

By 772 the church built here in the sixth century on the site of a pagan temple had become the church of the local Greek community, and it was they who called it Cosmedin (meaning lovely) because of its decor. It is also known as Santa Maria in Scuola Greca because people still come to celebrate Greek Orthodox Mass here.

It is most famous for the Bocca della Verità (Mouth of Truth), a large stone that was used as a drain cover by the ancient Romans. It's said that if a person places their hand inside its gaping mouth and tells a lie, the mouth clamps shut, severing the liar's fingers.

Between 1118 and 1123 the church was rebuilt and the elegant Romanesque bell tower was added. Inside, the nave and two aisles are divided by ancient Roman columns. There is fine cosmatesque marble-inlaid work in the floor, pulpits, screen and paschal candlestick. There is also a fragment of an eighth-century mosaic in the sacristy.

68 E7 Piazza Bocca della Verità, 00186 Roma (Piazza Venezia/Circo Massimo) 06 678 1419 Daily 9–6.30 Free Circo Massimo

SANTA MARIA MAGGIORE

⊳ 96.

SANTA MARIA SOPRA MINERVA

www.basilicaminerva.it

In 1280 two Dominican friars, Sisto and Ristoro, who designed Santa Maria Novella in Florence (⊳ 253), began building a church here on the site of a pagan temple to Minerva. The baroque-style refurbishment of the interior in the 16th and 17th centuries masked the church's medieval Gothic structure, a rarity in Rome, and the church was further embellished in the 19th century when the Dominican architect Girolamo Bianchedi added frescoes to its walls and vaults. Kept by Dominican friars, the Minerva offers a peaceful escape from the crowds.

St. Catherine of Siena is buried beneath the high altar. Frescoes in the Capranica Chapel illustrate her life. More famous are the frescoes by Filippino Lippi in the Carafa Chapel, depicting the life of the Dominican St. Thomas Aquinas and the Assumption. Other works of art include the statue of *Christ Risen* by Michelangelo. To the left of the altar is the tomb of the great Florentine artist and Dominican monk Fra Angelico, who died here in 1455.

Other noteworthy funerary monuments include tombs of the Medici popes, Leo X and Clement VII, sculpted by Antonio da Sangallo, and that of Maria Raggi, by Bernini. To the rear are the cloisters and the Dominican convent. It was here that Galileo was condemned for insisting that the earth moves around the sun (⊳ 37).

68 D5 Piazza della Minerva 42, 00186 Roma 06 679 3926 Daily 8–7; no visits during Mass Free Tram 8

Below *Santa Maria sopra Minerva*

SANTA MARIA MAGGIORE

In the fourth century, the story goes, Pope Liberius had a dream in which the Virgin Mary told him it would snow that night and that he was to build a church in her honour where the snow settled. That night, 5 August 356, it snowed on the Esquiline Hill, and Santa Maria Maggiore was constructed on top of it. In fact, it was probably commissioned by Sixtus III in AD432—the first basilica to be built by a pope rather than an emperor.

THE BASILICAN NAVE

The interior of this immense church has kept its original medieval structure. Above the Roman columns in the nave, 36 fifth-century mosaic panels illustrate Old Testament stories. Easier to see are the mosaics depicting scenes of Christ's life on the arch at the entrance to the Cappella Paolina. The nave's 16th-century coffered ceiling by Giuliano da Sangallo is said to be decorated with some of the first gold brought from America. The floor has 12th-century inlay work.

THE BALDACCHINO AND MOSAICS

The *baldacchino* (altar canopy) by Ferdinando Fuga is made of porphyry columns with bronze foliage. It stands over the Confession (crypt), where a silver urn is believed to contain fragments of Christ's wooden cradle. The chancel arch is decorated with a fifth-century Byzantine-style mosaic showing Jerusalem and Bethlehem, and Jesus as a child at the Feast of the Epiphany. The apse has a fine mosaic depicting the *Coronation of the Virgin Mary* (1295) by Jacopo Torriti. To the right of the apse is the humble tomb of the sculptor Gian Lorenzo Bernini.

THE CHAPELS

The Cappella Paolina is also known as the Cappella Borghese after the family of Pope Paul V, who commissioned the bejewelled surround to the altar and whose elaborate tomb is here. Next to this is the Cappella Sforza, designed by Michelangelo. Across the nave, the Cappella Sistina, commissioned by Pope Sixtus V and built by Domenico Fontana in 1585, is almost a church in its own right, with a dome, frescoes and papal tombs. The highlight is the *Presepe* (Nativity crib) by Arnolfo di Cambio, which stood outside from the sixth century but was moved on Sixtus's orders. During the process, unfortunately, much of it was broken.

INFORMATION

69 G5 Piazza Santa Maria Maggiore, 00184 Roma 06 483195 or 06 6988 6800 Basilica: daily 7–7. Cappella Sforza: Mon–Fri 9–5. Museum: daily 9.30–6. Sacristy: daily 7–12.30, 3–6 Basilica and Cappella Sforza: free. Museum: adult €4.50, child (under 18) €2 Cavour or Termini, Vittorio Emanuele Guided tours, tel 06 483058. Loggia delle Benedizioni: guided tours by appointment only, tel 06 6988 6802, €5; Presepe di Arnolfo di Cambio: Mon–Sat 9.30–1, €1.50. Audiotours, €1

TIPS

» Start in the Loggia delle Benedizioni, where a mosaic tells the story of the basilica.

» There is little information on site and parts of the basilica are closed to the public or can be seen only with a guide.

» The basilica is badly lit, so bring a torch (flashlight) to get a better view.

Above *An obelisk outside the church of Santa Maria Maggiore*

SANTA MARIA DEL POPOLO

Tucked into a corner of the Piazza del Popolo, Santa Maria del Popolo is famed for its collection of Renaissance art. Replacing an 11th-century chapel on the traditional site of Nero's grave, St. Mary of the People was built by Andrea Bregno in simple Renaissance style and paid for by the people of Rome, in 1472. The baroque embellishments to the interior were added later.

In the della Rovere chapel the altar painting *The Adoration of the Child* is by Pinturicchio, and frescoes of the life of San Girolamo are the work of his pupil Tiberio d'Assisi. In the choir are masterpieces by Andrea Sansovino, monuments to Cardinal Ascanio Sforza (1505) and Cardinal Girolamo Basso della Rovere (1507). The early stained glass is by the French artist Guillaume de Marcillat. In the little Cappella Cerasi are Caravaggio's two magnificent works of 1601, *The Conversion of St. Paul* and *The Crucifixion of St. Peter.* The Cappella Chigi was built in 1516 as a mausoleum for the Chigi family, with sculpture, paintings and mosaics all designed by Raphael.

67 D2 Piazza del Popolo 12, 00186 Roma 06 361 0836 Mon–Sat 7–12, 4–7, Sun 7.30–1.45, 4.30–7.30 Free Flaminio, Spagna

SANTA MARIA IN TRASTEVERE

The picturesque quarter of Trastevere, in which the medieval gem of Santa Maria stands, lies on the right bank of the Tiber. Legend has it that in 38BC a fountain of oil suddenly started flowing here, heralding the birth of Jesus Christ, and Pope Callixtus (217–22) built a sanctuary to commemorate the miracle. The present-day basilica was built in the 12th century, using materials from the Terme di Caracalla (▷ 98). The mosaics on the facade, probably 12th-century, have survived as Rome's only example of what all the city's medieval church facades once looked like. Inside, the mosaics in the apse are beautiful above all else. In the half-dome, 12th-century mosaics show Mary embraced by her son and flanked by popes and saints. Below this, Pietro Cavallini's masterpiece depicts scenes from the life of the Virgin (1290). More 12th-century mosaics on the chancel arch depict the prophets Isaiah and Jeremiah. The central panel of the 17th-century coffered ceiling has an *Assumption* by Domenichino. Visit after dark, when the basilica's facade is floodlit and you can sit at one of the outdoor cafés in the piazza.

68 C7 Piazza di Santa Maria in Trastevere, 00153 Roma 06 581 4802 Daily 8–8 (may close 12.30–3.30 in winter) Free Tram 8 9–5

SAN PIETRO IN VINCOLI

Fans of Michelangelo flock to the church of St. Peter in Chains to see its main treasure, the monument to Pope Julius II, dominated by the artist's statue of Moses (1515). Not content with keeping Michelangelo busy on the Sistine Chapel ceiling, Julius also wanted him to execute a vast tomb, complete with 40 statues of Old Testament prophets. This ambitious scheme was too much to ask, and Michelangelo only succeeded in completing Moses and part of the statues of Leah and Rachel on either side; the rest of the tomb was completed by less accomplished hands. It's far smaller than intended, making Moses quite out of proportion. The horns are the result of a bad translation, where the Hebrew word for 'radiant' was confused with that for 'horned'. The church itself is very old, a fifth-century structure that was altered in the eighth, 11th, 15th and 18th centuries. Most visitors come to pray at the high altar, beneath which are a set of prisoner's chains said to have been used to shackle St. Peter in Jerusalem, one of the most venerated relics in all Rome.

69 G6 Piazza San Pietro in Vincoli 4a, 00184 Roma 06 488 2865 Apr–Sep daily 8–12.30, 3.30–7; Oct–Mar 8–12.30, 3–6; no visits during Mass Sun 11am Free Colosseo

Left *Inside Santa Maria del Popolo*
Below *Santa Maria in Trastevere*

SANTA PRASSEDE

Santa Prassede houses one of Rome's most important Byzantine treasures, the San Zeno chapel, built by Paschal I as a mausoleum for his mother, Theodora, and known as the Garden of Paradise because of the beauty and richness of the gold mosaics. A house of worship has stood on this spot since AD489, rebuilt and restored many times before it was enlarged in 822 by Paschal I to house relics of martyrs taken from the catacombs. The highlights are the ninth-century mosaics in the San Zeno chapel, depicting Christ Pantocrator, the saints and Virgin Mary, but the apse and the triumphal arch are also covered with beautiful mosaics. These show St. Peter and St. Paul introducing St. Prassede and her sister, St. Pudenziana, to Christ and, in the arch, New Jerusalem, Christ and the saints. The Chapel of San Zeno also has an excellent example of ornamental *opus sectile* paving in multi-hued marble. In a corner stands the Column of the Flagellation, brought from Jerusalem in 1223.

Outside is Bernini's first work, of Bishop Giovanni Battista Santoni.

69 G5 Via di Santa Prassede 9/A, 00184 Roma 06 488 2456 Daily 7.30–12, 4–6.30; closed Aug Free; bring €1 for the light machine outside Chapel of San Zeno Cavour, Termini, Vittorio Emanuele 16, 70, 71

TERME DI CARACALLA

www.beniculturali.it

The Terme di Caracalla (Baths of Caracalla) in Celio are one of the most impressive ancient Roman complexes. Designed primarily to care for the body, the baths were also a cultural meeting place. Begun by Septimius Severus in AD206 and opened by Emperor Caracalla in AD217, they were functional until AD537, when the Goths destroyed the aqueducts that supplied the water. There was an immense pool for cooling the body called a *frigidarium*, a large, hot, circular room known as a *caldarium*, rooms for hot and warm baths, porticoes, halls, gymnasia, statues, libraries, gardens and a stadium. Up to 1,600 people were able to bathe at one time. All the rooms were decorated with alabaster, granite and mosaics, most of which are intact. Recent excavations have uncovered an underground Mithraic temple. Open-air opera is staged here in summer by the Teatro dell'Opera.

69 G9 Viale delle Terme di Caracalla 52, 00153 Roma 06 3996 7700 Mon 9–2, Tue–Sun 9–sunset; last entry 1 hour before closing €6; EU youths (18–24) €3; under 18s free Circo Massimo

VIA APPIA ANTICA

The Via Appia (Appian Way), also known as the Regina Viarum (Queen of Roads), was the first road built by the Romans. The magistrate Appius Claudius began building it in 312BC, and by the second century BC it reached Brindisi, a distance of 589km (366 miles). Now 212km (132 miles) long, running between Rome and Capua, it is closed to cars, and a green park lines the route—a popular spot with Romans at weekends. It is paved with *basoli*, basalt rock stones of polygonal shape, many of which are intact. You can walk on these ancient stones, passing venerable busts and statues, churches, catacombs and ancient villas.

In Rome, the road begins at Porta San Sebastiano. Look for the ancient column inserted in a modern wall marking the first mile. At the corner with Via Ardeatina is the Church of Domine Quo Vadis, Latin for 'Lord, where are you going?' It was here that St. Peter, escaping Nero's persecutions, was stopped by Jesus, who asked him to return to Rome and face his destiny.

On the other side of the Via Appia are the ruins of Maxentius's circus and imperial residence. The tomb of Cecilia Metella, wife of Marcus Crassus, son of the Republican Roman ruler, stands at a crossing with a road of the same name. From here pine and cypress trees, statues and funerary monuments flank the way. Farther along are the remains of a nymphaeum, the pleasure house of Villa dei Quintili, the largest villa in ancient Rome's suburbs. Along the way, look for the catacombs of St. Priscilla, St. Callisto and St. Sebastian.

69 off G9 Via Appia Antica, 00178 Roma Circo Massimo 118, 160, 628

Above left *Beautiful ninth-century mosaics depict Christ and angels in Santa Prassede* **Above right** *The Roman aqueduct on Via Appia Antica*

VILLA BORGHESE

The Villa Borghese's beautiful avenues and paths, embellished with ancient statues and fountains, make it one of the grandest parks in Rome. Cardinal Borghese created both it and the imposing Villa Pinciana, or Casino Borghese, in the early 17th century to house his art collection. Highlights are the Casino della Meridiana, the aviary and the lake with its little island, in the middle of which is an 18th-century Ionian-style temple to Aesculapius, the Greek god of medicine. At the heart of the park is Piazza di Siena, a popular venue for international horse-races. There is also a zoo (▷ 108).

67 F2 Villa Borghese, 00187 Roma 06 0608 Dawn–dusk. Zoo daily 9.30–5 Zoo: adult €8.50, child (3–12) €6 Flaminio, Spagna

VILLA GIULIA AND MUSEO NAZIONALE ETRUSCO

www.beniculturali.it

Built between 1550 and 1555 as a country house and garden for the hedonistic Pope Julius III, Villa Giulia, near Piazza del Popolo, was designed by some of the leading architects of the day, including Michelangelo. Surrounded by a series of courtyards, the villa has a loggia by Ammanati, sumptuous interiors and a nymphaeum with caryatids, rockeries, false grottoes and a Vasari fountain. Today it houses the world's greatest collection of Etruscan art and objects, piecing together the way of life and death of this mysterious civilization. .

The Etruscan museum houses the pre-Roman heritage of Latium, Umbria and southern Etruria, found in the necropolises of Cerveteri (▷ 323) and Veio. It contains treasures and objects from the Etruscan, Faliscan and Greek civilizations. Hall 7 houses statues from Veio made of polychrome terracotta, including one depicting Heracles in combat with Apollo for the doe, a masterpiece. These statues all come from one temple in Veio and are thought be the work of Vulca, who carved the statues for the Temple of Jupiter on the Capitol in 509BC. The most celebrated piece of Etruscan art is the Sarcophagus of the Spouses, found in the Cerveteri halls. It dates from the end of the sixth century BC and is a clear indication that the Etruscans believed in an afterlife. A vase decorated with the Etruscan alphabet is displayed in Hall 15, while the Room of Venus houses pieces that were found at the fifth-century BC temples of Pyrgi, the ancient Etruscan port of Lazio. Here are displayed hundreds of vases, models of buildings and items of furniture that were made to accompany the dead to their graves. Outside in the gardens there is also a reconstruction of an Etruscan temple.

67 D1 Piazzale Villa Giulia 9, 00196 Roma 06 32180 Tue–Sun 8.30–7.30 Adult €4, child (under 18) free Flaminio

Below *Geometric mosaic flooring in the Baths of Caracalla*

FROM TRASTEVERE TO THE VATICAN

This walk takes you through the vibrant Trastevere neighbourhood, then on to the Janiculum Hill where there's a chance to visit two superb galleries and enjoy some great city views en route to the Vatican.

THE WALK
Distance: 2.5km (1.5 miles)
Allow: 3 hours
Start at: Isola Tiberina
End at: Piazza San Pietro

HOW TO GET THERE
Take bus 23, 63, 280 or tram 8.

★ Start on the Isola Tiberina. The Tiber island has a long tradition of healing and much of it is still occupied by one of Rome's major hospitals. The Romans dedicated a temple here to Esculapio (Greek Asclepius), the god of healing, and transformed the island's shape to conform to a legend that the god, disguised as a water snake, swam here from a boat. The island is indeed boat-shaped and must have looked more so when it was panelled with travertine to form a stern and prow and had an obelisk to act as a mast. Both bridges leading to the island date from Roman times and are the oldest in the city.

Face the Trastevere bank and cross the Ponte Cestio to leave the island. Cross the busy Lungotevere dell'Anguillara and carry straight on to Piazza in Piscinula. Turn right on to the Via della Lungaretta and continue straight on until you come to Piazza di Santa Maria in Trastevere and the church of the same name (▷ 97).

❶ The Church of Santa Maria has some beautiful mosaics, both on the facade and inside.

Facing the church of Santa Maria, take the right-hand street out of the piazza: Via della Scala. When you reach the junction with Via Garibaldi cross this and continue straight ahead along Via della Lungara, passing the Villa Farnesina on your right.

❷ The beautiful Renaissance Villa Farnesina was designed and built in 1508 by Baldassare Peruzzi for Agostino Chigi, a wealthy banker from Siena. He wanted a showcase villa to impress his business guests; the result is 16th-century opulence at its height, with a frescoed walk and ceilings, shady loggias, gilding and precious stone. Raphael painted the Loggia di Galatea on the ground floor, and don't miss the *trompe l'oeil* frescoes of rural Italy in the Salone delle Prospettive on the upper floor. In 1580 the Chigi family sold the villa to the Farnese family; it has been known by their name ever since. The lovely gardens are a delightful refuge on a hot day.

Opposite, on the other side of the road, stands the Palazzo Corsini, designed by Fuga and built between 1732 and 1736; it houses part of the Galleria Nazionale d'Arte Antica, a rich collection of 16th- to 17th-century art, including works by Fra Angelico, Titian and Caravaggio.

After visiting the Palazzo Corsini, take the Via Corsini, and follow it to the end to the entrance of the Orto Botanico, Rome's wonderful botanic garden on the slopes of the Gianicolo (the Janiculum Hill).

❸ Although not one of Rome's original seven hills, it is generally agreed that the Janiculum is one of the city's finest vantage points. You can see across the city from almost anywhere on its slopes, though the best views are from the huge sweep of the Piazzale Garibaldi at the top. The hill is also home to Rome's Botanic Garden, whose history dates back to the 13th century, when Pope Nicholas III first cultivated medicinal plants on the site. Today, it's a shady oasis, filled with palms, pines, oaks, herbs and roses. The greenhouses have fine collections of orchids and tropical plants.

Leave the Orto Botanico by retracing your steps (as this is the only entrance and exit), and turn left onto Via della Lungara. Continue onto Lungotevere Gianicolense and then turn right onto Ponte Principe Amadeo Savoia Aosta.

❹ The equestrian monument you can see on the bridge commemorates Giuseppe Garibaldi, one of the key figures in the Risorgimento, the founding of modern Italy, who fought a battle nearby in 1849.

Follow the river by walking along the Lungotevere in Sassia, named after the medieval English pilgrims, the Saxons, who once lodged in this area. By the next bridge, the Ponte Vittorio Emanuele II, cross the road and turn left along Borgo Santo Spirito. This runs parallel with the Via della Conciliazione and will lead you to the Piazza San Pietro and the Pinacoteca Vaticana (▷ 86–87).

❺ Piazza San Pietro lies directly in front of the Basilica San Pietro (▷ 74–75) and was redesigned by Bernini in the 17th century. His impressive colonnade surrounds the piazza.

WHEN TO GO

Morning is the best time for this walk, when the shops in Trastevere and both museums are open, but before it gets too hot for the walk on to San Pietro.

WHERE TO EAT

ROMOLO NEL GIARDINO DI RAFFAELLO

It's claimed Raphael's mistress La Fornarina, the beautiful baker's daughter, lived here. The food is traditional, with innovative twists.
✉ Via di Porta Settimiana 8, 00153 Roma
☎ 06 581 8284 🕐 Tue–Sun 12–3, 7–11; closed Aug

Opposite *View of the Vatican City from the dome of St. Peter's*

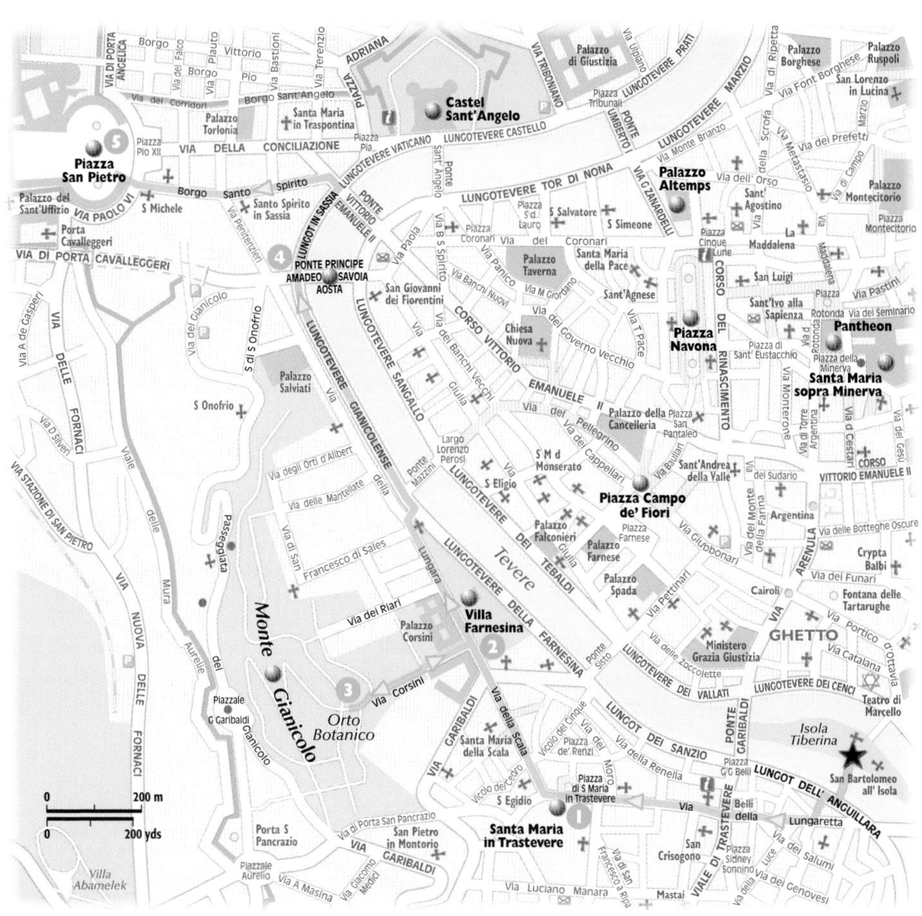

CENTRO STORICO

A walk through medieval and Renaissance Rome, with the chance to see some of Caravaggio's finest works, take in elegant shopping streets and explore some of Rome's loveliest piazzas.

THE WALK
Distance: 2.5km (1.5 miles)
Allow: 3 hours
Start at: Largo di Torre Argentina
End at: Piazza del Popolo

HOW TO GET THERE
Take bus 30, 40, 46, 62, 63, 81, 787, 492 to Largo di Torre Argentina.

★ With your back to the ruins in the Largo di Torre Argentina, turn left and go along the Corso Vittorio Emanuele towards the river. Then take the second or third left (following the brown tourist information signs on either of the turnings) to the Campo dei Fiori.

❶ One of Rome's most picturesque squares, Piazza Campo dei Fiori has a wonderfully vibrant daily fruit and vegetable market (▷ 104–105), while the surrounding streets are crammed with food and artisan shops and busy with locals shopping. Its name comes from its original role as grazing land for sheep and cattle—the 'field of flowers'. The statue in the centre shows the philosopher Giordano Bruno, who promoted the separation of political and religious power and was condemned to death for heresy on the strength of his beliefs. He was burned alive in the centre of the square in 1600, the first of a series of executions here that the Inquisition carried out throughout the 17th century. It's worth visiting the shops around the square for local goods.

From here, walk through Piazza della Cancelleria back to Corso Vittorio Emanuele II and cross the road diagonally right to Piazza San Pantaleo. Follow the brown signs to Piazza Navona (▷ 89).

❷ Piazza Navona is busy with outdoor cafés, street performers and fountains, one of which is the famous Fontana dei Quattro Fiumi.

Exit the piazza about halfway down by turning right down Corso Agonale; ahead you'll see Palazzo Madama. Built in the 17th century and named after Margaret of Austria, the illegitimate daughter of Emperor Charles V, it is now the seat of the Senate, the upper house of the Italian Parliament. Behind it, turn left down Via della Dogana Vecchia to the interesting church of San Luigi dei Francesi.

❸ San Luigi dei Francesi is the national church of France in Rome and was designed by Giacomo della Porta, who built it between 1523 and 1578. Its main draw is the little chapel of St. Matthew, at

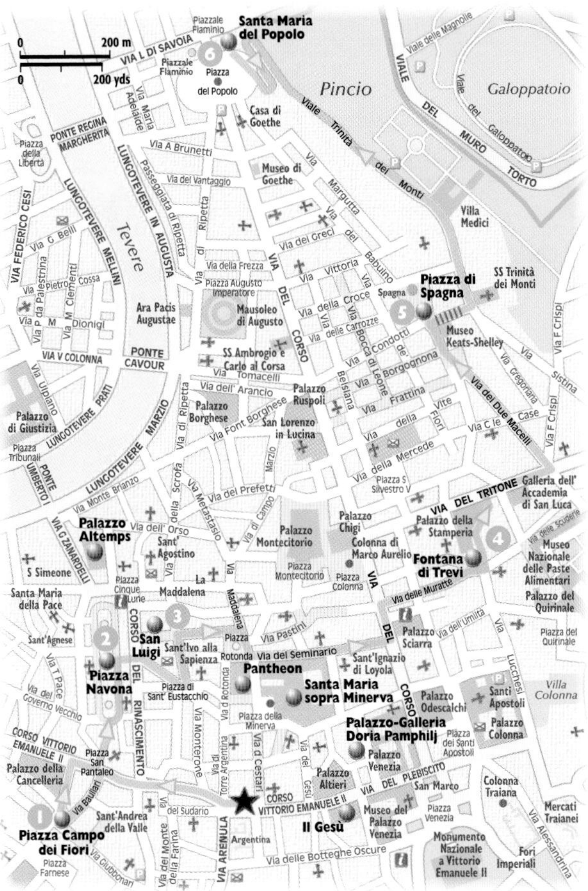

the bottom of the left-hand aisle, which is virtually covered with three outstanding paintings by Caravaggio, his first great religious pictures. They show, with outstanding realism and vitality, scenes from the life of the saint; the *Calling*, the *Martyrdom* and *St. Matthew with the Angel*, and all show the artist's obsession with light, shade and realism—he used local people as his models and their shabbiness and dirty feet often enraged his patrons. He lived life to the full and we know as much about him from contemporary police records as from any other source.

Cross the road and follow the brown signs to Piazza della Minerva and the Pantheon (▷ 90). Facing the Pantheon, go left up Via del Seminario and through Piazza Sant'Ignazio to the Via del Corso. Turn left, cross the Corso and follow the brown signs to the Fontana di Trevi (▷ 73).

❹ The dramatic Trevi Fountain was designed in 1762 by Nicola Salvi; throw a coin over your left shoulder if you want to return to Rome.

Turn left along Via Stamperia to Via del Tritone, where you cross and turn right to take the left hand turning into Via dei Due Macelli, which leads to Piazza di Spagna and the famous Spanish Steps (▷ 89).

❺ The Spanish Steps were designed by Francesco de Sanctis and built in the 1720s.

Opposite The Calling of St. Matthew *by Caravaggio, in the church of San Luigi dei Francesi*

Climb the steps. Pause at the top to take in one of Rome's best views, with domes and rooftops stretching away in front of you towards St. Peter's Basilica. Leave the steps via Viale della Trinità dei Monti. On the right, you'll pass the Villa Medici, home to the French Academy, which was founded in 1666 and still applies itself to studies in art and architecture, and walk along beneath the edge of the Pincio gardens until you see Piazza del Popolo, with its Egyptian obelisk, below you. Descend to the piazza to visit the church of Santa Maria del Popolo (▷ 97).

❻ The church was built originally in the 15th century and is packed with art by the masters. Raphael, Pinturicchio and Bramante all contributed to Santa Maria's interior, but today most people flock here to see the two paintings by Caravaggio, *The Conversion of St. Paul* and *The Crucifixion of St. Peter*, which are in a side chapel. They are superb examples of the artist's work, full of technical wizardry, drama and marvellous *chiaroscuro*.

WHEN TO GO

Morning is the best time, when the Campo dei Fiori market is in full swing and the churches are open.

PLACES TO VISIT

SAN LUIGI DEI FRANCESI

✉ 5 Piazza San Luigi dei Francesi, 00186 Roma ☎ 06 688271 🕐 Mon–Wed, Fri 10–12.30, 4–7, Thu 10–12.30 ✋ Free

WHERE TO EAT

BABINGTON'S TEA ROOMS

Opened in 1896 by two British ladies to cater for homesick tourists, Babington's is a Roman institution, serving snacks and light meals all day, including, naturally, an excellent cup of tea.

✉ Piazza di Spagna 23, 00187 Roma ☎ 06 678 6027 🕐 Wed–Mon 9–8.30

SHOPPING

AI MONASTERI

www.monasteri.it

Shops as special as this barely exist outside Italy. This 19th-century pharmacy specializes in products from monasteries all over the country, with a wide range of natural skin and body care products, as well as food and giftware.

✉ Corso del Rinascimento 72, 00186 Roma ☎ 06 6880 2783 🕐 Tue–Fri 9–1, 5–8, Sat 9–1 🚌 Any to either Corso Vittorio Emanuele II or Corso del Rinascimento

ANGLO AMERICAN BOOK CO.

www.aab.it

A short distance from the Scalinata di Triniti dei Monti, this is one of the better English-language bookshops in town, housed in a 19th-century building. The excellent selection includes music, cinema, philosophy, religion, science, fiction and children's books. They also stock visitors' guidebooks to Rome, Italy and most world destinations.

✉ Via delle Vite 02, 00187 Roma ☎ 06 679 5222 🕐 Tue–Sat 10.30–7.30, Mon 3.30–7.30. Closed Aug 🚌 40, 62, 64, 116

Above *Campo dei Fiori market*

BERTÈ

One of Rome's oldest toy shops, with a huge array of teddy bears, dolls, Lego and all kinds of other collectibles catering to children of all ages. Parents recommend it too for the very helpful staff and great attention-keeping selection of toys and gadgets.

✉ Piazza Navona 107–111, 00186 Roma ☎ 06 687 5011 🕐 Tue–Sat 9.30–1, 3.30–7.30, Mon 3.30–7.30 🚌 64, 87, 116 or any to Corso del Rinascimento

BRIGHENTI

Crystal chandeliers, marble floors and pastel decor are the setting for this glamorous shop trading in *lingerie di lusso*. Sensuous, silky nightwear, lavish underwear and beautifully crafted swimwear bring out the movie star in you.

✉ Via Frattina 7, 00187 Roma ☎ 06 679 1484 🕐 Tue–Sat 10–7, Mon 3–7 Ⓜ Spagna

BRIONI

www.brioniroma.com

Brioni has dressed royalty and celebrities since 1945, earning a well-deserved reputation as one of Italy's top tailors. Leave your measurements with them and you can call up to have a suit made anytime, anywhere. This, the oldest and largest of their stores, also stocks women's ready-to-wear items. Others can be found at Via Condotti 21a and Via Veneto 129.

✉ Via Barberini 79, 00187 Roma ☎ 06 484517 🕐 Mon–Sat 10–1.30, 3.30–7.30 Ⓜ Barberini 🚌 63, 116, 175, 492, 590, 630

BULGARI

www.bulgari.com

This is the most splendid jewellery shop in Rome, and it has prices to match. The 20th-century American artist Andy Warhol called it the most important museum of art in the Western world. It specializes in glittering Renaissance-inspired pieces that have graced Italy's most glamorous women over the decades.

✉ Via Condotti 10, 00187 Roma ☎ 06 696261 🕐 Daily 10–7 Ⓜ Spagna

CAMPO DEI FIORI

Probably the most expensive, and without doubt the liveliest market in Rome. Stall-holders collect their wares from the nearby medieval storage vaults and set up shop in

this charismatic location. There was a time when heretics were burned here, and traitors hanged. These days the only things hanging are the flowers and food.
✉ Piazza Campo dei Fiori, 00186 Roma
🕒 Mon–Sat 8–2 🚌 46, 62, 64, 116

LA DOLCEROMA
www.ladolceroma.com
This Viennese patisserie is an unobtrusive little shop right in the heart of the Jewish quarter. Once inside you'll understand why people make detours for it. Aside from the excellent chocolate Sacher cake, you can buy cheesecakes of all sizes and with different fillings—from yoghurt to Austrian cream cheese—and various other mouth-watering Austrian specialties. There are also cookies and brownies to munch on to keep you going while you sightsee. This is not the cheapest bakery in town, but it is among the most memorable.
✉ Via del Portico d'Ottavia 20/b, 00186 Roma ☎ 06 689 2196 🕒 Tue–Sat 8–1.30, 3.30–8, Sun 10–1.30 🚌 H, 23, 63, 280, 630, 780 to Lungotevere dei Cenci, or walk from Largo di Torre Argentina or Piazza Venezia

FABRIANO
www.fabrianoboutique.com/stores.asp
Minimalist in design, this store sells stacks of paper goods and stationery such as notepads, diaries and address books, enticingly arranged by colour. Shades run from yellow, green and blue to white, brown and black. The paper is of the highest quality and made by an 800-year-old firm; prices are predictably high. They sell briefcases, too.
✉ Via del Babuino 173, 00187 Roma
☎ 06 32600361 🕒 Mon–Sat 10–7.30
🚇 Spagna or Flaminio 🚌 81, 117, 119, 590, 628

FURLA
www.furla.it
Purveyors of chic bags and practical totes in bright shades, along with scarves, shoes and jewellery, Furla has some wild style combinations and original touches. Prices are moderate compared with other big-name designers. The company has a branches all over the world, including several more in Rome.
✉ Piazza di Spagna 22, 00187 Roma
☎ 06 6920 0363 🕒 Daily 10–8
🚇 Spagna 🚌 116, 117, 119, 590

GIORGIO SERMONETA
www.sermonetagloves.com
The shop is fairly small and may feel cramped, but don't be fooled—just look up! Top-quality gloves—thousands of them—decorate this shop, and come in bright shades and styles to fit every hand. Prices range from €23 to €100.
✉ Piazza di Spagna 61, 00187 Roma
☎ 06 6791960 🕒 Mon–Sat 9.30–8, Sun 10–7 🚇 Spagna 🚌 116, 117

LEAM
www.leam.com
Leam has three stores within a few doors of each other, with top designer fashion and accessories for men and women. The best of Italian design under one roof, there are Armani, Gucci, Dolce & Gabbana, Prada and even Philippe Stark dresses. The shop assistants can be over-attentive (not uncommon in Rome). There is a roof terrace and bar in the women's store.
✉ Via Appia Nuova 26, 30, 32, 00183 Roma
☎ 06 7720 7204 🕒 Mon 4–8, Tue–Sat 9.30–8 🚇 San Giovanni 🚌 87, 360

MATHERIA FARNESE
www.farnese.it
The owners of this shop create bright, handcrafted ceramic floor tiles inspired by Roman villas and 18th-century patrician houses. The group of architects and artisans also restore beautiful antique tiles, plates and jugs. Naturally, this kind of craftsmanship comes at a price.
✉ Via G. Garibaldi 53–55/a, 00153 Roma
☎ 06 581 7566 🕒 Mon–Fri 10–7, Sat by appointment 🚌 23, 280: stop closest to Via Garibaldi

NATOLLI
This specialist glass store near Piazza Navona sells every conceivable type of glass from Murano in Venice—tableware, mirrors, chandeliers and decorative pieces. Shipping can be arranged worldwide.
✉ Corso del Rinascimento 55, 00186 Roma
☎ 06 6830 1170 🕒 Mon–Sat 9–8 🚌 64, 87,116

PORTA PORTESE
Rome's most famous flea market stretches all the way from Porta Portese to Trastevere station. It also branches off down the side streets. From trendy clothes and antiques to junk, you can find all sorts here. Arrive early for the best buys, and beware of pickpockets.
✉ Porta Portese, 00153 Roma 🕒 Sun 6.30–1 🚌 Tram 3

RICORDI MEDIA STORE
www.lafeltrinelli.it
Rome's popular music store, part of Feltrinelli, an Italy-wide bookshop chain, is in a nicely designed building that once housed the Verdi archives. It has the largest classical DVD/CD collection in Rome. There is a large Italian music section and sheet music and musical instruments are also sold. They have two other outlets: Termini and Via del Corso.
✉ Via Vittorio Emanuele II Orlando 73/75, 00187 Roma ☎ 06 6290 8023 🕒 Mon–Sat 9.30–8, Sun 3.30–8; closed Jul, Aug Sun
🚌 116, 117

TAD
www.taditaly.com
Rome's first 'concept store', where old and new are beautifully combined for a full lifestyle experience. Browse among the chic fashions, rare perfume, designer homeware, books, sounds, have your hair cut perhaps, and then relax in the delightful café-restaurant.
✉ Via del Babuino 155a, 00187 Roma
☎ 06 9684 🕒 Tue–Fri 10.30–7.30, Sat 10.30–8, Sun–Mon 12–7.30 🚇 Spagna
🚌 117, 119

UNDERGROUND
Flea markets have sprung up all over Rome in the past few years. One of the best-established is this antiques and collector's market in the Ludovisi underground car park,

held once a month in the winter. More than 100 stands sell prints, small antiques, frames, comics, lace and old vases. There are also children's stands where toys are sold and exchanged.
✉ Via Francesco Crispi 96, 00187 Roma ☎ 06 3600 5345 🕓 Oct–Apr 1st Sun of the month 9–7; closed Feb Ⓜ Spagna 🚌 116, 119, 204, 630, 910 or any bus to Via Veneto

VALENTINO

Several of Italy's top fashion houses were founded in Rome, including Fendi and Valentino, who has been dressing the rich and famous since the late 1950s. Further branches are in Via del Babuino (haute couture) and Via Bocca di Leone.
✉ Via Condotti 13, 00187 Roma ☎ 06 679 5862 🕓 Mon 3–7, Tue–Sat 10–7 Ⓜ Spagna

VOLPETTI

www.volpetti.com
Volpetti is one of the best (though not the cheapest) delis in Rome. There is an astounding variety of breads, cheeses, hams, salamis, fresh pasta and ready-made dishes. Service is professional and cheerful and you can sample the cheese to help you decide. Whatever happens, you won't go away empty-handed, and it's good for gifts. There's another, more expensive branch in Via della Scrofa in the city centre.
✉ Via Marmorata 47, 00153 Roma ☎ 06 574 2352 🕓 Mon Sat 8–2, 5–8.15 Ⓜ Piramide 🚌 23, 30, 75, 280, 716 (or any to Piramide or Via Marmorata); tram 3

ENTERTAINMENT AND NIGHTLIFE

ALEXANDERPLATZ

www.alexanderplatz.it
Rome's most famous jazz venue hosts jazz festivals all year round, and organizes outdoor concerts at Villa Celimontana in summer. American bands are often on the bill. Creole cuisine is served in the busy restaurant.
✉ Via Ostia 9, 00192 Roma ☎ 06 3974 2171 🕓 Mon–Sat 9pm–1.30am; closed first 2 weeks of Aug Ⓜ Ottaviano 🚌 Bus to Piazza Risorgimento or Clodio

ANIMA

At the heart of Roman nightlife, west of Piazza Navona, this bar is a beloved hangout for foreigners and English-speakers. There are excellent fresh-fruit cocktails, ultra-modern decoration and highly respectable resident DJs.
✉ Via di Santa Maria dell'Anima 57, 00186 Roma ☎ 06 6889 2806 🕓 Tue–Sun 9.30pm–2am 🚌 46, 62, 64, 116, 81, 87, 492

AUDITORIUM PARCO DELLA MUSICA

www.auditorium.com
This concert hall building was designed by architect Renzo Piano and opened in 2002. The year-round, three-auditorium complex with an open-air arena is the city's biggest music venue, with a capacity of 4,600. Find it between Lungotevere Flaminio and Viale Tiziano.
✉ Parco della Musica, Viale Pietro de Coubertin 30, 00197 Roma ☎ 06 808 2058 🕓 Performances: Mon–Fri 7–9, 9–11; Box office: daily 11–6; Hello Ticket (credit card reservations): Mon–Fri 10–5 🎟 From €5 Ⓜ Piazzale Flaminio, and then tram 🚌 Bus to Auditorio

BAR SAN CALISTO

Tiny, spit 'n' sawdusty, even a little seedy, but this is where the locals hang out over a beer or glass of prosecco—or one of Marcello's delicious home-made ice creams, especially an *affogato* (drenched in liqueur). The outside tables are a good vantage point from where to observe Trastevere life.
✉ Piazza San Calisto, 00153 Roma 🕓 Mon–Sat 5.30am–2am 🚌 780; tram 8

BIG MAMA

www.bigmama.it
Big Mama is a famous Trastevere jazz club, where local and international bands play in the cavernous underground hideaway. The audience sits close to the band, and it is not uncommon to see dancing on the table tops.
✉ Vicolo San Francesco a Ripa 18, 00153 Roma ☎ 06 581 2551 🕓 Daily 9pm–1.30am; shows at 10.30. Closed

Above *There is a great atmosphere at the Big Mama jazz club*

Jul–Oct 🎟 Annual membership €14 🚌 75 or 170 to Viale Trastevere or Piazza Mastai

CARUSO

The best bet for Latin beats, ranging from salsa to hip-hop, Caruso has a mix of live bands and Rome's best DJs. It is always packed, especially on Sunday, which is disco night. There are Arabic music nights, too.
✉ Via di Monte Testaccio 36, 00153 Roma ☎ 06 574 5019 🕓 Tue–Sun 10.30pm–3am 🎟 €8–€15 Ⓜ Piramide 🚌 Bus to Testaccio

ESCOPAZZO

This wine and cocktail bar, loved by the younger crowd, is just off Piazza Venezia. Most nights see live music and a buzzing atmosphere. Other evenings feature DJs.
✉ Via d'Aracoeli 41, 00186 Roma ☎ 06 6920 0422 🕓 Daily 8.30–3am 🎟 Free 🚌 40, 64, 175

FRENI E FRIZIONI

www.freniefrizioni.com
This is the place for *aperitivi*—a spectacular buffet served along with your glass of beer, wine or cocktail in the early evening, including anything from pasta to guacamole. The name means 'brakes and clutches', as it was once a garage; now it is Trastevere's coolest bar.
✉ Via del Politeama 4–6, 00153 Roma ☎ 06 5833 4210 🚌 23, 280

THE GALLERY

www.thegallery.it

This is an enegetic, modern and elegant bar behind the Pantheon. Music from hip-hop to R&B to 1970s and 1980s revival draws a crowd that's young and ready to party.

✉ Via della Maddalena 12, 00186 Roma ☎ 06 481 8795 🕐 Tue–Fri 8pm–3am, Sat–Sun 8pm–4am 💳 €12 🚌 116

PALALOTTOMATICA

www.forumnet.it

The biggest venue in the city is this huge sports stadium-turned-concert hall in EUR. It hosts all the top international acts—everyone from Sting to the Rolling Stones has played here at some time.

✉ Piazzale dello Sport, Viale dell'Umanesimo, 00144 Roma 🕐 8pm (usually) Ⓜ Metro to EUR Palaeur and bus to Palazzo dello Sport

PALAZZO DELLE ESPOSIZIONI

www.palazzoesposizioni.it

This is Rome's all-round cultural centre where theatre, film showings and art exhibitions take place under one roof. If all of the city's artistic juices could be captured in a single space, this would be it. It can be found at the mouth of the huge tunnel that connects Via Nazionale to Via del Tritone.

✉ Via Nazionale 194, 00184 Roma ☎ 06 399 67500 🕐 9pm (usually);. box office: Wed–Mon 10–9 🚌 Bus to Via Nazionale

QUBE

www.qubedisco.com

The young crowd dance till they drop in Rome's biggest underground disco. Friday night is 'Muccassassina' night, once gay and transgressive, now more straight and mainstream.

✉ Via di Portonaccio 212, 00159 Roma ☎ 06 438 5445 🕐 Thu–Sat 11pm–4am 💳 Cover charge Ⓜ Tiburtina 🚌 71, 168, 204, 409, 492, 545, 649

TEATRO OLIMPICO

www.teatroolimpico.it

This Accademia Filarmonica-owned venue is very comfortable, although it has been upstaged by the Auditorium Parco della Musica (▷ 106). The main season runs from September to the end of May, and the acoustics and range of productions are always excellent.

✉ Piazza Gentile da Fabriano 17, 00196 Roma ☎ 06 326 599 Daily 10–1, 3–5.30; after 8pm for same-day tickets 💳 €20–€35 🚌 Bus or tram to Piazza Mancini or Stadio Olimpico

TEATRO DELL'OPERA DI ROMA

www.opera.roma.it

www. amitsrl.it (online booking)

The Teatro dell'Opera is a hidden gem, too often overlooked by the locals. The interior is adorned with all the trimmings of a true opera house, complete with velvet boxes. Not to be missed by those who love classical dance, the theatre is beautiful and attracts first-rate dance troupes from all over the world. You are certain to see the cream of Roman society here.

✉ Piazza B Gigli 1, Esquilino, 00184 Roma ☎ 06 4816 0255 🕐 Performances: Nov–end May 9pm; Box office: Tue–Sat 9–5, Sun 9–1.30 💳 €11–€130 Ⓜ Repubblica 🚌 40Exp, 60Exp, 64, 70, 117, 170

TEATRO DI ROMA–ARGENTINA

www.teatrodiroma.net

This is a leading year-round venue for beautifully staged productions in one of Rome's oldest theatres. A performance here is a night to remember. Dress to impress. There is a bar serving cocktails at the intermission. The theatre is on the Campo dei Fiori side of the square.

✉ Largo di Torre Argentina 52, 00186 Roma ☎ 06 6880 4601/800 013390 🕐 9pm; box office: Mon–Sat 10–2, 3–7 💳 €12–€27 🚌 Bus or tram to Largo Argentina

VILLAGGIO GLOBALE

This former slaughterhouse (the Mattatoio) is Rome's best-loved music venue. There's a huge outdoor courtyard for concerts and dancing. During larger events, food stands are set up inside.

✉ Via di Monte Testaccio 22, 00153 Roma ☎ 06 334 179 0006 🕐 6pm–3am (variable) 💳 €10 (varies) 🚌 Bus to Testaccio or Lungotevere Testaccio

WARNER VILLAGE SPACE CINEMA MODERNO

www.warnervillage.it

This multiplex screens premieres, major releases and Hollywood chart-toppers in both Italian and English. It also has screenings in 3D and late-night shows on Saturday.

✉ Piazza della Repubblica 45, 00185 Roma ☎ 06 892111 💳 €6–€11 Ⓜ Repubblica

SPORTS AND ACTIVITIES

CINECITTÀ

www.cinecitta.it

On warm summer nights, Rome's celebrated film studio opens to the public. Among the attractions are chariot races Ben Hur-style, when gladiators and their horses are dressed in the appropriate Roman attire.

✉ Via Tuscolana, 00173 Roma 🕐 Sat evenings, summer only 💳 €15 Ⓜ Cinecittà

CIRCOLO DEL GOLF DI ROMA

www.golfroma.it

This is an excellent 18-hole golf course surrounded by umbrella pines and Roman ruins. There is a great on-site restaurant.

✉ Via Appia Nuova 716/a, 00178 Roma ☎ 06 780 3407 🕐 Tue–Sun 8–sunset 💳 €80 weekdays, €110 weekends Ⓜ Colli Albani, then a taxi ride

CIRCOLO DELLA STAMPA

This friendly tennis club has both clay and synthetic-grass courts at reasonable prices. There are tennis lessons for all levels.

✉ Piazza Mancini 19, 00196 Roma ☎ 06 323 2452 🕐 Daily 8am–11pm 💳 €10–€30 per hour 🚌 Bus to Piazza Mancini

PISCINA DELLE ROSE

Rome's largest open-air pool is a great place to bring the kids at weekends. It's at the ultra-sleek Palasport facility built by Mussolini.

✉ Viale America 20, 00144 Roma ☎ 06 592 6717 🕐 Daily 9am–10pm 💳 €12 Ⓜ Palasport, EUR

STADIO FLAMINIO

www.federugby.it

Don't be fooled into thinking Italians only go mad for *calcio* (soccer). The

country is home to 24 rugby clubs, and the best games are in the capital, when club RDS Roma hits the field.
✉ Viale Tiziano, 00196 Roma ☎ 06 3685 7832 ✋ €10–€30 🚌 Bus or tram to Viale Tiziano

STADIO OLIMPICO
www.asroma-calcio.com
Football, football, football—no spectator sport is more important to Romans. The city has two rival teams: Roma fans sit on the south side of the stadium and Lazio fans on the north side.
✉ Viale dello Stadio Olimpico, 00194 Roma ☎ 06 323 7333 🕓 Sun throughout season ✋ €15–€100 🚌 Bus to Lungotevere Maresciallo Cadorna 🚇 Line A to Otaviano then bus 32

HEALTH AND BEAUTY

AVEDA SALON
www.aveda.com
Enjoy pampering at its finest by one of Europe's leading lotions-and-potions brands. Energize yourself with plant steam inhalation, skin hydration or mild aromatherapy. Renew yourself with a manicure, pedicure or a quick wax.
✉ Rampa Mignanelli 9, 00187 Roma ☎ 06 6992 4257 🕓 Mon 3.30–8, Tue–Sat 10–8 ✋ €35 manicure, €44 plant steam inhalation 🚇 Spagna

FOR CHILDREN

AQUAPIPER
www.aquapiper.it
This summer open-air park is one of Rome's best, fully equipped with water slides, a huge swimming pool and five other smaller ones, along with plenty of other water activities designed for family fun. There's also a *trenino* (little train), go-kart area and an ice-skating rink.
✉ Via Maremma Inferiore, Guidonia Montecello, Roma ☎ 0774 326538 🕓 May to mid-Sep daily 9–7 ✋ Adult €16 Mon–Sat, €20 Sun; one child (under 11) free with a paying adult, additional children €6 🚇 Ponte Mammolo then Cotral bus Roma/ Palombara to Aquapiper 🚌 Free bus from Piazza della Repubblica at 8.30, 9.30, 10.30, 11.30 (also 12.30 on weekends); return at 6pm

BIOPARCO DI ROMA
www.bioparco.it
Bioparco is one of the oldest zoos in Europe but it has modern aims to promote the conservation of endangered species. It also hopes to educate visitors about the animals, some of which have been rescued from illegal trading in rare species. The zoo is set in botanical gardens and contains over 1,000 animals.
✉ Piazzale del Giardino Zoologico 1, Villa Borghese, 00197 Roma 🕓 Apr–Oct daily 9.30–6 (7 on Sat, Sun, holidays); Nov–Mar 9.30–5 ✋ Adult €8.50, child 3–12 €6.50 🚇 Flaminio 🚌 52, 53, 926; tram 13,19

EXPLORA—IL MUSEO DEI BAMBINI
www.mdbr.it
Rome's first and only children's museum (best for those eight years and under) opened in 2001. There are four sections dedicated to the human body, the environment, communications, and society, with plenty of signs and material in English. Kids can star in their own TV show, work in a supermarket and find out about living ecologically. Advance reservations are required at the weekend.
✉ Via Flaminia 82, 00192 Roma ☎ 06 361 3776 🕓 Tue–Sun 9.30–7. Tours last 1 hour 45 mins and depart at 10, 12, 3 and 5 (not 10 in Aug) ✋ Adult and child over 3 €7, child (1–3) €3, under 1s free 🚇 Flaminio 🚌 95, 117, 119, 204, 231, 490, 495, 618, 916; tram 2, 3, 19

TIME ELEVATOR
www.timeelevator.it
Time Elevator is a multimedia experience illustrating the history of Rome from its founding to the present day. With headphones, a screen, a moving platform and surprise special effects, this is a genuinely fun (if occasionally factually weak) introduction to the city. Watch Rome burn and see Caesar's assassination; it's worth the rather high entrance fee.
✉ Via S.S. Apostoli 20, 00187 Roma ☎ 06 977 46243 🕓 Daily screenings 10–7.30 ✋ Adult €14–€22, under 12s €12–€19, depending on number of viewings 🚇 Colosseo or Barberini 🚌 40, 62, 63, 64, 916 or any bus to Via del Corso or Piazza Venezia

FESTIVALS AND EVENTS

DECEMBER–JANUARY

BEFANA

According to legend, the Befana was an old woman who refused the Magi shelter on the journey to Bethlehem. Befana is associated with the Christmas period, as is the wise old woman who flies from house to house delivering the good children's presents on 6 January—bad children get coal. A lively fair runs in Piazza Navona during Christmas time. Toys and sweets are the main attraction: look out for the sweet called *carbone*, which looks like lumps of coal.

December–6 January

MARCH

ROME CITY MARATHON

www.maratonadiroma.it

Each spring, runners flock to Rome and, like gladiators, they come down the avenue that cuts right through the Forum. This event is slowly gaining the status equivalent to those held in London and New York.

Via dei Fori Imperiali, 00186 Roma 06 3018 3022, 06 3018 3016 3rd Sunday in March Bus to Piazza Venezia

APRIL

SETTIMANA DEI BENI CULTURALI

www.beniculturali.it

A week when admission is free to many of Rome's museums.

mid-Apr

NATALE DI ROMA

Rome celebrates its birthday every April with feasting and fireworks displays over the Campidoglio.

21 Apr

MAY

CONCORSO IPPICO INTERNAZIONALE DI PIAZZA DI SIENA

www.piazzadisiena.com

Few know it, but Rome plays host to an important annual equestrian event that has all the trimmings of the big horse shows around the world. Show jumping is the main event.

Villa Borghese, Piazza di Siena, 00186 Roma 06 327 9939 Last week in May Adult €44–€78, child €5–€14 Bus to Via Veneto

CAMPIONATO INTERNAZIONALE DI TENNIS

Every May, Rome hosts the Italian Open tennis tournament. This is Europe's most competitive non-grand slam tennis event.

Foro Italico, Viale dei Gladiatori, 00194 Roma 06 323 3807 1st two weeks in May €12–€70 Bus to Lungotevere Maresciallo Cadorna

JULY

OPERA FESTIVAL AT THE TERME DI CARACALLA

www.operaroma.it
www.amitsrl.it (for online booking)

This is what grand opera and ballet are all about. Big productions such as Verdi's *Aida* are staged—complete with horses and elephants—inside the ruins of the ancient Roman Baths of Caracalla. Shows are staged in the largest area of the baths, not the smaller indoor ones. Bring a cushion to sit on.

Terme di Caracalla. Box office: Teatro dell'Opera, Piazza B. Gigli 1, Esquilino, 00184 Roma 06 4816 0255 Performances 8pm; booking office: Tue–Sat 9–5, Sun 9–1.30 €11–€130 FAO Bus to Terme di Caracalla

SEPTEMBER

NOTTE BIANCA

www.lanottebianca.it

An annual event at the end of the summer season, Notte Bianca is when theatres, palaces, art galleries and other venues open all night in a city-wide party celebrating Rome's art and cultural heritage. From 8pm to 8am the next morning, over 500 events are held at various locations and in the streets of central Rome and some suburbs. Municipal, state and private museums, historic squares, villas and gardens, cultural institutes, theatres, libraries, churches and other places of worship, cinemas, art galleries and sports centres remain open through the night. Restaurants and food shops remain open too and there is cheap public transport to get you around.

Saturday in mid-September

SEPTEMBER–NOVEMBER

ROMAEUROPA FESTIVAL

www.romaeuropa.net

This is a major annual arts festival of classical and contemporary theatre, music and dance, held in different venues across the city.

06 455 53050 20 September–30 November €5–€30, festival pass €135, 6-performance pass €60

OCTOBER–NOVEMBER

ROME JAZZ FESTIVAL

www.romajazzfestival.it
www.listicket.it (for online booking)

Another major festival that attracts international artists, the events take place at some of Rome's top music venues, including La Palma Club and the Auditorium, Parco della Musica.

199 109 783 (information) Last week in October, 1st week in November €10–€12

NOVEMBER

INTERNATIONAL FESTIVAL OF SACRED MUSIC

This is a festival of church music and art in which some outstanding musical events take place in some of the most beautiful basilicas in Rome. In previous years top orchestras like the London Philharmonic have taken part. The festival opens with the Holy Mass, complete with Gregorian chant performed by the choir of the Cappella Giulia at St. Peter's Basilica.

November (dates vary)

Left *Meeting an Etruscan lion*

PRICES AND SYMBOLS
Restaurants are listed alphabetically. The prices given are the average for a two-course lunch (L) and a three-course dinner (D) for one person, without drinks. The wine price given is for the least expensive bottle.

For the key to symbols, ▷ 2.

AL 34

Tucked away near the Spanish Steps, this friendly restaurant spills out onto the pavement in summer. Step inside, and you'll see the day's fresh fish displayed for you to choose, or sit and browse the menu of traditional dishes with an imaginative twist. *Primi* include a delicious chickpea soup with cuttlefish, raw marinated octopus with pistachios or home-made *maltagliata* (rough pasta) with green tomatoes and pecorino cheese. Main courses include roast suckling pig and different types of steak and fish such as skewers of swordfish or tuna served with radicchio. All the desserts are home-made—try the delicious *semifreddo* (soft iced dessert with honey and almonds).

✉ Via Mario de' Fiori 34, 00187 Roma ☎ 06 679 5091 🕐 Tue–Sun 12.30–3, 7–11 L €30, D €35, Wine €9 Spagna 🚌 116, 117, 119

Above *Dining alfresco in Rome is always pleasant in summer*

AL BRIC

www.bric.it

This is a very stylish *osteria* and wine bar. There are many small tables in the large room overlooking Via del Pellegrino, near Campo dei Fiori. The wine list is huge, with more than a thousand labels to choose from, while the menu has a wide selection of creative dishes matched perfectly with the wine suggestions. Try spaghetti with anchovies and pecorino or pears with Gorgonzola cheese. Among the home-made desserts, don't miss the strudel with cinnamon ice cream. The bread is home-made, too.

✉ Via del Pellegrino 51, 00186 Roma ☎ 06 687 9533 🕐 Tue–Sat 7.30–11.30pm, Sun 12.30–3 (Oct–Mar only), 7.30–11 D €60, Wine €10 🚌 64, 87, 492 to Largo Argentina. Tram 8

AL VANTAGGIO

Once a simple eating house for local carriage drivers, Al Vantaggio prides itself on serving truly Roman cooking. The interior is simple and traditional, with cool tiled floors, white table settings and frescoed walls. The cooking is straightforward, with plenty of Roman specialties to choose from, as well as excellent *salumeria* sourced by the owners from Calabria. Try local lamb, cooked to tender perfection and served with roast potatoes spiked with rosemary, artichokes done in the Roman style, or a splendid seafood *antipasto*. There's a wicked tiramisu on the dessert menu and good wine, either *sfuso* (carafe) or by the bottle. If you're watching the budget, the pizzas are recommended.

✉ Via del Vantaggio 35, 00186 Roma ☎ 06 323 6848 🕐 Thu–Tue 12–3, 7–11 L €25, D €35, Wine €8 🚌 95, 117, 119, 495, 628

ANTICA TRATTORIA POLESE

www.trattoriapolese.it

Run by the same family since 1960, the Polese started life as a simple restaurant and pizzeria. It's stuck to its guns, still specializing in excellent traditional dishes, lovingly made with fresh seasonal ingredients. You can choose from around 20 different *pizze*, or kick off with delicious

crostini (toasted ciabatta bread) topped with anchovies, mushrooms or ham, before moving on to the house specialties. These include home-made fettuccine with crab, tender roast lamb and a *tagliata* of beef (grilled sliced T-bone steak) served with rocket (arugula) and balsamic dressing. Wines are sourced from all over Italy and include the big names in Italian wine production.
Piazza Sforza Cesarini 40, 00186 Roma 06 686 1709 Wed–Mon 12.30–3, 7–11 L €25, D €35, Wine €8 30, 40, 46, 62, 63, 81, 787, 492

ANTICO CAFFÉ GRECO

www.anticocaffegreco.eu

This famous old café was founded in 1767 by a Greek, hence the name. It has always been popular with the rich and famous, and English poets John Keats and George Byron and German poet and scientist Johann von Goethe all sought refreshment here. Look out for the pictures of some of the café's well-known past customers in the back room.
Via dei Condotti 86, 00187 Roma 06 679 1700 Daily 9–7 Table service: coffee €6, cappuccino €5.50, cake €7 Spagna 119 to Piazza di Spagna, or 52, 53, 58, 61, 71, 85, 160 to Piazza San Silvestro

ANTONIO AL PANTHEON

A family-run restaurant in a pedestrian street near the Pantheon. You can be sure of good food and a warm welcome. The large, brick-vaulted room has 1960s paintings on the walls. Food is quintessentially Roman and the clientele local. Try the fresh fettuccine with creamy walnut sauce and for a main course the calves' liver cooked in chilli, olive oil and wine. The portions are very generous and the service is outstanding.
Via dei Pastini 12, 00186 Roma 06 679 0798 Mon–Sat 12–3, 7–11; closed 2 weeks in Aug L €20, D €38, Wine €8 30, 40, 46, 63, 116

AR MONTAROZZO

www.armontarozzo.itt

It's worth getting a taxi to this lovely restaurant on the Appia Antica with its cosy interior, complete with open fire for winter eating and lovely garden for summer dining. Many of the dishes are straightforward, featuring grilled meat and fish cooked on an open fire, but there are also Roman specialties, such as tripe and offal dishes, seasonal artichokes cooked in the Roman style, and a daily special that's typical of traditional Roman cooking. The huge wine list offers some 300 wines from all over the country, and desserts are home-made, often incorporating the best of lush seasonal fruit.
Via Appia Antica 4, 00179 Roma 06 7720 8434 Tue–Sun 12.30–3, 7.30–11 L €35, D €45, Wine €9 Taxi recommended

BAIRES

www.baires.it

Vibrant walls and floors and the sounds of tango create a South American mood just behind Piazza Navona. Argentinian grilled meat served with various sauces is the obvious dish of choice. First courses include Argentinian-style marinated chicken *(pollo all'escabeche)* and there's a choice of salads and soups. The wine list similarly focuses on Argentinian varieties.
Corso Rinascimento 1, 00186 Roma 06 686 1293 Daily 12–3.30, 7–midnight L €27, D €40, Wine €12 87, 116, 492

LA BUCCA DI RIPETTA

www.labuccadiripetta.com

Established in the 1900s, this perenially popular trattoria just off the Piazza del Popolo combines good Roman cuisine with creative flair at reasonable prices. Freshly baked bread and hand-made pasta feature daily—perhaps try the homemade ravioli filled with radicchio or, in season, truffles or the traditional Roman dish, *spaghetti alle vongole* (with fresh clams). Risotto with red pumpkin is also a house specialty. *Secondi* include swordfish, suckling pork or offal such as Roman tripe. For the sweet-toothed, the *millefoglie* or hot chocolate cake are both divinely decadent. There is a comprehensive wine list including the best Italian wines.
Via Ripetta 36, 00139 Roma 06 321 9391 Daily 12.30–3, 7–11. Closed 4–17 Aug L €30, D €40, Wine €12 Flaminio

CAFFÈ BERNINI

A lovely place to relax after some intensive sightseeing, this elegant bar-restaurant is set on one of Rome's most beautiful piazzas, with tables outside in summer and an elegant interior ranged with wine bottles. You can snack or enjoy a full meal, where dishes include swordfish sushi with lime, risotto with basil and pecorino cheese, and mozzarella with sun-dried tomatoes. Don't miss out on the fabulous cakes on display at the counter.
Piazza Navona 44, 00186 Roma 06 681 92998 Daily 9–midnight; closed Jan L €30, D €50, Wine €14 23, 30, 62, 70

CHECCHINO DAL 1887

www.checchino-dal-1887.com

This temple of Roman cuisine is rated by many as among the city's finest restaurants, and it's been in business for over 120 years, attracting clients from all over the world. Come here for a special dining experience in elegant and friendly surroundings, and sample cooking that's based on the traditional *cucina povera* (poor cooking) raised to new heights. Tasting menus range from €30–€60 and all include specialties rooted in tradition. Oxtail, wild boar, rabbit with rocket and tomatoes and tender milk-fed lamb are all on offer. Desserts include ricotta tart and creamy *panna cotta* (made with pure double cream). There are over 30 different cheeses and a wine list that covers the length and breadth of Italy and many other countries.
Via di Monte Testaccio 30, 00153 Roma 06 574 3816 Tue–Sat 12–3, 8–12 L €40, D €65, Wine €12 Piramide 75

CUL DE SAC

This atmospheric, very popular *enoteca* (wine bar) specializes in a cornucopia of antipasti, cold cuts,

cheeses, patés and salads, and, as you would expect, a splendid collection of wines—more than 1,500 labels. Wines can be sampled by the glass or bottle. A Roman institution.
✉ Piazza Pasquino 73, 00186 Roma ☎ 06 6880 1094 ⏲ Mon–Sat 12–4, 6–12.30 ✋ L €17, D €28, Wine €8 🚌 46, 62, 64, 87, 116, 492

DA BAFFETTO PIZZERIA
Eat early or prepare to queue outside one of Rome's best pizzerias. Don't miss the savoury *bruschetta al pomodoro* (toasted bread topped with tomato, basil and olive oil). Credit cards are not accepted.
✉ Via del Governo Vecchio 114, 00186 Roma ☎ 06 686 1617 ⏲ Daily 6.30pm–midnight ✋ D €20, pizza €6–€9, Wine €5 🚌 46, 62, 64, 87, 116, 492

DA MEO PATACCA
Old beams, a vaulted brick ceiling and red-and-white check table cloths characterize this Trastevere restaurant, a firm favourite with locals and tourists. Recognized for its genuine Roman cooking, the kitchen serves up local dishes such as home-made filled pasta, bean and chickpea soups, *bistecca* and *costata di manzo* (different cuts of well-hung steak), and a mean *spaghetti alla carbonara*, the great Roman staple of spaghetti with an egg and crispy bacon sauce. Desserts are simple but produced on the premises—try the *panna cotta* or a slice of fruit tart. The wine is all *sfuso* (in a carafe) and served by the litre.
✉ Piazza dei Mercanti 30, 00153 Roma ☎ 06 5833 1086 ⏲ Daily 12.30–3, 7.30–10.30 ✋ L €30, D €40, Wine €6 🚌 23, 44, 280, 780. Tram 8

DITIRAMBO
www.ristoranteditirambo.it
Close to the Campo dei Fiori, this little trattoria has a rustic appearance that belies its sophisticated, excellent menu and a wine list of more than 400 labels. The food is seasonal and fresh from the market and the pasta is prepared by hand. Try perhaps the *risotto marinato al prosecco con punte di asparagi, vellutata di parmiggiano* (risotto marinated with prosecco, asparagus and parmesan cream). Inspired vegetarian dishes include *maltagliati con i fiori di zucca* (pasta with courgette flowers), while meat, seafood and fish are always of the highest quality. Try to leave room for one of the delectable desserts such as *semifreddo* with pistachio and saffron cream.
✉ Piazza della Cancellaria 74/75, 00186 Roma ☎ 06 687 1626 ⏲ Tue–Sun 12.30–3.30, 7.30–11.30, Mon 7.30–11.30 ✋ L €30, D €35, Wine €12 🚌 46, 62, 64, 116

L'EAU VIVE
This restaurant is run by nuns. The cuisine is mainly French in origin and the wine list is excellent. Profits from the restaurant help the nuns raise funds for Third World missions.
✉ Via Monterone 85, 00186 Roma ☎ 06 6880 1095 ⏲ Mon–Sat 12.30–4, 7.30–11; closed Aug ✋ L €35, D €53, Wine €11 🚌 87, 492. Tram 8

GELATERIA SAN CRISPINO
This famous ice cream parlour just around the corner from the Trevi Fountain serves what many say is the best ice cream in Italy—if not the world—in lots of flavours. Pistachio, zabaglione, ricotta, or fresh fruit sorbet—the choice is vast. There is a no-cone policy so there is no distraction from the simple, divine tastes. Expect to queue.
✉ Via della Panetteria 42, 00187 Roma ☎ 06 679 3924 ⏲ Wed–Mon 12pm–12.30am (Fri–Sat till 1.30am) ✋ Ice creams from €3.50 🚌 52, 53, 62, 63, 95, 172, 492

IL MARGUTTA
www.ilmargutta.it
Founded in 1979, this modern restaurant, filled with artwork and clean stylish fittings, has been pulling in vegetarians and their friends since it opened. Lunchtime is dedicated to the 'Green Brunch', when, for €15, you can enjoy a choice of soup, a main course, dessert and coffee from a buffet of over 50 dishes. Things are more sophisticated in the evenings when dishes such as broad bean soufflé with pecorino and courgette flowers, ravioli with cheese and an aubergine and tomato sauce, and a tart of asparagus, eggs and truffles make an appearance on the menu. Over 70 per cent of the produce used is organic, as are many of the wines; oils are cold pressed and pasta and bread are made on the premises using organic flour. There's live music every Saturday evening and a special jazz evening on the last Tuesday of the month.
✉ Via Margutta 118, 00187 Roma ☎ 06 3265 0577 ⏲ Daily 12.30–3.30, 7.30–11.30; closed 2 weeks in Aug ✋ L €10–€16, D €40, Wine €15 Ⓜ Flaminio or Spagna 🚌 116, 117

LA PERGOLA
wwwromecavalieri.com
This is Rome's only three Michelin-starred restaurant, stunningly located at the top of the Rome Cavalieri Waldorf Astoria with breathtaking views of the Eternal City. Helmed by acclaimed chef Heinz Beck, it has maintained its three-star rating since being awarded the distinction in 2005. 'My intention,' says Chef Beck, 'is to transmit emotions through harmoniously balanced aromas, flavours and colours—sensory stimuli which are intertwined and blended in suffused and refined surroundings.' You will probably feel he has succeeded. Reservations essential.
✉ Via Cadlolo 101, 00136 Roma ☎ 06 3509 2152 ⏲ Tue–Sat 7.30pm–11.30pm; closed first 3 weeks Jan and 8–23 Aug ✋ D €122, Wine €20 Ⓜ Barberini 🚌 62, 492 to Via Quattro Fontane

PIERLUIGI
www.pierluigi.it
This excellent restaurant is reasonably priced considering its quality and setting—on the edge of a piazza, with plenty of tables outside. The scampi risotto is fantastically smooth and tasty, as is the carpaccio of tuna or swordfish. It aso caters well for carnivores: Try the *tagliata di manzo*—tender beef strips on a bed of rucola.
✉ Piazza de' Ricci 144, 00186 Roma ☎ 06 686 1302 ⏲ Tue–Sun 12–3, 7–midnight ✋ L €28, D €55, Wine €14 🚌 46, 62, 64, 87, 116, 492

PORTO DI RIPETTA

Just off the Piazza del Popolo, this family-run, up-market restaurant made its name from a steadfast refusal to use butter, cream or garlic in its cooking. The food, nevertheless, is delicious—artichokes stuffed with prawns, home-made pasta and wonderful desserts made on the premises. The oil and wine come from the owners' own property.

Via di Ripetta 250, 00186 Roma 06 361 2376 Mon–Sat 12.30–2.30, 7.30–10; closed 2 weeks in Aug L €44, D €65, Wine €15 Flaminio 95, 117, 119, 628, 926

LA ROSETTA

This stylish restaurant near the Pantheon is deservedly popular. Founded in 1966, it was the first and only restaurant in Rome to serve nothing but fish and seafood. That tradition continues today. Expect glamorous surroundings, beautifully prepared and presented dishes with a modern spin and accomplished service.

Via della Rosetta 8/9, 00186 Roma 06 686 1002 Mon–Sat 12.30–2.30, 7.30–11.30, Sun 7.30–11.30 L €60, D €85, Wine €18 Fontana del Tritone

SAN PIETRINO

A wooden ceiling, pink-washed walls and blue tiles are the backdrop here for family-style cooking at excellent prices. The menu has been updated while remaining loyal to tradition and you can expect to find old favourites still on the menu, as well as more innovative dishes. Among these are starters of lightly fried vegetables, pasta with pecorino cheese and peppers, and aubergine dumplings with tomatoes, while main courses include a piquant *baccalà* (salted cod) served with raisins and pine nuts, a daily fish special and tender *tagliata* with rocket and parmesan.

Piazza Costaguti 15, 00186 Roma 06 6880 6471 Mon–Sat 12.30–3, 7.30–11 L €30, D €40, Wine €11 23, 63, 280. Tram 8

SIMPOSIO

www.pierocostantini.it

This fine restaurant is run by the owners of the neighbouring Piero Costantini, one of Rome's finest wine merchants. The wine list is therefore superb, featuring wines from all over Italy, Europe and the New World, and you can enjoy wines by the glass as you eat classic meat and fish dishes or sample a *menu di degustazione* (tasting menu).

Piazza Cavour 16, 00193 Roma 06 320 3575 Mon–Sat 12.30–3, 7.30–11; closed Aug and Christmas L €44, D €65, Wine €15 Ottaviano San Pietro 23, 34, 62, 64

SORA LELLA

www.soralella.com

Set on Isola Tiberina, near Trastevere, this is possibly one of the most unusual places to eat in Rome. Here you will find Roman cuisine at its best. All the typical dishes, from oxtail with cinnamon, cloves, raisins and pine nuts to memorable fried artichokes. Reservations are recommended.

Via di Ponte Quattro Capi 16, Isola Tiberina, 00186 Roma 06 686 1601 Mon–Sat 12.30–2.30, 8–11pm; closed Tue lunch and Aug L €30, D €65, Wine €13 23. Tram 8

Below *Il Margutta's airy and light interior*

Above *Hotel de Russie has an unbeatable location between the Spanish Steps and Piazza del Popolo*

PRICES AND SYMBOLS

Prices are the lowest and highest for a double room for one night, unless otherwise stated. Breakfast is included, and all the hotels listed accept credit cards unless otherwise stated. Note that rates vary widely throughout the year.

For the key to symbols ▷ 2.

ACCADEMIA

www.travelroma.com

If you're looking for a combination of historic surroundings and modern design, the Accademia, near the Fontana di Trevi, is a good find. The building has retained its period exterior, but inside rooms have the clean and minimalist lines of an up-to-the-minute boutique hotel. Every comfort is on hand, there's WiFi internet access and a sleek and shiny bar for relaxation.

Piazza Accademia di Sa Luca 74, 00187 Roma 067 6992 2607 €190–€240 892 52, 53, 61, 204, 492 (alight at San Silvestro)

ALBERGO DEL SOLE AL BISCIONE

www.solealbiscione.it

Rome's oldest hotel, dating back to 1462, was built on the site of the ancient Pompeo's theatre, now very conveniently located between Piazza Navona and the Campo dei Fiori. Rooms are basic but very good value, and the delightful courtyard garden terrace exudes Roman charm.

Via del Biscione 76, 00186 Roma 06 6880 6783 €100–€160 59 40, 62, 64, 70, 87

ALIMANDI

www.alimandi.it

Alimandi is a superior 3-star, family-run hotel that is very good value. Close to the Vatican Museums and totally refurbished, the 19th-century building has kept some original features, including elegant Venetian stuccowork. The guest bedrooms are spacious, with modern furnishings and pastel hues. All have satellite and pay TV, spacious bathrooms with a hairdryer, and internet connection. The hotel also caters very well for visitors with disabilities. The Continental buffet breakfast is served on the roof terrace or in the dining room. Usefully, they provide a free airport shuttle service, and garage parking is available.

Viale Vaticano 99, 00165 Roma 06 3974 5562 €130–€220 25 Cipro-Musei Vaticani or Ottaviano 81, 95, 492

ANNE AND MARY

www.anne-mary.com

This welcoming bed-and-breakfast occupies part of an elegant 19th-century building near the Colosseum. Rooms are simple but they are dramatically appointed, with clean lines and swooping curtains. Each has a private bathroom with an enclosed shower. Via Cavour is a

large, somewhat busy road, but the proximity of this hotel to the major sights means it is worth putting up with the noise.
✉ Via Cavour 325, 00184 Roma
☎ 06 6994 1187 €100–€150 6
Cavour, Colosseo 75, 81, 85, 87, 116, 117

ATLANTE STAR
www.atlantehotels.com
Nestled between Vatican City and Castel Sant'Angelo, this establishment exudes class and nobility, with richly upholstered sofas, heavy drapes, stuccoed ceilings and plush carpets. The guest rooms are equally lush and spacious. Half of them have whirlpool baths. There is a bar and gourmet restaurant and you can enjoy views of the Basilica di San Pietro. The hotel provides a free airport shuttle service.
✉ Via G. Vitelleschi 34, 00193 Roma
☎ 06 687 3233 €175–€250; under 12s free 61 32, 81, 492
Ottaviano–San Pietro

CAPO D'AFRICA
www.hotelcapodafrica.com
This is a handsome 19th-century building close to the Colosseo in a trendy district. The hotel is a fusion of contemporary and classic design with Japanese touches. The rooms are a joy to behold, with warm ochre and saffron shades and perfectly fitted bathrooms in marble and wood. The breakfast room on the roof looks out over the Colosseo. There's a large, well-equipped gym and a solarium. The hotel is accessible for guests with disabilities. There is an American buffet breakfast.
✉ Via Capo d'Africa 54, 00184 Roma
☎ 06 772 801 €380–€400 65
Colosseo, San Giovanni 81, 85, 87, 117. Tram 3

CASA HOWARD
www.casahoward.com
This stylish boutique hotel is split into two houses offering elegantly furnished rooms, opulent with silky fabrics, fresh flowers and a Turkish bath. Both establishments are near the Spanish Steps—one on Via Capo le Case, the other in Via Sistina, the work of interior designer Tommaso Ziffer. The extremely good rates for such luxurious living are hard to beat in Rome.
✉ Via Capo le Case 18, 00187 Roma
☎ 06 6992 4555 €170–€250, excluding breakfast (€10) 10 Spagna

DEI MELLINI
www.hotelmellini.com
Two adjoining palazzi, right on the River Tiber, form this pleasant hotel, whose comforts are very much in the *stile inglese*, the admired English style. Expect tasteful furnishings and attractive fabrics. Relax after a day's sightseeing in La Terrazza, a lovely beauty solarium on the top floor.
✉ Via Muzio Clemente 81, 00193 Roma
☎ 06 324 771; fax 06 324 77801
€320–€355 66 rooms, 14 suites
Ottaviano San Pietro 23, 34, 62, 64

DUE TORRI
www.hotelduetorriroma.com
Once a cardinal's residence and later a brothel, there's plenty of history at what is now a cosy little hotel in the heart of the *centro storico*. As you'd expect in an old building, the rooms are on the small side, but book ahead and you might get one of the top floor rooms with a terrace overlooking the rooftops of Rome.
✉ Vicolo del Leonetto 23–25, 00186 Roma
☎ 06 687 5765; fax 06 68 65 442 €150–€240 26 Spagna 70, 81, 87, 116

THE DUKE
www.thedukehotel.com
The Duke is in the heart of the well-heeled Parioli district, between the parks of the Villa Borghese and the Villa Gloria. Inside, it looks like an English country home with classical flourishes and there is a delightful art nouveau glass cupola in the Polo lounge. The rooms are luxurious and intimate, spacious and light, with minibar, safe, satellite television and a games console. The large marble bathrooms are very luxurious. Children get welcome packs and free tickets to the zoo.
✉ Via Archimede 69, 00197 Roma
☎ 06 367 221 €140–€470 78
Flaminio 910 From Piazza del Popolo, train to Viterbo, 1st stop–Termini

EDEN
www.lemeridien.com /eden
This super-smart hotel just off the Via Veneto, built in 1889, has stylishly decorated reception and public rooms, while the sumptuous bedrooms live up to this promise. The roof terrace has exceptionally fine views. First-class service and a relaxed yet perfect attention to detail justify the reputation of this fine hotel.
✉ Via Ludovisi 49, 00187 Roma ☎ 06 478 121; fax 06 482 1584 From €680 per room, €1,900 per suite 121 rooms, 13 suites Barberini

FONTANELLA BORGHESE
www.fontanellaborghese.com
A hospitable welcome awaits in this comfortable hotel, attractively situated on the upper floors of a 16th-century palazzo. Modern comforts have been grafted on to traditional style, making a stay here a truly Roman experience.
✉ Largo Fontanella Borghese 84, 00186 Roma ☎ 06 6880 9504; fax 06 686 1295
€150–€255 24 Spagna
30, 70, 81, 91 204

GABRIELLA
www.gabriellahotel.it
There are good transport links from this excellent-value hotel near the Termini station. The rooms are a good size, with huge double beds and marble bathrooms with baths rather than showers. Run by the same family for over 50 years, it's a good example of a comfortable, mid-range hotel and makes a good choice if you're watching the budget.
✉ Via Palestro 88, 00185 Roma ☎ 06 445 0120 €80–€160 23 Termini
14, 38, 90, 105, 217

HOTEL FENIX
www.fenixhotel.it
An elegant, but not expensive, hotel in the Trieste residential area, away from the crowds but within

easy reach of Rome's centre and numerous historical and cultural attractions. The rooms are decorated and furnished in neoclassical style and the hotel has its own secluded garden off the restaurant/ breakfast room. The Fenix was built in the 1960s, so the architecture is bland and unimpressive, but inside the hotel is bright, with a mix of antique furniture and modern art, just like a private residence. The atmosphere is relaxed and comfortable, and the staff aim to make you feel at home.
Viale Gorizia 5/7, 00198 Roma 06 854 0741; fax 06 854 3632 €160–€280 73 rooms, 4 suites Bologna 36, 60, 62, 84 On the corner of Viale Gorizia and Via Nomentana

HOTEL QUIRINALE
www.hotelquirinale.it
Very centrally located and convenient for Termini Station, this grande dame hotel has hosted many famous people. Composers Puccini and Verdi were among them, as a private connecting door gives privileged access to Rome's Opera House.. High-ceilinged rooms are furnished in the classical style, complete with parquet floors, chandeliers, early empire furnishings and, often, huge marble bathrooms. There is a very pleasant shaded loggia overlooking the courtyard for breakfast or drinks.
Via Nazionale 7, 00184 Roma 06 4707 €140–€290 210 Repubblica

HOTEL DE RUSSIE
www.roccofortecollection.com
In the heart of the city amid all the top designer shops, this is one of the best hotels in Rome. The Bonaparte brothers lived and died here. It's a unique blend of contemporary and classic styles. The guest rooms have high ceilings and are well furnished, and the bathrooms are a work of art. If that's not enough, there is a spa with a hydropool, sauna, Turkish baths and beauty treatments. The first-class restaurant is elegant and, when open onto the gardens, one of the most romantic spots in Rome.
Via del Babuino 9, 00187 Roma 06 328 881 €490–€1,055 (suites more) excluding breakfast (€34) 97 rooms, 25 suites Flaminio 117

INTERNAZIONALE
www.hotelinternazionale.com
Wisteria winds up the front of this palazzo, which was a convent in the 16th and 17th centuries. The breakfast lounge has stucco and gilt ceilings and is painted blue and mauve. The scheme continues throughout the hotel, from the cupids in the cupola to the moiré wall coverings in the bedrooms.
Via Sistina 79, 00187 Roma 06 6994 1823 €180–€350 42 Spagna 62

LANCELOT
www.lancelothotel.com
Don't let the high-rise appearance put you off this welcoming hotel just above the Colosseum. The lounge and dining room have period furniture and Murano glass chandeliers. There is a bar, library and a delightful courtyard to relax in. The rooms are spacious and most have wooden floors and pastel walls. All have satellite television; some have terraces. Breakfast is continental style.
Via Capo D'Africa 47, 00184 Roma 06 7045 0615 €170–€200 60 Colosseo, San Giovanni 81, 85, 87, 117. Tram 3

LOCARNO
www.hotellocarno.com
Artists and intellectuals like Umberto Eco, author of *The Name of the Rose*, favour this art deco refuge on a sleepy street near Piazza del Popolo. The 1925 building still has some original features, including a cast-iron elevator. The decorating is delicate and deft, using period lamps, furniture and fabrics. Each room is different. The deluxe rooms in the eastern annex are lighter and more spacious than those in the main building. Guests can use the business facilities and vintage bicycles for free.
Via della Penna 22, 00186 Roma 06 361 0841 €215–€620 66 Flaminio 117

LORD BYRON
www.lordbyronhotel.com
The Lord Byron is a romantic hideaway in pastoral Parioli, overlooking the Villa Borghese. The art deco villa has been elegantly restored, with scarlet sofas, lacquered furniture, gilded mirrors and marble bathrooms. Rooms 503, 602 and 603 have spectacular views. The restaurant, Ristorante Sapori de Lord Byron, is considered to be one of Italy's finest.
Via Giuseppe de Notaris 5, 00197 Roma 06 322 0404 €230–€530 6 rooms, 6 suites Flaminio 117 West side of Via Giuseppe de Notaris 5, just north of Via Mangili

NAZIONALE A MONTECITORIO
www.hotelnazionale.it
This hotel is close to the Fontana di Trevi and the Scalinata di Trinità dei Monti. It has dark wood panelling and marble floors and columns in the lobby. The moderately sized rooms, with high ceilings and period furnishings, are decorated in gold and brown shades. All have private bathrooms, satellite/pay television, minibar and a safe. The restaurant serves Italian and Continental cuisine.
Piazza Montecitorio 131, 00186 Roma 06 695 001 €359–€380 100 rooms, 1 suite 46, 62, 116

PORTOGHESI
www.hotelportoghesiroma.it
This hotel is tucked away in the Tor di Nona area, north of Piazza Navona. From here you can feel the heartbeat of Rome as mopeds sputter and locals chatter nearby. It's easy to miss the unassuming entrance, but keep an eye out for the row of dainty flags. Highlights include the sunny breakfast room and the roof terrace.
Via dei Portoghesi 1, 00186 Roma 06 686 4231 €130–€200 27 Spagna 116, 280

RIPA
www.ripahotel.com
Fans of sleek minimalism will be thrilled to find a hotel for the 21st century right in the heart of trendy Trastevere. Streamlined public areas give a taste of the bedrooms,

where some might say style takes precedence over comfort. Classy and cool, this hotel will appeal to a very individual type of traveller.
✉ Via degli Orti di Trastevere 1, 00153 Roma ☎ 06 58611; fax 06 581 45 50 € €120–€270 ⓘ 170 ❄ Trastevere 🚌 Tram 3, 8

SAN FRANCESCO

www.hotelsanfrancesco.net
Trastevere is an atmospheric area and the San Francesco is a good choice here, a comfortable hotel that offers excellent value. Rooms are traditionally furnished with white walls and sombre, rich textiles, the public areas are delightful, with contemporary design, and the breakfast buffet generous and delicious. The big bonus is the rooftop terrace, where you can look over the rooftops to the trees on the Janiculum while you enjoy a drink. The hotel has a garage (€20–€25 per night, no booking necessary).
✉ Via Jacopa de' Settesoli 7, 00153 Roma ☎ 06 5830 0051 € €135–€240 ⓘ 24 ❄ 🚌 23, 44, 280

SANTA MARIA

www.hotelsantmaria.info
This charming hotel first opened in 2000, when a 16th-century convent, just off Piazza Santa Maria in Trastevere, was transformed. Tranquility is the keynote, with all the bedrooms opening out onto a central courtyard planted with orange trees. Rooms are pretty, with co-ordinated fabrics in light colours, and bathrooms are a good size.
✉ Vicolo del Piede 2, 00153 Roma ☎ 06 589 4626; fax 06 589 4815 € €140–€230 ⓘ 16 rooms, 2 suites ❄ 🚌 23, 44, 280, 780

SCALINATA DI SPAGNA

www.hotelscalinata.com
Reserve months—if not years—in advance at this boutique hotel at the top of the Scalinata di Trinita dei Monti. La Scalinata's 16 rooms are highly coveted (especially numbers 10 and 12). The breakfast terrace on the roof, overlooking the red-tiled roofs and cupolas, is a riot of blossom. Active visitors can jog in the nearby Villa Borghese park, which has a modern underground gym. You can also plug in your laptop, or try the free internet television with email.
✉ Piazza Trinità dei Monti 17, 00187 Roma ☎ 06 699 40896 € €130–€370 ⓘ 16 ❄ Spagna 🚌 116

SOLE AL PANTHEON

www.hotelsolealpantheon.com
Known to have been the site of an inn since 1467, the Sole is one of the world's oldest hotels, aptly situated in the same piazza as the iconic Pantheon, one of Rome's oldest functioning buildings. Terracotta floors, frescoed walls and ceilings and a tranquil inner courtyard, where summer breakfasts are served, help make this one of Rome's most memorable places to stay.
✉ Piazza della Rotonda 63, 00186 Roma ☎ 06 678 0441; fax 06 699 40689 € €210–€500 ⓘ 25 ❄ 🚌 30, 40, 62, 63, 787, 628

VISCONTI PALACE

www.viscontipalace.com
This hotel has recently had a complete refurbishment. The rooms are spacious and furnished in contemporary style, and there is a range of room types to suit your budget. The outside of the building is not impressive, but the interior is bright and airy with displays of modern art by Roman artists; the public areas also have fresh flowers every day. The lavish buffet breakfast in the spacious basement dining area makes a great start to the day. The Visconti Palace is popular with business visitors and there are good deals for leisure stays, especially in the summer months. The hotel now also offers splendid new designer penthouse suites with private terrace. Given that some of Rome's major attractions are within 10 minutes' walk, this is a near-ideal location. The hotel is adapted for disabled access throughout, with ramps wherever steps occur. WiFi and internet access is provided in rooms and the lobby bar. There is a valet parking service.
✉ Via Federico Cesi 37, 00193 Roma ☎ 06 3684 € €120–€380; suites from €400 ⓘ 242 rooms, 12 suites ❄ 🚌 23, 34, 40, 280

Below *Comfortable lounge, Hotel de Russie*

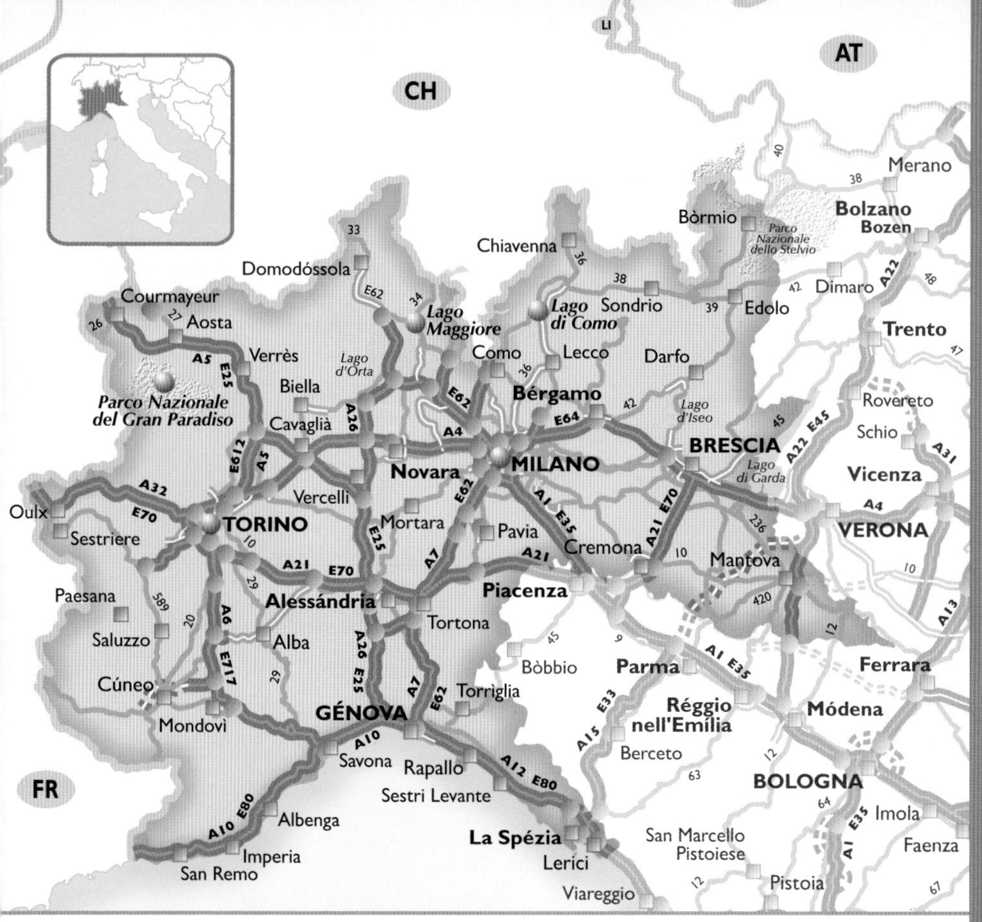

THE NORTHWEST

Stretching from the majesty of the Alps to the great fertile plains of Lombardy, and from the French border around a beautiful coastline to the northern boundary of Tuscany, northwest Italy packs in diversity in every way. This region is home to northern Italy's most thriving cities, Milano (Milan) and Torino (Turin), and its main port, Genova (Genoa). Its history is the story of independent states, great dukedoms and petty kingdoms, its artistic heritage in the form of cathedrals, churches, galleries, villas and museums immense, and its modern preoccupations, working and playing hard, essentially 21st century.

Away from the powerhouse cities, with their fast pace of life and blatant commercialism, the smaller towns are full of charm. In the west, in the green Alpine foothills, lie inland Asti, Alba, Bergamo and Brescia, while the coast is a string of pretty villages and resorts whose appeal ranges from the glitz of celeb-pulling Portovenere and Portofino on the Riviera di Levante to the laid-back way of life in the wine-producing communities along the Cinque Terre. North of here, there's winter and summer sport in the shape of skiing and hiking in the Valle d'Aosta and the grandeur of the Parco Nazionale del Gran Paradiso, Italy's oldest national park. To the east historic cities such as Cremona, famous for Stradivarius and his violins, Mantova (Mantua), offering no fewer than two vast palaces, and prosperous Pavia, are balanced by the beauties of the northern lakes of Como, Maggiore and Garda, where lemon trees flourish in sheltered micro-climates and thousands come for summer relaxation. It's a beguiling mix; factor in stylish design and living, great shopping wherever you go, some of Italy's finest wine and specialty foods including majestic Barolo and Europe's best truffles, and it's easy to fill idyllic days exploring the area.

ALBA

www.langheroero.it

Prized for its wines and white truffles *(tartufi bianchi),* the medieval town of Alba, 62km (39 miles) from Turin, is the main town in the Langhe, a beautiful region of vine-clad slopes and hills crowned by ancient castles. Here gastronomy reigns supreme: delicatessens are piled high with hams, wild boar, pastas, *funghi* and bottles of Barolo and Barberesco.

The old town is compact and its cobbled streets, arcades, red-brick medieval towers and historic monuments have been well preserved. The Piazza del Risorgimento, or Piazza del Duomo as it is known, is overlooked by the town hall and the Duomo di San Lorenzo (Mon–Sat 9–12, 3–5.30, Sun 9–1, 3–5.30). The 15th-century duomo has beautifully carved and inlaid choir stalls. From the square you can see the tallest and best-preserved of Alba's medieval towers; there were originally 100 in the town.

462 B4 Piazza del Risorgimento 2, 12051 Alba 0173 35833 Alba

ASTI

www.astiturismo.it

Asti is the home of, and synonymous with, *spumante*, the sweet sparkling wine. This large town, 60km (37 miles) east of Turin, is predominantly industrial, but its medieval past is evident in the historic buildings and churches that are scattered throughout the old centre.

In medieval times Asti was the largest town in Piedmont and a rival to Milan. The town's *palio*, a horse-race, similar to Siena's, is the oldest in Italy, dating from the 13th century. Asti once had around 150 towers but only 12 survive, of which one can still be climbed: Torre Troyana o dell'Orologio in the Piazza Medici.

The main cultural attraction is the medieval complex of the 15th-century church of San Pietro in Consavia, a Gothic cloister with a small circular baptistery dating from the 10th to 12th centuries and an archaeology museum (summer Tue–Sat 9–12, 4–7, Sun 10–12; winter Tue–Sat 9–12, 3–6, Sun 10–12). The large Gothic church of San Secondo on the piazza of the same name has a Romanesque bell tower and an altarpiece by Gaudenzio Ferrari (1475–1546).

462 C4 Piazza Alfieri 29, 14100 Asti 0141 530357 Asti

BERGAMO

Northeast of Milan in the southern foothills of the Alps, Bergamo could not be more different from Italy's business capital. The city is divided into the medieval Città Alta (Upper Town) and the relatively dull, modern Città Bassa (Lower Town).

The arches of the Palazzo della Ragione lead to the glorious Piazza del Duomo and the Cappella Colleoni (1470–76). Built as a mausoleum for Bartolomeo Colleoni, the famous Venetian *condottiere* (▷ 35), it has a pink and white marble facade covered with statues, reliefs and stuccowork, with a large rose window above the portal (daily 9–12.30, 2–6.30, to 4.30 Nov–Feb). To the right of the chapel is a copy of the 14th-century octagonal baptistery, complete with a red marble gallery. Inside are Flemish and Florentine tapestries, 15th- to 17th-century frescoes, the tomb of Bergamo's most famous son, composer Gaetano Donizetti, and a splendid wooden choir stall (1522–55) with inlaid panels depicting scenes from the Old Testament (Sun 3–6 or on request, tel 035 210223).

463 D3 (Lower Town) Piazzale Marconi, 24100 Bergamo 035 210204; (Upper Town) Via Gombito 13, 24100 Bergamo 035 242226 Bergamo

BRESCIA

www.provincia.bresica.it/turismo

Brescia may lack the charm of nearby Bergamo, but it is an ancient city with a strong cultural heritage. The most appealing of the three squares is the Venetian-style Piazza Loggia, where you will find the richly decorated Palazzo della Loggia (the town hall), with an arcade and cupola. An archway on the south side leads to the controversial Piazza della Vittoria (Victory Square), built in a Fascist style during Mussolini's rule (▷ 40–41). The archway brings you to Piazza Paolo VI, the religious heart of the city, overlooked by the great green cupola of the Duomo Nuovo (Mon–Sat 7.30–12, 4–7, Sun 8–1, 4–7). This towering modern baroque cathedral dwarfs its older and more interesting neighbour, the Duomo Vecchio, a rare example of a Romanesque cathedral with a circular plan—hence its nickname, La Rotonda (Apr–Oct Tue–Sun 9–12, 3–7; Nov–Mar 9–12, 3–6).

The remains of the Capitoline Temple around Piazza del Foro are a legacy of the Roman colony of Brixia, established here in AD73 by Emperor Vespasian (daily 11–4; free). Archaeological remains from the site are housed in the Museo della Città, in the nearby 16th-century Monastery of Santa Giulia. Highlights include a bronze Winged Victory discovered in 1826 and the eighth-century Lombard Desiderio Cross, studded with jewels and cameos (Tue–Sun 10–1, 2–5).

464 E3 Via Musei 32, 25121 Brescia 030 374 9916 Brescia

Opposite *Torre dell'Orologio at night, Piazza Loggia, Brescia*

Below *A statue in Bergamo*

Above *A boat on the Ligurian Sea, just offshore from Manarola in the Cinque Terre*

CINQUE TERRE

www.cinqueterre.it

The ravishing coastline of the Cinque Terre (Five Lands) is named after the five little fishing villages that cling precariously to the cliffs northwest of La Spezia. From here to Levanto the landscape is characterized by mountains cloaked in woods, terraces of vines and cliffs, which provide spectacular views over the turquoise sea. Tourism is growing rapidly here, but the area is a protected national park and the locals are encouraged to maintain their traditional occupations of fishing and viticulture. Grapes grown on the steep slopes produce the fragrant and fruity white Cinque Terre wine and the rarer, stronger and sweeter Sciacchetri.

The villages most easily reached by road, and hence the best-equipped and least charming, are Monterosso, the oldest village, and Riomaggiore. Vernazza is arguably the most beautiful of the five villages, a huddle of painted houses, narrow alleys and arcades. Genoese fortifications here include medieval bastions and a watchtower. Manarola is another highly photogenic village, with a cluster of pastel-washed houses, steep cobbled streets, a quaint harbour and the only sandy beach in the Cinque Terre. Corniglia, the smallest of the villages, clings to a ridge, with steps leading down to the sea. The clear blue waters and rocky coastline are home to a huge variety of fish and thriving underwater gardens, making this a popular destination for divers.

463 D6 Piazza Rio Finale 26, Riomaggiore 0187 920633 La Spezia–Monterosso line Apr–Oct Navigazione Golfo dei Poeti operates a regular boat service linking all the villages except Corniglia. Summer ferries and catamarans from Genoa to the Cinque Terre

CREMONA

www.aptcremona.it

The first modern violin, as opposed to the medieval fiddle, was made here by Andrea Amati in 1566, and Antonio Stradivarius, the great violin-maker, was born here in 1644. His life and work are commemorated in the Museo Stradivariano, where many of his tools are on display (Tue–Sat 9–6, Sun 10–6). The Sala dei Violini in the Palazzo Communale (same house as Museo Stradivariano) also has a collection of historic violins, including examples by Amati and Stradivarius.

This little market town on the north banks of the River Po, 95km (59 miles) southeast of Milan, revolves around the Piazza del Comune, with its ensemble of medieval monuments. The Romanesque and Gothic cathedral (1107–1332) has an ornately sculpted marble facade with a fine rose window. The frescoes inside by the Cremona school are the highlight. Particularly notable is Pordenone's *Crucifixion* (1520–21), prized for its bold spatial effects (Mon–Sat 10.30–12, 3.30–6, Sun and holidays 10.30–11, 3.30–5.30). The 14th-century Lombard-Gothic church of Sant'Agostino (1339–45) is also worth visiting to see its serene altarpiece by Perugino, *The Madonna and Saints,* in the fifth chapel on the south side (daily 9.30–12, 3.30–6).

463 E4 Piazza del Comune 5, 26100 Cremona 0372 23233 Cremona

GENOVA (GENOA)

www.apt.genova.it

Its outskirts are unattractive, but Genoa has a rich heritage and a wealth of historical palaces, churches and museums to explore. It was, and still is, Italy's principal seaport and was famously the birthplace of Christopher Columbus in 1451. Genoa enjoyed a major facelift when Renzo Piano, also a native of Genoa, revamped the harbour in preparation for EXPO 92. Its *carruggi* (narrow alleys) and lavishly decorated mansions and palazzi, especially along Via Garibaldi and Via Balbi, further soften its rough exterior.

The Galleria Nazionale di Palazzo Spinola on Via San Luca, an opulent 16th- to 18th-century palace, has original furnishings, frescoed ceilings and an art collection that includes works by Van Dyck, Antonello da Messina, Rubens and Pisano (Thu–Sun 9–7, Tue–Wed 9–1.30). The Museo Civico di Palazzo Bianco, housed in a 16th-century palace on Via Garibaldi, also has an exceptional collection of paintings by Genoese and other European artists, including Rubens, Van Dyck, Antonello da Messina, Caravaggio and Murillo (Tue–Fri 9–7, Sat–Sun 10–7).

The early 13th-century Cattedrale di San Lorenzo in the piazza of the same name has a Gothic black-and-white striped marble facade (Mon–Sat 9–12, 3–6). Opened for EXPO 92, the Acquario di Genova is Europe's largest marine park, with 71 tanks, 800 species and more than 10,000 specimens set against the incomparable backdrop of the Gulf of Genoa. It was built to commemorate the fifth centenary of Columbus's discovery of the New World (Mon–Fri 9.30–7.30, Sat–Sun and holidays 9.30–8.30).

462 C5 Piazza Acqua Verde—Stazione Porta Principe, 16126 Genova 010 246 2633 Genova

LAGO DI COMO

Surrounded by high mountains and rugged hills, Lake Como has inspired writers, artists and musicians from Pliny the Younger in Roman times to 19th-century Romantics such as French novelists Stendhal and Flaubert and the Italian composer Rossini. The first steamboat was launched from here in 1826 and visitors have been taking boat trips to enjoy the views of the lakeside ever since.

Como is smaller than lakes Maggiore and Garda, but it has the longest perimeter (over 170km/106 miles). Between Argegno and Nesso, it reaches a maximum depth of 410m (1,345ft), making it the deepest lake in Italy.

THE THREE LAKES

The sunny and gentle west coast of the Como branch of the lake is typified by patrician villas, elegant hotels, harbours and villages often presided over by an ancient campanile. The shadier Lecco branch, between the High Brianza to the west and the Grigna to the east, is less accessible, with fewer villages and harbours. At the southern tip, Lecco developed into a large industrial centre in the 19th century. The northern section of the lake, often referred to as Alto Lario, is different again. Here the lake widens and campsites dot both shores. In the north, Monte Legnone (2,609m/8,560ft) towers above Culico, south of which lies the main attraction along the coast—Piona's ancient abbey, on the tip of a peninsula. The 'three lakes' meet at the Punta Sparivento (the Point That Divides the Wind).

LAKESIDE TOWNS AND VILLAS

At this central headland is Bellagio, known as the pearl of the lake for its charming setting and beautiful villas. Geographically isolated, it has excellent boat connections, which make it popular for day trips. Against a backdrop of high mountains, the lively resort of Menaggio has some excellent walking, windsurfing, swimming, trekking and rock-climbing opportunities. Villa d'Este at Cernobbio (▷ 140–141) is the most famous of Como's villas. Built in the 16th century, it is now a sumptuous hotel. In a glorious wooded peninsula, Villa del Balbianello, in Lenno, is full of unusual treasures, including mementoes collected by the eccentric explorer who lived here.

INFORMATION

www.lakecomo.com

463 D2 Piazza Cavour 17, 22100 Como 031 269712; Mon–Sat 9–1, 2.30–6; also Sun 9.30–1 Jun–Sep Como town Car ferry service links Menaggio, Varenna, Bellagio and Cadenabbia

TIP

» Spring and autumn are the best times to visit as in peak season the main resorts and the narrow winding coastal roads are uncomfortably crowded.

» There are several options for touring the lake, hopping from village to village: a *batello* (ship), *servizio rapido* (fast service/hydrofoil) or an *autotraghetto* (car ferry). There are also full-day cruises starting from Como or Lecco. All are run by the Gestione Navigazione Laghi (www.navigazionelaghi.it).

» Silk has been processed in Como since the 16th century, and Italy's most beautiful silks are woven and designed here. There are plenty of shops and outlet stores—just look for the label *'pura seta di Como'*.

Below *Villa Balbianello near Lenno. Built as a palazzo of the Balbiati family, the villa was later a rest home for Franciscan monks and then remodelled by Cardinal Angelo Divini*

INFORMATION

www.stresaonline.com

462 C3 Piazza Marconi 16, 28838 Stresa 0323 31308 From Milan From Verona Boats run to the Borromean Islands every 30 minutes in high season. There are ferries to and from other lakeside destinations (Angera, Stresa, Pallanza, Intra)

TIP

» The best places to stay are Stresa, Baveno and Pallanza. The resorts further north are quiet but unexciting and, in comparison to the western shore, the eastern shore is scenically dull.

LAGO MAGGIORE

Maggiore is the second-largest and the most westerly of the three main lakes. Piedmont in the west, Lombardy in the east and the Ticon canton in Switzerland, in the north, all converge on its shores. With its southern tip approximately 55km (35 miles) northwest of Milan, the lake is 65km (40 miles) long, averages 2km (1.3 miles) across and has a perimeter of 170km (106 miles). The surface area is 212sq km (82sq miles) and the deepest point, in the Gulf of Borromeo, is 372m (1,220ft). The scenery ranges from wild, mountainous landscapes in the north to gentle Mediterranean views further south. Gardens flourish in the spring, when camellias, rhododendrons and azaleas brighten up the shores.

EARLY TOURISM

Maggiore has long been a popular holiday destination. In the 17th century, the illustrious Borromeo family of Milan built opulent palaces and gardens on Isola Bella and Isola Madre. The Lombard aristocracy followed in the 18th and 19th centuries with their splendid villas between Stresa and Arona and, thanks to the mild climate and fertile soil, their gardens flourished. Grand hotels were opened to accommodate wealthy Europeans, and Stresa became a stop on the Grand Tour. The shores also provided inspiration for musicians such as the Italian conductor Arturo Toscanini, and literati, including John Ruskin, Charles Dickens, Lord Byron and Percy Bysshe Shelley from Britain, and Gustave Flaubert and Stendhal from France. Queen Victoria and Sir Winston Churchill stayed in Baveno, and the Hôtel des Îles Borromées in Stresa was a popular choice with royalty, and with Ernest Hemingway, who was so enamoured of it that he wrote it into his book *A Farewell to Arms*.

STRESA AND THE BORROMEAN ISLANDS

In Stresa, Baveno and Pallanza, flower-filled promenades have delightful views of the Borromean Islands (Isola Bella, Isola Madre and Isola dei Pescatori). Rising above Stresa and accessible by cable car or toll road, the snowcapped peak of Monte Mottarone commands stunning views, while from the west-shore road between Arona and Stresa, known as The Riviera, you can see across to the eastern shore.

Below *View of Cannero Riviera, Lago Maggiore*

LAGO DI GARDA

www.lagodigarda.it

The largest and most visited of the Italian lakes, Garda stretches between the Dolomites and the Lombardy plain, where the regions of Trentino Alto-Adige, the Veneto and Lombardy meet. The landscape is remarkably diverse: in the north, narrow and fjord-like with dramatic rocks dropping sheer into the deep water; in the south, sea-like, with beaches lining the huge expanse of water. From the early Middle Ages, ruling dynasties identified the strategic importance of the lake, building splendid defences that are visible along its shores today. Although picturesque villages still dot the shorelines and medieval castles rise from the waters, the south in particular has become commercialized.

Lake Garda is 51km (32 miles) long and 17km (11 miles) across at its widest point. The waters are renowned for their clarity and are warm enough for summer swimming. The daily Ora del Garda wind ensures superb windsurfing and sailing conditions, particularly in the north. Mediterranean flora, including olive and citrus trees, flourishes in the warm climate and the lakeside promenades are lined with palms and pines. A cable car runs up to Monte Baldo. Rising above the eastern shore, the mountain is known for its wealth of botanical diversity, earning it the name 'Hortus Italiae' (Garden of Italy) in the 16th century.

464 F3 Via Roma 8, 25083 Gardone Riviera 0365 290411 Mar–Oct

LAGO D'ISEO

www.bresciaholiday.com

With its wild, mountainous scenery and peaceful villages, Lago d'Iseo—or Sebino, as it is sometimes still called—is a quiet alternative to the larger, more commercialized lakes. Between the provinces of Bergamo to the east and Brescia to the west, Iseo is the seventh-largest Italian lake. It is 24km (15 miles) long, averages 2.4km (1.5 miles) across and has the largest lake island (Monte Isola) in Italy. An Ice Age glacier created the lake's characteristic S shape, and the River Oglio feeds it from its source at Passo Gavia in the Camonica Valley.

The attractive hilly region of Franciacorta in the south, known for its champagne-style wines, lies between the lake and Brescia. The main town of Iseo, in the south, has a medieval centre, a long, pleasant, tree-shaded promenade, a lido with good sports facilities and the best choice of shops, hotels and campsites on the lake. Clusane, to the west, is a fishing village famous for *tinca ripiena* (stuffed tench), while Sarnico is popular for sports. Lovere, in the north, is the most appealing town close to Val Camonica, which is famous for its prehistoric rock art and majestically wild scenery. Pisogne, across the lake, is also worth a detour for the 16th-century frescoes of Girolamo Romanino in the Church of Santa Maria della Neve.

At the hamlet of Zone (turn off the eastern shore road at Marone) is the Riserva Naturale Piramidi di Zone, an amazing landscape of erosion pillars, created by weather-beaten debris from glaciers. Tapering at the top, these strange natural formations look like pinnacles, some spectacularly high and others with huge boulders on top. Cislano is the best place from which to admire them.

463 E3 Lungolago Marconi 2C/D, 25049 Iseo 030 980209; closed Sat pm and Sun winter Iseo Seasonal ferry links Sarnico with Lovere, calling at towns, villages and Monte Isola

LAGO MAGGIORE

▷ 124

LAGO D'ORTA

www.ortasangiulio.com

Separated from Lago Maggiore by the Mottarone peak, Orta is the westernmost lake in the northwest. With its island and beautifully preserved medieval village of Orta San Giulio, it is arguably the most enchanting of all the pre-Alpine lakes. Legend has it that in the fourth century St. Julius drove away the dragons and serpents from the island in the middle of the lake and founded a church there. From this site he preached to the fishermen and the island became the religious heart of the lake, a role that it maintains today.

Measuring 14km (9 miles) in length and around 3km (2 miles) at its broadest point, Orta is tiny compared to the lakes further east. The largest town on the lake is Omegna, in the north. Known chiefly for manufacturing and as HQ of design guru Alberto Alessi, it still preserves some of its old quarter around Piazza XXIV Aprile. The village of Quarno Sotto, 7km (4 miles) west of Omegna, stands 809m (2,654ft) above sea level and has spectacular views of the lake. In the 19th century the village was renowned worldwide for making wind instruments, some of which can be seen in the local Museo Etnografico e dello Strumento Musicale a Fiato. Some 20km (12 miles) west is Varallo, a predominantly industrial town dominated by the Sacro Monte, the prototype for the Orta San Giulio's Sacro Monte. This huge complex consists of 45 chapels, over 800 statues and 4,000 paintings of scenes from the life of Christ.

462 C3 Via Panoramica, 28016 Orta San Giulio 0322 905614 Orta San Giulio Ferry service links the main towns: Easter to mid-Oct daily; rest of year weekends only

Below *Lago d'Iseo*

sestante
CAMBIO
EXCHANGE
CHANGE
WECHSEL
FERT
FERT
FERT

INTRODUCTION

Milan is Italy's economic capital, where hard work and fast pace go hand in hand with style, money and 21st-century values. This is one of the few Italian cities where the siesta is unknown, and the pace of life is as fast as in London or New York. Throw in a stupendous cathedral, some ancient churches, the world's most famous opera house, fine neoclassical buildings and some world-class galleries and museums and it's clear that, retail therapy apart, Milan's got plenty to offer.

Milan achieved its affluence and style during industrialization in the 19th century, when the city emerged from 300 years of foreign rule and expanded from its historic core into a sprawl of wide streets and neoclassical and art nouveau buildings. In the historic centre, the main sights span the city's history. There are traces of the original Roman city of Mediolanum, once the seat of Emperor Constantine, and impressive buildings dating from the 13th to 16th centuries, when Milan was ruled by a series of dynastic families. The buildings devoted to culture and commerce—the opera house, the art galleries, the Galleria Vittorio Emanuele II (one of Europe's first malls)—are a testament to the 19th-century surge to prosperity that Milan enjoys today.

INFORMATION

www.milanoinfo.eu

463 D3 Piazza del Duomo 19A, 20123 Milano 02 7740 4343 Mon–Sat 8.45–1, 2–6, Sun 9–1, 2–5 Milano Centrale, Milano Garibaldi, Milano Lambrate, Milano Porta Genova, Milano Nord Milano Malpensa and Milano Linate

WHAT TO SEE

DUOMO

www.duomomilano.it

Milan's duomo is the hub of the city, the world's largest Gothic cathedral and the third-largest church in Europe. Building began in 1386 under Duke Gian Galeazzo Visconti and finally finished nearly 500 years later. The facade, built of marble from the Lake Maggiore area, is an unusual mix of Gothic and baroque. The brass strip on the pavement near the entrance is part of Europe's largest sundial, laid out in 1786. Above the chancel, the crucifix has a nail from Christ's cross, while the nearby crypt contains the remains of St. Charles Borromeo, who worked with Milan's poor in the 16th century. The highlight is the roof itself, a forest of statues and 135 spires, the tallest of which is topped with Milan's symbol, a gilded copper Madonnina (little Madonna); the views stretch as far as the Alps. There is a lift to the roof (daily 9–5.30; €8), or you can climb the 165 steps.

129 C2 Piazza del Duomo, 20123 Milano 02 7202 2656 Daily 9–6

PINACOTECA DI BRERA

www.brera.beniculturali.it

Right in the heart of the smart Brera district, the Pinacoteca di Brera is Milan's most prestigious art gallery, originally founded by Napoleon to display loot from churches and displaced aristocrats. The collection is huge, with more than 600 works exhibited in 40 rooms. The emphasis is on Italian Renaissance painting, and in particular the Venetian school. Early Renaissance Venetian works include pictures by Carpaccio and Giovanni and Gentile Bellini, and there is a striking *Dead Christ* by Andrea Mantegna, viewed from the soles of Jesus's feet. For a serene contrast to Venetian drama, don't miss Piero della Francesca's *Madonna with Saints and Federigo di Montefeltro,* all harmony and pellucid greys, and Raphael's sumptuously languid *Marriage of the Virgin.*

129 C1 Via Brera 28, 20121 Milano 02 722631 Tue–Sun 8.30–7.15 €5

SANTA MARIA DELLE GRAZIE

www.cenacolovinciano.org

The church of Santa Maria delle Grazie was begun in Gothic style in the mid-15th century, and altered considerably by Bramante in 1492 when he added the beautiful tribune, serene cloister and massive dome. What draws the crowds,

Opposite *Detail of a marble crest on the floor of an arcade within the Galleria Vittorio Emanuele II*

Above *Night falls over Milan's Gothic cathedral*

however, is Leonardo da Vinci's fragile fresco of *The Last Supper* on one wall of the Old Refectory in the adjoining monastery. This huge work portrays the moment when Christ announces that one of his disciples will betray him. Da Vinci applied the tempera and oil to dry plaster, rather than using the more stable, wet-plaster technique, so his work began to deteriorate five years after it was completed. Napoleonic troops used the fresco for target practice and the building was bombed in 1943, but amazingly the fresco survived. The work is fading fast despite continuous restoration, but against the odds, the brilliance of the artist's hand continues to shine through.

129 A2 Piazza Santa Maria delle Grazie, 20123 Milano 02 8942 1146 Tue–Sun 8–7.30; reserve at least a week in advance; visits restricted to 25 people and 15 minutes €8

CASTELLO SFORZESCO

www.milanocastello.it

The Castello Sforzesco, built originally by the ruling Visconti family in the 15th century, is one of Milan's major landmarks. Destroyed in the 1440s, it was rebuilt by the Sforzas and became the heart of one of Europe's most powerful and cultured courts. It was used as a barracks from the 15th century, when the Sforzas fell, until it was converted into a museum in the 19th century. Artistic highlights include Michelangelo's unfinished *Rondanini Pietà*, sculpted at the end of his life, works by Bellini and Mantegna, and Arcimboldo's 16th-century surrealistic portrait of *Primavera* (Spring), an image composed entirely of flowers.

129 B1 Piazza Castello 3, 20121 Milano 02 884 63700 (information); 02 884 63703 (museum) Oct–Mar Tue–Sun 7–6; Apr–Sep Tue–Sun 7–7 Castello: free. Museum €7

LA SCALA AND MUSEO TEATRALE ALLA SCALA

www.teatroallascalla.org

The Teatro alla Scala, named after the church that once stood on this site, is one of the world's most famous opera houses. Designed and built in the neoclassical style between 1776 and 1778 by Giuseppe Piermarini, it has a beautiful interior surrounded with four tiers of gilt and velvet boxes seating 3,600 people, superb acoustics and, despite its size, a real sense of intimacy. Tickets are expensive and hard to come by, but any visitor can take in the opera house museum, with its huge and fascinating collection of opera memorabilia.

129 C2 Largo Ghiringhelli 1, Piazzale della Scala, 20123 Milano 02 8879 7473 Daily 9–12.30, 1.30–5.30 €5

Above *The cathedral's intricate spires*

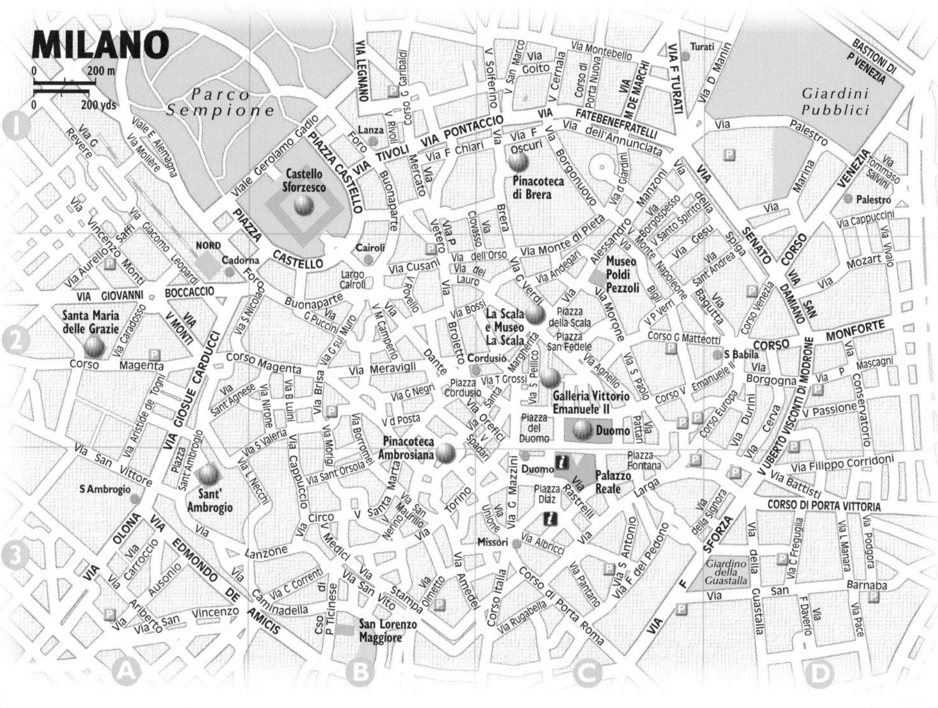

MORE TO SEE

SANT'AMBROGIO

www.santambrogio-basilica.it

An outstanding Lombard-Romanesque church, founded in the fourth century by St. Ambrose, patron saint of Milan, whose remains lie in the crypt. The simple church, with relics, carving and mosaics, is reached through a colonnaded courtyard; outside is Bramante's Cortile della Canonica.

129 A3 Piazza Sant'Ambrogio 15, 20123 Milano 02 8645 0895 Mon–Sat 7–12, 2.30–7, Sun 7–1, 3–8

GALLERIA VITTORIO EMANUELE II

A monumental glass-roofed shopping arcade, built in 1867, which links the Piazza del Duomo with the Piazza della Scala. The central mosaic shows the symbols of the cities of the newly united Italy. It is considered good luck to stand on the testicles of Turin's bull, then turn around three times; Turin and Milan have traditionally been arch rivals. Lined with expensive bars, cafés and shops, its is a great place for people-watching.

129 C2 Piazza del Duomo, 20123 Milano

PINACOTECA AMBROSIANA

www.ambrosiana.it

Cardinal Federico Borromeo founded this art gallery in the early 17th century. Highlights include Leonardo da Vinci's *Portrait of a Musician,* Raphael's cartoon for the *School of Athens* in the Vatican and Caravaggio's *Basket of Fruit*—purportedly Italy's first still life. The adjoining library also has exhibitions, and is Italy's oldest public library, founded in 1609.

129 B3 Piazza Pio XI 2, 20123 Milano 02 806921 Tue–Sun 10–5.30 €7.50

MILANO

0 200 m
0 200 yds

Parco Sempione
Castello Sforzesco
Pinacoteca di Brera
Giardini Pubblici
Santa Maria delle Grazie
Museo Poldi Pezzoli
La Scala e Museo La Scala
Galleria Vittorio Emanuele II
Duomo
Pinacoteca Ambrosiana
Palazzo Reale
Sant' Ambrogio
San Lorenzo Maggiore

LERICI

Surrounded by steep terraced slopes, Lerici is an attractive resort with a seafront lined with elegant villas, gardens, pines, palms and pebble beaches. A former fishing village, its sheltered cove and bay, in the Golfo dei Poeti, was immortalized by the 19th-century English Romantic poets Lord Byron and Percy Bysshe Shelley. Byron famously once swam from Portovenere across the gulf to visit Shelley, who had rented a house in the village of San Terenzo, 2km (1.2 miles) north of Lerici. In 1822, while returning from Livorno to his home on San Terenzo, Shelley drowned (aged 30) when his yacht capsized in a storm near Viareggio in Tuscany.

463 D6 Via Biaggini 6, 19033 Lerici 0187 967346

MANTOVA (MANTUA)

www.turismo.mantova.it

In the heart of the rather featureless Lombard plain, Mantua's uninspiring outskirts give few clues to the beautifully preserved medieval city, which, under the Gonzaga family (1328–1708), grew to be the centre of one of the greatest Renaissance courts in Europe.

Life here revolves around three squares. The spacious cobbled Piazza Sordello is flanked on one side by the formidable red-brick walls of the Palazzo Ducale. Once home of the Gonzagas, this is a vast complex of buildings, courtyards and gardens between Piazza Sordello and Lake Inferiore. The oldest parts are the Palazzo del Capitano and the adjacent Magna Domus, founded by the Bonacolsi family, who ruled Mantua from 1271 to 1328. There are over 500 rooms, the most famous being the Camera degli Sposi (Bridal Chamber), decorated with a cycle of frescoes (1474) by Mantegna, glorifying the Gonzaga family (Tue–Sun 8.45–7; €6.50, plus small extra charge for Camera degli Sposi). Opposite the Palazzo Ducale stand the Palazzo Bianchi (Archbishop's Palace) and the Cattedrale di San Pietro. South of the city centre, outside the old city, stands the extraordinary Palazzo del Tè, built between 1525 and 1535 by Giulio Romano as a summer palace for the Gonzaga dukes.

464 F4 Piazza Mantegna 6, 46100 Mantova 0376 432432 Mantova

MILANO (MILAN)

▷ 126–129.

PARCO NAZIONALE DEL GRAN PARADISO

▷ 132.

PAVIA

www.turismo.provincia.pv.it

Fine Romanesque and medieval buildings grace Pavia, but it is the nearby Certosa di Pavia, one of the most extravagant religious complexes in northern Italy, that draws the crowds. In medieval times emperors Charlemagne and Frederick Barbarossa were crowned here and in the 14th century it was taken by the Viscontis of Milan, who built the castle and founded both the university and the Certosa. Pavia's rich heritage of art and architecture is reflected in its Renaissance cathedral, whose architects include Leonardo da Vinci, Bramante and Amadeo, several fine medieval churches, and the Visconti castle.

The Certosa lies 8km (5 miles) north of Pavia, set in former hunting grounds. This monastery was originally founded as a mausoleum by Gian Galeazzo Visconti in 1396. The church's exuberant marble facade (1400s–1560) has a profusion of sculpture. Notable works include the polyptych by Perugino in the second chapel on the left (Tue–Sun 9–11.30, 2.30–4.30; later in summer).

463 D4 Piazza Petrarca 4, 27100 Pavia 0382 597001 Pavia and Certosa di Pavia

PORTOVENERE

www.portovenere.it

Portovenere has an old town and magnificent views to the offshore islets. Its tall, pastel-painted houses, built in defensive form, are wedged along the seafront and main street. The steep narrow stairways lead up from the port to the cobbled streets and alleys of the old town, where you'll find the Romanesque church of San Lorenzo. Its prized possession is a revered Madonna Bianca (White Madonna), reputedly washed up on the shores of Lerici.

On the clifftop are the ruins of the Genoese 12th-century Castello di San Lorenzo, worth visiting if only for the magnificent views across the Cinque Terre (▷ 122). San Pietro, the windswept sanctuary on the tip of the promontory, is said to stand on the site of an ancient temple dedicated to Venus.

Boat trips run from Portovenere to the Cinque Terre and the offshore islands of Palmaria, del Tino and del Tinetto.

463 D6 Piazza Bastreri 7, 19025 Portovenere 0187 790691 Catamarans link Genoa and Portovenere (summer)

Opposite *Palazzo Ducale in Mantova*
Below *The waterfront of Portovenere*

PARCO NAZIONALE DEL GRAN PARADISO

INFORMATION

www.parks.it/parco.nazionale.gran.paradiso

462 B3 Piazza Chanoux, 11012 Cogne 0165 74040 Mon–Sat 9–12.30, 2.30–5.30 Aosta and Pont Canavese For guided tours contact Società Guide Alpine Cogne, tel 0165 74835; www.guidealpinecogne.it

TIPS

» In summer the visitor centres organize activities, show films and run trips for children.

» The park offers many winter activities, including cross-country skiing, snow trekking and walking tours to see frozen waterfalls. Information is on the park website.

The Parco Nazionale del Gran Paradiso was established in 1922, the first national park in Italy. Surrounding the Gran Paradiso massif, the park extends over some 70,000ha (173,000 acres), shared between the Valle d'Aosta and Piedmont and linked to the Vanoise National Park across the French border. At the heart of the park, the Gran Paradiso massif rises to 4,084m (13,400ft). The scenery is extremely varied: snowcapped mountain peaks and glaciers, flower-filled slopes, high pastures, waterfalls, fast-flowing streams, and forests of larch, pine and fir in the valleys.

THE PARK'S RESORTS

Two of the most popular resorts are Valsavarenche, the main village in the valley of the same name and a starting point for the climb of Gran Paradiso and Grivola (3,969m/13,022ft), and Cogne, the main resort on the Aosta side of the park and another good base for excursions. The park has 450km (280 miles) of tracks. The most popular takes you from Valnontey, near Cogne, up a steep path to the Rifugio Vittorio Sella (2,599m/8,527ft), then on to the Rifugio Sella Herbetet and the head of the valley (full day).

FLORA AND FAUNA

The number of ibex in the park declined drastically in the 1940s, but careful protection has seen numbers rise to around 3,500, and they have now been reintroduced to other parts of the Alps. They are normally seen well above the tree line; one of the best places to observe them is from the pastureland of the Gran Piano di Noasca in the Piedmont section of the park (a beautiful path, with fine views of the Orco Valley, connects Nivolet and the Gran Piano). There are around 6,000 chamois in the park, as well as Alpine marmot and rare birds such as the bearded vulture, which disappeared from here in 1912 and is now returning, thanks to a reintroduction project. Many rare species of Alpine flora can be seen in the Giardino Alpino Paradiso at Valnontey near Cogne. Established in 1955, this garden now supports around 2,000 species of Alpine flora, including the mountain lily *(Paradisea liliastrum)*. Late spring is the best time to visit to see the flowers, while winter is ideal for cross-country skiing.

Below *Mountain peaks and glaciers in the Parco Nazionale del Gran Paradiso*

RAPALLO

www.apttigullio.liguria.it

Rapallo's bay overlooks the Gulf of Tigullio and is protected by the surrounding mountains. Its temperate climate and natural beauty attracted the wealthy in the early part of the last century, and in the 1920s it became a haunt of literati. The American poet Ezra Pound lived here for 20 years.

At the end of a promenade, lined with palm trees, orange trees and open-air cafés, stands the 16th-century castle. Built to protect the town against the Saracens, it is now an exhibition venue. In the hills behind Rapallo, overlooking the valley and bay, the Santuario di Montallegro was built in the 16th century to protect a Byzantine icon of the Madonna that miraculously appeared here in 1557 (daily 7–12.30, 2.30–6; until 8 in summer).

463 D5 Lungomare Vittorio Veneto 7, 16034 Rapallo 0185 230346 Mon–Sat 9.30–12.30, 2.30–5.30 Rapallo

RIVIERA DI LEVANTE

www.turismoinliguria.it

This stretch of coastline between Genoa and La Spezia is bordered by rugged mountains and hills cloaked in pine, olives and vines. Subtropical trees and flowers form a lush backdrop to the resorts and tiny fishing villages that cling to the cliffs.

The most attractive section of the Riviera is the Cinque Terre (▷ 122), whose fishing villages have kept their picturesque charm. East of Genoa most of the rugged Portofino promontory is a national park. A retreat for the rich and famous, Portofino has an idyllic natural harbour, with pastel-washed houses and a piazza overlooked by chic but notoriously pricey cafés, restaurants and designer boutiques. Down the road from Portofino is Santa Margherita Ligure, a fashionable, but slightly more affordable resort. La Spezia in the far east, the largest naval base in the country, is worth a visit for its Pinacoteca Civica Amedeo Lia, a Franciscan convent converted into an art gallery with works by Bellini, Titian, Tintoretto, Veronese and other great Italian masters (Via Prione 234; Tue–Sun 10–6; €6).

463 D5–6 Via XXV Aprile 2B, 16038 Santa Margherita Ligure 0185 287485 Via Roma 35, Portofino 0185 269024 Santa Margherita Ligure

Above *The bell tower and church of Santa Orsa in Aosta, Valle d'Aosta*

SACRA DI SAN MICHELE

www.sacradisanmichele.com

This ancient monastery perches spectacularly on a spur halfway up Monte Pirchiriano at 962m (3,156ft), 18km (11 miles) from the ancient town of Avigliana. Founded as a small church in 983–86 by Hugues de Montboissier from the Auvergne, the monastery was entrusted to five Benedictine monks. It was enlarged in the 12th century with the addition of a five-apsed church and soon became a pilgrimage church for worshippers en route to Rome. The complex began to decline in the 14th century and suffered French attacks in the 17th century, but it has undergone major renovations since. The fortress-like church is accessed via 154 steps cut into the rock, gruesomely named Scalone dei Morti (Stairway of the Dead) after restorers discovered skeletons of monks in the walls. Inside, the church has a high altar by the Piedmontese artist Defendente Ferrari.

462 A4 Abbazia Sacra di San Michele, 10651 Avigliana 011 939130 Jul–Sep Tue–Sat 9.30–12.30, 2.30–6, Sun–Mon 9.30–12, 2.40–6.30; mid-Mar to Jun, first half of Oct Tue–Sat 9.30–12.30, 2.30–6, Sun 9.30–12, 2.40–6.30; mid-Oct to mid-Mar Tue–Sat 9.30–12.30, 2.30–5, Sun 9.30–12, 2.40–5 Adult €4, child (under 14) €3 Avigliana (26km/16 miles west of Turin; 30 minutes' journey time)

TORINO (TURIN)

▷ 134–135.

VALLE D'AOSTA

www.regione.vda.it/turismo

The Aosta Valley, dominated by Alpine peaks, is a region of finely preserved medieval castles, traditional villages and monumental Roman remains. In 1948 it was granted semi-autonomous status in recognition of its French culture and language. Italy's smallest region encompasses the towering peaks of the French and Swiss Alps, Mont Blanc, Monte Rosa, the Matterhorn and Gran Paradiso, whose snow-covered slopes are ideal for winter sports. The most popular resort is Courmayeur, both for winter sports and as a summer base for excursions by car, foot or cable car. The south-eastern part of the valley is famous for its castles, built in the Middle Ages.

Aosta, capital of the Valle d'Aosta, is an industrial town and popular with visitors. The town, enhanced by its mountain setting, makes a good base for trips to the Parco Nazionale del Gran Paradiso (▷ 132) and Valle del Gran San Bernardo. It is often called the Rome of the Alps; its city walls, Roman theatre and forum all impressively illustrate its ancient past.

462 B3 Piazza Chanoux 2, 11100 Aosta 0165 236627

INFORMATION

www.turismotorino.org
www.comune.torino.it
462 B4 Stazione Porta Nuova, 10123 Torino 011 535181 (number operates 9.30–9.30) Daily 9.30–7
Also at Torino Caselle Airport and Piazza Castello (variable opening hours)
Torino's new metro (underground) line uses state-of-the-art technology and is adapted for people with limited mobility
The city is served by buses, trams and a funicular. Tickets are sold at stations, *tabacchi*, etc. A tourist bus takes visitors around the city with a guide (departs from Piazza Castello) The city is a major rail terminus. Regular trains run to and from Milan (1 hour 15 minutes)
Torino Caselle Airport is 16km (10 miles) north of the city, accessible by regular bus and train services Guided tours for individuals or groups tel 011 535181/535901

Above *Arcades on Via Roma, Turin*

INTRODUCTION

Viewed for years as a dour industrial city, Turin today has re-emerged into the sun as one of northern Italy's finest metropolitan destinations, an elegant centre that happily combines historic stylishness with 21st-century amenities. The capital of Piedmont, it lies within a seeming stone's throw of the Alps, a proximity that gained it the 2006 Winter Olympics. The Torinese made the most of their shot at fame, transforming the city's infrastructure and investing not only in impressive sports facilities, but in museums and attractions. There was already plenty to build on. Once through the dreary suburbs, you'll find yourself in a gracious city centre, rich in parks, boulevards and airy squares lined with serene palazzi. Pick of the bunch is the beautiful Piazza San Carlo, whose sweeping expanse is surrounded by arcades that house Turin's renowned *fin-de-siècle* cafés.

This lovely central core owes its existence to Turin's role as the base, from 1574, for the royal court of the French House of Savoy, owners of the Turin Shroud *(La Sacra Sindone)*. They made Turin their capital and their money paid for the baroque transformation of the city by 17th-century architects Guarini and Juvarra, making it a fitting setting as the first capital of a united Italy, when Vittorio Emanuele was proclaimed king here in 1861. Migrant labour flocked to the city, attracting industrialists such as Giovanni Agnelli, who founded the Fiat motor business in Turin in 1899. Though the Fiat factory has now been transformed by architect Renzo Piano into a cutting-edge designer exhibition, hotel and shopping centre, Turin is still an economic powerhouse.

WHAT TO SEE

MUSEO EGIZIO AND GALLERIA SABAUDA

www.museoegizio.it, www.museitorino.it/galleriasabauda

Within a vast baroque palace, this is the world's only museum outside Cairo dedicated solely to Egyptian art and architecture. Among the great treasures are a black granite statue of Ramses II, the tomb of the architect Kha, and the reconstructed temple of Ellesija. The Galleria Sabauda, in the same building, has

an exceptional collection of paintings by Piedmontese, Tuscan, Lombard and Venetian masters, plus major Flemish and Dutch works. The museum adjoins Piazza San Carlo, known as 'the drawing room of Turin'—a baroque square flanked at the far end by the twin churches of San Carlo and Santa Cristina.
✉ Palazzo dell'Accademia, Via Accademia delle Scienze 6, 10123 Torino ☎ 011 561 7776
🕘 Tue–Sun 8.30–7.30; Galleria Sabauda Tue, Fri–Sun 8.30–2, Wed 2–7.30, Thu 10–7.30
✋ Museo Egizio €7.50; Galleria Sabauda €4; combined ticket €8 ☛ Audioguide €4

PIAZZA CASTELLO

This is the historic heart of Turin, full of reminders of the House of Savoy, Turin's rulers for six centuries. It is also the site of the original Roman settlement, Augusta Taurinorum, founded in the first century BC. Dominating the piazza is the 13th-century Palazzo Madama, which stands on the site of the old Roman eastern gate. Within is the Museo Civico d'Arte Antica, with more than 3,000 works showing the rich complexity of Italian and European art spanning 10 centuries. Nearby is the Armeria Reale, one of the largest arms and armour collections in the world. Beyond, the 17th-century Palazzo Reale is one of Turin's most splendid baroque monuments, built for Carlo Emanuele II and home to the Savoy dukes and kings until 1865. Inside, the palazzo is filled with exquisite treasures, from chandeliers to chinoiserie, while the delightful garden was designed in the French style by André le Nôtre, creator of the gardens at Versailles.
✉ Piazza Castello, 10121 Torino

GALLERIA CIVICA D'ARTE MODERNA E CONTEMPORANEA

www.gamtorino.it

If you like modern art, seek out the Galleria Civica d'Arte Moderna e Contemporanea (GAM), northwest of the station. It has 15,000 works of art including pieces by Modigliani, De Chirico, Klee and Warhol.
✉ Via Magenta 31, 20100 Torino ☎ 011 442 9518 🕘 Tue–Sun 10–6 ✋ Adult €7.50, child/youth/students (10–25) €4, free all day Tue

MOLE ANTONELLIANA

www.museocinema.it

Turin's answer to Paris's Eiffel Tower is 167m (548ft) high, with a panoramic glass-walled elevator that soars up to a viewing platform 85m (280ft) up on the spire of the building. Built between 1798 and 1888, it houses an outstanding museum tracing the history of cinema.
✉ Via Montebello 20, 10124 Torino ☎ 011 813 8560; information line 011 217 8540
🕘 Tue–Fri, Sun 9–8, Sat 9am–11pm ✋ Museum: Adult €7, EU youths (18–25) €5, child (6–18) €2. Elevator: Adult €5, EU youths (10–25) €3.50, under 10s free. Combined ticket available

TIPS

» The Turin card (€20 for 48 hours, €25 for 72 hours) covers 120 museums, monuments, castles and palaces in Turin and Piedmont, plus urban and suburban transport and river trips. It also gives reductions on services such as guided tours, car rental and theatre tickets.

» TurismoBus Torino is a hop-on hop-off tour bus with live commentary on the sights, culture and history of Turin. A ticket lasting all day costs €20 for adults and €10 for children under 15. You can buy the tickets at tourist information offices in Piazza Castello and the Porta Nuova train station, at Torino Caselle Airport, in hotels or on board the bus. TurismoBus Torino is free if you have a Turin Card.

» The ChocoPass entitles you to sample the range of tastes and products around the city. It costs €12 for 10 tastings in two days, from Turismo Torino information points.

» If you want to see the Turin Shroud, a replica is displayed in the duomo; the original is only brought out rarely—its next scheduled appearance is in 2025.

» Just outside the city at Pessione di Chieri you can visit the premises of Martini & Rossi, makers of the famous aperitif since the mid-1800s. At the end of the visit you can relax on the Martini Terrace and savour a tasting of the four types of the famous drink. Visits daily 9.30–7. Via Piazza Luigi Rossi 1, Pessione di Chieri, tel 011 941 9217.

Below *Turin by night, with the striking Mole Antonelliana brilliantly illuminated*

THE CINQUE TERRE

This scenic route winds around a dramatic part of the Ligurian coastline, past secluded villages that cling to the steep cliffs (⊳ 122). The Cinque Terre (or Five Lands) is a national park and a UNESCO World Heritage Site. There are plenty of hairpin bends so this drive is not for the faint-hearted, but you will be rewarded with superb views.

THE DRIVE
Distance: 103km (64 miles)
Allow: 3 hours' driving time
Start/end at: Levanto

★ From Levanto, pick up the SP43 and drive through the industrial outskirts of the town. After 1km (0.6 mile) you reach a fork in the road where you turn left and begin to climb. Go through Busco, and then past Legnaro, where there is a very sharp bend. There are good views from here of the pretty village of Chiesanovo on the right. When you come to an intersection, turn left, following signs to La Spezia. Continue, passing the little church of Santuario di Soviore, and after another 1km (0.6 mile) take a right turn signposted for Vernazza.

❶ The views over the sea from now on are spectacular, with pink and toffee-coloured houses dotted over the hillsides below. The hills are terraced for the cultivation of vines, grown in small layered patches held up by dry-stone walls *(muri a secco)*.

After 3km (2 miles) you come to another intersection—keep straight on for La Spezia. The road dips, then after about 5km (3 miles) you come to another intersection where you turn left. (If you want to visit the village of Corniglia, turn right onto the SP30.)

❷ Corniglia is perched on the ridge of a rocky promontory at the foot of terraced vineyards. This fishing and farming community is similar architecturally to inland villages. The parish church of San Pietro, built in 1334 on the ruins of an 11th-century chapel, has a baroque exterior and is one of the most beautiful Gothic-Ligurian buildings in the Cinque Terre.

After thick patches of conifer woodland, the landscape opens out again with good views of Manarola, which juts out precipitously into the sea.

❸ While you drive you may occasionally see the monorail trucks used by farmers to help harvest their grapes from the terraced fields. The rare wine Sciacchetrà is produced in this area. The proximity of the vines to the sea and their exposure to the sun creates the ideal conditions for maturing grapes with high sugar content. The sweet flavour and golden colour of Cinque Terre wines make them an excellent accompaniment to cheese, seafood and desserts.

Now head downhill to another intersection where you turn right onto the SP59 to Manarola, or left to continue driving. This road, the SS370, climbs again for about 4km (2.5 miles), after which you enter a tunnel. Continue straight ahead

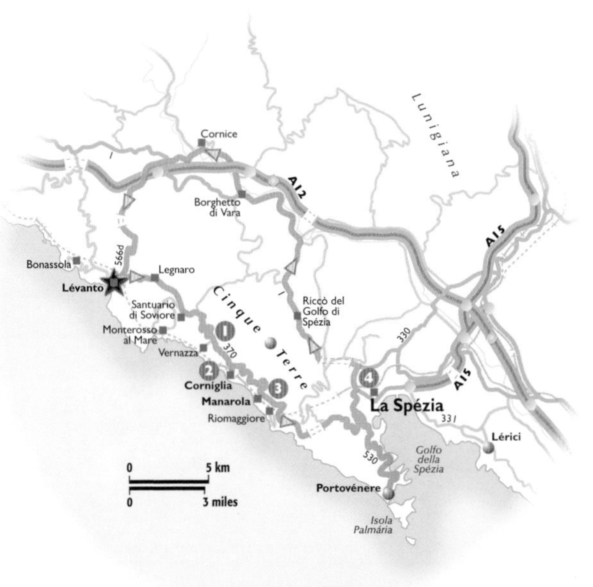

when you leave the tunnel and on your left you will see La Spezia, framed by mountains.

You soon come to an intersection, where you need to take a sharp right-hand turn at the traffic lights to join the SS530, which takes you to Portovenere. Follow this road as it climbs away from the harbour and after 8km (5 miles) you come to an intersection. Keep to the right, following signs for Portovenere.

After 3km (2 miles) you enter Portovenere (▷ 131), a pretty wedge of coloured houses. After exploring, follow the road back to La Spezia. There is a NATO base in the port, so be prepared for heavy traffic and large vehicles.

❹ La Spezia is the biggest naval base in Italy. The public gardens in the west of the town are just a short distance away from Piazza Chirodo and La Spezia's naval Arsenale, rebuilt after World War II. Just off the complex is the Museo Tecnico Navale, celebrating La Spezia's naval history with impressive displays of battle relics and models.

Follow the road going through the centre of La Spezia, then turn left at the next intersection and pick up the SS1 for Ricco del Golfo. You no longer overlook the coast now and the landscape has a quiet, rural feel. Drive through the village and on to Borghetto di Vara, where you follow signs for the SS1 and continue to Cornice. After 1.5km (0.9 mile) you will reach another intersection; turn left, following signs to 'Levanto 14'. Drive on for another 3km (2 miles), then turn left at the intersection onto the SS566d. In about 45m (50 yards) you turn right again, go under a road bridge, through a tunnel and emerge at Ponte d'Osso. Continue downhill, enjoying views of Levanto as you descend into the village.

WHEN TO GO

Late spring and early autumn are quieter than summer.

PLACE TO VISIT

MUSEO TECNICO NAVALE

✉ Viale Amendola, 19122 La Spezia
☎ 0187 783016 ⏲ Mon–Sat 8–6.45, Sun 8–1

WHERE TO EAT

Taverna Garibaldi in Levanto is an excellent pizzeria (Via Garibaldi 57, tel 018 7808098; 12–2, 7.30–11).

TIPS

» The villages of the Cinque Terre are car-free. You need to park in the car parks at the tops of the villages (most close at 10 or 11pm), or farther away on the roadsides.

» Roads in this area are rarely numbered, and you will find that local signs often only direct you as far as the next village.

Opposite *The coastal town of Portovenere*
Left *A street in Vernazza*

A WINE TOUR FROM ALBA TO CUNEO

A vast array of wines is produced in northwest Italy, and the best of them come from the Langhe hills in southern Piedmont. From the medieval town of Alba, this tour takes you through a picturesque landscape of hilltop villages and castles, passing many *enoteche*, *cantine* and private cellars en route, where you can sample the local produce.

THE DRIVE
Distance: 92km (57 miles)
Allow: 1 day
Start at: Alba
End at: Cuneo

★ Capital of the Langhe district, Alba is famous for wine and white truffles. It was formerly known as the 'City of 100 Towers', and though few of these survive, much of the town has kept its medieval appearance.

From Alba (▷ 121) follow the signs for Diano d'Alba, a village about 8km (5 miles) to the south, set among rolling vineyards.

❶ The vineyards here produce the fruity and fresh Dolcetto DOC table wine. This easy-drinking, sociable wine is renowned for its purplish colour, plum and cherry flavours and distinctive bitter-almond aftertaste.

Backtrack to the left turn for Grinzane Cavour in the Gallo d'Alba direction.

❷ Castello di Cavour, which used to belong to Count Camillo Benso di Cavour, offers tours. It is home to the Museo dell'Enoteca Regionale Piemontese (Museum of Piedmont Vintage Wines), with a collection of tools used in wine production and the finest *enoteca* (specialist wine shop) in the region. Established in 1967, it stocks an impressive range of Piedmont wines.

From the castle turn left for Gallo d'Alba, then left again, following signs for Serralunga d'Alba. Drive up the hillside to this medieval hilltop village, where the houses huddle around the foot of a 14th-century fortress. After exploring Serralunga, return in the direction of Gallo d'Alba. When you come to the main road turn left for Barolo.

❸ The medieval village of Barolo, home of 'the king of wines, the wine of kings', perches on the hill, its castle visible for miles around. The elaborately decorated rooms are open to visitors and include the famous Silvio Pellico Library. The antique wine cellar houses the prestigious Enoteca Regionale del Barolo (Regional Wine Store of Barolo), which represents 11 boroughs in the Barolo area. Here you can stop and sample the wines and discover why they are so popular. On the upper floors is the Farming Museum, which illustrates the meticulous care and attention involved in producing Barolo's wines.

Leave Barolo following signs for La Morra, about 6km (4 miles) to the north.

❹ La Morra is the capital of Barolo and produces a third of the wines; it also has superb views from the belvedere at the top of the town. Taste the local wines at the Enoteca Civica, which also has a wine exhibition, and at the Cantina Comunale (Via Carl Alberto 2, tel 0173 509204, Wed–Mon 10–12.30, 2.30–6.30).

Leave La Morra and take the road to Cherasco, crossing the River Tanaro.

❺ Cherasco has much to explore: a well-preserved 14th-century castle, historic palaces and churches. It is also the centre of the National Association of Snail Breeders and hosts special gourmet gastropod events in September.

From Cherasco, take the Bra road and turn left onto the SS231, which leads to Cuneo.

❻ Cuneo is the main town of southern Piedmont and is renowned for its Tuesday market, which fills the huge, arcaded Piazza Galimberti. The deconsecrated 13th-century Church of San Francesco houses the local museum and is also worth exploring.

WHEN TO GO

October is the best time to go, for the grape harvest and the famous white truffles, though fog and rain may dampen your trip. Alternatively visit in late spring.

WHERE TO EAT

The Piedmont region takes its food very seriously. Truffles, cheese, hazelnuts and Barolo wine are just a few of the regional items often found on menus. Try the Trattoria del Castello on the road up to Serralunga d'Alba (closed Wed) or the more expensive and elegant Locanda nel Borgo Antico in the centre of Barolo. This is a Michelin-starred restaurant so booking is essential (tel 017 356355; www.locandanelborgo.it; closed Tue and Wed lunch). If you prefer a picnic, there are some wonderful food shops in Alba.

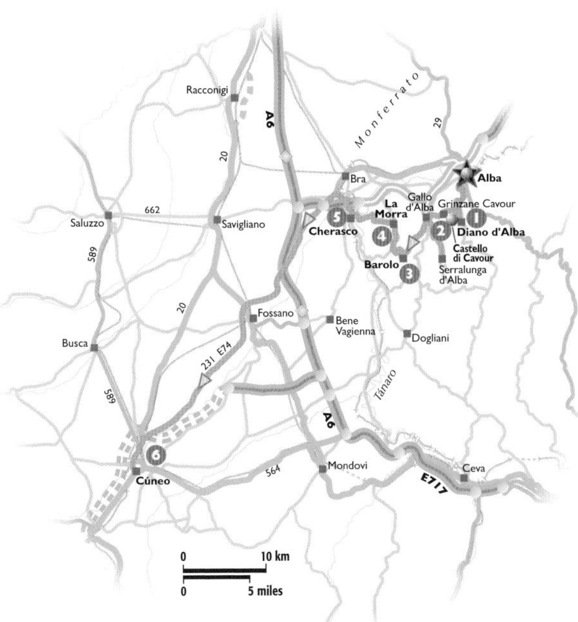

PLACES TO VISIT

ENOTECA REGIONALE AND MUSEO DELL'ENOTECA REGIONALE PIEMONTESE

www.castellogrinzane.com

✉ Via Castello, 5, 12060 Grinzane Cavour ☎ 0173 262159 🕒 Apr–Oct Wed–Mon 9.30–7; Nov–Mar 9.30–6; also open Tue 1 Sep–15 Nov

CASTELLO FALLETTI DI BAROLO

✉ Piazza Falletti, 12060 Barolo ☎ 0173 334030. Enoteca 0173 56277 🕒 Mar–Oct Fri–Wed 10–12.30, 3–6.30; Nov–Dec, Feb 10–4.30; closed Jan

Opposite *Barrels of wine in a cellar in one of the vineyards around La Morra*
Above *Bottles of Annunziata Barcio*

LAGO DI COMO—LOWER LARIO

This drive follows the shores of the southern arms of Lake Como, past sumptuous villas and gardens, historic towns, resorts and fishing villages. High points are the village of Varenna, the Villa Carlotta at Tremezzo and the ferry trip across the lake. The hills above the lake, easily accessed from many resorts, provide fine views and excellent opportunities for hiking.

THE DRIVE
Distance: 95km (59 miles)
Allow: 1 day
Start/end at: Lecco

★ From Lecco take the SS36 Sondrio road north, through a series of tunnels. Come off at the Mandello/Varenna exit (7km/4 miles). Drive along the shore to the village of Varenna, lying at the foot of the Grigna Mountains.

❶ Narrow alleys and stepped streets lead down to Lake Como and its promenade.

Take the car ferry (every 30–45 minutes in peak season) across to Menaggio, a lively resort with a pleasant lakeside promenade. Drive south along the SS340 to the Villa Carlotta, between the resorts of Cadenabbia and Tremezzo.

Above *Piazza Cermenati in Lecco*

❷ The famous Villa Carlotta was built by Marquis Clerici in the 18th century and was partially modified by Count Sommariva in the neoclassical style. Although it's now somewhat faded, you can still admire the original furniture and fine works of art inside. The villa has landscaped gardens, particularly lovely in spring, laid out by the subsequent owners, the dukes of Sachsen Meiningen.

Continue south to Ossuccio, with its distinctive Romanesque tower topped by an unusual late-Gothic belfry. Just beyond Ossuccio take a boat from Sala Comacina to Isola Comacina.

❸ Tiny Isola Comacina is Lake Como's only island, an influential political and military base in the Middle Ages. After siding with Milan in the 10-year war between Como and Milan, it was ravaged in 1169 by the people of Como. Ruins and a baroque oratory are all that remain of the strategic settlement.

Drive another 4km (2.5 miles) on the SS340 to Argegno, at the south of the delightful Val d'Intelvi. A cableway here climbs to the village of Pigra, commanding a splendid view of the lake. A stretch of fairly wild coastline leads to the pretty village of Moltrasio, via Brienno. Perched on the rugged lakeshore, it was once famous for the grey stone in its quarries, which is used in the buildings all around the shores of the lake. Now these villages are the site of luxury villas owned by the glitterati and celebrities, including George Clooney. The next resort is Cernobbio, famous for the exclusive luxury villas built here from the 16th to 18th centuries.

❹ The most famous is the 16th-century Villa d'Este, once the home of Princess Caroline, wife of King

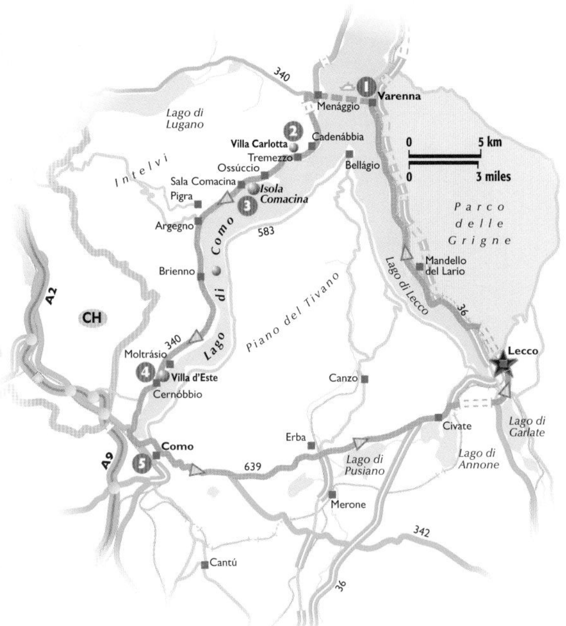

George IV of England. Since 1873 it has been a luxury hotel, and every one of the 161 sumptuously decorated rooms is unique. Overlooking the lake and surrounded by 10ha (25 acres) of parkland, the hotel has an 18-hole golf course and a wide range of outdoor and indoor sports and leisure facilities, including tennis courts, water-skiing, windsurfing, canoeing, squash courts, a gym and a spa.

The lakeside road leads south to Como.

❺ The fine walled city of Como is one of the most elegant places on the lake (▷ 123; town walk ▷ 144–145).

From Como follow the signs for Lecco, which bring you to the SS639. Fork left after 6km (4 miles), keeping to the SS639. The road bypasses Erba—a former resort, but now a major industrial hub. Another 10km (6 miles) brings you to Civate, departure point for San Pietro al Monte, a major Lombard Romanesque complex with fine views and rare 11th- and 12th-century frescoes. Return to the main road, which passes through several tunnels before reaching Lecco (7km/4 miles).

WHERE TO EAT

There are plenty of lakeside cafés and restaurants to choose from en route. In Sala Comacina the delightful La Tirlindana has wonderful home-made pasta (Piazza Matteotti 5, tel 0344 56637; daily 12.15–2.30, 7.30–11; closed Mon lunchtime).

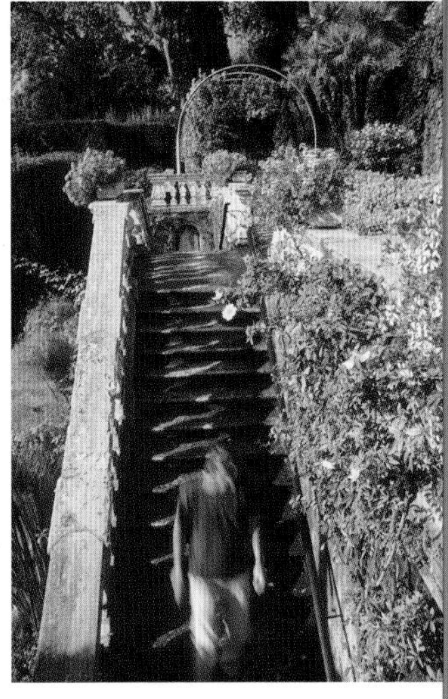

PLACES TO VISIT

VILLA CARLOTTA

www.villacarlotta.it

✉ Via Regina 2, 22019 Tremezzo

☎ 0344 40405 🕐 End Mar to mid-Oct daily 9–6; mid-Mar to end Mar, mid-Oct to Nov 10–4.30 💶 Adult €8.50, students €4.50, under 6s free

VILLA D'ESTE

www.villadeste.it

✉ Via Regina 40, 22012 Cernobbio

☎ 031 3481

Above *Villa Carlotta, Tremezzo*
Below *Ceiling detail by Ludovico Pogliaghi in Villa Carlotta*

LIMONE—SIRMIONE

This drive skirts the northern and eastern shores of Lake Garda (▷ 125), stopping at historic towns along the way, dominated by the imposing Scaligeri castles, built by the della Scala family from Verona. In the north, dramatic peaks rise sheer from the deep waters; in the south, the lake broadens into a vast expanse of blue water.

THE DRIVE
Distance: 93km (58 miles)
Allow: 1 day
Start at: Limone
End at: Sirmione

★ Limone sul Garda, which lies below white cliffs, is named after the lemon trees that once made it prosperous. A small resort, it has a centre of narrow alleys and a popular waterfront with lake-view cafés and restaurants.

From Limone sul Garda take the SS45 north through a series of tunnels to Riva del Garda.

❶ At the northern tip of the lake, sitting spectacularly below the mountains, Riva del Garda, formerly a trading port, is now a thriving resort with a prominent castle, home to the Museo Civico, and an attractive medieval core which is worth a stroll around.

Follow the signs for Torbole (4km/ 2.5 miles to the east), a small resort that is a magnet for windsurfers as the north winds guarantee action. Follow the main road (SS249) along the eastern shore of the lake, passing through tunnels, and continue as far as Malcesine.

❷ Dominated by the striking Castello Scaligero and set below the scenic Monte Baldo, Malcesine is the highlight of the lake's eastern shore. From the castle tower you can appreciate the sweeping views of the surrounding walls and steep cliffs. Inside the castle there is a museum featuring a collection of weapons, archaeological finds and objects from the Italian Risorgimento (resurgence), the 50-year struggle for liberation from foreign rule that culminated in the Unification of Italy in 1870. Malcesine's panoramic cable car will take you up to Monte Baldo, for excellent views and rare mountain flora, an ideal spot for a walk.

Continue south through a series of villages, the prettiest of which is Castelletto, where old houses group around Piazza dell'Olivio. Keep on this road to reach Torri del Benaco.

❸ Despite being a ferry terminus, Torri del Benaco still retains its old character—a charming port with a castle on the lakeside. The della Scala family rebuilt the castle between 1383 and 1393 on Roman foundations and it now houses a museum. From Torri del Benaco to Peschiera del Garda most of the lakeside has been developed for tourism. Stop at Punta di San Vigilio, occupied by the lovely Villa Guarienti, a church, park and beach. Beyond the resort of Garda is Bardolino.

❹ This area is synonymous with light, fruity red wine. Bardolino's wine museum, the Museo del Vino at the Cantina Zeni, has some interesting exhibits on the history of wine-making in the region, the highlight being the opportunity to taste (for free) the full range of wines made in the Gardesana area. Bardolino also has an olive-oil museum, with an exhibition illustrating the history of olive-oil production in rural society that stretches back more than 1,000 years. You can taste many different kinds of extra-virgin olive oil and then buy some in the museum shop, which is also stocked with a wide variety of Italian delicacies including spiced oils, aromatic vinegar, pesto and a selection of wines from the Garda region.

Continue south towards Peschiera del Garda.

❺ For many visitors the main attraction of Peschiera del Garda is the popular Gardaland (on the right before you reach the resort), northern Italy's answer to Disneyland. The town itself is a busy intersection, with a formidable fortress.

From Peschiera del Garda take the SS11, following signs to Sirmione.

❻ The loveliest of Garda's resorts and a mecca for day-trippers, Sirmione stands on the tip of a thin, craggy peninsula extending 4km (2.5 miles) into the lake; the remains of a huge Roman villa (Grotte di Catullo) occupy a spectacular position there. A beautiful 13th-century castle, surrounded by a moat, dominates the old quarter. Visitors' cars must be left outside the town.

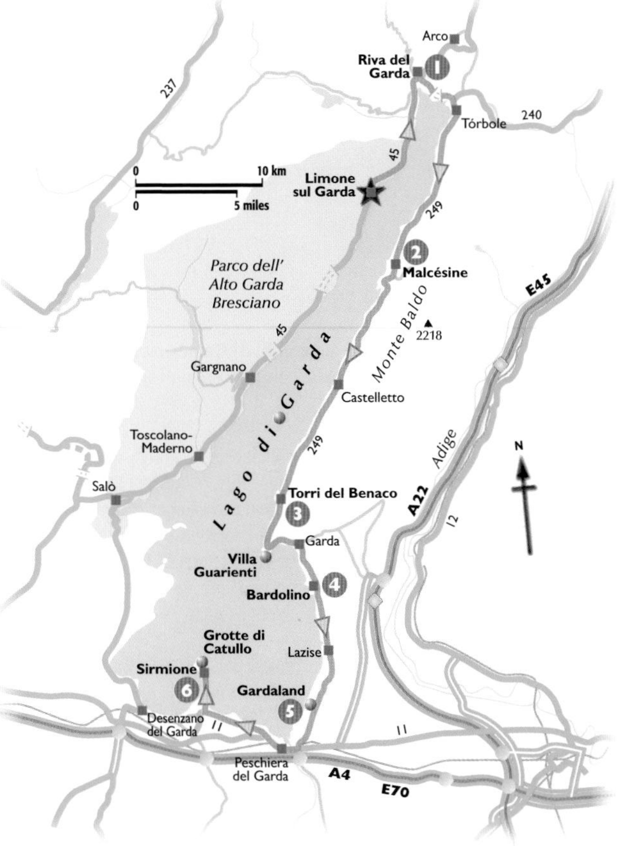

WHEN TO GO

Avoid July and August, when the roads are choked with traffic. Spring is the ideal time to go.

WHERE TO EAT

The lakeside resorts have no shortage of cafés, pizzerias and restaurants. There are also plenty of places by the lake where you can picnic. One of the prettiest spots to stop for a drink or meal is the old port in Torri del Benaco.

PLACES TO VISIT

MUSEO CIVICO

www.garda.com/museocivico

Piazza C. Battisti 3/A, 38066 Riva del Garda 046 457 3869 End Mar to early Nov Tue–Sun 10–12.30, 1.30–6; also open Mon Jul–Sep €2

MUSEO DEL CASTELLO SCALIGERO DI TORRI DEL BENACO

Viale Fratelli Lavanda 2, 37010 Torri del Benaco 045 629 6111 Apr–end May, Oct daily 9.30–12.30, 2.30–6; Jun–end Sep daily 9.30–1, 4.30–7.30 €3

ZENI MUSEO DEL VINO

www.zeni.it

Cantina Zeni, Via Costabella 9, 37011 Bardolino 045 721 0022 Mid-Mar to Oct daily 9–1, 2.30–7

OLEIFICIO CISANO DEL GARDA

www.museum.it

Via Peschiera 54, 37011 Cisano di Bardolino VR–Lago di Garda 045 622 9047 Mon–Sat 9–12.30, 2.30–7; Sun and public holidays 9–12.30; closed Jan, Feb, Sun, 15 Aug, 25–26 Dec, 1 and 6 Jan Free

GARDALAND

www.gardaland.it

Castelnuovo del Garda, 37014 Verona 045 644 9777 Late Mar to mid-Jun daily 10–6; mid-Jun to early Sep 9am–midnight; early Sep–end Sep 10–6; Oct–early Nov weekends only 10–6; closed early Nov–late Mar Adult €35, child under 10 €29, child under 1m tall free

Opposite *Hotel Locanda San Vigilio at Punta di San Vigilio*

COMO TOWN

Off the lakeside drive (▷ 140–141), this walk meanders through the old centre of Como town (▷ 123) past fine monuments, silk and leather shops and inviting *pasticcerie* and cafés, ending with a funicular ride up to the village of Brunate with fine views above and across the lake.

THE WALK
Distance: 2.7km (1.7 miles)
Allow: 2 hours
Start at: Piazza Cavour
End at: Brunate

★ From the 19th-century Piazza Cavour, with its open-air cafés and views of the lake, take Via Caio Plinio Secondo to the left of the Hotel Barchetta Excelsior. This leads into Piazza Duomo, the heart of the old centre and its finest square.

❶ Here you see the towering Torre del Comune, dating from 1215, the Broletto, a former law court from the same period, with stripes of pink, white and grey marble, and the magnificent Gothic/Renaissance duomo, with its lavish marble exterior and 15th- to 16th-century sculpture.

From the duomo head down Via Vittorio Emanuele II. Halfway down on the right is the five-sided apse of the church of San Fedele and the carved 'door of the dragon'. The building opposite (16th–17th century) has been the town hall since 1853. The street ends in Piazza Medaglie d'Oro, dominated by the archaeological and historical museums, occupying the palazzi Giovio and Olginati respectively. Pass under the arch on the left, along Via Serafino Balestra, formerly called Vicolo delle Orfanelli (Little Orphans Alley).

Follow the medieval wall to the Torre di San Vitale, an imposing tower in the city walls. Turn right when you reach the busy Viale Battisti, keeping to the old city walls. Continue south here and you come to the Basilica di Sant'Abbondio, a Romanesque construction that stands out in a rather dreary part of town. From Viale Battisti turn right by the medieval tower, best viewed from the far side. Turn right at the end of the road, down Via Giuseppe Rovelli, take the first left and turn right for Piazza San Fedele.

❷ The Piazza San Fidele was built on the site of the Roman forum, and until the 1800s the town market was held here. Today it is a small, intimate space, with cafés, arcades and a couple of finely preserved medieval buildings, which contrast with the uninspiring facade of the church of San Fedele, rebuilt in the early 20th century.

Exit the piazza on the side facing San Fedele, crossing Via Indipendenza, one of the main shopping streets. Continue straight ahead to return to Piazza Cavour. At the lakeside—a busy scene of boats and ferries—turn right, following the waterfront until you reach Piazza di Gasperi.

❸ The funicular here departs every 15 minutes and takes just over 6 minutes to reach Brunate, a village 720m (2,362ft) above the city, with magnificent views over Lake Como and the Alps.

WHEN TO GO

Avoid doing this walk between 12 and 3, when the churches and museums are closed.

WHERE TO EAT

There are plenty of good cafés and restaurants to choose from en route.

PLACES TO VISIT

DUOMO

✉ Piazza del Duomo 🕐 Daily 7–12, 3–7
✋ Free

FUNICOLARE COMO-BRUNATE

www.funicolarecomo.it
✉ Piazza de Gaspari 4 ☎ 031 303608
🕐 Mid-Apr to mid-Sep 6am–midnight
✋ Adult return €4.35, child €2.75

Opposite *Como Cathedral*
Below left *A sundial in Como town*
Below *Boats on the shores of Lake Como*

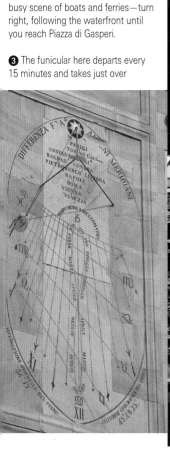

BERGAMO

TEATRO DONIZETTI

www.teatrodonizetti.it

A wide range of music is performed at this old theatre, from productions of musicals such as *Grease* to hard-hitting Verdi. It's also home to three big international music festivals: jazz in February, piano in May and opera every autumn.

✉ Piazza Cavour 15, 24121 Bergamo ☎ 035 416 0602; booking line 035 416 0601/2/3 (Mon–Sat 1–8.30) ⌚ 8.30pm; some Sun shows from 3.30pm

COMO

LIDO DI VILLA OLMO

This lakeshore bathing establishment is a great find for a lazy day; there are loungers and umbrellas, lake bathing, a whirlpool bath and adults' and kids' swimming pools, all set on a sandy beach beside Lake Como, backed by grassy slopes. You can have a drink or a full meal in the restaurant before hiring a boat for a lake outing.

✉ Via per Cernobbio 2, 22100 Como ☎ 031 570871 ⌚ Daily May–Sep 10–6 Adult all day €6, child (3–12) €3.50 Outside Como on road to Cernobbio

TEATRO SOCIALE

vwww.teatrosocialecomo.it

This 1,000-seat auditorium sits majestically in its own square, between the duomo and the Nord Lago rail station. The major theatre in town, the Sociale is the perfect venue for opera and classical music.

✉ Via Bellini 3, 22100 Como ☎ 031 270171 ⌚ Weekly performances Oct–end May €15–€70

LA TESSITURA

www.mantero.comt

This outlet/concept silk store is owned by Mantero, one of Como's largest silk producers, and is on the site of their former factory. Designers including Chanel and Louis Vuitton source their silk fabrics here and there is everything from home furnishings to ties, all displayed in suitably silky splendour.

✉ Viale Roosewvelt 2/A, 22100 Como ☎ 031 321666 ⌚ Tue–Sat 11–9

GARDONE

TEATRO DEL VITTORIALE

www.vittoriale.it

This is an open-air theatre operating in summer in the grounds of the magnificent Il Vittoriale villa. Performances range from ballets to classic musicals. Tickets are available from the box office outside.

✉ Via Vittoriale 12, 25083 Gardone Riviera ☎ 0365 296511 ⌚ Performances Jun–end Aug 7.30pm €25–€30

GENOVA (GENOA)

LA CITTÀ DEI BAMBINI

www.cittadeibambini.net

This is one of Genoa's few places specifically aimed at kids, from two to 14 years. The focus is on learning about technology and the world in a fun-fuelled and fully interactive way. Adults can leave their children to entertain themselves under the supervision of trained staff, and feel free to go shopping and explore Genoa's premier tourist district.

✉ Magazzini del Cotone, Area Porto Antico, 16128 Genova ☎ 010 234 5635 ⌚ Jul–Sep Tue–Sun 11.30–7.30; Oct–Jun 10–6; €7 1, 2, 3, 4, 7, 8, 12 or 15 to the Porto Antico complex

TEATRO CARLO FELICE

www.carlofelice.it

Teatro Carlo Felice has unmissable premises on Piazza dei Ferrari.

Opera dominates, but there are plenty of other classical and show performances woven into the schedule. There are some good cafés and bars around the corner from the theatre. Buy tickets online.
Passo Eugenio Montale 4, 16121 Genova
010 53811 Performances 8pm
€22–€100 17, 18, 19, 20, 30, 32, 35, 37, 39, 40, 41 or 46 to Piazza dei Ferrari

MILANO (MILAN)

AC MILAN AND INTER MILAN LIVE FOOTBALL

www.acmilan.com, www.inter.it
Catch one of Italy's most illustrious clubs, AC Milan or Inter Milan, at the San Siro stadium. Tickets for a match with either sell out fast, so buy your tickets in advance from their club shop in Via Turati, from FNAC in Via Torino, online on their website or through TicketOne.
Via Piccolomini 5, 20151 Milano
02 4009 2175 Sep–end Jun every other weekend From €17 Lotto (free before matches)

ALCATRAZ

www.alcatrazmilano.com
This live music and disco venue is rock oriented. One of the city's largest venues, it attracts more than 1,000 happy dancers at the weekend. It is frequented by the occasional famous face and the well dressed, so it's best to dress to impress, as with most Milanese clubs. It only really gets going after midnight.
Via Valtellina 25, 20121 Milano
02 6901 6352 Fri–Sat 11pm–4am
Disco from €6, live performances from €16 Garibaldi

ARMANI

www.emporioarmani.it
The flagship Armani Superstore has collections paying homage to the Milanese 'master of minimalism' Children's clothes, lingerie, accessories and the latest fashions are spread across eight floors, and there are also books, cutlery and designer chocolates to salivate over..
Via Manzoni 31, 20121 Milano
02 6231 2605 Mon–Sat 10.30–7.30
Monte Napoleone

CENTRO SPORTIVO MARIO SAINI

Hit a few tennis balls on an open-air clay court or have a game on one of the 12 indoor synthetic courts. Quality equipment is available to rent at the club. Non-members are welcome, but tennis whites are appreciated.
Via Corelli 136, 20134 Milano
02 756 1280 Daily dawn–dusk
€8 before 6, €12 after 6 38

ITALIAN GRAND PRIX

www.monzanet.it
The Italian Grand Prix at Monza is one of the highlights of the Formula One calendar. Phone for full details, or reserve on the Monza website.
Parco di Monza, 20052 Monza
039 248 2212 Mid-Sep €35–€500 Monza is clearly signed 20km (12 miles) northeast of Milan

LOUIS VUITTON

www.louisvuitton.com
Get your hands on the world's most distinctive luggage. There are branded bags, purses and cases for the international jet set. The nearby branches of Bruno Magli and Samsonite are also useful if you need extra luggage space to take your shopping home.
Via Monte Napoleone 2, 20121 Milano
02 777 1711 Mon–Sat 9.30–7.30, Sun 11–7.30 San Babila

MANDARINA DUCK

www.mandarinaduck.com
Mandarina Duck has two floors of funky, functional handbags and purses. The shop is close to Milan's central Piazza del Duomo, next door to the British Abbey National bank. Full sets of non-leather luggage start at around €350.
Via Orefici 10, 20123 Milano 02 8646 2198 Tue–Sat 10–7.30, Mon 3–7
Duomo

ODEON

A 10-screen multiplex cinema in the heart of town, the Odeon shows all the latest blockbusters. Many are screened in their original language. Half of the theatres provide access for people with disabilities, and all have air-conditioning. Less expensive tickets are available for daytime shows.
Via Santa Radegonda 8, 20121 Milano
02 892111 Thu–Tue (contact for details) €8 Duomo

PLASTIC

This buzzing disco for gay and straight revellers has a drag night on Tuesday. Even after 30 years it remains a popular and busy venue, but it's only open three nights a week.
Viale Umbria 120, 20123 Milano
02 733996 Fri–Sun 11pm–4am
€18 Duomo

PRADA

www.prada.it
The windows of this flagship store, near Via Monte Napoleone, are jam-packed—purses, bags and shoes beckon those with style and money. Immaculately turned-out staff are there to help you choose from Prada's reassuringly expensive range.
Via Sant'Andrea 21, 20121 Milano
02 7600 1426 Daily 10–7.30
San Babila

RADETZKY

This very popular bar in the Brera area attracts a cool, fashionable crowd for *aperitivi*/Happy Hour, people-watching and its famous long brunches on Sunday.
Largo La Foppa 5 (Corso Garibaldi 105), 20124 Milano 02 657 2645 Daily 8am–1.30am €10 Moscova
43, 94

ROLLING STONE

www.rollingstone.it
Listen to live rock, punk, indie and jazz at this hangout near the Porta Vittorio rail station. It is very relaxed and there is no dress code. Listings are in Milan's free newspapers.
Corso XXII Marzo 32, 20135 Milano
02 733172 Tue–Sat 7am–1pm, 8.30pm–4am Cover charge (depending on performances) Porta Vittorio

Opposite *Galleria Vittorio Emanuele II in Milan*

LE SAC FACTORY OUTLET

You can find bargain bags, belts and purses here (leather and snakeskin predominate). Many items come with chic labels, and prices range from €50 to €500—reasonable compared to some of the other big stores nearby.

✉ Via Carnevale 13, 20121 Milano ☎ 02 376 0399 ⏲ Tue–Fri 9.30–2, 3.30–7.30, Mon 3.30–7.30, Sat 9.30–1, 2.30–7.30 Ⓜ San Babila

SISLEY

www.sisley.com

This is very much a flagship fashion store for this smart-casual Italian label, part of the Benetton group. In sight of the duomo, Sisley's huge window displays and moderately priced clothes draw the shoppers in droves. Quality Italian shirts for men are around €40. T-shirts for women start from around €12. This branch also stocks Sisley's latest lingerie collection.

✉ Via Dogana 4, 20123 Milano ☎ 02 8699 6191 ⏲ Mon–Sat 10–7.30, Sun 11–7 Ⓜ Duomo

TEATRO ALLA SCALA

www.lascala.milano.it

Milan's most famous playhouse is the venue for a huge variety of classical music and operatic performances. The opera season opens on 7 December. As well as entertainment, this stunningly beautiful theatre has an on-site bookshop, bar and history museum to explore. You can reserve tickets and find details of up-and-coming events on their flash website.

✉ Piazza della Scala, 20121 Milano ☎ 02 7200 3744 ⏲ Most evenings from 8pm ✋ €20 upwards Ⓜ Monte Napoleone

TOCQUEVILLE 13

www.tocqueville13.it

This posh club is popular with footballers and you might spot a few famous faces. Thursday and Sunday are the big nights. Entry is easier on other nights. Pricey nibbles are available.

✉ Via de Tocqueville 13, 20154 Milano ☎ 02 2900 2973 ⏲ Daily 9pm–3am ✋ €15 Ⓜ Garibaldi

PESCHIERA

CANEVAWORLD

www.canevaworld.it

Canevaworld's Movieland Studios offers family fun in Hollywood studios where you can take part in shows, experience fire, waterfalls and earthquakes, or even the Stone Age in the new children's set—all from a safe distance. Or discover Peter Pan and Captain Hook in the Aquastudios, where you can float down rapids and dive-bomb down the waterslides. There are plenty of fast-food outlets and restaurants and in the evening the fun continues at Medieval Times (▷ below).

✉ Via Fossalta 1, 37010 Peschiera ☎ 045 696 9900 ⏲ Mid-May to end Sep Mon–Sat 10–6, Sun 10–7 ✋ Combined ticket: adult €34, child (1–1.4m) €29, child under 1m free. Movieland Studios or Movieland Aquastudios alone: adult €24, child (1–1.4m) €19, child under 1m free 🚌 Regular shuttle buses from train station 🚗 5km (miles) from Peschiera del Garda

MEDIEVAL TIMES

www.canevaworld.it

A whole evening of medieval fun and entertainment for all the family awaits you here. Walk around a Ruritanian castle, watch the jousters, then eat and drink all you can at the king's feast. Crazy court jesters and some serious sword fighting make this unsuitable for the very young.

✉ Via Fossalta 1, 37010 Peschiera ☎ 0457 590622 ⏲ May–Jun, Sep Mon–Fri show 7pm, Sat–Sun shows 7pm, 9.30pm; Jul–Aug shows daily 7pm 9.30pm; Oct, Mar Apr Sat–Sun show 7pm ✋ Adult €28, child (under 1.4m/4ft 6in) €18, child (under 1m/3ft 4in) free (discounts for additional entry into other Canevaworld entertainment sites, such as the adjoining aquapark) 🚌 Regular shuttle buses from train station 🚗 5km (3 miles) from Peschiera del Garda

STRESA

MOUNTAIN BIKE HIRE

You can rent mountain bicycles from the cable-car station (next to Stresa's Carciano harbour) and ride up to Mount Mottarone (1,455m/4,772ft). The long, slow descent is magnificent.

✉ Piazzale Lido, 28838 Stresa ⏲ Mar–end Oct daily 8–8 ✋ €20 for full day

TORINO (TURIN)

BALÔN MARKETS

www.balon.it

Just behind Porta Palazzo, one of Europe's largest open-air markets, the Balôn is a popular Saturday flea market. On the second Sunday of each month, its big cousin, the Grand Balôn antiques fair, occupies the same site.

✉ Borga Dora, near Piazza della

Below *San Remo hosts the World Fireworks Championship in July*

Repubblica, 10152 Torino ☎ 011 436 9741 ⌚ Balôn Sat, Grand Balôn Sun 8–7

CIRCOLO GOLF
www.circologolftorino.it
This is a classy 19-hole, 72-par golf course. The club has a practice field, swimming pool, bar, fine restaurant, and jewellery and fashion shops. The summer heat tends to be quite bearable up here too.
✉ Via Agnelli 40, Fiano, 10070 Torino ☎ 011 923 5440 ⌚ Mar–Dec 15 Tue–Sun 8–8 A round of golf is €90 on a weekday, €108 at the weekend. Equipment rental extra 🚗 Take the Venaria Reale exit from the Tangenziale Nord from Milan

GERLA
www.giandujotto.it
Thousands of chocolates vie for customers' attention, especially the *giandujotto*—the heavenly chocolate and hazelnut confection for which Turin is so famous. The ornate chocolate cakes cost around €20. Piedmontese savoury specials—as well as fruit tarts, sweet breads and pastries—complete the spread.
✉ Corso Vittorio Emanuele II 88, 10123 Torino ☎ 011 545422 ⌚ Mon–Fri 9–7.30, Sat 8.30–1, 3.30–7.30, Sun 8.30–1 🚌 15

JUVENTUS LIVE FOOTBALL
www.juventus.com
Italy's most decorated football (soccer) club, Juve play alternate weeks at the Stadio delle Alpi. Tickets start from €15 but you can pay up to several hundred euros for the best seats.
✉ Piazza Crimea 7, 10131 Torino ☎ 011 65631 ⌚ Sep–Jun every other weekend €15 (cheapest ticket) 🚗 The Stadio delle Alpi is clearly signed 4km (2.5 miles) southwest of the city centre

TEATRO REGIO TORINO
www.teatroregio.torino.it
You will find this unmissable theatre on the corner of Piazza Castello next to Via Giuseppe Verdi. It hosts musicals, plays and the occasional opera all year round.
✉ Piazza Castello 215, 10122 Torino ☎ 011 881 5241 ⌚ 7.30pm €20–€300 🚌 11, 12

FESTIVALS AND EVENTS

JANUARY

FIERA DI SANT'ORSO
www.fieradisantorso.it
Traditional street fair in honour of Sant Orso, a sixth-century Irish monk who lived in Aosta and was an expert woodworker, carving sandals for the poor. Today, more than 700 woodcarvers exhibit and sell their work, mostly traditional bowls and utensils, while artisan lace and fabrics are also available. Local restaurants serve regional specialties throughout the two-day fair.
✉ Aosta ⌚ 30–31 January

FEBRUARY

BATTLE OF THE ORANGES
www.carnevalediivrea.it
Dating from the 12th century, this festival commemorates the assassination of the tyrannical Count Ranieri by a miller's daughter. Today, a girl is chosen annually to lead the festivities, which include historical processions and pageants. The high point is a series of 'battles' fought between rival factions, with more than 400 tons of oranges used as ammunition and thrown from decorated horse-drawn carts.
✉ Ivrea ⌚ 21–24 February

JULY

WORLD FIREWORKS CHAMPIONSHIP
www.sanremo.it/fuochi
Italians are world famous for their firework displays and the major companies operate worldwide. There's no better place to see what they can do than at San Remo, when incredible fireworks burst noisily and spectacularly over the port for a whole week. Look out for the pyrotechnics on the water.
✉ San Remo ⌚ 1st week in July

AUGUST

FESTIVAL DEL MARE
The feast of the Assumption is celebrated all over Italy with processions and general jollity, but pyrotechnic-lovers should head for Diano Marina on the Piedmont coast to see the superb firework displays over the sea.
✉ Diano Marina ⌚ 15 August

SEPTEMBER

SETTEMBRE MUSICA
www.comune.torino.it
Most of September is devoted to this music festival, which combines classical, modern, jazz and world music at various venues around the city. As befits the home of the RAI National Symphony Orchestra, standards are high; great venues include the Lingotto centre and the Teatro Regio opera house.
✉ Torino ⌚ September

OCTOBER–NOVEMBER

GIOSTRA DELLE CENTO TORRI AND PALIO
A donkey race that dates from the 12th century when troops from Asti chased the Albese inside their walls and ran a *palio* outside. The Albese promptly organized their own race inside the walls—but used donkeys. This is re-enacted to mark the opening of the National Truffle Fair, which runs for three weeks—the most famous celebration of the delicacy in Italy.
✉ Alba ⌚ 1st Sunday in October–1st weekend in November

DECEMBER

MERCATO DI SANT'AMBROGIO
A festival in honour of the birthday of Sant' Ambrogio, Milan's ninth-century patron saint and the city's first mayor. Stands selling a bit of everything appear around the church of Sant'Ambrogio, and thousands of people take the day off work to attend. The festival is also called Oh Bej! Oh Bej! after the children's cries of delight in the 16th century.
✉ Milano ⌚ 7 December

PRICES AND SYMBOLS

The restaurants are listed alphabetically within each town. The prices given are the average for a two-course lunch (L) and a three-course dinner (D) for one person, without drinks. The wine price given is for the least expensive bottle.

For the key to symbols, ▷ 2.

ALBA

PIAZZA DUOMO

www.piazzaduomoalba.it

This two Michelin-starred restaurant is one of Italy's temples to haute cuisine, housed on two floors in a historic building on Alba's main piazza. The ground-floor La Piola offers less expensive local specialities with a modern twist; book upstairs in the main restaurant for some of northern Italy's most creative cooking, where 21st-century style meets centuries of local tradition.

✉ Piazza Risorgimento 4, 12051 Alba ☎ 0173 366167 🕐 Tue–Sat 12.30–3, 7.30–10; also Sun lunch Aug–May; closed 2 weeks in Jan, Aug, Dec 🖐 L €70, D €100, Wine €20

Above *Eating out in Menaggio, Lake Como*

AOSTA (GRAN PARADISO)

VECCHIO RISTORO

www.ristorantevecchioristoro.it

This quietly elegant restaurant offers top-notch cooking with plenty of local recipes—try the *polenta con funghi* (polenta with wild mushrooms) in autumn. There's an excellent *bollitto misto* (mixed boiled meat with sauce *verde*); or sample the *degustazione* menu for a full range of dishes. Great puddings; the amaretto-stuffed peaches with raspberry coulis shine. They have the best of Val d'Aosta wines and some good French varieties.

✉ Via Tourneuve 4, 11100 Aosta ☎ 0165 33238 🕐 Tue–Sat 12.30–2.30, 7.30–10.30, Mon 7.30–10.30; closed Jun 🖐 L €51, D €68, Wine €18

ASTI

GENER NEUV

www.generneuv.it

An old inn on the banks of the Tanaro is home to the Fassi family's lovely Michelin-starred restaurant, known throughout the north for its fine Piedmontese cooking. Father Piero is front of house, while his wife and daughters are the talents in the kitchen, from where a range of dishes such as fresh pasta with white truffles, snails with herbs, eels simmered in white wine and free-range duck and chicken issues. There's also a fine wine list with the accent on local vintages.

✉ Lungotanaro Pescatori 4, 14100 Asti ☎ 0141 557270 🕐 Tue–Sat 12.30, 3–7.30–10, Sun 12.30–3; closed 3 weeks Aug and Christmas 🖐 L €54, D €78, Wine €15

BELLAGIO

SALICE BLU

www.ristorante-saliceblu-bellagio.it

This long-established restaurant has been recently taken over by the son of the family, who has retained the accent on local dishes but given them a makeover for the 21st century, resulting in an altogether lighter approach. The specialty is fish from the lake. Desserts too, are special, and you can enjoy it all alfresco in summer, eating under the pergola.

✉ Via per Lecco 33, 22021 Bellagio ☎ 0319 50535 🕐 Thu–Mon 12.30–2.30, 7.30–10; closed 2 weeks Jan 🖐 L €30, D €50, Wine €12

BERGAMO

VINERIA COZZI

A 19th-century building in the upper town is home to this welcoming wine bar and restaurant, specializing in local dishes with a modern twist. The decor is traditional, with a splendid 6m-long (20ft) marble bar and two pretty dining rooms and garden terrace. Dishes include a *millefoglie* with aubergines and cheese, good *baccalà* and a mouthwatering *semifreddo* of blood oranges.

Via B. Colleoni 22, 24129 Bergamo
0352 38836 Thu–Tue 12.30–3, 7.30–10.30; closed 2 weeks in Jan and Jun
L €25 D €40, Wine €12

BRESCIA

NOCE

www.ristorantehotelnoce.com

Traditional cooking for the 21st century is the order of the day at this lovely restaurant, part of a hotel. The airy dining room offers Padroni family specialities such as pasta with meat or fish sauces and well-hung meat; go for the meat or fish tasting menu to experience the full range of the chef's expertise.

Via dei Gelsi 5, 25125 Brescia
030 349510 Mon–Fri 12.30–2.30, 7.30–9.30, Sat 7.30–10; closed Aug
L €45, D €60, Wine €14

CREMONA

ANTICA TRATTORIA BISSONE

www.bissone.it

Cremona's oldest and best-known restaurant is in the heart of the *centro storico* and retains a decor straight out of the 19th century. There's often live music here, including jazz and opera, which you can enjoy while eating local specialities plus a few dishes that have crept across the border from Emilia.

Via Pecorari 3, 26100 Cremona
0372 23953 Tue–Sat 11.30–4.30 (kitchen closes at 2), 7.30–10, Sun 12.30–3
L €22, D €35, Wine €11

GENOVA (GENOA)

LUPO ANTICA TRATTORIA

www.lupoanticatrattoria.it

This welcoming restaurant specializes in Genoese cuisine, including the fabled *pesto genovese* sauce with inventive twists and fishy delights. Service is very attentive and there is an excellent wine list.

Via Monachette 20/r, 16126 Genova
010 267036 Thu–Tue 12.30–3, 7.30–midnight; closed 20 Jul–10 Aug
L €30, D €45, Wine €12

LAGO DI COMO

RESTAURANT TERMINUS

www.albergoterminus.it

This is a fine restaurant overlooking Lake Como. First courses such as *penne arrabbiata* (pasta quills with a spicy tomato, onion and garlic sauce) are priced at around €15. Main courses, including tiger prawns, are around €22. In summer diners can enjoy views of the lake while seated outside on the large terrace. The restaurant seats just 20, so booking ahead is advised.

Lungo Lario Trieste 14, 22100 Como
031 329111 Wed–Mon 12–2.30, 7.30–10 L €35, D €50, Wine €13

LAGO DI GARDA

L'ARCIMBOLDO

This restaurant, with a terrace overlooking the lake, offers simple dishes made with the finest ingredients. Highlights include beef, rocket (arugula) and Parmesan cheese, grilled swordfish or trout fillet in white wine. The restaurant's jazzy music makes this a lively place to eat.

Via Vittorio Emanuele 71, 25019 Sirmione del Garda 030 916409 Wed–Mon 11.45–2.45, 7–10.45 L €28, D €50, Wine €14

AL FATTORE

www.gardalake.it/alfattore

The crusty pizzas here are loaded with Italian goodies, including olives, roasted courgettes (zucchini), aubergine (eggplant), Parma ham, mozzarella and crispy Parmesan cheese. Fine dining in the restaurant's modern interior includes specialties like lake fish, seafood and grilled meats. There is also plenty of room outside in the summer.

Via Roma 8, 25015 Desenzano 030 9141937 Thu–Tue 12–2.30, 7–11
L €20, D €33, Wine €10

MISTRAL, GRAND HOTEL VILLA SERBELLONI

www.ristorante-mistral.com

Lakeside opulence without comparison. This is one of the most prestigious hotels on Lake Como. The attached restaurant, the Michelin-starred Mistral, is one of the area's best. Predominantly meat-based, the menu choices range from carpaccio to succulent lamb and partridge. A jacket is required at dinner.

Via Roma 1, 22021 Bellagio 031 956 435 Mar–Nov daily 12.30–2.30, 8–10
L €80, D €130, Wine €20

LAGO MAGGIORE

IL CLANDESTINO

www.ristoranteilclandestino.com

Very centrally located and close to the lake, this elegant restaurant specializes in seafood and lake fish. Some of the recipes are also Sicilian. Allow the chef-patron to serve you a specially selected feast.

Vi Rosmini 5, 28838 Stresa 032 330399 Wed–Sun 12–2.30, 7–11, Mon 7–11; closed 10–30 Nov and 10Jan–Feb
L €30, D €42, Wine €13

LA TERRAZZA

www.ristoranteterrazza.com

This lakeside restaurant, just across the road from the water, is a special place to enjoy fantastic views and delicious fish dishes. The menu includes smoked herring, Norwegian salmon and grilled lake fish.

Via Mazzini 83, 28832 Belgirate
0322 7493 Thu–Tue 12.30–2.30, 7–11 L €26, D €40, Wine €14

MANTOVA (MANTUA)

IL CIGNO-TRATTORIA DEI MARTINI

Mantuan cooking returns to its roots in this long-established restaurant. Homely dishes such as *tortelli di zucca* (pasta stuffed with pumpkin) and *maccheroni con pancetta e fagioli* (macaroni with pancetta and beans) are gorgeous. Main courses are seasonal—expect *faraona* (guinea fowl), *piccione* (pigeon) and *rognone trifolate* (kidneys with garlic and herbs). Fantastic puddings and an excellent wine list.

✉ Piazza d'Arco 1, 46100 Mantova ☎ 0376 327101 ⓘ 12.30–1.45, 7.30–9.45 Wed–Sun; closed Aug and 31 Dec–5 Jan ✋ L €40, D €65, Wine €13

MILANO (MILAN)

ALLA CUCINA ECONOMICA

This friendly little restaurant changes its menu weekly to take advantage of seasonal produce. The pasta is home-made and served in various ways, simply grilled meat and fish dishes are nicely presented and there's a choice of desserts made on the premises. Excellent value in this expensive city.

✉ Via Guicciardini 8, 20129 Milano ☎ 02 783 256 ⓘ Mon–Fri 1–3, 8–11, Sat 8–11; closed Aug ✋ L €25, D €35, Wine €12

ARMANI/NOBU

www.armaninobu.it

This well-established fusion restaurant in the Armani flagship store is very popular with the chic Milano set. Choose between the ground-floor bar and glamorous upstairs, renowned for its stylish food and geometric decor.

✉ Via Pisoni 1, 20121 Milano ☎ 02 6231 2645 ⓘ Daily 12–3, 7–11; closed Sun lunch Jun–Sep, Sun dinner Aug and 25 Dec–7 Jan ✋ L €40, D €80, Wine €15 Ⓜ Montenapoleone

LE BICICLETTE

www.lebiciclette.com

Housed in a former bicycle shop, this restaurant is decorated with modern paintings by emerging artists. It is ultra-busy at aperitif time, when there is a giant buffet of pasta, sandwiches and tasty delights to accompany the €7 cocktails. The short menu includes dishes such as artichoke salad, fish ravioli with black butter, and Argentinian steak.

✉ Via Torti angolo Corso Genova, 20123 Milano ☎ 02 839 4177 ⓘ Sun–Thu 8pm–2am, Fri–Sat 8pm–1am ✋ L €26, D €58, Wine €14 Ⓜ Sant'Agosina 🚌 84

LA COZZERIA

Gigantic portions at competitive prices are served at this seafood restaurant. As well as every type of oyster, the menu has plenty of variety, with mussels, rich *zuppa de pesce* (fish soup), homemade pasta, prawns, squid and fish, including Ligurian sea bream.

✉ Via Muratori 7, 20135 Milano ☎ 02 5410 7164 ⓘ Tue–Fri 12.30–2.30, 7–11, Sat 7–11; closed Aug ✋ D €45, Wine €15 Ⓜ Porta Romana

GIULIO PANE E OJO

www.giuliopaneeojo.com

This buzzing rustic osteria specializes in typical Roman cuisine, presented and served by a young, enthusiastic staff. The lunchtime menu is more simple and good value, while dinner is more elaborate but still excellent value for money.

✉ Via Muratori 10, 20135 Milano ☎ 02 545 6189 ⓘ Mon–Sat 12–2.30, 7–11 ✋ L €25, D €35, Wine €11 Ⓜ Porta Romana

INNOCENTI EVASIONI

www.innocentievasioni.com

This place has a tiny garden where guests can dine in summer. The nouvelle cuisine is beautifully presented and the restaurant has one Michelin star. Four seasonal fixed-price menus are available, including one based on truffles. The restaurant is tricky to find, as it is on a street that looks like a private road. Reservations are advised.

✉ Via Privata della Bindellina 1, 20155 Milano ☎ 02 3300 1882 ⓘ Tue–Sat 8pm–10pm; closed Aug ✋ D €50, Wine €13 Ⓜ Certosa

SADLER

www.sadler.it

Push the boat out and experience some of Italy's greatest cooking at this superb two Michelin-starred restaurant in the Navigli district. Chef Claudio Sadler's food is creative and modern, expertly blending tradition with 21st-century style and presentation—look for the fish specialties and delicately-sauced *primi*, and follow it up with a new take on tiramisu, flavoured with green tea and chestnuts.

✉ Via Sforza 77, 20141 Milano ☎ 02 5810 4451 ⓘ Mon–Sat 8–11; closed 2 weeks in Jan and 3 weeks in Aug ✋ D €130, Wine €28

IL SAMBUCO, HOTEL HERMITAGE

www.ilsambuco.it

Rich colours and chintz are the backdrops to eating at this excellent fish restaurant, where you can enjoy traditional dishes such as *spaghetti all vongole* (spaghetti with clams) or try something more innovative such as shrimp and spelt salad or turbot with ratatouille. Desserts include a wicked *cassata* and a trio of ices; the wine list complements the food.

✉ Via Messina 10, 20154 Milano ☎ 02 336 10333 ⓘ Mon–Fri 12.30–3, 7.30–10; closed Christmas, 1–20 Aug ✋ L €75, D €125, Wine €20

TANO PASSAMI L'OLIO

www.tanopassamilolio.it

In this creative Michelin-starred restaurant dishes are made with one of some 40 types of oil. Main courses are a mix of creative and traditional: duck with truffles, king prawn tempura, and ravioli with ricotta. There is a dedicated smoking room. Reservations are advised.

✉ Via Villoresi 16, 20143 Milano ☎ 02 839 4139 ⓘ Mon–Sat –10.30pm; closed 24 Dec–6 Jan, Aug ✋ €75, Wine €15 Ⓜ Porta Genova

ZEN SUSHI

www.zenworld.it

Here at one of Milan's few sushi bars, you grab your rice, seaweed and raw fish as they revolve on a giant conveyor belt. The evening menu is à la carte only. This Italian-run Zen establishment is fun and friendly. Sake (rice wine) and Kirin beer are served, as well as some Italian wines.

✉ Via Maddalena 1, 20122 Milano ☎ 02 8901 3557 ⓘ Mon–Fri 12.30–3, 8–midnight, Sat 8–midnight; closed Aug ✋ L €28, D €45, Wine €14 Ⓜ Missori

PAVIA

HOSTARIA IL CUPOLONE

www.hostariailcupolone.it

This friendly trattoria has been satisfying hungry diners since the

1930s and continues to please with its well-priced local dishes. The à la carte menu changes monthly but specialities such as a trolley of boiled meats are always on offer. Risottos and homemade pasta are particularly recommended, as are the puddings.
✉ Via Cardinal Riboldi 2, 27100 Pavia ☎ 0382 303 519 🕐 Wed–Sun 12.30–3, 7.30–11, Mon 7.30–11; closed 2 weeks Jan and Aug 💰 L €24, D €37, Wine €9

RIOMAGGIORE

BAR A PIE' DE MA'

After a stroll along the Via dell'Amore, there's nowhere nicer to pause than this terrace bar, perched high above the sea. You can drop in for a drink, a snack or a full meal for a group if you reserve ahead. The emphasis is on fish, with whatever came off the boats that morning on the menu. Expect light meals such as mixed fried fish and shellfish and seafood salad with peppers, onions and piquant dressing. Wash it all down with a glass or two or Cinque Terre white wine, a flinty tipple.
✉ Via dell'Amore, Riomaggiore 55, 19010 Riomaggiore ☎ 0347 737 3985 🕐 Daily 10am–1am; Oct to mid-Nov, Mar, Apr closed Wed; closed mid-Nov to end Feb
💰 L €13, D €30, Wine €10

SANTA MARGHERITA LIGURE

IL FRANTOIO

www.ristoranteilfrantoio.com
When in Liguria eat basil and fish, and you'll find them both here; a delicate and intense *lasagne al pesto*, and a huge variety of risottos. Homemade pasta includes tagliolini served with a fish sauce. Wild strawberry tart and a bittersweet *semifreddo al caffé* stand out on dessert menu. The wine list is huge.
✉ Via Giuncheto 23, Santa Margherita Ligure, 16038 Genova ☎ 0185 187 0118 🕐 Thu–Tue 2.30–2.30, 8–midnight; closed Nov 💰 L €25, D €45, Wine €14

TORINO (TURIN)

AL GARAMOND

www.algaramond.it
There's an excellent range of traditional and more innovative dishes at this elegant restaurant, housed in a 19th-century building just off Piazza San Carlo. For the best dining experience, choose one of the tasting menus and enjoy artichoke flan, homemade pasta delicately flavoured with fish and herbs, and sea bass and well-hung meat. Puddings are sensational with chocolate especially taken extremely seriously.
✉ Via Pomba 14, 10123 Torino ☎ 011 812 2781 🕐 Mon–Fri 12.30–3, 8–10.30, Sat–Sun 8–10.30; closed 2 weeks Aug and Jan 💰 L €45, D €75, Wine €15

Above *Fresh fish and seafood fill the menus in the restaurants of Liguria*

LA BARRIQUE

www.labarriqueristorante.it
La Barrique is a very pleasant family-run restaurant under the watchful eye of Michelin-starred chef Stefano Gallo, who believes in using the freshest seasonal, regional produce. Happily, sublime homemade pastas feature in every season, as do heavenly chocolate puddings. The wine list is excellent and the service impeccable.
✉ Corso Dante 53, 10126 Torino ☎ 011 657900 🕐 Tue–Sat 12.30–3, 7.30–10.30, Mon 7.30–10.30 💰 L €54, D €82, Wine €15

C'ERA UNA VOLTA

www.ristoranteceraunavolta.it
This well-established but recently renovated restaurant serves Piedmontese cuisine but with light touches. *Al dente* risotto with truffles and cheese, little puff pastry tarts with porcini mushrooms and wild boar feature in season. There is also an excellent *menu degustazione* (tasting menu).
✉ Corso Vittorio Emanuele 11 41, 10125 Torino ☎ 011 650 4589 🕐 Mon–Sat 7.30–10.30pm 💰 D €42, Wine €12

PERBACCO

www.ristoranteperbacco.torino.it
There's an excellent range of classic dishes at this good value restaurant, where the menu changes every two months and the accent is on local produce. *Primi* include pasta and *risotti*, and there is both meat and fish dishes for main courses. The owner prides himself on a choice of vegetarian specials and all desserts are home-made.
✉ Via Mazzini 31, 10123 Torino ☎ 011 882 2110 🕐 Mon–Sat .30–10.30; closed Aug 💰 L €30 D €35 Wine €12 ❄

SOTTO LA MOLE

www.sottolamole.eu
Opposite the Mole Antoniella and the delightful Museo Nazionale del Cinema, this brick-vaulted little restaurant is deservedly very popular. Piedmontese classical and innovative dishes are on the menu, and it is a member of the Slow Food Movement. Reserving ahead is advised.
✉ Via Montebello 9, 10124 Torino ☎ 011 817 9398 🕐 Tue–Sun 12.30–2, 7.30–10.30 💰 L €32 D €55, Wine €11

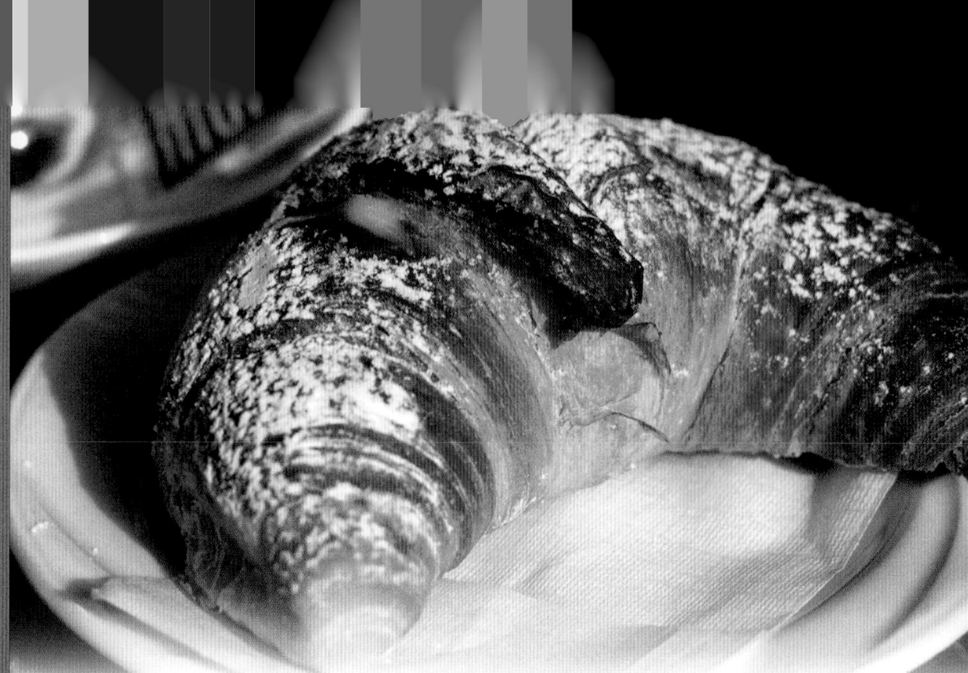

PRICES AND SYMBOLS

Prices are the lowest and highest for a double room for one night, unless otherwise stated. Breakfast is included, and all the hotels listed accept credit cards unless otherwise stated. Note that rates vary widely throughout the year.

For the key to symbols ▷ 2.

AOSTA (GRAN PARADISO)

HOTEL MILLELUCI

www.hotelmilleluci.com

Located above Aosta, with splendid views of the Alps and the Aosta Valley, the Milleluci is ideal for exploring the Parco Nazionale del Gran Paradiso. Most rooms have a balcony and are furnished with period pieces.

✉ Porossan Roppoz 15, 11100 Aosta
☎ 0165 235 278; fax 0165 235 284
€140–€190 24 rooms, 7 suites
Outdoor

RAYON DE SOLEIL

www.rayondesoleil.it

If you're looking for good value and peace and quiet, this mountain-style hotel, 10 minutes' drive from the centre of Aosta, is a good choice. It stands on a hillside near the cable car up to the Pila—ideal for high-altitude walking—and has a nice garden, outdoor pool and children's climbing frames. The rooms are a good size and adequately equipped, with tiled bathrooms; many have their own balconies with beautiful views, or you can sit outside on the terrace with a drink. The decor is a little old-fashioned, but at this price you couldn't do much better in the area.

✉ Viale Gran San Bernardo, 11100 Aosta (2km/1.2 miles from Aosta) ☎ 0165 262247; fax 0165 236085 Jan–Sep €40–€90 45

BERGAMO

SAN LORENZO

www.hotelsanlorenzobg.it

If you're staying in Bergamo, the *città alta*, the medieval town on the hill, is the place to be. The San Lorenzo overlooks the Cittadella right at the top of the town and is nicely set on a mainly quiet and peaceful tree-lined square, though it can be noisy at weekends. Inside, all is bright, modern comfort, with many of the rooms having access to the walkway that runs round the exterior. The bedrooms are light and a good size, some have views towards the lower town or to the hills. A buffet breakfast is served in a well-lit and designed downstairs room. You can drive right up to the hotel and park nearby.

✉ Piazza L. Mascheroni 9/A, 24129 Bergamo ☎ 0352 37383; fax 0352 37958 €140–€170 25

BRESCIA

ALBERGO OROLOGIO

www.albergoorologio.it

Right in the heart of the old town, the 'Clock' is housed in a well-converted medieval palazzo, where modern comfort merges happily with old style. It sells itself as a boutique hotel, and there's much to praise, from the charming bedrooms, with their beamed ceilings and terracotta floors, to the deep leather sofas and pretty breakfast room. The multilingual staff will do everything possible to look after you, including bringing you breakfast out to the internal, flower-hung courtyard in summer.

✉ Via C. Beccaria 17, 25121 Brescia
☎ 03037 55411; fax 03024 04805 From €125 16

Above *A Continental breakfast is usually included in the price of your stay*

CINQUE TERRE

LOCANDA LORENA

www.locandalorena.com

This restaurant with rooms is set in a delightful spot on the Isola Palmaria, 10 minutes away from Portovenere. This little establishment will send a boat over to collect guests, who can then enjoy the quiet, romantic retreat. The restaurant specializes in fresh fish.

Via Cavour 4, Isola Palmaria, 19025 Portovenere 0187 792370; fax 0187 766077 Closed Feb–Nov €120–€150 6

MARINA PICCOLA

www.hotelmarinapiccola.com

Literally a stone's throw from the sea, this is a simple seaside hotel, with quirky elegance and a touch of style. It combines good taste with a totally relaxed atmosphere. The rooms are plain but some have sea views. There is a great restaurant overlooking the sea, serving nothing but fish.

Via Birolli 120, 19010 Manarola 0187 920103; fax 0187 920966 Closed Nov €115 13 Take the SS566 from La Spezia, then head on the SS370 to Manarola. You will need a permit from your hotel to take the car into the village

LA TORRETTA

www.torrettas.com

Perched high above the sea and village this charming boutique hotel offers cool, airy rooms, marble bathrooms and a sense of relaxed style. Breakfast is served on the terrace above the sea, the staff speak English and the atmosphere is relaxed.

Piazza della Chiesa, Vico Volta 20, 19010 Manarola 0187 920 327 Closed Jan–Feb €120–€180 5 Take the SS566 from La Spezia, then head on the SS370 to Manarola. You will need a permit from your hotel to take the car into the village

COGNE

MIRAMONTI

www.miramonticogne.com

A good-size chalet-style hotel that's open all year gives guests a chance to explore the beautiful mountain countryside of the upper Aosta valley in the Parco Nazionale del Gran Paradiso. The style is firmly *gemütlich*, with wood panelling, pretty fabrics and fresh flowers. There's a good restaurant, cosy bar, indoor pool, beauty centre and an in-house cinema.

Viale Cavagnet 31, 11012 Cogne (Parco Nazionale del Gran Paradiso) 0165 74030; fax 0165 749 378 €140–€250 45

COURMAYEUR

MAISON LO CAMPAGNAR

www.maisonlocampagnar.com

A traditional chalet at the foot of the mountains offers a charming choice, either if you're driving south into Italy, or if you want a few days of Alpine air. Bedrooms are pretty, though some have low ceilings. The restaurant serves local dishes and there's a sauna and hydrotherapy suite—ideal to ease aching muscles after a day on the piste.

rue des Granges 14, Località Dolonne (1km/0.6 mile from Courmayeur), 11013 Courmayeur 0165 846 840; fax 0165 846 534 Dec–Apr, Jun–Sep Price €170–€310 12

CREMONA

HOTEL IMPERO

www.hotelimpero.cr.it

Right in the heart of town and overlooking the duomo, the Impero caters equally well for tourists and business travellers. A recent and comprehensive overhaul has ensured state-of-the-art technology, with WiFi access in the hall, internet points in the bedrooms and satellite TV. Visitors are also offered bicycles to get around town and the staff are a mine of local information. The rooms are big and comfortable, with huge beds, plenty of storage and work space, and excellent bathrooms. The breakfast buffet is varied and generous and guests will get a discount when dining in Cremona's best restaurants.

Piazza della Pace 21, 26100 Cremona 0372 413013; fax 0372 457295 €110–€160 53

GENOVA (GENOA)

GRAND HOTEL SAVOIA

www.grandhotelsavoia.it

This is the closest hotel to Genoa's Principe station. Spacious yet simple rooms have classic furniture and balconies. The large public facilities are shared with its 4-star sister hotel next door, the Savoia Majestic. The restaurant is somewhat uninspiring. Parking is available.

Via Arsenale di Terra 5, 16126 Genova 010 27721; fax 010 277 2825 €120–€840 40

HOTEL BRISTOL PALACE

www.hotelbristolpalace.com

This lovely old palazzo is situated on the elegant Via XX Settembre and is among Genova's most elegant hotels. Parquet floors, antiques, stucco and tapestry are among the opulent furnishings blended with every modern comfort in this temple to the belle époque.

Via XX Settembre 35, 16121 Genova 010 592541; fax 010 561756 €129–€350 128 rooms, 5 suites

LAGO DI COMO

ALBERGO FIRENZE

www.albergofirenze.it

A high-quality, affordable hotel in the heart of Como, the newly renovated rooms of Albergo Firenze are sleek and most have great views. The hotel also has rooms specially fitted for use by people with disabilities.

Piazza Volta 16, 22100 Como 031 300333; fax 031 300101 €115–€145 44

HOTEL FLORENCE

www.hotelflorencebellagio.it

There's more than a touch of the *fin-de-siècle* about this pretty, pink-washed hotel, with its wrought-iron balconies overlooking the lake in postcard-perfect Bellagio. The high-ceilinged bedrooms, with their parquet floors and luxury fabrics, are large and beautifully furnished—some have four-poster beds, many have lake views. Downstairs, there are lovely public areas, notably the wisteria-clad terrace above the lake, where breakfast is served in summer.

The hotel has its own excellent restaurant and also offers pampering in the form of a spa with sauna, whirlpool baths, Turkish baths and treatments. Half-board here is less than the room price; it's exceptional value for money.
Piazza Mazzini 46, 22021 Bellagio
031 950342; fax 031 951722 Apr–Oct
€140–€230 (room only) 30 rooms, 1 suite

LAGO DI GARDA

BELLEVUE

www.hotelbellevuegardone.com
This small, quiet lakeside hotel is brimming with amenities. The outdoor pool never gets too busy, as the hotel has just 30 rooms, most of which have balconies. Private parking is available.
Via Zanardelli 81, 25083 Gardone Riviera
0365 20235; fax 0365 290080
Apr–Sep €54–€80 30
Outdoor

FLAMINIA

www.hotelflaminia.it
Flaminia is a hotel with large rooms and a stunning location. The wooden terrace built over the lake is perfect for swimming and sunbathing.
Piazza Flaminia 8, 25019 Sirmione
030 916078; fax 030 916193 €125–€195 20 Mar–6 Nov, 26 Dec–10 Jan
41 rooms, 4 suites

MIRAMAR

www.hotelmiramar.it
Real value for money, especially in the low season. Most rooms have balconies, and all are very modern. A huge lounge and bar area caters for all the summer visitors and the gardens lead down to the water.
Via XXV Aprile 22, 25019 Sirmione
030 916239 €55–€90 including breakfast 30

LAGO MAGGIORE

GRAND HOTEL DES ÎLES BORROMÉES

www.borromees.it
Distinguished guests have been staying at this 5-star luxury hotel since 1861. Commanding fine views of the lake, the hotel offers watersports, mountain biking, horseback riding and golf. Rooms have fireplaces, giant balconies and huge baths.
Corso Umberto I 67, 28838 Stresa
0323 938938 Closed Dec–Jan
€275–€430 164 rooms, 15 suites

ROYAL

www.hotelroyalstresa.com
Palm trees, azaleas and hydrangeas are massed in the lovely garden surrounding this lakeside hotel, with its mountain views and easy access along the promenade to the town centre, some 800m (0.5 mile) away. Built in 1920, and run by the Rosa family as a hotel since 1958, this is a wonderfully typical villa of the époque, with big rooms, parquet floors, antique furnishings and lovely old rugs and pictures. The bedrooms, all of which have balconies overlooking the gardens or lake, are spacious; the pretty dining room spills outside onto the terrace in summer. As in many resort hotels, half-board is cheaper than the cost of room only.
Viale Lido 1, 28838 Stresa 03233 2777; fax 03233 3633 Apr–Oct
€100–€160 72

SPERANZA AU LAC

www.milansperanza.it
Overlooking both the lake and the main square, this 4-star hotel has the best location in town. The modern rooms have wide balconies. The hotel restaurant is recommended, although there are several places to eat within a minute's walk.
Piazza Marconi 6/9, 28838 Stresa
0323 31178 €90–€180 86 rooms, 3 suites

MANTOVA (MANTUA)

RECHIGI

www.rechigi.com
Contemporary art, polished marble and interesting lighting enliven the interior of this modern hotel, near the Palazzo Ducale. The rooms are comfortable and well equipped, though the bathrooms are small.
Via Calvi 30, 46100 Mantova
0376 320781; fax 3762 220291
€130–€235, excluding breakfast 60
From Parma take the SS343 to Mantova. Immediately before the station, turn right along Corso Vittorio Emanuele II and continue across the intersection at Piazza Cavalloti into Corso Umberto I. At the end (Piazza Marconi) turn right into Via Calvi

MILANO (MILAN)

ANTICA LOCANDA LEONARDO

www.anticalocandaleonardo.com
Set around an attractive internal flower-filled courtyard, this 19th-century family-run hotel is well furnished with antiques and parquet floors. It is also very conveniently located for Leonardo da Vinci's *Cenacolo*. Enjoy breakfast al fresco.
Corso Magenta 78, 20123 Milano
02 4801 4197 €165–€245 16
Conciliazione

BRISTOL

www.hotelbristolmil.it
Exit Centrale rail station via the stairs and you'll find yourself at the front door of this classic, stylish hotel. The style is refined, with modern amenities such as soundproofed rooms, direct-dial phones, in-room Jacuzzis and internet facilities. There is no restaurant, but the bar serves snacks and drinks until late at night.
Via Scarlatti 32, 20124 Milano
02 669 4141 €130–€230; closed August and 24 Dec–2 Jan 68
Centrale FS

CARLTON HOTEL BAGLIONI

www.baglionihotels.com
The Baglioni offers the ultimate in refinement and elegance, overlooking the ultra-glamorous Via della Spiga, in the heart of the Quadrilatero fashion area. Rooms are furnished with antiques and hung with exquisite silk brocades, and the bathrooms are marble. There is an outside terrace with a tented 'shisha bar' with hubbly-bubbly pipes. There is also fine dining in the hotel's restaurant, Il Baretto al Baglioni.
Via Senato 5, 20121 Milano 02 77077 €610–€765 83 rooms, 9 suites
San Babila

CARLYLE BRERA HOTEL
www.carlylebrerahotel.com
The stylish Carlyle Brera is a cut above most business hotels. The Moscova Metro station is a stone's throw from the front door. Bicycles are also available free of charge.
Corso Garibaldi 84, 20121 Milano 02 2900 3888 €290 94 rooms (2 suites) Moscova

MICHELANGELO
www.milanhotel.it
This modern business 4-star hotel offers hydrotherapy suites, opulent lounges and fine dining. The guest rooms are vast and most bathrooms have Jacuzzis.
Via Scarlatti 33, 20124 Milano 02 67551 €190–€400 300 rooms, 4 suites Centrale FS

RAPALLO

HOTEL CANALI
www.hotelcanali.com
Expensive Rapallo is well served by this value-for-money hotel, set in a pretty garden above the port. It's quiet up here, and the style of this early 20th-century villa makes the most of its situation, offering bedrooms furnished traditionally, garden and terrace chairs for lounging and an elegant dining room. From the hotel terrace, steps lead down to the garden, and there's a recently opened solarium and hydrotherapy suite. The hotel is noted for its restaurant, which offers a fish-based menu; half board is cheaper than the room-only rates.
Via Petrafraccia 15, 16035 Rapallo 01855 0369; fax 01852 2382 Feb–Nov €130–€170 21 rooms, 6 suites

MIRÒ
www.hotelmiro.net
Right on the water's edge, this small hotel is a good find. Its 10 rooms are all different from each other and feature sea views and original furnishings—some have four-poster beds.
Lungomare Vittorio Veneto 32, 16035 Rapallo 0185 234 100; fax 0185 237 224 €90–€160 10

SANTA MARGHERITA LIGURE

LIDO PALACE
www.lidopalacehotel.com
Redolent of gracious Edwardian days, all the rooms at this seafront Liberty-style hotel have sea views and many have balconies. The four-people suites are excellent value.
Via A. Doria 3, Santa Margherita Ligure, 16038 Genova 0185 285821; fax 0185 284708 Closed Nov to mid-Dec €150–€270 54 From north exit the A12 at Rapallo and follow signs to Santa Margherita Ligure. The hotel is on the seafront opposite the marina

MINERVA
www.hotelminerva.eu
Set back from the sea, but overlooking it from the roof terrace, the Minerva is set in a delightful garden and has its own parking. Rooms are comfortable, if a little on the small side, and the restaurant is noted for its local cuisine. You can eat outside in summer, or relax in the cool of the public rooms.
Via Maragliano 34/D, 16038 Santa Margherita Ligure 0185 286 073; fax 0185 281 697 €102–€162 38

TORINO (TURIN)

LE MERIDIEN TURIN ART+TECH
www.lemeridien.com
This monument to cutting-edge design in the refurbished former Longotto Fiat plant is the work of celebrated architect Renzo Piano, with input from style gurus Philippe Starck and Giò Ponti. From the glass-roofed Central hall, elevators whizz up to spacious, high-ceilinged rooms equipped with every amenity—from power showers and plasma screen TVs to allergy-free bed linen and carpets. From the jogging track on the roof there are glorious views of the snowy peaks of the Alps.
Via Nizza 230, 10126 Torino 011 664 2000 Closed Aug €130–€410 140 rooms, 1 suite Lingotto

VICTORIA
www.hotelvictoria-torino.com
Despite being in the middle of the city, the Victoria has a quiet situation. Each room is individually and imaginatively designed, reflecting the owners' love of world-wide travel in a symphony of colours and moods. There's also a wellness centre, equipped with a pool, sauna and Turkish bath.
Via Nino Costa 4, 10123 Torino 011 561 1909 €230–€280 106 rooms Porta Nuova

VARESE

BOLOGNA
www.albergobologna.it
A converted 18th-century monastery is now home to the Bologna, a family-run hotel that offers good value for money. The rooms are big, with parquet flooring and wide beds and it's well situated in the *centro storico*. The adjoining restaurant, where you'll eat well, is run by the same family.
Via Broggi 7, 21100 Varese 0332 234362 Closed 2 weeks in Feb and Aug €95 18 Off A8 Varese Milano Malpensa 25km (16 miles)

Below *Grand Hotel des Îles Borromées offers luxury on Lake Maggiore*

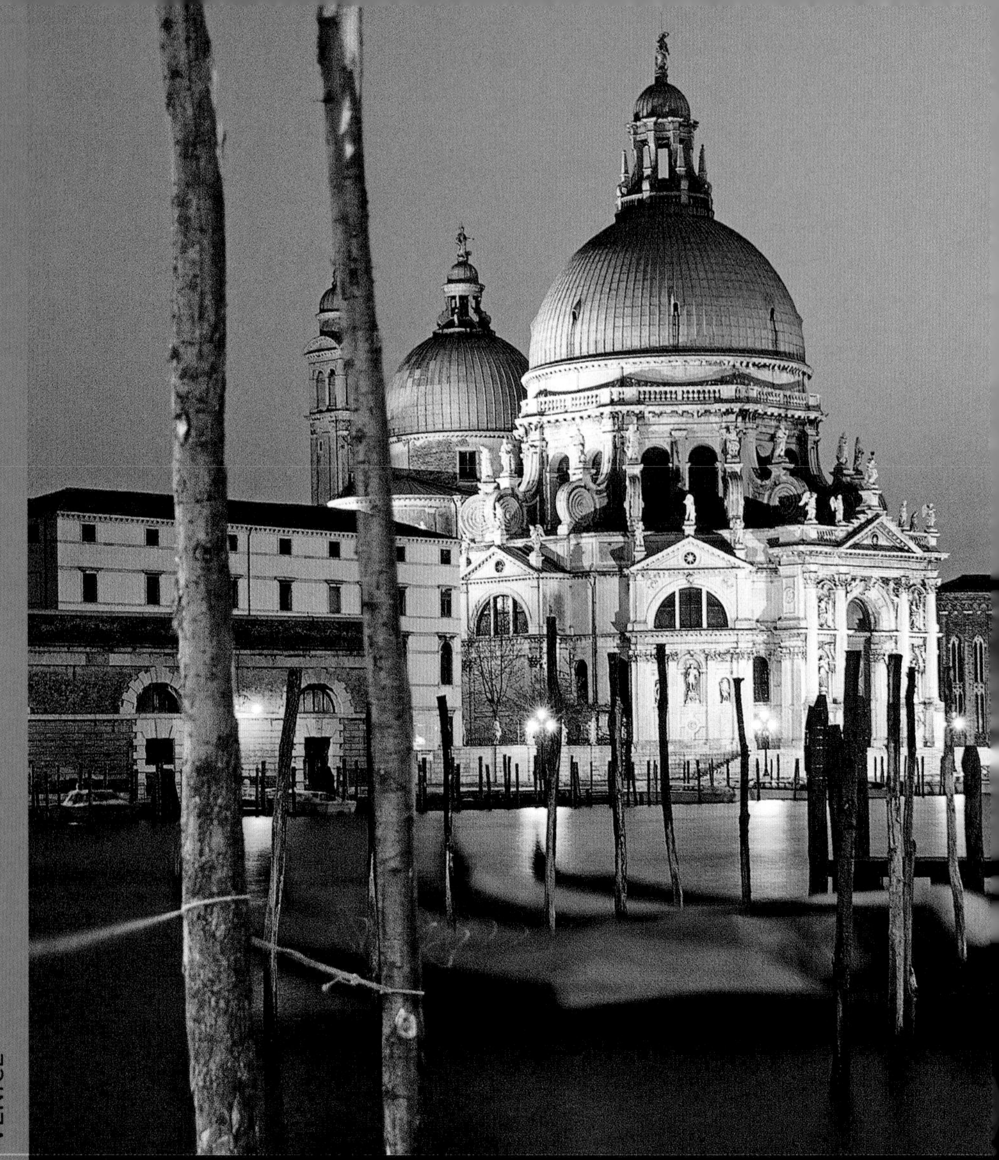

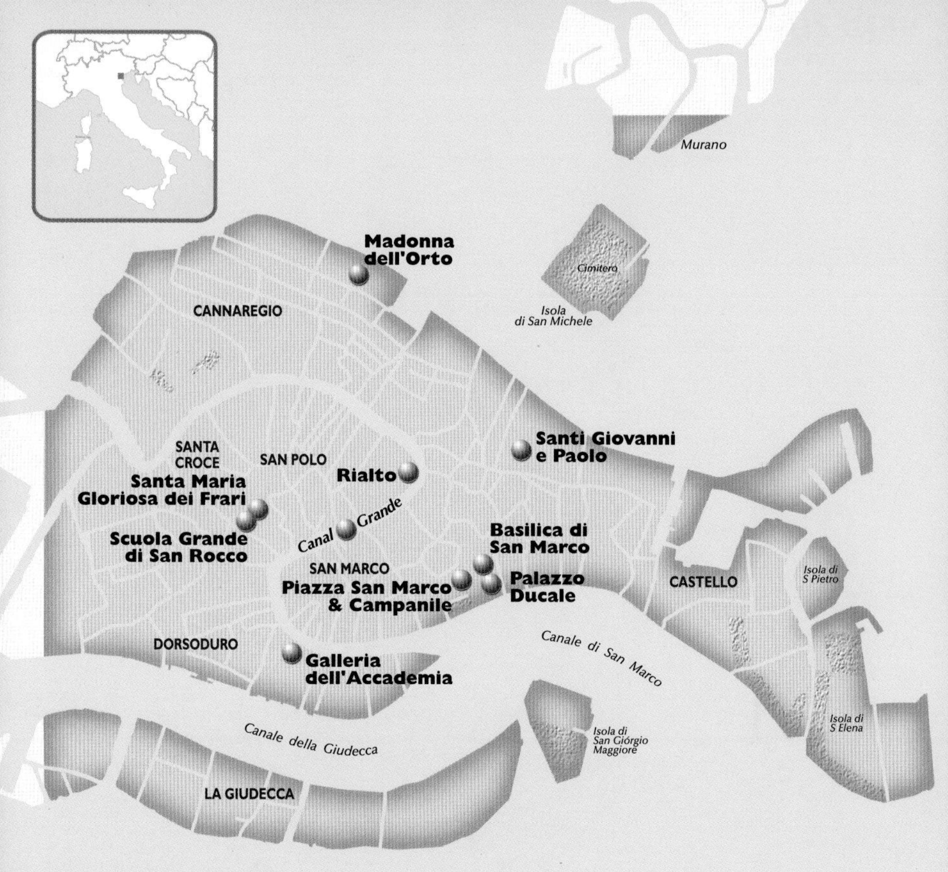

VENICE

Venice (Venezia), a city built on water in the heart of a lagoon, is unique. Here, shimmering light reflects off water to illuminate one of the world's greatest cityscapes, where canals, streets and squares are lined with palaces and churches containing some of the world's greatest mosaics, paintings and sculpture. Venice is linked to the mainland by a causeway and built on 118 tiny islands, divided from each other by numerous canals spanned by over 400 bridges. Most important is the Canal Grande (Grand Canal), a substantial waterway lined with superb monuments, dividing the northern and southern city areas.

Once the greatest and richest of all medieval sea and trading powers, Venice, founded in the fourth century by Romans fleeing the Barbarian hordes, commanded an empire that stretched throughout the Mediterranean and held the monopoly on the overland trade routes to the Far East. Spices, silk, gold and precious stones all reached Europe via the Venetian merchants, the profits funding the building and decoration of the city and the hedonistic lifestyle of its citizens. As the sea routes to the east opened up, Venice declined, losing its independence in 1797 and becoming part of united Italy in 1866. The city has been drawing visitors for over a thousand years. They still come to marvel at the treasures packed along its waterways and narrow streets, jostling shoulders with the Venetians themselves, who are accustomed to the inconveniences of a life dictated by tides. Today, modern Venice faces huge challenges, chief of which are the effects of the ever-increasing high tides and the rapidly shrinking population. The city must try to balance the needs of its citizens with those of the floods of tourists, drawn here by the incredible beauty of the city, its fascinating daily life, and great sightseeing, eating and shopping.

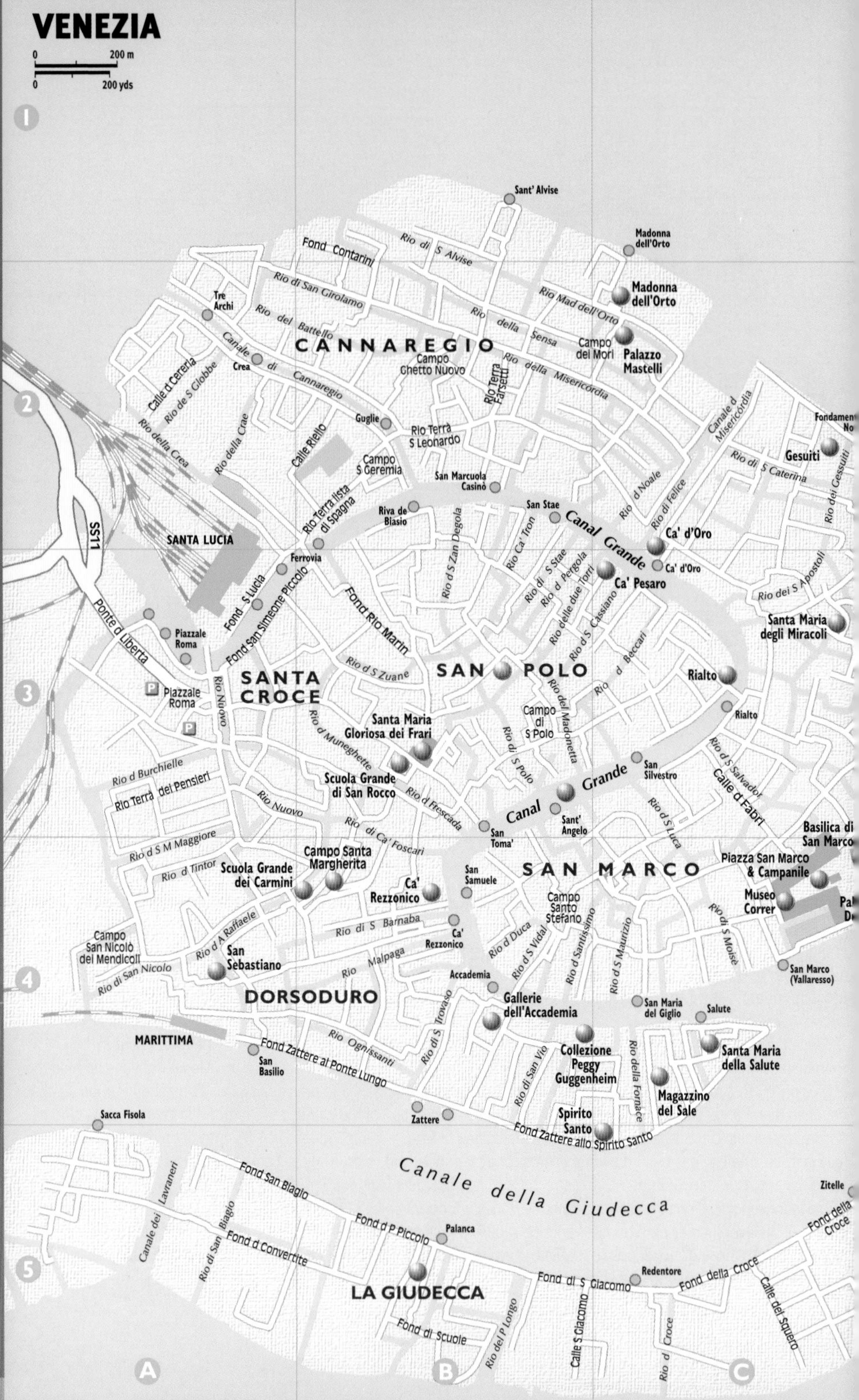

VENEZIA

0 200 m
0 200 yds

1
2
3
4
5

Sant' Alvise
Madonna dell'Orto
Fond Contarini
Rio di S Alvise
Rio di San Girolamo
Rio Mad dell'Orto
Madonna dell'Orto
Tre Archi
Rio del Battello
Rio della Sensa
Campo dei Mori
Palazzo Mastelli
CANNAREGIO
Canale di Cannaregio
Crea
Campo Ghetto Nuovo
Rio Terrà Farsetti
Rio della Misericordia
Calle d Cereria
Rio de S Giobbe
Rio della Crea
Rio della Crae
Calle Riello
Guglie
Rio Terrà S Leonardo
Canale d Misericordia
Fondamenta No
Gesuiti
Rio di S Caterina
Rio dei Gesuiti
Campo S Geremia
San Marcuola Casinò
Rio d Noale
Rio di Felice
Rio Terra lista di Spagna
Riva de Biasio
San Stae
Canal Grande
Ca' d'Oro
Ca' d'Oro
SS11
SANTA LUCIA
Ferrovia
Fond S Lucia
Fond San Simeone Piccolo
Fond Rio Marin
Rio d S Zan Degola
Rio Ca' Tron
Rio di S Stae
Rio d Pergola
Rio delle due Torri
Rio d S Cassiano
Ca' Pesaro
Rio dei S Apostoli
Santa Maria degli Miracoli
Ponte d Libertà
Piazzale Roma
Rio d S Zuane
SAN POLO
Rio d Beccari
Rialto
SANTA CROCE
Piazzale Roma
Rio Nuovo
Rio del Madonnetta
Campo di S Polo
Rialto
Santa Maria Gloriosa dei Frari
Rio d Muneghette
Rio di S Polo
San Silvestro
Rio d S Salvador
Calle d Fabri
Rio d Burchielle
Rio Terrà dei Pensieri
Scuola Grande di San Rocco
Rio Nuovo
Rio d Frescada
Canal Grande
Rio d S Luca
Rio di Ca' Foscari
San Tomà
Sant' Angelo
Basilica di San Marco
Rio d S M Maggiore
Rio d Tintor
Campo Santa Margherita
Scuola Grande dei Carmini
Ca' Rezzonico
San Samuele
SAN MARCO
Piazza San Marco & Campanile
Museo Correr
Campo Santo Stefano
Rio di S Barnaba
Ca' Rezzonico
Rio di S Moisè
Campo San Nicolò dei Mendicoli
Rio d A Raffaele
San Sebastiano
Rio di San Nicolo
Rio Malpaga
Rio d Duca
Rio d S Vidal
Rio d Santissimo
Rio d S Maurizio
Accademia
San Marco (Vallaresso)
DORSODURO
Rio di S Trovaso
Gallerie dell'Accademia
San Maria del Giglio
Salute
MARITTIMA
Rio Ognissanti
Collezione Peggy Guggenheim
Rio della Fornace
Santa Maria della Salute
Fond Zattere al Ponte Lungo
San Basilio
Rio di San Vio
Magazzino del Sale
Zattere
Spirito Santo
Fond Zattere allo Spirito Santo
Sacca Fisola
Canale della Giudecca
Fond San Biagio
Zitelle
Canale dei Lavraneri
Rio di San Biagio
Fond d P Piccolo
Palanca
Fond d Convertite
Fond della Croce
LA GIUDECCA
Fond di S Giacomo
Redentore
Fond della Croce
Calle del Squero
Fond di Scuole
Rio del P Longo
Calle S Giacomo
Rio d Croce

A B C

Fonda del Vetrai
Murano
Murano
Burano, Torcello
San Michele in Isola
Cimitero
Cimitero
Isola di San Michele
Nuove
ndicanti
Ospedale
Santi Giovanni e Paolo
Rio d Giustina
Celestia
Rio d S G Laterano
Rio di S Francisco
anta Maria ormosa
Rio d S Lorenzo
Scuola di San Giorgio degli Schiavoni
Canale d Galeazze
Canale di Porta Nuova
Darsena Grande
S Ternita
San Giorgio dei Greci
S Martino
Rio d Gorne
San Pietro
Rio d Vergini
S Pietro
San Zaccaria
Rio d Greci
Rio del la Pietà
Rio Ca di Dio
Rio San Daniele
Isola di S Pietro
CASTELLO
Canale di
Riva degli Schiavoni
Rio del Arsenale
Museo Storico Navale
San Zaccaria
Arsenale
Rio della Tana
Fond a Sant Ana
Rio di Quintavale
Via Giuseppe Garibaldi
Viale Garibaldi
Riva dei Sette Martiri
Canale di San Marco
Secco Marina
Rio di S Giuseppe
Vle 24 Maggio
San Giorgio Maggiore
San Giorgio
Viale del Giardini Pubblici
Viale Trento
Giardini
Rio dei Giardini
Viale 4 Novembre
Isola di S Elena
Viale Piave
Canale di S Elena
Via S Elena
Canale della Grázia
Isola di San Giórgio Maggiore
Sant Elena
D
E
F

VENICE STREET INDEX

VENICE CANAL INDEX

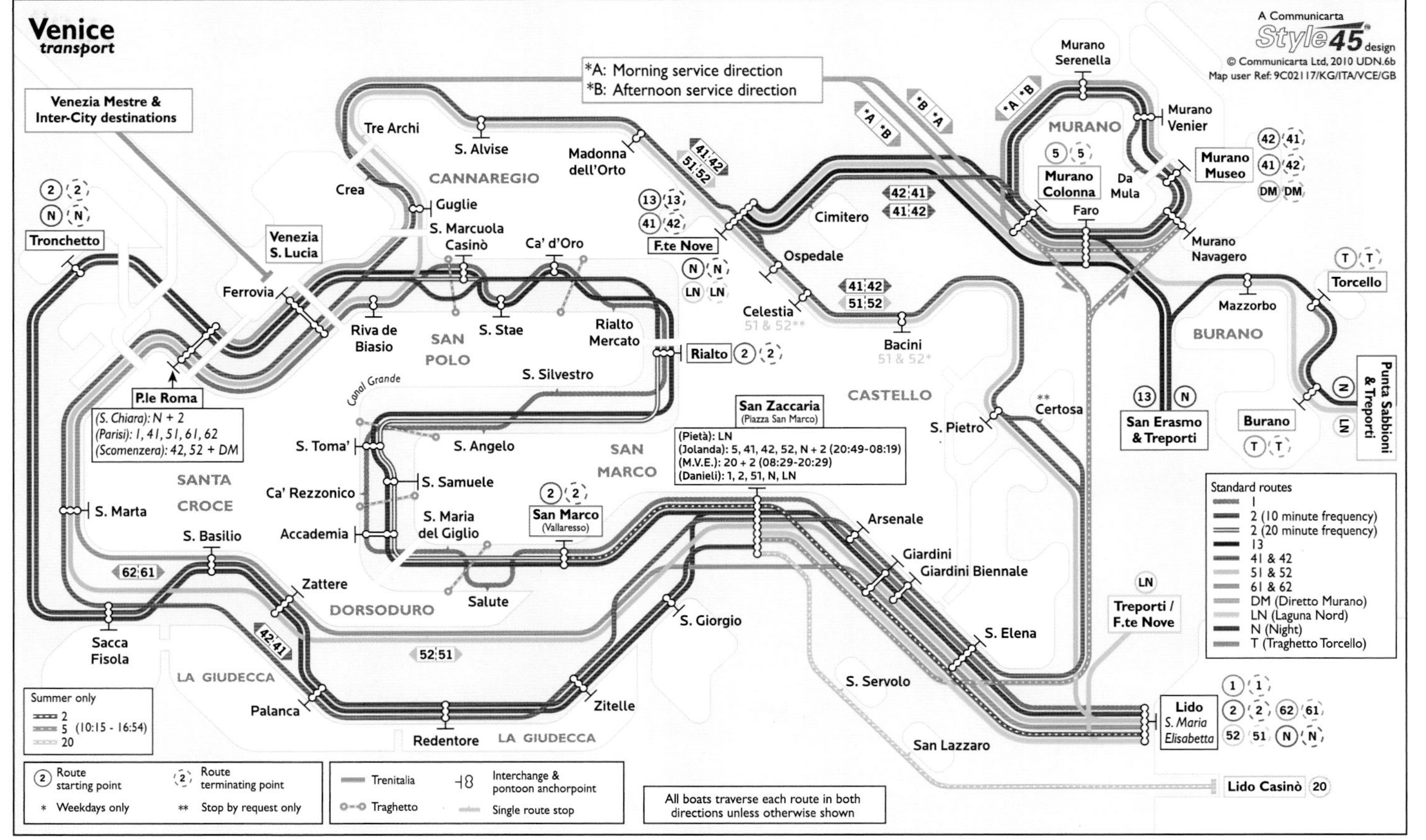
Venice
transport
A Communicarta Style45 design
© Communicarta Ltd, 2010 UDN.6b
Map user Ref: 9C02117/KG/ITA/VCE/GB
*A: Morning service direction
*B: Afternoon service direction
Venezia Mestre & Inter-City destinations
Tronchetto
Venezia S. Lucia
Ferrovia
P.le Roma
(S. Chiara): N + 2
(Parisi): 1, 41, 51, 61, 62
(Scomenzera): 42, 52 + DM
Tre Archi
Crea
S. Alvise
CANNAREGIO
Guglie
S. Marcuola Casinò
Ca' d'Oro
Madonna dell'Orto
F.te Nove
Cimitero
Ospedale
Celestia
51 & 52**
Bacini
51 & 52*
Riva de Biasio
SAN POLO
S. Stae
Rialto Mercato
Rialto
S. Silvestro
Canal Grande
S. Toma'
S. Angelo
S. Samuele
Ca' Rezzonico
S. Maria del Giglio
Accademia
SAN MARCO
San Marco (Vallaresso)
San Zaccaria (Piazza San Marco)
(Pietà): LN
(Jolanda): 5, 41, 42, 52, N + 2 (20:49-08:19)
(M.V.E.): 20 + 2 (08:29-20:29)
(Danieli): 1, 2, 51, N, LN
CASTELLO
S. Pietro
Certosa
Arsenale
Giardini
Giardini Biennale
S. Elena
SANTA CROCE
S. Marta
S. Basilio
Zattere
DORSODURO
Salute
S. Giorgio
Sacca Fisola
LA GIUDECCA
Palanca
Redentore
Zitelle
S. Servolo
San Lazzaro
MURANO
Murano Serenella
Murano Venier
Murano Colonna
Da Mula
Faro
Murano Museo
Murano Navagero
Mazzorbo
BURANO
Burano
Torcello
Punta Sabbioni & Treporti
San Erasmo & Treporti
Treporti / F.te Nove
Lido S. Maria Elisabetta
Lido Casinò
Standard routes
1
2 (10 minute frequency)
2 (20 minute frequency)
13
41 & 42
51 & 52
61 & 62
DM (Diretto Murano)
LN (Laguna Nord)
N (Night)
T (Traghetto Torcello)
Summer only
2
5 (10:15 - 16:54)
20
Route starting point
Route terminating point
* Weekdays only
** Stop by request only
Trenitalia
Traghetto
Interchange & pontoon anchorpoint
Single route stop
All boats traverse each route in both directions unless otherwise shown

Above *The courtyard of the Ca' d'Oro*
Opposite *Lion statues on the Ca' d'Oro*

BASILICA DI SAN MARCO

▷ 166–167.

BURANO

www.comune.venezia.it

For a change of pace, Burano is an island tucked away in the northern part of the lagoon, whose brilliantly painted houses and miniature canals provide some of Venice's best photographic opportunities. Burano, and Mazzorbo next door, were among the first settlements in the lagoon. As Venice proper boomed, Mazzorbo declined, but Burano thrived as a fishing community, where the men went to sea and the women stayed home to make gossamer-fine lace, once famous all over Europe. The *rii* (canals) are still busy with boats and all the paraphernalia of fishing, and the *fondamente* (streets along the canals) are lined with houses of varying colours. Lace is still on offer everywhere, although few women make the real thing now; you can see it at the Scuola e Museo del Merletto (Lace-making School), on Piazza Galuppi.

161 off E1 Piazza San Marco 71f, San Marco, 30120 Venezia 041 529 8711; daily 9.30–3.30 Burano

CA' D'ORO

www.cadoro.org

One of the city's finest and most flamboyant examples of a Gothic palazzo, the Ca' d'Oro (Golden House) stands on the Canal Grande just above the Rialto. It was built for the Contarini family in the early 15th century, but changed hands repeatedly until it was heavily (and badly) restored in the 1850s by the Russian Prince Troubetskoy. Forty years later, Baron Franchetti bought and restored it, filling it with his painting, sculpture and coin collections. As a result, the ground floor regained its medieval layout, with a courtyard, tiny pleasure garden and main door opening onto the water. An exterior staircase leads to the upper floors, where the family lived. These floors, imaginatively converted into light and airy galleries, now house the collections, and have beautiful Gothic loggias overlooking the canal. Artistic highlights include Andrea Mantegna's powerful *St. Sebastian* and the ghostly fragments of frescoes by Giorgione that once decorated the nearby Fondaco dei Tedeschi.

160 C2 Calle Ca' d'Oro, Cannaregio, 30121 Venezia 041 520 0345 Mon 8.15–2, Tue–Sun 8.15–7.15 Adult €5, student (18–25) €2.50, under 18s and over 65s free (EU citizens) Ca' d'Oro Overlooking the sculpture garden

CA' REZZONICO

www.museicivicivenezani.it

This grandiose palazzo on the Canal Grande is now a museum devoted to the hedonistic, dying days of the Republic (Museo del Settecento Veneziano). Emerging from a lengthy restoration in 2001, the Ca' Rezzonico, with its huge rooms, gilded stuccowork, frescoed ceilings and opulent textiles, is a fabulous expression of patrician wealth.

As you glimpse the facade from the canal or walk through the courtyard you can see why the palazzo's construction costs virtually bankrupted the Bons, who commissioned Baldassare Longhena to design the building in 1667. Seventy years later, the unfinished palazzo was acquired by the Rezzonicos, who poured money into the building and decor. Its most original architectural feature is the ballroom. Two floors high, this immense space was the scene of some of the 18th century's most prestigious events. From here, a series of ornately decorated, interconnecting rooms fans out, each furnished with fine contemporary pieces. Highlights include the Tiepolo ceiling panels in the Throne Room and Nuptial Room, the flower-decorated Murano glass chandeliers, and furniture designed by Andrea Brustolon. In the gallery look for the quirky genre paintings by Pietro Longhi and the superb Tiepolo panels from Villa Zianigo, the painter's home. The Pulcinella (Carnival Clown) scenes will charm, but it is the surreal Mondo Novo (New World) *trompe-l'oeil* panels that will linger in the memory.

160 B4 Fondamenta Rezzonico, Dorsoduro 3136, 30123 Venezia 041 241 0100 Apr–Oct Wed–Mon 10–6; Nov–Mar Tue–Sun 10–5 Adult €7, student (15–25) €5 Ca' Rezzonico

CAMPO SANTA MARGHERITA

At the heart of the *sestiere* (district) of Dorsoduro, Campo Santa Margherita is one of Venice's liveliest squares. Browse the morning market stands, sit in the cafés, eat one of the best ice creams in the city (at Causin), eavesdrop on raucous local conversations and mingle with the university crowd—all in all, a slice of Venetian life.

The square is surrounded by old Gothic houses, many dating from the 14th century. The central expanse is broken by market stands, trees and benches, while in the middle there is an oddly shaped small building, the Scuola dei Varoteri, once the headquarters of the tanners' guild. At the north end stands the church of Santa Margherita, which has been beautifully restored and now forms part of the university. Look for the St. Margaret's dragon on the campanile and, on the facade of a house at the same end of the square, the saint standing on the beast. At the opposite end, past the vegetable and fish stands and the interesting shops, you will find the entrance to the Scuola Grande dei Carmini (▷ 185).

160 B4 Campo Santa Margherita, Dorsoduro, 30123 Venezia Ca' Rezzonico

CANAL GRANDE

▷ 168–169.

BASILICA DI SAN MARCO

INFORMATION

www.basilicasanmarco.it

160 C4 Piazza San Marco, San Marco, 30124 Venezia 041 522 5697 Basilica Mon–Sat 9.45–5, Sun 2–5. Tesoro and Pala d'Oro Mon–Sat 9.45–4.45, Sun 2–5.; all close at 4pm Dec–Easter Basilica free. Pala d'Oro €2, reduced ticket €1. Tesoro €3, reduced ticket €1.50. Museum €4, reduced ticket €2 San Marco (Vallaresso)/San Zaccaria Wide range at various prices. *Electra* is the best of those published in Italy; it covers various specific sights in Venice (available at the Palazzo Ducale) Stands in atrium and loggia selling postcards, religious souvenirs and tourist guides to Venice

Above *The Byzantine Basilica di San Marco is the spiritual heart of Venice*

INTRODUCTION

There's nothing to beat the wow factor of your first glimpse of the Basilica di San Marco (St. Mark's Basilica), its domes and pinnacles etched against the sky, the facade glittering with mosaics. As you walk into the far end of the Piazza di San Marco (St. Mark's Square), the vast expanse of the square opens before you, with this wonderful building at the far end and the adjacent campanile rocketing skywards.

Eleventh-century Venice still looked culturally east to Byzantium, and this explains the decision to construct a church that is completely oriental in style, known as the *Chiesa d'Oro* (Golden Church). San Marco, with its centralized Greek cross plan and multiple domes, is modelled on two basilicas in Constantinople, and the interior, with its raised choir and gold-ground mosaics, also owes much to the East. The first basilica was built in 829 to house the remains of St. Mark the Evangelist, brought to Venice from Alexandria by merchants to become the city's new patron saint. Today's version, the third on the site, went up between 1063 and 1094. Inside, the shadowy spaces and mosaics are totally Byzantine in spirit, while the facade was altered between the 11th and 15th centuries with the addition of Gothic-style marble columns and carved stonework.

WHAT TO SEE

THE LOGGIA

For a superb overview of the basilica, climb the steep stairs from the atrium to the gallery, where you'll find yourself at eye level with the mosaics (▷ 167). From here you can gain access out onto the loggia, a splendid vantage point from which to view the piazza.

THE BRONZE HORSES

Also here are replicas of the famous bronze horses (the originals are inside). These powerfully evocative creatures were looted from Constantinople in 1204 and are the only surviving four-horse chariot group from antiquity. They were thought to have been made for the Hippodrome in the third century, but they could be as much as 500 years older. Apart from a brief spell in Paris in the Napoleonic years, they have stood at San Marco for 800 years.

THE MOSAICS

The Sant'Alipio doorway, one of five leading to the atrium, is the only door with an original 13th-century mosaic. In the glittering darkness, shafts of light and slanting sunbeams illuminate more than 4,000sq m (43,000sq ft) of mosaics illustrating stories from the Bible. The early Byzantine-Venetian examples are the finest and include the Pentecost dome, nearest the entrance, the Ascension in the central dome, and Christ Emmanuel in the eastern dome. Old as it looks, the great Christ Pantocrator above the apse is actually a faithful 16th-century copy of the 11th-century original.

THE PALA D'ORO

The focal point at ground level is the iconostasis, a Byzantine marble screen that hides the chancel and high altar. The remains of St. Mark lie beneath the altar, which is backed by the Pala d'Oro, an opulent gold and silver altarpiece. Made by a Sienese master in 1342, it is covered with more than 3,000 precious stones and 80 enamel plaques, many of which date from the 10th to 12th centuries.

CHAPEL OF THE MADONNA NICOPEIA AND THE TREASURY

To the left of the Pala d'Oro is the Chapel of the Madonna Nicopeia, a tiny, much-revered 12th-century Byzantine icon, and there is more Byzantine work in the Treasury (Tesoro). Look out for the 12th-century censer in the shape of a domed church.

TIPS

» Cover your arms and shoulders when visiting the basilica.

» Queues start to build up by about 9.30am and the wait can be more than an hour, so get there early. It tends to get quieter just before closing time.

» You can gain access to the basilica for prayers from 8am via the side door (off Piazzetta dei Leoncini).

» Stringent security means that all large bags need to be left around the corner at Ateneo di San Basso, off Piazzetta dei Leoncini, where there's a free left-luggage service for 1 hour (daily 9.30–5.30).

Below *View of a dome from inside the basilica*

INFORMATION

160 B2–C4 Piazzale Roma, Ferrovia, Riva de Biasio, San Marcuola, San Stae, Ca' d'Oro, Rialto Mercato, Rialto, San Silvestro, Sant' Angelo, San Tomà, San Samuele, Ca' Rezzonico, Accademia, Giglio, Salute. Lines 1 and 82 cover the whole canal; No 1 is the more leisurely route and takes about 40 minutes each way

Above *Palazzi and gondolas on the Grand Canal*

INTRODUCTION

The Canal Grande (Grand Canal) is Venice's main thoroughfare, a wide waterway running northwest to southeast that was originally the arrival route for merchant vessels approaching the Rialto. The best, and indeed, only, way to see the whole is by water, travelling from Piazzale Roma, where the causeway from the mainland ends. Grab a seat on a *vaporetto* and sit back to enjoy the constantly changing succession of palazzi and churches, their facades lapped by water, that line this sinuous water highway.

The Canal Grande is almost 4km (2.5 miles) long and varies in width from 30–70m (100–230ft), with an average depth of around 5m (16ft). The Venetians call it the *Canalozzo*, their high street, and it divides the city in half, with three *sestiere*, San Marco, Castello and Cannaregio, to the east, and another three, Santa Croce, San Polo and Dorsoduro, to the west. Along its length, merchants, aristocracy and trading communities built their palazzi, headquarters and warehouses, each with its main facade on the water. These were erected over five centuries, and their style covers the entire span of Venetian architectural development, the combination of water, stone and light one of the world's great visual experiences. Bridges were also constructed across the canal to link the two sides of the city. The Rialto bridge, dating from the late 12th century, was the earliest; the Scalzi, by the railway station, and the Accademia were both built in the 1850s during the Austrian occupation. In 2008 a fourth bridge was opened near Piazzale Roma. *Traghetti*, gondola ferries, also operate at fixed points along the canal; these have been in operation throughout the city's history.

WHAT TO SEE

FERROVIA TO RIALTO

The present 1950s railway station *(ferrovia)* replaced the original 1846 construction, built when the causeway to the mainland was created; the stone-built Ponte dei Scalzi went up in 1934. On the right is the domed church of San Simeone Piccolo (1738); on the left is the ornate facade of the Scalzi (1656) and the entrance to the wide Canale di Cannaregio, the gateway to Venice in its pre-causeway days. The brick church soon after this is San Marcuola, unfinished since funds ran out in the 18th century; the two impressive buildings opposite are the Fondaco dei Turchi, trading headquarters for the Turks in Republican days, and the Deposito dei Megio, once a granary. In winter, the Casino moves to the Renaissance Palazzo Vendramin Calergi, where Richard Wagner died in 1883. Opposite, to the left, is the white baroque facade of San Stae. Two highlights are Longhena's Ca' Pesaro on the right (1652), now housing the Museo d'Arte Moderna (Apr–Oct Tue–Sun 10–6; Nov–Mar Tue–Sun 10–5; tel 041 721127; adult €6.50, reduced ticket €4), and the Gothic Ca' d'Oro (▷ 165). Across the water lie the *pescheria* (fish market) and Rialto market stands; the long building beside them is the Tribunale Nuove (1555), now the Assize Court. Opposite is the Fondaco dei Tedeschi, once home to German merchants, and overhead is the graceful Ponte di Rialto.

RIALTO TO ACCADEMIA

Highlights on the next stretch are the Gothic 13th-century Palazzo Barzizza (on the right) and the Ca' Mocenigo (on the left), where Byron lived in 1818. Beyond a sweeping bend known as La Volta, are the huge Palazzo Giustinian and Ca' Rezzonico (▷ 165) on the right, along with the 18th-century Palazzo Grassi, one of Venice's prime exhibition venues. More Gothic facades follow before the Galleria dell'Accademia and its bridge (1932) come into view (▷ 170–171).

ACCADEMIA TO SAN MARCO

Below the bridge, Campo San Vio fronts the water on the right, followed by Palazzo Barbarigo, decorated with 19th-century mosaics, and the Palazzo Venier dei Leoni, home to the Peggy Guggenheim Collection (▷ 172). Opposite is Ca' Grande, designed by Sansovino in 1545, followed by some of Venice's grandest hotels. Look for the tiny Gothic Palazzo Dario on the right as the great plague church of Santa Maria della Salute approaches. The canal ends at the Dogana di Mare (customs), opposite which are the Giardini Reali, laid out by Napoleon, and the glories of San Marco.

TIPS

» The *vaporetto* is the cheapest and probably most entertaining way of seeing the Canal Grande. *Vaporetti* cross the Grand Canal where there is no bridge. The service costs €1 and you stand for the duration of the crossing.

» A gondola or water taxi is a more expensive option.

» It is best to begin at the station end and keep San Marco for the end of the trip.

» For the best chance of getting a good vantage point (and a seat) get on at Piazzale Roma.

» *Vaporetti* can be very crowded, particularly during the morning and evening rush hours. The best time is between 12.30 and 3 (siesta time), along with very early or late in the day.

» Few palazzi along the Canal Grande are floodlit, but a night ride is still a great experience.

Below *Palazzi and the Grand Canal illuminated at night*

GALLERIE DELL'ACCADEMIA

INFORMATION

www.gallerieaccademia.org

160 B4 Campo Carità, Dorsoduro 1050, 30123 Venezia 041 522 2247; call centre 041 520 0345 Tue–Sun 8.15–7.15, Mon 8.15–2 Adult €6.50, EU citizens (18–25) €3.25, plus €1 reservation fee under 18s and over 65s free Accademia Tours in English and Italian, Mon–Sat 11–1, 3.30–5, Sun 10–2, tel 041 520 0345. Audiotours in English, Italian, French, German, Spanish and Japanese €5 Full and short illustrated guides in Italian, English, French, Spanish, German and Japanese, €15.50 and €8.20 One shop and a stand selling good postcards, prints, good-quality gifts and art books (mainly on Renaissance art and artists)

Above *Room 23, with canvases by Bellini and Giorgione*

INTRODUCTION

If you want an overview of what Venetian art is all about, head for the Gallerie dell'Accademia, the city's main gallery, a splendid collection where you can compare works by all the great masters and revel in the richness of colour and light that typifies Venetian painting. Five hundred years of Venetian painting are covered by the Accademia's more or less chronologically arranged 24 rooms, where you can see the obsession with colour, texture and light emerge, and the development of the technical mastery of composition, perspective and anatomy. If these finer points aren't your thing, the pictures on display are also a window into Venetian life and preoccupations down the centuries—family, friends, lovers, clothes and good times, much the same as our own today.

The Accademia di Belle Arte, which houses the Accademia, as it's known, was founded in 1750 as the city's art school. It moved to its present home in 1807 under Napoleon, who, having suppressed dozens of churches and monasteries, needed somewhere to put their artworks. It was envisioned that the paintings would be as much used by art students as admired by the public, and this was the Accademia's initial role. The art school actually still exists, but today the Accademia is primarily known as one of Europe's finest specialized art collections.

WHAT TO SEE

THE SAN GIOBBE ALTARPIECE BY GIOVANNI BELLINI—ROOM 3

By the mid-15th century, the Bellini family had developed the concept of the *sacra conversazione*, a unified composition of the Madonna and saints. This superb altarpiece, all architectural detail, balance and warmth, is a prime example, painted at the time of the 1478 plague.

LA TEMPESTA BY GIORGIONE—ROOM 5

Giorgione's contribution to the development of Venetian painting was huge. In this, *The Storm,* his most enigmatic work (*c*1507), its iconography still unsolved, we see the growing importance of realistic landscape and light—a far cry from the rigid gold used just over a century before.

FEAST IN THE HOUSE OF LEVI BY VERONESE—ROOM 10

Figures stand out against a background of classical architecture in this stupendous set piece, dating from 1573. The painting, showing a banquet scene presided over by Christ with a motley assortment of drunkards, dwarfs and buffoons, was originally titled *The Last Supper*, but was judged so secular by its patrons that Veronese faced heresy charges if he failed to change it; cleverly, he simply changed the name.

MIRACLE OF THE SLAVE BY TINTORETTO

Tintoretto's technical wizardry still shocks in this picture of the hurtling figure of St. Mark swooping down to help a persecuted slave, painted for the Scuola Grande di San Marco in 1547 and the work that made his reputation.

DISCOVERY OF THE TRUE CROSS BY GIAMBATTISTA TIEPOLO—ROOM 11

Painted *c*1745 for a church in Castello, now destroyed, this ceiling panel perfectly embodies Tiepolo's style—dizzying perspective, startling light and sugary, light-hearted hues.

PROCESSION IN THE PIAZZA DI SAN MARCO BY GENTILE BELLINI—ROOM 20

Created in 1496, this work shows the Piazzà di San Marco as it was more than 500 years ago, with St. Mark's and the Doge's Palace much as they appear today. Carpaccio's painting of the Rialto nearby makes a good contrast, as there is little that's recognizable in the 21st century.

ST. URSULA CYCLE BY VITTORE CARPACCIO—ROOM 21

Crammed with charming anecdotes and details, the *St. Ursula Cycle* was painted in around 1498. It's the complicated tale, mixing reality and imagination, of a princess who, accompanied by her fiancé and 11,000 virgins, attempted to cross Europe to Rome, only to be massacred in Cologne.

PRESENTATION OF THE VIRGIN BY TITIAN—ROOM 24

This beautiful picture, painted between 1534 and 1539 for the Scuola della Carità, still hangs in its original position. The composition balances landscape, architecture and figures, with the small Virgin ascending the stairway.

GALLERY GUIDE

The rooms are arranged chronologically except for 19–24, which are specific collections. This is a selection of them:

Room 1: The Primitives—Byzantine and international Gothic gold-ground paintings, typified by Paolo Veneziano.

Rooms 2–3: 15th-century altarpieces and works by the Bellini family, Sebastiano del Piombo, Cima de Conegliano and Carpaccio.

Rooms 4–5: Giovanni Bellini, Mantegna, Piero della Francesca, Cosmè Tura and Giorgione.

Rooms 6 and 10: Titian, Jacopo Tintoretto and Paolo Veronese.

Rooms 7–8: Lorenzo Lotto, Romanino and Jacopo Palma il Vecchio.

Room 11: Veronese and Tiepolo.

Rooms 14–18: The 17th and 18th centuries: pictures and genre paintings by Tiepolo, Canaletto, Bellotto, Guardi, Pietro Longhi and Rosalba Carriera.

Rooms 19–20: Stories of the Relic of the Cross by Vittore Carpaccio, Gentile Bellini and other Renaissance masters.

Room 21: *St. Ursula Cycle* by Vittore Carpaccio.

Room 23: Former church of Santa Maria della Carità with 15th-century paintings by the Bellini and Vivarini families.

Room 24: Former Albergo Room of Santa Maria della Carità.

TIPS

» Staffing shortages mean that sometimes certain rooms are closed, so if there is something specific that you want to see, ask before you buy your ticket.

» The €11 (reduced rate €5.50) combined ticket for the Galleria dell'Accademia, Ca' d'Oro (▷ 165) and Museo Orientale is a good bargain, even with the €1 reservation fee.

» You can reserve timed tickets if you don't want to stand in line (Mon–Fri 9–6, Sat 9–2, tel 041 520 0345).

Below *A Madonna and Child by Bellini*

COLLEZIONE PEGGY GUGGENHEIM

www.guggenheim-venice.it

The Palazzo Venier is one of the Canal Grande's most eccentric buildings, an oddity whose construction began in 1759 but had progressed only as far as the first storey before the Venier money ran out. Its bizarre appearance appealed to American millionairess Peggy Guggenheim (1898–1979), who realized its potential as a showcase for her collection. She began collecting contemporary art in the 1920s, buying from and dealing in the works of a whole generation of innovative abstract and surrealist artists. She married Max Ernst, one of the greatest exponents of Surrealism, in 1941, but divorced him in 1946 and moved to Venice. Now administered by the Guggenheim Foundation, the collection is one of Venice's top attractions, its works the perfect antidote to the excess of Byzantine, Gothic and Renaissance art elsewhere in the city.

The light-filled rooms are approached through a garden court, tastefully scattered with sculptures by such artists as Alberto Giacometti (1901–66) and Henry Moore (1898–1986), all shaded by trees and greenery. Examples of work by all the big names of the early and mid-20th-century movements of Cubism, Surrealism, Abstract Expressionism and Constructivism adorn the walls. Included in the collection are works by Marc Chagall, Jackson Pollock, Paul Klee, Max Ernst, Alexander Calder, Joseph Cornell and Marino Marini.

160 B4 Palazzo Venier dei Leoni (entrance on Fondamenta Venier), Dorsoduro 701, 30123 Venezia 041 240 5411 Wed–Mon 10–6 Adult €10, over 65s €8, students with card €5, under 12s free Salute Snacks and lunches overlooking the sculpture garden

GALLERIA DELL'ACCADEMIA

▷ 170–171.

GESUITI

Fans of baroque architecture must not miss the Jesuit Church of Santa Maria Assunta, known as the Gesuiti (not to be confused with the Gesuati in Dorsoduro). The Jesuits, with their close ties to the papacy, were never popular in Venice and it was not until 1715 that they commissioned Domenico Rossi to build a church. He made up for the delay by going for maximum impact—a church with a vast facade and a mind-bogglingly ornate interior.

Inside you are struck by the baldachin over the altar, modelled on Bernini's version in St. Peter's in Rome (▷ 74–75), and festoons of drapery that billow from every corner and decorate every inch of wall space. What appear to be swags and drapes of figured damask and brocaded velvet are actually intricately carved and polished pieces of green and white marble. With scarcely a corner unadorned, it all adds up to a visual feast that is far more memorable than the comparatively pedestrian paintings by Palma il Giovane in the sacristy. The best painting, though badly lit and hard to see, is a night scene by Titian, the *Martyrdom of St. Lawrence,* over the first altar on the left.

160 C2 Campo dei Gesuiti, Cannaregio, 30121 Venezia 041 528 6579 Daily 10–12, 4–6 Fondamenta Nove

LA GIUDECCA

Take a boat across the Canale della Giudecca to escape the crowds, explore a unique part of the city and visit one of Palladio's finest churches. During the ninth century the Giudecca, an island, began to develop as a location for the richly decorated summer palazzi of the aristocracy. By the 19th century it had become the city's industrial area, filled with boatyards and factories. Over the past 50 years, industry has declined and the Giudecca is today largely a residential area, with a distinctive way of life. A broad *fondamenta* runs along the canal on the north side of the island, which is where you will find the main sights: the churches of the Redentore (Mon–Sat 10–5, Sun 1–5), built by Palladio in 1577 in thanks for Venice's deliverance from the bubonic plague, and the Zittelle and Santa Eufemia. You will also find rows of local food shops, bars and restaurants, modest houses and grand 14th-century *palazzi.*

160 B5 and C6 Palanca, Redentore, Zitelle

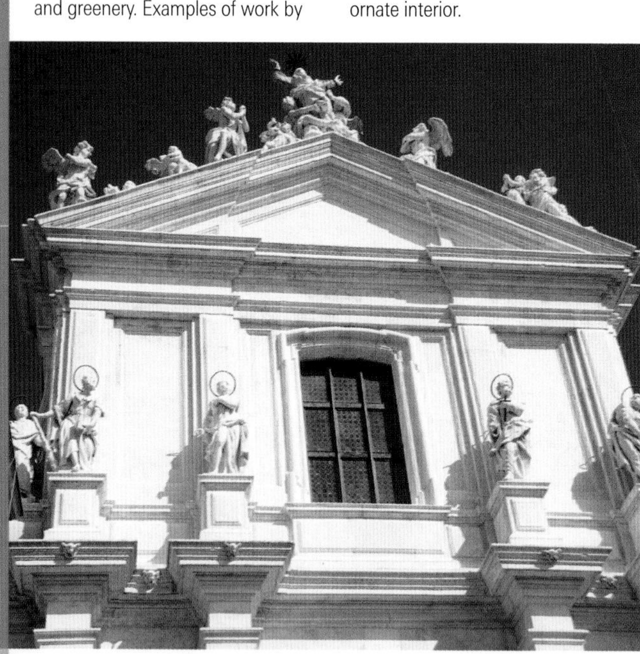

Below *Exterior of Gesuiti church*

MADONNA DELL'ORTO

The original church was founded at the end of the 14th century. It was dedicated to St. Christopher, the patron saint of voyagers, in the hope that he would keep an eye on the ferry service to the northern islands and the gondolas that ran from the jetty. He was demoted in 1377 when a statue of the Madonna and Child, which was said to have miraculous powers and which had been attracting a following in a nearby vegetable garden *(orto)*, was moved here. This Madonna still stands in the Chapel of San Mauro, while St. Christopher presides over the main door. The church was rebuilt between 1399 and 1473. Tintoretto's 16th-century paintings in the choir and apse and on the side walls represent 30 years of his working life. After the 1966 floods, this church was the first major restoration project funded by the British Venice in Peril Fund, and its first chairman, Sir Ashley Clarke, is commemorated by a plaque in the chapel near the main altar.

THE FACADE

Overlooking its own square and a canal, the beautiful Gothic facade has similarities to those of Santa Maria Gloriosa dei Frari (▷ 184) and Santi Giovanni e Paolo (▷ 182), but the false gallery at the top is unique. The figure of St. Christopher is by Nicolò di Giovanni and the portal by Bartolomeo Bon. Rising behind is a splendid onion-shaped cupola, balanced by a slender campanile, one of the prominent landmarks of the lagoon.

THE PAINTINGS

The three naves draw the eye towards the chancel, site of two huge canvases by Tintoretto, the *Making of the Golden Calf* and the *Last Judgement*. In the apse are the *Beheading of St. Christopher* and *St. Peter's Vision of the Cross,* both full of swooping angels, while the south aisle's mystical *Presentation of the Virgin in the Temple* provides a peaceful contrast. Radiant blues shine in *St. Agnes* in the Contarini Chapel, and there is a superb Cima da Conegliano over the first altar on the right. Be sure to find *Saints John the Baptist, Mark, Jerome and Paul* by Cima da Conegliano (1494) and Tintoretto's tomb in the chapel to the right of the chancel.

INFORMATION

www.chorus-ve.org
160 C2 Campo Madonna dell'Orto, Cannaregio, 30121 Venezia
041 719933 Mon–Sat 10–5
€3.50 Orto All CHORUS churches have audioguides €4

TIP

» Madonna dell'Orto is one of the CHORUS group of artistically important churches. A pass covering entry to all 16 churches costs €10 for adults and €7 for EU students up to 29 years (tel 041 275 0462). It is valid for one year.

Above *Decoration by Tintoretto in the vaulted apse of the church of Madonna dell'Orto*

MURANO

www.comune.venezia.it

Murano, 10 minutes by boat from Fondamenta Nuove, is a self-contained community of around 5,000 people, with a miniature Canal Grande, an excellent museum, old palazzi and fine churches. It has been the focus of the Venetian glass industry since the 13th century. There are many glass showrooms in the city proper, but if you want to see it being made, Murano is the place to go.

Five or six main canals thread their way through the island, lined with shops and houses and crossed by bridges—a miniature version of Venice itself. You can leave the boat at the Colonna or Faro, explore the island and then re-embark at Venier, at the other end of the main canal.

The big attraction is the glass, and there are workshops all over the island where you can see master craftsmen demonstrate the skills of flamework, twisting and blowing. Learn more in the Museo di Vetro (Glass Museum), in the splendid 17th-century Palazzo Giustinian, where the history and production of Murano's glass are explained (Apr–Oct Thu–Tue 10–6, Nov–Mar 10–4; €5.50). Don't overlook the 12th-century Basilica di Santa Maria e Donato, Murano's main church, with a colonnaded portico, a lively floor mosaic dating from 1140 and a grave Byzantine *Madonna* above the altar.

161 E1 Piazza San Marco 71f, San Marco, 30120 Venezia 041 529 8740; daily 9–3.30 Murano

MUSEO CORRER

www.museiciviciveneziani.it

The Museo Correr bills itself as the Museum of Venetian Civilization, focusing on city life during the great days of the Republic. Set in a series of grand and elaborate rooms, many overlooking the Piazza San Marco, it is now directly linked with the Museo Archeologico and the Biblioteca Marciana, so you can easily explore the whole complex (which occupies the upper floors of the Ala Napoleonica, the Procuratie Nuove and Sansovino's library).

At the museum's core are the 16th-, 17th- and 18th-century collections of Teodoro Correr, given to the city in 1830. Tours take you through halls devoted to the accomplished sculpture of Antonio Canova (1757–1822), including the famous *Orpheus and Eurydice*. Next is a series of princely rooms that provides an insight into the ducal elections, the workings of the Arsenale and everyday life and entertainment. Upstairs the Quadreria contains some fine works, notably *Two Venetian Noblewomen* by Vittore Carpaccio (1472–1526), erroneously known for years as *The Courtesans*. The route then leads through the Museo Archeologico (Greek and Roman art strictly for enthusiasts) before reaching the opulent state rooms of the Biblioteca Marciana. Here there is a huge variety of manuscripts and early books displayed beneath an impressive ceiling covered in allegorical painting.

160 C4 Ala Napoleonica, Piazza San Marco 52, San Marco, 30124 Venezia 041 240 5211 Apr–Oct daily 9–7; Nov–Mar 9–5 Adult €13 for combined ticket to Museo Correr and Palazzo Ducale (▷ 176–179), reduced rate €7.50 San Marco (Vallaresso)

MUSEO STORICO NAVALE

www.regione.veneto.it/cultura/musei

Venice's power and wealth came from the sea, and few places better demonstrate this than the Museo Storico Navale, a child-friendly museum devoted to the history of sailing. Four floors are crammed with model ships, uniforms, weaponry, navigational instruments and more.

The museum occupies an old granary building right on the water's edge, beside the Rio dell'Arsenale and a stone's throw from the entrance to the Arsenale. Highlights are the richly gilded Bucintoro, a model of the Doge's state barge, the huge 16th-century *galleass* (a large galley) and the last surviving private gondola, which once belonged to Peggy Guggenheim (▷ 172). There are other vessels from all over the world, cannons and torpedoes, dress uniforms, sextants and astrolabes—more than 25,000 exhibits in total.

Keep an eye out for the superb scale model of the *cammello,* a device used to lift ships from low water in the lagoon, and the naïve votive paintings, given in thanks for salvation from storm and shipwreck.

161 E4 Campo San Biagio, Castello, 2148 Venezia 041 520 0276 Mon–Fri 8.45–1.30, Sat 8.45–1 €3 Arsenale

PALAZZO DUCALE

▷ 176–179.

Below *A gondola on display in the Museo Storico Navale*

PIAZZA SAN MARCO AND THE CAMPANILE

As you emerge from the narrow surrounding streets into St. Mark's Square, its sheer scale is breathtaking—not for nothing did Napoleon describe it as 'the biggest drawing room in Europe'. Within the arcades that line three sides of the piazza are Florian's and Quadri's, two historic cafés with plush interiors, impeccable service and tables outside on the piazza. They are very expensive, but a drink here is quite an experience, often accompanied by an orchestra.

THE PIAZZETTA AND THE TORRE DELL'OROLOGIO

At the east end of the piazza's wide expanse stands the Basilica di San Marco (▷ 166–167). The open space runs down to the water's edge, St. Mark's Basin, and is flanked on the right by the Biblioteca Marciana and the Zecca, designed by Sansovino between 1527 and 1537, and the Palazzo Ducale (▷ 176–179) on the left. A winged lion, the symbol of Venice, and St. Theodore, the city's first patron saint, top its two columns. On the other side of the basilica, the tiny space fronted by ancient marble lions, known as the Piazzetta dei Leoncini, is overlooked by the Torre dell'Orologio. This clocktower, now unveiled once more after years of restoration, has a zodiacal clock with mechanical figures and is crowned with a golden lion. It was designed by Mauro Coducci and built between 1406 and 1506.

THE ARCADES AND THE CAMPANILE

The arcaded buildings that run down the long sides of the piazza are the offices of the Procurators of San Marco; the 16th-century Procuratie Vecchie, to the north, and the Procuratie Nuove, built a century later, to the south. After the fall of Venice in 1797, the two were linked by another arcaded building, the Ala Napoleonica, now home to the Museo Correr (▷ 174). In front of San Marco, the campanile (bell tower), a great place for city and lagoon views, was designed in 1514. What you see is a copy, as in 1902 the entire tower collapsed. No other buildings were damaged but the custodian's cat was killed. It was rebuilt *'Com'era, dov'era'* ('Like it was, where it was') and Sansovino's Loggetta at the foot of the tower was pieced together from the fragments.

INFORMATION

160 C4 Piazza San Marco, San Marco, 30170 Venezia Campanile: 041 522 5205. Torre dell'Orologio 041 520 9070 Campanile: Apr–Jun, Sep–Oct 9–7; Jul–Aug 9–9; Nov–Mar 9.30–3.45. Torre dell'Orologio by pre-booked tour only (tel 8480 820000; www.museicivicivenezia ni.it) Campanile lift €8. Torre dell'Orologio adult €12, reduced rate €7 San Marco (Vallaresso)

TIPS

» In peak season, come early or late to avoid the crowds.

» Choose a clear day to go to the top of the campanile as heat haze or mist significantly reduces visibility.

Above *Detail of the upper part of the campanile*

INTRODUCTION

Venice's number one sight, the Palazzo Ducale (Doge's Palace) adjoins the Basilica di San Marco at the east end of the Piazza San Marco and overlooks the Piazzetta to one side and, in front, the sparkling waters of the Bacino di San Marco. Built at a time when the rest of Europe cowered behind fortified walls, the fairy-tale pink-and-white facade of the Palazzo Ducale, light, airy and confident, turns outward to embrace the world.

This huge edifice, with its dozens of grand chambers and warrens of offices, incorporated both a residence for the Doge, the Venetian Republic's head of state, and the offices that housed the machinery of state. Here, in one building, were combined all the offices of government—councils, committee rooms, assembly chambers, diplomatic and foreign offices, and the judiciary, as well as the state prisons. From the 14th century Venetian government was in the hands of members of those patrician families whose names were inscribed in the so-called *Libro d'Oro* (Golden Book), and the building reflects their power, wealth and prestige as well as that of the Republic itself. The Doge, the Republic's figurehead ruler, was elected from this aristocracy, and once elected, remained in power until his death, leaving his home to live in the palazzo. Around him ground the machinery of state, as it had done from the 9th century, when the first government building was erected on the site. Today's complex dates from the 14th century, altered and reconstructed over the years, but always retaining its magical Veneto-Gothic facade. The block across the Canale della Paglia, approached via the Ponte dei Sospiri (Bridge of Sighs), is the exception, being built in the late High Renaissance classical style.

It's all mind-bogglingly splendid, with seeming acres of painted ceiling, miles of gilt and stucco corridors, wood carvings, marble, statuary, panelling and endless stairways, loggias and courtyards. Get it in perspective by realizing that all this over-the-top decor had a purpose: to render all visiting ambassadors, diplomats, foreign princes and merchants speechless with wonder, and to hammer home the point that Venice was very, very powerful and very, very rich.

WHAT TO SEE

THE EXTERIOR, THE PORTA DELLA CARTA AND THE COURTYARD

One of the world's finest examples of Gothic architecture, the exterior of the Palazzo Ducale runs along the water's edge and the piazzetta. The waterfront facade was finished in 1419 and the side on the piazzetta was built in the 15th century. The beautiful pink-and-white frontage has an airy arcade topped by a gallery supporting the mass of the upper storeys; the play of light and shade over the masonry enhances the impression of harmony. The columns and pillars at ground level are mainly copies of the 14th- to 15th-century originals, now housed in the Museo dell'Opera, off the interior courtyard.

The main entrance into the palazzo is the Porta della Carta, a grand piece of Gothic architecture built by Bartolomeo and Giovanni Bon between 1438 and 1442. This provides access through a portico to the courtyard, an enclosed space with a first-floor loggia. The most imposing approach to the loggia is via Sansovino's 1485 Scala dei Giganti (Giant's Staircase), used by the Doge at his inauguration. There is another flamboyant Sansovino stairway, the stucco-and-gilt Scala d'Oro (Golden Stairway), leading from the loggia to the upper floors.

THE DOGE'S APARTMENTS

The Doge, elected from Venice's patrician families, was the one politician to sit on all the major councils and the only one elected for life—a position of such potential power that it was hedged about with endless restrictions to

INFORMATION

160 C4 Piazza San Marco 1, San Marco, 30124 Venezia 041 271 5911 Apr–May daily 9–7; Jun–Oct 8.30–6.30; Nov–Mar 9–6. Itinerari Segreti (Secret Itineraries) tour must be reserved in advance Adult €13, child (6–14) €7.50 San Zaccaria, San Marco (Vallaresso) Guided tours in English Tue–Thu, Sat 11.30, €6; audioguides in Italian, English, French, German and Spanish, €6 Good Electra guidebooks available from bookshops in several languages Bar on ground floor serves drinks, coffee and snacks Excellent bookshop, with good range of guidebooks, art books, posters, postcards and souvenirs

Opposite *The magnificent ceiling of the Sala del Maggior Consiglio*
Below *Detail of a window on the Palazzo Ducale*

TIPS

» Expect parts of the Palazzo Ducale to be closed; a building of this age requires constant restoration.

» The Museum Card for the Musei della Piazza San Marco (€13) provides entrance to all the museums in Piazza San Marco (Palazzo Ducale, Museo Correr, Museo Archeologico Nazionale, Biblioteca Nazionale Marciana).

» A Museum Pass (€18) is available for all Venice's civic museums in the Musei della Piazza San Marco (Palazzo Ducale, Museo Correr, Museo Archeologico Nazionale, Biblioteca Nazionale Marciana), the Musei del Settecento (Ca' Rezzonico (▷ 165), Palazzo Mocenigo, Casa di Carlo Goldini, Ca' Pesara) and the Musei delle Isole (Museo del Vetro and Museo del Merletto). You may find the private museums of greater interest, and for these you will need to pay separately.

» Various Venice passes allow unlimited use of public transport, as well as museum and shop discounts, including www.veniceconnected.com. If you plan a vague itinerary before you go, pre-purchasing a pass online will save you money.

Below *Statue of Atlas at the foot of the Scala del'Oro*

prevent abuse of power. After his election, the Doge gave his entire life over to the service of the State, and his apartments reflect this lack of privacy. They comprise a series of surprisingly intimate rooms, magnificently if austerely decorated, with splendid ceilings and superb fireplaces. Here, the Doge received deputations and ambassadors and oversaw council deliberations. The finest and biggest chamber is the Sala delle Mappe (Map Room), painted with maps of the whole of the 16th-century known world, with Venice firmly as the central focus.

THE ANTICOLLEGIO, THE COLLEGIO AND THE SALA DEL SENATO

The extraordinarily rich decoration of the state rooms in the Palazzo Ducale is intended to illustrate the history of Venice and was painted by some of the greatest 16th-century Venetian artists. The aim was to impress visiting emissaries, many of whom passed through the palace on official business. The Anticollegio served as a waiting room for ambassadors hoping to see the Doge; four mythological paintings, created between 1577 and 1578 by Tintoretto (1518–94), hang on the walls, while facing the window is Veronese's *Rape of Europa*. From here, the ambassadors moved to the adjoining Collegio to be received. This was also the room where the inner cabinet met. The ceiling panels are by Veronese (1528–88), pure propaganda showing Justice and Peace as mere sidekicks to Venice herself. Venice triumphs yet again in Tintoretto's painting in the middle of the ceiling in the Sala del Senato next door, where the 300-strong senate met to receive reports from returning ambassadors and debate questions of commerce, war and foreign policy.

THE SALA DEL MAGGIOR CONSIGLIO

The first-floor Sala del Maggior Consiglio is the largest room in the palazzo, stretching almost the entire length of the waterfront side of the building. This lavishly decorated room was the great council chamber where the 2,600 patricians met. The paintings in this room were commissioned to replace those lost in a fire in 1577. *Paradiso* on the far wall was begun by Tintoretto, then aged 70, who was responsible for its complex iconography. It was completed after his death by his son, Domenico (1562–1637). The *Apotheosis of Venice* on the ceiling is by Veronese. Devoted to the concept of Venice the superpower, its meaning is more straightforward. Around the walls are portraits of the first 76 doges. Look for the gap, where there is a black veil instead of a doge; this space should have commemorated Doge Marin Falier, but he was executed for conspiring against the State in 1355. If the windows are open on the left side of the hall, step out onto the balcony for lovely views across St. Mark's Basin.

THE PONTE DEI SOSPIRI AND THE PRIGIONI NUOVE

Until the 16th century, all Venetian criminals served their sentences in either the attics or the waterlogged basement of the Palazzo Ducale. This changed after the construction of the Prigioni Nuove (New Prisons) in 1598; from then on petty villains enjoyed the comforts of what was considered to be Europe's most sophisticated prison accommodation. The prisons are separated from the main palace by a canal, which is crossed by the world-famous Ponte dei Sospiri (Bridge of Sighs). Designed by the aptly named Antonio da Ponte, it is probably Venice's (if not the world's) most photographed bridge. By the 19th century the romantic legend was firmly established that once prisoners crossed this enclosed first-floor bridge they would never return. In the prison block, steep stairs lead down to the warren of cells, some of which have their number and capacity painted over the door. At the bottom there is a small courtyard for exercise, once home to an unofficial tavern.

GALLERY GUIDE

Itinerari Segreti: A guided tour behind the scenes, taking in the warren of offices and small chambers that links the public rooms of the palazzo, as well as the old prisons in the basement (must be reserved in advance; tel 041 520 9070, or visit museiciviciveneziani.it; €16).

Museo dell'Opera: A ground-floor museum displaying, among other exhibits, the best of the palazzo's exterior arcade capitals. Twelve date from the 14th century and are outstanding examples of sculpture, especially the scene showing the creation of Adam and Eve.

Arco dei Foscari: A late Gothic arch in the courtyard, commissioned by Doge Francesco Foscari in 1438, designed and built by Antonio Bregno and Antonio Rizzo.

Sala del Magistrato: A small room housing some outstandingly bizarre paintings by the Flemish artist Hieronymus Bosch (*c*1450–1516), collected by the Grimani family.

Armoury: A huge and somewhat daunting collection of armour, weapons and instruments of war, mostly captured from Venice's enemies.

Bocche di Leone: 'Postboxes' adorned with lion's heads—in various parts of the palazzo, notably the loggia, the Sala della Bussola and the Sala della Quarantia Criminal—which served as delivery boxes for anonymous accusations made by Venetian citizens against each other.

Above and below *The Palazzo Ducale is the most opulent civic building in Venice*

INFORMATION

160 C3 *Vaporetto:* Rialto

TIP

» The fish market is closed on Mondays

» The Venetians know the two sides of the Rialto Bridge as *Rialto di quà* (this side) on the San Marco side, and *Rialto di là* (that side) on the San Polo side.

» The back streets around the Rialto Bridge are riddled with hole-in-the-wall wine bars *(bacari)* that are atmospheric and very good value. On offer are Venetian snacks *(cicchetti)* and glasses of wine. Some *bacari* date back to the 15th century.

» Just beyond La Salute on the point is Punta della Dogana (www.palazzograssi.it), the new flagship to the arty Dorsoduro district. The former Customs House exhibits a collection of contemporary art belonging to French fashion tycoon François Pinault.

Above *The Rialto Bridge illuminated at night*

RIALTO

The Rialto was one of the earliest parts of the lagoon to be settled: the word *Rialto* is a corruption of *Rivoaltus*, the upper bank, the highest area and thus less likely to be flooded. By the 10th and 11th centuries, the Rialto was Venice's commercial heart and one of Europe's most important trading areas. In 1097 the market became a permanent fixture. A pontoon of boats linked the two banks, but in the 12th and 13th centuries the first of five wooden bridges was built across the canal. Venetian merchants controlled trade between Europe and the Far East, while Europe's major banks and international trading companies set up offices here. The name Rialto was as familiar to medieval moneymen as that of Wall Street or the City of London is today.

PONTE DI RIALTO

The idea of a stone bridge at the Rialto was first mooted in 1557 and a competition was held to choose the best design, with big names such as Michelangelo, Palladio and Sansovino all submitting their plans. The prize went to the aptly named Venetian, Antonio da Ponte, for his revolutionary single-span suggestion. Two *fondamente* (canalside streets) stretch along either side of the water, one of the few places in Venice where you can actually stroll along the edge of the Canal Grande (▷ 168–169). The San Marco side is the Riva del Ferro, named after the iron that was once unloaded here, while opposite, the Riva del Vin is a reminder that this was originally the discharge point for wine barrels.

THE MARKET

Behind the Riva del Vin is a labyrinthine maze of narrow streets, many named after the goods sold during the great days of the Republic: Ruga de'Orefici (Goldsmiths' Row), Ruga Speziali (Spicemakers' Street), Riva dell'Olio (Oil Quay) and Campo della Pescheria (Fish Market Square). Nearby is the Rialto market and its surrounding specialist shops, the city's main place for food shopping, where people bargain for meat, fruit, vegetables and, above all, fresh fish and seafood.

The little church of San Giacomo, on the San Polo side of the bridge, is said to be Venice's oldest, founded, according to legend, on the same day as the city itself, 26 March 421. The clock above the church is famous for its inaccuracy; it has been incorrect since its installation in the 15th century.

SAN GIORGIO DEI GRECI

San Giorgio dei Greci is a tangible reminder of the foreign communities that lived and settled in Venice. Renaissance Venice had a large Greek population, particularly after Constantinople fell to the Turks in 1453, and the Greek community received permission to build their own church in 1539. The church was designed by Sante Lombardo, with an interior that is completely Orthodox in layout and design. Look for the *matroneo* (women's gallery) above the main door and the *iconostasis* (screen) that separates the high altar from the body of the church. The icons on the screen represent a mixture of dates and styles, the oldest dating back as far as the 12th century. The campanile, drunkenly leaning towards the canal, is one of the landmarks in this part of the city.

161 D3 Fondamenta dei Greci, Castello, 30122 Venezia 041 523 9569 Wed–Mon 9–1, 3–5 San Zaccaria

SAN GIORGIO MAGGIORE

The open waters of St. Mark's Basin frame the great Palladian church of San Giorgio Maggiore. The island of San Giorgio was home to a Benedictine monastery from the 10th century to 1806, and in 1565 Andrea Palladio was commissioned to design a church for the monks. He united two temple fronts in the facade: four central columns that rise to the full height of the nave are flanked by shorter, Corinthian columns, which match the height of the aisles—an arrangement echoed in the luminous interior and emphasized by the use of white marble and stucco. This is a triumphantly light and airy building, full of soaring space decorated with fine pictures by Tintoretto and his school. Stop to admire the works on either side of the chancel, *The Fall of Manna* and *The Last Supper,* both of which emphasize the importance of the Eucharist, before taking the elevator up the campanile for views over the city and lagoon.

161 D4 Isola di San Giorgio Maggiore, 30124 Venezia 041 522 7827 May–Sep Mon–Sat 9.30–12.30, 2.30–6.30; Oct–Apr 9.30–12.30, 2.30–4.30 San Giorgio

Below *The decidedly listing campanile of the Greek Orthodox church of San Giorgio dei Greci, designed in the 16th century by Sante Lombardo*

SANTI GIOVANNI E PAOLO

▷ 182.

SANTA MARIA DEGLI MIRACOLI

www.chorusvenezia.it

The exquisite church of Santa Maria degli Miracoli is tucked away in Cannaregio. It was built between 1481 and 1489 to house an image of the Madonna by Nicolò di Pietro, which still hangs over the altar. The church is entirely covered inside and out with polychrome marble, creating a jewel-casket effect, with one side of this perfect Renaissance church running along a quiet canal.

Begin by looking closely at the exterior, built, like the inside, by the Lombardo brothers, stoneworkers who uniquely fused architecture, decoration and sculpture. Marble in subtly different shades covers every surface, while graceful pilasters make the church appear longer. The interior has some of the most intricate carving in Venice, seen at its best when the sun streams in, illuminating the rose, white and silver-grey marble. The altar steps and balustrade leading to the raised choir are beautifully carved with figures, while fine filigree stonework covers the columns below the nuns' choir and a carved frieze runs right around the church.

160 C3 Campo Santa Maria Nuova, Cannaregio, 30121 Venezia 041 275 0462 Mon–Sat 10–5, Sun 1–5 €2.50. Santa Maria degli Miracoli is one of the CHORUS group of 15 artistically important churches; a pass covering entry to all 15 costs €10 Rialto

SANTA MARIA DELLA SALUTE

www.sacred-destinations.com/italy/venice-santa-maria-della-salute

An unmistakable feature of the Venetian cityscape, the gleaming white bulk of the great baroque 17th-century church of Santa Maria della Salute looms over the San Marco entrance to the Canal Grande. Built in thanksgiving for the end of the disastrous plague of 1630, which wiped out a third of the city's population, the church has outstanding paintings by Titian (*c*1490–1576). Baldassare Longhena designed the huge, domed, octagonal construction, his first commission.

From the canalside, a flight of steps leads up to the Palladian facade with its huge half-columns. The main dome is buttressed by circular volutes, affectionately known to Venetians as *orecchini* (little ears), surrounded by more than 120 exuberant statues and ornate decoration. By contrast, the interior is rather austere, with six chapels around the central space. On the high altar, the marble Virgin and Child are shown rescuing Venice from the plague. There are eight Titians in the sacristy, including *The Sacrifice of Abraham* and *David and Goliath,* and Tintoretto's *Marriage Feast at Cana*. The church is beautifully illuminated at night.

160 C4 Campo della Salute, Dorsoduro, 30123 Venezia 041 522 5558 Church: Apr–Sep daily 9–12, 3–6.30. Sacristy: Apr–Sep daily 3–5.30 Sacristy €1.50 Salute

INFORMATION

161 D3 · Campo Santi Giovanni e Paolo, Castello, 30122 Venezia · 041 523 5913 · Mon–Sat 9.30–6; Sun 1–6 · €2.50 · Ospedale · In Italian, English, French, German, €3.60

Above *View of the south transept of Santi Giovanni e Paolo, with the campanile of Santa Maria Formosa in the foreground*

SANTI GIOVANNI E PAOLO

Northern Castello is home to the huge Gothic church of Santi Giovanni e Paolo which, in Venetian dialect, combines into San Zanipolo. The L-shaped *campo* (square) that fronts the church is a good vantage point from which to appreciate the impressively large exterior: the church is 100m (330ft) long, 38m (125ft) wide and 33m (108ft) high. Constructed between 1246 and 1430, of red brick with stone ornamentation, Santi Giovanni e Paolo is among the most ambitious expressions of Gothic architecture in Venice, complete with a soaring façade and five apses at the east end.

The main portal has Byzantine reliefs and marble columns from an abandoned church on the island of Torcello (▷ 185). The most ornate of four tombs built into the facade is that of Doge Giacomo Tiepolo, who in 1234 reputedly dreamed that he should found a church here, on what was then a swamp.

THE INTERIOR

The vast, shadowy interior is a single spatial unit punctuated by simple columns. The walls are lined with tombs and monuments by some of Venice's most famous Renaissance artists and sculptors. They include some of the best pieces by the Lombardo family of sculptors. No fewer than 25 doges are buried here. Particularly striking are the Morosini, Vendramin, Nicolò Marcello and Corner monuments, and the Lombardo Mocenigo monuments on the rear entrance wall. Paintings to look for are the superb polyptych *St. Vincent Ferrer* by Giovanni Bellini, *St. Antonius Pierozzi Giving Alms to the Poor* by Lorenzo Lotto, in the south transept, and the ceiling paintings by Veronese in the Cappella del Rosario. There is some good stained glass in the transept, designed by Bartolomeo Vivarini and made at Murano (▷ 174).

THE COLLEONI STATUE AND SCUOLA GRANDE DI SAN MARCO

The Lombardo family were also responsible for the elaborate façade of the Scuola Grande di San Marco, which stands at right angles to the front of the church. Completed in 1495 with stunning marble *trompe l'oeil* panels, it was one of the major Venetian *scuole* (confraternities) and today houses Venice's main civic hospital. Opposite the entrance, and the focal point of the *campo*, is Andrea del Verrocchio's powerful equestrian statue of the *condottiere* Bartolomeo Colleoni (▷ 35).

SANTA MARIA FORMOSA

www.chorusvenezia.org

The church of Santa Maria Formosa gives its name to the surrounding *campo*, a typically Venetian square that is constantly busy with the comings and goings of both Venetians and visitors, a great place to experience life in Castello. This irregular space is bordered by a fine range of *palazzi.* The ancient church got its name from a seventh-century vision that appeared to St. Magnus, where he saw the Virgin as a buxom and shapely matron—*formosa*.

The present church was designed by Mauro Coducci in 1492; he retained the original 11th-century Greek-cross plan, threading a Renaissance design around a typically Byzantine layout. The campanile is baroque. The church has two facades, one on the canal (1542) and one on the *campo* (1604), both added after Coducci's death. The harmonious grey-and-white interior has three naves and barrel-vaulted side chapels. Look for the triptych in the first chapel on the right, showing the Virgin in her role as Our Lady of Mercy by Bartolomeo Vivarini, with scenes from her life on either side.

161 D3 Campo Santa Maria Formosa, Castello, 30122 Venezia 041 275 0494 Mon–Sat 10–5, Sun 1–5; Jul, Aug closed Sun €3 San Zaccaria, Rialto

SANTA MARIA GLORIOSA DEI FRARI

▷ 184.

SAN MICHELE IN ISOLA

The island of San Michele, a few minutes' journey across the lagoon from the Fondamente Nuove, is the final resting place for Venetians. But the cemetery is by no means a morbid place. Infused with a gentle melancholy, it is busy with Venetians bringing flowers for their loved ones. Today it is only a temporary resting place as it became full years ago. Bones are now removed after 10 years or so and taken to an ossuary.

Begin by pausing at Venice's first Renaissance church, the beautiful San Michele in Isola, designed by Mauro Coducci in the 1460s. From here a walkway leads through the cloisters of the monastery; the brothers look after the church and cemetery. It is covered in an array of stacked tombs, dramatic sculpture, photographs and flowers. Most tourists head for the Protestant section to visit the tomb of American poet Ezra Pound (1885–1972), before tracking down the graves of Russian composer Igor Stravinsky (1882–1971) and Russian ballet impresario Sergei Diaghilev (1872–1929) in the Greek Orthodox section. There is a corner dedicated to gondoliers, whose graves are decorated with stone gondolas.

161 D1 Isola di San Michele, 30121 Venezia Cemetery: daily 7.30–4. Church: daily 7.30–12.15, 3–4 Free San Michele (from Fondamente Nuove)

SAN POLO

www.chorusvenezia.org

The district of San Polo, the Venetian version of San Paolo (St. Paul), gets its name from this church, a ninth-century foundation. Tucked into a corner of the square of the same name, the church faces the canal, though it has lost its waterfront facade and entrance. The original building was Byzantine, but Gothic elements such as the side portal, the rose window and the wooden ceiling were added in the 14th and 15th centuries. In 1804 there were more alterations in an attempt to impose a neoclassical look; some were removed in the 1930s. The campanile, detached from the church, has suffered less since its construction in 1362; look for the pair of stone lions at the base. Inside, the main draw is Giambattista Tiepolo's *The Virgin Appearing to San Giovanni Nepomuk,* while in the oratory are dazzling paintings showing scenes from *The Stations of the Cross,* the work of Tiepolo's less famous but very gifted son Giandomenico.

160 B3 Campo San Polo, San Polo, 30125 Venezia 041 275 0494 Mon–Sat 9–6, Sun 1–6 €3 San Tomà, San Silvestro

SAN ZACCARIA

San Zaccaria, dedicated to the father of John the Baptist (said to be buried here), is the only Venetian church with an ambulatory and crypt. On a square off the Riva degli Schiavone, it is a Venetian mix of Gothic and Renaissance styles.

The ambulatory is instantly striking, an elegant ring of elliptical cupolas lit by long windows. The church is stuffed with 17th- and 18th-century paintings, of distinctly variable quality. Standing artistically apart from this mass is Giovanni Bellini's luminously stunning and serene *Madonna and Four Saints*, in the second chapel on the left. The Chapel of St. Tarasius was once part of the original church and houses three ornate *ancone* (volutes supporting a cornice) by Antonio Vivarini and Giovanni d'Alemagna, wonderfully hieratic pictures in sumptuous gold Gothic frames. This chapel also gives access to the permanently waterlogged crypt, the burial place of eight of the early doges. It is confirmation that the water continues to rise in Venice.

161 D4 Campo San Zaccaria, Castello, 30122 Venezia 041 522 1257 Mon–Sat 10–12, 4–6, Sun 4–6 Church: free. Chapels of St. Athanasius and St. Tarasius, sacristy and crypt: €1.50 San Zaccaria

Left *Santa Maria Formosa*

INFORMATION

www.basilicadeifrari.it
www.chorusvenezia.org
160 B3 Campo dei Frari, San Polo, 30125 Venezia 041 275 0494
Mon–Sat 9–6, Sun 1–5 €3. The Frari is one of the CHORUS group of 16 artistically important churches; a pass covering entry to all 15 costs €10 San Tomà Audioguides
Several versions, with differing levels of information, in English, Italian, French, German, Spanish, €4–€9

TIPS

» Enter via the north transept, but once inside start your visit from the back of the church.
» If you are visiting between Christmas and the end of January, don't miss the *presepio* (crib), one of the city's best, with sound and light effects and moving figures.
» Classical concerts are often held in the Frari.

Above *The long cruciform interior of the Franciscan church of Santa Maria Gloriosa dei Friari*

SANTA MARIA GLORIOSA DEI FRARI

The Franciscans, *frari* in Venetian dialect, came to Venice around 1222 and built their first church on the site in the 1270s. As the order developed, they outgrew it, and work started on a new church and bell tower in 1340. The latter was finished in 1396, but it was not until the 1430s that the church was completed. The adjoining cloisters, chapter house and convent (now housing the Archivio di Stato) were built at the same time. The convent was suppressed under Napoleon, but today the Frari is a parish church still in the care of the Franciscans..

GREAT PAINTINGS

Built of terracotta brick with a typical Gothic stone exterior and architectural details, the Frari is huge—102m (335ft) long, 48m (158ft) wide and 28m (92ft) high—and has one of the tallest bell towers in Venice. Enter the vast nave (the 12 pillars represent the Apostles) and you will be immediately drawn to Titian's famously radiant and dynamic *Assumption* (1518) over the high altar, one of the most important and innovative paintings of the Venetian High Renaissance. To the left of the main altar is Titian's *Madonna di Ca' Pesaro* (1526), commissioned by Bishop Pesaro and showing members of his family. In the sacristy, the inspiring and tranquil triptych *Madonna and Child* (1488) by Giovanni Bellini is noted for its skilful use of perspective; it is still in its original frame. Immediately to the right of the high altar is Donatello's sculpture of *St. John the Baptist,* the only work by the Florentine master in Venice. In the Monks' Choir *(Coro dei Frati)*, the 124 wooden choir stalls were carved by Marco Cozzi in 1468.

MONUMENTAL TOMBS

Less immediately appealing than the paintings but of equal interest are the monumental tombs. The rear section of the nave has a 19th-century monument to Titian and opposite there is a large neoclassical marble pyramid containing the heart of the sculptor Antonio Canova (1757–1822). Look for the late Gothic monument to Doge Foscari (1457) near the high altar, and the Renaissance monument to Doge Tron (1476) nearby. The composer Claudio Monteverdi (1567–1643) is buried in a chapel to the left of the high altar.

SCUOLA GRANDE DEI CARMINI

www.scuolagrandecarmini.it

The Scuola Grande dei Carmini was the only *scuola* to escape the maraudings of Napoleon's troops, and is thus the only surviving one to have kept an 18th-century appearance. Tucked away just off the atmospheric Campo Santa Margherita, this Carmelite confraternity base has flamboyant interior decoration.

Pause before you go in to admire the formal symmetry of the facade, designed by Longhena between 1668 and 1670. This was the Venetian headquarters of the Carmelites, a religious order devoted to the Virgin Mary. From here they practised their charitable works. In 1739 they employed the artist Giambattista Tiepolo (1696–1770) to decorate the upper hall, a task that occupied him for 10 years. Access upstairs is via an ornate staircase, and the hall itself is dominated by Tiepolo's nine audacious panels. Incomprehensible iconography aside, they can be appreciated for their swirling figures and off-beat composition and the extraordinary accomplishment of *trompe-l'oeil* perspective.

160 B4 · Campo dei Carmini, Dorsoduro 2617, 30123 Venezia · 041 528 9420 · Apr–Oct daily 10–5; Nov–Mar 11–4 · Adult €5, child (under 10) €2 · Ca' Rezzonico, San Basilio

SCUOLA GRANDE DI SAN ROCCO

▷ 186–187.

SCUOLA DI SAN GIORGIO DEGLI SCHIAVONI

This intimate little building houses one of the most appealing of all Venetian Renaissance picture cycles. After the splendours of the great set pieces, the low-key charm of Vittore Carpaccio's paintings is a great contrast. By the 15th century, the Slavs had established an important community in Venice, and obtained permission to found their own *scuola* here. In 1502 they commissioned Carpaccio (*c*1460–*c*1525) to decorate the interior with scenes from the lives of three special saints revered by the Slavs—St. George, St. Tryphon and St. Jerome.

The Carpaccio cycles occupy a dimly lit, wood-panelled chamber entered directly from the street. Much of their appeal stems from their meticulous detail. The iconography is confusing, but it is easy to spot St. George killing the dragon, while the princess looks on in rapture.

161 D3 · Fondamenta dei Furlani 3259a, Castello, 30122 Venezia · 041 522 8828 · Mon 2.45–6, Tue–Sat 9–1, 2.45–6, Sun 9–1 · €3 · San Zaccaria

TORCELLO

www.comune.venezia.it

On the marshy, neglected island of Torcello, 9km (5 miles) northeast of Venice in the northern part of the lagoon, you will find a handful of working Venetians, a single muddy canal and the oldest building in the lagoon, the superb ninth-century Basilica di Santa Maria Assunta.

Established in the fifth century, this was Venice's earliest settlement; by the 1300s the population numbered over 20,000. But the rise of the Rialto (▷ 180) and the mosquito-fed fevers took their toll in the 14th century, forcing the inhabitants to flee. All that remains is a few houses, an 11th-century church and the basilica.

The interior of Santa Maria Assunta (Piazza Torcello; Mar–Oct daily 10.30–6; Nov–Feb 10–5; €4), first built in 638, is serene and cool, with a superb marble pavement and a series of outstanding mosaics, dating from the ninth to the 12th centuries, including a melancholy *Madonna* in the apse and a magnificently detailed *Last Judgement* on the back wall. For spectacular views over the lagoon, climb the bell tower.

161 off E1 · Piazza San Marco 71f, San Marco, 30124 Venezia · 041 529 8740; Mon–Sat 9.30–3.30 · Torcello

Below *View over Torcello*

SCUOLA GRANDE DI SAN ROCCO

There is little in Venice so powerful as the picture cycle by Tintoretto in the Scuola Grande di San Rocco. The series of 54 staggering paintings was produced by the artist in three bursts of creativity over a period of 23 years. This colossal achievement covers the walls and ceilings of the three halls of the sumptuous headquarters of the richest of the 15th-century *scuole* (charitable confraternities), dedicated to San Rocco (St. Roch), who was the patron saint of the plague stricken and much revered in Venice. The Scuola was founded in 1478 and built its meeting house, designed by Bartolomeo Bon, between 1515–49. Tintoretto started work here in 1564, finally completing his paintings in 1588. The Scuola is still the seat of the Archbrotherhood of St. Roch, the only confraternity to have been spared dissolution under Napoleon. Today, it has about 350 members of both sexes, who meet annually in Council and continue to act as an active charity.

SALA DELL'ALBERGO AND UPPER HALL

A wonderfully elegant staircase leads to the upper floor where the Sala d'Albergo, the small meeting room, contains the *Crucifixion*, painted in 1565 and considered one of the greatest paintings in the world. It is a powerful and passionate work, packed with detail and drama, and bathed in light. The composition is extraordinary, the figure of the crucified Christ forming the central axis from which radiating diagonals spread out to encompass the other elements of the narrative. Next door the Upper Hall contains scenes from the Old Testament on the ceiling and a *Life of Christ* cycle on the walls. Here, the *Adoration of the Shepherds* is a perfect example of Tintoretto's unique style, where the composition, perspective, light and colour are used to heighten the inherent drama of the scene—these same elements are used in many of the other paintings, notably *The Last Supper*.

GROUND FLOOR HALL

The ground floor paintings were the last to be executed, and show Tintoretto at the height of his powers. In the *Annunciation*, the angel, a whirling mass of wings and drapery attended by a swarm of accompanying cherubs, crashes into the Virgin's chamber, while the *Flight into Egypt* is one of the few paintings containing landscape; it's tempting to believe Tintoretto based the scene on memories of his boyhood home in the foothills of the Dolomites. Don't miss the superbly carved wooden stalls and the gilded ceiling here.

INFORMATION

www.scuolagrandesanrocco.it

160 B3 Campo San Rocco, San Polo, 3052 Venezia 041 523 4864

Scuola and church daily 9–5.30

€7; youth ticket (under 26) €5

San Tomà In Italian, English, French, German and Spanish, €4.50–€15

▷ Tips

TIPS

» Audioguides are included in the ticket price and will help you make the most of your visit. Don't forget to pick up a plan and explanatory leaflet on you way in.

» Use the hand mirrors provided to examine the ceiling panels.

» Dress warmly for a winter visit—the Scuola is unheated.

» There are often baroque recitals performed here, in this grandest of the *scuole*.

Opposite Moses Striking Water from the Rock *by Tintoretto*

Below *The* Crucifixion *by Tintoretto*

THROUGH DORSODURO

This is a wonderfully varied walk through the heart of the *sestiere* of Dorsoduro. En route you'll explore off-the-beaten track areas, have the chance to visit superb churches and some of Venice's finest museums, and enjoy views that range from picturesque corners to sweeping vistas that encompass some of the city's great landmarks.

THE WALK
Distance: 4.5 km (2.8 miles)
Allow: 2–2.5 hours
Start at: Ca' Rezzonico *vaporetto* stop
End at: Accademia *vaporetto* stop

★ Get off the *vaporetto* at Ca' Rezzonico and walk straight down Calle Traghetto to Campo San Barnaba. Cross the square diagonally, walking past the vegetable boat and right over the bridge to head down Rio Terrà Canal, bearing left to Campo Santa Margherita, the focal point of Dorsoduro. Turn right into the Campo, then take the third left (yellow sign to Piazzale Roma) off the square, and cross the canal. Over the bridge, turn left and follow the canal. Keep on this *fondamenta* as it passes the church of Angelo Raffaele, then take the second right into Campiello Riello. Walk through to the next canal and then turn left along Fondamenta Tron to reach the church of San Nicolò dei Mendicoli and its *campo*.

❶ This charming little *campo*, situated in one of the earliest parts of the city to be settled, featured in Nicolas Roeg's cult 1970s movie *Don't Look Now*. The 13th-century Veneto-Byzantine church, founded in the seventh century, is one of the city's oldest churches, and has retained its original plan. It was formerly the artisans' and fishermen's church, and is a wonderful muddle of architectural elements, panelling and wooden sculpture, perfectly epitomizing the long history of the building.

Retrace your steps back through Campiello Riello and turn right over the first bridge. Turn left on the other side and walk along the Fondamenta de Pescheria to the church of Angelo Raffaele.

❷ Angelo Raffaele dates from the 17th century and contains paintings and sculptures connected to the story of Tobias and the Angel—the images, among them five panels by Guardi, depict the Archangel with Tobias and his dog; Tobias is always pictured holding a fish, which plays a key role in the biblical story. The church features in Salley Vickers' book *Miss Garnet's Angel*.

Exiting the side door of the church, turn left and walk down the side of the church into Campo Angelo Raffaelle which leads into Campo San Sebastiano and the church of San Sebastiano.

❸ The church is brilliantly and lavishly decorated by the late Renaissance genius Veronese, who worked here from 1555 to 1559 and 1565 to 1570. The decoration is a *tour de force*, full of visual ricks, dizzying perspectives and foreshortenings and glowing with colour. Veronese's genius lies not only in his technical ability and his use of *trompe l'oeil,* but also in his gift to portray realistic figures that are emoved from the everyday world by the clear, transparent tones and unearthly light.

Cross the bridge in front of San Sebastiano and go straight to emerge back in Campo San Barnaba, where you turn right under the *sottoportego*, and follow this main route to Rio San Trovaso. Cross the canal by the Ponte delle Maravegie and turn right down the *fondamenta*, from where you'll see the church of San Trovaso and a *squero* (gondola boatyard) across the water. At the bottom, turn left onto the Fondamenta Zattere. Walk along beside the Canale della Giudecca past the baroque church of the Gesuati and continue, crossing two bridges to reach the church of Spirito Santo.

❹ The church and convent of Spirito Santo were founded in 1483; the present church dates from the 16th century. The convent was constantly rocked by scandal, its foundress being accused of squandering community funds to entertain her over, the local priest. By the 16th century the foundation was so notorious the Inquisition had to step n several times to restore order.

Continue to the next bridge, cross it and turn left to walk beside the Rio de la Fornasa, with the walls of the old Magazzino del Sale on your right.

❺ This was where Venice's only raw material was stored. Salt was produced in salt pans near Chioggia, and the warehouses, first constructed during the 14th century, could store up to 44,000 tons. Today, they're used as *cantiere* (boat sheds) and for occasional exhibitions and events, such as the Biennale art festival.

Turn left down Rio Terra dei Catecumenii and walk to a small *campo*, with the facade of the 15th-century ex-church of San Gregorio to your right. Continue under the *sottoportego* to cross the wooden bridge and reach the great church of Santa Maria della Salute (▷ 181).

❻ The baroque Santa Maria has paintings by Titian, including *David and Goliath*.

Cross the bridge to the left of the Salute and follow the route round to Campiello Barbaro, with its three acacia trees, across another bridge, and walk round to the Fondamenta Venier where you'll find the entrance to the Collezione Peggy Guggenheim (▷ 172) on your right. Leaving the museum, turn right and follow the street along to emerge into Campo San Vio. Bear left and cross the bridge into the Calle Sant'Agnese; walk along this, then turn right to the Galleria dell'Accademia (▷ 170–171).

❼ The Galleria dell'Accademia is one of the world's great specialist collections and gives a comprehensive view of the best in Venetian painting.

WHEN TO GO

Choose a sunny day! But if you can't, try to avoid wet or windy weather as there's not much shelter in some areas en route.

WHERE TO EAT

The Fondamente Zattere makes a good stopping place; roughly halfway along the walk, it has a good choice of bars and cafés with outside tables and lovely views.

Above *Interior of San Sebastiano*
Opposite *Boat-building in Squero di San Trovaso*

THE BACKSTREETS OF CANNAREGIO

The wide, quiet canals and sun-drenched quaysides of northern Cannaregio are one of the least known, and loveliest, parts of Venice. Modest houses and low-key palazzi line the canals, there's plenty of local life and the area is scattered with a handful of superb and contrasting churches. This walk threads through narrow *calle*, beside the water and across tree-shaded squares to show you a Venice that's well away from the crowds.

THE WALK
Distance: 4km (2.5 miles)
Allow: 2 hours
Start at: Tre Archi *vaporetto* stop
End at: Ca d'Oro *vaporetto* stop

★ Walk off the Tre Archi landing stage and turn right down the Fondamenta di Cannaregio. Count the left turns and take the ninth, ducking under a *sotoportego* into the Soto de Ghetto Vecchio. This passes through two small *campi* to a bridge over the Rio di Ghetto Nuovo, the canal that surrounds the Ghetto. Cross the bridge to arrive in the Campo Ghetto Nuovo.

❶ The world's first ghetto was established here in 1516, when the Republic instituted the area as a compulsory place of residence for Jews, who were safer in Venice than elsewhere in Europe. As the community was augmented by influxes from more oppressive countries, taller buildings went up; these contain the Ghetto's seven remaining tiny synagogues, known as *schole*—counterparts to the *scuole*—and a Jewish museum. The Jewish population today is small, but the Ghetto is still the centre of the community and a place of pilgrimage for Jews from many countries.

Cross the *campo* diagonally to the right and take the bridge with the cast-iron balustrade over the Rio della Misericordia, turning left on the other side along the Fondamenta dei Ormesini. Take the first right up Calle Turlona, cross a bridge and turn right along the Rio della Sensa. Walk left along the *fondamenta* and cross a bridge, then take the next turning left (blue sign to Fratebenefratelli) up Calle Loredan. This leads through to the third of the three parallel canals in this part of the *sestiere*, the Rio Madonna dell'Orto. Cross the bridge and turn right along the *fondamenta* to reach the jewel-like church of Madonna dell'Orto (▷ 173). With the church behind you, bear left onto the bridge to take in the Palazzo Mastelli.

❷ The facade of this picturesque Byzantine-Gothic palazzo has a splendid relief of a man leading a heavily loaded camel. Legend says this refers to the builder of the house, an Eastern merchant, who, having made his fortune, sent home for a beautiful wife. 'How will I find your house in such a vast and strange city?' wrote the girl, to which he replied, 'Just look for a house with a reminder of home'. More prosaically, the camel probably simply refers to the trading links of the Levantine Mastelli family.

Opposite *Shop window displaying decorative glassware in the Ghetto*

Walk through into the Campo dei Mori, and detour a few steps left to Tintoretto's house at No. 3399, marked by a plaque.

❸ The Campo dei Mori contains four 13th-century statues of turbaned Moors; wonderfully naïve pieces associated with the Mastelli family, who used to live in the palazzo where two of the figures are embedded. They were a Greek trading family who originated in the Morea (the Pelopponese), and were known in the city as the Mori. No. 3399 to the left of the *campo* was occupied by Tintoretto for the last two decades of his life (1574–94), when he lived here with his daughter Marietta, also a painter.

Cross the canal and continue down Calle Larga to the next canal. Turn left along the Fondamenta della Misericordia; the huge buildings on the left at the far end are the defunct Scuola Nuova della Misericordia. Cross the bridge, turn right, then take the second bridge on the right and walk under two *sotoportegi* to emerge on the Calle Rachette and take a left. Walk on and cross another widish canal and head right along the Fondamenta Santa Caterina. This leads past mellow buildings into the Campo dei Gesuiti, home to the superb baroque church of the same name (▷ 172) at the far end on the right.

With your back to the church and the *carabinieri* station on your left, cross the bridge and walk down Salizzada Sereman. Bear right into Salizzada Spezier, then right into Rio Terra Ss Apóstoli, passing the Co-op on the right. Turn right along Rio Terra dei Francesci (past the cinema) and left onto Salizzada Pistor; this will lead you down into the Campo degli Ss Apóstoli. Follow the yellow signs to the Rialto, turning left up the narrow Salizzada San Canciano immediately before the next bridge. This leads through Campo San Canciano into the lovely *campo* Santa Maria Nova, with the church of Santa Maria degli Miracoli (▷ 181) at the far end.

❹ Santa Maria degli Miracoli was built in the 15th century to house Nicolò di Pietro's image of the Madonna.

Turn right as you leave the church, cross a canal, then take the third turning left back onto Salizzada San Canciano. This leads to the main Rialto–Ferrovia route, so turn right through Santi Apóstoli and along the Strada Nuova. You'll pass pretty Campo Santa Sofia, fronting the Grand Canal, on your left. Take the narrow *calle* straight after the *campo*, which leads past the Ca' d'Oro (▷ 165), and carry on on to the *vaporetto* stop.

❺ The Golden House is a Gothic palazzo with good views of the Canal Grande from its upper loggias.

WHEN TO GO

This is a good walk for either the morning or afternoon, though avoid the middle of the day when everywhere will be very quiet and some churches will be closed.

WHERE TO EAT

The cafés in and around Campo Santi Apostoli make a good place to pause. Alternatively make a short detour to Algiubagiò on the Fondamenta Nuova near the Gesuiti—great for sandwiches, pizzas and ice cream.

PLACE TO VISIT

MUSEO EBRAICO

✉ Campo Ghetto Nuovo, Cannaregio 2902b, 30121 Venezia ☎ 041 715 359
🕑 Jun–Sep Sun–Fri 10–7, Oct–May Sun–Fri 10–6; may close early on Fri
💶 Adult €3, students €2 ☞ Half-hourly from 10.30; €8.50

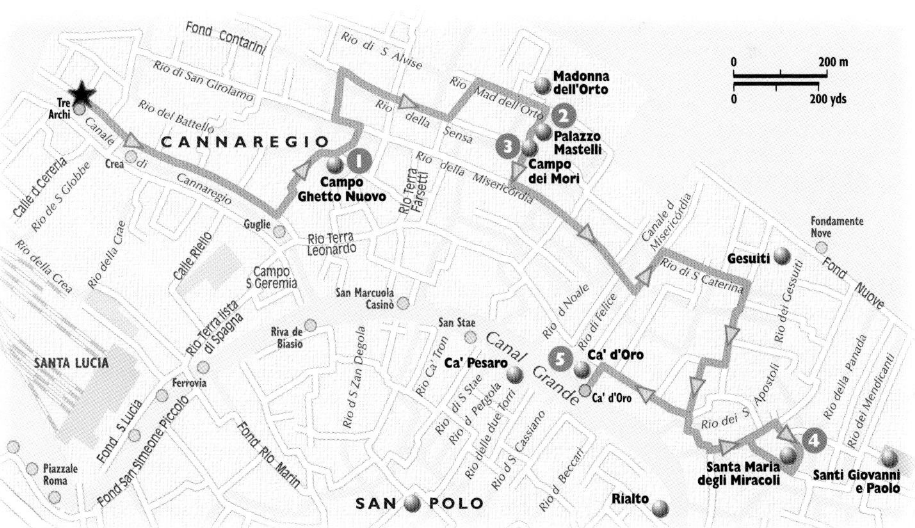

SHOPPING

BEVILACQUA

www.luigi-bevilacqua.com

The big Italian fashion houses come to Bevilacqua for their Venetian brocades, velvets, taffetas and damasks, still produced on 17th-century looms. The curtain ties, swags and key tassels make wonderful souvenirs.

✉ Fondamenta della Canonica, San Marco 337/B, 30124 Venezia and Campo Santa Maria del Giglio, San Marco 2520, 30124 Venezia ☎ 041 528 7581 and 041 241 0662 🕐 Tue–Sat 10–1, 4–7, Mon 4–7 ⛴ San Zaccaria, Santa Maria del Giglio

BOTTEGA VENETA

www.bottegaveneta.com

An elegant shop, famed for its superior leather goods. Kit yourself out with belts, bags and wallets. A great place to buy classic gifts that are practical and enduring.

Calle Vallaresso, San Marco 1337, 30124 Venezia ☎ 041 522 8489 🕐 Mon–Sat 10–7.30, Sun 11–7 ⛴ San Marco

CASA DEL PARMIGIANO

www.aliani-casadelparmigiano.it

Next to the fish market, this little shop sells big cheeses and even bigger prosciutto. Locals shop here too—watch what they buy for inspiration. A number of cheeses and salamis are vacuum-packed, ideal for taking home.

✉ Erberia, Rialto 214/215, 30125 Venezia ☎ 041 520 6525 🕐 Mon–Thu 8–1.30, Fri–Sat 8–1.30, 5–7.30; closed Sun ⛴ Rialto or San Silvestro

CLAUDIA CANESTRELLI

Tucked away near the Guggenheim, this tiny shop sells old prints, lamps and ornaments but is best known for its beautiful 18th-century-style earrings made by the owner. Each pair is unique and features pearls, tiny emeralds or rubies, all at remarkably good prices.

✉ Campiello Barbaro, Dorsoduro 364A, 30123 Venezia ☎ 041 522 7072 🕐 Daily 10–12.30, 3–6 ⛴ Salute

EBRÛ

www.albertovalese-ebru.com

Alberto Vallese's products are still the best—notebooks, photo frames, boxes and albums in marbled or stamped paper in a huge variety of colours. Superb value.

✉ Campo Santo Stefano, San Marco 3471, 30124 Venezia ☎ 041 523 8830 🕐 Tue–Sat 10–1, 4–7, Mon 4–7 ⛴ Accademia

LA FENICE ATELIER

If you're looking for beautiful lingerie or table linen, this is a good place to start. Cristina Linassi has nightgowns and dressing gowns in gossamer-fine cotton and smooth linens, all exquisitely finished, while table linens come in rich damasks in white, cream and a rainbow of colours.

✉ Calle dei Frati, San Marco 3537, 30124 Venezia ☎ 041 523 0578 🕐 Mon–Sat 10–1, 4–7 ⛴ Sant'Angelo

Above *Take to the canals in a gondola*

LIBRERIA TOLETTA
Huge selection of books of all kinds, including beautiful coffee-table books about Venice, guide books, art and cook books. The Studio across the street sells posters, more books and stylish souvenirs.
✉ Calle Toletta, Dorsoduro 1213, 30123 Venezia ☎ 041 523 2034 ⌚ Mon–Sat 9.30–1, 3.30–7.30; Oct–May Sun 3.30–7.30 ⛴ Ca' Rezzonico

MANEKI-NEKO
www.manekineko.it
Crisp cottons and linens are used here to make beautiful shirts and blouses ranging from strictly tailored to casual. They also stock pretty nightgowns and bathrobes.
✉ Campo Sant'Angelo, San Marco 3820, 30124 Venezia ☎ 041 520 3340
⌚ Apr–end Sep daily 10–6; Oct–end Mar Mon–Sat 10–6 ⛴ Sant'Angelo

MISTERO
Mistero is three shops next to one another: one sells items for the home, another sells fashion for the young and the third sells ladies' clothes (including bigger sizes). The ladies' shop—Atelier—has tops, trousers, dresses and scarves imported from India, and there's a huge selection of vibrant styles to choose from.
✉ Ruga Giuffa, Castello 4745, 30122 Venezia ☎ 041 523 1414 ⌚ Mon–Sat 9.30–12.30, 3.30–7.30 ⛴ San Zaccaria

MONDONOVO
www.mondonovomaschere.it
Venice's most famous *mascheraio* has been setting an example to other mask-makers for decades with its enormous variety of masks, handmade on the premises from papier mâché and beautifully gilded and painted.
✉ Rio Terà Canal, Dorsoduro 3063, 30123 Venezia ☎ 041 528 7344 ⌚ Daily 10–1, 4.30–7 ⛴ Ca' Rezzonico

PERLE E DINTORNI
www.perle-e-dintorni.it
It's easy to spend hours in this shop, choosing beads for a necklace. However, benefit from the experience of the staff, who are on hand to help you combine colours and effects which a novice would never have dreamed of. There is also ready-made jewellery at a range of prices.
✉ Calle della Mandola (Della Cortesia), San Marco 3740, 30124 Venezia ☎ 041 520 5068 ⌚ Mon–Sat 10–7 ⛴ Sant'Angelo

RIALTO MARKET
Wander around the Rialto for fruit and vegetables or head down to the *pescheria* (fish market), to see the strangest creatures in the lagoon. A great experience that hasn't changed for centuries.
✉ Near the Rialto Bridge, on the San Polo side ⌚ Mon–Sat 8am–noon ⛴ Rialto

RIGATTIERI
www.rigattieri-venice.com
This low-ceilinged shop is crammed with the best of decorative ceramics, as well as glass, silver and pewter, from all over Italy; choose from pyramids of fruit and vegetables, elegant pierced-work baskets and tureens or pick up an affordable take-home gift.
✉ Calle dei Frati, San Marco 3532–3535, 30124 Venezia ☎ 041 2523 1081
⌚ Mon–Sat 10–1, 3–8 ⛴ Sant'Angelo

TONOLO
Many Venetians rate this the best *pasticceria* in the city, and there's a vast assortment of mouthwatering cakes and pastries prepared daily with prime ingredients on offer. You can buy to take away or enjoy a sugary mouthful with a cappuccino at the bar.
✉ Calle San Pantalon, Dorsoduro 3764, 30125 Venezia ☎ 041 523 7209
⌚ Tue–Sat 7.45am–8.15pm ⛴ San Tomà

VENINI
www.venini.com
If you're serious about buying some Murano glass, spend an afternoon seeing how it's made. The great thing about Venini is that it's not too packed, so you can appreciate the craftsmanship. A good balance of traditional designs and artier pieces. There's another branch on the Piazzetta Leoncini, San Marco.
✉ Fondamenta Vetrai, Murano 47–50, 30141 Venezia ☎ 041 273 7211 ⌚ Mon–Sat 9.30–7.30 ⛴ Colonna, Murano

ENTERTAINMENT AND NIGHTLIFE

CANTINA DO MORI
Famous 15th-century *bacaro* (wine bar) in the Rialto, where Casanova was reportedly once a reveller. Today it's a great place for gossip and socializing over *cicchetti* (tapas-like snacks) and an *ombra* (glass of wine) or a luridly orange *spritz*, the Venetian aperitif (*spriss* in the local dialect), made with white wine, soda water and Aperol or Campari—all enjoyed standing up, as there are no tables.
✉ Calle do Mori, San Polo 429, 30121 Venezia ☎ 041 522 5401 ⌚ Daily 8.30am–10pm ⛴ Rialto

CASINO MUNICIPAL DI VENEZIA AND VENICE CASINO CA' NOGHERA
www.casinovenezia.it
If you want a flutter in the opulent surroundings of a palazzo on the Grand Canal, Ca'Vendramin is the place to come—though the Casino at Ca' Noghera near Mestre is flashier and more popular. Both offer table games such as roulette, baccarat and blackjack and banks of slot machines and electronic games. Wear a jacket and tie at the Vendramin.
✉ Palazzo Vendramin Calergi, Ca' Vendramin Calergi, Cannaregio 2040, 30123 Venezia ☎ 041 529 7111 ✉ Ca' Noghera, Via Pagliaga 2, near Mestre ☎ 041 529 7111
⌚ Casino slot machines daily 11am–3am, tables daily 3pm–3am; Venice Casino Mon–Fri, Sun 10am–4am, Sat 10am–5am
💶 €5 entry or €10 for entry plus €8 token
⛴ San Marcuola or private boat (Naveta Casino) from Piazzale Roma every 10 min; ACTV 4 or shuttle service from Piazzale Roma

CENTRALE LOUNGE
Funky lounge bar that is a celebrity haunt and one of the few sophisticated late-night spots outside the grand hotels. Chill to minimal house and lounge music over long, cool cocktails or one of the excellent wines. There's also a good restaurant and it's handy for the Fenice theatre.

San Marco, Piscina Frezzeria 1659/B, 30124 Venezia 041 296 0664 Daily 6.30pm–2am Calle Vallaresso, Zattere

GRAN TEATRO LA FENICE

www.teatrolafenice.it

The spiritual headquarters of 19th-century opera and classical ballet was ravaged by fire in 1996. After lengthy delays, the building reopened for the 2004–05 winter season. Tickets are available from the Cassa di Risparmio in Campo San Luca, from the theatre and online.

Campo San Fantin, San Marco 1965, 30124 Venezia 041 786511 €20–€1,000 Santa Maria del Giglio

SCUOLA GRANDE DI SAN ROCCO

www.scuolagrandedisanrocco.it

This famous 16th-century guild has a rich musical tradition. Its splendid interior contains famous Tintoretto paintings—an ideal venue for the regular and popular baroque music concerts. You can reserve tickets in person or over the telephone.

Campo San Rocco, Santa Croce, 30135 Venezia 041 523 4864; 041 962999 for tickets €30 San Tomà

SCUOLA GRANDE DI SAN TEODORO

www.imusiciveneziani.com

This magnificent guild building hosts baroque and operatic concerts all year round. Vivaldi's *The Four Seasons* is often performed, as is music by Mozart, Donizetti and Verdi, with the added bonus that the orchestra and singers dress in 18th-century costume.

Campo San Salvador, San Marco, 30124 Venezia 041 521 0294 All year Tue–Sun. Contact for times €21–€35 Rialto

TEATRO FONDAMENTE NUOVE

Venice's premier avant-garde dance and ballet theatre is not far from the church of the Gesuiti (▷ 172). Check out a modern production here, then head for Paradiso Perduto and the other night spots. It also stages alternative rock gigs.

Cannaregio 5013, Fondamente Nuove, 30121 Venezia 041 522 4498 Fondamente Nuove

TEATRO MALIBRAN

www.teatrolafenice.it

This wonderful building stages well-known operas such as *La Traviata* and more modern works, as well as classical concerts and ballet. There is a full theatrical and musical programme.

Calle dei Milion, Cannaregio 5873, 30121 Venezia 041 786 603; box office 041 899 909 090 €35 Rialto

TORINO@NOTE

Only three minutes from St. Mark's Square, this pub draws in a young crowd at night, buzzing with regular live jamming sessions and DJ sets—reggae, jazz, even karaoke singalongs.

Campo San Luca, San Marco 4591, 30125 Venezia 041 522 3914 Mon–Sat 10pm–2am San Zaccaria

VENICE JAZZ CLUB

www.venicejazzclub.com

Aficionados flock here to lap up the sounds by the Venice Jazz Club Quartet, who are among the best of all the Veneto's musicians. Expect tributes to the greats, including Miles Davis, classic jazz and plenty of modern improvisations. Cold meats and sandwiches are served before the concerts (from 8pm).

Ponte dei Pugni, Dorsoduro, 30123 Venezia 041 523 2056 Doors open 7pm; concerts start at 9 €20 (including first drink) Ca' Rezzonico

SPORTS AND ACTIVITIES

AC VENEZIA

www.veneziacalcio.it

The open-air Stadio Penzo is on the island of Sant'Elena, to the east of San Marco. AC Venezia are a Serie B outfit who have also played in the top-flight Serie A. Expect firecrackers, flag-waving, singing and a lot of gesticulating and moaning. Tickets are available from the ground, ACTV and Vela offices.

Isola Sant'Elena, 30122 Venezia 041 238 0711 *Curve* (behind the goal) €10, *distinti* (side of pitch) €20 Sant'Elena

AEROCLUB DI VENEZIA

Fancy flying over the lagoon and looking down on San Marco from above? This club has 20 years' experience. One-off jumps are available after a short but thorough introduction course. The price includes tuition and equipment.

Aeroporto G. Nicelli, San Nicolò, 30126 Venezia 041 526 0808 By appointment only Phone for details of the latest courses (Signor Michele Zanella, tel 041 961154) Santa Maria Elisabetta (Lido), then bus A to San Nicolò

CIRCOLO GOLF VENEZIA

www.circologolfvenezia.it

At the far end of the island, near the fortress, is the well-groomed 18-hole, par 72, Alberoni golf course. It has practice greens, a club house, restaurant and equipment rental.

Via Strada Vecchia 1, Alberoni, 30126 Lido di Venezia 041 731333 Apr–Sep Tue–Sun 8–8; Oct–Mar 8.30–6 €72 weekdays, €84 weekends Santa Maria Elisabetta (Lido), then bus B

GONDOLA RIDE

A gondola ride, the ultimate in Venetian romance, allows visitors to see the city at its most magical and is an unforgettable experience—even though the price may be high. If you're planning a trip, you can discuss the itinerary beforehand with the gondolier; the route will depend on where you're boarding, but most gondola trips will cover either the Bacino di San Marco and some side canals, or a section of the Grand Canal and some smaller *rii*. Fares are set by the gondola board (tel 041 528 5075, www.gondolavenezia.it), and are based on six passengers, with no reductions for smaller numbers. Prices are fixed—€80 for 40 minutes or €100 after 7pm— with extra for songs. Additional time is charged in 20-minute tranches—€40 daytime, €50 at night. If funds are short, you can ride in a gondola for just €1 by taking one of the *traghetti* (gondola ferries) across the Grand Canal. There are eight routes, each taking a couple of minutes, and using *traghetti* will often save a long hike to one of the bridges.

Gondola Stations

- Bacino Orseolo (behind Piazza San Marco)
- Campo San Moïse (in front of Grunwald hotel)
- Ferrovia (railway station)
- Piazzetta San Marco
- Piazzale Roma
- Riva degli Schiavoni (in front of Hotel Danieli)
- Riva del Carbon (south end of Rialto Bridge)
- San Marco (Vallaresso) (next to *vaporetto* stop)
- San Tomà (near *vaporetto* stop)
- Santa Maria del Giglio (next to *vaporetto* stop)

REALE SOCIETÀ CANOTTIERI BUCINTORO

www.bucintoro.org

Experienced rowers as well as novices are welcomed by the famous Reale Società Canottieri Bucintoro. Try your hand at *voga veneta* (Venetian rowing standing up), *canotaggio* (ordinary rowing) or sailing.

Fondamenta Dogana e Salute 15, Dorsoduro, 30123 Venezia 335 667 3851 Tue–Sat 9–6, Sun 8.30–1 Enrolment €90 then €250 standard fee La Salute

REYER VENEZIA AND APG BEARS BASKETBALL

www.reyervenezia.it
www.bears.shineline.it

Basketball is very popular in Italy. Reyer is one of the leading female clubs and the APG Bears are the local men's team. Games are played at the Palasport Taliercio on Sundays.

Via Vendramin 10, Mestre, 30173 Venezia 041 534 5250 Sun 6pm Free (usually) To Mestre, then bus 12 to Via Vendramin

TENNIS CLUB CA' DEL MORO

Bring your tennis kit and a supple wrist to this fantastic club on the Lido. Phone in advance to reserve one of the dozen or so floodlit clay courts and to rent equipment. Gym and pool also available.

Lido 6, Via Ferruccio Parri, 30126 Lido di Venezia 041 770 965 Mon–Sat 8.30–8.30, Sun 8.30–8 €12 per hour Santa Maria Elisabetta (Lido), then bus B

FESTIVALS AND EVENTS

FEBRUARY

CARNEVALE

www.carnevale.venezia.it
www.meetingeurope.com (The Ball)

Carnevale was Republican Venice's ultimate anything-goes festival. It has been revived to become a hugely successful 10-day festival, with costumes,masks and fun and games all over the city. One of the hottest carnival tickets is for the official Baroque Ball (Il Ballo Tiepolo), which takes place at the splendid Palazzo Pisani-Moretta. If you can't afford this, there are four other balls to choose from and various other events.

041 522 5150 (tourist office); 041 717065 (Carnival Committee) 10 days preceding Shrove Tuesday Ballo Tiepolo €420

APRIL

SETTIMANA DELLA CULTURA (WEEK OF CULTURE)

www.comune.venezia.it/turismo/feste

For one week in the middle of April entrance to national museums is free for everybody.

Mid-Apr

JUNE–NOVEMBER

BIENNALE INTERNAZIONALE D'ARTE

www.labiennale.org

Venice's Biennale began in 1895 as a showcase for the best in modern art, an aim it still pursues. It's based around a series of pavilions in Castello, in the east of the city, each designed and maintained by an exhibiting country and only open during the festival.

041 521 8711 In odd-numbered years. The Biennale of Architecture and Biennale Danse are held in even years

JULY

IL REDENTORE

www.comune.venezia.it/turismo/feste

A two-day festival celebrating Venice's deliverance from the plague of 1576, in honour of which the church of the Redentore was built on the Giudecca. A pontoon bridge spans the Giudecca canal so people can cross to the church, and there's a huge party on the Saturday evening with spectacular fireworks.

3rd weekend of July

AUGUST

VENICE INTERNATIONAL FILM FESTIVAL

www.labiennale.org

A stylish film festival that attracts both big-budget movies and uncommercial art-house films. Held on the Lido, where the big stars occupy the ornate *fin-de-siècle* hotels, there's plenty of razzmatazz. The Palazzo del Cinema is the venue for the main-screen auditorium, but tickets get snapped up for the premières. During the festival the Arena Estiva di Campo San Polo becomes an open-air cinema.

Lungomare Marconi, 30126 Lido di Venezia 041 272 6501 1 week, late August €8 before 6pm, €45 for premières Casino 61 and San Silvestro

SEPTEMBER

REGATA STORICA

www.comune.venezia.it/turismo/feste

Venice's biggest water festival, which kicks off with a superb costumed procession in ornate boats down the Canal Grande. This is followed by big-money rowing races.

1st Sunday in September

NOVEMBER

FESTA DELLA SALUTE

www.comune.venezia.it/turismo/feste

A truly Venetian festival that commemorates the deliverance of the city from the plague of 1631, which triggered the construction of the great church of the Santa Maria della Salute. A pontoon bridge crosses the Grand Canal opposite the church, and people cross to light candles and attend Mass.

21 November

Above *Dining with a view of the water*

PRICES AND SYMBOLS

The restaurants are listed alphabetically. The prices given are the average for a two-course lunch (L) and a three-course dinner (D) for one person, without drinks. The wine price given is for the least expensive bottle.

For the key to symbols, ▷ 2.

AI GONDOLIERI

www.aigondolieri.it

The accent here is firmly on well-hung, beautifully cooked meat served in elegant surroundings. Reservations essential for dinner.

✉ Fondamenta Venier, Dorsoduro 366, 30123 Venezia ☎ 041 5286396 🕐 Wed–Mon 12–3, 7–10 L €50, D €70, Wine €15 Accademia

ALLA VEDOVA

Very near the Ca' d'Oro ferry stop, the restaurant's official title is Ca' d'Oro, but it is known as Alla Vedova (Widow's Place). This typical Venetian old-world, cheap-and-cheerful *bacaro* (wine bar) serves great *cicchetti* as well as excellent pasta dishes and main courses. If you want to sit at a table rather than propping up the bar, reserve ahead.

✉ Ramo Ca' d'Oro, Cannaregio 3912, Venezia ☎ 041 528 5324 🕐 Mon–Wed, Fri–Sat 11.30–2.30, Sun 6.30–11pm; closed Aug L €15, D €35, Wine €12 Ca' d'Oro

AL PONTE

Affectionately known as La Patatina—after its specialty chunky chips (fries)—this bustling place offers bar snacks and table service. It's busy day and night with workers and students, filling them up with straightforward Venetian fare, such as *polpette* (meat balls), seafood risotto and *fritto misto*. Eating at the bar is excellent value—you'll pay more for table service.

✉ Ponte San Polo, San Polo 2741, 30135 Venezia ☎ 041 523 7238 🕐 Mon–Sat 9.30–2.30, 5–10 L €28, D €45, Wine €10 San Tomà

ANTICA LOCANDA MONTIN

www.locandamontin.com

The tempting menu here includes an impressive steak tartare and a tantalizing tiramisu.

✉ Fondamenta di Borgo, Dorsoduro 1147, 30123 Venezia ☎ 041 5227151 🕐 Thu–Mon 12.30–2.30, 7.30–10pm, (also open Wed Mar–Jun and Sep, Oct, Christmas and Carnevale); closed 2 weeks Jan, 1 week Aug L €22, D €45, Wine €12 Accademia

ANTICHE CARAMPANE

www.antichecarampane.com

Carampane is dedicated to the history of Venetian cooking. Medieval and Renaissance dishes are cleverly reinterpreted—try the shellfish with olive oil and Parmesan or the filleted St. Peter's fish with Treviso chicory.

✉ Rio Terra delle Carampane, San Polo 1911, 30125 Venezia ☎ 041 524 0165 🕐 Tue–Sat 12.30–3.30, 7.30–10.30 L €25, D €52, Wine €12 San Silvestro

CORTE SCONTA

One of Venice's finest and most famous restaurants focuses on fresh fish. Superbly imaginative *antipasti* are followed by light fish dishes, homemade pasta and traditional puddings. The wine list is admirably matched with the cuisine. Reservations are essential.

✉ Calle del Pestrin, Castello 3886, 30122 Venezia ☎ 041 522 7024 🕒 Tue–Sat 12–3, 6–10; closed 7–30 Jan, 20 Jul–16 Aug 🖐 L €40, D €70, Wine €14 ⛴ Arsenale

DO FORNI

www.doforni.it

An elegant-rustic trattoria near to St. Mark's with a warren of snug, interlinked rooms that all have a different atmosphere, though all have the same menu. The cuisine covers a broad range from typical Venetian to classic Italian and some international touches too. There is also an outstanding wine list.

✉ Calle dei Specchieri, San Marco 457/467, 30124 Venezia ☎ 041 523 2148 🕒 Daily 12–2, 7–10.30 🖐 L €35, D €60, Wine €15 ⛴ San Marco

DONA ONESTA

www.donaonesta.com

Tucked beside the bridge of the same name, the 'Honest Woman' is indeed an honest Venetian restaurant offering all the local staples. House specialties include a light *insalata di mare* (seafood salad), *risotto alle seppie nero* (black cuttlefish risotto) and a selection of plain grilled fish. There's a good choice of vegetables and the desserts are home-made.

✉ Ponte della Donna Onesta, Dorsoduro 3922, 30123 Venezia ☎ 041 710 586 🕒 Daily 12.30–2.30, 7.30–10 🖐 L €28, D €40, Wine €10 ⛴ San Tomà

FIASCHETTERIA TOSCANA

www.fiaschetteriatoscana.it

One of Venice's finest restaurants has shown consistent quality over the years—although some say the service in this old merchant's wine store makes you feel slightly hurried. Enjoy classic Venetian dishes of seafood (of course), meat and game, all well prepared and beautifully presented. The extensive wine list includes robust Tuscan reds and whites, a contrast to the fresher wines from the Veneto and Friui. The smooth, professional service makes eating here a real pleasure.

✉ Salizzada San Giovanni Grisostomo, Cannaregio 5719, 30121 Venezia ☎ 041 528 5281 🕒 Thu–Mon 12.30–2.30, 7.30–10.30, Wed 8–10.30; closed Aug 🖐 L €55, D €75, Wine €18 ⛴ Rialto

HARRY'S BAR

This stylish restaurant is very popular with Americans, and is famous for its bellinis and carpaccio of beef.

✉ Calle Vallaresso, San Marco 1323, 30124 Venezia ☎ 041 528 5777 🕒 Daily 10.30am–11pm 🖐 L €44, D €105, Wine €24 ❄ ⛴ San Marco

LINEADOMBRA

www.ristorantelineadombra.com

Near to La Salute, from the pontoon terrace there is one of Venice's most romantic views. Expect light, modish yet classically oriented Italian food, together with Venetian options and specials including tuna tartare and sea bass. If you don't fancy eating outside, the inside restaurant has an appealing funky, arty vibe.

✉ Dorsoduro 19, 30100 Venezia ☎ 041 241 1881 🕒 Thu–Tue 12–2.30, 7.30–11; closed 9 Dec–14 Feb 🖐 L €60, D €80, Wine €18 ⛴ Salute

NARANZARIA

www.naranzaria.it

A mixture of traditional and modern, this 16th-century *osteria* still contrives to be more cosmopolitan than most Venetian options. Choose between familiar Venetian dishes, the chef's Mediterranean take on sushi and fine meat and vegetarian dishes, all accompanied by views of the Grand Canal and Rialto Bridge.

✉ San Polo 130, 30125 Venezia ☎ 041 724 1035 🕒 Tue–Sun noon–2am; closed 3 weeks in Jan, 1 week in Aug 🖐 L €34, D €60, Wine €15 ⛴ Rialto

OSTERIA ALLE TESTIERE

www.osterialletestiere.it

This tiny *bacaro* (wine bar) restaurant has a sky-high reputation for innovative and creative cooking. Local seafood and fish are imaginatively cooked with spices and herbs. The cheeseboard is well-chosen and the wine list is excellent. There are two sittings nightly; choose the later one (9pm) for a more relaxed evening.

✉ Calle del Mondo Novo, Castello 5801, 30122 Venezia ☎ 041 522 7220 🕒 Tue–Sat 12–2, 7–10.30; closed last week Dec, 2 weeks Jan, ug 🖐 L €50, D €70, Wine €14 ⛴ Rialto

OSTERIA OLIVA NERA

The menu here shows that Venetian cooking can be given a contemporary edge. Delicious examples include scallops with wild mushrooms, and lamb cooked in thyme. The dessert menu includes a rich mascarpone cheesecake.

✉ Calle della Madonna, Castello 3417/18, 30122 Venezia ☎ 041 522 2170 🕒 Fri–Tue 12–2.30, 7–10.30 🖐 L €28, D €50, Wine €15 ⛴ San Zaccaria

VECIO FRITOLIN

www.veciofritolin.it

Set in the Rialto market area, this quirky, seemingly old-fashioned, fish restaurant is the place for a seafood extravaganza and Venetian-style pasta dishes. Chef Irina Freguia personally chooses the fish and seafood from the market each day.

✉ Calle della Regina, Rialto 2262, Santa Croce, 30135 Venezia ☎ 041 522 2881 🕒 Wed–Sun 12–2.30, 7–10.30, Mon–Tue 7–10.30 🖐 L €35, D €65, Wine €15 ⛴ Rialto

VINI DA GIGIO

www.vinidagigio.com

This increasingly famous place is one of the best-value restaurants in Venice, known for its superlative antipasti, fresh fish, meat and game; in season, try the wild duck from Burano. The wines come from all over the world. Reservations are essential.

✉ Fondamenta San Felice, Castello 3628A, 30122 Venezia ☎ 041 528 5140 🕒 Wed–Sun 12–2.30, 7.30–10.30; closed 3 weeks Jan, 3 weeks Aug 🖐 L €35, D €60, Wine €14 ❄ ⛴ Ca' d'Oro

PRICES AND SYMBOLS

Prices are the lowest and highest for a double room for one night, unless otherwise stated. Breakfast is included, and all the hotels listed accept credit cards unless otherwise stated. Note that rates vary widely throughout the year.

For the key to symbols ▷ 2.

BISANZIO

www.bisanzio.com

This restored 16th-century palazzo hotel is near the so-called 'Chiesa di Vivaldi'. Guest rooms have parquet flooring, beamed ceilings and unfussy Venetian touches. The most expensive rooms have charming balconies with rooftop views. All have telephone, satellite television, hairdryer and minibar. The Brown Lounge, bar and breakfast room share a functional, understated appearance. A continental breakfast is included.

✉ Calle della Pietà, Castello 3651, 30122 Venezia ☎ 041 520 3100 €180–€390 50 San Zaccaria

LA CALCINA

www.lacalcina.com

A perennial favourite along the Zattere, this hotel has wonderful views of the Giudecca. The simple rooms have parquet flooring and attractive period touches. Each has a private bathroom, telephone, hairdryer and safe. There are no televisions or minibars in the bedrooms. Take breakfast on the canalside platform, then relax on the roof terrace. La Piscina bar/restaurant serves Venetian fare.

✉ Fondamenta Zattere ai Gesuati, Dorsoduro 780–783, 30123 Venezia ☎ 041 520 6466 €90–€310 22 Zattere

CA' MARIA ADELE

www.camariaadele.it

Right next to Santa Maria della Salute and barely a minute's walk from the *vaporetto*, this luxurious little hotel provides the ultimate in sybaritic and romantic living. You can choose between one of the themed suites, where the decor ranges from cosy fireside to Oriental, or relax in the comfort of a more conventional room.

✉ Rio Terà dei Catecumeni, Dorsoduro 111, 30123 Venezia ☎ 041 520 3078 €340–€715 12 rooms, 2 suites Salute

CA' PISANI

www.capisanihotel.it

Smooth lines, exposed beams and art deco furnishings mix with modern minimalist touches here. Each room is individually designed and has a relaxing, sophisticated charm. The facilities, including sauna, are excellent and the bathrooms ultra-modern. La Rivista restaurant continues the modern theme with simple Italian cuisine.

✉ Rio Terra dei Foscarini, Dorsoduro 979/a, 30123 Venezia ☎ 041 240 1411 €220–€360 29 Access to Accademia

CENTRALE APARTMENTS

www.centrale-lounge.com

Choose between several trendy or time warp apartments near St. Mark's and the Rialto.

☎ 339 760 9136 From €120

CHARMING HOUSE DD 724

www.thecharminghouse.com

This little *locanda* is a discreet designer den overlooking the Collezione Peggy Guggenheim. This is an art curator's paradise, full of opulent comfort, for when those frou-frou brocaded beds get too much.

✉ Ramo da Mula, Dorsoduro 724, 30123 Venezia ☎ 041 277 0262 €150–€330 7 Salute

Above *Stay in a canalside palazzo*

LOCANDA LA CORTE

www.locandalacorte.it

Within easy reach of many shops, restaurants and entertainment venues, this pleasant hotel is in an attractive part of the Castello *sestiere*, near Chiesa Santi Giovanni e Paolo. The rooms have been completely restored and refurbished using rich fabrics and luxury Venetian furniture. Facilities include private bathroom, television, hairdryer and telephone. The secluded courtyard full of trees and flowers is a great place to enjoy the buffet breakfast.

Calle Bressana, Castello 6317, 30122 Venezia 041 241 1300 €80–€200 16 San Zaccaria or Fondamente Nuove

LOCANDA ORSEOLO

www.locandaorseolo.com

This diminutive boutique hotel only a few steps from St. Mark's Square, overlooking the Orseolo canal, is a treasure trove of delights. Decorated in the style of a traditional, elegant Venetian home, the elegance is matched by the warmth of the welcome from the hosts. Superb breakfasts include homemade pastries, eggs, meat and cheeses.

Corte Zorxi, San Marco 1803, 30124 Venezia 041 5204827 €170–€300 11 rooms, 1 suite San Marco

LONDRA PALACE

www.hotellondra.it

This handsome 19th-century palazzo along the busy Riva was renovated in 1999. In 1877, Tchaikovsky composed his fourth symphony in room 106, while gazing out towards San Giorgio Maggiore. Dark wood furniture and marble floors blend with the light walls and modern lighting, creating an air of calm and restrained elegance. Enjoy the stunning views from the terrace while you dine at Do Leoni, which serves regional dishes. Rooms are comfortable, if a little characterless. The ample pink marble bathrooms come with a bathrobe, shower and Jacuzzi.

Riva degli Schiavoni, Castello 4171, 30122 Venezia 041 5200533 €365–€625 53 San Zaccaria

LUNA HOTEL BAGLIONI

www.baglionihotels.com

Glide by gondola to the entrance, just off St. Mark's Square, and step into the opulence of Venice's oldest hotel—the palazzo has its origins in the 15th century. Impeccable service is complemented by marbled halls, beautiful antiques, silk-panelled walls and sheer luxury that are trademarks of the Baglioni style.

Calle Larga dell'Ascencione, San Marco 1243, 30124 Venezia 041 528984 €250–€800 89 rooms, 15 suites San Marco

NOVECENTO

www.locandanovecento.it

This San Marco gem is another stunning boutique hotel that's right up with the best of Venice's new-wave designer lodgings. There's a tiny courtyard, a breakfast room and honesty bar, but you'll probably want to spend time in your room, equipped with every comfort.

Calle delle Dose, Campo San Maurizio, San Marco 2683, 30124 Venezia 041 241 3765 €140–€260 9 Giglio

PAUSANIA

www.hotelpausania.it

This 14th-century palazzo, complete with quadruple lancet windows, stunning staircase and an original well, was refurbished in 2002. Public areas have marble floors, understated furnishings, Murano glass chandeliers and frescoed ceilings. The similarly decorated bedrooms are spacious and well equipped, all with a private bathroom, telephone, television, radio and minibar. The buffet breakfast is served in a room overlooking the wonderful garden—a rarity in Venice. Make sure you reserve a room in plenty of time, as this is a very popular hotel.

Fondamenta Gheradini, Dorsoduro 2824, 30123 Venezia 041 522 2083 €65–€340 24 Ca' Rezzonico

PENSIONE ACCADEMIA VILLA MARAVAGE

www.pensioneaccademia.it

Verdant courtyard gardens, Grand Canal views and helpful staff complement this hotel, which is in a great location for art-lovers. Once called Villa Maravege, it is a former Russian embassy. The stately rooms have wooden floors, 19th-century furniture and chandeliers. All rooms have private bathroom, television and phone. The Continental breakfast spread provides a bountiful choice and can be enjoyed on the tranquil canalside terrace. Early reservations are recommended.

Fondamenta Bollani, Dorsoduro 1058, 30123 Venezia 041 521 0188 €140–€280 27 Accademia

LA RESIDENZA

www.venicelaresidenza.com

This handsome palazzo hotel is reasonably priced by Venetian standards. The Gothic facade, with its 10th-century sculptural details, overlooks the peaceful Campo Bandiera e Moro to the south. Request one of the refurbished rooms, which have a fresh, bright feel and period pieces. Facilities include a television, safe and minibar.

Campo Bandiera e Moro, Castello 3608, 30122 Venezia 041 528 5315 €80–€180 15 Arsenale

SAN CLEMENTE PALACE

www.sanclementepalacevenice.com

Set on its own little island, close to St. Mark's yet far away from the throngs, this elegant hotel is spiritually on another plane. A complimentary shuttle boat whisks you to this haven of elegance, where every pampering comfort awaits, including a spa. The rooms are luxurious yet restrained, a reminder of the San Clemente's monastic heritage. There are lagoon-side terraces for taking the air, and a very good restaurant, Le Maschere.

Isola di San Clemente, private dal pontile San Marco, 30124 Venezia 041 244 5001 €215–€430 172 rooms, 28 suites San Marco (private shuttle)

VENETIAN APARTMENTS

www.venice-rentals.com

This British company offers a wide range of exclusive apartments

From €650 for 3 nights for a studio

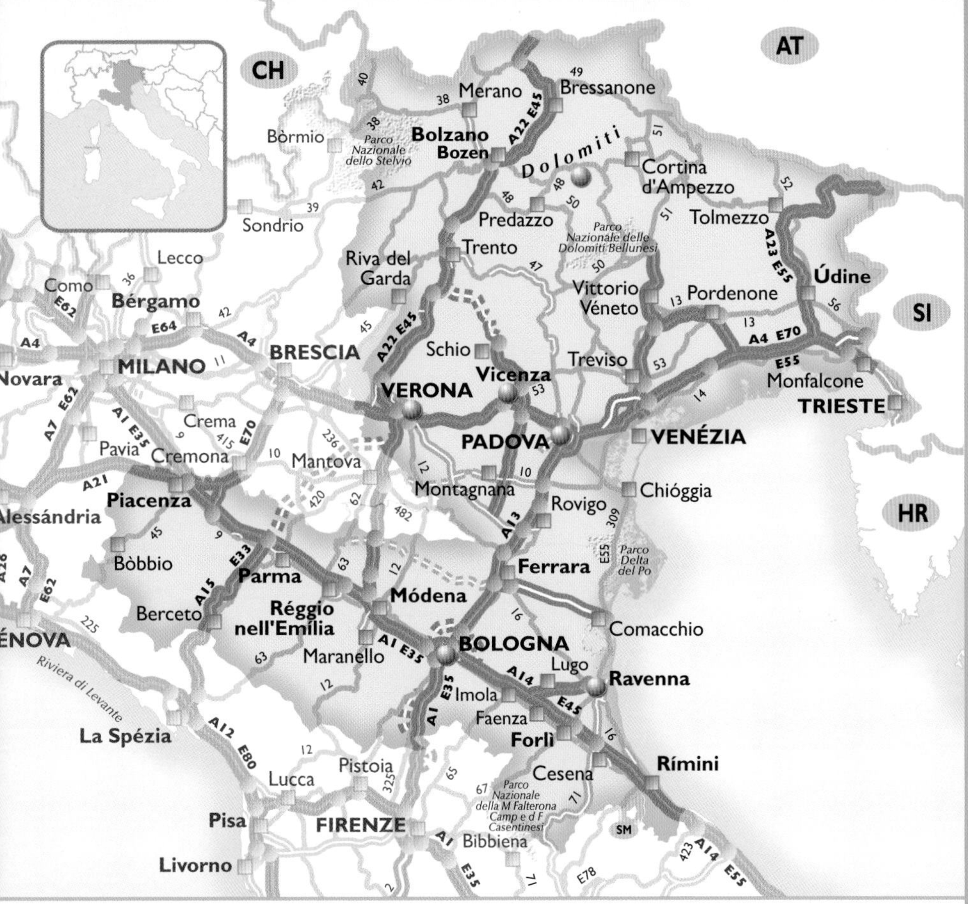

THE NORTHEAST AND EMILIA-ROMAGNA

The landscape of Emilia-Romagna and northeast Italy packs in the delights: mountains and plains, rivers and coastlines. In the north, the Alps, seen at their most spikily dramatic in the chain of the Dolomites, fall away via green and fertile valleys to the flatlands of the Veneto, Venice's hinterland, and the eastern plains that stretch to the borders of Slovakia. The Dolomites are among Europe's most splendid peaks, at their best in the Parco Nazionale dello Stelvio, with its ridges, valleys, lakes and glaciers and wonderful skiing and hiking. South of here, across the plains, the coastline is flat and sandy, with a series of lagoons, the marshy and serpentine estuary of the great River Po, swathes of aromatic pines and long beaches running south to the border with the Marche. Behind this coast lie softer valleys and hills, while Emilia-Romagna's green and gold landscape is gentle and intensely agricultural.

The towns and cities echo the land. In the north, the German-speaking towns of Bolzano, Merano and Bressanone, all deep in the Dolomites, are essentially Alpine, northern settlements, where pasta and a decent cup of coffee are more difficult to come by, while Trieste (home of Illy coffee, Italy's leading brand), Udine and Cividale dei Friuli have historically always looked east into central Europe, with its stolid architecture, noodles and cream cakes. Lovely Trento, lying in an Alpine valley in the southern Dolomites, and Treviso, in the foothills, mark the return to the Veneto and Emilia-Romagna and 'real' Italy, where rose-red Verona boasts one of Italy's greatest Roman monuments and sleepy Ravenna preserves some of the world's finest and oldest mosaics. Up the coast, wealthy Padova (Padua) is a historic university city, while to the east, Emilia-Romagna's capital, Bologna, seamlessly combines historic, intellectual and artistic heritage with a role as one of Italy's most vibrant business centres. Bologna's lovely satellite cities of Vicenza, Modena, Parma and Ferrara perfectly illustrate the long history and modern prosperity of this part of Italy.

AQUILEIA

www.turismo.fvg.it

Most great Roman cities were transformed into settlements that survive as modern cities, but Aquileia (33km/20 miles south of Udine), once the fourth most important centre in Italy (after Rome, Milan and Capua), is little more than a tangle of ruins, a few houses and a superb Romanesque basilica. Founded in 181BC as a defensive and trading hub, it is now a peaceful town with a rich heritage.

In AD314, a Christian patriarchate was founded here and Theodore, the first patriarch, built a basilica. A devastating earthquake in 1348 destroyed most of the exterior, but inside is a different matter. A fabulously preserved swathe of 750sq m (8,000sq feet) of the richly coloured original fourth-century mosaic has been uncovered, stretching the entire length of the nave. It was discovered only 100 years ago, having lain under rubble for centuries. In 2000 a major restoration was carried out, and the mosaics were painstakingly polished stone by stone. Christian and pagan themes are combined, with heavy emphasis on fish mosaics, the symbol of God. Other symbols include the cock, representing the church of Rome, and the lowly tortoise, depicting heresy.

Around the basilica and bell tower lie the grassy ruins of the Roman city, much of whose stone was stolen by the Venetians for their buildings. You can climb the bell tower and see the Roman finds in the Museo Archeologico and the Museo Paleocristiano.

Nearby, the lagoon resort of Grado, 12km (7 miles) away, was known as the official health resort for the Hapsburg Empire at the end of the 19th century. The thermal baths and spa are as popular now as then, basking in the gentle microclimate, with long stretches of beach lapped by warm, shallow waters.

465 J3 Via Julia Augusta, Piazzale Terminal, 33051 Aquileia 0431 919491 Viale Dante Alighieri 72, Grado 0431 877111; fax 0431 83509

BOLOGNA

▷ 204–205.

BOLZANO (BOZEN)

www.bolzano-bozen.it

Residents of Bolzano enjoy one of the highest standards of living in Italy. The town is a good starting point for a trip into the Dolomites (▷ 207, 216–217). It is strongly Tyrolean—it was only after World War I that it became part of Italy. It lies at the heart of an excellent wine-producing region, and has a handful of sights, plenty of cafés and one of the best museums in the Alto-Adige (Südtirol).

The town stands at the confluence of the rivers Talfer (Talvera) and Eisack (Isarco), 86km (53 miles) northeast of Trento and surrounded by mountains whose lower slopes are planted with vines and apple trees. West of the Talfer sprawls the 'Italian' town, laid out by Mussolini in the late 1920s. Most visitors concentrate on the old town to the east, where arcaded streets spread out from the central Waltherplatz (Piazza Walther). The duomo stands on one side, a distinctive building whose tower is a local landmark.

Ötzi, nicknamed 'the Iceman', the 5,000 year-old body of a man frozen in the ice and discovered in 1991, can be seen in the Museo Archeologico (Tue–Sun 10–6; www.iceman.it).

464 G2 Waltherplatz/Piazza Walther 8, 39100 Bolzano 0471 307000 Bolzano/Bozen

BRESSANONE (BRIXEN)

www.brixen.org

Bressanone makes a good stopping-off point en route to the Brenner Pass. It is a popular year-round resort, with winter access to miles of pistes and excellent summer walking.

Founded in 901 as the seat of an important bishopric, the town stands on the River Eisack, 47km (29 miles) northeast of Bolzano. The heart of the town is focused on the duomo, with porticoed streets and frescoed medieval buildings. The duomo was ruthlessly modernized in the 18th century, but the Romanesque cloisters are intact. Local artists created the frescoes in the 1390s and there are more examples in the 11th-century baptistery. There is a collection of crib figures in the crypt. The duomo's treasure is kept in the Museo Diocesano, in the 13th-century Bishop's Palace.

You can sample a local wine at the Abbazia di Novacella, just north of town.

465 G2 Viale Stazione/Bahnhofstrasse 9, 39042 Bressanone 0472 836401 Bressanone/Brixen

CIVIDALE DEL FRIULI

www.cividale.com

A few miles from the Slovenian border, delightful Cividale (7km/10 miles east of Udine), founded by Julius Caesar in 50BC, is little known to visitors. Its medieval streets and squares line the banks of the River Natisone, and it is one of the few places in Italy with tangible reminders of the Lombards (▷ 33). This Teutonic race invaded in the sixth century, embraced Christianity and left behind some of the finest Lombard carvings in Italy.

Simply walking around Cividale is a pleasure; it is small enough to get your bearings but big enough to have some great architecture. The river, spanned by the Ponte del Diavolo (Devil's Bridge), is particularly pretty. Cividale's sights lie west of the river; the pearl is the Tempietto Longobardo (Lombard Temple), whose eighth-century stucco arch, with gently smiling saints, is a peerless example of Lombard art. There is more Lombard carving in the Museo Cristiano (in the precincts of the 15th-century duomo), notably the baptismal font of Callisto and the altar of Ratchis, a haunting masterpiece.

The main museum is the Museo Archeologico Nazionale (Mon 9–1.30, Tue–Sun 8.30–7), where finds from Lombard tombs include stunning carvings and intricate jewellery.

465 J3 Piazza Paolo Diacono 10, 33043 Cividale del Friuli 0432 710460; Mon–Fri 9–1, 3–6 Cividale del Friuli

Opposite *Karneid Castle at the end of the Eggental, with Bolzano in the distance*

INFORMATION

www.bolognaturismo.info
466 F5 Piazza Maggiore 1, 40124 Bologna 051 239660 Daily 9–8 Bologna

Above *Café in a portico on Via Rizzoli by the Torre Garisenda (one of the two surviving leaning towers)*

INTRODUCTION

Inner Bologna is endowed with beautiful streetscapes—arcades of mellow brick and stone and wide piazzas that contrast with the outlying stark shapes characteristic of the high-tech industry that generates the money sustaining the expensive restaurants and shops. It is a classic Roman city that, after the Dark Ages, became a free commune and subsequently, in the 15th century, gave way to rule by an individual family, the Bentivoglio, until annexed by the Papal States. It has earned many nicknames, from La Dotta (the Learned), for having one of Europe's oldest universities, to La Rossa (the Red), as much for its buildings as for its politics, and La Grassa (the Fat), for its gastronomic excellence.

WHAT TO SEE

THE MEDIEVAL CORE

The compact historic core is medieval in plan, scattered with churches, monuments, civic buildings and museums. Elegant porticoed streets radiate from the two main squares, Piazza Maggiore and Piazza del Nettuno, with most of what you'll want to see lying on the eastern side of the city. Around Piazza del Nettuno, named after Giambologna's 16th-century Fontana del Nettuno, rise medieval civic palaces and, to the east, the Torre Pendenti (Leaning Towers) two surviving towers of the dozens that once bristled up from the heart of the city. Both lean alarmingly; you can climb the 498 steps of the 97.6m (320ft) Torre degli Asinelli (Apr–Oct daily 9–6; Nov–Mar 9–5; €3), built around 1120, and take in the stupendous city views. Next to the Piazza del Nettuno lies Piazza Maggiore, Bologna's civic heart since the 13th century, dominated by the Gothic Basilica of San Petronio. Its central doorway is decorated with wonderful statues by the Sienese sculptor, Jacopo della Quercia, while the interior is rich in marble screens, majolica tiling and stained glass. Opposite is the Palazzo dei Notai, home to 14th-century lawyers, and the Museo Civico Archeologico (Tue–Fri 9–3, Sat–Sun 10–6.30; free).

Farther east are some of the loveliest streets and buildings—a series of porticoes punctuated by attractive squares. Head for Via Clavatura, with tempting food stands displaying all that's best of local produce, before exploring the Arciginnasio complex, a beautiful 16th-century palazzo and courtyard that was once part of the university. Its chief draw is the Teatro Anatomico (Anatomy Theatre, 1637), the old medical school's dissection theatre, where students sat in tiered seats to watch the dissection of human corpses, and the first place in Europe to introduce this method. More arcades lead south to the church of San Domenico, built in 1251 to house the relics of the saint, which are enclosed in the superb Arco di San Domenico, sculpted by Pisano and the young Michelangelo. Head north from here to take in the trio of ancient churches known as Santo Stefano (daily 9–12.30, 3.30–6.30). No complex better illustrates Bologna's long history than these lovely churches, dating from the 10th to 12th centuries. The Crocifisso, on the right and heavily restored, is the oldest, San Sepolcro, in the centre, was built in the 11th century, while San Vitale e Agricola is Romanesque and dedicated to the city's first martyrs; it stands on the site of a Roman temple. A lovely early courtyard, centred around an eighth-century basin, and a serene 12th-century Benedictine cloister add to the sense of tranquillity.

AROUND THE UNIVERSITY

Behind the Torre Pendenti, Via Zamboni is the heart of the university. It was founded in the 11th century, making it one of the oldest universities in the world. Along this street lie lecture halls, administrative buildings and some of the university's museums, covering everything from astronomy to obstetrics. You can wander in and out of the various buildings, and you shouldn't miss Palazzo Poggi (Nos. 31–33, museums Tue–Fri 10–1, 2–4, Sat–Sun 10.30–1.30, 2.30–5.30; free), built in 1549. Its main entrance leads to a handsome courtyard, surrounded by the Aula Carducci, a fine lecture theatre, and the Specola, one of 18th-century Europe's leading observatories. The Museo Ostetrico (Obstetric Museum) is fascinating for its meticulously modelled wax replicas of foetuses and the various instruments used to help women in childbirth. Stop off at No. 35 to take in the University Library before heading for the Pinacoteca Nazionale (Via Belle Arti 56, Tue–Sun 9–7; €4), Bologna's main art gallery, packed with medieval, Renaissance and baroque works.

NORTH FROM THE CENTRE

North from Piazza Maggiore, Via dell'Indipendenza, a long, beautifully porticoed street, was built in the 19th century to link the centre with the railway station. It is home to Bologna's Metropolitana (Cathedral), an ancient foundation that was remodelled in the early 17th century; its Romanesque campanile and crypt are highlights. Farther down, the street is lined with good, mid-range shops, where you can browse for leather goods, clothes and food products. At the far end, just inside the line of the old city walls, is the city's main park, the Montagnola, a formally laid out green space that is approached by a fine staircase.

TIPS

» Bologna makes few concessions to tourists, so don't expect cheap accommodation or restaurants, other than in the university area. It is vital to reserve a hotel in advance as rooms are in constant demand during trade fairs.

» Two organizations provide 2-hour guided walks (in English) from the tourist office in Piazza Maggiore. No reservations required.

» There are 40-minute tours of the Museo della Specola at the university. For information about tours in English, tel 051 209 9398.

Below *Piazza Maggiore by night*

CONEGLIANO

www.tourism.provincia.treviso.it

Low-key but prosperous, Conegliano is a beguiling mix of simple buildings and expensive antique shops. It's an excellent stop en route north through the Veneto. The town perches on the edge of the hilly area, 33km (20 miles) north of Treviso, surrounded by vineyards that produce the best *prosecco,* a light, dry, sparkling wine. In 2009 Conegliano's *prosecco* earned DOCG status (Denominazione di Origine Controllata e Garantita), the highest award to be given to Italian wines. You can follow the Strada del Prosecco west to Valdobbiadene.

Conegliano neatly splits into a medieval and Renaissance old town and a grander, neoclassical quarter. In the old section, the Contrada Grande/Via XX Settembre, is an arcaded street lined with *palazzi,* restaurants and shops. The duomo, with a 14th-century frescoed portico, lies west of the main square, Piazza Cima. Farther uphill is the birthplace of Conegliano's most famous resident, the High Renaissance painter Giambattista Cima (*c*1459–1517). Look for his *Sacra Conversazione* in the duomo. Above town looms the *castello* (castle), now the town's museum. The collection is unexciting, but the views enjoyed while strolling uphill are superb.

465 H3 Via XX Settembre 61, 31015 Conegliano 0438 21230 Conegliano

DOLOMITES

▷ 207

FERRARA

www.ferrarainfo.com

A major player on the Renaissance political scene, Ferrara was ruled by the dynamic d'Este family. Their court was one of Europe's most prosperous, and their money paid for the palaces and artistic treasures that are scattered around. Beautiful Romanesque facades, excellent museums, medieval streets and gracious piazzas make up the city.

Ferrara stands on the banks of the Po di Volano, an offshoot of the River Po, 55km (35 miles) northeast of Bologna. Within the walls, which can be explored on foot or by bicycle, the city is divided by the Viale Cavour/Corso Giovacca. Most sights of interest lie in the *centro storico* to the south. Start at Castello Estense (Tue–Sun 9.30–5.30; €2), a bulky, moated 14th-century fortification with sumptuous state apartments and spooky dungeons. The cathedral has a beautiful Romanesque-Gothic facade and an interior of 18th-century ornate gold. Follow the vaulted Via delle Volte south to the Palazzo Schifanoia, a former Este summer palace, or cross the Viale Cavour to the Palazzo dei Diamanti, where there are four museums, including the Pinacoteca Nazionale, tracing the history of painting in Ferrara.

464 G5 Castello Estense, 44100 Ferrara 0532 209370 Ferrara

MERANO (MERAN)

www.meran.eu

If you plan to explore the Alto-Adige (Südtirol) and want a base with a touch of sophistication, Merano is a good choice. It has chic shops (with an Austrian accent), restaurants and hotels, a lively cultural scene, gracious architecture, promenades and pretty gardens. This mountain-ringed town, with an unexpected Mediterranean-type microclimate, found a new role for itself in the 1800s as a major spa resort. Elegant thermal buildings, solid villas and civic buildings were built around its medieval heart.

The town lies on the banks of the Passirio River, 30km (19 miles) northwest of Bolzano (▷ 203). The buildings of the medieval core cluster around the duomo, while 13th- and 14th-century arcaded streets run parallel to the river. Passeggiata d'Estate and Passeggiata d'Inverno are two beautiful garden walks laid out in the 1860s and the 1870s. The terraced Trautmansdorff Botanical Gardens are planted with shrubs and trees from all over the world.

464 F2 Corso Libertà 45, 39012 Merano 0473 272000 Merano/Meran

MODENA

www.turismo.comune.modena.it

Modena, a quietly prosperous town along the Via Emilia, makes a good outing from Bologna, 55km (35 miles) southeast (▷ 204–205). Historically Modena is a rival to Bologna, but it has an entirely different atmosphere. It has a splendid Romanesque cathedral, tranquil arcaded squares, baroque palaces and an excellent museum complex. Today's money comes from the knitwear, ceramics and Ferrari car factories on its outskirts. Modena's most famous modern citizen, the late opera singer Luciano Pavarotti, used to give the occasional summer concert here. It is good for shopping and there are some excellent restaurants and bars.

The town's historic core is split by the Via Emilia. To the south is Piazza Grande, with arcades and elegant cafés. Alongside is the magnificent 12th-century Romanesque duomo, with a leaning tower and fine carving. The web of medieval streets and pleasant squares makes Modena a serendipitous place to explore.

466 F5 Via Scudari 8, 41100 Modena 0592 032660 Modena

Below *Castel Tirolo (Schloss Tirol) near Merano was built in the 12th century*

DOLOMITES

Fertile green valleys, villages of wooden houses with window boxes dripping with geraniums, swathes of mountain flowers and air like champagne make the Dolomites an outdoor feast. Geologically different from the rest of the Alps, the Dolomites are composed of ancient coral reefs, formed beneath the seabed 250 million years ago and uplifted 190 million years later. Wind, ice and storms acted on the relatively soft, pinky-orange limestone, creating the astounding shapes that are so distinctive. The lower slopes are wooded or covered in alpine pasture, and vines and apples are cultivated in the fertile valley.

YEAR-ROUND ACTIVITIES

In the 20th century the massifs developed into a year-round recreational area. There are ski resorts and a good network of cable cars and lifts. There are pistes to suit all levels and there is cross-country skiing, sledging and tobogganing in the valleys. The walking is some of the best in Europe, with a network of scenic trails. Accessed by cable cars and lifts, they are linked by *rifugi alpini* (mountain refuges, end Jun–Sep). By using the refuges, you can walk the *alte vie*, eight long-distance trails.

THE DIFFERENT REGIONS

The Italian-speaking Cadore Dolomites lie north of Belluno in the Veneto. The main resort is the glitzy Cortina d'Ampezzo, venue for the 1956 Winter Olympics.

In the western Dolomites, Trento (▷ 211) and Bolzano (▷ 203) are two beautiful main towns. The Val di Fassa is the heart of the old Ladino region. An exhibition at the Castel de Tor Museum is dedicated to this unique culture; the Ladino language is still alive, and each valley has its own dialect. To the west rises the Catinaccio/Rosengarten Massif, one of the most dramatic ranges.
The main areas of the Brenta group are Madonna di Campiglio and Molveno. Dramatic rock formations, summer walking and winter sports make the area very popular. The most important valleys are the Val di Sole, with meadows and pretty villages, and the wooded Val di Non.

INFORMATION

www.dolomiti.com
www.vinschgau.suedtirol.com
www.dolomitipark.it
465 G2 Piazza Duomo 2, 32100 Belluno 0437 940083 Piazzetta San Francesco 8, 32043 Cortina d'Ampezzo 0436 3231 Daily 9–12.30, 3.30–6.30 Trento, Bolzano/Bolzen, Merano/Meran

TIPS

» If you plan some serious walking, invest in good maps (available in most villages—Kompass maps are excellent) and take proper equipment and provisions.
» Remember that even over short distances driving can take time as the roads are twisty.
» It is worth learning a few basic German phrases.

Above *Cortina d'Ampezzo is surrounded by splendid peaks and is a great base for skiing holidays*

INFORMATION

www.turismopadova.it
465 G4 Railway station: Stazione Ferroviaria, 35100 Padova 049 875 2077 Galleria Pedrocchi, 35100 Padova 049 876 7927 Mon–Sat 9–1.30, 3–7 Padova

TIPS

» Driving in Padua is confusing and parking a problem, so come by train. The station is about 10 minutes' walk from the centre and there are buses.
» The main tourist office is in the station, so pick up a map as soon as you arrive.
» Access to the Cappella degli Scrovegni is limited to 25 people at a time; advance reservations are compulsory. Book online or by phone at least 24 hours in advance (tel 049 201 0020, Mon–Fri 9–7, Sat 9–6; www.cappelladegliscrovegni.it). Admission costs €12 for adults, €5 for children, plus €1 reservation fee. Evening visits are less expensive.

Above *The Basilica di Sant'Antonio was dedicated to St. Antony of Padua*

PADOVA

Historic Padova (Padua), the Veneto's most important economic hub and an ancient university city, combines lively, spacious squares and narrow medieval streets with important works of art and monuments, elegant shops, buzzing markets and green spaces. With its efficient transport connections, it is also a good base for exploring the region.

WHERE TO GO

Padua's overlords were the Da Carrara family from 1337 until the capture of the city by the Venetian Republic in 1405. Great cultural patrons, they attracted stars such as Giotto, Dante and Petrarch, and Padua remained a cultural focus even after the fall of the city. Many people come only to see Giotto's frescoes in the Cappella degli Scrovegni and the Venetian art collections in the Musei Civici; others head straight for the attractive squares, Piazza della Frutta and Piazza dell'Erbe. The two are divided by the bulk of the 13th-century Palazzo della Ragione or Il Salone (Tue–Sun 9–7), ringed with cafés, bars and shops. The Caffè Pedrocchi on Via VIII Febbraio was once Padua's main intellectual salon (Tue–Fri 9.30–12.30, 3.30–6, Sat–Sun 9.30–12.30, 3.30–7; bar: daily 8am–11pm).

BASILICA DI SANT'ANTONIO

The Basilica di Sant'Antonio (or Il Santo) is one of Italy's main pilgrim shrines (Apr–end Oct daily 6.30am–7.45pm; Nov–end Mar daily 6.30am–7pm, tel 049 824 2811), begun after the death in 1232 of St. Anthony of Padua. In the square is Donatello's equestrian bronze statue of the mercenary Erasmo de Narni, known as *Gattamelata* (Honey Cat).

GIOTTO AND THE VENETIAN SCHOOL

Padua's most precious jewels are in Cappella degli Scrovegni (daily 9–7, plus some evening visits, 7–10pm; reserve ahead—see Tips) and the adjoining Museo Civico on Piazza Eremitani (daily 9am–7pm). Between 1303 and 1309 Giotto painted a series of scenes in the chapel from the life of Christ and the Virgin. Like his Assisi cycle (▷ 271), this marked a turning point in Western art, introducing a naturalism not seen in the stylized art of the Middle Ages. The museum's excellent collection of works by Paduan and Venetian artists includes a Giotto crucifix and two exquisite Giorgione paintings.

PARCO NAZIONALE DELLO STELVIO

www.stelviopark.it

The Parco Nazionale dello Stelvio embraces the entire Ortles range, sprawling across Lombardy, Trentino and the Alto Adige (Südtirol). It is one of Italy's most important and largest national parks, ideal for winter sports and spectacular summer walking. The landscape includes high peaks, fertile valleys, woodland, more than 50 lakes and 100 glaciers. There is a great deal of diversity in the animal and plantlife here. The park is criss-crossed with superb hiking trails, and many visitors head away from the roads, spending nights in *rifugi alpini* (mountain refuges).

The Ortles (3,950m/12,960ft) are south of the Val Venosta (Vinschgau), a broad valley east of Merano (▷ 206). Three roads thread through the foothills from the valley into the massif: Val Martello, Val d'Ultimo and Val di Solda. These are jumping-off points for the park. In summer drivers can cross the park via Passo dello Stelvio (2,758m/ 9,050ft), the second-highest pass in the Alps (early Jul to mid-Sep). Begin your explorations at the park's main information office in Glorenza, a miniature walled city. The whole area is very Austrian so away from the tourist areas it helps if you speak German.

✚ 464 F2 ℹ Comitato di Gestione per la Provincia Autonoma di Bolzano, Piazza Municipio 1, 39020 Glorenza ☎ 0473 830430

PARMA

www.turismo.comune.parma.it

Parma's name is synonymous with *prosciutto* (Parma ham) and *parmigiano* (Parmesan cheese). But this rich, cultured provincial city also has artistic treasures and a strong musical tradition. The old city has a beautiful cathedral, Renaissance palaces, and a famous opera house. It also has good designer shops.

Parma's three most famous residents are the artists Correggio (*c*1490–1534) and Parmigianino (1503–40) and the musician Artur Toscanini (1867–1957).

The elegant, pedestrianized streets at the heart of the city are on the east of the River Parma. The three main piazzas—della Pace, Duomo and Garibaldi—are as different in themselves as Parma's most important monuments. Most notable are the 11th-century duomo (daily 9–12.30, 3–7), a lovely Lombard-Romanesque church with interior frescoes by Correggio, and the beautiful octagonal 12th-century baptistery, built of pink Verona marble with sculpted friezes. This simple ensemble contrasts with the Renaissance magnificence of Santa Maria della Steccata and its frescoes by Parmigianino (daily 9–12, 3–6). Also important are the artistic pieces in the Palazzo della Pilotta, the perfectly restored Renaissance Teatro Farnese and, across the river, the Palazzo Ducale (Mon–Sat 9–12). The Casa Natale e Musei di Arturo Toscanini, the birthplace of Tocanini, is on Via Rodolfo Tanzi.

✚ 463 E5 ℹ Via Melloni 1, 43100 Parma ☎ 0521 218889 🚉 Parma

PIACENZA

www.provincia.piacenza.it

Piacenza is a perfect example of Emilia-Romagna's unostentatious, prosperous provincial towns. It is off the main tourist trail, near the Lombardy border. The Roman town marked the end of the Via Emilia, a major military road. In the Middle Ages it flourished as a free city, then came under the control of the Farnese and the Bourbons, and was the first town to join the embryonic Italian state in 1848 (▷ 40). It has fine medieval buildings and churches, a couple of museums and good shops and restaurants. The Lombard-Gothic, red-brick Palazzo del Comune dates from 1280, as does the church of San Francesco. Piazza del Duomo is the scene of a weekly market.

Note, however, that lying in the flat Po Valley, the town is misty and raw in winter and baking hot in summer.

✚ 463 D4 ℹ Piazza dei Cavalli 7, 29100 Piacenza ☎ 0523 329324 🚉 Piacenza

RAVENNA

▷ 210.

RIMINI

www.riminiturismo.it

Rimini's beaches, 51km (32 miles) south of Ravenna, stretch for more than 16km (10 miles), a strip of hotels, arcades, shops, restaurants and clubs. In peak season the resort heaves with noisy crowds day and night; off-season, it is very quiet. The beach has very few free areas but many privately owned *stabilimenti,* fenced-off areas that you pay to use. The hotels are good, but there is virtually no accommodation available in August, as Italian families pour in.

If hedonism doesn't appeal, explore the amphitheatre, palazzi and the Renaissance Tempio Malatestiano, an unusual building that served as a chapel and a monument to Sigismondo Malatesta, a 15th-century mercenary. The town is also the birthplace of film director Federico Fellini (1920–93), and you can visit the Museo Fellini in the Via Nigra.

✚ 467 H6 ℹ Piazza Federico Fellini 3, 47900 Rimini ☎ 0541 56902 🚉 Rimini

Below *Orderly ranks of sunbathers along Rimini's long stretch of sandy beach*

INFORMATION

www.turismo.ra.it
www.ravennamosaici.it
467 G6 Via Salara 8–12, 48100 Ravenna 0544 35755 Mon–Sat 8.30–7 (till 6 Oct–Mar), Sun 10–4
Ravenna

Battistero Neoniano, Mausoleo di Galla Placidia, Sant'Apollinare Nuovo, San Vitale 0544 541 688 (for advance booking)

TIPS

» The Ravenna Visitcard is a combined ticket for all the main sights. Buy it at any of the sights in low season or reserve in advance.

» To see the mosaics at Sant'Apollinare in Classe, take bus 4 or 44 (hourly) from outside the railway station.

» The main sights are floodlit and open on Friday evenings throughout July and August.

» After his expulsion from Florence in 1302, Dante spent the last 19 years of his life in Ravenna and wrote most of his *Divine Comedy* here. You can see his tomb at Via d'Alighieri 9 (daily 9.30–6.30). The oil for the perpetually burning lamp is provided by Florence.

Above *One of the early mosaics in the chapel of the Mausoleo di Galla Placidia*

RAVENNA

In AD402, with the imperial court installed at Milan and the Roman Empire threatened by invaders from the north, Emperor Honorius decided to move his capital to Ravenna, an easily defensible marshland town near the important naval base of Classis, on the Adriatic coast. After the fall of Rome in AD410, Ravenna became the imperial capital, fittingly ornamented with lavish monuments. The city fell to the Goths in AD476, but they, too, were Christian and pursued the building design, a process continued by the Byzantines after their annexation of Ravenna in the sixth century. The city later came under Venetian control, but was sacked in the 16th century and absorbed into the Papal States, becoming part of Italy after 1870. Ravenna was heavily bombed in World War II and it has been extensively rebuilt, but it still has an important port, 12km (8 miles) from the old city.

THE MOSAICS

The most important sites date from fifth- and sixth-century Roman, Ostrogoth and Byzantine eras, and are UNESCO World Heritage Sites. They are scattered around the Piazza del Popolo, where shoppers on bicycles weave in front of outdoor cafés. A few minutes' walk south is the complex of the Basilica of San Vitale, the Mausoleum of Galla Placidia and the Museo Nazionale.

San Vitale (Via Fiandrini; Nov–Feb daily 10–5; Mar and Oct daily 9.30–5.30; Apr–Sep daily 9–7) was begun in 525 under the Roman Emperor Theodoric and completed by the Byzantine ruler Justinian in 548. It is typically Byzantine, with a central dome supported by eight columns. The apse is covered with glowing mosaics showing Christ, the Apostles, and biblical scenes in the choir, while the side walls are covered in processional scenes. Across the grass is the Mausoleum of Galla Placidia, half-sister of Honorius (▷ 33; Via Fiandrini; Nov–Feb daily 10–5; Mar and Oct daily 9.30–5.30; Apr–Sep daily 9–7). Tiny and jewel-like, it is richly ornamented with blue and gold mosaics, the oldest in Ravenna. Also important is the Basilica of Sant'Apollinare Nuovo (Via di Roma; Nov–Feb daily 10–5; Mar and Oct daily 9.30–5.30; Apr–Sep daily 9–7), built in the sixth century by Theodoric; mosaics high above the nave show martyrs bearing gifts for Christ and the Virgin. There are more mosaics in the baptisteries (Via Battistero; Nov–Feb daily 10–5; Mar and Oct daily 9.30–5.30; Apr–Sep daily 9–7), and a short bus ride away, at Classe, in the evocative Basilica di Sant'Apollinare (Apr–Sep daily 9–7; Mar, Oct 9.30–5.30; Nov–Feb 10–5).

TRENTO

www.apt.trento.it

Capital of Trentino, and 150km (93 miles) north of Verona, Trento stands on the River Adige, surrounded by green hills. Ruled for centuries by prince-bishops, the town rose to prominence when Bishop Bernardo Cles made it the meeting place for the 16th-century Council of Trent, the Counter-Reformation movement. He opened up the old medieval town with the construction of Via Belenzani, which cuts a straight line through to Piazza Duomo, site of the Romanesque duomo.

At the foot of the hills is Castello del Buonconsiglio, the prince-bishops' residence and one of the first castle-palaces in Italy. Its courtyards, loggias and sumptuous state apartments form the perfect setting for Trento's greatest artistic work, the ravishing fresco cycle *The Months of the Year* (*c*1400), full of images of flirting nobility and working peasants.

For a change of pace, take the cable car up Monte Bondone to see the alpine plants in the botanical garden at Viotte.

464 F3 Via Manci 2, 38100 Trento 0461 216000 Trento

TREVISO

www.provincia.treviso.it
www.marcatreviso.it

With frescoed facades, porticoed streets and shimmering waterways, historic Treviso is quite different from nearby towns. Modern money comes from knitwear—Treviso is home to Benetton (▷ 19)—while past glories are reflected in fine early Gothic buildings and Renaissance churches. The city was painstakingly rebuilt after bombing in World War II, and there is a great sense of the new Italy here, with relics of the past co-existing happily with casual, stylish wealth. The excellent shops include tempting delicatessens, and the nightlife buzzes.

Treviso is ringed by Venetian-built walls, bordered by the River Sile. Willow-fringed branches of the river weave through the old town, at the heart of which is the Piazza dei Signori. Here is the Palazzo dei Trecento, first built in 1217, and behind are the churches of San Vito and Santa Lucia, with superb frescoes by the 14th-century Tommaso da Modena, considered the finest artist of his age after Giotto. To the east is a maze of streets and waterways around the bustling market (don't miss the *pescheria*, fish market). Calmaggiore is an attractive arcaded street with fine shops. At the far end, the duomo has a Titian *Annunciation*, but more interesting artistically is the Dominican church of San Nicolò, which is rich with frescoes.

465 G3 Piazza Monte di Pietà 8, 31100 Treviso 0422 547632 Treviso

TRIESTE

www.turismo.fvg.it

Trieste was built by the Austrians as a port. Its slightly battered neoclassical streets and buildings contrast with a clutch of Roman remains and a dramatic medieval castle and cathedral. With its café culture, literary associations (Irish writer James Joyce lived here in the 1920s) and contrasting socialist and right-wing politics, Trieste is border territory—a mix of cultures, languages and allegiances that straddles the bridge between the Mediterranean world and that of Teutonic and Slavic central Europe. With exceptionally friendly people, great food and a thriving café society, it is an ideal base for exploring the Carso, a plateau that stretches into Slovenia.

Trieste's position is stunning, with a grid of 18th-century streets, the Borgo Teresiano, nestling between the sea and a limestone plateau. Piazza Unità d'Italia is a splendid square, open on one side to the sea. Behind rises the hill of San Giusto, where you find the city's oldest buildings with the best sea views. Highlights are the Romanesque Cattedrale di San Giusto, Venetian mosaics and a 13th-century fresco cycle in the Capella di San Giusto, and the Risiera di San Sabba, a thought-provoking museum in a World War II concentration camp.

435 K4 Piazza Unità d'Italia 4B, 34121 Trieste 040 347 8312; daily 9.30–7 Trieste Trieste R dei Legionari (TRS)

UDINE

www.turismofug.it

More Italian in spirit than Trieste, Udine is the second city of Friuli-Venezia Giulia. It is a provincial town with more than a touch of Venetian style—arcaded streets, canals, restaurants and a relaxed pace make it worth exploring. It is also a stronghold of Friulian nationalism—listen for Slovenian influences in the dialect.

As in many Italian cities, the sprawling outskirts might put you off, but the *centro storico* is unspoiled. It is overshadowed by the *castello*, said to have been built with soil carried in the helmets of Attila's invading Huns (▷ 32). Reach it from Piazza della Libertà, described as the most beautiful Venetian square on *terra firma*: the striped Loggia del Lionello echoes the Doge's Palace (▷ 176–179); there is a lion of St. Mark, and a fine Palladio gateway leading past a Venetian Gothic gallery to the castle.

465 J3 Piazza I Maggio 7, 33100 Udine 0432 295972 Udine

Below *Treviso's old town is filled with attractive 15th- and 16th-century streets*

INTRODUCTION

Beautiful Verona—Roman ruins, rose-red medieval buildings and romantic dreams of young love—is the largest city in mainland Veneto, a quietly prosperous, cultured place where tourism plays second fiddle to the rest of the economy. Most of its historic heart is enclosed by a loop of the River Adige, with a few other important sights on the north bank. Wonderful churches and buildings are scattered throughout the pleasant streets.

Verona is on the River Adige, 50km (30 miles) west of Vicenza, at the bottom of an Alpine pass, and was first colonized by the Romans in 89BC. It became a regional capital and survived the Ostrogoth and Frankish invasions of AD489 and AD754, becoming a free *comune* in 1107. Feuds and vendettas between the city's noble families dominated the next century or so and provided the basis for William Shakespeare's tale of doomed love, *Romeo and Juliet,* set in Verona. By the late 1200s one family had emerged as top dogs, the Scaligeris, a terrifyingly successful mercenary clan who named themselves after dogs. They were ousted in their turn by the Milanese Viscontis in 1387. In 1402, having had their fill of lords, Verona turned to republican Venice, and remained part of *La Serenissima* (the Venetian Republic) until 1797, after which the city passed to the Austrians, who retained control until 1866, when Verona and Venice became part of the new Kingdom of Italy. The city was badly bombed during World War II, but quickly recovered to become one of Italy's outstanding economic success stories.

INFORMATION

www.tourism.verona.it
464 F4 Via degli Alpini 9 (Piazza Brà), 37121 Verona 045 806 8680
Mon–Sat 8.30–7, Sun 9–5 Verona

WHAT TO SEE

THE ARENA

Piazza Brà should be your first stop, an irregular open space dominated by one of the city's best-known monuments, the great Roman amphitheatre, the Arena. Built in the first century AD, it is the third-largest of the surviving Roman amphitheatres in Italy. A 13th-century earthquake destroyed most of the exterior arcade, but the interior is intact, with steeply pitched tiers of pink marble seats and dizzying views from the top. Since 1913 people have flocked to Verona to catch a performance during its summer opera season.

Piazza Brà, 37121 Verona 045 800 3204; www.arena.it Sep–end Jun Mon 1.45–6.30, Tue–Sun 8.30–6.30; Jul, Aug (opera season) daily 9–3.30; closed to visitors during performances
Adult €6, child €2

BASILICA DI SAN ZENO MAGGIORE

Farther west from Castelvecchio stands San Zeno Maggiore, a Romanesque church founded in the fourth century that attained its present form around 1398; a set of superb 11th-century bronze doors open into a lofty interior with Roman columns and an altarpiece by Andrea Mantegna (*c*1431–1506). The church is the burial place of Pepin the Short, king of the Franks. Father of Charlemagne and founder of the Frankish dynasty of the Carolingians, he led his army into Italy to defeat the Lombards in AD754.

Piazza San Zeno, 37121 Verona Mon–Sat 8.30–6, Sun 1–6 €2.50

PIAZZA DELLE ERBE

From Piazza Brà, Via Mazzini, an elegant and tempting pedestrian-only shopping street, leads north to Piazza delle Erbe, the setting for a lively daily market, and Piazza dei Signori, the heart of medieval Verona. Piazza delle Erbe is surrounded by exquisite buildings: the Torre dei Lamberti, which you can ascend on foot or by elevator, soars above the brightly frescoed Casa Mazzanti, and there is a loggia, a 14th-century fountain and a fine Lion of St. Mark.

Opposite *The Torre dei Lamberti and Piazza delle Erbe at night*
Below *The Roman amphitheatre*

TIPS

» The historic heart is closed to traffic for most of the day, so come by train or use the parking area near the station.

» You can rent a bicycle in Piazza Brà (tel 333 536 7770).

» The Verona Card, valid for a day or a week, includes unlimited travel and museum admissions and is available from the tourist office. Pick up a free copy of *Passport Verona* for up-to-date listings.

» Verona is the venue for plays and musical events all year round, including great jazz and rock concerts, often in historic monuments and in open spaces outdoors. In July and August there is opera in the amphitheatre.

» Verona has a great café scene and is much livelier in the evenings than Venice. It is also a better bet for buying clothes.

PIAZZA DEI SIGNORI

From Piazza delle Erbe an arch leads to the old civic area, the Piazza dei Signori, the focus of which is a statue of the Renaissance poet Dante Alighieri (1265–1321). The candy-striped Palazzo della Ragione has a fine Romanesque-Gothic courtyard. The building behind Dante is the Renaissance Loggia del Consiglio dating from 1493, with the Tribunale next to it. Don't overlook the Scaligeri tombs, next to the Tribunale, covered with statuary and Scaligeri emblems, dogs and ladders.

CASA DI GIULIETTA

From Piazza delle Erbe, Via Cappello leads southeast to the so-called Casa di Giulietta (House of Juliet), a graffiti-adorned mecca for love-sick teenagers and bus tours; the balcony was added in 1935.

✉ Via Capello 23, 37121 Verona ☎ 045 803 4303 🕐 Tue–Sun 9–7, Mon 1.30–7.30 ✋ €4

LA CATTEDRALE

On the northern point of the promontory is the Romanesque cathedral, which has a beautiful apse and a fine *Assumption* by Titian in the first chapel of the north aisle.

✉ Piazza del Duomo 🕐 Mon–Sat 10–5.30, Sun 1–5; reduced hours in winter ✋ €3

VICENZA

In 1404, under threat from stronger forces in Padua, Verona and Milan, the free *comune* of Vicenza offered itself to Venice and became a satellite city. As a Venetian possession, the city was given Gothic palaces, but its big architectural makeover came in the 16th century, when Andrea Palladio (1508–80) started to develop his own classical style. Palladio was born in Padua, but found his major patron, the humanist nobleman Trissino, in Vicenza. Between 1549 and his death in 1580 he transformed the face of the city, and all his work in Vicenza and around has been designated a UNESCO World Heritage Site.

PALLADIO'S CLASSICAL MASTERPIECES

Corso Andrea Palladio, lined with superb palazzi, ends at Piazza Matteoti. Palazzo Chiericati, designed by Palladio in 1550, now contains the Museo Civico, with paintings by Tintoretto, Tiepolo, Veronese and local artist Jacopo Bassano, one of the big names of the later Renaissance (Tue–Sun 9–5). Across the piazza is the Teatro Olimpico, Europe's oldest indoor theatre, opened in 1585 (Tue–Sun 9–5). Palladio died before it was complete, but his designs inspired the astonishing *trompe l'oeil* backdrop—it appears to be hundreds of metres deep, but it only stretches back 15m (50ft).

At the heart of the *centro storico* is Piazza dei Signori, site of Palladio's dazzling basilica, his first major project and the one that made his reputation, and the stunning double-tiered Loggia del Capitaniato.

PALAZZI

Fruit and vegetables have been sold in the Piazza dell'Erbe since medieval times. Near here on Contrà Porti and Contrà Riale are several palaces, the finest of which are the Palazzo Thiene, Palazzo Barbaran (Museo Palladiano, Tue–Sun 10–6) and Palazzo Colleoni Porto. Notable churches include the reconstructed duomo (the original was destroyed in World War II), 13th-century Santa Corona, notable for its paintings by Bellini and Veronese, and Santo Stefano. The hill to the south is Monte Bérico, an important plague shrine topped by a 17th-century basilica. Nearby, is Andrea Palladio's famous Villa Capra (1567), also known as the Villa Rotonda (Mar–Nov: villa Wed 10–12, 3–6; garden Tue–Sun 10–12, 3–6).

INFORMATION

www.vicenza.org

464 G4 Piazza Matteotti 12, 36100 Vicenza 0444 320854 Piazza dei Signori 8, 36100 Vicenza 0444 544 122; daily 9–1, 2–6 Vicenza

TIPS

» Reserve hotels in advance—Vicenza has surprisingly few and it is a big conference city.

» A Vicenza Card, a combined ticket, costs €10 and gives entrance to all the main attractions at big reductions.

» There are parking areas at the east and west ends of town—catch the shuttle bus into town.

» Touring Club Italiano has produced a guidebook to the villas of Andrea Palladio in Vicenza and its province. It is available from tourist information offices, bookshops or direct from the TCI (www.touringclub.it).

Opposite *Statue of Shakespeare's Juliet at the Casa di Giulietta (House of Juliet)*
Below *Relief work on the pediment of a building in Vicenza's Piazza dei Signori*

GRANDE STRADA DELLE DOLOMITI

This drive follows the Grande Strada delle Dolomiti (Great Dolomites Road), which was constructed in 1909 to link Bolzano and Cortina d'Ampezzo. It cuts through some of Europe's most breathtaking mountain scenery, navigating high passes and fertile alpine valleys. Pretty villages line the route, and cable cars and chairlifts give access to the higher slopes.

THE DRIVE
Distance: 90km (56 miles)
Allow: 3 hours' driving time
Start at: Bolzano
End at: Cortina d'Ampezzo

★ Leave Bolzano/Bozen and head northeast in the direction of Bressanone/Brixen (▷ 203). Take the SS241, which is signposted in brown for the Eggental, and head along the Valle d'Ega (Eggental) towards Lago di Carezza.

The SS241 twists and climbs as it cuts through a narrow gorge into the mountains. It gradually opens up and the high peaks of the Latemar and Catinaccio/Rosengarten massifs begin to appear, giving you the first taste of the area's scenic glories. Your first stop is Carezza al Lago.

❶ Carezza al Lago is beside a beautiful lake whose turquoise waters reflect the surrounding dark fir trees and mountain ridges. You can stretch your legs by following the well-made track around the lake, approximately a 30-minute stroll.

From the lake the road continues to climb up to the Passo di Costalunga (1,745m/5,725ft), the first of the high passes along this route, which forms the boundary between the Alto Adige and Trentino regions. Continue on the SS241 over the Passo di Costalungo, which drops down into the beautiful Val di Fassa.

❷ Once over the pass, the road descends into the Val di Fassa, a lovely alpine valley that attracts mountain sports enthusiasts in summer and winter. The River Avisio runs through the valley past a string of pretty villages, among them Vigo di Fassa, all catering to holidaymakers. From Vigo di Fassa you can head up into the hills for a high-altitude walk through the beautiful Catinaccio Mountains (▷ 218–219).

About 1.5km (0.9 mile) past Vigo di Fassa turn left onto the SS48 towards Canazei. Drive up the valley past Canazei and stay on the SS48 towards the Passo Pordoi (2,239m/7,346ft).

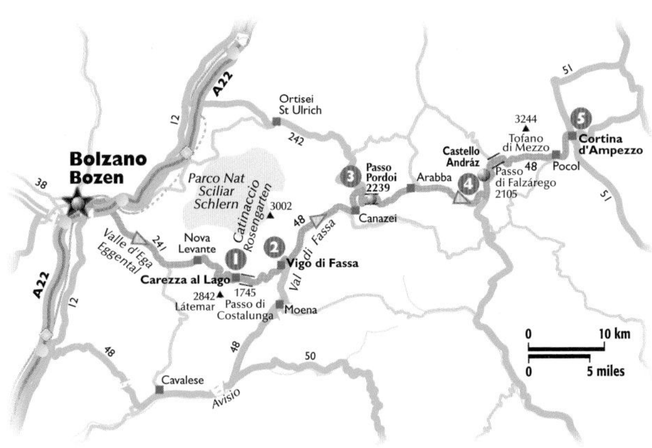

For the next 12km (7.5 miles) you will wind around 27 hairpin bends and the road becomes increasingly challenging, with dramatic views of mountains all around and the green meadows of the Val di Fassa below.

❸ Passo Pordoi is the highest pass along the drive and you're likely to find yourself above the snowline at most times of year.

More hairpins snake down to Arabba, a mountain village that is a popular resort with winter skiers. Stay on the SS48 through Arabba. From Arabba the road threads its away along the sides of a heavily wooded valley, where houses are few and far between and there's a real sense of isolation amid the upland countryside. Another steep section of road snakes up to the Passo di Falzarego (2,105m/6,906ft).

❹ Look for the stark outline of the ancient Castello Andraz on your left and the relatively rare stone pines that dot the slopes of the high meadows around here.

At Falzarego the views open up across new mountain ranges and peaks before the road begins its descent. Stay on the SS48 towards Cortina d'Ampezzo. The contrasts of landscape are stark on this last section of the drive, where rocky mountain slopes tower above deciduous forests and alpine pastures. The road passes through the village of Pocol and emerges into the mountain bowl that encircles Cortina d'Ampezzo.

❺ Affectionately known as both the pearl and the queen of the Dolomites, Cortina d'Ampezzo is Italy's most glamorous winter resort. It hosted the first televised Winter Olympics in 1956, and the awesome peaks formed the backdrop for some jaw-dropping scenes in the James Bond film *For Your Eyes Only* (1981) and *Cliffhanger* (1993), starring Sylvester Stallone. There are pistes for all skiing abilities, but if that doesn't appeal, you can glide around the Olympic skating rink or ride on a horse-drawn sleigh or dog sled. Thrill-seekers can rent skidoos or experience an Olympic bobsleigh run via the Taxi-bobsleigh (tel 0436 860808), which takes you to speeds of over 120kph (75mph).

TIPS

» The roads are good, but the route can be crowded with tour buses.
» This route is twisty—best avoided by sufferers of vertigo
» Take snow chains as you will be above the snow line on several stretches of this route..

Opposite *Mountains around Lago di Carezza*
Below *Sassolungo range near Canazei*

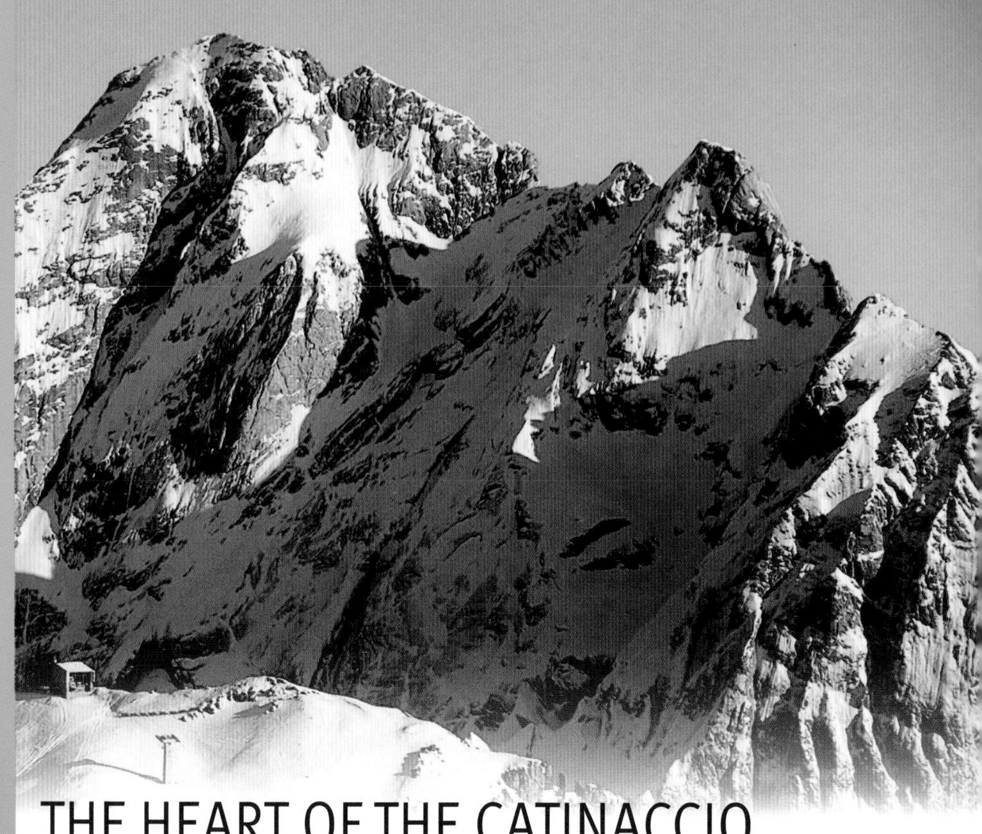

THE HEART OF THE CATINACCIO

This straightforward walk is one of the easiest and most spectacular of the high-altitude Dolomite trails, giving you a true taste of the power and beauty of the mountains (▷ 207). The route plunges deeper and deeper into the peaks of the Catinaccio (Rosengarten), lined with alpine flowers, trees and shrubs and all without struggling on foot from the valley bottom.

THE WALK
Distance: 6km (3.7 miles)
Allow: 1.5–2 hours
Ascent: 100m/328ft
Start/end at: Vigo di Fassa
Paths: Excellent, wide stony mountain trails. Can be slippery in icy/snowy conditions. Late spring and early autumn snow can hang around in patches, so shoes or walking boots with good grip are essential outside the peak summer season
Parking: Funivia Ciampedie (Ciampedie cable car) parking in Vigo di Fassa
Toilets: At *rifugi alpini* (mountain refuges)

★ After parking the car at Funivia Ciampedie, buy a return ticket for the *funivia* (daily, every 15 minutes, 8.30–1, 3.30–6; €11). The cable car takes the strain, whisking you over 600m (1,970ft) up the mountain. As it ascends there are ever-widening views over the Val di Fassa and the Monzoni massif to the southeast. At the top walk out onto the Ciampedie plateau (1,998m/ 6,555ft).

Look for the waymark signpost (a little to the left) showing 540 and follow the trail down the hill with the *rifugio alpino* (mountain refuge) on your right. About 200m (218 yards) after the path flattens, take trail 540 (way-marked), which contours to the right. This splendid path leads right into the heart of the Catinaccio (Rosengarten) range, some of the Dolomites' most impressive mountain scenery.

❶ The German name for these peaks means 'Rose Garden', an apt reference to the blush pink of the stone, which looks its deepest at dawn and by twilight. Legend has it that, betrayed by the colour and splendour of his roses, the king of the dwarves was dragged away from his mountain kingdom. He cursed the roses, binding them with a spell to make them invisible by day and night. While he ranted, he forgot to mention dawn and dusk, which is when the mountains glow a vibrant pink.

Follow the trail through the woods, across two ski slopes, grassy in summer, and under the cables of two ski lifts.

❷ The woods are pine, carpeted with alpine shrubs. The most common are juniper, alpenrose *(Rhododendron ferrugineum)*, whose lovely pink azalea-like flower blooms from late June to August, and bilberry. Bilberries have small dark berries with a lustrous bloom and intense flavour; look for ripe fruit in late August and September. The juniper berries that grow here have been used for centuries to flavour spirits and liqueurs and are still used today in many of the locally distilled *aperitivi* and *digestivi*.

Head deeper into the circle of peaks where the path undulates and the summits grow ever more dramatic.

❸ The highest peaks of the Catinaccio/Rosengarten group are the Cima Scalieret (2,887m/9,472ft), to your right, and Punta Emma (2,919m/9,577ft), ahead and to your left. All these peaks are popular with rock climbers and many of them have *vie ferrate* (fixed iron ladders) to help mountaineers on the precipitous rock walls (▷ 15).

The path descends out of the woods and ahead of you stands the pink-washed building of the Rifugio Catinaccio (1,960m/6,430ft), where you can rest and admire the mountain peaks.

❹ There are hundreds of *rifugi alpini* throughout the Dolomites, some

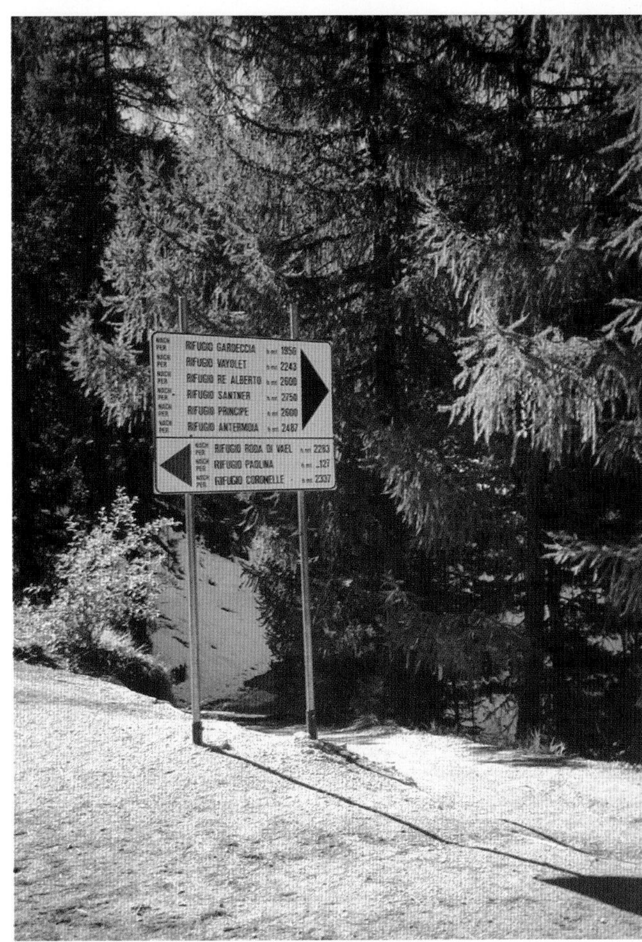

providing food and drinks, others offering accommodation for hikers following the long-distance paths through the mountains.

Retrace your route back to the cable car. With the Catinaccio behind you, wide views open out to the mountains of the southeast.

❺ The lumpy peak is the unmistakable silhouette of Marmolada, at 3,246m (10,650ft) the highest peak in the Dolomites, with its retreating glacier draped down one side. Pieces of timber from old buildings are often visible on the newly exposed slopes that were part of the 'City of Ice' hacked out by Austrian troops during World War I.

If you are feeling fit you can tackle the other side of the range. Take the Paolina chairlift from Passo di Carrezza and follow trails 539 and 549 to Baita Pederiva. This is a 5km (3-mile) walk with yet more stunning views along the way.

WHERE TO EAT

Rifugio alpino at Ciampedie (top of the cable car) or *Rifugio Catinaccio* at the end of the walk.

WHEN TO GO

The path is open all year, but the less sure-footed should avoid the route during late autumn and winter, when the trail can get icy and slippery.

Above *A sign in the pine woods of Catinaccio*
Opposite *Marmolada mountain*

BOLOGNA

CANTINA BENTIVOGLIO

www.cantinabentivoglio.it

This large bar in the university district is one of the top jazz venues in town, with music every night from 10 and good, cheap food. There is music outdoors in July and August.

✉ Via Mascarella 4b, 40126 Bologna
☎ 051 265416 🕐 Daily 8pm–2am
✋ €4

CLURICAUNE

An Irish-themed bar on the edge of the university district, near the two towers. It is regularly packed to bursting with young people.

✉ Via Zamboni 18, 40126 Bologna
☎ 051 263419 🕐 Mon–Fri 12–2am, Sat 2pm–2am

MERCATO DI MEZZO

This has been Bologna's traditional market for at least two millennia. Shops and stalls display the finest-quality products in a dizzying parade of pasta, velvety sauces, meat, Parma and Culatello hams, salamis, cheeses and pungent balsamic vinegars from Modena. Look too for the traditional tortellini, modelled, as legend has it, on the shape of a local inn-keeper's mistress's belly button; you can also get chocolate tortellini—perfect replicas of the Bolognese-stuffed pasta shape but filled instead with silky praline.

✉ Via Peschiere Vecchie, Piazza Maggiore area, 40100 Bologna 🕐 Mon–Wed, Fri–Sat 7–1, 4.15–7.30, Thu 7–1

NUOVO CINEMA NOSADELLA

www.nosadella.it

The two-screen cinema shows films in English on Mondays and in other languages on other days.

✉ Via Ludovico 2/7, 40123 Bologna
☎ 051 521550 🕐 Four screenings daily, 4pm–midnight ✋ Adult €7.50, child €4.50

LA SCUDERIA

www.lascuderia.bo.it

In the heart of the university area, this ultra-hip nightspot is much loved by the students and the sophisticated young. Live music most nights and themed dance nights with DJs.

✉ Piazza Verdi 2, 40126 Bologna
☎ 051 656 9619 🕐 Wed–Mon 10pm–4am

SODA POPS

www.sodapops.it

Hidden behind a plain steel door, this little club is a favourite with clubbers who go for somewhere small, hot, and very crowded. Things get going late, the sound system is superb and the friendliness of the habitués is a real bonus.

✉ Via Castel Tialto, 40125 Bologna
☎ 051 272 079 🕐 Daily 10pm–4am

SOTTOTETTO SOUND

Music here varies from night to night, covering sounds that range from ska to pop, jazz and reggae, with Juke Box on Fridays. Mondays are for indie, hard rock and punk fans, while Thursday dishes up something quieter in the shape of background music. There is live music occasionally and you can even get tattooed here on Saturdays.

✉ Via Viadagola 16, 40127 Bologna
☎ 051 633 5555 🕐 10pm–4am

TAMBURINI

www.tamburini.com

This is the finest delicatessen in what is considered the gastronomic capital of Italy. The large display of local produce includes fresh pasta (such as black pasta coloured with squid ink and tortelloni stuffed with pumpkin), cheeses, hams and salamis. There is also a self-service café (open 12–2.30).

Above *Cantina Bentivoglio in Bologna*
Opposite *Masks for sale in Verona*

Via Caprarie 1, 40124 Bologna
051 234726 Mon–Wed, Fri–Sat 8–7, Thu 8–2

TEATRO COMMUNALE

www.tcbo.it
Wagner preferred to premiere his operas here in Bologna's leading venue, an auditorium in the heart of the university district that first opened in 1763. You can buy tickets online.
Largo Respighi 1, 40126 Bologna
051 529958; 199 107070 (ticket office)
Sep–end Jun €30–€100

PADOVA (PADUA)

AUDITORIUM POLLINI

www.amicimusicapadova.org
One of the main concert venues in Padua, hosting performances by, among others, the Orchestra di Padova e del Veneto. It has capacity for 600 people.
Via San Massimo 37, 35138 Padova
049 875 6763 (Mon–Fri 9–4)
Oct–end Mar €15–€40

PRATO DELLA VALLE MARKET

Every Saturday the Prato della Valle—claimed to be the largest town square in Italy, and a marketplace since the 11th century—is turned into an open-air market selling clothes, kitchenware, shoes, woven baskets and more. An antiques fair takes place on the third Sunday of the month.
Prato della Valle, 35137 Padova
Sat dawn–dusk

ROBERTO CALLEGARI

www.robertocallegari.com
Padua's top jewellery shop—in a town with a large number of jewellers—is less than 10 minutes' walk north of the middle of town. It sells watches, jewellery and antique silver.
Via Davila 8, 35137 Padova 049 875 5803 Tue–Sat 9.30–12.30, 3.30–7.30

TRIESTE

CAFFÈ DEGLI SPECCHI

The Mirror Café is one of Trieste's oldest and most lavish symbols of the belle époque. It has always been patronized by intellectuals and writers, from the 'Irredentist' literary figures that were part of the Italian nationalist movement, to former resident James Joyce.
Via Mascarella 4b, 40126 Bologna
051 265416 Daily 8pm–2am
€4

VERONA

ARENA

www.arena.it
This is one of the best-preserved Roman amphitheatres in Italy (▷ 213). When the opera is not taking place (▷ Festivals and Events, above), kids can discover what it was like to be a gladiator in this ancient playground, running around the high-vaulted corridors and through the arches into the arena.
Piazza Brà, 37121 Verona 045 800 3204 Opera: Jun–Aug from 7.30pm
Adult €4, child €1

ASTRA

This city-centre cinema shows all the latest releases of the blockbuster variety as well as occasional indie and art house movies. There is Dolby sound, a bar and cafeteria and an air-conditioned auditorium.
Via Oberdan 13, 37121 Verona
455 96327

CINECITY

This mulitiscreen, not far from the centre of town, shows all the latest movies, with occasional original language screenings.
Via Bonporti, 37121 Verona 0498 774 325 Daily 4, 7, 10pm €8

L'ENOTECA DELL'ISTITUTO ENOLOGICO ITALIANO

www.enotecaverona.com
Near the river on the east side of the old town, these old wine cellars lie beneath a 17th-century palace. Here is an excellent selection, and afternoon wine-tasting sessions take place daily, with a different wine to sample every week.
Via Sottoriva 7, 37100 Verona
045 590366 Tue–Sat 9–12.30, 3.30–7.30, Mon 9–12.30

GIARDINO GIUSTI

This is a magnificent Renaissance garden, across the river from the heart of town. Get lost in the hedge maze or climb up to the grotto below a fearsome stone face and enjoy the view across to the city.
Via Giardino Giusti 2, 37129 Verona
045 803 4029 Apr–Sep daily 9–8; Oct–Mar 9–dusk €5

FESTIVALS AND EVENTS

FEBRUARY

CARNEVALE

www.comune.cento.fe.it/carnevale
One of Italy's oldest carnivals (1615), twinned with Rio de Janeiro's extravaganza. More than 500 floats throw out 15,000kg (33,000lb) of sweets into the crowd lining the streets of Cento.
Shrove Tuesday

JUNE–AUGUST

INTERNATIONAL OPERA FESTIVAL

www.arena.it
Opera in the arena of Verona. There is a great choice of operas, all very popular, so reserve well in advance—and take a cushion.
Piazza Brà, 37121 Verona 045 800 5151 €20–€200

PRICES AND SYMBOLS

The restaurants are listed alphabetically within each town. The prices given are the average for a two-course lunch (L) and a three-course dinner (D) for one person, without drinks. The wine price given is for the least expensive bottle.

For the key to symbols, ▷ 2.

BOLOGNA

AL CAMBIO

Housed inside the Hotel Maxim, but independently run, this beautiful restaurant has been scooping plaudits since it opened 15 years ago. Chef Massimiliano chooses his ingredients with care, makes his own bread and turns out imaginative dishes such as scampi with cucumber and tomato sorbet, bream with violet potatoes and coffee mascarpone cream.

✉ Via Stalingrado 150, 40128 Bologna ☎ 051 328118 🕑 Mon–Fri 12.30–3, 7.30–10.30, Sat, Sun 7.30–10.30; closed Aug and Christmas 🖐 L €35, D €54, Wine €11

BROCCAINDOSSO

At this rustic establishment, with rough tables and long wooden benches, they only serve one course and desserts, and there is no menu; although you can order pasta, it's better to wait and see what the staff bring you. Reservations are essential. Credit cards are not accepted.

✉ Via Broccaindosso 7/a , 40125 Bologna ☎ 051 234153 🕑 Mon–Sat 8.30pm–2am; sometimes closed Aug 🖐 L €22, D €30, Wine €8 🚌 14, 27

FANTONI

This small, lively trattoria serves simple local dishes with home-made pasta and wines and fresh fish from Thursday to Saturday. The small menu changes daily. You can sit out on the terrace in summer. Be prepared to queue at the door if you haven't made a reservation. Credit cards are not accepted.

✉ Via del Pratello 11, 40122 Bologna ☎ 051 236358 🕑 Tue–Sat 12–2.30, 8–10.30, Mon 12–2.30 🖐 L €16, D €28, Wine €9

MARCO FADIGA BISTROT

www.marcofadigabistrot.comt

Atmospheric French-style bistro with an oyster bar. As well as seafood, the specials include popular regional dishes like homemade tortellini and *coniglio con polenta morbida al tartufo nero* (rabbit with polenta and black truffle). The fine wines complement the excellent food.

✉ Via Rialto 23/c, 40124 Bologna ☎ 051 220118 🕑 Tue–Sat 7.30pm–11pm 🖐 D €40 Wine €14

VICTORIA STATION

www.victoriastation.it

Easily recognized by the red London bus standing outside, this is a lively party place where British style meets old-fashioned Bolognese hospitality. A popular hangout for trendy young Bolognesi and celebrity visitors to the city, there's a large garden area and seating for 500 guests. The daily menu can be viewed on the website.

✉ Via Zanardi 76, 40131 Bologna ☎ 051 634 6062 🕑 Mon–Thu 12–3, 7.30pm–2am, Fri 12–3, 7.30pm–2am, Sat 7.30pm–2am 🖐 D €17 Wine €8

BOLZANO/BOZEN

VÖGELE

One of the oldest and most traditional restaurants in the Alto-Adige occupies a series of cosy and totally diverse *Stuben* (rooms), where local groups have gathered since the 19th century. The accent is firmly Austrian, with *canerderli* (dumplings), *Speck* (peppered smoked ham), and gnocchi being firm menu favourites.

✉ Via Goethe 3, 39100 Bolzano ☎ 0471 973938 🕑 Mon–Sat 9am–1am 🖐 L €19, D €35, Wine €9

BRESSANONE/BRIXEN

FINK

This pretty place, the 'Finch', is both an excellent restaurant and superb *Konditorei* (patisserie) serving up a huge range of melt-in-the-mouth pastries and cakes oozing cream. The menu offers typical Austrian specialties, such as a carpaccio of venison, various noodles and dumplings, delicate *Speck* and both lamb and veal dishes. The desserts, as you'd expect, are wicked.

Via Portici Minori 4, 39042 Bressanone 0472 834883 Wed–Mon 12.30–2.30, 7.30–10; also Tue evening Jul to mid-Sep L €33, D €45, Wine €14

CANAZEI

RISTORANTE DE TOFI

www.hotel-astoria.net

Good restaurants are rare in this area, and locals consider the restaurant at the Hotel Astoria to be the best. Local dishes include *polenta al ragù* (polenta with meat sauce), *funghi* (mushrooms) in autumn, and game.

Via Roma 88, Canazei, 38032 Trento 0462 601302 Daily 12.30–1.30, 7–8.30; closed May to mid-Jun and Oct, Nov L €13, D €30, Wine €9 From the A22 (Brennero) exit Egnaora then follow signs for Cavalezei and Val di Fassa. From here follow signs to the hotel

CIVIDALE DEI FRIULI

ANTICA TRATTORIA DOMINISSINI

www.anticatrattoriadominissini.it

Make your way through the bar area and down a couple of steps into this traditional restaurant, decorated with local pottery and with a delightful alfresco terrace. The menu is faithful to straightforward Friulian cooking, so you'll be able to try traditional cheese and potato cakes, thick vegetable soups and grilled meat. The owner doubles as the waiter and he is passionate about wine; ask his advice on local vintages or try the smooth white Tocai.

Stretta Jacopo Stellini 18, Cividale dei Friuli, 33043 Udine 0432 733763 May–Oct Tue–Sun 10.30–3, 6–11; Nov–Apr Tue–Sat 10.30–3, 6–11 L €22, D €35, Wine €7

FERRARA

OSTERIA DELLA CAMPANA

You can savour to the full the traditional dishes of the area at this pleasant city-centre restaurant, a happy survivor of a different age. Panelled walls, white linens and tiled floors herald a serious attitude to enjoying good food; try the home-made *cappellacci* (little hats) of pasta stuffed with pumpkin and the pasta with unctuous *ragù*.

Via Borgo dei Leoni 26, 44100 Ferrara 0532 241256 Tue–Sun 12.30–3, 7.30–10 L €25, D €40, Wine €10

MERANO (MERAN)

SISSI

www.sissi.andreafenoglio.com

Chef Andrea Fenoglio has earned a Michelin star for this elegant Liberty-style restaurant in the heart of town. Dishes are based on traditional regional specialties but with a modern and creative twist. There is an excellent wine list and a good selection of wines by the glass. The restaurant is both popular and small, so reservations are strongly advised.

Via Galilei 44, 39012 Merano 0473 231062 Wed–Sun 12.30–2.30, 7.30–10.30, Tue 7/30–10.30; closed 3 weeks between Feb and Mar L €50, D €65, Wine €16

MODENA

L'ERBA DEL RE

The food in this Michelin-starred restaurant is firmly rooted in tradition, but the style of cooking and presentation are up to the minute. Local specialities are beautifully cooked with a light touch; dishes include risotto with smoked ricotta and red leaves, slow-cooked milk-fed pork and a mixed plate of 10 local cheeses. The tasting menus include a vegetarian option.

Via Castel Maraldo 45, 41100 Modena 0592 18188 Tue–Sat 12.30–3, 7.30–10, Mon 7.30–10; closed 1–6 Jan and 1–20 Aug L €35, D €55, Wine €15

PADOVA (PADUA)

ANFORA

This is a lively place with a bohemian air. Anfora concentrates on local produce and fish dishes, and its prices are very reasonable. Arrive early or make a reservation.

Via dei Soncin 13, 35122 Padova 049 656629 Mon–Sat 9am–midnight L €13, D €27, Wine €9

BELLE PARTI

www.ristorantebelleparti.it

A charming restaurant with wooden beams, white tablecloths and art nouveau stained glass. The menu includes regional and international dishes such as steamed mullet with potatoes and olives, cuttlefish with polenta, *bigoli* pasta with duck *ragù* and foie gras, and risotto with prawns and saffron. The wine list is excellent. Reservations are advisable.

Via Belle Parti 11, 35122 Padova 049 875 1822 Mon–Sat 12.30–2.30, 8–11; closed Aug L €40, D €53, Wine €14

DONNA IRENE

The emphasis is on the wine in this *enoteca*/restaurant, with a superb list that features over 1,200 vintages, but the food has been carefully chosen to match the wine. Ingredients and dishes are local, nicely prepared and there's the bonus of a pretty garden for summer dining.

Vicolo Pontecorvo 1, 35100 Padova 049 656852 Tue–Sun 10.30am–3.30pm, 6pm–1am; closed 2 weeks in Jan and Aug L €25, D €45, Wine €12

NANE DELLA GIULIA

This friendly *osteria*, reputed to be the oldest in town, is in the university quarter. The menu is strong on Veneto and vegetarian dishes, making good use of local cheeses and vegetables, including the popular pasta with beans. Credit cards are not accepted.

Via Santa Sofia 1, 35121 Padova 049 660742 Tue–Sun 12–2.30, 7–midnight L €12, D €30, Wine €8

PEPEN

There's a wide range of pizzas, as well as other dishes at Pepen. Try the fish and puff pastry with cream

Opposite *Eating out near the Porta Borsari in Verona*

cheese, barley and candied fruit. A reservation is essential, even at lunchtime, as it's hugely popular with local office workers.
Piazza Cavour 15, 35100 Padova
049 875 9483 Mon–Sat 12–3, 7–11; closed Aug L €17, D €47, Wine €10

PARMA

SANTA CROCE

Restrained elegance in three rooms—glowing damask, polished wood floors and fresh flowers, all warm and welcoming. They serve up authentic Parma cuisine with a twist; try the mixed *salumi* to sample Parma ham in its birthplace, or delicate crab roulade, then move to seasonal dishes like prime fillet steak and mousses and *semifreddi* for dessert. The wine list is huge.
Via Pasini 20, 43100 Parma 0521 293529 Mon–Fri 12.30–2, 8–10, Sat 8–10 L €35, D €60, Wine €150

PIACENZA

VECCHIA PIACENZA

www.ristorantevecchiapiacenza.it
An 18th-century palazzo, complete with frescoed ceilings, is home to this good and very popular restaurant; book ahead. The good-value menu includes risotto, with truffles in season, homemade pasta and excellent beef and veal. Desserts are the stars of the menu—try the champagne sorbet or the *zabaione* with strawberries. There is also a long and good wine list.
Via S. Bernardo 1, 29100 Piacenza
0523 305462 Mon–Sat 12.30–3, 7.30–10; closed 1 week in Jan and Jul
L €38, D €60, Wine €15

RAVENNA

ANTICA TRATTORIA AL GALLO 1909

www.trattoriagallo1909.it
Run by the same family for just about 100 years, this little Liberty-style restaurant is renowned for its superb *primi;* try the artichoke tart, cheese profiteroles with truffle sauce or *cappelletti* (a type of meat-filled ravioli) before moving on to fresh fish or perhaps a vegetarian dish.
Via Maggiore 87, 48100 Ravenna
0544 213775 Wed–Sat 12.30–3, 7.30–10, Sun 12.30–3.30; closed Easter and Christmas L €25, D €42, Wine €8

BABALEUS

www.ristorantebabaleus.com
Very good-value pizzeria/restaurant in the pedestrianized *centro storico*. From Monday to Friday there's a self-service lunch menu for €7, while at other times there is pizza, drink and entrance to the nearby Cinema Astoria for €11. As well as pizza and pasta there are more substantial meat and fish dishes too.
Vicolo Gabbiano 7, 48100 Ravenna
0544 216464 Mon–Tue, Thu–Fri lunch, dinner; Sat–Sun dinner L Pizza from €4, D €25, Wine €8

BELLA VENEZIA

You'll find classic Emilian cooking at this fine establishment, where the accent is on local ingredients and recipes. Here are traditional dishes such as ravioli stuffed with young nettles, risotto with *funghi* and parmesan cheese and excellent and super-fresh fish.
Via IV Novembre 16, 48100 Ravenna
0554 212746 Mon–Sat 12.30–3, 7.30–10, closed mid-Dec to mid-Jan
L €33, D €44, Wine €11

BIZANTINO

A self-service restaurant on the big market square in the centre of old Ravenna, Bizantino is ideal for a quick bite while you're out sightseeing. Expect good, simple food with plenty of fresh produce. Credit cards are not accepted.
Piazza A. Costa, 48100 Ravenna
0544 32073 Mon–Fri 11.45–2.45
L €7–€8, Wine €4

AL RUSTICHELLO

Just outside the old town walls west of Ravenna, Rustichello has gained a reputation for both the quality of its food and the size of its portions. The restaurant has a modern, light and elegant interior. English is spoken and the owner comes and tells you what's on the menu. Top dishes here include a marvellous *cappelletti* with asparagus. Reservations are recommended. Credit cards are not accepted.
Via Maggiore 21/23, 48100 Ravenna
0544 36043 Mon–Fri 12–2, 7–10, Sat 7–10pm L €27, D €35, Wine €6

RIMINI

TAVERNA DEGLI ARTISTI

www.tavernadegliartisti.com
Have a look in the tanks as you enter this bustling restaurant, and choose fish or seafood that couldn't be fresher. The accent here is marine, but they do simple grills well. Pasta and bread is home-made and there's an excellent selection of pizza if you're watching the budget.
Viale Amerigo Vespucci 1, 47900 Rimini
0541 28519 Daily 12.30–3, 7.30–10.30 L €48, D €75, Wine €14

TRENTO

LA CANTINOTA

A pretty vaulted dining room in a 16th-century building and a garden for summer eating make this a good choice for sampling some nicely cooked local dishes. Eat à la carte or choose from one of the three set menus, which offer a chance to taste dishes such as feather-light polenta, local *funghi*, risottos and a range of homemade desserts.
Via S. Marco 22–24, 38100 Trento
0461 238 527 Fri–Wed 12.30–2.30, 7.30–10 L €22, D €42, Wine €12

TRIESTE

ANTICA TRATTORIA SUBAN

This old coaching inn serves the best food in Trieste, and is well worth a trip out to the suburbs. Try the bean soup, ham and sauerkraut, or risotto with wild local herbs. Follow it up with veal simmered in wine and a thoroughly modern chocolate soufflé.
Via Comici 2/D, 34128 Trieste
040 54368 Wed–Sun 12–3, 7–10.30, Mon 7–10.30; closed Aug L €30, D €50, Wine €15 35

UDINE

VITELLO D'ORO

www.vitellodoro.com
Just off the central piazza, this long-established restaurant has a warm, wood-panelled interior and

a lovely garden for summer dining. The accent is on fish, but meat also appears on both the traditional and tasting menus. The wine list has some interesting Friuli wines from small local producers.
✉ Via Valvason 4, 33100 Udine ☎ 0432 508 982 ◷ Thu–Sun, Tue 12.30–3, 7.30–10, Mon 7.30–10, closed Sun Jun–Sep
L €38, D €60, Wine €14

VERONA

ANTICA TRATTORIA DA L'AMELIA

www.trattoriaamelia.com
Three rooms in a riverside building house this well-regarded eating place, where care is taken with the traditional local food—look out for the salted meat carpaccio and the feather-light gnocchi flavoured with radicchio from Treviso. They have an excellent selection of oil and cheese and the wine list is a serious affair.
✉ Lungadige Rubele 32, 37121 Verona ☎ 045 800 5526 ◷ Tue–Sat 12.30–3, 8–11, Sun 12.30–3; closed 2 weeks in Jan and Aug L €20, D €43, Wine €10

LA BOTTEGA DEL VINO

www.bottegavini.it
A major player on the Veronese gastronomic scene, this elegant *enoteca*/restaurant, with its flamboyant interior, is always crowded and bustling, but the service is slick and professional. As the name suggests, they have a very good wine list. The excellent Italian cheese is served with honey.
✉ Via Scudo di Francia 3, 37121 Verona ☎ 045 800 4535 ◷ Jul–Aug daily 10.30–3, 6–midnight; Sep–Jun Wed–Mon 10.30–3, 6–midnight; open until 3am on opera nights L €45, D €70, Wine €17

AL CARRO ARMATO

www.carroarmato.it
This is a delightful bar/restaurant near the Gothic church of Santa Anastasia, with its mysterious name meaning 'armoured car'. Delicious *antipasti* are served from the narrow bar or on large trestle tables in the adjoining high-ceilinged hall. The good-humoured staff occasionally burst into song. Card games are often played here, and there's occasional live music. The clientele is young. Credit cards are not accepted.
✉ Vicolo Gatto 2/a, 37121 Verona ☎ 045 803 0175 ◷ Thu–Tue 11–3, 6pm–2am, Sun 1–5, 6–midnight L €15, D €35, Wine €8

DODOCI APOSTOLI

www.12apostoli.com
A beautiful vaulted room, complete with a Roman cellar beneath where the wine is stored, is the setting for one of Verona's most famous and long-established restaurants. The food is classical Veronese, using local seasonal produce and concentrating on quality and freshness. The restaurant's specialty is duck breast cooked in a wine sauce.
✉ Vicolo Corticella San Marco 3, 37121 Verona ☎ 045 596999 ◷ Tue–Sat 12.30–3, 7.30–10.30, Sun 12.30–3; closed 1 week in Jan, and Jul and Aug L €55, D €75, Wine €18

OSTERIA LA PIGNA

www.osteriapigna.it
At this large and elegant restaurant diners are given a glass of sparkling *prosecco* while they peruse the menu. Try the duck *pappardelle*, risotto with Amarone or *stracotto* (beef stew) and Amarone wine. A good range of wines is available.
✉ Via Pigna 4, 37121 Verona ☎ 045 800 4080 ◷ Mon–Sat 12–3, 7–11 L €25, D €40, Wine €10

PIZZERIA LEON D'ORO

www.pizzerialeondoro.com
Relax with pizza and pasta in the garden of this unpretentious pizzeria, just a short walk from the Arena, and away from the crowds of Piazza Brà. Popular at lunchtime with locals; German beer is served more than wine. In the late evenings there is live music and a disco at weekends.
✉ Via Pallone 10a, 37121 Verona ☎ 045 595076 ◷ Daily 11.30am–2am; closed lunch Tue and Wed L €15, D €30, Wine €12

VICENZA

ANTICA TRATTORIA TRE VISI

www.ristorantetrevisi.com
This lovely 15th-century building has a great team of staff making this a particularly enjoyable place to eat. The food is firmly mainland Venetian, made with top-quality seasonal ingredients, raised and grown locally. Try *porca l'oca in pignatti con funghi*, a traditional dish of long-simmered goose with wild mushrooms, or *bigoli al radicchio di Treviso con acciughe*, the bittersweet long red radicchio from Treviso served with homemade pasta and anchovy—an intense and rich dish.
✉ Corso Palladio 25, 36100 Vicenza ☎ 0444 324868 ◷ Tue–Sat 12.30–2.30, 7.30–10.30, Sun 12.30–2.30 L €30, D €50, Wine €12

Below *Wheels of Parmesan cheese*

PRICES AND SYMBOLS

Prices are the lowest and highest for a double room for one night, unless otherwise stated. Breakfast is included, and all the hotels listed accept credit cards unless otherwise stated. Note that rates vary widely throughout the year.

For the key to symbols, ▷ 2.

BOLOGNA

CENTRALE

www.albergocentralebologna.it

Centrale is a small, central, third-floor hotel with lift, the most pleasant of the city's cheaper hotels. The hotel is simply furnished, but there is a TV in all the rooms.

✉ Via della Zecca 2, 40121 Bologna ☎ 051 225114 €85–€140 excluding breakfast 20

GRAND HOTEL BAGLIONI

www.baglionihotels.com

Housed in the Palazzo Ghisilardi Fava, rooms here are luxuriously furnished and superbly equipped, with 24-hour room service, satellite television, minibar and safe. Other facilities include a restaurant, parking and computer access.

✉ Via Indipendenza 8, 40121 Bologna ☎ 051 225445 €340–€520 103 rooms, 6 suites

OROLOGIO

www.bolognarthotels.it.

The elegant rooms are well equipped, and service is excellent. Pets are allowed. Bicycles are available and there is garage parking. Reservations are essential.

✉ Via IV Novembre 10, 40123 Bologna ☎ 051 1745 7411 €190–€370 33 rooms, 6 suites

CIVIDALE DEI FRIULI

LOCANDA AL POMO D'ORO

www.alpomodoro.com

There are plenty of traditional touches here but the bathrooms are modern and the rooms spacious.

✉ Piazza San Giovanni 20, Cividale dei Friuli, 33043 Udine ☎ 0432 731489 €80 17 From the north exit the A23 at Udine and follow signs to Cividale dei Friuli (S54). Turn right opposite the station and follow signs into town and the hotel. From the south exit A23 Udine Sud and follow signs to Cividale (S54)

MERANO (MERAN)

EINSIEDLER EREMITA

www.einsiedler.com

This hotel is a good base for families, with tennis courts, a sauna and a playground. There's a good bus service into town 5km (3 miles) away and a cable car nearby.

✉ Via Val di Nova 29, Merano, 39012 Alto Adige ☎ 0473 232191; fax 0473 256407 Feb–end Oct €66–€102 37 Outdoor and indoor Exit the A22 at Merano Sud. The city is divided into six hotel zones. The Einsiedler is in the yellow zone, so follow the yellow arrows to the correct zone, where you will pick up signs directing you to the hotel

PADOVA (PADUA)

AL FAGIANO

www.alfagiano.it

If you're looking for good value in Padua, the Pheasant fits the bill. Situated in a quiet area close to the Basilica of St. Anthony, this recently modernized hotel has smallish but comfortable rooms, a bar and breakfast room. It's a few minutes' walk from the heart of the city and has its own garage.

✉ Via Locatelli 45, 35123 Padova ☎ 049 853396 €75–€80 40

MAJESTIC TOSCANELLI

www.toscanelli.com

This is the best of the city's 4-star hotels. The rooms are equipped with satellite television and a safe. Other services include laundry, parking and child-minding.

✉ Via dell'Arco 2, 35122 Padova ☎ 049 663244 €160–€190 34

Opposite *Giardino Giusti, Verona*

SANT'ANTONIO

www.hotelsantantonio.it

This hotel is on the northern edge of the town, overlooking the old stone bridge that spans the river. Rooms are large and pleasant, and there is a bar and a lift. Pets are welcome.

Via San Fermo 118, 35137 Padova 049 875 1393 €82–€94 excluding breakfast (€7) 33

PARMA

VERDI

www.hotelverdi.it

A stylish, traditional Italian hotel of the old school, Verdi has private parking and a good restaurant.

Via Pasini 18, 43100 Parma 0521 293 539; fax 0521 293 559 Closed 3 weeks Jul and over Christmas €155–€190 excluding breakfast (€12) 20 Take the *viale* that circles the *centro storico*. Via Pasini is the section opposite the Parco Ducale

RAVENNA

ALBERGO CAPPELLO

www.albergocappello.it

This is an elegant hotel with very stylish rooms. Some are accessible for guests with disabilities. A babysitting service is also available.

Via IV Novembre 41, 48100 Ravenna 0544 219813 Closed 10 days Feb and 10 days Aug €130–€150 7

TRENTO

ANDES

www.hotelandes.com

Facilities at this chalet-style hotel include a wellness and beauty centre and a kids' playground.

Piazza Massar 3, Vigo di Fassa, 38039 Trento 0462 764575; fax 0462 764598 Closed end Oct–30 Dec €50–€100 per person half board, minimum 3 days. Special rates Christmas and Easter 31 From SS 48 take the N242 to Vigo di Fassa. Turn left in village to Funivia Catinaccio; hotel is on left

VILLA MADRUZZO

www.villamadruzzo.it

If you don't have a car, there are regular buses up the hill to this beautiful 18th-century villa. Bedrooms are classy and the rooms airy and well equipped. The restaurant is excellent and good value.

Via Ponte Alto 26, Cognola, 38050 Trento 0461 986220; fax 0461 986 361 €100–€140 51 Exit the A22 at Trento or Trento Nord and follow signs to Padua. Climb the hill and go through the tunnel, then turn almost immediately left towards Cognola. At the roundabout turn right to Via Ponte Alto, continue for about 100m (109 yards) then take the sharp right between the walls into the hotel

TREVISO

VILLA ABBAZIA
HOTEL DEI CHIOSTRI

www.hotelabbazia.it
www.hoteldeichiostri.com

These are two hotels well located for exploring the Veneto Alpine mountains and Venice, Vicenza and Treviso. The Abbazia is a cosy romantic hotel, in the style of a private house. The Hotel dei Chiostri is a light, airy boutique hotel furnished in contemporary style. They share a classy restaurant.

Piazza IV Novembre 3, 31051 Follina, Treviso 0438 971277; fax 0438 970001 Abbazia: €195–€330; dei Chiostri: €80–€150 Abbazia: 12 rooms, 4 suites; dei Chiostri: 15 rooms Located in Follina, north of Treviso, off the A27 motorway taking the exit for Conegliano. Conegliano Treviso

TRIESTE

DUCHI D'AOSTA

www.duchi.eu

A great combination of old-world style and modern comforts makes this elegant hotel Trieste's top choice.

Piazza Unità d'Italia 2, 34121 Trieste 040 7600011 €188–€267 55 Follow the signs to *centro città;* the hotel is on the main piazza facing the sea

UDINE

LÀ DI MORET

www.ladimoret.it

Immensely comfortable, with classically simple, large bedrooms, Là di Moret has one of the best restaurants in Italy.

Viale Tricesimo 276, 33100 Udine 0432 545096; fax 0432 545096 €70–€160 88 rooms, 4 suites Outdoor and indoor Exit the A23 at Udine Nord and follow signs to Tarvisio, then Udine –Cividale; the hotel is on the right at the second set of traffic lights

VERONA

COLOMBA D'ORO

www.colombahotel.com

There is beautiful antique furniture in many of the rooms at this luxury hotel. Parking is free or you can pay €18 to park in the hotel garage.

Via Carlo Cattaneo 10, 37121 Verona 045 595300 €290 41 rooms, 10 suites

HOTEL DUE TORRI BAGLIONI

www.baglionihotels.com

This luxurious hotel occupies a 13th-century palazzo in central Verona, right next to Sant'Anastasia church. It is spread over five floors, and the public areas and guest rooms are magnificently furnished.

Piazza Sant'Anastasia 4, 37121 Verona 045 595044 €570–€1,025 90

IL TORCOLO

www.hoteltorcolo.it

The rooms at this small, friendly hotel are simply equipped but elegantly furnished and include a television and a refrigerator. Parking costs €8 per day.

Vicolo Listone 3, 37121 Verona 045 8007512 €70–€125 excluding breakfast 19

VICENZA

CRISTINA

www.hotelcristinavicenza.it

This modern family-run hotel is ideal for an overnight stay. A stroll away from the *centro storico*, there's plenty of parquet flooring, marble-clad walls and deep sofas in the public areas. The bedrooms are well equipped but some are a little small.

Corso SS Felice e Fortunato 32, 36100 Vicenza 0444 323751; fax 0444 324297 Closed 24 Dec–2 Jan €85–€170 33 From the A4 follow signs to the city; you will arrive on the Corso SS Felice e Fortunato

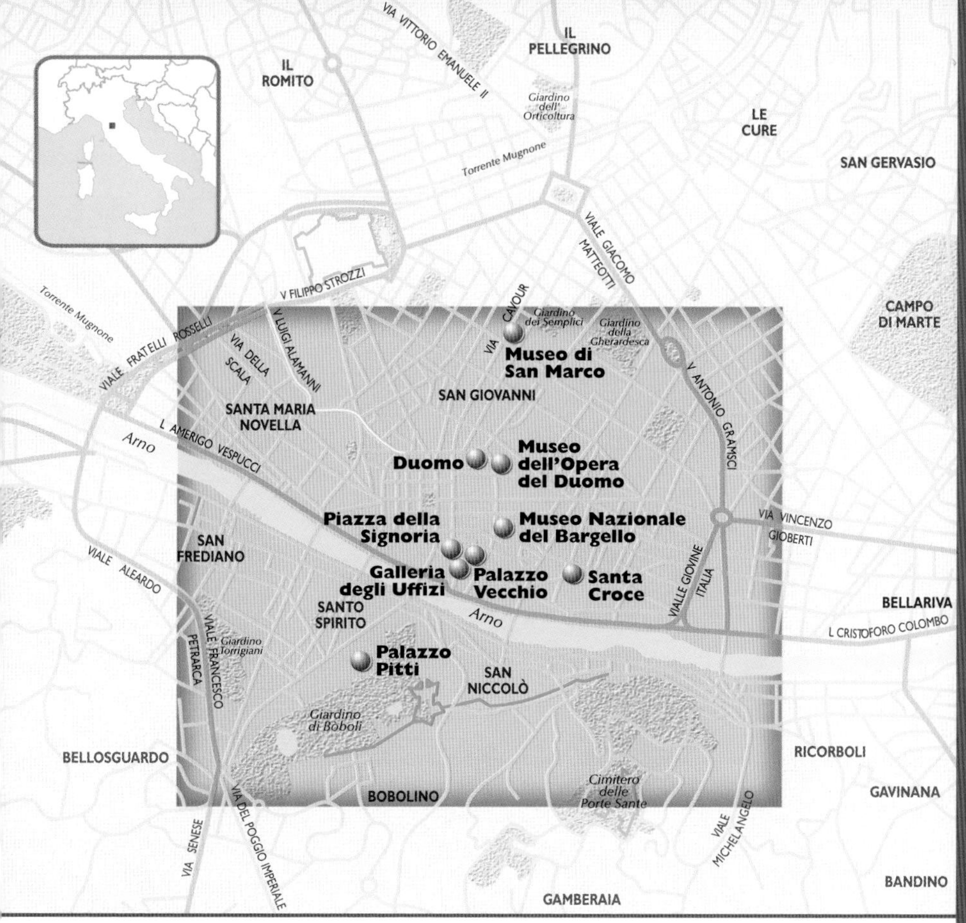

FLORENCE

It is stern and stony, impossibly crowded and often airless, but Florence (Firenze) still wins hands down for packing so much into so small an area. This tiny city—its centre measures barely a kilometre (0.6 mile) across—contains buildings, churches, paintings and sculpture which changed the face of the world forever and still influence our modern ideas of aesthetic beauty. It's the birthplace of the Italian Renaissance, that vivid and heady flowering of ideas and art that signalled the end of the Dark Ages and the entry into the light of a new, more rational world. Whatever you see in Florence illustrates a mood of optimism that today is hard to grasp, and a sense of humanity's potential and capability that continues to encourage so many of the millions who flock here.

The string of great names that worked in Florence is well known—Giotto, Brunelleschi and Ghiberti, Botticelli and Donatello, Michelangelo, da Vinci and dozens of others. All were brought here by the commissions and money of Florence's thriving and well-heeled bankers and merchants, men who surrounded themselves with beautiful things and fine minds, and were as interested in philosophy as the price of commodities. No family more perfectly symbolizes these Renaissance patrons than the Medici, Florence's leading money men, whose power and wealth gave them control of the city by the 14th century and kept them at the top of the heap until the 1700s. Their money and that of their associates, financed the building of the palazzi, the decoration of the churches and the sculptures and paintings they wanted for their town houses and country villas. The miracle is that it's all still here, endowed to the city by the last Medici, and waiting to be discovered.

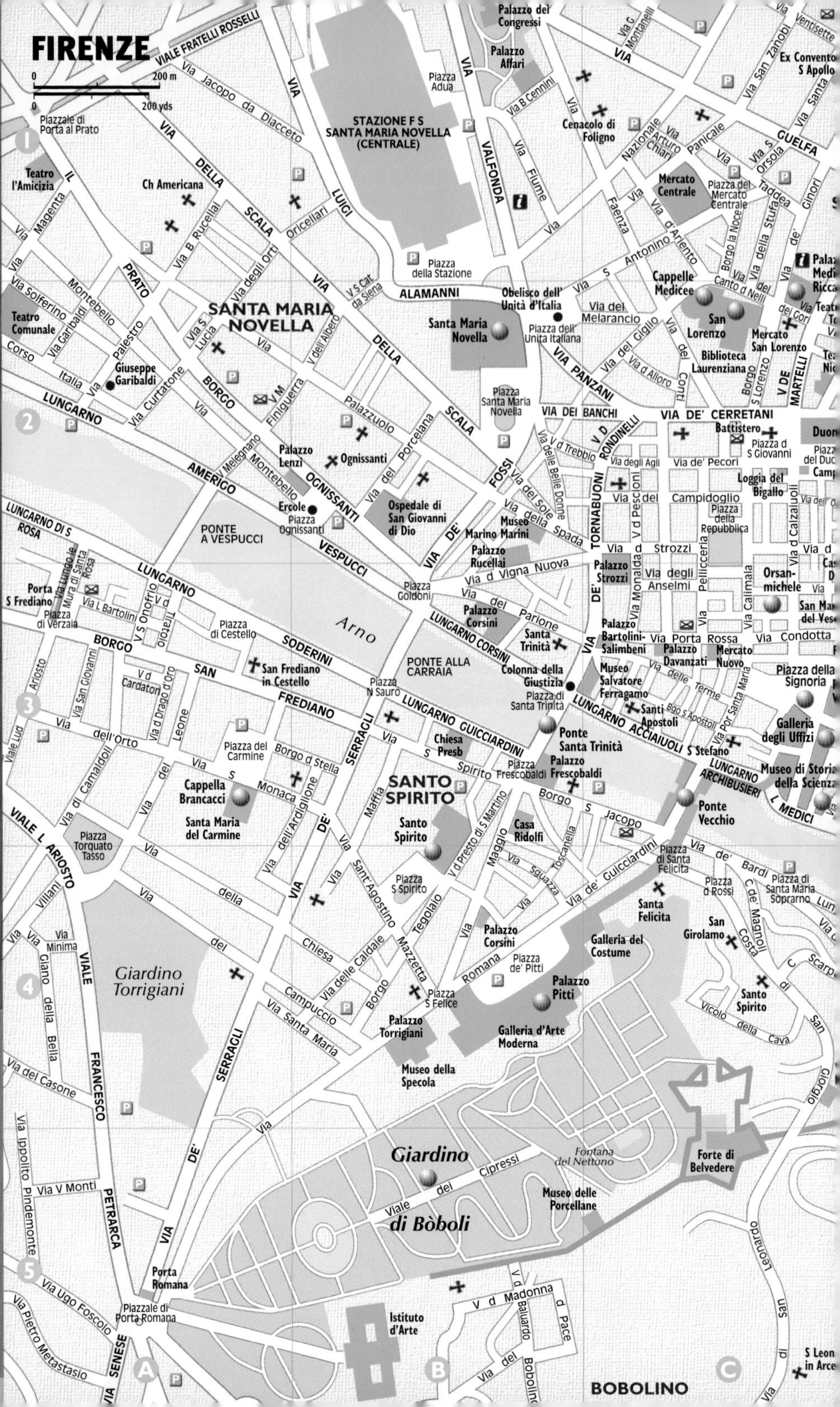

FIRENZE

0 200 m
0 200 yds

Piazzale di Porta al Prato
Teatro l'Amicizia
Ch Americana
Viale Fratelli Rosselli
Via Jacopo da Diacceto
Via della Scala
Via Il Prato
Via Magenta
Via B Rucellai
Via degli Orti Oricellari
Via Luigi
Stazione F S Santa Maria Novella (Centrale)
Piazza Adua
Palazzo dei Congressi
Palazzo Affari
Via Valfonda
Via B Cennini
Via Fiume
Via G Montanelli
Cenacolo di Foligno
Via Nazionale
Via Arturo Chiari
Via Panicale
Via Guelfa
Via S Orsola
Via San Zanobi
Via Ventisette
Ex Convento S Apollo
Mercato Centrale
Piazza del Mercato Centrale
Via Taddea
Via Ginori
Via Faenza
Via d'Ariento
Borgo la Noce
Via della Stufa
Via de' Ginori
Palazzo Medici Riccardi
Piazza della Stazione
Via S Antonino
Cappelle Medicee
Canto d Nelli
Via Teatro
Via Solferino
Via Montebello
Teatro Comunale
Via Garibaldi
Via Palestro
Corso Italia
Giuseppe Garibaldi
Via Curtatone
Santa Maria Novella
Via S Lucia
Borgo Ognissanti
V dell'Albero
Via Alamanni
V S Cat da Siena
Via della Scala
Obelisco dell' Unità d'Italia
Piazza dell' Unita Italiana
Via del Melarancio
Santa Maria Novella
Via Panzani
Via del Giglio
Via d Alloro
Via dei Conti
San Lorenzo
Mercato San Lorenzo
Biblioteca Laurenziana
Borgo S Lorenzo
V de Martelli
Via dei Gori
Piazza Santa Maria Novella
Via dei Banchi
Via de' Cerretani
Battistero
Piazza d S Giovanni
Duomo
Piazza del Duomo
Campanile
Lungarno Amerigo Vespucci
V M Finiguerra
Palazzuolo
Via del Porcellana
Via de' Fossi
Via delle Belle Donne
V d Trebbio
V D Rondinelli
Via degli Agli
Via de' Pecori
Loggia del Bigallo
Via dell' Oche
V Melegnano
Montebello
Palazzo Lenzi
Ognissanti
Ercole
Piazza Ognissanti
Ospedale di San Giovanni di Dio
Via del Sole
Via della Spada
Museo Marino Marini
Via Tornabuoni
Via del Campidoglio
V d Pescioni
Piazza della Repubblica
Via de' Calzaiuoli
Ponte a Vespucci
Lungarno di S Rosa
Via Lungo le Mura di Santa Rosa
Porta S Frediano
Piazza di Verzaia
Via L Bartolini
V S Onofrio
V d Tiratoio
Lungarno Soderini
Palazzo Rucellai
Via d Vigna Nuova
Palazzo Strozzi
Via Strozzi
Via Monalda
Via degli Anselmi
Via Pellicceria
Orsanmichele
Via Calimala
San Martino del Vescovo
Piazza Goldoni
Via del Parione
Palazzo Corsini
Santa Trìnità
Palazzo Bartolini-Salimbeni
Via Porta Rossa
Palazzo Davanzati
Mercato Nuovo
Via Condotta
Arno
Piazza di Cestello
Borgo San Frediano
San Frediano in Cestello
Lungarno Corsini
Ponte alla Carraia
Colonna della Giustizia
Piazza di Santa Trìnità
Museo Salvatore Ferragamo
Via delle Terme
Piazza della Signoria
Via Ariosto
Via San Giovanni
V d Cardatori
Via d Drago d'Oro
Via del Leone
Piazza N Sauro
Via de' Serragli
Lungarno Guicciardini
Ponte Santa Trìnità
Lungarno Acciaiuoli
Santi Apostoli
Bgo S Apostoli
Via Por Santa Maria
S Stefano
Galleria degli Uffizi
Viale Lud Ariosto
Via dell' Orto
Via di Camaldoli
Piazza del Carmine
Borgo d Stella
Via S Spirito
Chiesa Presb
Piazza Frescobaldi
Palazzo Frescobaldi
Lungarno Archibusieri
Museo di Storia della Scienza
Lungarno Medici
Via del Leone
Cappella Brancacci
Via S Monaca
Santa Maria del Carmine
Via dell'Ardiglione
Via Maffia
Santo Spirito
Via d Presto di S Martino
Borgo S Jacopo
Casa Ridolfi
Via Toscanella
Ponte Vecchio
Viale L Ariosto
Piazza Torquato Tasso
Via della Chiesa
Via Sant'Agostino
Piazza S Spirito
Via Maggio
Via Sguazza
Via de' Guicciardini
Piazza di Santa Felicita
Via de' Bardi
Piazza di Santa Maria Soprarno
Piazza d Rossi
Santa Felicita
Costa de' Magnoli
San Girolamo
Costa Scarpuccia
Via Villani
Via Minima
Via Giano della Bella
Viale Francesco Petrarca
Giardino Torrigiani
Via del Campuccio
Via delle Caldaie
Via Tegolaio
Via Mazzetta
Borgo
Via Romana
Palazzo Corsini
Piazza de' Pitti
Galleria del Costume
Palazzo Pitti
Galleria d'Arte Moderna
Piazza S Felice
Palazzo Torrigiani
Via Santa Maria
Museo della Specola
Santo Spirito
Vicolo della Cava
Costa di San Giorgio
Via del Casone
Via Ippolito Pindemonte
Via V Monti
Via de' Serragli
Giardino di Bòboli
Viale dei Cipressi
Fontana del Nettuno
Museo delle Porcellane
Forte di Belvedere
Via Leonardo
Porta Romana
Piazzale di Porta Romana
Via Ugo Foscolo
Via Pietro Metastasio
Via Senese
V d Madonna d Pace
V d Baluardo
Istituto d'Arte
Via del Bobolino
Via di San Leonardo
S Leonardo in Arcetri
Bobolino

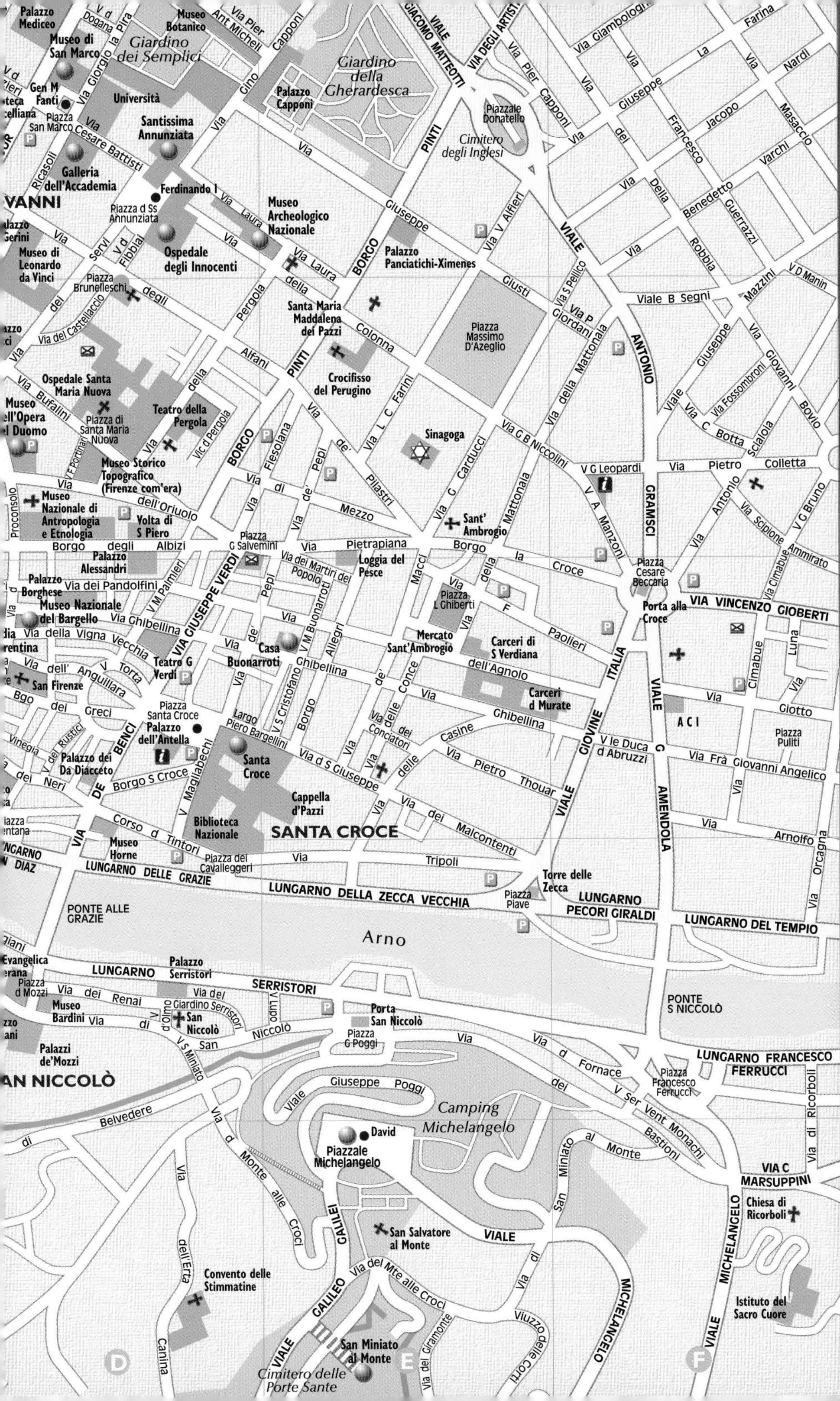

Palazzo Medici
Museo di San Marco
Gen M Fanti
Piazza San Marco
Giardino dei Semplici
Museo Botanico
Università
Santissima Annunziata
Galleria dell'Accademia
Via Cesare Battisti
Ferdinando I
Piazza d Ss Annunziata
Museo Archeologico Nazionale
Ospedale degli Innocenti
Museo di Leonardo da Vinci
Piazza Brunelleschi
Giardino della Gherardesca
Palazzo Capponi
Piazzale Donatello
Cimitero degli Inglesi
Palazzo Panciatichi-Ximenes
Santa Maria Maddalena dei Pazzi
Crocifisso del Perugino
Piazza Massimo D'Azeglio
Sinagoga
Ospedale Santa Maria Nuova
Piazza di Santa Maria Nuova
Teatro della Pergola
Museo dell'Opera del Duomo
Museo Storico Topografico (Firenze com'era)
Museo Nazionale di Antropologia e Etnologia
Volta di S Piero
Borgo degli Albizi
Palazzo Alessandri
Piazza G Salvemini
Loggia del Pesce
Sant' Ambrogio
Piazza L Ghiberti
Mercato Sant'Ambrogio
Carceri di S Verdiana
Carceri d Murate
Piazza Cesare Beccaria
Porta alla Croce
Via Vincenzo Gioberti
Palazzo Borghese
Museo Nazionale del Bargello
Casa Buonarroti
Teatro G Verdi
San Firenze
Piazza Santa Croce
Palazzo dell'Antella
Palazzo dei Da Diacceto
Santa Croce
Cappella d'Pazzi
Biblioteca Nazionale
SANTA CROCE
Museo Horne
Piazza dei Cavalleggeri
Lungarno delle Grazie
Lungarno della Zecca Vecchia
Torre delle Zecca
Piazza Piave
Lungarno Pecori Giraldi
Lungarno del Tempio
Piazza Puliti
A C I
Ponte alle Grazie
Arno
Lungarno Serristori
Palazzo Serristori
Piazza d Mozzi
Museo Bardini
Palazzi de'Mozzi
San Niccolò
Porta San Niccolò
Piazza G Poggi
SAN NICCOLÒ
Ponte S Niccolò
Lungarno Francesco Ferrucci
Piazza Francesco Ferrucci
Camping Michelangelo
David
Piazzale Michelangelo
San Salvatore al Monte
Viale Galileo
Viale Michelangelo
Via C Marsuppini
Chiesa di Ricorboli
Convento delle Stimmatine
Istituto del Sacro Cuore
San Miniato al Monte
Cimitero delle Porte Sante
D
E
F

FLORENCE STREET INDEX

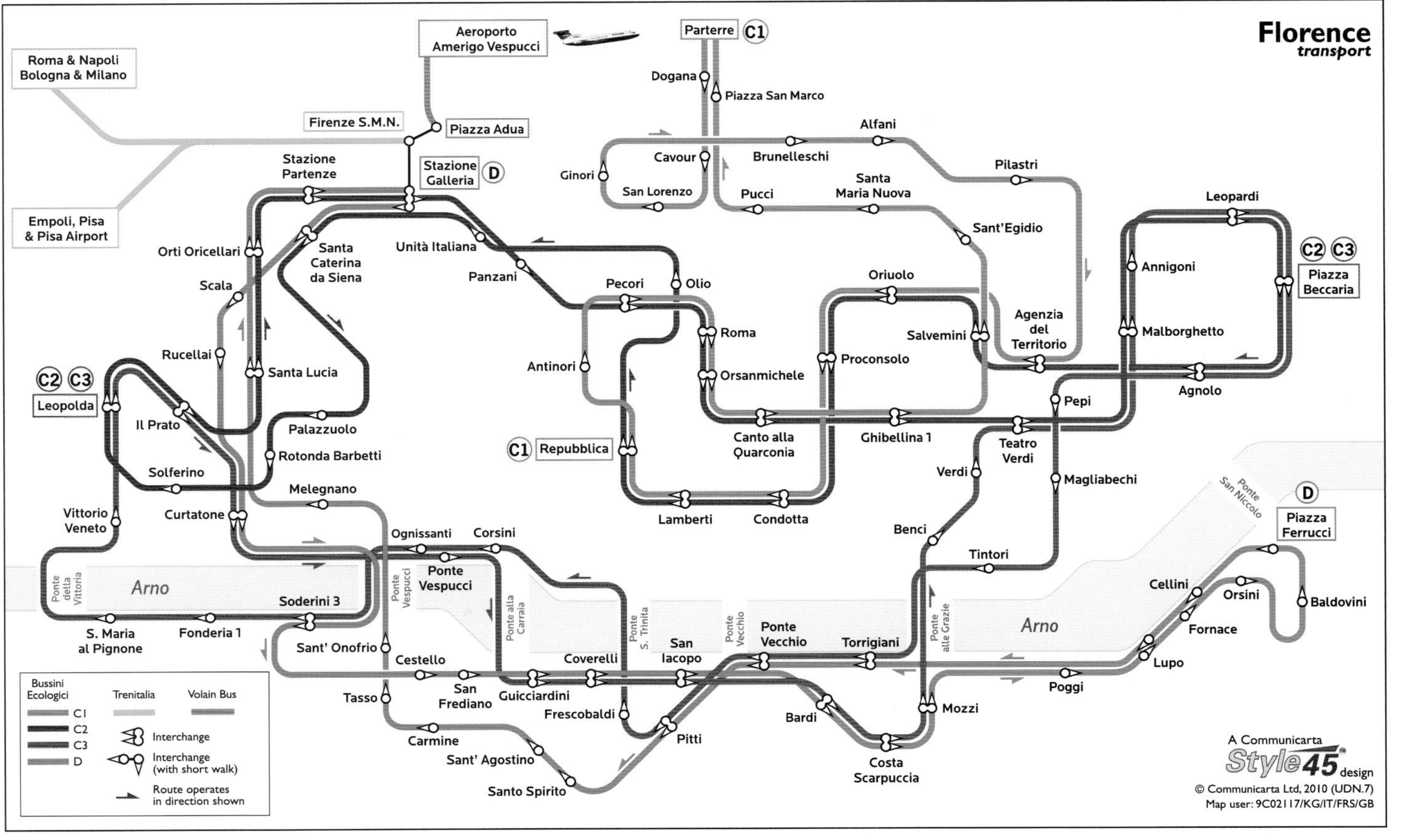
Florence
transport
Roma & Napoli
Bologna & Milano
Empoli, Pisa
& Pisa Airport
Aeroporto
Amerigo Vespucci
Firenze S.M.N.
Piazza Adua
Stazione
Partenze
Stazione
Galleria
D
Parterre
C1
Dogana
Piazza San Marco
Cavour
Ginori
San Lorenzo
Brunelleschi
Alfani
Pucci
Santa
Maria Nuova
Pilastri
Sant'Egidio
Leopardi
Annigoni
C2
C3
Piazza
Beccaria
Malborghetto
Agnolo
Orti Oricellari
Santa
Caterina
da Siena
Unità Italiana
Panzani
Scala
Pecori
Olio
Roma
Orsanmichele
Oriuolo
Salvemini
Agenzia
del
Territorio
Proconsolo
Rucellai
Santa Lucia
Antinori
Leopolda
Il Prato
Palazzuolo
Rotonda Barbetti
Repubblica
Canto alla
Quarconia
Ghibellina 1
Teatro
Verdi
Pepi
Solferino
Melegnano
Lamberti
Condotta
Verdi
Magliabechi
Vittorio
Veneto
Curtatone
Ognissanti
Corsini
Benci
Tintori
Ponte
San Niccolo
Piazza
Ferrucci
Ponte
della
Vittoria
Arno
Ponte
Vespucci
Ponte
Vespucci
Ponte alla
Carraia
Ponte
S. Trinita
Ponte
Vecchio
Ponte
alle Grazie
Soderini 3
S. Maria
al Pignone
Fonderia 1
Sant' Onofrio
Cestello
San
Frediano
Guicciardini
Coverelli
San
Iacopo
Ponte
Vecchio
Torrigiani
Cellini
Orsini
Baldovini
Fornace
Lupo
Poggi
Tasso
Frescobaldi
Pitti
Bardi
Mozzi
Carmine
Sant' Agostino
Santo Spirito
Costa
Scarpuccia
Bussini
Ecologici
C1
C2
C3
D
Trenitalia
Volain Bus
Interchange
Interchange
(with short walk)
Route operates
in direction shown
A Communicarta
Style 45 design
© Communicarta Ltd, 2010 (UDN.7)
Map user: 9C02117/KG/IT/FRS/GB

BADIA FIORENTINA

The Benedictine abbey of Badia Fiorentina was founded by Willa, the widow of the Margrave of Tuscany, at the end of the 10th century to commemorate her husband. The church bell, mentioned by Dante in the *Paradiso*, sits inside the beautiful hexagonal bell tower (1310–30), one of the landmarks of Florence.

On the left of the entrance is Filippino Lippi's enchanting *Madonna Appearing to St. Bernard*. On the opposite wall is a sculpted marble altarpiece by Mino da Fiesole, the artist also responsible for the marble monument to Ugo, Willa's son and the benefactor of the church, in the left transept. A door to the right of the choir leads to the upper loggia of the Chiostro degli Aranci (Cloister of Oranges), a reminder that monks once grew orange trees in this peaceful setting. Designed by Bernardo Rossellino between 1432 and 1438, it has a well-preserved series of frescoes of scenes from the life of St. Benedict.

231 D3 Via del Proconsolo, 50122 Firenze 055 264402 Tue–Sat 6.30–6.30, Sun–Mon 4.30–6.30

CAPPELLA BRANCACCI

This small chapel at the end of the right transept of the church of Santa Maria del Carmine has some of the most significant works of Florentine Renaissance painting—the Cappella Brancacci frescoes. The church's exterior is dull—a rough stone facade rebuilt after a fire in 1771. The frescoes survived the fire and, thanks to restoration in the 1980s, are vibrant once again.

The chapel, so small that only 30 people can enter at one time, is covered with paintings by Masolino, Masaccio and Filippino Lippi. Certain sections date back to 1425. In particular, look for Masolino's *Temptation of Adam* and *Healing of the Cripple*, and Masaccio's *Expulsion of Adam and Eve*. The image of Adam and Eve being expelled from the Garden of Eden, and their consequent anguish, is particularly emotive.

230 A3 Piazza del Carmine 14, 50125 Firenze 055 238 2195 Mon, Wed–Sat 10–4.30,Sun 1–4.30 Adult €4, under 18s €1.50. Advance reservations required in person at the entrance or by phone on 055 276 8224 or 055 276 8558

CAPPELLE MEDICEE

www.firenzemusei.it

The Medici's main monument, the Cappella dei Principi, is awesome in its dimensions and kitsch opulence, and provides ample proof of their wealthy egotism. This gloomy monstrosity can be appreciated for its sheer size. The other chapel, Sagrestia Nuova, is modest in comparison and has statues by Michelangelo.

The chapels are at the eastern end of the church of San Lorenzo (▷ 253), where most of the Medici family are buried. Glass cases display gold and silver objects from the church treasury, including beautifully crafted reliquaries and a 16th-century pearl-encrusted mitre. Stone steps lead to the entrance to the Cappella di Principi; the Grand Duke's octagonal mausoleum was begun in 1604, and is lined with marble and gems.

The Sagrestia Nuova has some superb examples of tombs and statues by Michelangelo. The tomb of Lorenzo, Duke of Urbino, is decorated with the famous reclining figures of *Dawn* and *Dusk*. The statues on the tomb opposite, that of Giuliano, Duke of Nemours, of *Day* and *Night* are considered by some to be Michelangelo's finest. The beautiful *Madonna and Child* is also by Michelangelo, along with the two candelabra on the altar.

230 C2 Piazza Madonna degli Aldobrandini 6, 50123 Firenze 055 238 8602 Tue–Sat 8.15–4.50; closed 2nd and 4th Sun and 1st, 3rd and 5th Mon of each month, 1 Jan, 1 May Adult €6, under 18s free

CASA BUONAROTTI

www.casabuonarotti.it

The Casa Buonarotti is a typical Renaissance town house. Now the Michelangelo museum, it provides an interesting insight into the life and times of one of the world's most famous artists.

Michelangelo Buonarotti (1475–1564) bought the house in 1508. On his death he left the property and several works of art to his nephew Leonardo, who in turn left it to his son, also named Michelangelo. He was an art collector and in 1612 he turned part of the house into a gallery dedicated to his great-uncle. The last direct descendant of the family founded the present museum in 1858. Three of Michelangelo's sculptures and a few of his drawings are displayed, along with various works of art collected and created by his descendants.

There are several portraits of Michelangelo and the marble bas-relief of *The Madonna of the Steps*, his earliest known work. Particularly charming are the Camera degli Angeli, a chapel, and the library with a frieze portraying famous Florentines.

231 E3 Via Ghibellina 70, 50122 Firenze 055 241752 Wed–Mon 9.30–2; till 4 during temporary exhibitions €6.50

Opposite *The tomb of Giuliano, Duke of Nemours, by Michelangelo in the Sagrestia Nuova, Cappelle Medicee*

Below *The spire of the Benedictine monastery of Badia Fiorentina and the 13th-century tower of the Palazzo del Bargello, viewed from the Campanile di Giotto*

INFORMATION

Duomo

www.duomofirenze.it
www.operaduomo.firenze.it
230 C2/D2 Piazza del Duomo, 50122 Firenze 055 230 2885
Mon–Wed, Fri 10–5, Thu 10–3.30, Sat 10–4.45, Sun and holidays 1.30–4.45; Easter 3.30–4.45; closed 1 Jan, Easter Day, 15 Aug and 25 Dec Free Free guided tours. Fixed audioguide points in the duomo, €1 Guidebooks cover the whole complex, in Italian, English, French, German and Spanish, €10 Duomo bookshop sells guidebooks, art books, postcards, gifts and posters

Above *The duomo is a masterpiece in marble and an icon of the city*

INTRODUCTION

North of Florence's civic heart, at the other end of Via de' Calzaiuoli, stands the city's spiritual focus, the wondrous complex of the duomo (the cathedral, properly called Basilica di Santa Maria del Fiore), campanile (bell tower) and battistero (baptistery). The buildings stand in their own piazza, a clear space that's constantly thronged with visitors. These are some of the most beautiful buildings of the early Renaissance, a tribute to the imagination of their architects, who pushed contemporary engineering skills to the limit to achieve these soaring, richly decorated structures. Outside and in, the scale of the decoration is mind-blowing, a proliferation of coloured and contrasting stone that's inlaid and carved, adorned with stone columns and delicate tracery, glittering with mosaics and enriched with sculpture, bronze and terracotta.

There has been a cathedral here since early Christian times. The baptistery, built in the sixth to seventh centuries, first acted as the city's main church and was later replaced by the church of Santa Reparata whose remains lie beneath the present duomo. In the 1200s, the city fathers decided to build a new cathedral, largely to flaunt the city's growing wealth and political clout. Arnolfo di Cambio was the designer, and throughout the 14th century a succession of master builders followed the plans he drew up in 1294. The campanile was completed by 1334 and in 1418 the duomo awaited the massive dome planned for the crossing of the nave and transepts, largely because nobody had yet worked out how to erect a freestanding dome. Step forward Filippo Brunelleschi (1377–1446), an architect who exuded confidence but refused to explain his plans. The nervous building committee gave him the go-ahead but insisted he work with his rival Lorenzo Ghiberti (1378–1455), who had already made his name with the bronzes he cast for the baptistery doors. Year by year the dome grew, and by 1436 it was complete, and the cathedral was consecrated.

WHAT TO SEE

THE DUOMO

The Duomo di Santa Maria del Fiore is huge—there is room inside for 20,000 people. It is worth walking right around its green-and-white striped marble exterior to appreciate the vast proportions. Several doors punctuate the walls, the most elaborate being the Porta della Mandoria with its relief of the Assumption sculpted by Nanni di Banco in 1420. By contrast, the ornate Gothic facade dates from the 19th century; the original was destroyed in the late 1500s.

Compared with the outside, the interior is remarkably austere. Over the years many of the finest artworks have been moved to the Museo dell'Opera del Duomo, leaving the duomo relatively bare. This enables you to appreciate the soaring space beneath the Gothic arches, the patterned marble pavements, the scale of the dome itself and the superb mid-15th-century stained-glass windows.

There are two equestrian memorials dedicated to two of Florence's most famous *condottieri:* a monument to Niccolò da Tolentino (1456) by Andrea del Castagno, and a far sharper-edged portrait (1436) of Sir John Hawkwood, an English mercenary, by Paolo Uccello. Terracotta reliefs by Luca della Robbia decorate both north and south sacristy doors, and a superb bronze reliquary urn by Ghiberti stands in the central apse.

INSIDE THE DOME

Climbing the rather claustrophobic 463 steps of the dome is a must; it is the high point of this great building, rewarded with sweeping views.

The interior of the dome glitters with Florence's only mosaic cycle, the earliest dating from 1225. Begin by looking above the entrance door and follow the history of the world from the Creation to John the Baptist, before taking in the main image of Christ and the Last Judgement, together with the Apostles and the Virgin.

Sun–Fri 8.30–7, Sat 8.30–5.40 (last admission 40 min before closing) €6

SANTA REPARATA (CRYPT)

From the south aisle of the duomo steps lead down to the crypt with the remains of the ancient church of Santa Reparata. Excavated in the 1960s, this ancient and confusing space has archaeological finds and, more importantly, the tomb of Filippo Brunelleschi, architect of the dome.

Mon–Wed, Fri 10–5, Thu 10–3.30, Sat 10–4.45 €3

Above *The marble interior of the duomo*
Below *A statue on the facade of the duomo*

MUSEO DELL'OPERA DEL DUOMO

The Museo dell'Opera del Duomo contains the sculptures and paintings of the duomo complex, too precious to be left to the mercy of modern pollution. Ghiberti's *Gates of Paradise* (▷ below) probably steal the show, but there is a *Pietà* by Michelangelo that many see as equally exquisite. The sculptor was 80 when he created it, his last work, and intended it to be for his own tomb, but never finished it; the figure of Nicodemus is said to be a self-portrait. Donatello, the greatest of Michelangelo's precursors, is represented by two works: a gaunt and bedraggled *Mary Magdalene* and the powerful figure of the prophet *Habbakuk*. Donatello carved this for the campanile and it is so realistic he is said to have seized it, crying 'Speak, speak'. His lighter side emerges in the choir loft from the duomo, carved with capering *putti* (children), the perfect contrast to Luca della Robbia's version, ornamented with earnest angels.

231 D2 Piazza del Duomo 9, 50122 Firenze 055 230 2885 Mon–Sat 9–7.30, Sun and holidays 8.30–1.45; closed 1 Jan, Easter Day, 8 Sep, 25 Dec Adult €6, under 6s free

GHIBERTI'S BAPTISTERY DOORS IN THE MUSEO DELL'OPERA

Having finished the north doors in the baptistery in 1425, Ghiberti set to work on the doors for the east side, a work of such beauty that Michelangelo named them the 'Gates of Paradise'. Completed in 1452, they are made up of 10 relief panels of

Opposite *The duomo and campanile viewed from the Piazza del Duomo*

TIP

» Shorts and sleeveless tops are frowned upon.

» The views from the gallery of the dome are breathtaking. The climb is best negotiated early in the day, and, once up there, try to give yourself half an hour to maximize your enjoyment.

biblical subjects, exquisitely carved in low relief. Their artistic importance is in their use of perspective, extending the scenes far into the background—a totally new concept at the time that became typical of the Renaissance. The composition is far more naturalistic than the earlier baptistery doors, with figures grouped off-centre to intensify the drama of each scene. The baptistery doors are Ghiberti's finest achievement. On the frame of the left-hand door is his self-portrait—the smug-looking gentleman with a bald head.

THE BATTISTERO

The octagonal baptistery, entirely encased in green and white marble, is one of Florence's oldest buildings, probably dating from around the sixth to seventh century, and remodelled in the 11th century. It is most famous for the three sets of bronze doors, the south set dating from the 1330s by Andrea Pisano, and the north and east by Lorenzo Ghiberti. Ghiberti, aged 20, won the commission for the north doors in a competition and worked on them from 1403 to 1424, embarking on his finest achievement, the east set (▷ 237), immediately afterwards. The panels in the doors you see are reproductions; the originals are kept away from 21st-century pollution in the Museo dell'Opera del Duomo.

230 C2 · Piazza del Duomo, 50122 Firenze · 055 230 2885 · Mon–Sat 12.15–7, Sun and holidays 8.30–2 · €4 · Audioguide

THE CAMPANILE

Giotto designed the campanile in 1334, but he died in 1337, before it was completed. Both Andrea Pisano, who took over after Giotto's death, and Talenti altered the original design considerably, strengthening the walls and adding large windows. The building is covered with bands of green, white and pink marble and is decorated with copies of sculptures and reliefs showing prophets, patriarchs and scenes from the Old Testament; the originals are in the Museo dell'Opera del Duomo. There are 414 steps to the top of the campanile, well worth it for the views of Florence and the hills.

230 C2 · Piazza del Duomo 9, 50122 Firenze · 055 230 2885 · Daily 8.30–7.30; closed 1 Jan, Easter Day, 8 Sep, 25 Dec · Adult €6, under 6s free

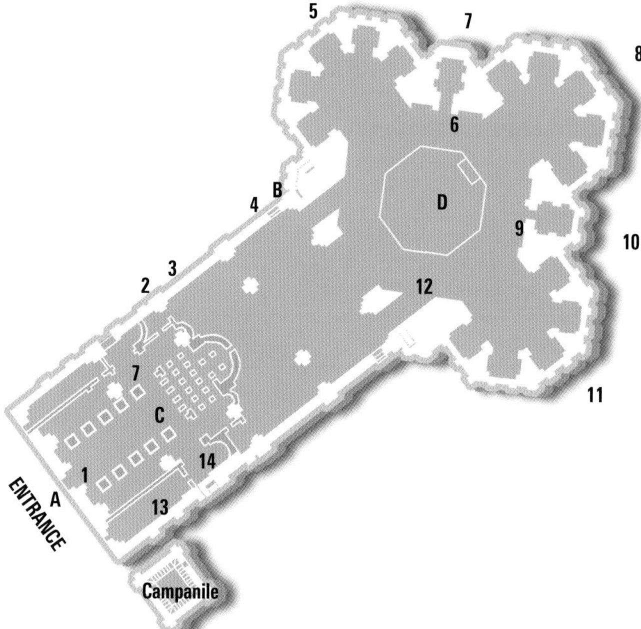

KEY

A Portale Maggiore with relief Maria in Gloria by A. Passaglia
B Porta dell Mandoria
C Crypt, with remains of old cathedral
D Chancel and High Altar
1. L'Assunta window by Ghiberti Incoronazione di Maria
2. Equestrian portrait of Niccoló da Tolentino, by A. del Castagno
3. Equestrian statue of Giovanni Acuto (John Hawkwood) painted by P. Uccello
4. 14th-century window, and below, Dante and the *Divine Comedy* by D. di Michelino
5. Marble altar (Buggiano)
6. In the door,*Lunette, Risurrezione,* by Luca della Robbia
7. Sagrestia Nuova o della Messe
8. Above the altar, two angels (Luca della Robbia), below the altar reliquary of St. Zenobius by Ghiberti
9. *Lunette, Risurrezione*, terracotta by della Robbia
10. Sagrestia Vecchia o dei Canonici
11. Altar by Michelozzo
12. Entrance to the dome
13. Bust of Brunelleschi, by A. Cavalcanti
14. Stairs to the Crypt

GALLERIA DEGLI UFFIZI

Above *The Ponte Vecchio links Palazzo Pitti with the Galleria degli Uffizi*

INFORMATION

230 C3 Piazzale degli Uffizi, 50122 Firenze 055 238 8651, 294 883 (reservations) Tue–Sun 8.15–6.50 (Jul–end Sep 8.15am–10pm); reservations in advance Mon–Fri 8.30–6.30, Sat 8.30–12.30, tel 055 294883, www.firenzemusei.it Adult €6.50, reservation fee €4, under 18s free Audio tours in English, French, Spanish, German, Japanese, Italian, from €4.65 Official guidebook from €4.50 Café overlooking Piazza della Signoria

INTRODUCTION

Entering the Uffizi and confronting the endless queues, the crowds, the pictures obscured by tour groups and the noise, may tempt you to wonder if it's worth it. It is. This is one of the world's greatest collections, the cream of the Renaissance, a procession of rooms crammed with masterpieces that illustrate one of the most remarkable periods in the history of world art. These are images familiar from a thousand reproductions, the output of a group of artists working over a couple of centuries in this small city.

The galleries of the Uffizi were built between 1560 and 1574 by Giorgio Vasari for Cosimo I de' Medici, who designed the U-shaped complex to house the city offices—or *Uffizi.* Cosimo's son, Francesco I, had the upper floor converted to house his art collection, and his successors added to it over the years. The collection was left to the people of Florence by Anna Maria Lodovica, the last Medici, in 1737, on condition the works never leave the city.

Superb museum though it is, the Uffizi's *Sopraintendenza* have long been aware of its shortcomings in terms of display areas and visitor facilities. In the first years of the 21st century a huge redevelopment plan was launched, which will eventually almost double the museum's space, as well as provide much-needed extra tourist infrastructure in the shape of better access and more cloakroom and refreshment facilities. Works of art now in storage will emerge, with the aim of opening up the Corridoio Vasariano, which links the Uffizi with the Pitti and is now used for storage, on a regular basis. The work continues into the second decade of the century, although progress seems to be very slow; the museum remains open as usual, though, as always, some galleries will close on a rotating basis due to lack of staff. For more information see www.nuoviuffizi.it.

WHAT TO SEE

MAESTÀ: GIOTTO—ROOM 2

A painting of the Madonna enthroned, combining Byzantine tradition with the first crucial steps towards the realism of Renaissance painting.

ADORATION OF THE MAGI: GENTILE DA FABRIANO—ROOM 6
This intricate picture (1423), with its sumptuously portrayed fabrics, epitomizes the zenith of the International Gothic movement.

PORTRAIT OF THE DUKE AND DUCHESS OF URBINO: PIERO DELLA FRANCESCA—ROOM 7
A double portrait showing the sitters in profile; the Duke lost his right eye in battle and was always portrayed from the left.

MADONNA AND CHILD WITH ANGELS: FILIPPO LIPPI—ROOM 8
Painted in 1465; the beautiful model for the Virgin was Lucrezia Buti, a nun, with whom the painter eloped.

Above *Detail of the* Madonna and Child with Angels *by Fra Filippo Lippi*

THE BOTTICELLI WORKS—ROOMS 10–14
The Uffizi's most famous paintings are *Primavera* and *The Birth of Venus*. *Primavera* symbolizes spring, with a Zephyr chasing Flora, transforming her into spring and covering her with flowers. *The Birth of Venus* (▷ 37) is inspired by Politia's poem and shows Zephyrus and Chloris blowing Venus ashore on a scallop shell.

LEONARDO DA VINCI—ROOM 15
This room contains early works painted by Leonardo when he was living in Florence. See his large *Annunciation* (1475), along with the *Adoration of the Magi* (1481), noted for its busy composition, remarkable character studies and curious symbolism. Left unfinished when Leonardo moved to Milan, it is in its preparatory state, sketched out in red-earth pigment.

THE HOLY FAMILY: MICHELANGELO—ROOM 25
Also known as the *Doni Tondo*, this painting was created between 1504 and 1505 for the marriage of Agnolo Doni and Maddalena Strozzi. It is Michelangelo's only completed work in tempera, a precursor to the Sistine Chapel frescoes in Rome.

THE RAPHAEL PAINTINGS—ROOM 26
Several important works hang here, including the luminous *Madonna of the Goldfinch*, a self-portrait, and the portrait group *Leo X with Giulio de' Medici*, painted shortly before the artist's death.

SALA DI PONTORMO E DEL ROSSO FIORENTINO—ROOM 27
Mannerism at its most startling, with attenuated forms and vivid shades.

VENUS OF URBINO: TITIAN—ROOM 28
This sensuous nude, painted in 1538, is unapologetically erotic, yet there is something innocent and trusting in the frankness of her gaze. Lord Byron described her as 'the definitive Venus'.

GALLERY GUIDE
Rooms 2–6: Giotto, 14th-century Florentine, International Gothic
Rooms 7–9: Early Renaissance
Rooms 10–14: Botticelli
Room 15: Leonardo da Vinci
Rooms 16–24: Perugino, Signorelli, Giorgione, Correggio
Rooms 25–26: Michelangelo, Raphael and Andrea del Sarto
Rooms 27–29: Mannerism
Room 30: Emilian painting
Room 31: Veronese
Room 32: Tintoretto
Rooms 33–45: 16th- to 18th-century—Rubens, Caravaggio and Rembrandt

Above David *by Michelangelo, in the Galleria dell'Accademia*

230 B5 Palazzo Pitti, Piazza Pitti, 50125 Firenze 055 265 1838 Jun–Aug daily 8.15–7.30; Apr–May, Sep 8.15–6.30; Mar, Oct 8.15–6; Nov–Feb daily 8.15–4.30; closed 1st and last Mon of each month Adult €8, under 18s free. Tickets are also valid for 3 days for the Museo delle Porcellane, Galleria del Costume and the Museo degli Argenti in the Palazzo Pitti (▷ 246–248)

GALLERIA DELL'ACCADEMIA

www.firenzemusei.it

Michelangelo's powerful *David* is the main draw of this gallery of the art school. Transferred here from Piazza della Signoria (▷ 250), where it was replaced with a full-scale marble replica, this depiction of *David* in a pensive mood before his battle with Goliath is a symbol of liberty to the Italians. Completed in 1504, when the sculptor was only 29, *David* immediately established Michelangelo as the leading sculptor of his day. In the adjoining corridor stand five other remarkable Michelangelo sculptures. The four celebrated *Slaves*, created between 1519 and 1536, intended for the tomb of Pope Julius II in Rome, appear to be unfinished, hence their alternative name of *Nonfiniti*. The fifth is a statue of St. Matthew.

Elsewhere in the gallery are early Florentine paintings, including works by Botticelli and Lippi. Also here is the Medici family's collection of musical instruments, as well as the plaster cast for *Rape of the Sabine Women*, in the Loggia dei Lanzi at Piazza della Signoria.

231 D1 Via Ricasoli 58–60, 50122 Firenze 055 294 883 (reservations) Tue–Sun 8.15–6.50 (hours often extended in summer); Easter Sun and Mon 8.15am–10pm Adult €6.50, reservations fee €4, under 18s free

GALLERIA DEGLI UFFIZI

▷ 240–241.

GIARDINO DI BOBOLI

This green space in the middle of Florence, a cool oasis on a hot summer's day, is the perfect fresh-air antidote to the many indoor sights in the city. Even at the height of summer, the warren of small lanes and pathways provides a welcome refuge from the tourist crowds. Elaborate fountains, grottoes, elegant buildings and formal gardens sit happily alongside lichen-covered statues and secluded glades, a playground for local cats.

The gardens are laid out on a hillside behind the Palazzo Pitti (▷ 246–248) and stretch from the palace up to Forte Belvedere. They were designed by Niccolò Tribolo (1500–50) for Cosimo I de Medici and were opened to the public in 1766. Near the main courtyard of the Palazzo Pitti is the magnificent Grotta Grande. In each of the four corners are copies of Michelangelo's unfinished *Slaves* (the originals are in the Galleria dell'Accademia). Walk up the terraces to the Neptune Fountain (1571), where you can either take a detour to the elegant, frescoed Kaffehaus for wonderful views and refreshments, or continue up to the top of the garden to the large statue, *Abundance*.

Off the beaten track, follow the magnificent Viottolone, a wide, steep path lined by cypress trees and statues leading to the lower part of the garden. At the bottom is the magical Isolotto, an island surrounded by a moat, adorned with statues, lemon trees and the Oceanus Fountain. Before you leave, pass by the Bacchus Fountain, a comic sculpture of Cosimo I's pot-bellied dwarf riding a turtle.

MUSEO ARCHEOLOGICO NAZIONALE

www.comune.firenze.it

The Museo Archeologico Nazionale has an excellent collection of art and ancient items, including the most important Etruscan and Egyptian collections in Italy—a welcome relief from the potential overload of Renaissance art in the city.

The museum is in the elegant 17th-century Palazzo della Crocetta on a busy street east of Piazza della Santissima Annunziata. One of the most important pieces in the museum, the restored bronze *Idolino*, is exhibited in a room on the ground floor. The torso of this statue of a young man, probably once used as a lampstand, is thought to date from the first century BC.

The Etruscan collection includes the famous bronze *Chimera*, part lion, part goat and part snake, dating from the late fifth to the early fourth century BC. Here also is the monumental *Arringatore*, or *Orator*, dating from the Hellenistic period, and a statue of *Minerva*.

The Egyptian collection includes mummies, statuettes, sarcophagi and vases, along with a 14th-century Hittite chariot made of bone and wood. On the second floor is a collection of Attic vases dating from the sixth and fifth centuries BC. Outstanding among these is the famous François Vase. Made in Athens around 570BC, this huge, highly decorative piece is one of the earliest examples of its kind.

231 D–E1 Via della Colonna 36, 50121 Firenze 055 23575 Mon 2–7, Tue, Thu 8.30–7, Wed, Sat–Sun 8.30–2 €4, 18–26 years (EU nationals) €2, under 18s, over 65s (EU nationals) free

MUSEO NAZIONALE DEL BARGELLO

The crenellated Palazzo del Bargello, home to the Bargello Museum, was built in 1255 as the Palazzo del Popolo, the seat of the city's government. In the 16th century the police headquarters was here, along with a prison, which was in use until 1858. The museum was first opened to the public in 1865.

GROUND FLOOR

Begin in the Gothic courtyard with its fine statues and sculptures. Until 1786, executions were carried out here, and condemned prisoners would spend their last night in the chapel on the first floor.

Off the courtyard, the spacious hall has the most celebrated sculptures, by Michelangelo and his contemporaries. Michelangelo's works include an early *Bacchus Drunk* (c1497), a humorous portrayal of the god of wine, and the marble tondo of the Madonna and Child with the infant St. John, known as the *Pitti Tondo* (*c*1503). Important works by Benvenuto Cellini include *Narcissus*, carved from a block of Greek marble, and *Apollo and Hyacinth*, once in the Boboli Gardens (▷ 242). There is also a life-size bronze cast of his famous *Perseus*.

FIRST FLOOR

The loggia has a group of bronze birds by Giambologna, made for the Villa di Castello. The Gothic Salone del Consiglio Generale contains works by Donatello and his contemporaries. His *Marzocco Lion*, the symbol of Florence carved in *pietra serena*, is the focus of the room. On the walls hang two of the trial bronze panels made by Ghiberti and Brunelleschi for the baptistery doors (▷ 237), a marble relief of the *Madonna and Child with Angels* by Duccio and a number of delightful glazed terracotta Madonnas by Luca della Robbia.

DECORATIVE ARTS

There are several rooms dedicated to European and Middle Eastern decorative art, including fabrics, carpets, ceramics, jewellery and clocks, and a large room filled with characteristically lively glazed terracottas by Giovanni della Robbia. Also worth seeing are the Renaissance bronzes, the most important collection of its kind in Italy.

INFORMATION

www.firenzemusei.it

231 D3 Via del Proconsolo 4, 50122 Firenze 055 238 8606

Daily 8.15–1.50; closed 1st, 3rd and 5th Sun, and 2nd and 4th Mon of every month, 1 Jan, 1 May and 25 Dec Adult €4 (€7 for special exhibitions), reservation fee €3, EU youths (18–26) €2, under 18s, over 65s (EU nationals) and art history students free Self-guided audio tours from €4.65 Official guide €7.50

TIP

» Look for Donatello's small bronze of David (1430–40), a work of extraordinary, melancholy beauty and the first naked sculpture since antiquity. It is so very different from Michelangelo's *David* in the Accademia (▷ 242).

Below *The courtyard of the Museo Nazionale del Bargello*

Above *Frescoes by Luca Giordano decorate the ceiling of the Palazzo Medici-Riccardi*

MUSEO GALILEO

www.museogalileo.it

This fascinating and informative museum, formerly the Museo di Storia della Scienza, explores the history of physics, chemistry, astronomy and medicine through more than 1,000 devices of major scientific importance and beauty. The renovated museum reopened in 2010.

The central figure is Galileo Galilei (1564–1642), one of Tuscany's famous sons, who was born in Pisa and died in Florence, having spent years in the service of the Medici family. Under the rule of the Medici and Lorraine, the city and region were a centre of excellence for scientific knowledge, as well as a cradle for the arts.

One of Galileo's many achievements was the perfection of the telescope, and here you can see the one through which he observed Jupiter's four satellites for the first time. Room VII is devoted to 'Galileo's New World', charting the progressive improvement of the telescope from Galileo's first examples, perfected in 1610 (▷ 37). There's a room dedicated to the development of the mechanical clock, with beautiful examples of pocket watches. Elsewhere, 'Science at Home' charts the use of scientific instruments used as home furnishings, while 'Therapy and Preventive Care' displays everything from lotions and potions to apparatus for self-administered electrotherapy. The museum also pioneers the use of portable interactive video-guides, making the most complex of instruments fully understandable even to non-specialist visitors.

230 C3 ✉ Piazza dei Giudici 1, 50122 Firenze ☎ 055 265311 ⏲ Wed–Mon 9.30– 6, Tue 9.30–1 Adult €8, child (7–18) €5

MUSEO NAZIONALE DEL BARGELLO

▷ 243.

MUSEO DI SAN MARCO

▷ 245.

ORSANMICHELE

Orsanmichele was built as a market in 1337, and the original building had a granary on the upper floor. When the market was moved in 1380, the ground floor became a church. The city's guilds commissioned some of the best artists of the day to make statues of patron saints to sit in the canopied niches, and so created a permanent exhibition of 15th-century Florentine sculpture. Some of the original statues are still here, including Ghiberti's bronzes of St. Matthew (1419–22) and St. Stephen (1427–28).

Inside, faded frescoes of patron saints decorate the walls. The jewel here is Andrea Orcagna's Gothic tabernacle, a large decorative work commissioned by the survivors of the Black Death in 1349.

230 C3 ✉ Via Arte della Lana, 50122 Firenze ☎ 055 284944 ⏲ Tue–Sun 10–5

OSPEDALE DEGLI INNOCENTI

The Ospedale degli Innocenti opened as a foundling hospital in 1445. It was the first of its kind in Europe and remained open as an orphanage until 2000. The building is an important architectural landmark—its beautiful loggia by Filippo Brunelleschi is an early Renaissance masterpiece.

A portico with nine arches borders Piazza della Santissima Annunziata, one of the loveliest squares in Florence. The spandrels are adorned with the familiar blue and white *tondi* (glazed terracotta medallions) of babes in swaddling clothes by Andrea della Robbia, while at one end of the loggia is the window-wheel where babies were left by their mothers. In the Museo dello Spedale are fine paintings, including Domenico Ghirlandaio's vivid *Adoration of the Magi* (1488). At one end of the room is a poignant collection of identification tags left by mothers in the hope that one day they might see their children again.

231 D1 ✉ Piazza della SS Annunziata, 50122 Firenze ☎ 055 249 1708 ⏲ Mon–Sat 8.30–7, Sun and holidays 8.30–2 Adult €4, child (6–18) €2

PALAZZO MEDICI-RICCARDI

www.palazzo-medici.it

The massive Palazzo Medici-Riccardi was built by Michelozzo between 1444 and 1462 for Cosimo il Vecchio, and was the residence of the Medici until 1540. The Riccardi family bought the palace in 1659 and enlarged it. Now it is the headquarters of the provincial government.

The main, columned courtyard is suitably impressive, and the adjacent gardens are filled with lemon trees in huge terracotta pots. The main staircase off the courtyard leads to the chapel, which is covered by Benozzo Gozzoli's beautifully restored frescoes of the *Procession of the Magi to Bethlehem* (1459–63). Gozzoli also dotted the scene with members of the Medici family and other celebrities of the day. The gallery is a large and elaborate baroque room decorated with mirrors and ceiling frescoes by Luca Giordano (1683). Look out for the restored *Madonna and Child* by Filippo Lippi in the smaller adjoining room.

230 C2 ✉ Via Cavour 3, 50129 Firenze ☎ 055 276 0340 ⏲ Daily 9–7 Adult €5, child (6–12) €3.50, under 6s free

MUSEO DI SAN MARCO

The Convent of San Marco, home to the museum, is next to the church of the same name. The original convent on the site was of the Silvestrine Order, but it was given to the Dominicans by Cosimo il Vecchio, who commissioned the architect Michelozzo to enlarge the existing buildings. Fra Angelico (*c*1400–55), also known as Beato Angelico, was a monk here from 1436 to 1447. The museum was founded in 1869 and in 1921 most of Fra Angelico's panel paintings were transferred here from other museums in Florence.

THE CLOISTERS AND THE PILGRIMS' HOSPICE

A visit starts in Michelozzo's peaceful Cloister of Sant'Antonio. In the middle is an ancient cedar of Lebanon and at each corner is a small lunette fresco by Fra Angelico. Off this cloister is the Pilgrims' Hospice, a long room full of beautiful paintings by Fra Angelico, glowing in bright jewel shades and gold leaf. At one end of the room is the superb *Deposition from the Cross* (*c*1435–40), while at the other is the famous *Linaiouli Tabernacle* (1433) with its *Madonna Enthroned and Saints.* The border consists of musical angels, often reproduced on Christmas cards. In this room is also the great *Last Judgement* altarpiece (1431) and a series of charming reliquary tabernacles in gold frames featuring 35 tiny scenes from the life of Christ.

Other paintings here are by Fra Bartolomeo, Giovanni Sogliani, Lorenzo Lippi and others. Before climbing the stairs to the monks' quarters, visit two more frescoes: Fra Angelico's large *Crucifixion and Saints* (1441–42) in the Chapter House and Domenico Ghirlandaio's *Last Supper* in the small refectory.

THE MONKS' CELLS

At the top of the stairs to the dormitory is one of Fra Angelico's most famous frescoes, the *Annunciation* (1442). The 44 tiny cells where the monks lived each has a shuttered window and a small fresco by Fra Angelico or his assistants. Those by the master himself are in cells 1 to 9. Note the beautiful angel in Cell 3 and the Nativity scene in Cell 5. Girolamo Savonarola, the rebel priest who was prior in 1491, occupied the Prior's Cell. Other famous inhabitants include the Florentine painter Fra Bartolommeo, who was a friar.

INFORMATION

www.polomuseale.firenze.it
231 D1 Piazza San Marco 3, 50121 Firenze 055 238 8608, 055 294883 (reservations) Tue–Fri 8.15–1.50, Sat–Sun 8.15–4.50; closed 1st, 3rd and 5th Sun and 2nd and 4th Mon of each month and 25 Dec, 1 Jan, 1 May Adults €4, reservation fee €3, 18–26 years (EU nationals) €2, under 18s and over 65s (EU nationals) free Official guidebook €7.50

TIPS

» The museum can be busy; a visit out of peak season allows you to experience the spirituality of the place, which may be compromised by the crowds.
» Only 120 people are allowed up to the dormitories at one time, so reserve your visit in advance (tel 055 294 883), arrive early in the morning or be prepared to wait.

Above *Paintings by Fra Angelico, displayed on the first floor of the Museo di San Marco*

REGIONS FLORENCE • SIGHTS

INFORMATION

www.polomuseale.firenze.it
230 B4 Piazza Pitti, 50125 Firenze 055 265 4321 Palatina, Appartamenti and Carrozze: Tue–Sun 8.15–6.50. Argenti: Jun–Aug daily 8.15–6.50; Apr–May, Sep–Oct daily 8.15–6.30; Nov–Mar 8.15–4.30. Arte Moderna: Daily 8.15–6.50. Porcellane: Jun–Aug daily 8.15–6.30; Apr–May, Sep 8.15–6.15; Mar, Oct 8.15–5.15; Nov–Feb 8.15–4.15; closed 1st and last Mon of the month. Costume: Jun–Aug daily 8.15–6.50; Apr–May, Sep 8.15–6.30; Mar, Oct 8.15–5.30; Nov–Feb 8.15–4.30; closed 2nd and 4th Sun, and 1st, 3rd and 5th Mon of the month Palatina and Appartamenti: Adult €8.50, under 18s (EU nationals) free. Boboli, Porcellane and Argenti: Adult €6, under 18s (EU nationals) free. Arte Moderna and Costume: Adult €8.50, under 18s (EU nationals) free Palatina audiotours €3.50 Café with a terrace in the main courtyard In Palatina and main courtyard

Above *A fountain at the Palazzo Pitti*

INTRODUCTION

Walk across the Ponte Vecchio from the Piazza della Signoria and Via Guicciardini leads to the wide piazza that fronts the looming bulk of the Palazzo Pitti. This huge Renaissance palace, as much a symbol of new money as a modern footballer's mansion, was home to the Dukes of Tuscany, the ennobled Medici family, who ruled Florence and Tuscany until 1737. It's a vast building, sprawling across a huge hillside plot, whose sheer scale dwarfs the crowds of visitors who come here. They come to see the eight museums now housed in different wings of the Pitti and to enjoy the green shade of the palace garden, the Giardino di Boboli (▷ 242), Florence's largest park.

The Palazzo Pitti, although by 1549 the Medici official residence, was actually built by a rival banking family. In 1457, Luca Pitti embarked on the construction of a palazzo, supposedly designed by Filippo Brunelleschi, that aimed to outshine anything else anyone owned in Florence. The enormous palace was certainly the city's largest, but it was also expensive to build and expensive to run. Pitti funds ran out and the palazzo was purchased by the Grand Duchess Eleonora, the wife of Cosimo I, a member of the very family Pitti had been trying to impress. The palace became the official residence of the Medici—by this time Grand Dukes of Tuscany rather than a simple banking family. They lived here until the death of the last family member in 1737. The Palazzo Pitti was then occupied by ruling families until its presentation to the state in 1919. It was the Medici who commissioned the alterations and extensions that brought the Pitti to its present size, and they were also responsible for amassing its collections. These are extremely varied, ranging from Renaissance and modern art to clothes and porcelain, and are housed in the various wings and state apartments of the palace. Pick of the bunch for most visitors is the Galleria Palatina, a suite of 26 rooms whose walls display a fabulous picture collection hung just as it was in the 17th and 18th centuries.

WHAT TO SEE

THE COURTYARD

The main entrance to the palace leads you to a grand courtyard (1560–70), an excellent example of Florentine Mannerist architecture by Bartolomeo Ammanati (1511–92) who was also responsible for the graceful Ponte Santa Trinità over the Arno. It was used as a stage for lavish spectacles between the 16th and 18th centuries, and is still the venue for concerts and ballets during the summer. It gives access to the Giardino di Boboli (▷ 242) and also houses the Pitti's café, a relaxing place for a break.

APPARTAMENTI REALI

The Royal Apartments were, from 1865 to 1870, briefly home to Italy's first monarch, Umberto I. Their extraordinary opulence is due to his taste in interior decoration rather than that of the Medici or the Dukes of Lorraine, who had previously used the apartments. Everything that can be gilded or decorated is done so with over-the-top extravagance; there's gilt and stucco, enormous mirrors, rich multicoloured textiles, vast chandeliers, marbles and precious stones. It's not exactly homelike, but it's certainly impressive. Among the hundreds of objects in questionable taste, it is worth tracking down the beautiful *pietra dura* tables, whose tops are inlaid with designs of flowers, fruit, birds and animals entirely composed of different coloured marbles and precious stones from all over the world.

GALLERIA PALATINA

Take your time in this spectacular series of state rooms. The walls are covered in damask and hung four or five deep with 16th- and 17th-century paintings by artists such as Tintoretto, Andrea del Sarto, Veronese, Caravaggio, Bronzino and Rubens. The approach is through the Sala di Venere, whose centrepiece is a perfect marble *Venus* by Canova, considered among the finest of 18th-century sculptors.

Madonna and Child: Filippo Lippi—Sala di Promoteo

Painted in 1452 and known as the *Pitti Tondo*, Lippi's famous work perfectly combines exquisite painting and intense spirituality. The eye is drawn to the pure face of the Virgin, the central point, surrounded by scenes from the life of her mother, St. Anne, and the Christ Child lying on her knee.

Madonna della Seggiola: Raphael—Sala di Saturno

Raphael painted this *tondo* in Rome in 1514, and it has been at the Pitti since the 18th century. Although heavily influenced by Venetian painting, evident in its use of light and shade, the painting follows a strictly Florentine form, its shape emphasizing the tender curves of the Virgin and Child.

Pietro Aretino: Titian—Sala di Apollo

Portraiture gained importance during the High Renaissance, as the Church lost its total control on subject matter, and new money brought self-made men to prominence. Titian painted this portrait of the satirical poet Pietro Aretino in 1545, after Aretino had moved from Mantua to Venice, Titian's native city.

Sleeping Cupid: Caravaggio—Sala dell'Educazione di Giove

This plump little sleeping Cupid is full of allegorical references to passion and lost love. Caravaggio painted it when he was in Malta in 1608. By this time he had already lived in Rome, where he had studied and grasped the fine details of human anatomy and was beginning to concentrate on the development of *chiaroscuro*, the contrast of light and dark, a technique expertly employed in his later work.

TIPS

» The Royal Apartments are closed for maintenance every year during January.

» The Galleria Palatina contains more than 1,000 paintings by Europe's greatest artists, representing the Renaissance to the Baroque. The quality and richness of its art collection make it easily a competitor for the Uffizi—and unlike the Uffizi, queues are not usually a problem.

» The Galleria d'Arte Moderna has a remarkable collection of Macchiaioli—an important late 19th-century movement that was a forerunner of Impressionism. The Macchiaioli wanted to break with convention and paint outdoors, capturing natural light, believing that patches of colour *(macchia)* were the most significant aspect of painting.

MUSEO DEGLI ARGENTI

In a series of sumptuous state rooms, this museum, located on the ground and mezzanine floors of the palace, concentrates on the luxury items amassed by the Medici dukes. Ferdinando I decorated these rooms in 1635, and the mind-blowing *trompe l'oeil* frescoes are the perfect backdrop for some wonderful treasures. Here you'll find the antique semi-precious stone vases collected by Lorenzo il Magnifico, Cosimo I's cameos, ivory vases and a fabulous jewellery collection, which includes 20th-century pieces from Italy's most famous jewellers. Don't miss the Salzburg Treasure, a huge collection of Austrian-made silver.

GALLERY GUIDE

Galleria Palatina: The main collection, strong on 16th-century works, particularly Raphael, Titian and Andrea del Sarto. In a wing of the main palace.
Galleria d'Arte Moderna: Works spanning the 19th to mid-20th centuries. In the main building on the floor above the Galleria Palatina.
Museo degli Argenti: *Objets d'art*, gold and jewellery from the Medici collections. Accessed from the main courtyard.
Museo del Costume: Rotating exhibitions of clothes from the early 16th to mid-20th centuries, including the burial clothes of Cosimo I, discovered when the Medici tombs were recently reopened. In Palazzina Meridiana in the south wing.
Museo delle Porcellane: French, Italian, German and Viennese porcelain and ceramics. In a pavilion at the top of the Boboli Gardens.
Appartamenti Reali: Lavishly decorated state apartments following on from the Palatina.
Collezione Contini Bonacossi: A picture collection on long-term loan, strong on Spanish painting. Next to the Museo del Costume in the Palazzina Meridiana.
Museo delle Carozze: Carriage collection—currently closed.

Below *A state apartment in Palazzo Pitti*

PALAZZO VECCHIO

The palace stands on the site of the medieval Palazzo dei Priori, rebuilt to Arnolfo di Cambio's design. Designers of *palazzi comunali* throughout Tuscany based their designs on its battlemented structure. Cosimo il Vecchio was imprisoned in the asymmetrically placed tower before his exile in 1433. Savonarola was also imprisoned here in 1498, but went on to be burned at the stake in Piazza della Signoria.

THE COURTYARD

Past the main entrance is the courtyard, reconstructed by Michelozzo in 1453. It was elaborately decorated by Giorgio Vasari in 1565 to celebrate the marriage of the son of Cosimo I to Joanna of Austria.

FIRST FLOOR

The largest room is the Salone del Cinquecento, a meeting room for the 500-member Consiglio Maggiore. Vasari painted the frescoes to celebrate Cosimo I's triumphs over Pisa and Siena. The most notable sculpture is Michelangelo's *Victory*.

Next door, the tiny, windowless Studiolo di Francesco I has allegorical paintings by Vasari and small bronze statues by Giambologna and Ammanati. It was here that the melancholic son of Cosimo I pursued his interest in alchemy. On the same floor, Vasari and Cosimo I's assistants decorated the Quartiere di Leone X with ornate illustrations of the history of the Medici family.

SECOND FLOOR

Access to the Quartiere di Eleonora di Toledo, the private apartments of Cosimo I's wife, is via a balcony across the end of the Salone del Cinquecento, providing a close-up view of the ceiling. The chapel, decorated with frescoes of various saints, is one of Bronzino's most important works. The Sala dei Gigli owes its name to the lily *(gigli)* motif, a symbol of the city. Here also is Donatello's bronze statue *Judith and Holofernes* (1455). Niccolò Machiavelli used the Cancellaria next door as an office from 1498 to 1512, when he was a government secretary. The *guardaroba*, or wardrobe, contains a fascinating collection of 57 detailed maps of the world as it was then known.

INFORMATION

www.comune.fi.it
www.museoragazzi.it
230 C3 Piazza della Signoria, 50122 Firenze 055 276 8224
Fri–Wed 9–7, Thu 9–2 Adult €6, child (3–17) €2 Audiotours in Italian, English, French, German, Japanese, €4.10.
From €5.50

TIP

» There is a wide range of guided tours geared towards both adults and children, often led by costumed guides and to places that are not usually accessible. Older children can attend workshops on fresco painting or experience the Renaissance in Florence 'live', while for adults the 'Secret Passages' tour is a fascinating look behind the scenes, including secret chambers and staircases. These tours are best booked in advance by phone or email to info.museoragazzi@comune.fi.it.

Above *An arcade decorated with frescoes by Vasari surrounds the courtyard of the Palazzo Vecchio*

INFORMATION

230 C3 Piazza della Signoria, 50122 Firenze

TIPS

» An elegant, expensive table at the Café Rivoire is a good place to people-watch. Or perch on a stone bench under the Loggia dei Lanzi.

» Free open-air concerts are held here in summer.

Above *Piazza della Signoria with its equestrian statue of Cosimo*

PIAZZA DELLA SIGNORIA

This wide, open square marks the heart of the *centro storico* and is next to the Galleria degli Uffizi (▷ 240–241). The Piazza della Signoria has been the political focus of Florence since the Middle Ages. Surrounded by tall buildings, notably the vast, sombre Palazzo Vecchio (▷ 249), this is where the ruling city fathers called open-air public assemblies in times of crisis. The crowd was often provoked by speeches on the *arringhiera* (oration terrace), a raised platform, and the gatherings frequently degenerated into violence. The area in front of the Palazzo Vecchio was named Piazza del Popolo (People's Square) in 1307.

THE SCULPTURES

The enormous Loggia dei Lanzi (also known as the Loggia della Signoria) was designed to be used by dignitaries for formal meetings and ceremonies. It was completed in 1382 and has been used as an open-air sculpture museum since the late 18th century. Dominating the front is Cellini's mannerist bronze *Perseus* (1545). Considered his greatest work, it shows Perseus triumphantly holding aloft the severed head of Medusa. Near it is Giambologna's last work, the *Rape of the Sabine Women*, completed in 1583. Donatello's *Judith and Holofernes* was the first of the statues to be placed in the piazza (this is a copy—the original is in the Palazzo Vecchio).

In front of the main entrance to the Palazzo Vecchio stands a copy of Michelangelo's *David* (the original is in the Galleria dell'Accademia, ▷ 242). The other large statue nearby is Bandinelli's *Hercules and Cacus* (1534), described by his rival Cellini as an 'old sack full of melons'. At the corner of the Palazzo Vecchio is Ammanati's massive fountain (1575), with the undignified figure of Neptune. The large equestrian bronze, Giambologna's monument to Cosimo (1595), shows detailed scenes of Cosimo's coronation and victory over the Sienese. The plaque in the pavement in front of the fountain marks the spot where Girolamo Savonarola was burned at the stake as a traitor on 23 May 1498.

PIAZZALE MICHELANGELO

On a hillside south of the Arno, Piazzale Michelangelo's wide, open space is bordered by a stone balustrade on the northern side overlooking the city. It is about halfway along the broad, leafy *viale* that winds through this part of the city and traffic can be heavy.

It is worth making the climb, or taking a bus, up to the square, for the unrivalled views over Florence. Here you can marvel at the full-scale replica of Michelangelo's *David* in the middle of the square or enjoy the view and a drink at one of the terraced bars. On a clear day, views extend way beyond the city to the surrounding hills, and the sunsets are fantastic.

231 E5 Piazzale Michelangelo, 50125 Firenze

PONTE SANTA TRINITÀ

The Santa Trinità bridge has the best view of the Ponte Vecchio and is a fine monument in itself. It is also remarkable, for in 1944 it was destroyed—along with all the other bridges in Florence except the Ponte Vecchio—by bombing, and was carefully reconstructed using stone from the original quarries. What you see today is a faithful replica of Ammanati's 1567 bridge.

Three wide, graceful arches make up the bridge, which links elegant Via Tornabuoni to the north and the characterful Oltrarno to the south. In each of the four corners stands a statue, the original *Four Seasons*. They fell into the river during World War II bombing, but were salvaged and reassembled (the last piece, the head of *Spring*, was fished out in 1961).

230 B3 Piazza Santa Trinità, 50123 Firenze

PONTE VECCHIO

If you can ignore the crowds and the modern gold shops, the Ponte Vecchio gives you a taste of what the medieval city was like—as well as a good view of the River Arno, its palaces and the adjacent Ponte Santa Trinità.

The present bridge was built in 1345, a reconstruction of an earlier structure washed away by a flood. Until 1218 this had been the only access across the river. At the end of the 16th century, Grand Duke Ferdinand I replaced the evil-smelling hog-butchers' shops that lined the bridge with gold- and silversmiths' shops, and they have remained here ever since. The bridge has survived two major traumas in recent history: in 1945, while all the other bridges in Florence were destroyed by bombing, the Ponte Vecchio was saved on Hitler's orders; then in 1966 the waters of the Arno rose so high that a fortune in gold was washed away in the floods.

Small shops and houses line the bridge on both sides, supported on brackets that overhang the river. They are painted in mellow shades of ochre, and with their wooden shutters, ancient wrought-ironwork and awnings they have retained their medieval appearance. Vasari's 1565 corridor is clearly visible running over the top of the eastern shops. Originally designed to be a secret passageway for Cosimo I, it joins the Galleria degli Uffizi (▷ 240–241) and the Palazzo Pitti (▷ 246–248).

230 C3 Ponte Vecchio, 50123 Firenze

SANTISSIMA ANNUNZIATA

www.ss-annunziata.it

In the mid-15th century this grand church was one of the most important in the whole of Florence. It was founded in 1250 to protect a miraculous picture of the Virgin, and expanded between 1444 and 1481 by Michelozzo, who also designed the Chiostrino dei Voti in front of the church, an unusual glass-roofed atrium decorated with frescoes by Andrea del Sarto (1486–1531) and some of his contemporaries.

The church's facade is made up of a graceful portico that leads into the Chiostro dei Voti. On the right are frescoes by Rosso Fiorentino of the *Assumption* and to the left is Jacopo Pontormo's *Visitation*. The interior is dark, yet lavishly decorated with marble and gold leaf. The tabernacle commissioned by the Medici family in the 15th century contains the miraculous painting of the Virgin, said to have been painted by a monk with help from an angel. Unusually, entry to the large apse behind the main altar is through a triumphal arch.

More notable works of art in the main body of the church include, in the north aisle, an *Assumption* by Perugino (*c*1450–1523) and *The Holy Trinity with St. Jerome* by Andrea del Castagno (*c*1421–57). The splendid organ in the nave, built between 1509 and 1521, is the oldest in the city and the second-oldest in Italy.

231 D1 Piazza Santissima Annunziata, 50123 Firenze 055 239 8034 Daily 7.30–12.30, 4–6.30 Free

Below *Ponte Vecchio spans the River Arno and was built in the 14th century*

INFORMATION

www.santacroce.firenze.com
231 D3 Piazza Santa Croce, 50122 Firenze 055 246 6105 Mon–Sat 9.30–5.30, Sun 1–5.30 Adult €5 (also covers museum); child (11–18) €3; child (under 11) free Free tours in English, French, German, Spanish, Italian tours given by volunteers, so times and availability of languages may vary). Audioguides at fixed points: English, French, Spanish, Italian, €1 €8

TIP

» The Calcio Storico, an established football (soccer) match, is played in medieval costume in Piazza Santa Croce or Piazza della Signoria on St. John's Day, 24 June (St. John is the patron saint of Florence). Other dates are picked from a hat on Easter Sunday.

Above *The facade of Santa Croce*

SANTA CROCE

In the heart of one of Florence's most attractive areas, the present Santa Croce was begun in 1294 and completed in the 1450s. The original plain front was replaced in the 19th century with an elaborate neo-Gothic one. The interior is vast, with a wide nave and superb stained-glass windows by Agnolo Gaddi. Although some frescoes were damaged in the 1966 flood, there are some exceptional works.

THE NORTH AISLE

Lorenzo Ghiberti (1378–1455) is buried under the tomb-slab with the eagle on it. There is also the tomb of Galileo Galilei (1564–1642), the great scientist who spent his latter years in Florence (▷ 37, 244).

THE EAST END

The polygonal sanctuary in the east end is covered with vivid frescoes by Gaddi. On either side are small chapels, each dedicated to an eminent Florentine family of the day, with frescoes by Giotto. The Bardi di Libertà Chapel has frescoes by Bernardo Daddi and an altarpiece by Giovanni della Robbia. The Bardi di Vernio Chapel has frescoes by Masi di Banco, while Donatello's wooden crucifix hangs in the Bardi Chapel in the north transept. The frescoes in the Castellani Chapel are by Gaddi, whose father Taddeo was responsible for the beautiful paintings in the Baroncelli Chapel. Next to the Baroncelli Chapel a corridor leads to the Medici Chapel by Brunelleschi.

THE SOUTH AISLE

In the south aisle are the tombs of Michelangelo (designed by Vasari), the poet Dante and Niccolò Machiavelli (▷ 37).

CAPPELLA DEI PAZZI

From the south aisle there is access to Brunelleschi's Cappella dei Pazzi. He was still working on this masterpiece of tranquillity when he died in 1446. Inside, in contrast to the elaborate Gothic tendencies of the age, grey *pietra serena* stone, simply carved in classical lines, is set against a white background. At the base of the elegant dome, 12 terracotta roundels by Della Robbia depict the Apostles.

SAN LORENZO

www.sanlorenzo.firenze.it

The principal members of the Medici dynasty from Cosimo II to Cosimo il Vecchio III are buried in this church. The basilica that once stood on the site was consecrated in 393 and is thought to have been the oldest church in Florence. The Medici commissioned Brunelleschi to rebuild it in 1425, enlisting Michelangelo's expertise for certain projects. There are fewer important works of art here than elsewhere in Florence, but the church is a shining example of archetypal Renaissance architecture.

The basilica dominates the bustling market area of San Lorenzo, rising above the lively and sometimes tawdry stands that attract bargain-hunters. The interior is dominated by the grey shades of *pietra serena* stone columns and the grey-white marble floor designed by Brunelleschi. Donatello's massive rectangular pulpits in the nave were his last work. Off the north transept is the Sagrestia Vecchia by Brunelleschi, featuring vaulting with terracotta tondi by Donatello, who also made the bronze doors. The small dome above the altar is decorated with frescoes of the zodiac in midnight blue and gold. Out of the main door on the left the graceful two-tiered cloisters frame a garden planted with orange trees.

230 C2 Piazza San Lorenzo, 50123 Firenze 055 216634 Church: Mon–Sat 10–5., Sun 1–5.30. Cloister: Sun–Fri 9.30–1 Adult €3.50; under 6s free

SANTA MARIA NOVELLA

www.smn.it

This Gothic church has numerous works of art but it attracts significantly fewer visitors than San Lorenzo and Santa Croce. It is a beautiful building, with outstanding stained-glass windows, chapels with important frescoes and peaceful cloisters.

The church stands on Piazza Santa Maria Novella, and has a striking black-and-white marble facade. Its lofty interior, with high stone vaulting decorated with stripes, is calm and uncluttered. The church's most famous fresco, Masaccio's *Trinità* (*c*1425), is remarkable for its use of perspective. The sanctuary is decorated with delightful frescoes by Domenico Ghirlandaio (1485–90). Next to it is the Filippo Strozzi Chapel in which there are some frescoes by Filippino Lippi.

There are more important frescoes in the Museo di Santa Maria Novella, in the convent.

230 B2 Piazza Santa Maria Novella, 50123 Firenze Church: 055 219257; museum: 055 282187 Church: Mon–Thu, Sat 9.30–5, Fri, Sun 1–5. Museum: Sat–Thu 9–5 Church: Adult €2.50, under 18s free. Museum: Adult €2.70, under 12s free

SAN MINIATO AL MONTE

The church of San Miniato al Monte, on a hill to the south of the city, is the finest example of a Romanesque church in Tuscany. The site also provides wonderful views across the Arno and the *centro storico* as far as Fiesole and the hills. A visit requires an uphill walk from town or a bus ride.

Built in 1013, the famous facade can be seen from all over the city. White and green geometrical marble designs surround a glittering 13th-century mosaic of Christ between the Virgin and St. Minias. Little has changed inside the church since the 11th century. In the middle of the nave the 1207 marble floor is made up of intarsia panels decorated with animals and signs of the zodiac. At 5.30pm (4.30pm in winter) you can hear the Benedictine monks singing Gregorian chants in the convent next door.

231 E5 Via Monte alle Croci, 50125 Firenze 055 234 2731 May–Oct daily 8–7; Nov–Apr 8–12, 3–6 Free

SANTO SPIRITO

www.firenzeturismo.it

The massive Santo Spirito was the last church designed by Filippo Brunelleschi (1377–1446). Its most notable feature is the simple 18th-century facade, now an emblem for the Oltrarno district of Florence. This is a great place to escape the crowds and discover artistic gems.

Brunelleschi began designing the church in 1444 and the work was finished in 1481. The huge structure, with its strange, blank facade, dominates pretty Piazza Santo Spirito. In spite of its grandeur, it is still a parish church.

Inside, grey *pietra serena* stone dominates, with massive columns, arches and vaults creating a harmonious space. The walls are lined with 38 chapels.

230 B3–4 Piazza Santo Spirito, 50125 Firenze 055 210030 Church: Mon–Tue, Thu–Sat 10–12, 4–5.30, Sun 4–5.30. Cenacolo: Summer Tue–Sun 9–2; winter 10.30–1.30 Church: Free. Cenacolo: Adult €2.50, child (under 20) €1.70

Below *The Gothic church of Santa Maria Novella*

THE HEART OF FLORENCE

This walk starts and ends with two of Florence's great churches and is a good way to get a general feel of the city. Weaving in and out of the main tourist route, it takes in some of the *centro storico's* quieter lanes, lesser-known churches, palaces and small museums along the way.

THE WALK
Distance: 2km (1.3 miles)
Allow: 1.5 hours
Start at: Duomo
End at: Piazza Santa Maria Novella

★ Begin at Piazza del Duomo, Florence's religious heart and one of the city's three main squares. The duomo (▷ 236–238) is one of Italy's most familiar landmarks, while the ancient Battistero (▷ 238) holds a significant place in Florence's spiritual history. The views from the top of Giotto's campanile (▷ 238) are stunning. At the top right-hand corner is the 14th-century Loggia del Bigallo, built for the Misericordia, a charitable institution whose members cared for plague victims in the 13th and 14th centuries. The beautifully carved porch served as a leaving place for abandoned babies.

On the southwest side of the square is Via de' Calzaiuoli, (Shoemakers' Street), built on the site of a Roman road. Follow this pedestrianized, shop-lined street, the medieval city's main thoroughfare, to Piazza della Signoria, passing the unusual church of Orsanmichele (▷ 244) on your right.

❶ Piazza della Signoria is one of two large piazzas in the city and has been home to Florence's civic forum since medieval times.

Leave the square on Via Vacchereccia, which emerges near the top of Via Por Santa Maria, once lined with medieval palaces that were destroyed by German bombing in 1944. A right turn brings you out to the Mercato Nuovo.

❷ The Mercato Nuovo is also known as the Straw Market or 'Il Porcellino', after the famous bronze statue of a boar, a copy of the original by Pietro Tacca (1612)—its snout is worn shiny by the daily affections of thousands of tourists who believe that touching it will ensure their return to Florence. There has been a market on this site since the early 11th century. The elegant loggia was built by Cosimo I in 1547 and has been restored; it now shelters stands selling souvenirs and leather goods.

Pass the market, turn left and walk down Via Porta Rossa. On the left is the Palazzo Davanzati or the Museo della Casa Fiorentina Antica, complete with top-floor loggia. At the end of the street lie Piazza Santa Trinità and its eponymous church, full of artistic treasures. In the middle of the square is the tall Column of Justice, a monolith brought from the Baths of Caracalla in Rome and given to Cosimo I in 1560 by Pope Pius IV. On the left stands the fine Palazzo Bartolini-Salimbeni, built between 1520 and 1523 by Baccio d'Agnolo, and beyond this the splendid

Palazzo Spini-Feroni, one of the best-preserved medieval palaces in Florence, now housing Ferragamo's flagship store and shoe museum (▷ 257). To its left, Borgo Santi Apostoli leads to the tiny sunken Piazza del Limbo, so-called because it stands on the site of a cemetery for unbaptized babies, and the Church of Santi Apostoli.

❸ Founded in the 11th century, Santi Apostoli is one of the oldest churches in the city with a series of marble columns and capitals and a carved tomb by Benedetto da Rovezzano inside.

Once back in Piazza Santa Trinità, take the Via del Parione to the right of the church, then head down one of the two narrow alleys on the right. This emerges onto the intriguing Via del Purgatorio (Road of Purgatory). Turn left into Via della Vigna Nuova.

❹ The elegant facade of the Palazzo Rucellai, designed by Leon Battista Alberti and built by Bernardo Rossellino between 1446 and 1451, faces you across a little square *(piazzetta)*. The lovely Loggia dei Rucellai, now home to a fashion store, is on your right.

Cross over Via della Vigna Nuova, turn right up Via dei Palchetti (at the corner of the Palazzo Rucellai), then right again into Via dei Federighi. This leads into Piazza San Pancrazio.

❺ Here you will find the ancient, deconsecrated Church of San Pancrazio, now home to the Museo Marino Marini, which is dedicated to the work of the Florentine sculptor Marino Marini (1901–80). Just around the corner, on the right at Via della Spada 18, is the tiny Cappella di San Sepolcro. Built by Alberti in 1467 for the Rucellai family, it features a superbly carved marble inlay model of the Church of the Holy Sepulchre in Jerusalem.

From the Cappella di San Sepolcro, walk back a little way along Via della Spada and turn left down Via del Moro, which is full of antique shops. At Piazza Goldoni, turn right and continue along Borgo Ognissanti.

❻ No. 60r is one of Florence's more unusual buildings, a well-preserved example of art deco architecture. A few doors down are the church and convent that give the street its name. It faces the river across the wide Piazza Ognissanti. To the right side is the 15th-century Palazzo Lenzi. Covered in elaborate sgraffito (incised patterning), it now houses the French Consulate. Across the river you can see the Church of San Frediano in Cestello, one of the many in Florence whose facade was left unfinished.

Backtrack a little and turn left up Via della Porcellana, lined with artisan workshops, then turn right at the top to emerge into the huge Piazza Santa Maria Novella. At the north end stands the magnificent Gothic church of the same name (▷ 253).

WHEN TO GO

Morning is the best time to explore Florence, when all the churches and museums are open. During the afternoon many of the smaller churches are closed and you will not be able to appreciate their remarkable interiors.

WHERE TO EAT

There are plenty of bars and cafés to choose from in this part of town. One of the nicest is Caffè Rivoire with its beautiful terrace (Piazza della Signoria 4r, tel 055 293045, Tue–Sat 8am–midnight), renowned for its delicious chocolate. The Cantinetta dei Verazzano (Via dei Tavolini 18–20r, tel 055 268590, Mon–Sat 8am–9pm), just off Via Calzaiuoli, serves coffee and cakes along with excellent wines and snacks.

PLACES TO VISIT

SANTI APOSTOLI

✉ Piazza del Limbo, 50122 Firenze
🕐 Mon–Sat 10–12, 4–6, Sun 4–6

MUSEO MARINO MARINI

✉ Piazza San Pancrazio, 50123 Firenze
🕐 Wed–Mon 10–5; closed in Aug

CAPPELLA DI SAN SEPOLCRO

✉ Via della Spada 18, 50123 Firenze
🕐 Mon–Fri 10–12

Opposite *A statue of a wild boar in the Mercato Nuovo*

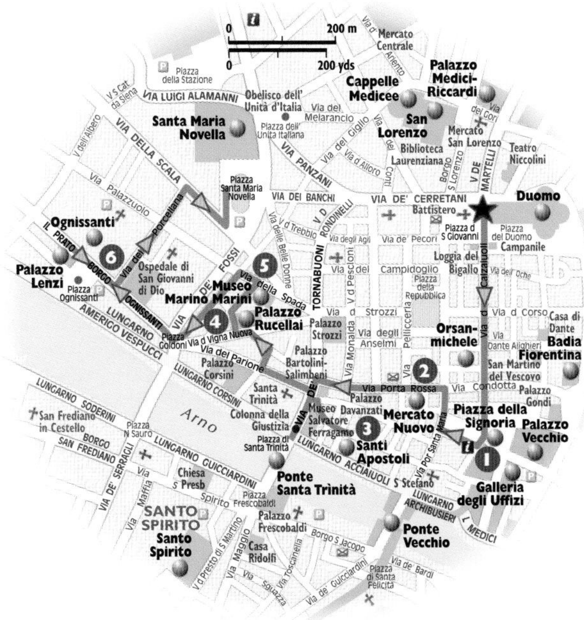

WHAT TO DO

Above *Freshly cut flowers at Florence's Mercato Centrale di San Lorenzo*

SHOPPING

ALICE'S MASKS

www.alicemasks.com

Masks in exquisite detail and infinite numbers fill every corner of this shop/studio. Not only can you buy masks here, you can join in a workshop to learn the art of papier mâché mask-making.

✉ Via Faenza 72r, 50126 Firenze ☎ 055 287 370 🕘 Mon–Sat 9–1, 3.30–7.30 🚌 4, 12, 25, 31, 32, 33

ALINARI

Alinari is Italy's oldest photographic archive, with a mouth-watering selection of beautiful photos and books, which you can buy in the shop or order online. This is the best place in Florence for photographic books, postcards, prints and photos.

✉ Largo Alinari 15, 50123 Firenze ☎ 055 23951 🕘 Mon–Sat 9–1, 2.30–6.30; closed 2 weeks Aug 🚌 6, 3, 36

ARGENTERIA BRANDIMARTE

www.brandimarte.com

The late Brandimarte Guscelli's dedicated apprentices continue his unusual designs in silver, and you can see them at work here in the silver factory. Plates and goblets are decorated in relief with fruits, vines and leaves.

✉ Factory: Via Ugo Foscolo 6, 50124 Firenze. Shop: Viale L Ariosto 11/C6, 50124 Firenze ☎ Factory: 055 239381. Shop: 055 23041 🕘 Mon–Fri 9–1, 2.30–6; closed Aug 🚌 D

FLORENTINE MARKETS

Florence has a huge number of markets selling everything from food to antiques. There are also some superb flea markets. The most famous is in and around Piazza San Lorenzo, where you'll find leather and other assorted goods. There are stands daily at Santo Spirito, selling bedding, shoes, clothing and haberdashery. On the second Sunday of the month there is an ethnic flea market, and on the third Sunday there are organic foods, Tuscan clothing and herbal remedies on sale. On the last Sunday of each month there's an antiques market in Piazza dei Ciompi (9–7). Head towards Via dell'Ariento and the Mercatone delle Cascine (Tue 7–2) for a morning of browsing and bartering. Even though you can't take plants back home, a walk around the plant market on Thursday mornings around the Piazza della Repubblica is a memorable experience. Mercato Nuovo (Porcellino) on Via Porta Rossa (daily 9–7) has leather bags and shoes and is full of inexpensive reproductions of Florentine classics, which makes it a great place for souvenir-hunters. The covered Mercato Centrale di San Lorenzo is full of mouth-watering Florentine delights—feast your eyes on the wonderful fruit and vegetable stands, and the *salumeria* counters brimming with meats and cheeses.

✉ Piazza San Lorenzo, Piazza Santo Spirito, Piazza dei Ciompi and Via dell'Ariento, Piazza Lorenzo Ghiberti, Piazza della Repubblica, Via Porta Rossa, Piazza del Mercato Centrale ☎ 055 234 0444 (tourist office) 🕘 Mon–Sat 8.30–7, 8.30–2 in winter

FRATELLI PICCINI

www.fratellipiccini.com

If you want to go jewellery shopping on the Ponte Vecchio, make sure you take in Piccini's. Their lovely gold charms make a nice gift.

✉ Ponte Vecchio 23r, 50125 Firenze ☎ 055 294768 🕘 Apr–Oct daily 9.30–7.30; Nov–Mar 9.30–1, 3.30–1 🚌 B, D

PINEIDER

www.pineider.it

Pineider remains Italy's original and most prestigious stationer—the letters of Napoleon, Byron and Dietrich were

scribed using Pineider's beautifully crafted tinted papers and inks. It also stocks exquisite leather-bound notebooks and accessories, from gloves to seals.
Piazza della Signoria 13–14r, 50122 Firenze 055 284655 Tue–Sat 10–7, Mon 3–7 23

ROMANO
There's something for literally everyone at this long-established store—everyday shoes, sandals, boots, both high fashion and comfort for older feet. They also sell bags and other leather accessories, with two collections of these and footwear twice a year.
Via degli Speziali 10r, Borgo San Lorenzo 13r, 50122 055 216535 or 055 284725 Tue–Sat 10–7.30, Mon 3.30–7.30 A

SALVATORE FERRAGAMO SHOP AND MUSEUM
www.museoferragamo.it
Florence is home to several fashion heroes, including Gucci, Cavalli and Pucci—and to Salvatore Ferragamo, the first celebrity shoemaker, creating shoes for movie stars and royalty. Set in the Palazzo Spini-Feroni, the shop and museum are utterly palatial and give a fascinating insight into the world of Ferragamo. In the shop the employees are so skilled they can fit clients into shoes without having to measure them first.
Piazza Santa Croce 16, 50122 Firenze 055 244533 Mar–Nov Mon–Sat 9.30–6, Sun 10–5 B, C, 23

SCUOLA DEL CUOIO (LEATHER SCHOOL)
www.leatherschool.it
This workshop, at the back of the famous church, was once run by Franciscan monks. If you intend to shop for leather goods, come here first to learn how to spot quality and craftsmanship. If you make a purchase at the on-site shop, they'll personalize the goods for you with a stamp.
Piazza Santa Croce 16, 50122 Firenze 055 244533 Mar–Nov Mon–Sat 9.30–6, Sun 10–5 B, C, 23

ENTERTAINMENT AND NIGHTLIFE

CAFFÈ CONCERTO PASZKOWSKI
This wonderfully traditional and elegant café, with its marble-topped bar and outside tables, is a favourite haunt of smart Florentines. Come to see and be seen and enjoy perfectly mixed drinks, coffee and a wide range of wines.
Piazza della Repubblica 31–35r, 50123 Firenze 055 210236 Tue–Sun 7am–1am A, 6, 22

CENTRAL PARK
This is a true house music complex, complete with garden, eight bars, four dance floors, restaurant and a VIP terrace. Italian house dominates but there's also plenty of room for chilling out with loungecore and smooth piano-bar music.
Via del Fosso Macinate 1, 50144 Firenze 055 353505 Wed–Sat 11pm–4am €20 1, 9, 12, 80

CINEMA GOLDONI
The Goldoni is one of only three Florentine cinemas to show movies in their original language.
Via Serragli 109, 50124 Firenze 055 222437 Adult €18, child €5 36, 37

CRISCO
One of Florence's leading gay clubs, for men only, Crisco is near the duomo in Santa Croce. In a city famed for its cross-dressing, expect to see the most glamorous of transvestites here.
Via Sant'Egidio 43r, 50122 Firenze 055 248 0580 Sun–Mon, Wed–Thu 9pm–3am, Fri–Sat 10.30pm–5am €15 A, 14, 23

ESTATE FIESOLANA (OPEN-AIR SUMMER CONCERTS IN FIESOLE)
www.estatefiesolana.it
Sunset concerts and operatic productions are held at the first-century Teatro Romano during the summer months. Reserve in advance and then head for the verdant, tranquil Fiesole hills, above the city. Tickets also available at Via Alamanni 39 (tel 055 210804).
Piazza del Mercato 5, Fiesole, 50014 Firenze 055 596 1293 Jun–end Sep €52 7 Fiesole central

FIDDLER'S ELBOW
www.thefiddlerselbow.com
The original Florentine Irish pub in Campo Santa Maria Novella is popular with students and tourists. Enjoy a Guinness and catch up on the latest premiership football action on the wide-screen TVs.
Piazza Santa Maria Novella 7r, 50123 Firenze 055 215056 Daily 11am–2am A, 1, 14, 17, 36, 37

JARAGUA
www.jaragua.it
Italy's first exclusively Latino music club is fun and free to get into. The spicy South American food also appeals to the 30-something crowd. For those who don't know how to dance salsa or merengue, there are lessons available as well as many willing tutors on the dance floor.
Via Erta Canina 12/r, 50125 Firenze 055 234 3600 Daily 9.30pm–3am C, D

MARACANÀ
Six levels, a carnival stage and a party crowd make this club a winner with lovers of all things Brazilian. It's the place to watch carnival dancers, samba, sip *caipirinhas* (a cocktail made with lime juice and cachaça, Brazilian sugar cane liquor) and try some of the enormous *churrasco* (Brazilian barbequed meats). The bar staff juggle bottles while some of the crowd attempt dance-floor soccer acrobatics.
Via Faenza 4, 50123 Firenze 055 210298 Tue–Sun 8pm–4am €15; free entry for women Tue, Thu and Sun 31, 32

PINOCCHIO LIVE JAZZ
www.pinocchiojazz.it
Jazz musos will love this place as it attracts some of Italy's top artists, who can be heard during the club's annual two-season schedule. Members nod approvingly while the musicians blow, brush and noodle their instruments into the night.

Viale Giannotti 13, 50126 Firenze 055 683388 Concerts begin 10pm Membership fee plus €10 31, 32

SASCHALL
www.saschall.it
Florence's leading music theatre venue hosts big-name rock/pop acts and famous musicals. Expect to see international artists like Tori Amos and Italian stars such as Luca Carboni and PFM. It also stages weekend craft and antiques fairs.
Lungarno Aldo Moro 3, 50136 Firenze 055 650 4112 €27, €19 3, 14, 31, 32, 34

TEATRO COMMUNALE
www.maggiofiorentino.com
Florence's major venue for all things orchestral, balletic and operatic. The winter concert season runs from January to March, while opera and ballet is staged from September to March. Expect old favourites like *Macbeth* and *Coppelia* as well as seminal composers' work from Wagner to Bach.
Corso Italia 16, 50123 Firenze 055 277 9350 for tickets (Tue–Fri 10–4.30, Sat 10–1) €15–€115 A, B

TEATRO PERGOLA
www.pergola.firenze.it
Well-known theatre productions are regularly held in the sumptuous main *Sala* and the elegant *Saloncino*. In addition to staging Italian classics by the likes of d'Annunzio and De Filippo, many English- and French-language playwrights, including Wilde, Berkoff, Hugo and Feydeau, are also showcased.
Via della Pergola 12–32, 50121 Firenze 055 226 4335 Theatre productions Wed–Sat, concerts Sat afternoons, Sun evenings €14.50–€29 C, 14, 23

TEATRO DEL SALE
www.edizioniteatrodelsalecibreofirenze.it
Part English-style club with a wood-panelled library, part theatre and part restaurant, this highly innovative place is run by well-known chef Fabio Picchi (owner of the legendary Cibreo, ▷ 261) and his comic actress wife Maria Cassi. Dinner is served from 7 to 8.45 before performances begin at 9.30pm. The entertainment is first-rate—as is the food—and the whole experience is superb value for money. Booking is essential for dinner/performance.
Via dei Macci 111/r 055 200 1492 Tue–Sat 9am–3pm, 6pm–midnight €5 annual membership; dinner and performance €30 11, 36, 37

TENAX
www.tenax.org
Florence's premier house-music club attracts big international names and live acts like Dimitri from Paris, Thievery Corporation, Grace Jones and Groove Armada. It has mind-blowing lighting and sound technology, as well as some very curious art installations.
Via Pratese 46, Quartiere di Peretola Aeroporto, 50127 Firenze 055 308160 Daily 11pm–4am €20 5, 29, 30, 56

YAB
www.yab.it
Theatrical decor and renowned DJs make this one of Florence's most popular clubs. House music dominates the schedule, with hard house on Fridays and happy house on Saturdays. Monday's Smoove Night sees electric boogaloo acrobatics on the dance floor and hip-hop tunes aplenty in a 1980s-style disco scene.
Via Sassetti 5, 50122 Firenze 055 215160 Mon–Tue, Thu–Sat 11pm–4am €14 A, 1, 6, 14

SPORTS AND ACTIVITIES

AUTODROMO DEL MUGELLO
www.mugellocircuit.it
Regular motor-sport events are held at this circuit owned by Ferrari. The biggest motorcycle races, including the Italian Grand Prix for 125cc and 250cc motorcycles, as well as the Superbike World Championship, draw large crowds, who fill the banks alongside the track.
Mugello 055 849 9111 €40–€160 (depending on race) including parking Take the 302 Faentina road, passing Scarperia for Mugello, or the A1 (Bologna–Firenze) motorway and exit at Barberino di Mugello

BALLOONING IN TUSCANY
www.balloningintuscany.com
If you are feeling flush and have three companions, you can book a balloon ride over Tuscany. This small company, run by an English couple, organizes personalized balloon trips with a champagne breakfast. It is an hour's drive south of Florence, but the views are worth it.
Podere La Fratta, 53020 Montisi 0577 845211 Contact for details €230 per person (minimum 4 adults) A1 towards Siena, Montisi exit

CANOTTIERI COMUNALI FIRENZE
www.canottiericomunalifirenze.it
Try your hand at kayaking at this club on the River Arno, where there are a number of courses available for all ages. There's also the chance to try dragon boating, Polynesian canoeing or even a game of canoe polo.
Lungarno Ferrucci 4, 50126 Firenze 055 681 2151 Mon–Sat 8.30–9, Sun 8.30–1 €95 joining fee (free for women) 8, 31, 32

CIRCOLO DEL TENNIS
www.ctfirenze.org
Florence's oldest tennis club (1898) has excellent facilities including 10 clay courts, swimming pool, football pitches, gym, sauna, restaurant/bar and even a bridge room. Check the press for the latest details of upcoming tournaments and events.
Viale del Visarno 1 (entrance on Viale degli Olmi), 50144 Firenze 055 332651/2 Daily 10–10 1, 9, 12, 16, 26, 27, 80

FIORENTINA NUOTO PISCINA SAN MARCELLINO
www.fiorentinanuoto.it (Italian only)
This swimming club welcomes visitors at its practice sessions and also offers Aquagym classes. There's a friendly café to stoke up after your swim. Call the office (Mon–Fri 10–9, Sat 10–7) for full details. The association also runs the Piscina

Bellariva in summer (Lungarno Aldo Mono 6, tel 055 677521).
✉ Via Chiantigiana 28, 50126 Firenze ☎ 055 653 0000 🕒 Mon–Sat 10–9, Sun 9.30–12.30 🚌 31, 32

FIORENTINA VIOLA
www.fiorentina.it
Watch the reborn Viola—complete with new name and owners—at the open-bowl, 47,000-capacity Stadio Communale Artemio Franchi. Expect fervent support for the club (formerly known as Fiorentina) who have fought back to Serie A from demotion in 2002.
✉ Sport-Santo Marte Viale Manfredo Fanti 14, 50137 Firenze ☎ 055 262 5537 🕒 Sep–May alternate Sun 💰 €15–€120 🚌 3, 10, 11, 17, 20, 34

FLORENCE BY BIKE
www.florencebybike.it
Florence by Bike has a good selection of bicycles and scooters to choose from should you wish to whizz around town or explore the countryside. reserve a place on the daily 32km (20-mile) bicycle tour in advance.
✉ Via San Zanobi 120, 50129 Firenze ☎ 055 488992 🕒 Mon–Sat 9–1, 3.30–7.30 💰 €3 per hour or €21 per day for mountain bike 🚌 20, 25, 31, 32, 33

MANDELA FORUM
www.mandelaforum.it
Various sports events are staged at this sports arena near the home of football club Fiorentina Viola. Check the local press for upcoming roller- and figure-skating, skateboarding, archery, water polo, volleyball and six-a-side football tournaments.
✉ Palazzetto dello Sport, Viale Pasquale Paoli 3, 50137 Firenze ☎ 055 678841 🚌 17

PARCO DELLE CASCINE
The Ippodromo della Mulina is the place to go for horse racing in Florence. If you fancy a flutter on a *galoppo* (flat race) or *trotto* (trotting race), many *tabbachi* (tobacco shops) have easy-to-use betting facilities.
✉ Ippodromo della Mulina, Viale dell'Aeronautica/Viale del Pegaso 1, 50144 Firenze ☎ 055 411107 💰 €15 🚌 17c

FESTIVALS AND EVENTS

MARCH/APRIL

SCOPPIO DEL CARRO
Florence's Scoppio del Carro (Explosion of the Cart) dates back to the 11th century when a carousel of fireworks was lit to spread the good news of Easter. Today, a ceremonial cart, stuffed with fireworks, arrives in the Piazza del Duomo, and a wire is run to the statue of the Virgin on top of the duomo and into the cathedral itself. At about 11pm, the wire is lit and a mechanical dove slides down to the cart, causing a huge explosion and igniting all the fireworks.
🕒 Easter Sunday

MAY/JUNE

MAGGIO MUSICALE FIORENTINO
www.maggiofiorentino.it
Florence's major music festival is held in indoor and outdoor venues across the city. Founded in 1933, it's Italy's longest-running music festival, with a good mix of opera, ballet and classical music. Tickets are also available online.
✉ Biglietteria Teatro Communale, Via Solferino 15, 50123 Firenze ☎ 055 211 1158; 199 109910 🚌 GB, D, 1, 9, 13

JUNE

GIOCO DI CALCIO
This is a no-holds-barred version of football that is played between the four city quarters, originally used to keep the city militia in fighting form and to weld the various factions into a united force. The final day is celebrated with a costumed procession and a flotilla of candlelit boats and fireworks on the River Arno.
✉ Ufficio Valorizzazione Tradizioni Popolari Fiorentine, Piazzetta di Parte Guelfa 1r, 50123 Firenze ☎ 055 261 6050/1/6 🕒 Sundays in June 💰 €10–€25 🚌 C, 23

OCTOBER

MUSICA DEI POPOLI FESTIVAL
www.flog.it/mus_pope.htm
In October each year, artists from around the globe descend on Florence for this international folk music festival. Italy's finest world music event has been running for more than 25 years and attracts a friendly crowd to its main venue, the Auditorium Flog.
✉ Via Maestri del Lavoro 24b, 50134 Firenze ☎ 055 422 0300 🚌 4, 8, 14

HEALTH AND BEAUTY

OFFICINA PROFUMO FARMACEUTICA DI SANTA MARIA NOVELLA
www.smnovella.it
One of the world's oldest pharmacies, this atmospheric and splendidly frescoed apothecary is operated by Dominican friars, in a 14th-century chapel. The sultry scents, potpourris and potions are still prepared to the Dominican monks' recipes.
✉ Via della Scala 16, 50123 Firenze ☎ 055 216276 🕒 Mon–Fri 9.30–7.30, Sun 10.30–6.30 🚌 A, 11, 36, 37

Right *The opening ceremony of the Gioco di Calcio in Piazza della Signoria*

PRICES AND SYMBOLS

The restaurants are listed alphabetically. The prices given are the average for a two-course lunch (L) and a three-course dinner (D) for one person, without drinks. The wine price given is for the least expensive bottle.

For the key to symbols, ▷ 2.

ALLE MURATE

www.allemurate.it

The charismatic owner Umberto Montana recently moved his restaurant to this historic palazzo, which formerly belonged to the Judges and Notaries' Guild and has fine frescoes to admire. Admirable, too, is the contemporary regional cuisine prepared by chef Giovanna Iorio, including fine classic dishes such as *bistecca alla fiorentina* (Florentine T-bone steak); there's also a tasting menu for €90. A fine wine list complements the darkly elegant, candlelit ambience.

✉ Via del Proconsolo 16r, 50122 Firenze
☎ 055 240618 🕒 Tue–Sun 8pm–midnight
💳 D €75, Wine €15

ANGELS RESTAURANT AND WINE BAR

www.ristoranteangels.it

It's rare to find a trendy, streamlined restaurant and bar in the heart of historic Florence, but Angels fits the bill and combines an ultra-modern interior with cooking that's long on local food and tradition—with a distinctly modern twist. Upstairs, you'll find the American Bar, with live music and great cocktails.

✉ Via del Proconsolo 29–31r, 50122 Firenze
☎ 055 239 8762 🕒 Variable closing days
💳 L €45, D €70, Wine €14

BACCAROSSA

www.baccarossa.it

This intimate restaurant right in the heart of Florence specializes in fish, with line-caught bass and tuna on the menu. Pasta dishes are light—try the gnocchi with scampi and asparagus—and there's tender steak from the Val di Chiana also on offer. You can sample the chef's full range by opting for the tasting menu.

✉ Via Ghibellina 46r, 50122 Firenze
☎ 055 240 620 🕒 Tue–Sun 12.30–3, 7.30–10; closed 2 weeks Aug–Sep
💳 L €40, D €60, Wine €15

BALDOVINO

A bustling yet relaxed trattoria not far from Piazza Santa Croce that is especially good for those with children, as it serves great pizzas. The changing menu includes lots of soups, beef, various grilled meats and some inventive plates of *pastasciutta*. The wine list includes many Tuscan classics.

✉ Via San Giuseppe 22r, 50122 Firenze
☎ 055 241773 🕒 Mar–Oct daily 12–2.30, 7–12; Nov–Feb Tue–Sun 12–2.30, 7–12
💳 L €14, D €25, Wine €14 🚌 C, 14

BUCA MARIO

www.bucamario.it

This solid Florentine restaurant, with its vaulted ceiling, terracotta floors and nicely furnished, old-fashioned tables, has been pleasing the customers since 1886 with its classic Tuscan dishes. Respect for tradition is the keynote here, with meticulously cooked favourites such as *ribollita* (thick vegetable soup), *pappa al pomodoro* (tomato soup thickened with Tuscan bread) and *ossobuco* (shin of veal) always on the menu. Starters include a delicate courgette, rocket, parmesan and pine nut salad, delicious homemade *crostini* (toasted bread with different toppings). The pasta is all home-made and main dishes include beef, veal and Tuscan rabbit, and tripe

Above *Eating alfresco on Piazza della Signoria*

if you're adventurous. Good service, friendly staff and a fine wine list complete the experience.
Piazza degli Ottaviani 16r, 50123 Firenze 055 214179 Fri–Tue 12.30–3, 7.30–10, Wed–Thu 12.30–3; closed 11–22 Dec L €40, D €52, Wine €7

CAFFÈ RIVOIRE

The Rivoire opened in the 1870s and is a must for the chocolate connoisseur. It produces arguably the best chocolate in town. Have an exquisite ice cream or sample the famous hot chocolate.
Piazza della Signoria 3r, 50122 Firenze 055 293045 Tue–Sun 8am–midnight; closed for 2 weeks in Jan Cappuccino €6, ice cream from €6 to eat in A, B

CAMILLO

The owners serve olive oil from their own trees at this classic Tuscan restaurant, where the cooking is traditional, the pasta all home-made and the ingredients seasonal and high quality. It's one of the best places in Florence to eat fish, simply grilled; wash it all down with a bottle from the comprehensive list of Tuscan wines.
Borgo San Jacopo 57r, 50125 Firenze 055 212427 Thu–Mon 12.30–2.30, 7.30–10; closed mid-Dec to mid-Jan and end Jul–end Aug L €35, D €55, Wine €12

CAPOCACCIA

This upper-crust café bar serves finger foods, sandwiches and light fare, and is famed for its sumptuously filled *panini* and American-style brunch menu. There are more than 200 wines available.
Lungarno Corsini 12–14r, 50123 Firenze 055 210751 Tue–Sun noon–2am, Tue–Fri dinner Filled *panini* €5–€14, smoked salmon and salad €16 B

LA CARABACCIA

A low-ceilinged, vaulted room houses this good restaurant, specializing in wonderful Florentine beef, grilled over charcoal. There's much else on the menu, with imaginative starters such as pears and pecorino, and *zuppa di faro* (spelt) and *ribollita* soup, while the vegetable selection is more varied than in many other places.
Via Palazzuolo 190, Firenze 50123 055 214782 Tue–Sat 12.30–3, 7.30–10, Mon 7.30–10; closed Christmas L €22, D €45, Wine €11

CARABÈ

www.gelatocarabe.com
This Sicilian *gelateria* sells ice cream reminiscent of the first ice dessert recipes that arrived in southern Italy from the ancient Arabic world. The tastes of pistachio, fig, apricot and vanilla make for a stimulating change. Credit cards are not accepted.
Via Ricasoli 60r, 50121 Firenze 055 289476 Summer daily 10am–1am; winter closed Sun Ice cream cone €2–€6 1, 6, 11, 14, 17, 22

IL CIBREO

www.edizioniteatrodelsalecibreofirenze.it
This legendary restaurant with owner/chef Fabio Picchi at the helm is still among Florence's best. Traditional Tuscan specialties are on the menu, including the Florentine favourite, *trippa* (tripe), which, even if never tempting before, could well convert you here. You will find no standard grilled meat or pasta here nor written menus, but the culinary creations are as delicious as they are inventive and the attentive young staff are multilingual.
Via A. del Verrocchio 8/r, 50122 Firenze 055 234 1100 Tue–Sat 12–2.30, 7–10.30; closed 31 Dec–6 Jan and Aug L €60, D €75, Wine €16

COCO LEZZONE

Come here for the best of Florentine cooking the way it used to be—shared tables, fast and friendly service and genuine cooking *alla casalinga*. The *ribollita* and *pappa col pomodoro*, two typical Florentine soups, are exceptional; there's a daily roast and vegetables from the market. The Paoli family have been running this well-kept secret since 1970. Credit cards not accepted.
Via Parioncino 26r, 50123 Firenze 055 287178 Mon, Wed–Sat 12–2.30, 7.30–10; Sun, Tue 7.10–10; closed late Jul–Aug and 23 Dec–7 Jan L €30, D €45, Wine €7

DINO

The cooking in this traditional restaurant, with is wood-beamed ceilings and internal courtyard garden, is spot-on Tuscan, with specialties such as homemade *pici* (thick handrolled pasta without eggs) and *panzanella*, the Tuscan bread, onion, tomato and herb salad on the menu. You can enjoy wine by the glass and don't miss the ice cream flavoured with *vin santo*, the local sweet dessert wine.
Via Ghibellina 47r, 50122 Firenze 055 241452 Mon 7.30–10, Tue–Sat 12.30–3, 7.30–10 L €30, D €50, Wine €10

DOLCI E DOLCEZZE

This old-style bakery deserves its international renown. If you are only in Florence for a day, make sure you come here for a cake break, but note there are no tables.
Piazza Beccaria 8r, 50121 Firenze 055 234 5458 Tue–Sat 8.30–8, Sun 9–1 A, 6, 31, 32

DON CHISCIOTTE

www.ristorantedonchisciotte.it
Lunchtime sees this restaurant near the station crammed with Florentine businessmen, always a good sign. The quality of the ingredients shines here and chef Gianni Molti struts his stuff with some original takes on classic Tuscan dishes. Fish and seafood are taken seriously, with scallops, scampi and prawns on the menu; sauces are delicate and nicely judged. Pasta could be served with an artichoke or asparagus sauce and stuffed with oxtail or seafood. Tables are well spaced, the lighting good and the staff discreet and professional. Wine buffs can choose from over 300 labels, mainly from Tuscany and Friuli, a great wine area in the north of Italy.
Via Ridolfi 4r, 50129 Firenze 055 475430 Tue–Sat 12.30–3, 7.30–10.30, Mon 7.30–10.30; closed Aug L €45, D €65, Wine €15

ENOTECA PINCHIORRI
www.enotecapinchiorri.com
Arguably Italy's finest restaurant, this establishment has three Michelin stars—one of only six in the whole country. It is run by world-famous foodies Giorgio Pinchiorri and Annie Feolde, who oversee a kitchen brigade of 18. Their food is a representation of Tuscan flavours and techniques enhanced by the application of French methods and modern imagination. This is very serious and expensive food, a culinary experience of a lifetime. Flavours, despite their complexity, remain clear and fresh. Dishes include fish served with a lemon marmalade, scampi with *cavolo nero*, and desserts that sound and taste like poetry—green tea, rose petals, vanilla all make their appearance among the selection of sorbets and ices, while chocolate desserts are rich and dark. The wines are superb, and the service excellent. There is a tasting menu on offer. You must reserve ahead.
Via Ghibellina 87, 50122 Firenze 055 242777 Thu–Sat 12.30–3, 8–10.30pm, Tue–Wed 8–10.30; closed 3 weeks Aug and 15–27 Dec L €210, D €300, Wine €30 A, 14

LA GIOSTRA
www.ristorantelagiostra.com
Named after the merry-go-round that was once a feature of this neighbourhood, tucked away in the centre of Florence, this little restaurant is intentionally difficult to find as it has no sign outside the front door. But a culinary treat awaits inside, presided over by the twin sons of the late Prince Dimitri Alberto Leopoldo of Hapsburg. The menu is Tuscan but with rich Austrian touches, such as the sublime Sacher Torte. The menu changes with the seasons and caters well for vegetarians and carnivores alike. The hand-rolled pasta is superb—try the signature dish with pear and pecorino cheese. A good selection of Italian wines includes many of the top Tuscans. The atmosphere is clubby, cosy and romantic and, with only 16 tables, reservations are advised.
Borgo Pinti 12r, 50121 Firenze 055 241341 Mon–Fri 1–2.30, 7–11, Sat-Sun 7pm–late L €40, D €90, Wine €16 A to Salvemini

IL LATINI
www.illatini.com
Latini started life in the 19th century as a wine bar serving food to local workers and was transformed into a restaurant in 1950—and it's still run by the same family. The accent is on Tuscan cooking, so expect the classics such as *ribollita*, *pappa al pomodoro*, tender roast pork and excellent steaks. This is a good place to try *cinghiale in dolceforte*, a very old recipe for wild boar that combines sweet and sour flavours—the meat is slow cooked with tomatoes, onions, celery and red wine with the addition of pine nuts, candied peel and chocolate. The wine list is extensive, there's a good selection of local hams and salami—including *finocchiona*, salami flavoured with wild fennel, and local *pecorino* (sheep's milk cheese).
Via de' Palchetti 6r, 50123 Firenze 055 210916 Tue–Sun 12.30–3, 7.30–10; closed 24 Dec–5 Jan L €30, D €45, Wine €10 A, 6, 14, 17, 26

OLIVIERO
www.ristorante-oliviero.it
Excellent service and superb Tuscan food are the main characteristics here. Specialties include wild boar, guineafowl and rabbit. Sublime soups, exquisite vegetables and innovative pasta creations make up the rest.
Via delle Terme 51r, 50123 Firenze 055 212421 Mon–Sat 7.30pm–1am; closed Aug D €60, Wine €17 A, B, 6, 11, 36, 37

OSTERIA DEL CAFFÈ ITALIANO
www.caffeitaliano.it
Classic Tuscan fare, including wild boar and chunky soups, is served at this *osteria*. There's an excellent choice of pasta dishes. The wine list includes lots of Chiantis and 'Super Tuscans'.
Via Isola delle Stinche 11/13r, 50122 Firenze 055 289020 Tue–Sun noon–1am L €20, D €55, Wine €14 A

OSTERIA DEL CINGHIALE BIANCO
Tucked away on one of the most atmospheric streets across the Arno, you'll find the White Boar. A series of brick and whitewashed rooms are furnished with plain wooden tables. This is a buzzing, lively place, where you can enjoy specialties such as *strozzapreti* (feather-light gnocchi made with spinach and ricotta), or homemade *taglierini* (ribbon noodles) with fresh truffles, before moving on to roast veal and pork, wild boar or rabbit. Vegetables and salads are nicely presented and desserts include *panna cotta al cioccolato* (cooked cream with chocolate) or a mousse of mascarpone. Serious Tuscan wines such as Brunello di Montalcino and Morellino di Scansano feature on the long list.
Borgo San Jacopo 43r, 50125 Firenze 055 215706 Thu–Fri, Mon–Tue 6.30–10.30, Sat–Sun 12–3, 6.30–10.30 L €30, D €40, Wine €10

OSTERIA SANTO SPIRITO
A trendy *osteria* that excels in creating adventurous, mountainous salads—chunks of Parmesan and *prosciutto crudo* ham are mixed with pine nuts and various leaves such as rocket (arugula). There's a superb choice of cheeses and a decent wine list. Reserving ahead is advisable.
Piazza Santo Spirito 16r, 50125 Firenze 055 238 2383 Daily 12.30–2.30, 8–12 L €15, D €30, Wine €12 D, 11, 36, 37

RISTORANTE RICCHI
www.ristorantericchi.it
Choose to eat alfresco in the gloriously leafy Piazza Santo Spirito, or opt for the clean, contemporary dining rooms inside. The menu is a feast of all-fresh fish and seafoods, together with imaginative salads and vegetables as accompaniments.
Piazza Santo Spirito 8–9r, 50125 Firenze 055 280830 Mon–Sat 7.30–11pm,

café 7am–1am; open 2nd Sun of month; closed last 2 weeks Aug L €18, D €40, Wine €15 D, 11, 36, 37

SABATINI
www.ristorantesabatini.it
This elegant restaurant serves solid Tuscan dishes with international touches, and the restaurant is known for *bistecca alla fiorentina* (steak). Seafood enthusiasts can opt for the *risotto con scampi*. There is an excellent wine list and multilingual service.
Via dei Panzani 9a, 50123 Firenze
055 282802 Tue–Sun 12.30–3, 7–11
L €35, D €80, Wine €14 A, 1, 4, 7, 10, 11, 22, 23, 36, 37

SERGIO GOZZI
Four generations of the same family have run this busy restaurant, known to the locals as Da Sergio, near San Lorenzo in the heart of Florence; the welcome is warm and *mamma* is busy in the kitchen while her sons look after the guests. Favourites such as *ribollita* and *pappardelle* (ribbon pasta with meat sauce) are on offer, and they pride themselves on the seasonal specials. Try the *cantuccini* (hard sweet biscuits) with *vin santo* (dessert wine) to finish.
Piazza San Lornezo 8r, 50123 Firenze
055 382941 Mon–Sat 12.30–2.30
L €20, Wine €8

LA SPADA
The deceptively simple menu here offers well-prepared dishes, from rabbit or pork roasted on a spit to delectable homemade pastas. The service is friendly and the atmosphere informal.
Via della Spada 62, 50123 Firenze
055 218757 Tue–Sat 12–3, 6–10.30
L €15, D €25, Wine €15 A, 11, 36, 37

TARGA BISTROT FIORENTINO
www.targabistrot.net
For a change from traditional cooking, head for the Targa, where you can dine on a veranda above the River Arno and enjoy local produce served with a 21st-century twist. Presentation here is important and a mouth-watering selection of local ham and tiny pickled vegetables could be followed by a wonderfully pink duck breast, a deeply flavoured risotto with broccoli or a beautifully cooked steak. As well as a trolley selection, desserts include hot chocolate soufflé and lemon crêpes. There are over 20,000 wines in the cellar, including a good selection of burgundies.
Lungarno Cristoforo Colombo 7, 50136 Firenze 055 677377 Mon–Sat 12.30–2.30, 7.30–11; closed Aug and 1–8 Jan L €30, D €50, Wine €19 14, 31, 32

TRATTORIA ENZO E PIERO
www.trattoriaenzoepiero.it
A solid 19th-century palazzo not far from the station is home to this restaurant, where the tables spill outside in summer. Here you'll find traditional Florentine cooking at its best, with local ham and salami featuring as starters, followed by a good selection of home-made pasta, including *ravioli burro e salvia* (ricotta and spinach-stuffed ravioli served with sage butter) and a light, well-balanced lasagne. Main courses are all meat-based, with pork, roast meat and steak featuring, but they are happy to knock up an omelette for vegetarians. Desserts are basic, but there's always a good selection of fruit. This is a truly typical Florentine restaurant that offers excellent value.
Via Faenza 105r, 50123 Firenze 055 214901 Mon–Sat 12.30–2.30, 7.30–10
L €25, D €40, Wine €8

TRATTORIA MARIO
www.trattoriamario.com
Come to this simple, family-run restaurant close to San Lorenzo food market for a take on traditional eating; dishes are classic Tuscan with *bistecca alla fiorentina* (steak), rabbit cooked with white Tuscan beans. and an excellent *ribollita* (vegetable soup) all on the menu. You may have to share a table, and it's better to stick to the *vino sfuso* (wine by the carafe), but eating here is a true reminder that the real Florence still exists outside the tourist trail. No reservations and no credit cards.
Via Rosina 2r, 50123 Firenze 055 218550 Mon–Sat 12.30–2.30; closed Aug L €22, Wine €4

VINOLIO
www.vinolio.com
Not far from Piazza San Marco, this cheery restaurant pleases locals and visitors like. At first glance a traditional wine bar serving food, you'll find the cooking far from everyday, with dishes such as maize pancakes with *baccalà* (dried salt cod), home-made pasta with a rabbit sauce and gnocchi delicately flavoured with pesto made using pistachios rather than pine nuts. You could stick with a *piatto di affettati*, a plate of mixed Tuscan ham and salami, or a selection of cheese. Vegetarians will find dishes such as aubergine bake with tomatoes and smoked cheese. Chocolate tart and a citrus ice are among the desserts, and the wine list is impressive, with a huge range of Chianti and wines from Montalcino.
Via San Zanobi 126r, 50129 Firenze
055 489957 Mon–Sat 12.30–3, 7.30–10 L €20, D €30, Wine €9

ZIBIBBO
www.zibibbonline.com
It's worth heading to the edge of the city to experience this charming and simply furnished little eating house surrounded by trees. Lunchtime sees a procession of excellent snacks on offer, as well as the restaurant menu. The menu is completely seasonal and changes frequently; there are always vegetarian dishes on offer. Pasta dishes range from a richly flavoured tagliatelle with meat sauce to spaghetti with mussels and clams or radicchio and smoked cheese, while main courses include pigeon, duck and fresh fish, as well as solid Tuscan roasts. All the produce is locally sourced direct from the producers; many of the vegetables served are organic.
Via di Terzollina 3r, 50139 Firenze
055 433383 Mon–Fri 12.30–3, 7.30–10, Sat 7.30–10pm; closed 1 week Aug L €35, D €45, Wine €10
14c, 40

PRICES AND SYMBOLS

Prices are the lowest and highest for a double room for one night, unless otherwise stated. Breakfast is included, and all the hotels listed accept credit cards unless otherwise stated. Note that rates vary widely throughout the year.

For the key to symbols ▷ 2.

CASCI

www.hotelcasci.com

This family-run hotel, near the duomo, was the home of the opera composer Gioacchino Rossini in the early 1850s. There are some original 14th-century touches, but overall it has been thoroughly modernized, with immaculate, functional rooms. The triple-glazed windows deaden street sounds. The hotel is especially good for families. Many of the simple but comfortable rooms have balconies. Facilities include private bathroom, safe, telephone, cable television and minibar.

✉ Via Cavour 13, 50129 Firenze
☎ 055 211686 €90–€165 24 1, 6, 7, 10, 11, 17, 31, 32

CRISTINA

www.hotelcristina-florence.com

This friendly, small hotel with largish rooms is a great place for families, as the owners go out of their way to make children and their parents feel at home. The rooms are clean and spacious, and four have private bathrooms. It's great value for money, so you'll need to reserve well in advance.

✉ Via della Condotta 4, 50122 Firenze
☎ 055 214484 €55–€105 (with bathroom) 9 A, 14, 23

GOLDONI

www.hotelgoldoni.com

Hotel Goldoni is great value for money. The well-tended rooms have 19th-century style touches and co-ordinated decor. Each guest room has a private bathroom, telephone, internet access, television and safe.

✉ Borgo Ognissanti 8, 50123 Firenze
☎ 055 284080 €65–€200 20 A, B, 6, 11, 36, 37

GRAND HOTEL MINERVA

www.grandhotelminerva.com

Locations don't get much better than this one, where guests step out to face the church of Santa Maria Novella, behind which is the main train station. Rooms have modern decor, with good views. Amenities include internet access, free WiFi, and garage parking.

✉ Piazza S Maria Novella 16, 50123 Firenze
☎ 055 27230 €140–€250 102 A, 11, 36, 37

HELVETIA & BRISTOL

www.royaldemeure.com

Once popular with English ladies on the Grand Tour, this hotel preserves the refined air of the 19th century. Each room has been individually designed. Modern amenities include private bathroom, hairdryer, television, telephone, minibar and safe. The Hostaria Bebendum restaurant serves contemporary Tuscan food.

✉ Via dei Pescioni 2, 50123 Firenze
☎ 055 26651 €280–€640 excluding breakfast (€26) 67 A, B, 6, 11, 22, 36, 37

JOHANNA AND JOHLEA

www.johanna.it

These are four elegant B&B residences in the centre of

Florence—charming homes from home with all the facilities of a good hotel at hand. The rooms here are small but beautifully furnished, with private bathrooms, coffee- and tea-making facilities, television and telephone. There is a comfortable communal room with a fridge. Credit cards are not accepted.
✉ Via San Gallo 80, 50129 Firenze ☎ 055 463 3292 € €70–€100 ⓘ 11 🚌 8, 11, 12, 20

LOGGIATO DEI SERVITI
www.loggiatodeiservitihotel.it
This former Servite monastery, with vaulted ceilings, dark wood antiques and rich fabric, is in a charming square. Many of the rooms look onto the arcades of Piazza Santissima Annunziata. Rooms have a private bathroom, telephone, minibar, safe, hairdryer and television.
✉ Piazza Santissima Annunziata 3, 50100 Firenze ☎ 055 289592 € €140–€220, including breakfast ⓘ 38 ❄ 🚌 C, 6, 31, 32

MALASPINA
www.malaspinahotel.it
Right on the beautiful Piazza Indipendenza, the elegant Malaspina Hotel was built in the 14th century. The soundproofed rooms are quite modern but they have kept some of their traditional touches and are spotlessly clean. Each room has a telephone, television, minibar and safe.
✉ Piazza Indipendenza 24, 50129 Firenze ☎ 055 489869 € €70–€245 ⓘ 31 ❄ 🚌 7, 10, 20, 25, 31, 32, 33

MONNA LISA
www.monnalisa.it
This 15th-century palazzo is a wonderful mix of old and contemporary design. The reception has stuccoed walls and a striking staircase. Many rooms have elaborate ceilings, wall hangings and antiques. Facilities include private bathroom, hairdryer, television, telephone, minibar and safe. The flower-filled garden is perfect for relaxing with a drink.
✉ Borgo Pinti 27, 50121 Firenze ☎ 055 2479751 € €265–€380 ⓘ 45 rooms, 4 suites ❄ 🚌 14, 23

PENSIONE SCOTI
www.hotelscoti.com
This impressive 15th-century building stands opposite the Palazzo Strozzi in the shopping mecca of Via Tornabuoni. It is small with simple but light-filled bedrooms, none of which have private bathrooms. The lounge has beautiful 18th-century frescoes depicting an Arcadian landscape. Electric fans are available in the summer.
✉ Via dei Tornabuoni 7, 50123 Firenze ☎ 055 292128 € €80–€110 ⓘ 11 🚌 A, 6, 11, 36, 37

PLAZA HOTEL LUCCHESI
www.plazalucchesi.it
Very centrally located on the right bank of the River Arno, just a few steps away from the Uffizi, Sante Croce and the Ponte Vecchio, the Lucchesi has elegant rooms furnished with parquet floors and good-size bathrooms. Many of the superior rooms have magnificent views over the Arno.
✉ Lungomare della Zecc Vecchia 38, 50122 Firenze ☎ 055 26236 € €96–€150 ⓘ 87 rooms, 10 suites ❄ 🚌 23

RELAIS CERTOSA HOTEL
www.florencehotelcertosa.it
Near the Certosa exit of the A1, this guesthouse is set in wooded grounds. It has spacious rooms and suites, some in rustic Tuscan style, others modern. Tuscan dishes predominate at lunch and dinner, served in the garden in good weather. The hotel's occasional complimentary shuttle or a bus takes guests to the city in 10 minutes.
✉ Via di Colle Ramole 2 (off Via Chiantigiana, Certosa), 50124 Firenze ☎ 055 204 7171 € €90–€250 ⓘ 69 ❄

RELAIS SANTA CROCE
www.relaisantacroce.com
Part of the luxury Baglioni group, this elegant small hotel in the heart of Florence blends tradition with cutting-edge design. Opulent furnishings, frescoed ceilings, Murano chandeliers and marbled walls are all part of rooms that are individually and exquisitely designed. The guestbook reads like a who's who of celebrities (recent guests include Brad Pitt and Angelina Jolie). Next door but belonging to the hotel is Florence's only three Michelin-starred restaurant, the Enoteca Pinchiorri (▷ 262). The restaurant in the hotel proper, Guelfi e Ghibellini, offers seasonal, regional menus.
✉ Via Ghibellini 87, 50122 Firenze ☎ 055 234 2230 € €300–€500, excluding breakfast (€25) ⓘ 20 rooms, 4 suites ❄ 🚌 A, 14

RIVOLI
www.hotelrivoli.it
Close to Santa Maria Novella, the Rivoli is a beautifully renovated Franciscan monastery. The public spaces have cross vaulting, arches and pillars, which recall its serene and austere past. The rooms are simple with large marble bathrooms, and some have a balcony or terrace. Expect 24-hour room service, laundry, coffee- and tea-making facilities, television, radio, telephone and trouser press. On fine days, breakfast is served on the flower-filled patio.
✉ Via della Scala 33, 50123 Firenze ☎ 055 27861 € €350 ⓘ 80 ❄ 🏊 Outdoor heated whirlpool 🚌 A, 11, 36, 37

SOGGIORNO ANTICA TORRE
www.anticatorre.com
The Soggiorno Antica Torre is part of an 11th-century tower beside the Piazza della Signoria, the venue for many of the city's most notable historical events. Even after extensive refurbishments and renovations, the original ceilings remain intact, complemented by handsome parquet floors. The distinctly Florentine rooms are beautifully furnished. Each one has a private bathroom (with shower or bath), hairdryer, minibar, television and telephone.
✉ Piazza della Signoria 3, 50122 Firenze ☎ 055 216402 € €90–€120 excluding breakfast (€3) ⓘ 6 ❄ 🚌 A, B, 23, 13, 62

TUSCANY AND UMBRIA

Rolling hills, vines, olives, solitary cypresses and warm stone glowing in the sun create the quintessential image of Italy, an image that truly exists in Tuscany and Umbria. Here is a landscape that is miraculously little changed in its essence since the Renaissance, where fertile farms are scattered about the land and tiny hilltop villages are home to undiscovered artistic treasures. Set in the heart of Italy, these two regions have the lot—mountains and a beautiful coastline, historic towns and postcard-perfect villages, and some of Italy's most luxurious hotels, best restaurants and most tempting shopping.

Away from Florence, Tuscany's capital, you'll find medieval towns and cities such as Siena and many-towered San Gimignano; thriving centres like Perugia, Umbria's main city; the empty landscape of the Maremma on the east coast, dotted with Etruscan villages like Sovana; and holy Assisi, Umbrian birthplace of St. Francis, and its neighbouring wine- and oil-producing towns. The landscape of Tuscany and Umbria is idyllic, ranging from the golden fields of southern Tuscany through the serene beauty of Lake Trasimeno, to the dramatic mountain scenery of Umbria's Valnerina, where the Nera rushes through a soaring gorge, and the upland splendours of the Sibillini Mountains, carpeted with wild flowers in early summer. This is country for exploring at leisure, devoting a few days to Umbria, Italy's only land-locked region, before moving on to take in southern Tuscany, home to the hilltop villages of Montalcino, famed for its wine, and Montepulciano. North of Siena lies Chianti, a wine-producing area that's home to many foreigners, and towns such as Prato and Pisa with its Leaning Tower. North again, the hills of the Garfagnana are a well-kept secret, a little-developed area where you can ski in winter and walk for miles on mountain trails in summer.

ABBAZIA DI MONTE OLIVETO MAGGIORE

www.monteolivetomaggiore.it

Near Chiusure, 9km (6 miles) northeast of Buonconvento, the isolated and beautiful medieval monastery of Monte Oliveto Maggiore is still home to a thriving monastic community. Set on a tree-covered hillside, the abbey draws numerous visitors who come to see the fresco cycle, one of the finest in Tuscany, in the Chiostro Grande (Grand Cloister). The abbey was founded by Bernardo Tolomei, a member of a wealthy Sienese family, and the delightful old buildings date from 1272. The Chiostro Grande has a fresco cycle on the life of St. Benedict, founder of the Benedictine order. It was created by Luca Signorelli, who began the work in 1498, and by the Milanese artist, Sodoma, who completed the majority of the work between 1505 and 1508. The church has a 15th-century layout. The monks have a library of 40,000 books and other documents, along with a workshop where they restore old books.

466 F8 Località Monteoliveto Maggiore, 53041 Asciano 0577 707611 May–Sep daily 9.15–12, 3.15–6; Oct–Apr 9.15–12, 3.15–5 Free

ABBAZIA DI SAN PIETRO IN VALLE

Set in idyllic surroundings, with its tall campanile rising above woods, San Pietro in Valle is steeped in history. Founded by Faroaldo II, the Lombard Duke of Spoleto, in 720, this abbey has some exceptional frescoes and beautiful cloisters. The restored fresco cycle in the nave depicts biblical scenes, and is famous for the variety of scenes depicted and the complexity of the work (late 12th to early 13th century). Look for the lively images of Noah being called to Eternity and Adam naming the animals. More frescoes cover the apses—those in the right-hand apse are by followers of Giotto. A small fresco in the left aisle illustrates the *Dream of Faroaldo*; it shows Faroaldo being visited by St. Peter, who is instructing him to build a monastery on this holy spot.

Also to be found in the open nave are a rare seventh-century Lombard altar showing the signature of the original craftsman (Ursus), and Roman sarcophagi carved with mythological scenes and reused as tombs for Faroaldo and his family.

468 H8 05034 Ferentillo Terni 0744 780316 Daily 10–5; closed occasionally 1–2 Free Custodian in the village will show you around (her family has been providing the service free for 100 years)—in Italian only, but she speaks very slowly

AREZZO

www.apt.arezzo.it

Arezzo thrived during the Middle Ages as a major hub of goldwork and jewellery manufacture and its historic old town still survives. About 80km (50 miles) southeast of Florence, it sits on a hilltop overlooking a fertile plain near the Arno, dominated by its cathedral and fortress. Many people come simply to enjoy Piero della Francesca's famous fresco cycle, *The Legend of the True Cross*, in the Church of San Francesco (Apr–Oct Mon–Fri 9–6.30, Sat 9–5.30, Sun 1–5.30; Nov–Mar Mon–Fri 9–5.30, Sat 9–5, Sun 1–5. Closed 1 Jan, 13 Jun, 4 Oct, 25 Dec. Reserve in advance online at www.pierodellafrancesca.it or tel 0575 352727).

One of Italy's most famous paintings, on the walls around the high altar in the Cappella Bacci (open as for Church of San Francesco) between 1453 and 1466, illustrates the legend of the cross on which Christ was crucified. There is another fresco by Piero della Francesca in the Duomo (daily 7–12, 3–6.30).

A short stroll away is the Passeggio del Prato, an attractive park overlooked by the Fortezzo Medicea (1538–60), a castle built by the town's Medici rulers. The Museo Archeologico (daily 8.30–7.30), in the Roman amphitheatre, has some priceless collections of local pottery.

The alleys around the main square, Piazza Grande, are full of dark workshops smelling of wood, where artisans restore antique furniture. On the first Sunday of the month the town is taken over by an excellent antiques fair.

466 G7 Piazza della Repubblica 28, 52100 Arezzo 0575 377678 Arezzo

ASSISI

▷ 270–271.

BAGNO VIGNONI

www.terresiena.it

Bagno Vignoni is one of Tuscany's most fascinating sights, a village whose old stone buildings cluster around a large, open-air pool filled with water from a natural hot spring. When the air is cool, a mist rises from the warm water and drifts over the village square. The spring was known in Etruscan times, and the waters were enjoyed over the years by the Romans, along with popes and saints, including Catherine of Siena. In medieval times the baths became a resting place for pilgrims going along the Via Francigena, the pilgrims' route over the St. Bernard Pass and through Italy to Rome. Today this is still a great place to stop and rest, with plenty of restaurants. You are not allowed to bathe here now, but there are baths open in the Hotel Posta Marucci for a fee (www.hotelpostamarucci.it) or at the 5 -star *benessere* (wellness) resort Hotel Adler Terme (www.adler-toscana.com), where the minimum stay is three nights.

466 F8 Strada di Bagno Vignoni, 53027 S. Quirico d'Orcia 0577 888975

Above *Piero della Francesca's fresco cycle in Arezzo*

Opposite *Abbazia di Monte Oliveto Maggiore*

ASSISI

Assisi, the birthplace of St. Francis (1182–1226), stands on the whalebacked slopes of Monte Subasio, above the Vale of Spoleto. Founded by the Umbrians, it became an important Roman *municipium*, and in the Middle Ages fell into the hands of the Baglioni family of Perugia. Plague, famine and tight ecclesiastical control later turned Assisi into a moribund backwater. Its economic decline was reversed when St. Francis was made patron saint of Italy in 1939. As a result, Assisi became one of the most prosperous towns in the region.

BASILICA DI SAN FRANCESCO

Combining Umbrian Romanesque with French-inspired Gothic architecture, the complex consists of two churches, one above the other. The dimly lit lower church (1228–30) has frescoes by Cimabue and Giotto. The four frescoes over the main altar depict St. Francis in glory and the virtues of the Franciscan order—poverty, chastity and obedience. Don't miss Cimabue's simple portrait of St. Francis in the right transept. St. Francis is buried in the crypt.

By contrast, the upper church, superbly restored after the 1997 earthquake, is drenched with light, its soaring arches providing the perfect backdrop for Giotto's fresco *Scenes from the Life of St. Francis*.

BASILICA DI SANTA CHIARA

St. Clare (1193–1253), founder of the Order of the Poor Clares, dedicated her life to the Franciscan movement. The Romanesque basilica, with its pink and white striped stonework and huge flying buttresses, was built between 1257 and 1265. The highlight is the iconic painting of *St. Clare and Eight Scenes from Her Life* behind the altar, painted in 1283 by an unknown Umbrian artist. St. Clare's remains are in the crypt.

PIAZZA DEL COMUNE

At the heart of Assisi is the Piazza del Comune, the site of the Roman forum. Here the imposing Torre del Popolo stands next to the Temple of Minerva, intact with its elegant Corinthian columns. Erected in the first century BC, it has been a church since 1539. Overlooking the town is Rocca Maggiore, a fearsome 14th-century fortress (daily 9–8).

INFORMATION

www.sanfrancescoassisi.org
467 H8 Piazza del Comune 22, 06082 Assisi 075 813 8680 Mon–Fri 8–2, 3–6, Sat 9–1, 3–6, Sun 10–1 Tickets for Rocca Maggiore, Pinacoteca and Foro Romano from €3, www.sistemamuseo.it Official guides can be hired in English, French, Spanish, German, Russian and Swedish (tel 075 815228,www.umbria.org./tourguides) Assisi, Santa Maria degli Angeli

TIPS

» Shorts, miniskirts, sleeveless tops, mobile phones and flash photography are not permitted in the churches.

» *Calendimaggio,* a medieval costume festival with street parades and music, takes place on the first Thursday, Friday and Saturday in May. The Festa di San Francesco is on 3 and 4 October.

Above *A ceramic panel depicting St. Francis on an external wall in Assisi*
Opposite *Some of the buildings of the ancient city of Assisi, set on a ridge of Monte Subasio*

BARGA

www.comune.barga.lu.it

Off the beaten track, yet easily accessible, Barga makes an ideal trip into the country for anyone staying in Lucca (▷ 275) or Pisa (▷ 282–283). Stroll through its attractive, winding streets, shop for local produce, or simply enjoy a drink in one of its historic cafés.

Barga sits on a hill above the Serchio Valley, 28km (17 miles) north of Lucca, with lovely views of the Alpi Apuane. The town has strong links with Scotland, as many of its residents emigrated to Glasgow. The town even has its own fish-and-chip fair in August.

It has kept much of its medieval appearance and layout, with remnants of the old walls and narrow, steep streets stretching down from the imposing duomo. It is a steep climb to the duomo, but worth it for the views.

466 E6 Piazza Salvo Salvi, 55051 Barga 0583 72471 Fornacci di Barga or Barga Gallicano (nearer to town); long uphill climb from both

BEVAGNA

The serenely beautiful walled town of Bevagna, lying 8km (5 miles) southwest of Foligno on the edge of the Vale of Spoleto, is an ancient settlement that once straddled the Roman Via Flaminia. Five gates pierce the walls, from which a warren of medieval streets converges on the irregular Piazza Filippo Silvestri, home to two of Umbria's finest Romanesque churches, San Michele and San Silvestro (daily 10–1, 3–6). Both were built in 1195 by an architect known as Maestro Binello, who also worked in Spello (▷ 290), and have a similar interior layout, with a raised presbytery and sunken crypt. The naves are lined with sturdy columns, whose Egyptian-style capitals were perhaps copied from those of a Roman temple, and both churches are faced with pink stone from Monte Subasio across the plain. These splendid buildings are balanced by the 12th-century Palazzo dei Consoli. In the 19th century its interior was adapted to house the charming Teatro Torti, a minuscule theatre complete with balconies and boxes. East of here, down the Corso Matteoti, Bevagna's Roman past is still present in the shape of a magnificent black-and-white Roman mosaic, the remains of a Roman temple and the tunnels that once lay beneath the stage of the amphitheatre.

467 H8 Pro Loco I.A.T Bevagna, Piazza Filippo Silvestri 1, 06031 Bevagna 0742 361 667 Guided tours of the town, theatre and Roman remains: daily 10.30–1, 2.30–5 Adults €3.50, child (6–14) €1, under 6s free. Reserve by telephone or fax on 0742 360 031

BUONCONVENTO

www.museoartesacre.it

Buonconvento is a small historic town, an important trading post in the mid-13th century and a prominent stopping-off point for pilgrims along the Via Francigena. The town is at the confluence of the Arbia and Ombrone rivers, between Siena and Montalcino. Its outskirts are unattractive but well-preserved medieval parts are surrounded by walls built between 1371 and 1381.

The Museo d'Arte Sacra (summer Tue–Sun 10.30–1; winter Sat–Sun 10–1, 2–5) is a museum of religious art displaying Sienese paintings from the 14th to the 17th century. It also has displays of jewellery, wood and marble sculptures. The 14th-century Church of Santi Pietro e Paulo has a *Madonna and Child* (1450) by Matteo di Giovanni.

466 F8 Museo d'Arte Sacra della Val d'Arbia, Via Soccini 18, 53020 Buonconvento 0577 807 190 Buonconvento

CHIANTI

www.chiantinet.it

The Chianti region, between Florence and Siena, is generally explored by driving down the Chiantigiana (SS222), a designated scenic wine road that runs through the heart of the district. This seductive area of rolling hills has produced wine since Etruscan times. The landscape is often wild, characterized by rich farmland, heavily wooded slopes, isolated villas and numerous vineyards. Visit some of the region's towns, such as Castellina in Chianti, Greve in Chianti (the unofficial capital) and Radda in Chianti.

Castellina in Chianti was once of great strategic importance, as it sits on the border between the territories of Siena and Florence. You can still see its ancient fortress and walk along the Via delle Volte, a tunnel-like road that runs right around the walls.

Radda in Chianti (tel 0577 738 494) is a hilltop town offering great views over the region, with fine buildings dating from the 15th and 16th centuries.

The lovely town of Greve in Chianti (tel 055 854 6287) has plenty of wine shops, cobbled streets and alleyways to explore.

466 F7 Via Ferruccio 40, 53011 Castellina in Chianti (Siena) 0577 741 392

Below *A farmhouse set amid vineyards near the small town of Greve in Chianti*

Above *View over Città di Castello from the Torre Civica*

CITTÀ DI CASTELLO

www.regioneumbria.eu
www.guideinumbria.com

Città di Castello has an interesting range of ancient and modern art housed in its elegant palazzi and former tobacco-drying sheds, where traditional crafts continue to thrive. Surrounded by medieval walls, the town occupies a central position in the Upper Tiber Valley. The Pinacoteca Comunale, in the Palazzo Vitelli alla Cannoniera, is an important gallery in Umbria. The oldest painting here is a large altarpiece by Maestro di Città de Castello, *Madonna in Trono col Bambino*, surrounded by six angels (13th century). In Room 6 is the only painting by Raphael to remain in the Pinacoteca, the *Gonfalon of the Holy Trinity*, one of his first works. It has been used for hundreds of years as a *gonfalone* (banner) during religious festivals and has suffered wear and tear. In Piazza Gabriotti, the newly restored ecclesiastical museum, the Museo del Duomo (Oct–Mar Tue–Sun 10–1, 2.30–6.30; Apr–Sep Tue–Sun 9.30–1, 2.30–7; €5), houses the Treasure of Canoscio from the palaeo-Christian period (sixth century), a rare collection of embossed silver ceremonial objects used during Mass.

✚ 467 G7 ℹ Logge Bufalini, Piazza Matteotti, 06012 Città di Castello ☎ 075 855 4922 ? CartaMusei (€7), valid for one week, gives reduced entry to certain museums (including Pinacoteca Comunale, Collezione Burri, Museo del Duomo and Centro Documentazione Tradizioni Popolari)

CORTONA

Perched on a hillside overlooking the Valdichiana and Lake Trasimeno, Cortona, with its medieval streets and good hotels and restaurants, makes a perfect overnight stopping point heading from southern Tuscany into Umbria. Substantial parts of the town's Etruscan walls are incorporated into the medieval structure, and churches and fine museums grace the precipitous cobbled streets. For the best views, climb up to the ruined Fortezza Medicea, built by Cosimo I in 1556.

From the focal point, Piazza della Repubblica, it is a short stroll to Piazza del Duomo, the setting for the Museo Diocesano (daily 10–7). The highlights include two masterpieces by Fra Angelico, an *Annunciation* and a *Madonna and Child with Saints*, along with works by Sassetta, Bartolomeo della Gatta and Luca Signorelli. The archaeological star is a second-century Roman sarcophagus carved with scenes depicting Dionysus's battle with the Amazons, a work much admired by the Renaissance sculptors Donatello and Brunelleschi. The town's Etruscan past is recalled in the Museo dell'Accademia Etrusca (daily 10–7), which has a huge fifth-century bronze lamp, exquisite jewellery, urns and vases, and an impressive, if incongruous, ancient Egyptian collection.

✚ 467 G7 ℹ Via Nazionale 42, 52044 Cortona ☎ 0575 630352

DERUTA

Deruta has been famous for its ceramics and majolica since the 14th century. Shops selling pottery abound, and in the old town you can visit the Museo Regionale della Ceramica (Apr–Jun daily 10.30–1, 3–6; Jul–Sep daily 10.30–1, 3.30–6.30; Oct–Mar Wed–Mon 10.30–1, 2.30–5, tel 075 971 1000). This restored museum building traces the history of ceramics from the earliest examples of terracotta to lavish Renaissance majolica. Among the fascinating exhibits is a display of plates presented as wedding gifts, devotional plaques, spouted drug jars and even a shoe-shaped handwarmer. The museum also contains fragments of floor from Perugia's Rocca Paolina and Priors' Chapel. In the old town many of the facades of the shops and buildings are covered in ceramic tiles. Next to the museum is the 14th-century church of San Francesco, which has Umbrian frescoes.

✚ 467 G8 ℹ Piazza dei Consoli 4, 0653 Deruta ☎ 075 971 1559 🕐 Mar–Jun

ISOLA D'ELBA

www.aptelba.it

Most people visit the mountainous island of Elba to explore the place where Napoleon lived in exile from May 1814 to February 1815, but others come to enjoy the delightful scenery, unspoiled beaches and bustling resort towns. There are plenty of historic sites to visit, including Napoleon's former villa and ancient, abandoned mines. The island is also an excellent place for walking.

About 10km (6 miles) west of the mainland and an hour's ferry ride from Piombino, Elba is a natural mosaic made up of gulfs, headlands, a precipitous coastline, peaceful bays, maquis scrub, wooded mountains and terraced vineyards. It is the largest island in the Tuscan archipelago, a group of islands once described as the 'necklace that slid from the neck of Venus'. There are several walking trails as well as a cable car to the top of Mount Capanne, from where you can enjoy excellent views.

In Portoferraio, the Palazzina dei Mulini, Napoleon's home while he was exiled, is now a museum (Wed–Mon 9–7, Sun and holidays 9–1) housing period furniture and Napoleon's library. The ticket also allows entry to Napoleon's summer villa, the Villa Napoleonica di San Martino, set in the hills 5km (3 miles) to the southwest (Wed–Sat 9–7).

✚ 466 E8/D8 ℹ Calata Italia 43, 53037 Portoferraio ☎ 0565 914 6711 ⛴ From Piombino

Above *The remains of the Roman amphitheatre in Fiesole*

FIESOLE

www.commune.fiesole.fi.it

On a hilltop 7km (4 miles) northeast of Florence, Fiesole offers sweeping views. Originally an Etruscan settlement, Fiesole grew in importance under the Romans; in the Area Archeologica east of the main square, Piazza Mino da Fiesole, there is a Roman amphitheatre, baths and temple and sixth-century Etruscan ruins. Piazza Mino da Fiesole is where you'll find the duomo, shops and restaurants. From here you can climb Via San Francesco for views of Florence. The Museo Bandini (Apr–Sep daily 9.30–7, reduced hours in winter) has ivories, ceramics and paintings on display, while the church of San Domenico has Fra Angelico's *Madonna with Saints and Angels*.

466 F6 Via Portigiani 3/5, 50014 Fiesole 055 597 8373 7 from Santa Maria Novella in Florence

GARFAGNANA

www.garfagnanaturisto.info

This delightful, undiscovered area north of Lucca is dotted with historic little towns and laced with a range of walking trails. If you have a car, you can visit the spa town of Bagni di Lucca, visited by Lord Byron, the area's main hub of Castelnuovo di Garfagnana, and the remote hamlet of San Pellegrino in Alpe. Even without a car, you can reach towns such as Barga (▷ 272).

The area is perfect for wildlife-lovers, as the surrounding Alps are home to many species of bird, including the golden eagle. The Garfagnana is on the eastern side of the River Serchio, which forges a path between the rugged Alpi Apuane and the gentler, more rounded slopes of the Garfagnana. The most rugged part of the area is the nature reserve of Orecchiella, near Castelnuovo di Garfagnana, a pleasant, bustling town at the heart of the Garfagnana. It has an open-air market every Thursday.

San Pellegrino in Alpe is an ancient pilgrimage area, and has a good folk museum. The winding roads mean that the area cannot be explored quickly, but it is easily accessible from Lucca (▷ 275) and Pisa (▷ 282–283).

463 E6 Centro Visite Parco Alpi Apuane, Piazza delle Erbe 1, 55032 Castelnuovo di Garfagnana 0583 65169 Castelnuovo di Garfagnana

GUBBIO

www.gubbio-altochiascio.umbria2000.it

Gubbio's grey limestone medieval buildings are built on a series of terraces against the backdrop of Mount Ingino, 40km (25 miles) from Perugia (▷ 281).

The spectacular Palazzo dei Consoli (town hall) is home to the Museo Civico (daily 10–1, 3–6, tel 075 927 4298) and its unique treasure, the *Tavole Iguvine* (Eugubine Tablets). The seven bronze plaques (second- to first-century BC) are written in the ancient Umbrian language, using the Etruscan and Latin alphabets. Discovered in 1444, they are the most important sacred texts in the whole of Italian classical antiquity, comparable in importance to the Rosetta Stone. They provide information about worship, legal systems, the city state structure and the religious ceremonies of the ancient Gubbian community.

A centuries-old ritual, *Corsa dei Ceri*, takes place here on 15 May, the eve of the feast of St. Ubaldo (Gubbio's patron saint, ▷ 310). The *ceri* are three 4m (13ft) wooden structures, each weighing about 200kg (440lb), made of two octagonal prisms joined by a central mast and crowned with statues of St. Ubaldo, St. George and St. Anthony. The *ceri* bearers race up the streets to the Basilica di Sant'Ubaldo on Mount Ingino. Near the Roman theatre is the 13th-century church of San Francesco, where St. Francis once took refuge.

467 H7 Via della Repubblica 2, 06024 Gubbio 075 922 0693

LAGO TRASIMENO

www.castiglionedellago.it

Lake Trasimeno is the largest inland lake on the Italian peninsula, but it is also one of the shallowest, with an average depth of 6m (20ft). Its bays, capes and islands are surrounded by fertile hillsides dotted with castles and olive groves. There are beaches, a wild nature reserve, jetties for boating, fishing and day trips by ferry to its two main islands, Isola Polvese and Isola Maggiore. Isola Maggiore is small, with a pretty 14th- to 15th-century village. It is inhabited by fishermen, and the women still make traditional 'Irish stitch' lace. St. Francis spent Lent here in 1211, and Castello Guglielmi (Villa Isabella), on the southern tip is built over a former Franciscan convent. On the eastern shore of the lake, San Feliciano is a pretty fishing village. From here take a summer ferry to Isola Polvese, the lake's largest island, which is being made into a nature reserve.

467 G8 Piazza Giuseppe Mazzini 10, 06061 Castiglione del Lago 075 965 2484 Castiglione del Lago

LUCCA

Lucca lies in the heart of a fertile plain in northwest Tuscany, an hour's drive from Florence (▷ 228–265) and 22km (14 miles) northeast of Pisa (▷ 282–283). Piazza San Michele is the site of the old Roman forum, hence the name of the Romanesque church here, San Michele in Foro. The church (daily 7.40–12, 3–6) dates from 1070 and has a dazzling exterior of striped marble walls and an intricate medley of tiny loggias, decorated columns and lavish carvings. A few minutes' walk away is the Casa di Puccini (still closed for very lengthy restoration), the birthplace of Giacomo Puccini, composer of operas such as *Tosca* and *Madame Butterfly.* His former home is now a museum where you can see the piano at which he composed his last work.

THE CATHEDRAL

Lucca's cathedral, the Duomo di San Martino (mid-Mar to Oct daily 7–7; rest of year daily 7–5), has 13th-century reliefs on and around the three principal doors, including some by Nicola Pisano, a noted 13th-century Pisan sculptor. Inside is Lucca's most important artwork, the *Volto Santo (Holy Face).* A cedarwood crucifix, it is said to be an exact likeness of Christ, carved by Nicodemus. In the sacristy (mid-Mar to end Oct Mon 9.30–5.45, Sat 9–6.45, Sun 11.20–11.50, 1–4.45; rest of year Mon 9.30–4.45, Sat 9.30–6.45, Sun 11.20–11.50, 1–4.45) is the tomb of Ilaria del Carretto, a sublime funerary monument by the Sienese sculptor Jacopo della Quercia, depicting the wife of Paolo Guinigi, a medieval ruler of the city.

Next to the cathedral is the Museo della Cattedrale (mid-Mar to end Oct daily 10–6; rest of year Sat–Sun 10–2), which displays paintings and religious objects.

ARTISTIC TREASURES

The Museo Nazionale di Villa Guinigi (Tue–Sat 8.30–7.30, tel 0583 496033) has an eclectic collection of paintings, sculpture, textiles, Roman and Etruscan archaeological finds, silverware and important works by the painter Fra Bartolommeo and the sculptor Matteo Civitali. The Pinacoteca Nazionale di Palazzo Mansi (Tue–Sat 8.30–7.30, Sun 8.30–1.30), also in a former palace, is worth visiting to see the sumptuous apartments, tapestries, precious *objets d'art* and fine furniture. Particularly impressive is the 18th-century bridal chamber, richly decked with gold.

INFORMATION

www.comune.lucca.it

466 E6 Main office: Piazza Santa Maria, 55100 Lucca 0583 919931 Daily 9–7 Piazzale Verdi, 55100 Lucca 0583 583150 Mar–Oct daily 9–7; Nov–Feb 9–5 Lucca

TIPS

» Lucca is easily explored on foot. The station is only 10 minutes' walk away and parking is not easy, so it is worth visiting by train.

» Do as the locals and get around by bicycle; they can be hired from the tourist office or numerous places around town (look for *noleggio de bici*).

» Walk along the famous encircling walls (4km/2.5 miles).

» For great views over the city, climb the Torre Guinigi, easily recognized by the tree sprouting improbably out of the top.

Above *The flower market in Piazza del Anfiteatro, Lucca*

MAREMMA

www.parcomaremma.it

Cowboys on horseback herd long-horned bulls in this area of empty, melancholy countryside, often referred to as the Wild West of Tuscany. The Maremma is the name given to the coastal plain that stretches from Cecina (south of Pisa) to Civitavecchia in Lazio. It includes the Monte Amiata range. Unspoiled coastal areas with wide, sandy beaches dominate the western part, while the landscape inland has been covered for centuries in wild, marshy tracts of maquis—fragrant scrub containing a variety of herbs (such as thyme), wildflowers and low bushes. The Etruscans started draining the region, but it reverted to malarial swamp until it was finally drained by Mussolini.

The area between Principina a Mare and Talamone on the Tyrrhenian coast is a nature reserve, where you might spot porcupines, wild boar and deer, as well as migratory birds. The park visitor centre is in Alberese, about 14km (9 miles) south of Grosseto, capital of the Maremma and a walled town with a 13th-century red and white cathedral and an archaeological museum.

466 F8 Parco Regionale della Maremma, Via Besagliari 7–9, 58010 Alberese 0564 407098 Summer only

MASSA MARITTIMA

A former mining town might not have much to offer the visitor in most countries, but this ancient city has some fascinating artworks, a fine 12th-century cathedral, an archaeological museum and a museum commemorating the town's mining history.

South of Volterra, 66km (41 miles) east of Centro Carapax, Massa Marittima overlooks the valley of the River Pecora. The town is divided in two: the lower, Città Vecchia (Old Town), and the upper, Città Nuova (New Town), the sense of which is debatable, as it dates from 1228.

There is a fortress between the two, built after the area was conquered by Siena in 1335. The old town has a striking, sloping medieval square, dominated by the cathedral, while the new town has a 13th-century tower with far-reaching views over the surrounding metal-rich hills.

The duomo was initially built in Romanesque style and later enlarged in the Gothic style. Dedicated to St. Cerbone, it has a baptismal font dating from 1267 and a sculpture carved in 1324 by Giraldo da Como. The Palazzo Podestà (Tue–Sun 10–12.30, 3.30–7; till 5 Nov–Mar), a 13th-century palazzo housing the museum of archaeology, has many not particularly interesting Etruscan finds and a small collection of medieval works of art, including a superb *Maestà* (Majesty) by Ambrogio Lorenzetti.

466 E8 Via Ximenes 14, 58024 Massa Marittima 0566 902243

MONTALCINO

www.prolocomontalcino.it

Montalcino is one of Tuscany's most important wine-producing towns, the home of the excellent rich red Brunello, the lighter Rosso di Montalcino and the fragrant Moscadello di Montalcino. The streets are liberally scattered with wine shops *(enoteche),* where you can often taste before purchasing.

High on a hilltop 40km (25 miles) south of Siena, the town is dominated by its *rocca* (fortress), a picture-perfect 14th-century castle (daily 9–8). From the battlements you can look out over southern Tuscany. The Palazzo Comunale, a fine civic palace built in 1292, dominates the Piazza del Popolo, the main square. The Fiaschetteria Italiana (daily 7.30–midnight) here is a bustling café established in 1888 with an ornate mirrored interior.

The Museo Civico (Apr–Oct Tue–Sun 10–6; Nov–Mar Tue–Sun 10–1, 2–6), the town's principal museum, is in the former convent of Sant'Agostino; it has medieval and late Gothic artworks, and wood sculptures dating from the 14th and 15th centuries.

Montalcino is a good place from which to explore the abbey of Sant'Antimo and the villages of the Val d'Orcia.

466 F8 Via Costa del Municipio 8, 53024 Montalcino 0577 849331

MONTE ARGENTARIO

If you would like to see where the Italian jet set hides out, this is one place worth visiting. Southwest of Grosseto, Monte Argentario was once an island, but the shallow waters silted up and the promontory is now linked to the mainland by causeways. It was on one of the beaches here that the painter Caravaggio died in 1609.

At one time owned by the Spanish, it became part of Tuscany in the 19th century. Its Spanish heritage can be seen in Porto Santo Stefano, where a Spanish fortress still stands, and in Porto Ercole, where there are three Spanish forts.

The harbours of the nearby villages are filled with expensive yachts, while the southern tip of the promontory is less developed. The highest point is Monte Telegrafo, from where there are good views over the Maremma.

468 F9 Via Sant'Andrea 10, 58019 Porto Santo Stefano 0564 814208 Orbetello

Below *Perched on the cliffs, these villas have a view of the bay from Monte Argentario*

MONTEFALCO

www.montefalcodoc.it

High up in rolling countryside, Montefalco is known as *La Ringhiere dell'Umbria* (Balcony of Umbria). Extensive views of the green Valle Umbra unfold from its majestic circular piazza. The medieval walls form a solid circle around the town.

Enter via the second-century gate of Sant'Agostino and climb the Corso to Piazza del Comune. Streets branch off downwards from this irregular-shaped square. The Museo Pinacoteca di San Francesco (Mar–May, Sep–Oct daily 10.30–1, 2–6; Nov–Feb Tue–Sun 10.30–1, 2.30–5; Jun–Jul daily 10.30–1, 3–7; Aug daily 10.30–1, 3–7.30), in the former 14th-century church, has paintings dating from the 13th to the 17th century, including works by Perugino. The highlights are the world-famous 15th-century frescoes by Benozzo Gozzoli in the central apse, illustrating scenes from the life of St. Francis.

Montefalco is famous for traditional linen crafts, red wine (particularly Sagrantino) and gastronomy. The excellent wine shop Enoteca di Benozzo, in the main square, specializes in wine, truffles and oil.

467 H8 Museo Civico de San Francesco, Via Ringhiera Umbra 6, 06037 Montefalco 0742 379598

MONTEPULCIANO

www.prolocomontepulciano.it

On a narrow ridge, with medieval streets, Montepulciano attracts lovers of art and culture, who come to admire the cathedral, palaces and Renaissance architecture. Wine buffs also enjoy the local Vino Nobile. When the town sided with Florence in 1511, it underwent a Renaissance overhaul, a vast building project that involved leading architects, including Antonio Sangallo and the mannerist master Vignola. Today Montepulciano plays host to various cultural events, including an International Arts Workshop every summer.

The Museo Civico (Apr–Sep daily 10–1, 3–7; Oct–Mar 10–1, 3–6, tel 0579 717300) has an impressive collection of ancient pottery, medieval sculpture, Etruscan tombs and cinerary urns, along with paintings by Sienese artists. The main square, Piazza Grande, is dominated by the duomo (daily 9–12, 4–6), whose altarpiece is an *Assumption* by Taddeo di Bartolo. In the baptistery are numerous reliefs, terracottas and other sculptures by an array of medieval and Renaissance artists, including Andrea della Robbia. There are plenty of wine shops and restaurants in town, including the elegant Caffè Poliziano, with its art nouveau interior.

466 G8 Via di Voltaia nel Corso 27, 53045 Montepulciano 0578 757341 Summer daily 9.30–12.30, 2.30–8; winter 9.30–12.30, 3–6 Chiusi-Chianciano Terme (24km/15 miles away)

Above *The bronze fountain in Piazza Garibaldi, Narni*

MONTERIGGIONI

www.monteriggionicastello.it

Set on a hill with its grey walls punctuated with towers, Monteriggioni has the appearance of a granite crown. This perfectly preserved Tuscan village is in better condition than the more popular San Gimignano (▷ 285) and, although there is not much to visit inside the walls, the defensive walls themselves are remarkable.

The town was founded by the Sienese in 1203 to defend the northern approach to Siena from the Florentines. The enclosing walls were built between 1213 and 1219, destroyed in 1244 by invading Florentines and rebuilt between 1260 and 1270. The 14 grim towers were described in Dante's *Inferno* as resembling giants.

466 F7

NARNI

www.comune.narni.tr.it

The ancient hill town of Narni is built on a rocky spur overlooking the Nera gorge. From the grid of ancient Roman streets, a road climbs up to two labyrinthine medieval districts and the spectacular *rocca* (fortress), a papal stronghold built in 1370.

From Piazza Garibaldi, past the bronze fountain and the medieval tower, is the cathedral of San Giovenale (1145). The main doorway has a graceful Renaissance portico with a frieze of garlands above the arcade, and the interior is a fusion of Romanesque and baroque styles. From here on, Via Garibaldi, which has been the main street since Roman times, becomes Piazza dei Priori, once the Roman forum. The square was narrowed in medieval times with the construction of two tower-houses, the Palazzo della Podestà and Palazzo dei Priori. The latter has a fine 14th-century loggia attributed to Gattapone.

468 G9 Piazza dei Priori 1, 05035 Narni 0744 715362 Narni

NORCIA

www.norcia.net

Norcia, in a fertile valley at the foot of the Sibillini Mountains, is a town of wide streets and low stucco-fronted buildings—many built after the 1859 tremors, when a maximum height of 12.5m (41ft) was set. In Piazza San Benedetto, the main square, you can see a statue of St. Benedict, the father of Western monasticism, who was born here in 480. The Basilica di San Benedetto, the Palazzo Comunale and the Castellina are all on the piazza.

The Castellina houses Norcia's Civic Museum (summer daily 10–1, 5–7.30; winter 10–1, 3–5), and was built in 1554 as a cross between a fortress and a government palace. There are archaeological displays and a diocesan collection with a fine 13th-century *Deposition from the Cross*, a *Risen Christ* by Nicola da Siena, a *Madonna and Child* by Antonio da Faenza and a glazed terracotta *Annunciation* by Luca della Robbia.

Well known for their expert knifework, Norcia's butchers were often employed as surgeons in the Middle Ages. Today, Norcia is still famous for its *norcinerie* (pork butchers' shops). Around the square there are food shops bursting with local delicacies like wild boar sausages, black truffles and cheese.

467 H8 · Via Solferino 22, 06047 Norcia · 0743 817090

ORVIETO

▷ 279

PARCO NAZIONALE DEI MONTI SIBILLINI

▷ 280.

PARCO REGIONALE MONTE SUBASIO

www.parks.it/parco.monte.subasio

Monte Subasio rises behind Assisi (▷ 270–271), overlooking the Valle Umbra, and has played a part in the town's history and culture. It was from here that the timber and rose-pink Subasio stone, so characteristic of the area, was taken to construct the city. St. Francis, who had a passion for nature, is said to have walked here.

The Subasio mountain range is a protected area, reaching heights of 1,290m (4,232ft), and extending over 7,500ha (18,532 acres). Monte Subasio was once entirely covered by a forest of tall holm oaks. Today a splendid group of these oaks remains around the Franciscan hermitage, the Eremo delle Carceri.

From the Porta Cappuccini on the edge of Assisi you can drive over the broad, flat mountain beyond Spello (▷ 290) to Collepino, densely covered with olive trees. The unsurfaced road over the top has potholes; it is not recommended in winter, but in spring there are huge spreads of narcissi, wild orchids, fritillary and wild peonies.

467 H8 · 0742 301144 · Closed to traffic 8pm–6am · Spello or Assisi

PERUGIA

▷ 281.

PIANO GRANDE

Remote, wild and beautiful, the Piano Grande (Great Plain) is a high plateau in eastern Umbria, overshadowed by Monte Vettore, at 2,476m (8,127ft) the highest summit in this stretch of the Apennines, the Monti Sibillini (▷ 280). The plain is ringed with whaleback hills, which still support a unique agricultural and pastoral way of life, with sheep, cattle and wild horses constantly moving across the grassland, and strip fields where lentils, one of Italy's most renowned products, are grown. In spring and early summer, the plain and surrounding hills are covered in a thick carpet of wildflowers; numerous types of orchid, wild peony, wild tulip, fritillary, narcissus and spreads of thyme and globularia are among the many species. In July these give way to drifts of poppies, cornflowers and marigolds, drawing visitors from miles around to admire the Fioritura dei Piani (Blossoming of the Plains).

At the far end of the plain is the weather-beaten village of Castelluccio. At about 1,450m (4,757ft) above sea level, it is the highest village in Umbria and the last outpost of the region. Castelluccio is a good base from which to explore the Sibillini Mountains National Park (▷ 280). There is also a hang-gliding and para-sailing school here.

467 H8 · Via Solferino 22, 06047 Norcia · 0743 817090

PIENZA

www.turismo.toscano.it

Pienza lies in ravishing, rolling countryside in the southeast corner of Tuscany, close to the hilltop town of Montepulciano and 55km (34 miles) southeast of Siena. Barely more than a village, it consists of a maze of small lanes that run parallel with the main square. You will be enchanted by its timeless atmosphere and crisp beauty, qualities recognized by UNESCO, which has ensured that Pienza will be preserved for future generations.

The duomo (daily 8.30–1, 2.30–7) has paintings by five prominent Sienese painters, commissioned by Pope Pius II. Behind it, from the lanes and alleyways that run along the top of the walls, there are beautiful views towards Monte Amiata. The Museo Diocesano (mid-Mar to mid-Oct Wed–Mon 10–1, 2–7; weekends only mid-Oct to mid-Mar), in Corso Rossellino, brings together medieval and Renaissance pieces of art from various churches in the area, including a 14th-century priest's cope embroidered by English monks.

466 G8 · Piazza D. Aligheri 18, 53026 Pienza · 0578 748852

Below *The city wall and duomo, Pienza*

ORVIETO

Orvieto is one of the oldest settlements in Umbria, already in existence when the Etruscans arrived in the eighth century BC. Corso Cavour winds up from Piazza Cahen to Piazza della Repubblica, where it runs over the Roman *decumanus* (the main east–west thoroughfare) and the site of the Etruscan, and later Roman, forum. The Museo Claudio Faina (Apr–Sep daily 9.30–6; Oct–Mar Tue–Sun 10–5), in the Palazzo Faina, has an impressive collection of Etruscan finds. Orvieto produces one of the most ancient wines of Italy, with the vines benefitting from the mild climate and the volcanic minerals in the soil.

THE DUOMO

The duomo (Mar–Oct daily 7.30–12.45, 2.30–6.15; Nov–Feb 7.30–12.45, 2.30–5.15) was built to commemorate the miracle of Bolsena. In 1264 a priest from Prague visiting Bolsena (▷ 325) on his way to a pilgrimage to Rome witnessed blood dripping from the communion host on to the altar cloth. Pope Urban IV was so impressed that he ordered the blood-stained linen to be brought to a shrine built to house the holy cloth, the Cappella del Corporale. The cathedral's striking facade was begun by Lorenzo Maitani in 1304 but not completed for 300 years. At the top of the steps, bas-reliefs depict biblical scenes. In the right transept is the Cappella di San Brizio (separate ticket required); its cycle of frescoes, unique in Renaissance Italy, was worked on first by Fra Angelico, with help from Benozzo Gozzoli, and then by Luca Signorelli.

CURIOSITIES

Near the funicular station and the Rocca dell'Albornoz, in Piazza Cahen, is the Pozzo di San Patrizio (daily 10–6.45), a vast well with a shaft dropping 62m (203ft) constructed to guarantee a supply of water during a siege. Spendthrifts in Italy are said to have 'pockets as limitless as the Pozzo di San Patrizio'. The Necropoli Etrusca del Crocifisso del Tufo (daily 8.30–7) is a necropolis that dates back to the sixth century BC. The alleys are lined with chamber tombs made from blocks of tufa (porous limestone).

INFORMATION

www.orvietoturismo.it

467 G8 Piazza Duomo 24, 05018 Orvieto ☎ 0763 341772 Mon–Fri 8.15–1.50, 4–7, Sat 10–7, Sun and holidays 10–6 Carta Orvieto Unica, €18/€15, includes entrance to Cappella di San Brizio in the duomo, Museo Claudio Faina, Orvieto Underground and the Torre del Moro; it also covers up to 5 hours' free parking and free city transport. Valid for 1 year. Available from above sites and the tourist information office Orvieto

TIPS

» The Orvieto Underground takes you on a guided journey through the tunnels and caves under the city (tel 0763 340688; www.orvieto underground.it).

» The centuries-old *Festa La Palombella* (Festival of Doves) takes place at Pentecost each year in and around the cathedral square.

» The Enoteca Regionale (Mon–Fri 11–1, 5–7, Sat–Sun by appointment) in Piazza San Giovanni runs guided tours and wine tastings.

Above *A cobbled lane in the medieval town of Orvieto*

INFORMATION

www.sibillini.net

467 H8 Main park office: Piazza del Forno 1, 62039 Visso 0737 95262 Apr–Sep Mon–Fri 9.30–1, 3.30–6, Sat and Sun 10–1; Oct–Mar Mon–Fri 9.30–1, 3–5, Sat and Sun 10–1. Other offices at Norcia and Preci; opening hours erratic Mountain refuges (not always open or manned) at Forca Canapine and at ski resorts 0743 823012; Rifugio Perugia 0743 8323015; Monti del Sole 0743 823002

TIPS

» Pick up a map of the area at any of the park's offices or tourist information points.
» The park's noticeboards and literature carry a distinctive blue and green emblem.
» There are many refuge points, ideal for picnic stops.
» For serious trekking, the Grande Anello dei Sibillini is a 120km (75-mile) itinerary. On average it takes nine days to walk and covers the whole mountain chain.

Above *Monte Vettore and the Piano Grande in the Parco Nazionale*

PARCO NAZIONALE DEI MONTI SIBILLINI

The Sibillini Mountains National Park extends across 70,000ha (173,000 acres) of protected land in Umbria and the Marche, with more than 20 summits higher than 2,000m (6,562ft). The highest, Monte Vettore, rises to 2,476m (8,123ft). As can be seen in the massive limestone outcrops, sheer slopes, steep cliffs and deep escarpments scored by springs and waterfalls, this is a karstic landscape—limestone with cavities, passages and underground drainage, created by the dissolution of the rock.

ANIMAL AND PLANT LIFE

The wild, open spaces make the park a winner with wildflowers. To date, around 1,800 botanical species have been recorded. Above the tree line extremely rare species of plants, such as the Apennine edelweiss *(Leontopodium nivale)* and gentians grow in the grazing areas.

Wildcats, wolves, deer and porcupine are just some of the wildlife that roam the park, but you are more likely to see flocks of grazing sheep, known as the white gold of the Sibillini Mountains, or shaggy white cattle. Eagles, peregrine falcons, goshawks and Alpine chough all nest in the park and there is a very wide range of butterflies, moths and insects.

FACT OR FICTION?

The Saracens came up from Sicily and raided the Valnerina region around the end of the ninth century. In the Upper Nera Valley there are many castles and watchtowers from where the inhabitants of the valley defended themselves against the raids. In the 15th and 16th centuries, the Sibillini Mountains were known all over Europe as a land of myth and legend. The rugged, magical landscape has inspired many popular romance tales, including the story of Sibyl, a divine soothsayer who lived in the caves in the mountain of the same name near Montemonaco and was thought to be able to foresee the future.

Another legend concerns Pontius Pilate: buffaloes are said to have pulled the lifeless body of the Roman procurator into the waters of a demoniac lake, which turned red. In reality, the reddish waters of the circular Lago di Pilato come from a tiny crustacean—*Chircephalus marchesonii*—that inhabits the lake.

PERUGIA

The capital of Umbria was originally a settlement from the ninth century BC, which then became part of the Roman state under Emperor Augustus in the first century BC. A series of monastic complexes developed in the 13th and 14th centuries, and during the Renaissance and baroque period the new nobility built showy palaces. Today you can make a journey into the bowels of medieval Perugia by escalator: it takes you from Piazza Partigiani to Piazza Italia via a network of underground streets. Or take respite in the Orto Botanico Medievale, the old monastic garden behind San Pietro Convent, laid out with medicinal plants and herbs.

HEART OF THE CITY

The hub of Perugia is Piazza IV Novembre. The duomo, on the square, was begun in 1300 by Fra Bevignate and has an exterior pulpit from where San Bernardino preached. Inside, the chapel of St. Bernardino contains Federico Barocci's *Deposition* (1567), and the Cappella del Santo Annello has the Virgin Mary's prized wedding ring.

HIGHLIGHTS

The top floors of the Palazzo dei Priori, just off Piazza IV Novembre, house the Galleria Nazionale dell'Umbria, Umbria's finest art gallery (Tue–Sun 8.30–7.30, closed first Mon of the month; www.gallerianazionaleumbria.it). It traces the development of Umbrian painting from its Byzantine-influenced roots through the Renaissance, which is particularly strongly represented by Umbria's two great masters, Perugino and Pinturicchio. Born Pietro Vannucci but known simply as Perugino after his birthplace, Perugino was also responsible in 1496 for the superb fresco cycle in the Collegio del Cambio (Mar–Oct Tue–Sat 9–12.30, 2.30–5.30, Sun 9–12.30; Nov–Feb Tue–Sat 8–2), headquarters of Perugia's banking fraternity in Corso Vanucci, the city's classy main street. From here, steep and narrow streets lead to other churches and museums; the best include San Severo, which contains one of Raphael's earliest works, the simple fifth-century church of Sant'Angelo, the ornate San Pietro, and San Domenico, whose cloisters house the Museo Archeologico Nazionale dell'Umbria with its fine collection of Etruscan and prehistoric finds (Mon 10–7.30, Tue–Sun 8.30–7.30).

INFORMATION

www.turismo.comune.perugia.it

467 G8 Piazza Matteoti 18, 16121 Perugia ☎ 075 573 6458 Daily 8.30–1.30, 3.30–6.30 (holidays 9–1); no lunch break in high season Perugia

TIPS

» The legendary Bar Pasticceria Sandri (Corso Vannucci 32) serves mouth-watering pastries and has been voted one of the top 10 *pasticcerias* in Italy.

» An antiques market is held in the Giardini Carducci on the last Sunday of the month.

» Perugia has also given the world its very own chocolate *baci* (kisses), and around the third week of October lovers of chocolate throng the Corso Vannucci for Eurochocolate—a nine-day celebration of the delicious cocoa bean (www.eurochocolate.com).

Below *View of Perugia looking towards San Domenico church*

PISA

Pisa reached the peak of its power in the 11th and 12th centuries, but this golden age was followed by naval defeats, the collapse of its commercial empire and the silting up of the harbour. In 1406 it was taken over by Florence, and the Medici embarked on major rebuilding while turning Pisa into a focus for science and learning. Sadly much of the city's former glory was destroyed during World War II.

THE LEANING TOWER OF PISA

Pisa's most important treasures stand on the Campo dei Miracoli and include the Torre Pendente (Leaning Tower; mid-Jun to mid-Aug daily 8.30am–11pm; Apr to mid-Jun, mid-Aug to Sep 8.30–8; Oct 9–7; Mar 9–5.30; Nov–Feb 9.30–5.30), the duomo, the baptistery and the Camposanto, a medieval cemetery. Begun in 1173, the Leaning Tower was intended as the cathedral's bell tower. As it was built on sandy soil, it began to lean before it had been completed. By 1284 the lean was 90cm (35in) from the vertical, and medieval engineers were attempting to correct it. By 1350, when the tower was completed, the lean was 1.45m (4.75ft). In 1990 the tower was closed to allow scientists to stabilize it—it was now 4.5m (14.75ft) from the vertical, and getting worse. Tons of lead were attached to the northern side, steel cables were attached to hold it in place, and a wedge of soil was removed. Gradually the structure began to settle into the cavity and within five months had returned to the position it held in 1890.

OTHER HIGHLIGHTS

The duomo, dating from 1064 (Apr–Sep daily 10–8 Oct 10–7; Mar 10–6; Nov–Feb 10–12.45, 2–5), has an ornate marble-striped exterior and carvings depicting New Testament stories. The Portale di San Ranieri (1180), facing the Leaning Tower, was once the main entrance; its bronze panels portray stories form the New Testament and the architrave has Roman reliefs. Inside, the carved pulpit is by Giovanni Pisano. Begun in 1152, the baptistery is the work of Giovanni and Nicola Pisano, with a pulpit carved with scenes from the life of Christ. The Camposanto (Apr–Sep daily 8.30–8; Oct 9–7; Mar 9–6; Nov–Feb 10–5), a medieval cemetery within a Gothic cloister, was decorated with some of Tuscany's most important frescoes, but only a few survived a World War II bomb.

INFORMATION

www.pisaturismo.it

466 E6 Campo dei Miracoli, 56100 Pisa 050 560 464 Apr–Sep Mon–Sat 9–7, Sun 10.30–4.30; Oct–Mar Mon–Sat 9–5.30 Piazza della Stazione (left on exiting the railway station), 56100 Pisa 050 42291 Apr–Sep Mon–Sat 9–7, Sun 9.30–3.30; Oct–Mar Mon–Sat 9.30–1, 3–5.30 Tower: €15 on site or €17 booked online at www.opapisa.it. Duomo €2 but free Nov–Feb. For the other sights in Campo dei Miracoli combined tickets are available: €5 for one (Baptistery, Cemetery, Museo dell'Opera or Museo delle Sinopie), €6 for two, €8 for four or €10 for five Leaning Tower guided tour (30 min). Timed tickets should be reserved in advance at the ticket office or online (€15) Pisa Centrale

TIPS

» It is much cheaper to buy a combined ticket for the Campo dei Miracoli sights than pay individually for each one.
» Public transport to the city is excellent, so leave the car.
» Children under eight are not allowed up the Leaning Tower.

Opposite *The Leaning Tower of Pisa with the Fontana dei Putti in the foreground*
Below *The pulpit in Pisa's duomo*

PISTOIA

www.pistoia.turismo.toscana.it

The heart of Pistoia is the Piazza del Duomo, with its 14th-century baptistery and sumptuous cathedral. The town has several other churches worth visiting, a museum and the historic Caffè Valiani. Every Wednesday and Saturday morning one of Italy's largest markets is held on the Piazza del Duomo.

Pistoia's surroundings are uninspiring, but the town has a Renaissance heart. It sits at the foot of the Apennine Mountains, 47km (29 miles) east of Lucca, and its name probably derives from the Latin *pistores*, meaning 'bakers'—it was a town that supplied provisions to the Roman troops. The opulent cathedral has a striking silver altarpiece, the *Dossale di San Jacopo*, made between 1287 and 1456, with figures by Filippo Brunelleschi. The 14th-century Church of the Baptistery of San Giovanni has a font made in 1226 and a 16th-century, gold-painted wooden altar. The Church of San Giovanni Fuorcivitas is proud of its *Visitation* by Luca della Robbia. The Museo Civico's collection includes paintings that chronicle Pistoia's art, ranging from Romanesque to 19th-century works.

466 F6 Palazzo dei Vescovi, Piazza Duomo 4, 51100 Pistoia 0573 21622 Pistoia

PITIGLIANO

www.collidimaremma.it

Pitigliano, 8km (5 miles) south of Sovana, is a medieval town that was once an Etruscan settlement. Its main attraction is the 16th-century Palazzo Orsini, which displays an impressive collection of Etruscan finds in the beautifully decorated rooms. Elsewhere you can see the remains of a large 14th-century aqueduct.

Pitigliano's jumble of mellow buildings is delightfully set on a volcanic ridge that rises dramatically from the countryside. The village was once owned by the powerful Orsini family and was home to a thriving Jewish community until World War II. The synagogue is a poignant reminder of the town's Jewish heritage. Explore the many cobbled streets and interesting alleyways that surround the Palazzo Orsini on the main square inside the fortress, and enjoy the views of Monte Amiata. The cathedral has a lovely 18th-century baroque facade and a medieval belfry.

468 F8 Piazza Garibaldi 51, 58017 Pitigliano 0564 617111

PRATO

www.prato.turismo.toscana.it

Prato, nestling between Pistoia and Florence, has several good museums and galleries and some interesting churches. Romantics might also be attracted by the news that Prato is where the monk and artist Filippo Lippi met and fell in love with a nun, Lucrezia Buti, whom he married.

Prato means 'meadow', but today the town is surrounded by industry. It has a long association with textile manufacturing and has been famous for its fabrics since the 13th century. Most of the sights are within the medieval walls that enclose the old part of the town. The mighty turreted walls of the Castello dell'Imperatore, built by Frederick II between 1217 and 1248, are reminiscent of castles of the Swabian period, when Frederick II, King of Sicily, controlled Puglia and Sicily, at which time there were huge developments in literature, then science and poetry.

The duomo, at the heart of the city, was built in the 12th century. The *Pulpit of the Sacred Girdle* by Michelozzo and Donatello graces its exterior, while the interior contains frescoes by Filippo Lippi, including a famous depiction of Salome dancing at Herod's feast. You can see more works from the duomo in the Museo dell'Opera del Duomo.

The church of Santa Maria delle Carceri, built in the form of a Greek cross, is a masterpiece of Renaissance architecture and contains terracotta works by Andrea della Robbia.

466 F6 Piazza delle Carceri 15, 59100 Prato 0574 24112 Prato

SAN GIMIGNANO

▷ 285.

Above *Bacchus Fountain in Prato*

SAN QUIRICO D'ORCIA

San Quirico, 15km (9 miles) east of Montalcino and 10km (6 miles) west of Pienza, is a strange mixture of the enchanting and the banal, with bland, post-World War II housing next to exquisite medieval churches and 16th-century gardens. It stands on the Via Francigena, the pilgrim route to Rome, and fine medieval houses line Via Poliziano.

The main attraction is the Collegiata, a 12th-century church off Piazza Chigi, built on the ruins of an eighth-century church. Of note are the Lombard-influenced carvings around the doors. Highlights inside include inlaid Renaissance choir stalls and a *Virgin and Child Enthroned with Four Saints* by Sano di Pietro. The Church of Santa Maria di Vitaleta features a terracotta *Madonna* by Bartolomeo della Robbia. The Horti Leoni were laid out in 1580 and are made up of a flower garden and a natural woodland area. If you have time to wander around this partly walled village, you can also take a look at the Palazzo Chigi, decorated with baroque frescoes.

466 F8 Via Dante Alighieri 33, 53027 San Quirico d'Orcia 0577 897211 Apr–Oct, 19 Dec–6 Jan only

SAN GIMIGNANO

San Gimignano flourished throughout the Middle Ages, largely due to its position on the Via Francigena pilgrim route. The town split into factions over allegiance to the papacy and the empire—those supporting the pope were known as Guelphs, those supporting the emperor, Ghibellines—and during these years of conflict, the wealthy families in the town built 72 protective towers, 14 of which still stand. Torre Grossa is the only tower you can climb. Now the town is a UNESCO World Heritage Site.

THE COLLEGIATA

From the Porta San Giovanni, the main gate, Via San Giovanni runs up to the town's two main squares, the Piazza della Cisterna and Piazza del Duomo. In the latter is the Collegiata, the principal church. The interior is covered with dazzling frescoes (Mar–Oct Mon–Fri 9.30–7.30, Sat 9.30–5, Sun 1–5; Nov–20 Jan Mon–Sat 9.30–5, Sun 1–5; 21 Jan–28 Feb open for Mass only). On the rear wall is a *Last Judgement* by Taddeo di Bartolo, alongside an *Inferno*, a *Paradiso* and a *St. Sebastian.* The second cycle on the right wall is now attributed to Lippo Memmi and the Old Testament cycle opposite is by Bartolo di Fredi. The Cappella di Santa Fina has frescoes by Domenico Ghirlandaio.

PALAZZO DEL POPOLO

To the left of the Collegiata stands the Palazzo del Popolo, the main museum (Mar–Oct daily 9.30–7; Nov–Feb 10–5.30). Within are paintings by Florentine, Umbrian and Sienese artists such as Filippo Lippi. The Sala del Consiglio (or Sala di Dante, because it was here that Dante, as a Florentine diplomat, met members of San Gimignano's council) is dominated by Lippo Memmi's *Maestà* (1317).

MUSEO D'ARTE SACRA AND MUSEO ARCHEOLOGICO

The Museo d'Arte Sacra (Apr–Oct daily 9.30–7.30; Nov–Dec, Mar 9.30–5) is a museum of religious art in the old Rectai Palace, while the Museo Archeologico (Mar–Oct daily 11–6; Nov–Dec Sat–Thu 11–6; Jan–Feb Fri–Mon 11–6) houses a small collection of Etruscan objects in a former convent.

INFORMATION

www.sangimignano.com
www.comune.sangimignano.siena.it
www.terresiena.it
466 F7 Piazza Duomo 1, 53037 San Gimignano 0577 940008 Mar–Oct daily 9–1, 3–7; Nov–Feb 9–1, 2–6
Combined tickets for the Museo Civico, Museo Archeologico and Torre Grossa, Spezeria di Santa Fina, Museo Ornitologico and Galleria d'Arte Moderna: Adult €10; child (6–18) and over 65s €7
The tourist office can provide an audioguide which covers a tour of the town and its main monuments and museums for €7.50 per day

TIPS

» Do not try to park in town.
» A stiff climb up the Torre Grossa—54m (177 feet) high—rewards you with spectacular views.

Above *The medieval town of San Gimignano, with some of the surviving towers*

INFORMATION

www.terresiena.it

466 F7 Piazza del Campo 56, 53100 Siena 0577 280551 Mar–end Nov Mon–Sat 9.30–7.30; rest of year Mon–Fri 8.30–1, 3–7, Sat 8.30–1 Combined tickets for: Museo Civico and Torre del Mangia (€9.50); Ospedale di Santa Maria della Scala, Centro di Arte Contemporanea (€9); Museo dell'Opera del Duomo (Metropolitana), Libreria Piccolomini, Battistero di San Giovanni (€7.50), Museo dell'Opera del Duomo (Metropolitana), Libreria Piccolomini, Battistero di San Giovanni, Oratorio di San Bernardino, Museo Diocesano (€9.50) Siena

Above *The famous Piazza del Campo*

INTRODUCTION

The beautifully preserved, homogenous medieval city of Siena is a magical mix of narrow streets, open spaces and superb buildings focused round the great central square of the Campo. This lies at the convergence of the city's three main streets, each of which runs along a ridge through Siena's medieval *terzi* (districts), which are divided into *contrade* (wards). This central core is tiny and traffic-free, running uphill from the Campo, with its clutch of superb medieval civic buildings, towards the black-and-white striped duomo (cathedral), the Ospedale di Santa Maria della Scala, the city's major exhibition space, and the Pinacoteca, home to great examples of the serene Sienese school of painting. Thousands come here as day visitors, but once evening comes, the city reverts to itself, a quiet backwater that preserves all that's best about medieval cities.

Siena wasn't always a backwater; in the 14th century this was one of Europe's richest centres, a prosperous banking city, permanently at odds with Florence, with an important wool industry, whose wealth paid for the construction of great buildings and funded major artists. The good times ended with the onslaught of the Black Death in 1348; the city's population dropped from 100,000 to around 30,000. Siena never really recovered, becoming part of the Medici Grand Duchy of Tuscany in 1557, the start of an era that saw the city become little more than a minor provincial town, albeit a proud one. The upside of this was the preservation of its medieval core, with little building or demolition after the 1400s. Slumbering in the countryside, it was untouched by 20th-century war, only seeing regeneration as tourists discovered its charms and the Monte dei Paschi di Siena, the city's oldest bank, founded in 1472, became one of Italy's major financial players.

Today, it is prosperous, its citizens proud of their city and fiercely loyal to their *contrade*, whose traditional rivalries are played out annually in the Palio (▷ 311), the world's most exciting and dangerous horse race, run against the stunning backdrop of the Campo itself.

WHAT TO SEE

THE CAMPO

Every year, on 2 July and 16 August, the beautiful shell-shaped piazza known as the Campo fills up for the Palio, a vital part of Sienese life since the Middle Ages. The three-lap horse race is ridden by 10 jockeys representing 10 of the city's 17 *contrade*, and is preceded by spectacular parades of *contrade* members in medieval costumes, beating drums and throwing huge silken banners in intricate patterns.

Whatever the time of year, the Campo is a space to linger, but you shouldn't miss the Palazzo Pubblico, once the seat of Sienese government and today home to the Museo Civico. Its series of chambers were the backdrop to council meetings and decisions of state, the iconography of the frescoes reflecting the building's role. Don't miss the Sala del Mappamundo, with its wonderful equestrian portrait of one of Siena's mercenary soldiers, Guidoriccio da Fogliano, and superb *Maestà* by Simone Martini, a quintessential Sienese Gothic masterpiece. The Sala della Pace contains Ambrogio Lorenzetti's beguiling portrayal of *Good and Bad Government*, painted in 1338 to remind the councillors how their decisions would affect the city's inhabitants. From the museum, you can access the soaring Torre della Mangia and climb its 503 steps for sweeping views over the city to the countryside beyond.

THE DUOMO

Siena's cathedral has been the city's religious focus for over 800 years, a Romanesque and Gothic building that was largely built in the 13th century. It is crammed with sculpture, frescoes, stained glass and decorative marble. These treasures are hidden behind a magnificent facade, designed by the sculptor Nicola Pisano, who was also responsible for the octagonal pulpit with its sculpted panels (1268). One of the duomo's greatest treasures is its marble paving, a series of decorative and narrative panels produced between 1369 and 1547 and worked on by practically every well-known artist of the day. Don't miss either the Piccolomini Library, built in the 1490s by Renaissance Pope Pius III and covered with glowing and colourful frescoes of scenes of the life of Pius II, Pius III's uncle, by Pinturicchio. In the Cripta (crypt), accessed through the superb Battistero (baptistery), there are important wall paintings dating from the 1270s.

✉ Piazza del Duomo, 53100 Siena ☎ 0577 283048 🕐 Mar–Oct daily 7.30–7.30; Nov–Feb 7.30–5 ✋ Free

TIPS

» Buy one of the combined tickets to save money.

» For a great view of the Campo and excellent ice cream, head for Gelateria La Costerella on Via di Città (corner of Costa dei Barbieri and Via di Fontebranda).

» Tickets for seats for the Palio are hard to come by and expensive, but you can, like most Sienese, watch free from the Campo. It can be very hot and crowded. The event is televised live on RAI 1. Palio tickets sell out months ahead but can be reserved through Palio Viaggi, Piazza Gramsci 7, tel 0577 280 828 (€150–€300).

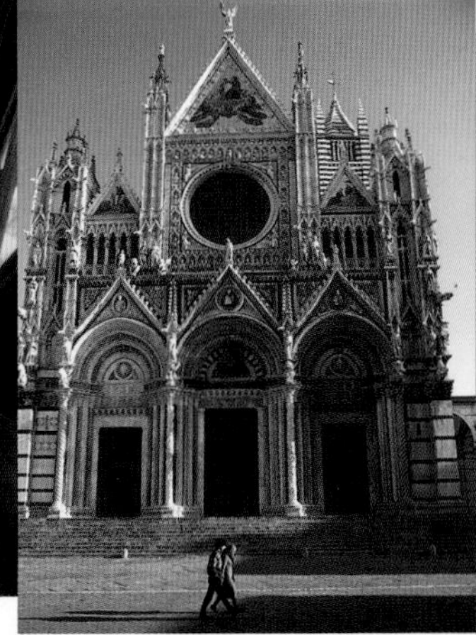

Left *The Libreria Piccolominea in the duomo*
Below *The facade of Siena's duomo*

MUSEO DELL'OPERA DEL DUOMO

www.operaduomo.siena.it

Treasures in the Museo dell'Opera del Duomo (or Museo dell'Opera Metropolitana) include a relief of the *Madonna and Child* by Donatello and Duccio's vast *Maestà*. In the Battistero di San Giovanni the font has bronze panels by Jacopo della Quercia, Donatello and Ghiberti.

✉ Piazza del Duomo 8, 53100 Siena ☎ 0577 283048 ⏲ Mar–May daily 9.30–7; Jun–Aug 9.30–8; Sep, Oct 9.30–7; Nov–Feb 10–5 ✋ €6

PINACOTECA NAZIONALE

Siena produced some of the greatest Italian painters of the 13th and 14th centuries, and the Pinacoteca Nazionale has the city's best collection of paintings by this influential school. Artists represented include Duccio di Buoninsegna, the first to move painting on from the austere traditions of Byzantine art, Simone Martini, and brothers Pietro and Ambrogio Lorenzetti.

✉ Via San Pietro 29, 53100 Siena ☎ 0577 281161 ⏲ Mon 8.30–1.30, Tue–Sat 10–6, Sun 8.30–1.30 ✋ €4.15

OSPEDALE DI SANTA MARIA DELLA SCALA

Opposite the duomo stands the great complex of Santa Maria della Scala, founded in the 11th century as a pilgrim hostel, charitable foundation, orphanage and hospital. It remained Siena's main hospital until 1995, when a new one was opened on the city outskirts, and today it is being transformed into the city's foremost museum and cultural space. It contains the archaeological museum, stages big temporary art shows and will eventually be home to the Pinacoteca. Its main draws are a series of frescoed rooms, used as hospital wards right up until the 1990s, that were painted in the 15th century by the artists Vecchietta and Domenico del Bartolo. The huge Sala del Pellegrino has 11 frescoes, crammed with wonderful details of everyday Sienese life, subject matter that was extremely rare at this date. Elsewhere you can explore the rest of the Ospedale with its chapels, churches, halls and endless corridors.

✉ Piazza del Duomo 2, 53100 Siena ☎ 0577 334811 ⏲ Apr–Oct daily 10.30–6.30; Nov–Mar 10.30–4.30 ✋ €6

Below *View from the Torre del Mangia across the rooftops of the city towards the duomo and campanile and the Tuscan hills beyond*

SPOLETO

ROMAN HERITAGE

Roman Spoletium was founded in 241BC, and the upper town's main square, the beautiful Piazza del Mercato, stands on the site of the forum, its entrance still straddled by the Arco di Druso, built in AD23. Nearby is the much-restored Roman theatre, used for performances during the summer festival, with an adjoining archaeological museum (daily 8.30–7.30; €4). In the lower town are the remains of the amphitheatre and a Roman bridge.

SANTA MARIA ASSUNTA

Up the hill in the old town, a sloping piazza fronts the elegant facade of the cathedral of Santa Maria Assunta (consecrated 1189). The exterior is a sublime blend of Romanesque and Renaissance elements, while the interior is dominated by glowing frescoes showing scenes from the life of the Virgin, painted by Filippo Lippi.

THE REST OF THE TOWN

Near the cathedral is Spoleto's most famous church, Sant'Eufemia, built in the 12th century and unique in Umbria for its *matroneum*, a high gallery above the nave where women heard Mass. Beside the church is the Museo Diocesano d'Arte Sacra (Apr–Sep Mon, Wed–Sat 10–1.30, 3–5; Oct–Mar Mon, Wed–Sat 10.30–1, 3–5; €3), a fine collection of paintings and *objets d'art* from churches across the diocese. From here, an uphill walk leads to the Rocca, a postcard-perfect fortress complete with crenellations, towers and soaring walls, which was built from the late 14th century. Below the Rocca's walls, a leafy lane leads to the Ponte delle Torri, a magnificent medieval aqueduct, whose 10 arches span the Tessino gorge; it was designed by Gattapone and built towards the end of the 13th century. Walk across the Ponte delle Torri through olive groves to the 12th-century church of San Pietro.

Other churches to visit include San Salvatore, an ancient church built from Roman stone in the style of a temple; the 12th-century church of San Ponziano and the Romanesque church of San Gregorio.

INFORMATION

www.visitspoleto.it

467 H8 Piazza della Libertà 7, 06049 Spoleto 0743 238 920 Apr–end Sep Mon–Fri 9–1, 4–7, Sat–Sun 10–1, 4–7; Oct–end Mar Mon–Fri 9–1, 3.30–6, Sat 10–1, 3.30–6, Sun 10–1 Terni, Perugia, Roma. Buses run from station to city. Tickets can be bought at newsstands and *tabacchi*

TIPS

» The Basilica di San Salvatore has no lights, so try to visit before sundown.

» Have an ice cream or coffee at Bar La Portella, on a little promontory with views down the valley.

» The annual theatre Festival dei Due Mondi, founded in 1958, usually takes place in June/July (www.festivaldispoleto.com).

» There is an antiques fair in Piazza della Libertà on the morning of the second Sunday of the month.

Above *Looking up to Spoleto's Rocca, with the campanile of Santa Maria Assunta on the right*

SANSEPOLCRO

www.comune.sansepolcro.it (Italian only)

This small and delightful town is filled with Renaissance buildings and churches. Along with its artistic heritage, the town is noted for its lace-making and jewellery. It is also the setting for the Palio of the Crossbow, a famous crossbow shooting event.

At the foot of the Apennines in the Tiber Valley, 8km (5 miles) northeast of Anghiari, Sansepolcro is said to have been founded by two 10th-century monks returning from the Holy Land with relics of Christ's sepulchre. It is packed with medieval palazzi and stone-built towers surrounded by ancient walls. The town's major claim to fame is as the birthplace and home of the Renaissance artist Piero della Francesca (1416–92). The Museo Civico (Jun–Sep daily 9–1.30, 2.30–7.30; Oct–May 9.30–1, 2.30–6) has a collection of works by him, including *The Resurrection*, *The Madonna della Misericordia* and *San Giuliano*. It also has works by Raffaellino del Colle and Santi di Tito, who were also local artists. The church of San Lorenzo has a *Deposition* by Rosso Fiorentino.

467 G7 Via Matteotti 8, 52037 San Sepolcro 0575 740536

SIENA

▷ 286–288.

SOVANA

Sleepy Sovana might be small but it has several striking reminders of its illustrious past. On the border with Lazio, 80km (50 miles) southeast of Grosseto, the village consists of little more than a single street, Via di Mezzo, with the ruins of a fortress at one end. There are Etruscan, Roman and medieval relics scattered about, and the limestone cliffs are dotted with ancient tombs.

The birthplace of Hildebrand, who became Pope Gregory VII in 1073, Sovana has a fine cathedral. A highlight is the church of Santa Maria, a 13th-century church with a Romanesque exterior, frescoes by the Sienese school, and a carved *ciborium* (altar canopy)—a rare palaeo-Christian work dating from the eighth or ninth century. There is an Etruscan graveyard on the outskirts of the village dating from the seventh century BC.

466 F8 Pitigliano (▷ 284)

SPELLO

www.comune.spello.pg.it

The enchanting town of Spello (Roman Hispellum) lies under the slopes of Monte Subasio. It is a smaller version of Assisi (▷ 270–271), with cobbled streets and medieval houses built from pinkish stone. The town's Roman origins are immediately visible as you approach Porta Consolare, one of five remaining gates. The town was founded at the beginning of the first century BC and enjoyed prosperity right through the imperial period.

Climb up to Via San Angelo and you pass the tiny Cappella Tega, which houses, behind glass, a Crucifixion fresco by Nicolò Alunno. From Via Consolare the street becomes Via Cavour, and in a small square to the right is the town's main church, Santa Maria Maggiore (13th to 17th century). It was built over the ruins of a Roman temple and is decorated with three delightful frescoes by Pinturicchio telling the story of the early life of Jesus.

The Pinacoteca Comunale (town art gallery) is in the Palazzo dei Canonici, next to Santa Maria Maggiore (summer Tue–Sat 10.30–1, 3–6.30; winter Tue–Sat 10.30–12.30, 3–5). Among the works on display are an enamelled silver processional cross by Paolo Vanni and a diptych by Cola Petruccioli, both late 14th century.

467 H8 Piazza Matteotti 3, 06038 Spello 0742 651408 or 0742 301009 Spello

SPOLETO

▷ 289.

TODI

www.umbria2000.it

www.comune.todi.pg.it

Todi's museum, churches and palaces make it a popular, but unspoiled, hilltop town.

Above *The medieval town of Todi*

The main square, the Piazza del Popolo, is bordered by magnificent buildings. On the south side is the battlemented Palazzo dei Priori, opposite the sweeping steps of the cathedral, whose Gothic facade features an early 14th-century rose window above carved wooden doors. The interior is fairly simple, with a 14th-century altarpiece and choir stalls of inlaid wood. In the crypt are three sculptures by Pisano.

On the east side of the piazza, the Palazzo del Popolo (1213), stands next to the Palazzo del Capitano (1293). The two are connected by a broad external stairway and the top floors together house the Museo Pinacoteca (Mar–Oct Tue–Sun 10–1.30, 3–6; Nov–Feb 2.30–5). Exhibits trace the history of Todi; in the grand hall is an outstanding altarpiece by Lo Spagna, *The Coronation of Mary with Choir of Angels and Saints* (1511).

The Tempio di San Fortunato (Tue–Sun 10.30–1, 3–6.30, Mon 3–6.30) on Piazza Umberto has frescoes by Umbrian painters from the 13th and 14th centuries and the crypt houses the tomb of the poet St. Jacopone, who died in Todi in 1306. There is a bronze sculpture of him at the foot of the steps of San Fortunato. You can climb the 153 steps of the Campanile di San Fortunato, accessed from the interior of the church, for views over the city and the surrounding countryside.

467 G8 Piazza del Popolo 37, 06059 Todi 075 894 5418

TREVI

www.protrevi.com

Halfway between Assisi (▷ 270–271) and Spoleto (▷ 289), Trevi is known as the City of the Olive. This warm-stoned hilltop town is surrounded by olive groves—there are about 200,000 trees on the slopes. The town celebrates the new season's oil with a festival every autumn.

Trevi has Roman origins and its heart is enclosed by medieval walls and gates. The former convent adjoining the church of San Francesco makes an interesting museum space, comprising the Museo della Civiltà dell'Ulivo di Trevi (Museum of Olive Oil Cultivation) and the Raccolta d'Arte di San Francesco di Trevi (San Francesco Collection) (Apr–May, Sep Tue–Sun 10.30–1, 2.30–6; Jun–Jul Tue–Sun 10.30–1, 3.30–7; Aug Tue–Sun 10.30–1, 3–7.30; Oct–Mar Fri–Sun 10.30–1, 2.30–5). The vaulted area downstairs has olive presses and huge antique storage jars. Upstairs, the San Francesco art collection includes an altarpiece by Lo Spagna, *The Coronation of the Virgin*, which was formerly in the 14th-century church of San Martino.

Facing Sant'Emiliano in Palazzo Lucarini is the Trevi Flash Art Museum (Tue–Fri 10–1, 3–7, Sat–Sun 3–6), which has a renowned contemporary art collection. Also worth visiting is the church of the Madonna delle Lacrime, which has an *Adoration of the Magi* by Perugino and a painted altarpiece by Lo Spagna.

467 H8 Piazza Mazzini 5, 06039 Trevi 0742 781150 Trevi

VALNERINA

www.paesaggi.regioneumbria.eu

The Valnerina, the Valley of the River Nera, begins in Visso, in the north of the Marche, and winds its way down to Terni, in the southern reaches of the region. Against a backdrop of rugged mountains, the river has carved deep ravines through the countryside, providing views around every bend. Fortress villages, towers and churches perch either side of the river, underlining the importance of this ancient route that has for centuries connected the Tyrrhenian Sea with the Adriatic.

Syrian monks fleeing persecution during the early period of Christianity hid in the caves and woods here. The monks set up hermitages in the Valnerina and Castoriana valleys, and these became the nucleus of the abbeys and monasteries that were founded later, including Sant'Eutizio and San Pietro in Valle.

The Nera River Park protects the area around the river's lower reaches, along with its tributary, the Velino. The region is famous for its black truffles, herbs, wild asparagus, river trout and crayfish. At various points along the valley there are opportunities for river sports such as canoeing and rafting, rock-climbing and even bungee-jumping, and as you travel along the SS209, the road that follows the river, you can easily visit any of a string of historic villages and hamlets.

The clear, cold waters of the river feed the 165m (540ft) Cascata delle Marmore waterfalls. The highest waterfalls in Europe, they are, surprisingly, a man-made phenomenon: they were created in 271BC by a Roman consul, Manius Curius Dentatus, who diverted the River Velino into the Nera.

467 H8 Piazza Garibaldi 1, 06043 Cascia 0743 71147 Mon–Sat 9–1, 4–7

VOLTERRA

www.olterratur.it

Volterra lies high in the volcanic hills, 50km (31 miles) west of Siena, in the triangle formed by Siena, Pisa and Florence. On a clear day you can see the islands of Corsica and Elba (▷ 273) off the Tuscan coast.

The town was founded by the Etruscans as an important stronghold and its medieval heart is the Piazza dei Priori, with its 12th-century duomo and 13th-century octagonal baptistery. Volterra also has a good art gallery (Mar to mid-Nov daily 9–7; mid-Nov to Feb 9–1.30), housing a *Deposition* by Rosso Fiorentino and a very well-preserved Roman theatre. This was built in the first century BC and unearthed only in the 1950s.

The Parco Archeologico is the site of an Etruscan and Roman acropolis, while the Museo Guarnacci (summer daily 9–7; winter 8.30–1.45) exhibits one of the most important collections of Etruscan works in the world.

Another highlight in the town is the Porta all'Arco, an Etruscan arch.

466 E7 Piazza dei Priori 19/20, 56048 Volterra 0588 87257

Below *Trevi, the City of the Olive.* **Right** *The Roman theatre in Volterra*

SIENA–VOLTERRA AND SAN GIMIGNANO

The delightful rolling countryside that characterizes Tuscany features on this drive. You travel along quiet roads through gently undulating hills, past olive groves, cypress trees and immaculately preserved hilltop towns and villages, many of which are generally overlooked by visitors.

THE DRIVE
Distance: 154km (96 miles)
Allow: 8 hours
Start/end at: Siena

★ From Siena, follow the road from Porta Romana and turn right at the sign for the A1. Turn left shortly afterwards, signposted Firenze, and follow the road *(tangenziale)* around the outskirts of Siena. After 6km (4 miles) go through a tunnel and follow the signs on the right for Monteriggioni (▷ 277).

You will soon see the walls of Monteriggioni sitting high on the hill. Park at the bottom of the village and climb to the top.

❶ The climb is worth it to see this extraordinarily well-preserved medieval fortified town, encircled by tower-studded walls.

From Monteriggioni follow the signs saying 'Firenze 46'. Turn left at the sign for Colle di Val d'Elsa.

❷ The landscape now becomes flatter and is covered with vineyards —this area is known as Chianti Colle Senesi (Sienese hills, Chianti).

When you reach a roundabout (traffic circle) you will see a large sign on the left saying CALP—one of the biggest producers of rock crystal in the world. Drive into Colle di Val d'Elsa, going uphill to reach Colle Altao, the old part of town, and parking in the parking area on Via della Porta Vecchia.

❸ Defined by three levels—Borgo, Castello and Piano (the Town, Castle and Plain)—Colle di Val d'Elsa is renowned for the production of fine handcrafted crystal. The town is entered through the monumental Porta Nuova that forms the gateway to a string of fine 16th- and 17th-century noble houses: the town hall, Palazzo Usimbardi, Palazzo Buoninsegni and the magnificent, but unfinished, Palazzo Campana, which marks the entrance to the castle, the oldest part of Colle di Val d'Elsa. The Piazza del Duomo is overlooked by the Praetorial Court, the seat of the Museo Archeologico (Archaeological Museum), the 17th-century cathedral, the Bishop's Palace, housing the Museo Civico e d'Arte Sacra (Museum of Religious Art), and the Via delle Volte, easily the most evocative corner of the town.

From Colle take the SS68, following signs for Volterra. After 6km (4 miles) the road starts to climb into the heart of the country. Go through Castel San Gimignano, after which there are glorious views of vine-dotted hills, olive groves, dark cypresses and fields of sunflowers. There is a thermal electric plant at Lardarello, 33km (21 miles) from Volterra. Look in the distance for steam rising from the underground thermal springs that spurt from these hills. After about 8km (5 miles) you should begin to see Volterra on the horizon as you reach the top of the hill and shortly you will see a sign saying 'Casciana Terme/Pontedera 44', where it is possible to turn right and make a diversion for a short walk up Monte Voltraio.

❹ After 1km (0.6 mile) you come to Volterra, a delightful Etruscan town containing fine medieval buildings and a Roman theatre (▷ 291).

Leave Volterra and follow signs for Pontedera. After 4km (2.5 miles) you will see a yellow sign on the left-hand side for San Cipriano, a little church that is an ideal spot for taking some photographs of the extensive views. Alternatively, keep going and follow the SP15 as it winds its way downhill, taking the right-hand fork and going over a modern bridge until you reach an intersection. Take the turn for Firenze and follow the SP4 for about 9km (6 miles). Turn right and follow the signs for San Gimignano. You will soon see the town perched on a hill in the distance; drive up and if possible park outside the town walls. This will be difficult unless you arrive early in the day.

❺ San Gimignano (▷ 285) is frequently referred to as the medieval Manhattan, due to its striking crown of towers. It's worth stopping to walk around the streets.

Drive around the town walls to reach an intersection, where you turn right for Poggibonsi. Go straight over the next roundabout towards Poggibonsi. When you reach the uninspiring industrial town, go left at the next roundabout, and get on the SS2 (Cassia) back to Siena.

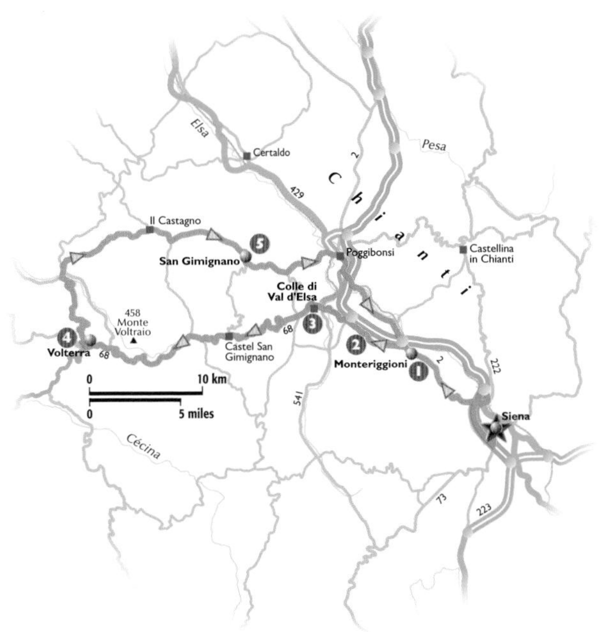

WHERE TO EAT

There are several places to choose from in Volterra, including the Trattoria da Bado (Borgo San Lazzero 9, tel 0588 86477; 12–2, 7–9.30; closed Wed) at the entrance to the town, which serves typical Tuscan dishes. Alternatively, if you just want a snack, there is an internet café on Via Porte Lago, which has a glass floor revealing the remains of a Roman grain silo. Just outside the town, off the SR439, is Villa Palagione, an elegant villa that is happy to cater for non-residents—a lovely rural spot for a snack or a meal. You have several choices of restaurants, cafés and pizzerias in San Gimignano. The Gelateria di Piazza in Piazza della Cisterna has a reputation for serving the best ice cream in town.

WHEN TO GO

The scenery makes this drive good at any time of the year, but to miss the crowds you should try to visit in early spring or late autumn. Arrive early in San Gimignano to park your car in one of the four car parks.

PLACES TO VISIT

MUSEO ARCHEOLOGICO

✉ Palazzo del Duomo, Piazza del Duomo 42, 53034 Colle di Val d'Elsa ☎ 0577 922954 🕐 May–Sep Tue–Fri 10–12, 5–7, Sat–Sun 10–12, 4.30–7.30; Oct–Apr Tue–Fri 3.30–5.30, Sat-Sun 10–12, 3.30–6.30 ✋ €3

Opposite *Olive groves in Volterra*
Right *Piazza della Cisterna in San Gimignano*

MUSEO CIVICO E D'ARTE SACRA

✉ Via del Castello 33, 53034 Colle di Val d'Elsa ☎ 0577 923888 🕐 May–Sep Tue–Sun 10.30–12.30, 4.30–7.30; Oct–Apr 11.30–5 ✋ €3

SIENA AND SOUTHERN TUSCANY

From Siena, this drive takes you south past the ancient abbeys of Sant'Antimo and Monte Oliveto Maggiore and the hilltop towns of Montalcino, Pienza and Montepulciano. Some of Italy's finest wines are produced in this region, so look for *enoteche* (specialist wine bars and shops).

THE DRIVE
Distance: 261km (162 miles)
Allow: 11 hours (tour is best spread over 2 days)
Start/end at: Siena

★ From Siena take the SR2. In 3km (2 miles) you will see signs saying 'Buonconvento 25'. After another 8km (5 miles) turn left, staying on the SR2 for Buonconvento. When you come to a crossroads, keep driving along the SR2 to Buonconvento. Bear right after the bridge to park outside the town.

❶ Buonconvento (▷ 272), unusual in this area in that it is not perched on a hill, has a medieval old town and a small museum of religious art, the Museo d'Arte Sacra. It was once an important stop on the Via Francigena, the historic pilgrims' route that stretched from Canterbury to Rome. The steam 'Nature Train' puffs its way here and to surrounding villages (www.terresiena.it).

Leave Buonconvento, following the SR2 past the outlying *zona industriale*. Turn right and take the SP45 for Montalcino. The scenery becomes prettier and you will soon see Montalcino on the hill ahead of you.

❷ As you climb uphill you will start to notice a large number of signs for *enoteche*, many of which offer free wine-tasting.

After about 9km (6 miles), bear right at the top of the hill and join the SP14, following signs for Montalcino. Follow the city wall counterclockwise until you arrive at the roundabout (traffic circle) at the top of the hill. There is free parking to the left of the roundabout. Alternatively there is pay parking on the right-hand side next to La Fortezza.

❸ Montalcino (▷ 276) is particularly famous for its rich ruby red Brunello wine, characterized by an intense aroma and delicate, warm flavour. After exploring Montalcino, follow the brown signs from the roundabout at the top of the hill for the Abbazia di Sant'Antimo, joining the SP55. The road now starts to wind downhill to the valley bottom and in about 2km (1.3 miles) you should spot the abbey, nestling below the hills on the right-hand side. Shortly turn right to reach the abbey, a good starting point for a walk, where there is parking and a shop on the access road.

From here, return to the road and drive up the hill to Castelnuovo dell'Abate. Turn right at the top of the hill, following the sign saying 'Stazione Monte Amiata' on the SP22. You will now traverse the Val d'Orcia, from where the road begins to wind downhill. Pass over a level-crossing by Monte Amiata train station and cross the River Orcia and you will come into the hamlet of Monte Amiata, after which the road begins to climb uphill again. When you reach the intersection, go to the left towards Castiglione d'Orcia. From here the road climbs even more steeply, with rewarding views. When you come to an intersection, take a left turn and join the SR323. Continue driving towards Castiglione d'Orcia.

❹ At the centre of Castiglione d'Orcia is Piazza il Vecchietta, dedicated to sculptor and painter Lorenzo di Pietro (1412–80), called 'Il Vecchietta'. It is overlooked by the Palazzo Comunale, home to a fresco of the Madonna and Child with two saints (Sienese school) taken from the nearby Rocca d'Orcia. There are two churches worth seeing here: the Romanesque Church of Santa Maria Maddalena, and the Church of Santo Stefano with its 16th-century facade and two Madonnas by Simone Martini and Lorenzetti.

Drive through the village, then head downhill. After 5km (3 miles) turn left at the intersection to join the SR2. Continue until you reach the side road to Bagno Vignoni. Turn left to park just outside town, on top of the hill.

❺ This ancient spa has been used since Etruscan times and is dominated by an enormous outdoor pool of warm, sulphurous water (▷ 269).

Go back downhill from the town, turn left at the end of the road and then take the next right to join the SP53 for Pienza. Turn left onto the SP18 and drive uphill. The striking golden sandstone town of Pienza is in front of you. Park outside the walls. There is off-street parking around Via degli Archi in the modern part of town.

❻ The focal point of Pienza (▷ 278) is the Piazza Pio II. The square, a UNESCO World Heritage Site, is lined by the Palazzo Piccolomini and Palazzo Borgia and the cathedral. With a pure Renaissance exterior, the cathedral has a Gothic interior similar to those of German churches.

Leave Pienza and continue uphill until you come to an intersection. Turn right here for the SR146 and Montepulciano. Follow the road until you reach Montepulciano, again parking outside the city walls.

❼ Montepulciano (▷ 277) has sweeping views and a maze of steep, winding streets and alleyways. Besides the Renaissance church of San Biagio, the town has many wine shops where you can purchase bottles of Vino Nobile, the famous local wine, made mainly from the superb Sangiovese grape. Aged in oak barrels for two years (three years for Reserva), this dry wine has a delicate bouquet with violet scents.

From Montepulciano, drive downhill. Turn right for Pienza on the SS146 and after 7km (4 miles) turn right to join the SP15, a twisty road heading towards Torrita di Siena. Turn left just in front of a bar on the corner to join the SP57. Follow the road to an intersection where you take a sharp left past Petroio and then drive on for another 4km (2.5 miles), after which you turn right towards Montisi.

The road now winds tightly downhill, passing through the woods until you reach an intersection. Turn left here and follow the SP14 through Montisi, on to the outskirts of San Giovanni d'Asso. When you come to the next intersection, turn right towards the remote Abbazia di Monte Oliveto Maggiore. Follow this road to Montefresco, then turn left at the intersection and drive for another 3km (2 miles). At the next intersection go left, then shortly turn off to visit the late 13th-century Abbazia di Monte Oliveto Maggiore.

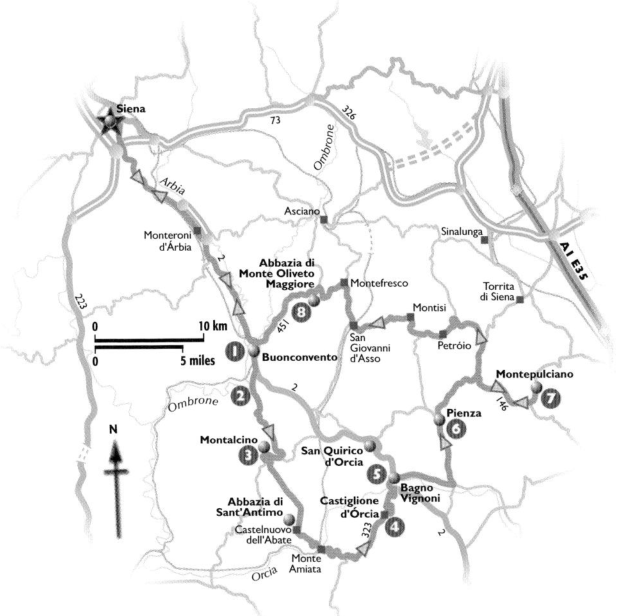

❽ This Benedictine abbey (▷ 269) stands in a wooded park on a scenic rise and is still inhabited by monks. Pause a while to admire the famous frescoes in the main cloister.

Leave the abbey and continue along the SR451 until you reach Buonconvento. From here, pick up the SR2 that leads back to Siena.

WHERE TO EAT

In Montalcino, the Fiaschetteria Italiana (Piazza del Popolo 6; 7.30am–midnight) serves coffees, cakes, light meals and wine. In Bagno Vignoni La Parata (tel 0577 887508; Thu–Tue 10.30–2.45, 7.30–9.30) serves *panini* and cakes.

Opposite *The landscape around Monte Oliveto Maggiore*

OLD SIENA

Wander through the heart of old Siena, beginning in the north of the city and winding south past medieval churches and palaces to the Campo (▷ 286–288). The route then takes you through the city's less-visited southern quarters, finishing in Piazza del Duomo, overlooked by the cathedral and the Ospedale di Santa Maria della Scala.

THE WALK
Distance: 2km (1.3 miles)
Allow: 2–3 hours
Start at: Piazza San Domenico
End at: Piazza del Duomo

★ Begin your walk in Piazza San Domenico, home to the church of the same name, containing frescoes by Sodoma (1477–1549). With your back to the church, walk down Via della Sapienza opposite San Domenico, and after 100m (110 yards) you will come to the Biblioteca Comunale degli Intronati.

❶ This library was founded in 1759 in what was probably a 13th-century hospital. It contains more than 500,000 books and other documents, including letters by St. Catherine of Siena and many medieval Sienese painters and architects. At the next minor crossroads is the church of San Pellegrino alla Sapienza, built in 1767 over the site of a much older chapel.

Continue straight on at the church to emerge on Banchi di Sopra, a major street that follows the path of the Via Francigena, a centuries-old pilgrimage route between Rome and northern Europe. On the corner of Banchi di Sopra you will see the Monte dei Paschi di Siena—the world's oldest bank, founded in 1472.

❷ Ahead is Piazza Salimbeni, home to a trio of fine palaces: Palazzo Tantucci (1548) on the left, the 14th-century Palazzo Salimbeni to the rear, and Palazzo Spannocchi (1470) to the right (only open to the public during the Palio, ▷ 311). The Salimbeni family were prominent bankers and silk and grain traders, while Ambrogio Spannochi was the treasurer to the Sienese Pope Pius II. A short diversion left on Banchi di Sopra brings you to the church of Santa Maria delle Nevi (rarely open), renowned for its high altarpiece, the *Madonna della Neve* (1477) by Stefano di Giovanni. Known as Sassetta, he was considered to be the first person to paint a cloudy sky.

Retrace your steps on Banchi di Sopra and look for the church of San Cristoforo on the left.

❸ Romanesque in origin, San Cristoforo was rebuilt in the late 18th century after earthquake damage. Opposite is the Palazzo Tolomei, part of the original fortress-home of the Tolomei, one of Siena's most powerful medieval dynasties of bankers and merchants. It is the oldest surviving private residence in the city, dating from 1205. Pause to admire the statue of the she-wolf suckling Romulus and Remus.

Continue south to the intersection with Banchi di Sotto and Via di Città, where you will find the Loggia della Mercanzia (1428–44), an attractive Gothic three-arched loggia. Little alleys either side take you into Piazza del Campo. Here you can admire the Campo from a café or visit the Museo Civico. Leave the piazza by Vicolo dei Pollaiuoli or Via dei Rinaldini. Both bring you to Banchi di Sotto, where you turn right. Immediately on your right stands the Palazzo Piccolomini.

❹ The Palazzo Piccolomini is a majestic palace begun in 1469. Inside, on an upper floor, is the little-known Archivio di Stato (State Archive), full of fascinating works of art. Beyond the palace is the Logge del Papa (Loggia of the Pope) built in 1462 on the orders of the Tuscan-born Pope Pius II (Enea Silvio Piccolomini).

Take the right-hand fork in front of the loggia and follow it around to the intersection with Via del Porrione, named after the *emporium*, the marketplace that stood nearby in Roman times. Cross Via del Porrione and walk through the arch down the Vicolo delle Scotte, passing Siena's Sinagoga (synagogue) on the right, the heart of the city's Jewish ghetto, created in 1571 by Cosimo I de Medici. Turn left on Via di Salicotto, then take the first right to emerge on Piazza del Mercato. Cross the square and bear right to pick up Via del Mercato, then turn left almost immediately to follow Via Giovanni Dupré, with attractive alleys branching off either side. At the Chiesa di San Giuseppe on the left take Via Sant'Agata straight onto a gravel area on your left towards the 13th-century church of Sant'Agostino, which contains paintings by Sodoma and Ambrogio Lorenzetti.

Opposite *Piazza Salimbeni*

Head through the arch to Via San Pietro and the church of San Pietro (set back on your right) and the red-brick Pinacoteca Nazionale beyond. Just before the church take a sharp left onto Via di Castelvecchio (an easily missed alley) and bear right for Via di Stalloreggi. Turn left towards the Arco delle Due Porte, an arch that formed part of the city's 11th-century walls, passing a house on the left (No. 91–93) where Duccio (*c*1260–1320) painted his famous *Maestà*. Turn right after the arch and follow the peaceful Via del Fosso di San Ansano to Piazza della Selva, where either Via Franciosa or Via Firolamo leads you to Piazza del Duomo or Piazza San Giovanni.

❺ In Piazza San Giovanni you can visit the Battistero di San Giovanni to admire works by local artist Jacopo della Quercia and other Florentine masters including Donatello and Ghiberti. Then walk up the steps to your right to see the duomo, and the Ospedale di Santa Maria della Scalla.

WHERE TO EAT

The Nannini café at Banchi di Sopra 95–99 is a good place for a break, as is Bar Il Palio on Piazza del Campo (tel 47 0577282055).

Below *Cafés line the edge of the Campo—expensive, but great for people-watching*

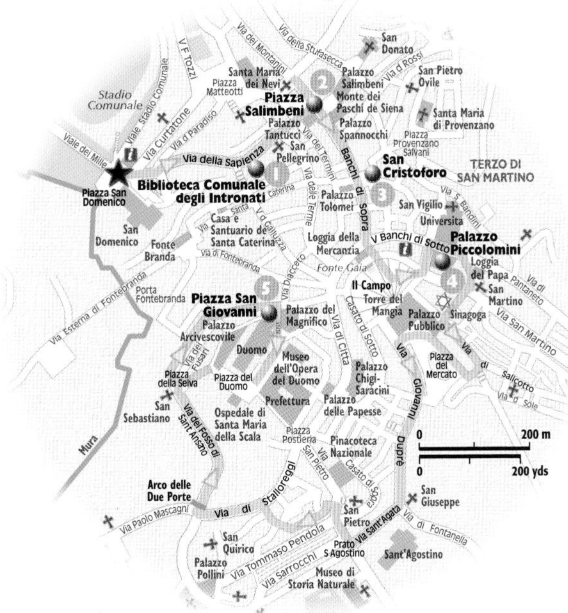

THE VALLE UMBRA

This drive through undulating, fertile countryside intersects with the Roman Via Flaminia, an ancient trade route that contributed to the prosperity of the towns that face each other across the valley. Saints, poets and painters have all lived and left their mark in this area.

THE DRIVE
Distance: 122km (76 miles)
Allow: 4.5 hours' driving time
Start/end at: Piazza Garibaldi, Santa Maria degli Angeli, near Assisi

★ From Piazza Garibaldi take the road south for Foligno, following signs for Perugia and Roma. Pass under the *superstrada* (main road), following signs for Costano and Bettona. Shortly after the *superstrada*, turn left at the intersection towards Bettona on the SP404 and head for Passaggio. Turn right at the roundabout (traffic circle), which is signposted for Bettona, Torgiano and Deruta and take a left, signposted for Bettona. Continue up the narrow SP403, with views to the north of the plain and Assisi, and drive through the terraced olive groves until you reach Bettona. Go clockwise around the town and park by the town walls.

❶ Overlooking the River Chiascio to the north, Bettona is an unspoiled town enclosed by medieval walls, dubbed the 'Etruscan Balcony' because of its beautiful vistas out over the Spoleto Plain toward the Apennine Mountains. It was the only Etruscan settlement on the east bank of the River Tiber.

Leaving Bettona, drive down the hill signposted for Torgiano. Turn right at the main road heading for Montefalco, Passaggio and Assisi, and continue to the roundabout at Passaggio. Go straight over the roundabout, towards Bevagna on the SP403. The road gently climbs as you near the town. Use the parking area on the right in front of the large tower, with its arched entrance that leads into the town.

❷ Bevagna's asymmetrical Piazza Silvestri is a well-preserved example of medieval town planning. The 13th-century Palazzo dei Consoli, with its theatre and 12th-century church of San Silvestro, are highlights of the town, as are the Roman remains, including mosaics of sea creatures on the floor of a bath house visible from outside Via Porta Guelfa.

Drive out of Bevagna, following signs for Montefalco (7km/4.5 miles away), passing down an avenue of trees. About 100m (110 yards) beyond the town limit sign, fork left onto the SP443, past vineyards and farmland dotted with trees. Turn right at the intersection and continue through Montepennino up towards Montefalco. Turn left at the intersection outside the town and at the walls bear right. Park in the large parking area on your right.

❸ With its panoramic views, Montefalco (▷ 277) is known as the 'Balcony of Umbria' and is renowned for its Sagrantino DOCG wine. The former church of San Francesco (now the Museo Civico) contains world-famous Renaissance frescoes by the artist Benozzo Gozzoli.

From Montefalco, take the road for Spoleto and Terni which heads down through thick olive groves onto the SP445, with views of Trevi across the valley. Drive through Turrita, passing the ornate Madonna della Stella sanctuary on the left (8km/5 miles from Montefalco). Go straight across at the lights and at the intersection turn right onto a long straight road. Bear left at the next intersection at Mercatello. In Bruna go over the bridge and take the sharp left signposted for Trevi. Drive 7km (4 miles) along the SP457, across the valley floor and past Castel San Giovanni. Go straight across the roundabout, following the signs for Trevi. About 600m (650 yards) farther along, turn left at the intersection onto the busy SS3, in the direction of Fano, Perugia and Foligno.

❹ Shortly on the right, you will come to the ancient springs at Fonti del Clitunno and the Tempio sul Clitunno, a church built on the site of a Roman temple, using some of its stones.

Continue north along the SS3 for a further 6.5km (4 miles), and at the traffic lights and petrol (gas) station turn right onto the road signposted for Parrano and Trevi. Drive up the SP425 past the church of the Madonna delle Lacrime and Bovara turning. Head through the gates of Trevi and circumnavigate the town towards the large parking area above in Piazza Garibaldi.

❺ Trevi (▷ 291) is known as the City of the Olive, and the old town is surrounded by olive groves. In nearby Bovara there is an olive tree dedicated to St. Emiliano, which, at around 1,700 years old, is thought to be the oldest in Italy.

Leave Trevi, following signs for Foligno. Continue up the hill and turn left at the top. Drive down through Santa Maria in Valle towards the SR3. Follow the signs for Perugia at the roundabout, heading up onto the *superstrada* north. This fast road takes you past the industrial area around Foligno. About 8km (5 miles) from the roundabout, take the right towards Perugia onto the SS75. Come off the *superstrada* at the Spello exit. Turn right into the centre of Spello. Park in Piazza Kennedy near Porta Consolare at the south end of town, or around the corner on the Collepino road.

❻ The winding alleyways of Spello (▷ 290) are constructed from the local pink stone quarried from Monte Subasio. There are more Roman remains here than in any other Umbrian town. The frescoes by Pinturicchio (1454–1513) in the church of Santa Maria Maggiore are considered to be the artist's finest.

Take the road to the right of Porta Consolare and follow the signs for Collepino and Monte Subasio. Continue around the east side of town, branching up to the left after 1km (0.6 miles) to the town's Porta Montanara. Follow the signs for Monte Subasio and head up the narrow SP249. Just past the fortified hamlet of Collepino, turn left at the Monte Subasio sign onto a white (rough) road.

❼ St. Francis retreated to the Eremo delle Carceri near the top of the massive limestone summit that forms the backdrop to Assisi. The top is 1,290m (4,232ft) above sea level, and 4.5km (3 miles) past the summit, the Eremo delle Carceri comes into view.

Continue down the hairpins of the SP251, past Assisi's 14th-century Porta Cappuccini. Turn left at the intersection at the bottom. Bear right past the petrol (gas) station towards Perugia along the SS147 and follow the road beneath the massive ramparts of the Basilica di San Francesco. Turn left to Santa Maria degli Angeli (3km/2 miles from the intersection), cross the level crossing (grade crossing) and drive straight on towards the basilica until you arrive back in Piazza Garibaldi.

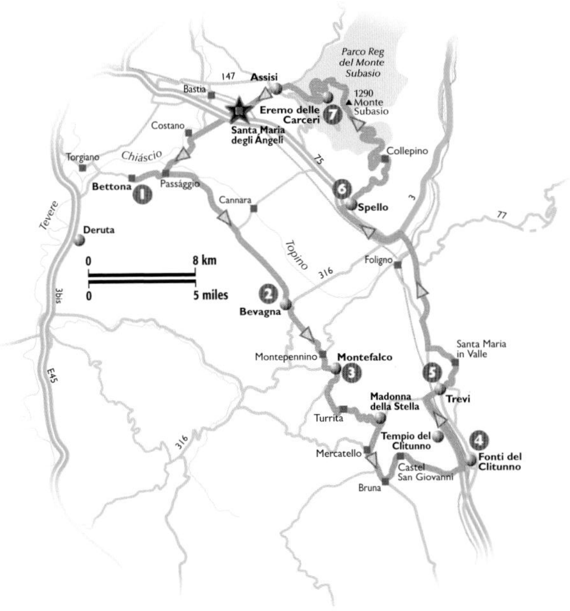

WHERE TO EAT

The Taverna del Guillare in Bettona serves traditional Umbrian dishes (Via Caterina 2; tel 075 987114; Easter–Nov daily 12–2.30, 7.30–10).

Opposite *View of Assisi across the vineyards*

THE VALNERINA AND PIANO GRANDE

Beginning in Spoleto, this drive takes in the dramatic upper sections of the Nera Valley–the Valnerina (▷ 291), the lower Corno Valley and the Piano Grande on the southern edge of Monti Sibillini National Park (▷ 280).

THE DRIVE
Distance: 183km (114 miles)
Allow: 5.5 hours' driving time (best spread over 2 days)
Start/end at: Spoleto
Overnight stop: Norcia

★ From Piazza della Vittoria on the north side of Spoleto follow the signs for Flaminia SS3, and Norcia and Foligno. Continue along the SS3, following signs for Fano, Perugia and Foligno for 2.5km (1.5 miles) and then bear right towards Cascia and Norcia. Passing Eggi on your left, drive into the long tunnel. You will emerge in the Valnerina. Follow the signs for Norcia, heading along the SS209 and up the valley for 14.5km (9 miles). The breadth of the valley fluctuates, sometimes narrowing dramatically to a gorge. Poplars and oaks border the Nera, and fortified towers and settlements punctuate the sides of the valley, pointing to its turbulent past.

❶ Castel San Felice, with its lovely 12th-century Romanesque church, is up to your right. High up on the left above Borgo Cerreto stands Cerreto di Spoleto and its tower.

About 500m (550 yards) past Borgo Cerreto, turn right at the intersection towards Norcia, over the elevated bridge into the tunnel. You will emerge on the SR320, which takes you along the narrow Corno Valley. The road cuts through tunnels and narrow gorges and passes under concrete galleries. At the sign for Cascia, where the main valley heads south, continue for a further 6km (4 miles) on the SS685 towards Norcia. The valley widens into a fertile bowl at the foot of the Sibillini Mountains, with the walled town of Norcia set on a mound before you (▷ 278).

❷ Park outside Norcia's city walls at Porta Romana, and walk into town. Have a coffee in Piazza San Benedetto, or sample some of the best salami in Umbria. Throughout Italy the word *norcineria* indicates a specialist pork butcher.

Drive around the town walls clockwise and turn left towards Pescara, down a long straight avenue, following signs for Castelluccio. Turn left after 2.5km (1.5 miles) and head for Castelluccio, climbing up the SP477, enjoying views of the green valley below and the steep slopes of the Monti Sibillini foothills. Where the main road continues to the Adriatic, turn left for Forca Canapine and Castelluccio.

As you climb you can admire the dramatic views of Norcia below and the Monti Reatini to the south. Around 17km (11 miles) from Norcia the landscape becomes more rugged as you rise above the tree line. A little farther on, turn left towards Castelluccio, past a modern restaurant and over the brow of the hill. The massive slopes of Monte Vettore greet you, with the Piano Grande (▷ 278) overlooked in the distance by Castelluccio, below. Cross the plain following the sign for Visso. Drive into the village and park by the low wall facing the Sibillini.

❸ Castelluccio, the last outpost in Umbria, is famous for the tiny lentils grown by local farmers.

From here, drive north on the SP477 towards Visso. After 5km (3 miles), from the pass above the village, there is a good viewpoint suitable for a picnic. As you continue into the Marche, down below the tree line the landscape becomes increasingly steep. Deep ravines cut through the white rock, and the conically shaped Monte Cardosa rises up on your left. About 11km (7 miles) from Castelluccio, just above the pretty village of Gualdo, turn left to Dell'Erborista Ristorante and Pizzeria, a good lunch stop. Continue down to Visso, bearing left onto the SP134 at Castelsantangelo sul Nera. Park in Piazza Garibaldi.

❹ The small town of Visso, with its square towers, nestles in a valley, surrounded by steep, mountainous terrain. The parish church of Santa Maria contains some interesting remains of old frescoes.

Leaving Visso, follow the signs for Rome and Terni and drive out via Il Gole della Valnerina ('the throat of the Valnerina', a narrow gorge between high rocks) on the SR209, to emerge into a wild, narrow valley with overhanging rock formations. The valley floor opens up gradually as you drive on, and more settlements come into view. A further 11km (7 miles) down the Valnerina, take the turning left to Norcia if you are staying there for the night.

Otherwise continue on the SR209 past the tall, bleak towers of Triponzo that rise precariously from the cliff face. Ignore the turning to the right to Spoleto and continue in the direction of Terni through Scheggino, with its crumbling towers. Continue past Ceselli, where hamlets dot the hillside to the south. Slow down as you approach Sambucheto, and turn sharply right uphill to San Pietro in Valle at the battered yellow sign just inside the village limits. Drive up the narrow lane past the cottages at Macenano and park in the parking area down past the abbey.

❺ The Abbazia di San Pietro in Valle was founded in 720. Steeped in history, it contains some of the most important examples of Romanesque frescoes in Italy (▷ 269).

Rejoin the main road, and continue south past Ferentillo as far as the intersection. Before turning right to Spoleto, make a detour and have a quick stop at Arrone to the left.

❻ Arrone's church, Santa Maria Assunta, contains frescoes by Vincenzo Tomagni and Giovanni da Spoleto. The immaculate upper village has a medieval close with a tree growing out of the clock tower.

Return to Spoleto, crossing the SR209 and Via Montefranco on the SP4, a winding road with good views of the distant hills. Turn right onto the fast Flaminia SR3 and after 15.5km (9.5 miles) you will see Spoleto's unmistakable Rocca.

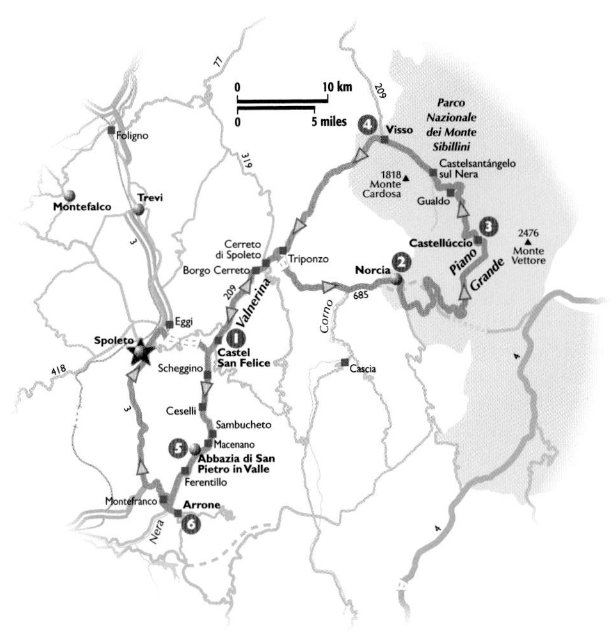

WHEN TO GO

The best time to see the Piano Grande (Great Plain) is in May and early June, when the wild flowers are at their best. Check the weather with the tourist information office in Norcia before you head off (tel 0743 816090; Sep–May closed Wed). Don't cross the Piano Grande in snow—Castelluccio can be cut off.

WHERE TO EAT

In Castelluccio: Bar del Capitano (Via della Bufera Castelluccio 10, tel 0743 821159).

WHERE TO STAY

Hotel and Restaurant Grotta Azzura (Via Alfieri 12, 06046 Norcia, tel 0743 816513). Local wild boar and truffles feature on the menu.

Opposite *Delta gliding in Monte Sibillini*

OLD PERUGIA

From the medieval Via dei Priori this walk around old Perugia (▷ 281) winds out to the northerly Porta Sant'Angelo and one of the oldest churches in Italy. You return to the city along the 13th-century aqueduct, ending the walk on Piazza IV Novembre.

THE WALK
Distance: 3.7km (2.3 miles)
Allow: 2–3 hours
Start at: Via dei Priori (from Palazzo dei Priori)
End at: Piazza IV Novembre

★ Begin by walking down Via dei Priori, the steep street that descends from the Arco dei Priori beneath the Palazzo dei Priori tower. As you go along, passing the baroque Chiesa Nuova on your right, you will walk over a fragment of the *decumanus*, a thoroughfare through the Roman town. As you continue, you will pass the Sciri tower and the Oratory of San Francesco on Via degli Sciri on your left.

The street now bends past the Piazzetta della Madonna della Luce, with its two churches.

❶ Stop and go inside the Church of the Madonna della Luce to take in the miraculous *Vision of the Virgin* by Tiberio d'Assisi, and the cupola covered in frescoes by Giovan Battista Caporali.

Go down the steps to the left, through the Etruscan Porta Trasimeno, the old exit to Trasimeno and Tuscany, and turn right to enter Piazza San Francesco.

❷ The Oratorio di San Bernardino, with its softly tinted facade, has a grassy area in front of it where students often relax in the sun—a good picnic spot on a sunny day.

Go back up Via San Francesco and take the next left up the steps along Via del Poggio. From here you can look down onto the front of the Church of San Francesco al Prato, built in 1230, and undergoing a lengthy restoration. Turn right up Via della Tartaruga, passing Piazza San Paolo on the right. At the top turn left and join Via Francolina towards Piazza Giuseppe Ermini and continue right onto Via del Verzaro. This narrow street, with tall buildings on both sides, runs along the back of the Teatro Morlacchi, built in 1778.

Before you emerge onto Piazza Morlacchi, part of the university, pass by the little Church of San Martino del Verzaro on your left (1163), which has frescoes by Giannicola di Paolo inside.

Bear left and you will come to Piazza Cavalotti. Cross over and walk down Via Baldeschi. Pass the steps marked Via Appia on your left and continue until you join Piazza Ansidei. Cross the square and walk down to the left along Via Ulisse Rocchi, following the signs to the Arco Etrusco. As you continue down, go through the Etruscan Arch and cross the road with the big red 18th-century Università per Stranieri building on your left. Cross over to Corso Garibaldi.

❸ This area is evidence of the city's expansion in medieval times, and is where the artisan quarters sprang up during the 13th and 14th centuries. On your right are Piazza Lupatelli and the Church of Sant'Agostino, with its pink-and-white checked front.

Continue walking along Corso Garibaldi and you will pass a little *madonnina* (shrine) on your left and the Complesso della Mercanzia.

❹ This 14th-century building belonged to one of the powerful guilds—you can still make out a granary sign above the door lintel. It was also used as a hospital for the poor.

As you wander along the Corso you will pass a series of monastic settlements, each with its own church. The Benedictine Santa Caterina on your right was restructured by Galeazzo Alessi in 1547, and the Dominican monastery of Beata Colomba at No. 191 was where St. Francis and St. Dominic allegedly met in 1220.

Go straight on under a brick arch and you immediately find the graceful approach to the Tempio Sant'Angelo, the oldest church in Umbria, to your right.

❺ Stop and admire the views from this peaceful spot, which marks the end of the medieval boundary. You can see over towards the restored Convent of San Francesco del Monte outside the city walls. Cassero di Porta Sant'Angelo has a little museum and panoramic terrace.

Return to Corso Garibaldi, passing the monastery of Santa Lucia. About two-thirds of the way down, just after the Complesso della Mercanzia building, turn right down Via Domenico Lupatelli, a narrow street lined with houses and picturesque side alleys. At the end of Via Lupatelli turn right. Go along Via Fabretti until you come to Via dell'Aquedotto on the left. Walk along the aqueduct, looking down onto the houses and gardens below.

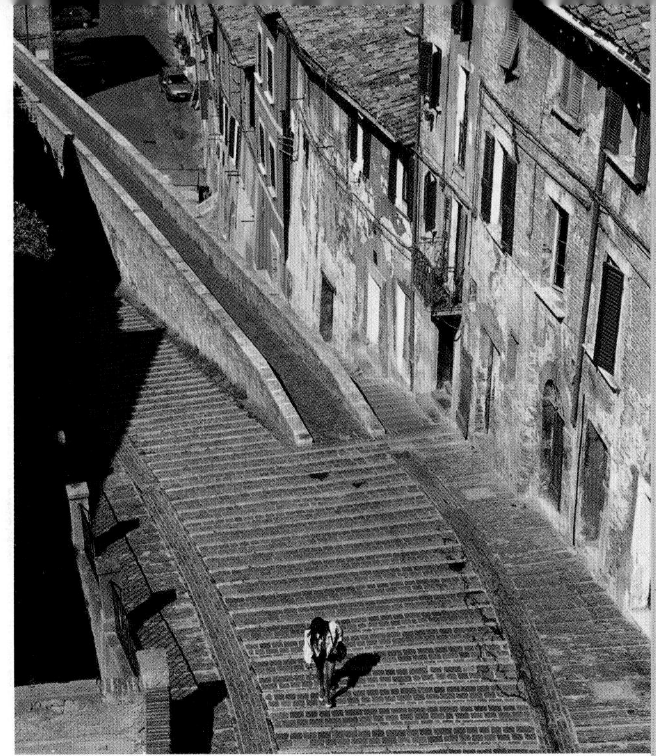

Above *A cobbled street in Perugia*
Opposite *Piazza IV Novembre, with Palazzo dei Priori on the left and the Fontana Maggiore in the centre*

❻ The aqueduct was built between 1254 and 1276 by Fra Bevignate to bring water down from Monte Pacciano to the city's Fontana Maggiore, 5km (3 miles) away. It became a pedestrian way in the 1830s after a new water supply was built. This is a popular spot with artists and photographers. Turn around to admire the rooftops and buildings behind you.

The ancient Via Appia merges with Via dell'Aquedotto, and 200 steps take you up through the arch of the aqueduct to Via Baldeschi. Return to Piazza Cavalotti and bear left up Via Maestà delle Volte.

❼ A fresco of the Virgin and Child was painted on this dark medieval thoroughfare in 1297. The Maestà delle Volte Oratory was built in 1335 to protect the fresco, but was rebuilt in 1576 after a fire. The medieval archway is a remnant of the portico, and Angelini built the fountain in the hollow beneath the church. On the right is a wall fresco by Beletti (1945).

Walk through the arches to Piazza IV Novembre, where you will find many cafés and bars selling ice cream to refresh you.

WHERE TO EAT

Il Padrino serves fish dishes and is a good lunch stop (Via Baldeschi 5; tel 075 572 7739; closed Sun and Aug). There is also the Osteria del Gambero (Via Baldeschi 9, 075 5735461; daily 12.30–2.30, 7.30–11; closed Mon pm).

PLACE TO VISIT

CASSERO DI PORTA SANT'ANGELO

www.sistemamuseo.it
✉ Porto Sant'Angelo, Corso Garibaldi, 06122 Perugia ☎ 075 41670 🕐 Jul–Aug daily 11–1.30, 3–6.30; Apr–Jun, Sep–Oct Wed–Mon 11–1.30, 3–6.30; Nov–Mar Wed–Mon 11–1.30, 3–5 💶 €4

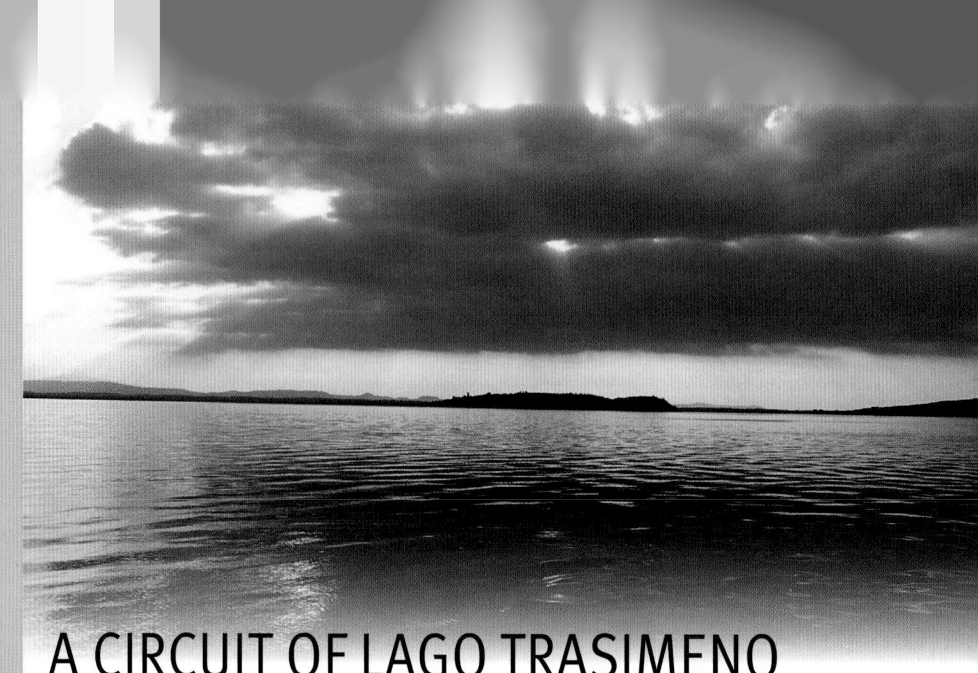

A CIRCUIT OF LAGO TRASIMENO

From Passignano this drive takes you counterclockwise around Lago Trasimeno (▷ 274), Italy's largest inland lake south of the River Po. You will pass by olive-studded slopes north of the lake, through the lowlands and marshy areas near the Tuscan border, and the gentle undulating countryside in the south.

THE DRIVE
Distance: 80km (50 miles)
Allow: 5.5 hours' driving time
Start/end at: Passignano

★ From the ferry pier drive west and north out of town, over the level crossing (grade crossing) on the old road (SR75) following signs for Tuoro and under the *superstrada*. After 6km (4 miles) turn right at the intersection and start climbing up, past the characteristic umbrella pines and cypress trees, to Tuoro, which is approached up an avenue.

❶ Park at the top and admire the view of Isola Maggiore from Piazza Municipio. This unassuming village is historically famous as the site of the bloody massacre of the Roman legions by Hannibal at the Battle of Lago Trasimeno in 217BC.

Turn back down the hill, and after 300m (330 yards) take a right, following the battle signs, then turn right again at the intersection to Castiglione del Lago. You will pass occasional signs for battle sites as the old road meanders past reed beds to the lake. Farther along from the intersection (at a bend in the road to the right), turn left, following the signs for Borghetto, Chiusi and Castiglione del Lago. Drive over the level crossing, and under the dual carriageway (divided highway). At Borghetto, turn right onto the SR75 then turn left at the intersection onto the SR71. Continue for 8km (5 miles) across the low-lying country near the lake's shore as far as Castiglione del Lago, which can be seen jutting out into the lake. Turn left and drive up to the large intersection just outside the town and park by the ramparts.

❷ This fortified town was an island on the lake in Etruscan and Roman times. Later, it was defended by the Tuscia Lombards against Byzantine Perugia and subsequently fought over by Arezzo, Cortona and Perugia. Its present form dates from the middle of the 13th century. On Wednesday mornings there is a very good market.

Drive out from town on the SR71, following signs for Chiusi, and continue along the long straight road towards Città della Pieve. Come off at the exit sign for Paciano and turn left onto the SP310, which goes under the main road. The landscape becomes more undulating and the fields widen to reveal vineyards, oaks and occasional red-brick houses. Approach Paciano up a road lined with cypresses and olives, turning left and driving up towards the centre. Park at the side of the road and walk up through the red-brick Porta Fiorentina.

❸ Set among olive groves and oak woodland, Paciano is a quiet, well-preserved medieval village dating back to the 13th century. With its extensive views, this is a good base for walking and there are plenty of places to enjoy picnics in the surrounding countryside.

Leave Paciano and return down the hill. Turn right onto the SP310 and shortly afterwards turn right again towards Panicale. After 2km (1.2 miles) turn right at the intersection and up, past olive trees, to the attractive *borgo*. Park immediately outside Panicale, near the lace museum, and walk up through the gate.

❹ Panicale once belonged to the Etruscan town of Chiusi, which became strategically important to the Perugians in controlling the Nestor Valley to the south as well as Lago Trasimeno. From its vantage point it provides lovely views over to Isola Polvese. The town's street layout has developed in a circular pattern, with its three main squares on different levels.

Continue driving around the town; turn left at the intersection and drive northwest through Macchie. At the SR599 turn right for Magione. Go through Panicarola, past reed-fringed ditches, and the Sant'Arcangelo ferry stop on your left. After some 13km (8 miles), turn left for San Feliciano onto the SP316 and past San Savino. Follow the signs for the village, past the turning for the *traghetti* (ferries) to Isola Polvese, and park where you can or in the square.

❺ San Feliciano is a traditional fishing village. Its fishing museum, the Museo della Pesca, is at the end of a narrow cul-de-sac near the lakeside and boatyards. It's possible to hire fishing boats from the Fishermen's Co-operative on the lakefront here (tel 075 847 6005).

Take the SP316 north out of the village, through Monte del Lago, and follow the signs for Torricella. Go over the level crossing and follow the signs for Passignano, which take you up onto the fast *superstrada.* Come off at the next exit at Passignano Est, cross the level crossing and head back to the start point.

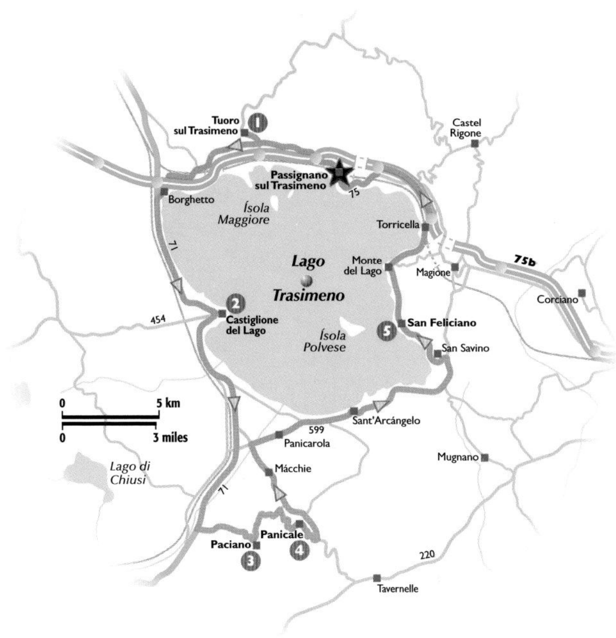

WHERE TO EAT

In Castiglione del Lago there are several café-bars and the restaurant La Cantina (Lione del Lago, Centro Storico, Via Vittorio Emanuele 93, tel 0759 652436; daily 12.30–3.30, 6.45–11; Oct–Mar closed Mon). For refreshment in Panicale visit Bar del Gallo. About 2km (1.3 miles) south of San Feliciano is Da Massimo, specializing in lake fish (Via dei Romani 16, San Savino, tel 075 8476094/075 8476269, daily 11–11; closed Mon). Back in Passignano, Del Molo (Via A Pompili 7, San Savino, tel 075 827151; Tue–Sun 12.30–2.30, 7–10) is a reasonably priced restaurant and there is a good pizzeria opposite the ferry stop and lakeside kiosks selling paninis and ice cream.

PLACE TO VISIT

MUSEO DELLA PESCA

✉ Via Lungolago della Pace e del Lavoro 20, 06063 San Feliciano, Magione ☎ 0758 479261 🕒 Jul–Aug daily 10.30–1,4–7; Apr–Jun, Sep Tue–Sun 10–12.30, 3–6; Feb–Mar, Oct Thu–Sun 10.30–12.30, 2.30–5.30; Nov–Jan Sat–Sun 10.30–1,2.30–5.30 💶 €3.50

TIPS

» Time your drive to enjoy the evening views across the lake from the east and north.

» If you want to follow the wine route (Strada del Vino), the Associazione Strada del Vino Colli del Trasimeno has suggested itineraries. Look online at www.stradadelvinotrasimeno.it or pick up a brochure at Castiglione's tourist office.

Opposite *Passignano sul Trasimeno on Lago Trasimeno*

Above *Rafting in Umbria*

AREZZO

FIERA ANTIQUARIA

This leading antiques fair floods Piazza San Francesco, Piazza Grande and the Logge Vasari. Filled with more than 600 dealers, and with some items dating back to the Renaissance, the fair lures both serious collectors and browsing visitors.

✉ Piazza San Francesco, 52100 Arezzo 🕑 1st Sun of the month Apr–Sep 7.30–7; rest of year 7.30–3

GRACE

www.grace.it

This trendy club, discotheque and sushi restaurant, run by three friends, verges on kitsch with its art deco seating and 1970s lighting. There's no denying it's got style.

✉ Via Madonna del Prato 129, 52100 Arezzo ☎ 0575 403669 🕑 Fri–Sat midnight–5am ✋ €20

LFI LIGHT-GAUGE RAILWAY

www.trenitalia.com

The LFI (La Ferrovia Italiana) railway linking Arezzo with Stia, Bibbiena and Sinalunga is a rolling train museum. Its antique fleet of electric locomotives and steam engines takes you through the surrounding countryside, past wonderful views. Reserve a seat on the steam train.

✉ Stazione Ferroviaria, Piazza della Repubblica 1/A, 52100 Arezzo ☎ 0575 39881 🕑 Jun–Sep

PRADA FACTORY OUTLET

Montevarchi, near Arezzo, is home to the Prada factory and its bargain outlet. You can get Prada bags, lingerie and shoes at up to 80 per cent discount. When you arrive, pull a ticket from the machine and wait your turn to enter. It also stocks Miu Miu, Helmut Lang and Jil Sander.

✉ Località Levanella SS 69, 52025 Montevarchi ☎ 055 919 6528 🕑 Mon–Sat 9.30–7.30, Sun 2–7.30 🚆 From Firenze to Montevarchi (about 1 hour), then taxi 🚗 Take the A1. Turn off at Valdarno intersection and follow the signs

ASSISI

CEROGIÀ

This is a treasure trove of Italian style, traditional and contemporary, for the house is showcased in this beguiling shop, where you'll find home accessories and gifts of all descriptions.

✉ Corso Mazzini 21, 06081 Assisi ☎ 075 815 144 🕑 Mon–Sun 9–7

ENOTECA LOMBARDI

A food store and *enoteca* (wine shop) selling more than 50 types of wine, priced €10 to €80. Truffle paste, roast peppers, artichoke pâté and dried porcini mushrooms also sold.

✉ 11 Via Borgo Aretino, 06081 Assisi ☎ 075 816697 🕑 Daily 9–7 🚌 Linea C every half hour from Assisi's rail station to Piazza Unità d'Italia (3km/2 miles)

BEVAGNA

AZIENDA AGRARIA E FRANTOIO RONCI

www.olioronci.it

Umbria's olive oils are internationally famous, and the Ronci family ranks among the best producers of high-quality, cold-pressed, extra-virgin organically produced oils.

✉ Voc Sasso 14/A, 06031 Bevagna ☎ 0742 360 501 🕑 Mon–Fri 10–6, Sat 10–1; shout if no one around 🚗 3km (2 miles) west of Bevagna on Gualdo Cattaneo road; follow yellow signs

COLLE VAL D'ELSA

TERRECOTTE TESI

Everything from giant terracotta garden urns to hand-painted plates is produced at this small ceramics factory near Colle. Prices, compared with town-centre outlets, are excellent, and there are usually

marked-down 'seconds' whose flaws are impossible to spot. Shipment can be arranged for large orders.
✉ Località Pian dell'Olmino, 53034 Colle Val d'Elsa ☎ 0577 928 130 ⏲ Mon–Fri 9–6, Sat 12–4 🚗 3km (2 miles) south of Colle Val d'Elsa on the SS541

COLLODI

PARCO DI PINOCCHIO

www.pinocchio.it

The Pinocchio Park is based on the famous wooden puppet, with mosaics, statues and fountains incorporating all the story's characters. Watch the entertaining puppet shows or explore the maze, playground or exhibition centre. There is a children's restaurant.
✉ Via San Gennaro 3, 51014 Collodi ☎ 0572 429342 ⏲ Daily 8.30–dusk 🎫 Adult €11, under 16s €8, under 3s free 🚌 From Lucca to Collodi 🚗 15km (9 miles) from Lucca on the SS435

LUCCA

CERAMISTI D'ARTE

Tuscan artists Stefano Seardo and Fabrizio Falchi sculpt and paint at this workshop. Pick up decorative tiles, terracotta sculptures and marble mosaics made from prized Massa Carrara marble. Everything is produced using traditional techniques. Browsers are welcome to just have a look around.
✉ Via Mordini 74–78, 56100 Lucca ☎ 0583 492700 ⏲ Mon–Sat 9.30–1, 3.30–8

LA CORTE DEI VINI

Centrally located, very close to Piazza San Michele, this is a very welcoming and popular *enoteca* (wine bar), where you need to arrive in good time to get a table at the front terrace, particularly at *aperitivo* time. Enjoy a feast of little dishes with a glass or two in the early evening, or a drink with lunch or dinner of cold cuts, regional dishes and cheeses.
✉ Corte Campana 6, 55100 Lucca ☎ 0583 55364 ⏲ Mon–Sat from 10am

LUCCA BOOK FAIR

Just behind the Chiesa di San Giusto and running towards Piazza Napoleone and Piazza San Michele, Lucca's old bookstalls sell anything and everything that is printed. Shoppers will find old prints of Lucca and other Italian cities, modern postcards and comic books in various languages.
✉ Off Via Beccheria, 56100 Lucca ⏲ Daily 10–6

NICOLAS

Known for its live music concerts, Nicolas gives local musicians the chance to perform everything from jazz and blues to reggae, as well as the odd traditional Italian song.
✉ Viale S. Concordio 887, 55100 Lucca ☎ 0583 582378 ⏲ Tue–Sun 8pm–2am 🎫 Free

MARINA DI PIETRASANTA

TRENINO DELLE VACANZE

With fantastic views of the Versilia coast, this *trenino delle vacanze* (little holiday train) runs from the middle of town along the coast of Marina di Pietrasanta during the summer season. The hour-and-a-half journey takes in several towns.
✉ Fratelli Verona ☎ 0584 745737 ⏲ Jun–end Sep daily 5.30pm and 9pm 🎫 Adult €8, child €4 🚆 Pietrasanta or Viareggio 🚗 Versilia exit off the A12

NORCIA

BALLA COI MULLI

www.lamulattiera.it

Children and adults can enjoy the tranquillity and scenic grandeur of the Monti Sibillini from the back of a friendly donkey by joining one of the treks organized by a local team based in the Sibillini National Park. Routes vary from a gentle morning's ramble across the Piano Grande to whole-day treks high into the mountains.
✉ Casteluccio di Norcia, 06040 Norcia ☎ 0743 820051 ⏲ Apr–Sep daily, but can arrange trips outside these months. Phone or email info@lamulattiera.it for details 🚗 Treks usually start from Casteluccio, on the Piano Grande east of Norcia

BRANCALEONE DA NORCIA

The town is famous for its black truffles and wild boar, hence the abundance of stores selling these delicacies. Brancaleone excels in *salse al tartufo* (truffle pastes) and loose truffles for sale. Local *pecorino di Norcia* (hard cheese) and Umbrian ricotta sit waiting to be popped into heavenly sandwiches.
✉ Corso Sertorio 17, 06046 Norcia ☎ 0743 828311 ⏲ Daily 8–8

GEOSTA

www.geosta.net

Hikers and outdoor enthusiasts will find everything they need in this specialist shop. There's a good selection of walking and climbing equipment, boots and clothing, an excellent range of local and other maps, guidebooks and picture books devoted to the great outdoors in both English and Italian, as well as postcards and stationery.
✉ Via Foscolo 10, 06046 Norcia ☎ 0743 828470 ⏲ Apr–Sep Mon–Sat 10–7; Oct–Mar Mon–Sat 10–1, 4–6 🚗 Inside city walls, down side street off right of main *corso*

RAFTING UMBRIA

www.raftingumbria.it

Rafting Umbria offers 2-hour rafting expeditions on 7km (4 miles) of the River Corno, with all equipment provided and expert guides. The trip runs through gentle stretches interspersed with exciting, but safe, white-water rapids, and there are stops for swimming. The company can also arrange hang-gliding, paragliding, caving, climbing and high-altitude trekking, and many of the guides speak good English.
✉ Serravalle di Norcia, 06040 Norcia ☎ 348 351 1798 ⏲ Mar–Oct daily. Phone to reserve 🚗 On SS396 6km (4 miles) west of Norcia

PERUGIA

AMICI DELLA MUSICA DI PERUGIA

www.perugiamusicaclassica.com

Weekly classical recitals at this theatre in the heart of Perugia. Violin and piano soloists feature as well as artists playing in small groups.
✉ Palazzo dei Priori, 06123 Perugia ☎ 075 572 2271 ⏲ Oct–Jun once a week 🎫 €7–€30 🚌 6, 7, 9, 11 to Piazza Italia

GOLF PERUGIA

www.golfclubperugia.it

This is one of Perugia's most beautiful, and tricky, 18-hole golf courses.

Località S. Sabina, Ellera Umbra, 06074 Perugia 075 517 2204 Tue–Sun 8.30–6 €50 weekdays, €60 weekends

ERUGINA CHOCOLATE FACTORY

Chocoholics can gorge themselves at the Museo Storico della Perugina. Antique chocolate-making equipment as well as packaging from the 20th century are on display. Tours of the factory can be reserved in advance.

Via Pievaiola, San Sisto, 20143 Perugia 075 527 6796 or 075 527 6635 Mon–Fri 9–1, 2–5.30; also Oct–Jan, Mar–May Sat 9–1. Factory tours 11–5 by appointment Free

ST. ANDREWS

This disco has an international clientele and a cave-like interior.

Via della Cupa 2, 06123 Perugia 075 609522 Daily 9pm–2am €12

VIA OBERDAN FABRICS MARKET

In between the stores on Via Oberdan, more than 20 stands sell a wide range of fabrics. Scarves, throws and ornamental pieces come in all shades, fabrics and sizes. Crystals and jewellery are also sold, as well as bags, incense and rugs.

Via Oberdan, 06121 Perugia Mon–Sat 4–8 6, 7, 9, 11 to Piazza Italia

PIENZA

LA BOTTEGA DEL GHIOTTONE

Pienza's food shops are numerous, and the superb selection here is the best in town. Your senses will be assaulted by the aroma of local *pecorino* (sheep's cheese), prosciutto and salami, while the shelves are packed with local oils, vinegars, jams, honeys and a range of spice mixes.

Corso Rossellino, 53026 Pienza 0578 748 686 Mon–Sat 10–7, Sun 11–7 On right of main *corso* before the Duomo

OLEIFICIO CHIANTI

If you're passionate about olive oil, make a detour from Pienza to buy direct from the producers of some of southern Tuscany's smoothest cold-pressed oils, still produced by stone-grinding. Four varieties are on offer, and they also sell locally sourced wines, honeys, jams and dried porcini mushrooms. Prices are excellent and they will make up a variety pack on the spot.

Via M. Cappelli 33, 53020 Monticchiello, Pienza 0578 755 075 Mon–Fri 9.30–1, 3.30–6 8km (5 miles) southeast of Pienza off Acquapendente road

PIEVE SAN STEFANO

NAZIONALE TURISMO EQUESTRE

Umbria's mountainous environs provide some impressive terrain for horseback riding. The National Equestrian Tourism bureau can help you arrange a day's ride with a recommended establishment. There is also an extensive choice of horseback-riding schools, stables and trails in Tuscany.

ANTE (Associazione Nazionale per il Turismo Equestre e per l'Equitazione di Campagna), Via Ponte Castel Giubileo 27/A, 00100 Roma 06 382 8060 Contact individual establishments for details Approximately €35 for half a day/€60 per day

PISA

OFFSIDE

Themed evenings range from Friday's gay-and-lesbian night to live music gigs on Wednesday and Saturday nights, and a cocktail and dance club on Sundays. Karaoke, the best night, is on Thursday.

Ospedaletto, Uscita Pisa Nord Est, Via Emilia, 56100 Pisa 340 496 4845 Mon–Thu 8pm–2am, Fri–Sat 8pm–4am, Sun 6pm–4am

PAUL DE BONDT

A Dutch-born pastry chef, Paul de Bondt creates handmade chocolates to order with meticulous attention to detail. De Bondt won the Euro-chocolate award in 1999 and the *tavoletta d'oro* (the golden bar) in 2003 for the best dark chocolate and the best milk chocolate bar in Italy. This Pisa outlet has everything from animal-shaped chocolates filled with almond paste to simple, rich truffles. But the *ganascia* chocolates, made with fresh cream and butter, are what de Bondt is most famous for.

Lungarno Pacinotti 5, 56125 Pisa 050 316 0073 Tue–Sat 10–1, 4–8; closed Jun–Sep

TENNIS CLUB PISA

www.tennisclubpisa.it

Five outdoor clay courts (three with lighting for night games) and two indoor courts can be rented at this year-round tennis club.

Piazzale dello Sport 7, 56122 Pisa 050 530313 Daily 8.30–8.30 €16 per hour

POPPI

ZOO FAUNA EUROPA

www.parcozoopoppi.it

Opened in 1972 by vet Dr. Roberto Mattoni, this zoo preserves European species, including deer, wolves, bears, birds of prey, and species in danger of extinction, such as the Asinara donkey. There are also a botanical garden, pony rides and a children's play area. There is a restaurant, a bar, picnic areas and free parking.

52015 Poppi 0575 504541/2 Daily 9–7 Adult €6, child (2–10) €5 Regular service from Firenze Trains to Poppi on the Arezzo–Stia line A 30-minute drive from Arezzo along the SS71. Follow signs for Bibbiena, then Parco Nazionale Casentinese or Parco Zoo Poppi

RAPOLANO TERME

ANTICA QUERCIOLAIA THERMAL BATHS

www.termeaq.it

Antica Querciolaia has been a spa resort since Etruscan and Roman times. Its spring fills the thermal baths and there is an adjoining park with three open-air pools. Try a mud wrap or an inhalation treatment. Water erupts from the famous 'intermittent fountain' every 10 minutes.

Via Trieste 22, 53040 Rapolano Terme 0577 724091 Oct–Mar daily 10–6; May–Sep Sun–Fri 9–7, Sat 9–midnight Treatments vary. Swimming pool €12, child (4–10) €8 Mon–Fri, €15 Sat–Sun (child

€10) Rapolano Terme railway station is on the Siena–Chianciano Terme line Valdichiana exit on the A1 or on the Firenze–Siena Valdichiana SS 326

SAN GIMIGNANO

AVALON

www.avalon-pub.com

Avalon appeals to all tastes with its *birreria* (pub), *enoteca* (wine bar) and internet café spread across three buildings in the old town. There are occasional live music and karaoke nights. The minimum age is 18.

Viale Roma 1, 53037 San Gimignano 0577 940023 Jun–Aug Tue–Sun noon–2am; Sep–May Tue–Sun 8pm–2am

GELATERIA DI PIAZZA

www.gelateriadipiazza.com

Sergio Dondoli's marvellous ice-cream emporium has scooped just about every award Italy has to offer and made it into numerous publications. You'll find all the classic tastes on offer, along with a changing range of specialties that mark the passing of the seasons; popular options in summer include pink grapefruit or mango sorbet, bittersweet cherry *amareno*, coconut and at least three or four chocolate-based flavours.

Piazza della Cisterna, 53037 San Gimignano 0577 942 244 Apr–Sep daily 9.30–10pm; Oct–Mar daily 9.30–7 On the main square

PODERI DEL PARADISO

www.poderidelparadiso.it

If you're buying wine in San Gimignano, head away from the town's tourist outlets and buy direct from the producers. Paradiso wines, both *vernaccia* (white) and full-bodied reds, have won the coveted *Tre Bicchiere* (Three Glasses) award at major wine exhibitions in Italy and abroad, and you can see the state-of-the-art production area housed in a centuries-old building. They also sell olive oil and arrange tasting sessions.

Località Strada 21/A, 53037 San Gimignano 0577 941 500 Daily 10–1, 4–6 Take Certaldo road north out of town and turn off onto side road at Strada (2km/1.3 miles), then follow signs

SAN GIULIANO TERME

SAN GIULIANO TERME

www.sangiulianoterme.net

This 18th-century building, once used by the Grand Dukes of Tuscany, is in a beautiful park of olive trees in the Pisan foothills. The year-round spa specializes in facial and body treatments as well as sessions to revitalize the respiratory and immune systems. The hotel has a bar and restaurant.

Largo Shelley 18, 56017 San Guiliano Terme 050 88501 Daily Mon–Sat 8.30–1, 2.30–6.30, Sun 8.30–1 €65 for a 30-min massage. Day spa packages start at €163 The Pisa–Lucca line stops at San Giuliano 7km (4 miles) from Pisa on the Brennero Road (SS12) towards Lucca

SIENA

BIANCHI STAMPE E CORNICI

www.siena-art.com

The wonderfully cluttered interior of Bianchi, one of Italy's oldest print and frame shops, is a treasure trove of prints, engravings, posters and reproductions, where you can be sure to find the perfect image to take home as a souvenir or gift. Designs range from 18th-century engravings and maps to vibrant posters featuring Palio scenes and architectural details, along with modern prints and postcards.

Via di Città 112, 53100 Siena 0577 282152 Mon–Sat 10–7 On right-hand side of Via di Città heading from the Campo to the duomo

BIRRERIA IL BARONE ROSSO

www.barone-rosso.com

Offering food, drink and live music in the heart of Siena, Il Barone Rosso is a regular haunt of Sienese beer-drinkers.

Via dei Termini 9, 53100 Siena 0577 286686 Daily 9pm–3am

DROGHERÍA MANGANELLI

A member of the Slow Food movement (▷ 26) and something of a local institution, the Droghería Manganelli has been selling local produce since 1879. Today it continues to sell regional foods including cured meats, cheese, vinegar, wine, olive oil, cakes, *ricciarelli* (almond biscuits) and pasta sauces.

Via di Città 71–73, 53100 Siena 0577 280002 Mon–Sat 9–8

PISCINA COMUNALE

In the north of Siena, this public swimming pool has diving boards and ample space for sunbathing.

Via Coppi, Località Acquacalda, 53100 Siena 0577 47496 Outdoor pool: Jun–Aug daily 9.30–7. Indoor pool all year Mon–Sat, times vary Outdoor pool: adult €6.40, child €4.90. Indoor pool: adult €4.90, child €3.90 10

STADIO COMUNALE

Crowded with passionate and vocal residents on match days, this football ground is home to AC Siena. The cheapest seating is in the *curva* (▷ 443).

Via Mille 3, 53100 Siena 0577 281084 €18

SPELLO

ARTE LEGNO

www.artelegnospello.com

At this fantastic shop, close to the Teatro Comunale Subasio in the highest lanes of Spello, most of the items are hand-carved from olive wood. Bowls, spoons, puppets, dolly pegs and breadboards are all on sale. Look up at the wonderful old beams supporting the roof.

Via Giulia 18, 06038 Spello 0742 302028 Mon–Sat 10–1, 4–7

TIRRENIA

PARCO GIOCHI FANTASILANDIA

Fantasilandia is brimming with attractions for kids. Split into two sections, the park has one free area with an electric car track, miniature train and mechanical bull. The other area has water slides and various swings. There's also a park for younger children.

Viale Tirreno 42, 56018 Tirrenia 050 30326 End May to mid-Sep daily; rest of the year Sun and public holidays Pay section: Adult €12, under 16s €8.50, under 3s free Regular service between Pisa and Tirrenia Take the Pisa Centro exit on the A12 motorway, then follow signs to Tirrenia

FEBRUARY–MARCH

VIAREGGIO CARNEVALE

www.viareggio.ilcarnevale.com

Viareggio's carnival is among Italy's biggest and best, with floats holding 200 people that wend their way along the waterfront. Gigantic moving puppets reflect current events and poke fun at famous people. It's all accompanied by music, dancing and food, and the national lottery awards a huge prize to the best float.

✉ Piazza Mazzini, 22 c/o Palazzo delle Muse, 55049 Viareggio ☎ 0584 962568 🕘 Four consecutive Sundays ✋ Free 🚆 Hourly from Pisa 🚗 Take the Versilia exit off the A12

MARCH–APRIL

SETTIMANA SANTA

Assisi, birthplace of St. Francis, celebrates Holy Week with religious processions throughout the town commemorating the passion and death of Christ. This is a serious religious occasion, and the atmosphere of piety in this holiest of Umbrian towns is almost tangible.

✉ Assisi 🕘 Week before Easter

APRIL

EUROCINEMA FESTIVAL

www.europacinema.it

A film awards festival including movie premieres, European TV and animated short films. Screenings are in a variety of languages with Italian subtitles.

✉ Via A. Pucci 138/A, 55049 Viareggio ☎ 0584 30750 🕘 3rd week in April ✋ Free 🚆 Trains run from Pisa to Viareggio every hour 🚗 Take the Versilia exit off the A12

MAY

FESTA DEI CERI

www.ceri.it

A direct descendant of a pagan festival, Gubbio's Festa dei Ceri is unique. The three *ceri* (candles) are 4m (13ft) high, immensely heavy wooden constructions, which are paraded through the town's streets before being raced up the steep slopes of Monte Ingino behind the town. It's all in honour of Gubbio's patron saint, St. Ubaldo, but there are plenty of pagan phallic undertones surrounding this springtime celebration.

✉ Gubbio 🕘 15 May

PALIO DELLA BALESTRA

Watch the medieval custom of the Eugubian (from Gubbio) and Sansepolcran (from Sansepolcro) battling it out to be crossbow champions. Don't miss the flag-throwing that precedes it.

✉ Piazza Grande, 06024 Gubbio 🕘 Last Sunday in May

MAY–JUNE

CHIANTI WINE FESTIVAL

One of the wine capitals of Tuscany, Montespertoli is the perfect place to taste the best of the year's vintage. Piazza San Pietro in the heart of the town is taken over by wine-lovers and professional buyers alike who flock to this well-established event.

✉ Montespertoli 🕘 Last Sun in May–1st Sun in June

JUNE

CORPUS DOMINI

www.orvietoturismo.it

The feast of Corpus Christi (known as Corpus Domini in Italy) is marked in Orvieto by superbly costumed processions through the town's streets, many of which are decorated with elaborate carpets of flower petals. A deeply moving experience.

✉ Orvieto 🕘 Mid-June

LUMINARIA AND GIOCO DEL PONTE

Pisa's main festival focuses on tug-of-war games between 12 teams from the north and south banks of the River Arno, who attempt to push a 7-ton carriage over the Ponte di Mezzo—while dressed in Renaissance costumes. The highlight of the Luminaria are the blazing torches that light the houses and streets on either side of the river.

✉ Pisa 🕘 Last Sun in June

PALIO DI SAN RANIERI

www.comune.pisa.it

In celebration of Pisa's patron saint, this festival features eight oarsmen, a steersman and a climber who races to the top of a 10m (33ft) mast to grasp the winning banner at the finish. The race can be seen along the River Arno between the railway bridge and the Palazzo Medici. Try to get a spot at the Palazzo Medici to watch the mast-climbing finale.

✉ Pisa ☎ 050 560464 (Pisa tourist board) 🕘 17 June ✋ Free

JUNE–JULY

FESTIVAL DEI DUE MONDI

www.spoletofestival.it

A major performing arts festival encompassing music, dance and theatre, was founded in 1958 by the composer Carlo Menotti. It attracts world-class Italian and international companies who perform in settings both indoors and out. It also has a lively fringe, with some alternative performances.

✉ Spoleto ☎ 0743 44700 🕘 End May–July

OPERA THEATRE OF LUCCA FESTIVAL

www.ccmoperalucca.org

In summer Lucca's piazzas are filled with some of the world's best amateur and semi-professional singers and musicians. Sponsored by the Opera Theatre of Lucca and the Music College of the University of Cincinnati, this is always a great event and a showcase for new talent.

✉ Vecchia Porta San Donato, 55100 Lucca ☎ 0583 583150 🕘 15 June–15 July ✋ Free

JUNE–AUGUST

ESTATE SAN GIMIGNANO

This summer arts festival has a strong musical element, including open-air opera recitals, classical concerts and film screenings in the ruins of the Rocca (fortress).

Piazza del Duomo 1, 53037 San Gimignano 0577 940008 Mid-June to August €14–€40

JULY

AREZZO WAVE

www.arezzowave.com

Arezzo rocks for a week when Arezzo Wave comes to town. It's a huge rock festival that attracts nearly 250,000 people. Around 150 events take place over the week. It's noisy and fun, with a good range of bands.

Corso Italia 236, 52100 Arezzo 0575 911005 1st week in July Free

ESTATE MUSICAL LUCCHESE

www.summer-festival.com

The Lucca Summer Music Festival is one of Tuscany's best-attended music festivals, and attracts major international artists. There are plenty of Italian bands, too.

Piazza Napoleone and Piazza Anfiteatro, 55100 Lucca 0584 46477 €15–€90 depending on performance

UMBRIA JAZZ

www.umbriajazz.com

Jazz is big in Italy and Perugia has been staging a major international festival since 1973, with a huge diversity of styles and top artists. Events take place all over the city—a must for serious jazz-lovers.

Perugia 10 days in July

VOLTERRA TEATRO

www.volterrateatro.it

Held in Volterra and the surrounding towns, this is Italy's leading avant-garde theatre festival. The schedule includes experimental drama, dance and film. A variety of international acts perform in English.

La Fortezza, 56048 Volterra 0588 80392 12–20 July Adult €15, child €10

JULY–AUGUST

IL PALIO

www.comune.siena.it/contenuti/palio
www.ilpaliodisiena.com

The Palio—a bareback horse race around the Campo in Siena in honour of the Virgin Mary—is probably Italy's most famous festival. The high speed, confined space and lack of rules make it hazardous for horse and rider alike, if exhilarating for spectators. The race is over in a moment, but it takes weeks to prepare the accompanying pageantry, feasting and drama. This is a festival that the Sienese are immensely proud of, evoking passion on an extraordinary scale.

Il Campo, 53100 Siena. Headquarters: Piazza Gramsci 7, 53100 Siena 0577 280551 2 July and 16 August Free standing in centre of Campo

PUCCINI FESTIVAL

www.puccinifestival.it

Close to Villa Puccini (where Puccini wrote his most famous works), Torre del Lago's opera festival draws 40,000 spectators every year to its performances of Puccini classics.

Teatro all'Aperto, 55048 Torre del Lago Puccini 0584 359322 €45–€100 A20—20 min drive from Lucca on the A11/SS1

SIENA JAZZ FESTIVAL

www.sienajazz.it

Since 1977, Siena Jazz has presented jazz performances and held seminars and masterclasses. Concerts are held in Piazza del Campo, Enoteca Italiana and Piazza Jacopo della Quercia.

Fortezza Medicea Anfiteatro, 53100 Siena 0577 271401 24 July–7 August Free

AUGUST

BARGA JAZZ FESTIVAL

www.bargajazz.com

This international festival revolves around a jazz orchestra competition. Performances are held in the Teatro dei Differenti and on Piazza Angelio in Barga, as well as in Lucca's Palazzo Ducale and in Castelnuovo di Garfagnana's Piazza Umberto.

Lucca and Barga 0583 711044 Last week in August Adult €12, child €7.50 Barga A40—45–55 min drive from Lucca (SS439 onto SS12, then onto SP2 and SP7)

BRAVIO DELLE BOTTE

www.valdichiana.it/montepulciano

This bizarre race sees a two-man team from each of Montepulciano's eight *contrade* (districts) rolling 80kg (176lb) wine barrels, mainly uphill, through the town's streets to Piazza Grande. There is dancing and drinking in the crowd and plenty of encouragement for the rollers.

Montepulciano Last Sun in August

AUGUST–SEPTEMBER

GIOSTRA DEL SARACINO

www.giostradelsaracino.arezzo.it

A vibrant medieval celebration of chivalry and jousting, which dates back to the Crusades combat training in the 14th century. The four teams, from the four quarters of Arezzo (Crucifera, Foro, Sant'Andrea and Santo Spirito), compete for the Lancia d'Oro (Golden Lance) trophy.

Piazza Grande, 52100 Arezzo 0575 377262 Last Sunday in August and 1st Sunday in September Free

SEPTEMBER

RENAISSANCE DAY

Scenes from the 16th century come to life as music, archers, artisans, serfs, guards, and noblemen and women take over the streets for the day. Renaissance food can be sampled and paid for in florins.

Scarperia in Mugello 1st Sun in September

SAGRA MUSICALE UMBRA

www.bellaumbria.net/Perugia/eventi

Umbria's summer season culminates in this prestigious music festival based in Perugia, with performances taking place in venues throughout the region. Orchestras and soloists come from all over Europe.

Perugia Middle 2 weeks of September

Above *A tempting dish of grilled polenta with vegetables*

PRICES AND SYMBOLS

The restaurants are listed alphabetically within each town. The prices given are the average for a two-course lunch (L) and a three-course dinner (D) for one person, without drinks. The wine price given is for the least expensive bottle.

For the key to symbols, ▷ 2.

AREZZO

LE TASTEVIN

Le Tastevin is buzzing with local life. One room resembles a traditional trattoria, another, with pictures of film stars, is a jazz bar where the owner performs at weekends. There's also outside seating in summer. The restaurant claims Roberto Benigni, among other celebrities, as a regular. The food is traditional with some modern additions such as truffle and asparagus risotto. It is so popular that it is advisable to make a reservation.

Via de Cenci 9, 52100 Arezzo 0575 28304 Tue–Sun 12.30–2.30, 7.30–11.30; closed Aug L €25, D €39, Wine €10

TRE BICCHIERE

www.itrebicchieri.it

There's a modern take on Tuscan cooking at this elegant restaurant in the heart of the *centro storico*, with up-to-the-minute presentation of traditional ingredients. Try the potatoes with a *pecorino e tartufo* (sheep's cheese and truffle) sauce or the beautifully cooked venison; desserts include a wonderfully unctuous burnt cream with raspberries. There's also an excellent wine list.

Piazzetta Sopra I Ponti 3–5, 52100 Arezzo 0575 26557 Mon–Sat 12.30–3, 7.30–10; closed 2 weeks in Aug L €45, D €65, Wine €12

ASSISI

LA BUCA DI SAN FRANCESCO

Despite the huge numbers of tourists, La Buca still retains, and deserves, its reputation as one of Assisi's best restaurants. The ambiance plays its part, with a cosy, stone-walled interior and airy pergola for hot-weather dining, but the food can be outstanding, with a touch of elegance given to traditional Umbrian meat and vegetable dishes. A good wine list and highly professional service add to the experience.

Via Brizi 1, 06081 Assisi 075 812 204 Tue–Sun 12–2.30, 7.30–10; closed 1st 2 weeks Jul L €35, D €50, Wine €12

RISTORANTE MEDIO EVO

This is a good option if you want to try out Umbrian delicacies. Truffles and wild boar are on the list of hearty local dishes. The fabulous grilled beef fillet with truffles as a main course costs €22, and the tasty homemade *strangozzi* (spaghetti with tomatoes) is €10 as a first course. Tasting menus are €30 per person. Dust from the 13th-century roof covers the vast range of wines, some of which are priced up to €60 and beyond.

Via Arco dei Priori 4, 06081 Assisi 075 813068 Thu–Tue 12–2.30, 7.30–10.30 L €25, D €40, Wine €10 The Linea A bus runs the 3km (2 miles) from Assisi's rail station into Piazza Unità d'Italia every half hour

BARGA

ALPINO

Attached to a hotel, the Alpino has been run by several generations of the Castelvecchi family, who pride themselves both on the quality of the local produce they serve, and the superb wine list. Enjoy freshly made pasta, local *funghi* in season, vegetables from the garden and

nicely cooked meat dishes, and wash it down with one of their wine suggestions—the list is particularly strong on 'super-reds'.
✉ Via Pascoli 41, 55051 Barga
☎ 0583 723336 ⌚ Dec–Mar Tue–Sun 12.30–3, 7.30–10; Apr–Oct daily 12.30–3, 7.30–10; closed Nov L €20, D €35, Wine €10

BEVAGNA

ENOTECA PIAZZA ONOFRI

More than 900 splendid Italian wines are carried by this winery-cum-restaurant, with the accent firmly on some of Umbria's great wines. The food lives up to the vintages, with all pasta made on the spot daily and dishes such as a cheese mousse with broad beans, grilled steak and braised pigeon on the menu. The ambience is cosy, with beams, vaulted ceilings, terracotta flooring and some fine old country furniture. There is also a specially designed smoking zone.
✉ Via Onofri 2, 06031 Bevagna
☎ 0742 361926 ⌚ Thu–Tue 12.30–3, 6.30–10 L €25, D €30, Wine €12

CASTELLINA IN CHIANTI

ANTICA TRATTORIA LA TORRE

www.anticatrattorialatorre.com
This is a lovely, everyday family-run restaurant in one of Chianti's most popular villages, with a traditional interior and tables outside for summer eating. The menu features all the Tuscan classic—*pasta fatt'in casa* (homemade pasta), huge steaks, beans and *ribollita* (vegetable soup) and a good selection of *crostini* (bread with different spreads). Desserts are simple, but the ricotta and walnut tart is worth trying.
✉ Piazza del Comune 15, 53011 Castellina in Chianti ☎ 0577 740236 ⌚ Sat–Thu 12.30–3, 7.30–10; closed 2 weeks Feb and Sep L €20, D €35, Wine €10

CITTÀ DI CASTELLO

IL POSTALE DI MARCO E BARBARA

www.ristoranteilpostale.it
Quiet Città di Castello is a surprising place to find a restaurant of this quality and innovation. It even has a Michelin star. The chef, Marco Bistarelli, is the president of the European Confederation of Young Chefs and his passion and creativity shine through into every dish on the menu. Opt for a tasting menu for the full experience or go à la carte and sample delights such as parmesan tortelli with an asparagus sauce, roast lamb with citrus and sweet onions, roast suckling pig or duck breast with foie gras. Barbara will help you with choosing from the list, featuring foreign as well as Italian wines.
✉ Via Raffaele dei Cesare 8, 06012 Città di Castello ☎ 0758 521356
⌚ Tue–Fri, Sun 12–3, 7.30–10, Sat 7.30–10; closed Sun pm Oct–May L €50, D €70, Wine €14

CORTONA

LA GROTTA

Tucked away from the crowds, this restaurant, which has courtyard tables for summer eating, is a real find. A friendly family cooks the best of straightforward Tuscan food, with robust meat dishes and specialities such as *ribollita*, a twice-cooked vegetable broth, and *fagioli in fiasco*, white beans cooked in a covered flask. The restaurant's diminutive size and popularity make advance reservations essential.
✉ Piazzetta Baldelli 3, 52044 Cortona
☎ 0575 630271 ⌚ Wed–Mon 12–2.30, 7.30–9.30; closed 1 week Feb, 10 days Jul L €20, D €36, Wine €10

IL PRELUDIO

www.ilpreludio.net
Just down the hill from Cortona's main piazza, an intimate old palazzo is the setting for one of southern Tuscany's best restaurants. Start with a selection of their hot *antipasti*, before moving on to traditional pasta, stuffed *crespelle* (pancakes) or fine cuts of meat served with a modern twist. The staff are friendly and will advise on a choice of wine from the comprehensive and interesting list.
✉ Via Guelfa 11, 52044 Cortona ☎ 0575 630 104 ⌚ Tue–Sun, 7.45–9.30 D €40, Wine €8

GUBBIO

LA FORNACE DI MASTRO GIORGIO

This elegant restaurant is named after the oven of Gubbio's famous ceramicist, Mastro Giorgio, which is a splendid feature here among the medieval stone walls and wooden beams. This is the place for a leisurely meal, feasting on freshest local, seasonal ingredients such as duck with pecorino cheese, game and porcini mushrooms in season and excellent homemade pasta and bread. The wine list contains more than 500 labels. Next door there is an *enoteca* for light bites washed down with a glass or two from the huge selection in the cellar.
✉ Via Mastro Giorgio 2, 06024 Gubbio
☎ 075 922 1836 ⌚ Thu–Mon 12.30–2.30, 7.30–10; also Wed lunch Jun–Oct; closed 1st 2 weeks Jan L €38, D €60, Wine €11

GREVE IN CHIANTI

TRATTORIA DEL MONTAGLIARI

www.montagliari.it
An idyllic wine estate, founded in 1720, lies 5km (7 miles) from Greve. It has a big dining room, with a beamed ceiling, checked cloths and old prints; tables outside in summer. Go for the *pappardelle al cinghiale* (wide pasta ribbons with a rich wild boar sauce), the homemade ravioli or the *faraona al vinsanto* (guineafowl with an intense wine sauce). Wines are serious; the estate produces Chianti Classico and Riserva, grappa, Vinsanto and Amaro—you can buy them in the estate shop.
✉ Via Montagliari 29, Panzano in Chianti, 50020 Firenze ☎ 0558 52014 ⌚ 12.30–2.30, 7.30–9.30; closed Mon and Jan 7–Feb 10 L €20, D €35, Wine €7 Take the SS222 from Firenze. The restaurant is on this road, at the 28.800km marker, 1km (0.6 mile) before Panzano

LUCCA

BUCA DI SAN ANTONIO

This is one of the oldest and most popular restaurants in Lucca. The à la carte menu focuses on Lucchese cuisine and changes with the season. Offerings generally include grilled and

roasted meats such as filleted and stuffed oven-cooked rabbit, pork with rosemary and garlic, and grilled beef with rocket (arugula) and parmesan. The waiters are happy to recommend something from the extensive wine list. Reservations are recommended for dinner.
Via della Cervia 1/5, 56100 Lucca 0583 55881 Tue–Sat 12.30–2.30, 7.30–11, Sun 12.30–2.30; closed 10–17 Jan, 4–11 Jul L €33, D €44, Wine €13

RISTORANTE GAZEBO

www.locandalelisa.com
In the stately conservatory of the 5-star Locanda l'Elisa hotel, Il Gazebo prides itself on using local produce in its menu of classic regional dishes. Main courses like *costolette d'agnello al rosmarine con purea di patate al tartufo* (lamb with rosemary served on mashed potato with truffles) reflect the chef's aim to serve traditional country food with a modern twist. Reservations are essential.
Via Nuova per Pisa 1952, 55050 Massa Pisana 0583 379737 Mon–Sat 12.30–2.30, 7.30–10; closed Jan–8 Feb L €45, D €55, Wine €20 From Pisa during the day A11 Firenze/Pisa Lucca exit, drive 4.5km (2.5 miles) towards San Giuliano Terme/Pisa

MONTALCINO

GRAPPOLO BLU

Down some steps from the main piazza you'll find this great little restaurant, serving up real Montalcino cooking. Terracotta floors, scrubbed tables and rush-seated chairs marry happily with the white walls and beamed ceiling—true Tuscan style. Try the *zuppa di fagioli* (Tuscan bean soup), *crostini* (toasted bread with different toppings) and *stinco all'aceto balsamico* (shin of beef in balsamic vinegar)—but leave room for the delicious *crostata di limone* (lemon tart). The local wines are excellent value. This is a small and deservedly popular restaurant, so reservations are recommended.
1 Via Scale di Moglio, Montalcino, 53024 Siena 0577 847150 12–3, 7–10; closed Fri and mid-Jan to mid-Feb L €17, D €30, Wine €8

ORVIETO

GROTTE DEL FUNARO

www.grottedelfunaro.it
Orvieto has no more stunning restaurant than the Grotte del Funaro. This giant cellar with views over the Umbrian valleys below has been open for business for more than 20 years. Several chambers with hefty stone walls are great for groups. More than 1,000 wines are stacked up in front of the huge casks. Sliced wild boar with truffles on toast is a first course at €12. Suckling pig, roasted on an open fire, is €14.
Via Ripa Serancia 41, 05018 Orvieto 0763 343276 Tue–Sun 12–2.30, 8–midnight L €25, D €45, Wine €9 Five minutes' walk from the funicular rail station at Piazza Cahen. The funicular connects the *città alta* with Orvieto's main rail station

I SETTE CONSOLI

www.isetteconsoli.it
This excellent restaurant is blessed with a garden at the back, ideal for summer dining, with splendid views of the duomo. The young brigade here is passionate about food, and it shows, with Umbrian specialties and the freshest possible produce served with a modern take. The wine list features over 700 vintages, and the staff will enjoy matching your wine to your menu choice; service can sometimes be slow, but eating here is an experience to enjoy at leisure.
Piazza Sant'Angelo 1/A, 05018 Orvieto 0763 343911 Thu–Sat, Mon–Tue 12–2.30, 7.30–9.30, Sun 12–2.30 L €35, D €45, Wine €12

PERUGIA

IL CANTINONE

Cantinone is a stunning restaurant in a 500-year-old dining hall with brick ceilings, stained with decades of wine residue, as this cellar was once used as a fermentation area. Several small rooms provide private dining away from the huge main medieval chamber. Chicken in white wine and the beef with Umbrian truffles are great main courses. There's also a good choice of pizzas, a wide range of cheeses and more than 50 wines. No credit cards.
Via Ritorta 6, 06123 Perugia 075 573 4430 Wed–Mon 12.30–2.30, 7.30–11; closed 22 Dec–5 Jan L €20, D €35, Wine €10 6, 7, 9, 11 to Piazza Italia

GRANARO DEL MONTE

The Granaro del Monte was once a tithe barn for offerings to the church. Today its lovely vaulted rooms are a national monument and home to one of Umbria's best restaurants. Every local dish appears on the menu—mountain lentils from Castelluccio, pork products and hams from the town, black truffles and *funghi* from the wooded valleys. *Degustazione* menus let you sample the lot. The wine list is serious, the welcome friendly, and there's a roaring log fire where you can watch your grilled meat cooking.
Via Alfieri 12, Norcia, 06046 Perugia 0743 816513 12.30–2.30, 7.30–10 L €20, D €35, Wine €10

OSTERIA DEL GAMBERO

www.osteriadelgambero.it
Among Perugia's best eateries, this moderately priced restaurant matches soothing, artistic decor and soft jazz sounds to good, creative Umbrian cuisine. Fish and seafood feature and, in season, there's a tasting menu with Norcia's prized black truffles; at other times a *degustazione* menu including *antipasto, primo*, *secondo* and *dolce* courses costs just €31. All the pasta, breads and desserts are lovingly handmade in the kitchens and the wine list is an encyclopaedic romp through Italy (with some foreign wines as well).
Via Baldeschi 8a, 06123 Perugia 075 573 5461 Tue–Sat 7.30–11.30pm, Sun 12.30–3, 7.30–11.30; closed 2 weeks Jan and 2 weeks Jul L/D €28, Wine €10

LA TAVERNA

A narrow medieval street leads to this big popular restaurant. It offers a superb range of elegant dishes, created for the 21st century while

paying homage to the region's culinary traditions. Expect subtle tastes and beautifully prepared meat dishes, and be sure to sample the *mousse di Baci Perugina*, a featherlight confection based on Perugia's own chocolate specialty.
✉ Via delle Streghe 8, 06100 Perugia
☎ 075 572 4128 ⏲ Tue–Sun 12.30–2.30, 7.30–11 L €20, D €35, Wine €10

PIENZA

LATTE DI LUNA

This little restaurant lies at the far end of Pienza's main street, with a few tables outside. In this tourist honeypot of a town, it's inevitably packed with foreigners, but remarkably few shortcuts are taken and the food, classic Tuscan with the emphasis on beans, bread and meat, is straightforward, well-sourced and nicely cooked. Try the house delicacy, *maiellino arrosto* (roast suckling pig).
✉ Via S. Carlo 2–4, 53026 Pienza
☎ 0578 748606 ⏲ Wed–Mon 12.30–3, 7.30–10; closed Feb to mid-Mar and Jul
L €22, D €38, Wine €9

PISA

OSTERIA DEL PORTON ROSSO

www.osteriadelportonrosso.com
Tucked away down a lane 10 minutes' walk from the Campo dei Miracoli, this popular rustic restaurant offers gastronomic menus of both *terra* (land) and *mare* (sea) at non-touristy prices. *Risotto al nero di seppia* (risotto with squid) is cooked to perfection, as is the *ravioli melanzane e pomodorini* (ravioli with aubergine and baby tomatoes). For *secondi*, mixed seafood or one of the local variations of *baccalà* (salt cod) are delicious choices, not forgetting of course the classic Tuscan steaks..
✉ Via Porton Rosso 11, 56126 Pisa
☎ 050 580566 ⏲ Mon–Sat 12.30–3, 7.30–10.30; closed 10–30 Aug L €27, D €37, Wine €10

SAN GIMIGNANO

RISTORANTE DORANDÒ

www.ristorantedorando.it
This restaurant is tucked away in the heart of San Gimignano, between Piazza del Duomo and Piazza della Cisterna. Some of the dishes on the menu are based on recipes from the Middle Ages and Etruscan times. Meals are given a modern twist, each accompanied by an intriguing story. The homemade desserts are also delicious. Exclusively Tuscan wines on the wine list. It is essential to reserve in advance.
✉ Vicolo dell'Oro 2, 53037 San Gimignano
☎ 0577 941862 ⏲ Tue–Sun 12.30–2.30, 7.30–9.30; also open Mon Easter–Oct; closed 10 Jan–10 Feb L €43, D €54, Wine €10

LE TERRAZZE

www.hotelcisterna.it
In San Gimignano's most central hotel, this restaurant has amazing views over the town's striking towers and defensive walls. Although the restaurant does not have outdoor seating, one wall in the 14th-century dining room is made entirely from glass, providing panoramic views. Traditional Tuscan and San Gimignano cuisine and a wide selection of wines.
✉ Albergo la Cisterna, Piazza della Cisterna 24, 53037 San Gimignano
☎ 0577 940328 ⏲ Fri–Mon 12.30–2.30, 7.30–9.30pm, Wed–Thu 7.30–9.30pm; closed 7 Jan–15 Mar L €25, D €50, Wine €10

SIENA

AL MARSILI

www.ristorantealmarsili.it
This restaurant in Siena's old town occupies a medieval building dating from the 14th century and is furnished with traditional heavy wood. There's a large main dining room and smaller brick niches with banqueting tables for larger parties. The wine bar is in a cellar carved out of rock below the Marsili Palace. Classical Tuscan cuisine is on the menu, including *gnocchetti* (little potato dumplings) with duck, homemade *crespelle* (crêpes) and vegetarian options. Reservations are advised.
✉ Via del Castoro 3, 53100 Siena
☎ 0577 47154 ⏲ Tue–Sun 12.30–2.30, 7.30–9.30 L €35, D €55, Wine €12

GUIDORICCIO

A few paces from the Campo, this elegantly furnished restaurant serves good traditional Tuscan and Sienese food with a modern accent—expect dishes such as ravioli stuffed with mushrooms and walnuts, a green vegetable lasagne or pork medallions flavoured with wild fennel. The extensive (Herculean, even) wine list was compiled by the knowledgeable owner, Ercolano. The restaurant is much favoured by local businessmen, a recommendation in itself.
✉ Via G. Dupré 2, 53100 Siena ☎ 0577 44350 ⏲ Mon–Sat 12.30–2.30, 7.30–9.30; closed 2 weeks in Nov L €25, D €50, Wine €12

OSTERIA LE LOGGE

www.osterialelogge.it
The building housing this famous Sienese restaurant was an *alimentari* (food store) in the 1800s, and it still retains its original furnishings. Eat in or outside on the street in summer and enjoy totally correct Sienese cuisine, with tasty dishes such as ravioli with mozzarella and *funghi porcini* (cep mushrooms) and lamb cooked with dried fruit. The wine and olive oil come from the proprietor's own estate.
✉ Via del Porrione 33, 53100 Siena
☎ 0577 48013 ⏲ Mon–Sat 12.30–2.30, 7.30–10; closed 9 Jan–2 Feb L €36, D €46, Wine €12

SPOLETO

IL TEMPIO DEL GUSTO

www.iltempiodelgusto.com
Eros Patrizi's lovely restaurant concentrates on the best of Umbria, with impeccable oils, local grains and vegetables, cheese and *salumeria* (cured meats), and well-hung meat. Truffles and *porcini* (cep mushrooms) appear in season, and all ingredients are transformed into innovative dishes that remain true to Umbrian roots. This is excellent cooking at a very good price and reservations are recommended.
✉ Via Arco di Druso 11, 06049 Spoleto
☎ 0743 47121 ⏲ Fri–Wed 12.30–3, 7.30–10; closed Feb or Mar and Jun or Sep
L €29, D €38, Wine €9

PRICES AND SYMBOLS

Prices are the lowest and highest for a double room for one night, unless otherwise stated. Breakfast is included, and all the hotels listed accept credit cards unless otherwise stated. Note that rates vary widely throughout the year.

For the key to symbols ▷ 2.

ASSISI

FONTEBELLA

www.fontebella.com

This slightly crumbling 16th-century palazzo can be found between Piazza del Pool and the Basilica di San Francesco. Golden swags, old paintings and tapestries cover the walls, and the rooms are traditionally furnished. The garden restaurant is the perfect place for dining if you don't fancy venturing farther afield.

✉ Via Fontebella 25, 06081 Assisi
☎ 075 812883 €60–€290 46

SAN FRANCESCO

www.hotelsanfrancescoassisi.it

This hotel, opposite the basilica, is perfectly positioned for exploring Assisi. There are both spacious and cramped rooms in this old building so chose your room wisely, but they are all comfortable and cheerful. The owners take great delight in making you feel welcome, and make a particular effort to ensure you start the day well fed. Don't miss the views over the rooftops from the terrace upstairs.

✉ Via San Francesco 48, 06081 Assisi
☎ 075 812281 €76–€130 44

BEVAGNA

HOTEL PALAZZO BRUNAMONTI

www.brunamonti.com

Right in the heart of Bevagna, this charming hotel combines 18th-century elegance in the public rooms with low-key Umbrian traditional style in the well-equipped bedrooms. There are splendid parquet floors and frescoed ceilings, while the dining room oozes a great combination of formality and style. Staff are friendly, and all rooms are equipped with everything you'd expect from a top-class hotel.

✉ Corso Matteotti 79, 06031 Bevagna
☎ 0742 361932 €70–€125 21

L'ORTO DEGLI ANGELI

www.ortoangeli.it

This stunning Residenza d'Epoca (Historic Hotel) comprises two old palazzi, surrounded by beautiful courtyards and gardens, in the heart of the walled town of Bevagna. Every bedroom is different, those in the Palazzo Andreozzi having frescoed ceilings, those in the Palazzo Alberti a more rustic style. A loggia overlooks the garden, and there are comfortable public rooms, an excellent restaurant, a fitness and beauty centre, and helpful multilingual staff.

✉ Via Dante Alighieri 1, 06031 Bevagna
☎ 0742 360130 €200–€350 5 rooms, 9 suites

CORTONA

RELAIS VILLA BALDELLI

www.villabaldelli.com

Dating from the 1600s, this 4-star country villa built of *pietra serena* (the local grey stone) sits in peaceful parkland. Rooms are simple but elegant with beamed ceilings and wrought-iron beds. The shared lounge has a large, original fireplace. Facilities include a bar and wine-tasting room. Traditional breakfasts are served on the terrace in summer. Walks, horseback riding and excursions can be arranged. There is also an on-site golf academy and driving range.

San Pietro a Cegliolo 420, 52044 Cortona 0575 612406 €140–€230 15 Outdoor Camucia, then taxi 2km (1.3 mile) Take the Valdichiana exit on the A1 and follow signs for Cortona. At Camucia take the SS71 in the direction of Arezzo. The Villa Baldelli is on the right just after Sodo, 2km (1.2 miles) from Arezzo, 5km (3 miles) northwest of Cortona

LUCCA

ALBERGO SAN MARTINO

www.albergosanmartino.it

This three-star hotel in Lucca's old town is only a brief stroll from the cathedral from which it takes its name. Bedrooms are comfortably furnished and have a television and refrigerator. An English speaker comes into the hotel at 6pm every evening to give guests a talk on what to see and do in Lucca. The talk comes with a complimentary afternoon tea or summer drink. Parking is €10 per day and bicycle rental is also available.

Via della Dogana 7/9, 55100 Lucca 0583 469181 €80–€130 9 300m (330 yards) from the central rail station Drive into the old city through Porta Eliza. Turn left at Via dei Fosso until you get to Corso Garibaldi where you take the first left

VILLA ROMANTICA

www.villaromantica.it

Villa Romantica is an imposing town house surrounded by trees only a few minutes' walk from Lucca's famous walls. The rooms are brightly decorated with busy fabrics in the fashion of the period. For a romantic trip, reserve the 'suite' with its four-poster bed, living room and terrace. There is a shuttle service to the town that runs four times an hour. You can also park here for free and rent a bicycle (at Località Stadio, 0.5km/550 yards away).

Via Barbantini 246, 55100 Lucca 0583 496872 Closed 1 week Feb and 1 week Dec €110–€140 excluding breakfast 6 Outdoor 5 minutes' walk from Lucca. At the city walls, just before the football stadium, turn right into Via dello Stadio. The hotel is at the end of the road

MASSA MARITTIMA

DUCA DEL MARE

www.ducadelmare.it

Massa is a good base for exploring southwest Tuscany and you could do a lot worse than basing yourself at this quiet hotel, overlooking the glorious landscape beyond the town. Rooms are simple and spotless; all have balconies, complete with window-boxes, many overlook the hotel garden and pool. There's ample lounge space downstairs and a comfortable breakfast room.

Piazza Alighieri 1–2, 58024 Massa Marittima 0566 902284; fax 0566 901905 Closed 20 Jan–end Feb €85–€110 28

MASSA PISANA

VILLA LA PRINCIPESSA

www.hotelprincipessalucca.it

This four-star hotel is one of the most elegant lodgings in Tuscany. The luxurious guest rooms are decorated with antiques and period furnishings. Facilities include a lounge, bar and restaurants. Bedrooms come equipped with telephone, satellite television and minibar.

Via Nuova per Pisa 1616, 55050 Massa Pisana 0583 370963 Closed early Nov to mid-Mar €240–€290 42 Outdoor Regular buses run from both Lucca and Pisa. From Pisa, there is a stop near the hotel

MONTALCINO

AL BRUNELLO DI MONTALCINO

www.hotelalbrunello.it

Don't let the modern brick exterior put you off this ultra-comfortable hotel, in a peaceful location just outside Montalcino. Rooms in the new wing are huge and beautifully appointed, with traditional Tuscan furniture and sumptuous bathrooms; many have private balconies with superb views. Less expensive rooms in the original building are smaller, though equally well equipped. There's a pool ideal for relaxing in at the end of a hot day. The restaurant serves local specialities.

Strada Provinciale Traversa dei Monti, 53024 Montalcino 0577 849304 €100–€120 (new wing); €60–€90 (original building) 35 Outdoor 2km (1.3 mile) southeast of Montalcino on Grosseto road

DEI CAPITANI

www.deicapitani.it

Almost all the rooms in this beautifully converted late medieval building have sweeping views over the archetypal Tuscan landscape of the Val d'Orcia. The bedrooms are lofty and come in cool shades with lovely beamed ceilings and plenty of space. Family-run, the hotel prides itself on personal service. The buffet breakfast could keep you going all day, and if the private parking is full, they'll help you find a space in town.

Via Lapini 6, Montalcino, 53024 Siena /Fax 0577 847227 Closed 5 Jan–15 Feb €120 29 Outdoor Exit the Autosole (A1) at Firenze Certosa from the north, Chiusi Chianciano from the south, and follow signs to Montalcino. On arrival follow the yellow signs to the hotel in the *centro storico*

MONTEPULCIANO

IL MARZOCCO

www.albergoilmarzocco.it

You'll be right in the heart of the old town if you stay at the Marzocco, one of Montepulciano's oldest hotels. This 15th-century palazzo has been a hotel since 1870 and owned by the same family for over 100 years. The public areas, furnished with Tuscan antiques, are beautiful; some bedrooms are smallish, but it's worth staying in for the atmosphere, the terrace and value.

Piazza Savanarola 18, 53045 Montepulciano 0578 757262 €90–€95 16 Take N146 from A1 autostrada to Montepulciano; the hotel is inside the walls at the bottom of the town

MONTERIGGIONI

MONTERIGGIONI

www.hotelmonteriggioni.net

This pleasing small hotel is inside the walls of one of Italy's most-photographed medieval villages. The rustic-style hotel is beautifully

Opposite *Santa Maria Maggiore in Assisi*

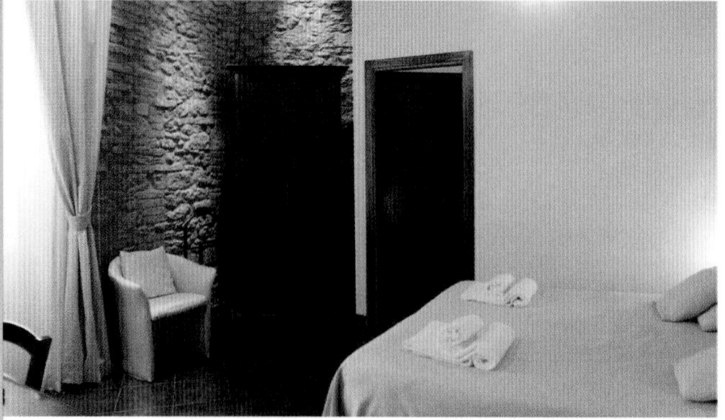

Above *There are dozens of lovely places to stay throughout Tuscany and Umbria*

furnished with Tuscan antiques, bedrooms are a good size with impressive marble bathrooms, and you can relax by the small pool in the garden. Breakfast is outstanding.
✉ Via I Maggio 4, Monteriggioni 53035
☎ 0577 305009; fax 0577 305 011
Closed 7 Jan–28 Feb €180–€230
12

NORCIA

GROTTA AZZURRA

www.bianconi.com

The building's beautiful stuccoed walls, cavernous rooms and fabulous furnishings create comfortable surroundings. Suits of armour preside over those eating in the impressive dining rooms, where local roast lamb is served. Most of the bedrooms are fairly simple, but the slightly pricier rooms look like film sets and are worth paying extra for.
✉ Via Alfieri 12, 06046 Norcia ☎ 0743 816513 €65–€115 46
Follow signs for the hotel from Spoleto

ORVIETO

VIRGILIO

www.orvietohotelvirgilio.com

You won't find better value in one of Orvieto's most popular areas. The sound of church bells can always be heard in this hotel, set right on the main piazza, never letting you forget you're in a small Italian town. The rooms are small but cared for, and every room has private facilities. Try to get a room with a view of the magnificent duomo. The breakfasts are simple but tasty.
✉ Piazza del Duomo 5, 05018 Orvieto
☎ 0763 394937 Closed Feb
€120–€160 13 Funicular from railway station and then take a taxi or hop on the city-circuit bus

PASSIGNANO SUL TRASIMENO

HOTEL LA VELA

www.hotellavela.it

The lakeside village of Passignano makes a good stop-off point heading into Umbria from Tuscany, and you'll find a warm welcome at this family-run, well-priced hotel. On a quiet street a few minutes' walk from the heart of town and the water's edge, the hotel has comfortable, simple bedrooms, all with bathrooms, telephone and television, a pleasant bar and breakfast room and a good restaurant serving everything from pizza to Umbrian specialties.
✉ Via Rinascita 2, 06065 Passignano sul Trasimeno ☎ 0758 28211 €60–€90
29

PERUGIA

SANGALLO PALACE

www.sangallo.it

This modern hotel is in Perugia's old heart. Almost all rooms have balconies, allowing guests to enjoy splendid views of the city and the hills that surround the property. The guest rooms are slightly impersonal since they are geared towards business visitors, but they have every standard amenity. There is a state-of-the-art gym and an impressive indoor pool.
✉ Via Masi 9, 06121 Perugia ☎ 075 5730202 €100–€180 100
Indoor

PIENZA

RELAIS IL CHIOSTRO DI PIENZA

www.relaisilchiostrodipienza.com

Walk through the luminous cloister of this 15th-century ex-monastery to one of southern Tuscany's most atmospheric hotels. The restoration has been beautifully done, leaving the vaulted ceilings, beams and architectural details untouched, while sensitively adding 21st-century comfort. The bedrooms are big and antique pieces enhance the public areas. A good restaurant, dreamy terraces and geraniums add to the magic, all a minute's walk from Pienza's main piazza.
✉ Corso Rossellino 26, Pienza, 53026 Siena
☎ /Fax 0578 748400 Closed 7–31 Jan; Feb–20 Mar weekends only €120–€215
37 Outdoor Exit the Autosole (A1) at Valdiciana from the north, Chiusi Chianciano Terme from the south, and follow signs to Pienza. The hotel is inside the town walls on the right

PISA

FRANCESCO

www.hotelfrancesco.com

Close to the Leaning Tower and the botanical gardens, this small hotel and restaurant is in the heart of Pisa. Rooms are whitewashed, with wooden furnishings, and most have panoramic views. Bedrooms have a television and minibar. Facilities include a family-run pizzeria, bicycle rental and a courtesy airport shuttle.
✉ Via Santa Maria 129, 56126 Pisa
☎ 050 555453 €60–€150 13
4

RADDA IN CHIANTI

RELAIS FATTORIA VIGNALE

www.vignale.it

Fattoria Vignale started life as the manor house of a big wine estate; today, it is one of Italy's top hotels, aimed at well-heeled foreigners. The conversion is very successful—expect traditional Tuscan architecture, well-polished antiques, fireplaces big enough to roast an ox

and huge sofas. The bedrooms, some with private terraces, are opulent and luxurious, with service to match. The vaulted wine cellars house a taverna, and there's a smarter restaurant near the main building.
Via Pianigiani 9, Radda in Chianti, 53017 Siena 0577 738300; fax 0577 738592 Apr–Oct €230–€280 37 rooms, 5 suites Outdoor From the Autosole (A1): from the north, exit Firenze Certosa, take the superstrada Firenze–Siena towards Siena. Exit at S Donato (22km/14 miles) and follow signs to Radda in Chianti. From the south, exit at Valdarno, take the N408 to Gaiole in Chianti. After 17km (11 miles) take the road to Radda in Chianti. The hotel is signposted (yellow signs) and is in the middle of Radda

SAN GIMIGNANO

L'ANTICO POZZO

www.anticopozzo.com

This three-star hotel, in a superbly restored 15th-century town house, is located in the middle of San Gimignano. The building sits on a cobbled street near the Piazza della Cisterna. The interior is medieval in character and contains a well-preserved lobby with a high, vaulted ceiling. There's an atmospheric bar in the brick cellar and a first-floor garden terrace. Rooms have satellite television, minibar and safe. Guests get a discount when parking in lot 3.
Via San Matteo 87, 53037 San Gimignano 0577 942014 Closed 20 Jan–20 Feb €110–€180 18 From Florence, Siena, Volterra Poggibonsi then bus to San Gimignano Take the Poggibonsi Nord exit of the Firenze/Siena highway and follow signs to San Gimignano

SIENA

BEL SOGGIORNO

www.hotelbelsoggiorno.it

Set within the walls of the *centro storico*, the Bel Soggiorno represents about the best value to be found for quality accommodation in this tourist honeypot. The refurbishment of this 14th-century building has been sensitively accomplished to provide spacious rooms with clean lines, light colours and antique touches. Many have panoramic views and you can drink them in at the hotel's own restaurant, with its brick-lined walls and huge windows looking over the countryside. You can drive to the hotel to unload luggage but must park outside the walls.
Via San Giovanni 9, 53037 Siena 0577 940375 €90–€170 21

GRAND HOTEL CONTINENTAL

www.royaldemeure.com

This luxurious hotel in a former aristocratic home is part of Siena's cultural heritage. It has recently been faithfully restored to its former glory right down to the magnificent frescoes, a wall painting of St. Christopher dating from the 15th century, and the ornamental motifs from the 19th century. A covered courtyard has been coverted into a winter garden. Full leisure facilities are available at the nearby Park Hotel via a courtesy bus service.
Via Banchi di Sopra 85, 53100 Siena 0577 56011 €473–€690 49 rooms, 2 suites 3, 9, 10, 5 from Florence to La Lizza

MINERVA

www.albergominerva.it

A 10-minute walk from Piazza del Campo and the rail station, this three-star hotel has good views over the city and hills beyond. It's good value and has basic but modern, fully equipped bedrooms.
Via Garibaldi 72, 53100 Siena 0577 284474 €96–€114 59 3, 4, 7, 8, 10, 17, 77

SPELLO

PALAZZO BOCCI

www.palazzobocci.com

Built in the 18th century and renovated in the 1990s, this romantic hotel is set in the heart of one of Umbria's prettiest towns. You'll find high frescoed ceilings, public rooms with deep sofas and terracotta floors scattered with Persian rugs, a pretty breakfast room and terraces with views over the plain below. The bedrooms are all different and spacious, with luxury fabrics, huge beds and state-of-the-art bathrooms. The staff are charming, efficient and multilingual.
Via Cavour 17, Spello, 06038 Perugia 0742 301021; fax 0742 301464 €130–€160 21 rooms, 2 suites Spello old town is a short walk from the rail station Exit the Autosole (A1) from the north at Valdichiana, from the south at Orte, and follow signs to Spello. Follow the signs to *centro storico* and then the yellow hotel signs. The hotel is on the left up the main street

SPOLETO

PALAZZO DRAGONI

www.palazzodragoni.it

Next to the cathedral, this 14th-century building was the home of the Dragoni family, who more than contributed to the prosperity of Spoleto. Now owned by the local bakers, the Diotallevi family, it has kept much of its original charm with the added bonus of modern facilities and the best breakfast pastries in town. The rooms are all different, but each is comfortable and well kept. The dining area has wonderful views of the city.
Via del Duomo 16, 06049 Spoleto 0743 222220 €125–€250 15 CA from station

TODI

FONTE CESIA

www.fontecesia.it

The Fonte Cesia was originally an 18th-century palazzo, complete with private chapel—today, it's a top-class luxury hotel. Bar, breakfast room and lounge all retain their brick vaulting. The bedrooms are decorated with heavy brocades and have ultra-comfortable beds and marble bathrooms. The staff are friendly, the breakfast excellent, and there's a smart, expensive restaurant on the premises. Free parking is available.
Via L. Leonj 3, Todi, 06059 Perugia 0758 943737; fax 0758 944677 €100–€172 32 bedrooms, 5 suites Ponte Rio (Terni/Perugia line) Route C Exit the Autosole (A1) at Orvieto and take the SS448 to Todi. Follow the yellow signs to the hotel in the *centro storico*

LAZIO AND THE MARCHE

The regions of Lazio and the Marche straddle the Italian peninsula from coast to coast. Rome, the capital of Lazio, pulls in the crowds, but the rest of this low-key region, with its gentle landscape and little-known towns, bridges the gap between the thriving, prosperous north and the poorer but vibrant south. Across the Apennines the remote Marche, like Lazio once part of the Papal States, is a whole other world, a region of hills, wooded valleys, and undiscovered towns and villages that contrast with the string of some of Italy's most lively resorts along the coast.

Lazio's history is long; this was the power base of the Etruscan tribes, forerunners of the Romans, whose cities have long gone but whose necropoli, the cities of the dead, remain at Tarquinia and Cerveteri. There's an entire Roman city to explore at Ostia Antica, once classical Rome's port, and the legacy of papal and aristocratic power lives on in the great villas and gardens surrounding Rome—Tivoli, with its wonderful fountains, Frascati, where water is again used to full effect at the Villa Aldobrandini, and Castel Gandolfo, the summer home of the Pope, in the Colli Albani, whose white wine is served at every Roman restaurant. North of here lies the historic and under-visited town of Viterbo and peaceful Lago di Bolsena, a lovely lake surrounded by laid-back resort villages. To the east of Lazio a narrow pass, home to the medieval town of Ascoli Piceno, leads through the Apennines to the Marche, once the seat of the dukes of Urbino, Renaissance princelings whose court was among Europe's most brilliant. Their palace survives intact, a dream-like Renaissance gem in a quiet university town, which contrasts with the cheerful holiday-time bustle of the coastal resorts of Ancona, Fano and Pesaro, and the commercialism of the tiny republic of San Marino to the north.

LE ARTI NELLE MARCHE
AL TEMPO DI SISTO V

ABBAZIA DI MONTECASSINO

www.montecassino.it

St. Benedict, supposedly guided by three ravens, chose this dramatic site to found a monastery in 529. High on a mountain top, 200km (125 miles) south of Rome, the huge white bulwarks of the abbey of Montecassino can be seen for miles around. This strategic position meant that the abbey was frequently involved in conflict, and it has been destroyed and rebuilt many times. During World War II the Nazis made the abbey their regional headquarters, and on 15 February 1944 it was destroyed by Allied bombing. The rest of the abbey was reconstructed in a medieval style. It has a slightly sterile appearance, but the views from here are superb (much of the abbey is closed to the public). Large parts of the town of Cassino were also destroyed during World War II. The ruins of the Roman town of Casinum, however, can still be seen.

469 J10 Via G. di Biasco 54, 03043 Cassino 0776 311529 Mon–Sat 8.30–12.30, 3.30–5.30, Sun only between Masses. Abbey: daily 9–12.30, 3.30–6 Cassino, then bus to the abbey

ASCOLI PICENO

▷ 324.

CASTEL GANDOLFO AND LAGO ALBANO

Castel Gandolfo, 24km (15 miles) south of Rome, is named after the powerful Genoese Gandolfi family, who originally built a castle here in the 12th century. The palace, built over the ruined castle in 1624 and later remodelled by Pope Pius XI, comes into its own in July, August and September, when the papal court transfers here from the Vatican. The palace can be seen only from the outside, but the Pope generally appears in the palace's courtyard at noon on Sundays during this period to address the public.

The palace is the dominant feature of the town, but don't overlook the Church of San Tommaso di Villanova, designed by Bernini, with frescoes by Pietro da Cortona.

Castel Gandolfo looks out over the waters of Lake Albano. Along the Via Appia, which runs down the length of the lake's west shore, are ancient towns and a number of restaurants and cafés.

468 G10 Piazza Libertà 5, 00040 Castel Gandolfo 06 932 4081 Cotral bus runs approx. every 30 min from Anagnina metro station in Rome

CERVETERI

Cerveteri was one of the wealthiest Etruscan towns in Italy and dates back to the 7th century BC. Known as Kysry (Roman *Caere*) in ancient times, it accumulated its wealth by trading the rich mineral deposits found in the Tolfa hills nearby. Today the heart of the town is largely medieval in appearance and the Etruscan remains for which it is famous are found 3km (2 miles) to the west. The Necropoli della Banditaccia were laid out to create a 'city of the dead', providing space for 5,000 tombs dating from the seventh to first century BC. With streets and houses like a town, this extraordinary burial site and the archaeological finds here give a fascinating insight into Etruscan culture. The tombs are carved into the rock or covered by earth, and several are elaborately constructed, including the Tomba degli Scudi e delle Sedie, in the form of an Etruscan house. The Museo Nazionale di Cerveteri (Tue–Sun 8.30–7.30) displays some of the many Etruscan objects that were buried with the dead. Other finds from these tombs are on display in Rome's Villa Giulia (▷ 99).

468 G9 Necropoli della Banditaccia, Piazza Libertà 5, 00052 Cerveteri 06 3996 7150 Daily 8.30–dusk Cerveteri-Ladispoli, then bus to town

FANO

www.turismofano.com

Fano's beaches make it a popular, but not overcrowded, resort, with a good choice of either sandy beaches sprinkled with sun umbrellas, or pebbly stretches with promenades.

Fano is 11km (7 miles) south of Pesaro on the Adriatic coast. It was once a Roman port on the Via Flaminia, but little of its Roman heritage remains visible. Today it is split by the railway, with the modern resort on one side and the old town on the other. In addition to some imposing palaces, Fano has a museum and art gallery, the Museo Civico and Pinacoteca, in the 15th-century Palazzo Malatesta. The impressive Biblioteca Federiciana has on display more than 200,000 volumes and two 17th-century globes, one of the earth and one of the skies. The highlight of the historic heart is the Arco di Augusto, an arch built by Emperor Augustus in AD2 to mark the city's foundation.

467 H7 Via Battisti 10, 61032 Fano 0721 803534 Fano

Opposite *The 13th-century Palazzo dei Capitani, Ascoli Piceno*
Below *Church of San Tommaso di Villanova, Castel Gandolfo*

INFORMATION

www.le-marche.com
467 J8 Piazza Arringo 7, 63100 Ascoli Piceno 0736 253045 Daily summer 9–6.30; winter 9–1, 3–7
Ascoli Piceno

ASCOLI PICENO

Some 65km (40 miles) southwest of Fermo, Ascoli is today a prosperous town relatively untouched by tourism. It began as a strategic Roman settlement founded after the defeat of the local Piceni tribe. During medieval times wealthy families living in the town, like those in San Gimignano (▷ 285), built defensive towers as a symbol of their wealth and dominance. At one time there were around 200 spearing the skyline; many were destroyed on the orders of Frederick II, but about 50 remain.

THE WHITE CITY

Architecturally, Ascoli is striking, built largely from white travertine stone. At its heart is the Piazza del Popolo, lined with an elegant Renaissance portico, reminiscent of those in Bolgona (▷ 204–205). It is dominated by the 13th-century Palazzo dei Capitani, once the seat of the *comune* (town council), and the Church of San Francesco. Visitors and locals are also drawn to this square by the delightful Caffè Meletti, an art deco café with huge mirrors on the walls, wooden floors and marble tables. Various famous people have sought refreshment here over the years since it opened in 1903, including novelist Ernest Hemingway; try the local liqueur, the aniseed-tasting Anisetta Meletti. Piazza Arringo, built over the Roman forum, is home to the 15th-century duomo, dedicated to St. Emidius, whose relics are kept in the crypt. In a chapel on the right of the nave is a polyptych considered to be one of Carlo Crivelli's finest works.

MUSEUMS

The Museo Diocesano (Mon–Fri 9.30–1, Sat 9.30–1, 3.30–6), in Piazza Arringo, displays a collection of prehistoric and Roman archaeological finds, while the Pinacoteca Civica (Mar–Sep Tue–Sun 10–7; Oct–Feb 10.30–5), an art gallery in the Palazzo Comunale, also on the square, is worth visiting just to see the palace's rich red drapes, marble floors and chandeliers. Among the pieces on show are an *Annunciation* by Guido Reni and Titian's *St. Francis Receiving the Stigmata*, along with works by Carlo Crivelli, Pietro Alemanno, Van Dyck and Rembrandt.

Below *Fountain outside the Palazzo Comunale in Piazza Arringo*

FRASCATI AND COLLI ALBANI

A popular destination with both Romans and tourists, Frascati has been a retreat for the rich for centuries and is still dominated by one of their villas, Villa Aldobrandini, begun by Giacomo della Porta in 1598 but not completed until 100 years later. The villa is not open to the public, but you can visit the grounds for free with a permit obtained at the visitor centre at Piazza G. Marconi (grounds: Apr–Sep Mon–Fri 9–1, 3–6; Oct–Mar Mon–Fri 9–1, 3–5; visitor centre: closed Sat afternoon and all day Sun).

The Colli Albani, the hills to the south of Frascati, 21km (13 miles) southeast of Rome, form a backbone to the Castelli Romani towns, so called because they grew up around the feudal castles of Rome's wealthy families. The soil of this 60km (37-mile) chain of volcanic hills is very fertile and produces many good wines, the best known being, naturally, Frascati. Give it a try in one of the local bars, where it is often available from huge wooden barrels.

There are a number of little towns to visit in the area besides Frascati, including Nemi and Rocca di Papa—the most dramatically positioned town in the Collini Albani.

468 G10 Piazza G. Marconi, 00044 Frascati Frascati Point (for information on local vineyards and wine cellars) 06 9401 5378 Frascati

GROTTE DI FRASASSI

www.frasassi.com

This is one of the most interesting cave complexes in Italy, situated next to the Church of San Vittore delle Chiuse, near Genga. The intriguing underground world of silent lakes and countless stalactites and stalagmites, 61km (38 miles) from Ancona, provides an arresting contrast to the surrounding countryside.

Discovered in 1971, the caves opened to the public in 1974. So far, 13km (8 miles) of limestone caves have been explored, and the complex is thought to extend a further 35km (22 miles). Less than 2km (1.3 miles) is open to the public, but it is sure to

Above *Villa Aldobrandini, Frascati*

impress. The Grotta Grande del Vento (Great Cave of the Wind) is possibly the largest cave of its kind in Europe, so huge that Milan Cathedral could fit inside. The warrens of other caves bear such evocative names as the Hall of the Candles, the Hall of the Bear and the Hall of Infinity.

467 H7 Genga 0732 90080 or 90090 Guided tours (Italian, 75 mins): Mar–Oct daily 10, 11, 12, 2.30, 4, 5 (also 6 Jul to mid-Sep); Nov–Feb Mon–Fri 11.30, 3.30, Sat 11.30, 2.30, 4.30, Sun 10, 11, 12, 2.30, 4, 5. Tours in English, French and German Jun–Sep daily 11.15, 12.45, 2.45, 4.15 Adult €15, child (6–14) €13 Genga, then shuttle bus in summer

LAGO DI BOLSENA AND BOLSENA

www.lagodibolsena.org

Lago di Bolsena, 112km (70 miles) north of Rome, is the largest volcanic lake in Italy and the fifth-largest in the country. It is lined with busy towns such as Capodimonte, where the waters lap the edge of the town, Gradoli, which lies at the heart of a large wine region, Etruscan Montefiascone and medieval Bolsena. Guided tours by boat run from Capodimonte and Bolsena to Isola Bisentina (daily 11 and 5, Sun 11, 3 and 5), an island in the middle of the lake where you can visit the Farnese family gardens.

On the hillside overlooking the lake, Bolsena's medieval castle dates back to the 13th century and today contains a museum displaying archaeological finds from the lake and objects from the Roman city of Volsinii (Bolsena). On Piazza Santa Cristina stands the collegiate Romanesque Church of Santa Cristina. The oldest part of this church is the grotto, where the miracle of Corpus Christi is said to have taken place in 1236. The grotto contains a 15th-century polyptych attributed to Sano di Pietro and Benvenuto di Giovanni, and frescoes by painters from the Umbrian-Sienese school.

468 G8 Piazza Matteotti 9, 01223 Bolsena 0761 799923

LORETO

Loreto, 22km (14 miles) southwest of Portonovo, is a place of pilgrimage—thousands make the journey every year to see the Virgin Mary's house. It was transported here from Nazareth by the Angeli family during the 13th century. In the 16th century an enormous church, the Santuario della Santa Casa, was built over the house to protect it. The Santa Casa (Holy House) is directly beneath the dome, protected by an ornate marble screen by Bramante. Around the Santa Casa are the sacristies of San Marco, San Giovanni and San Luca, which contain works by Melozzo da Forli and Luca Signorelli. Outside in the Piazza della Madonna is the Fontana della Madonna, a fountain designed by Giovanni Fontana and Carlo Maderno.

Opposite the church is the Palazzo Apostolico, begun by Bramante in 1509 and now occupied by the town's museum and art gallery.

467 J7 Via Solari 3, 60025 Loreto 071 970276 Loreto

OFFIDA

Easily reached from Ascoli Piceno and the coastal towns of the region, Offida is famous in the Marche for its fine lace, which has been produced by the women of the town for generations. There are plenty of places to purchase their craftwork, and the Lace Museum has examples of local lace, including a 19th-century tablecloth, dainty bridal shoes and an exquisite dress modelled by Naomi Campbell in 1997 for Antonio Beraddi.

Offida is surrounded by vineyards and the gently rolling hills to the west of San Benedetto del Tronto. It has a pleasant, unhurried atmosphere, with streets that invite exploration. The town's main focus is the square, which is flanked by the 14th-century Palazzo Comunale, home to the archaeological museum, a small art gallery and the Teatro Serpente Aureo.

From here it is about five minutes' walk to the Church of Santa Maria della Rocca, on an exposed hillside overlooking the countryside. The monks used its crypt as a hospital from the 12th century. During restoration in the 1980s, it was discovered that cavities in the walls had been used to bury the dead.

467 J8 Museo di Offida, Corso Serpente Aureo 66, 63035 Offida 0736 888609 Summer only

OSTIA ANTICA

▷ 327.

PARCO DEL CONERO

www.parcoconero.it

This is one of the most beautiful areas on the Adriatic and a good destination for those wanting to enjoy the outdoors. There are numerous coastal resorts where you can swim, sail, scuba-dive and windsurf, and for walkers there are 18 waymarked tracks around Monte Conero. There are many rare plants and excellent birdwatching opportunities, as well as some sites of cultural and geological interest to explore.

The park covers 5,800ha (14,300 acres) and is dominated by Monte Conero (572m/1,877ft). At the top of the mountain are the remains of a Palaeolithic settlement dating back 100,000 years.

To its north is Portonovo, a pretty bay that is home to the 11th-century church of Santa Maria di Portonovo, mentioned by Dante in *La Divina Commedia*. To the south is Sirolo, the area's main resort, with good beaches that are safe for children. Close by is Numana, where you can visit the Santuario della Croce, a shrine containing a wooden crucifix dating from the 12th or 13th century that is said to have miraculous powers.

On the road to Numana, Sirolo is home to the Villa Vetta Marina, the site of a convent founded by St. Francis in 1215.

467 J7 Centro Visite Parco del Conero, Via Peschiera 30/a, 60020 Sirolo 0719 331879 Mid-Jun to mid-Sep daily 9–1, 4–7; mid-Sep to Dec, Mar to mid-Jun Mon–Sat 9–1

PESARO

www.turismo-marche.com

www.turismo.pesarourbino.it

Founded by the Romans in 184BC, Pesaro is a busy provincial town characterized by a pleasant old town, elegant streets and a waterfront lined with white-stucco hotels overlooking sandy beaches. The hub is Piazza del Popolo, where you'll find the most impressive building, the 15th-century Palazzo Ducale.

Pesaro's beaches make it a great place for anyone simply wanting to relax in the sun. It also attracts opera-lovers, as it was the birthplace of the composer Gioachino Rossini (1792–1868), and is the venue for a festival celebrating his works every August. His birthplace, Casa di Rossini (Via Rossini 34; tel 0721 387537), is a small museum, which preserves the original furnishings and memorabilia of the composer. Heavy bombing in World War II destroyed much of the town, so it lacks the charm of other Italian towns, but it still has its art treasures.

Paintings in the Museo Civico (Piazza Toschi Mosca; tel 0721 387541) include Giovanni Bellini's masterpiece, *The Coronation of the Virgin*. The ceramic collection includes a terracotta work by Andrea della Robbia.

467 H6 Viale Trieste 164, 61100 Pesaro 0721 69341 Pesaro

Below *A sandy beach in Portonovo*

OSTIA ANTICA

Ostia Antica is Italy's best-preserved Roman settlement after Pompei. The sprawling remnants of this once-bustling town include shops, shrines, barracks, workshops, tombs, grain warehouses *(horrea)*, baths, inns and houses.

ROME'S PORT

In about 335BC a small fishing community settled on this site 25km (15 miles) west of Rome. The settlement grew to become Rome's principal port, trading commodities from all over the empire. With the outbreak of the First Punic War, the port also became an important naval base and by the second century it had a population of nearly 500,000. Excavations of the site began in the 19th century and have so far revealed about one half of the town.

EXCAVATIONS

The Terme di Nettuno (Baths of Neptune), the first main building on the right after the Porta Romana, was built by Hadrian and preserves a series of elaborate mosaics depicting Neptune and Amphitrite. The mill is equally well preserved, with millstones, basins and kneading machines. The amphitheatre was built in the age of Augustus, with capacity for 3,000 people. At the end of the second century its capacity was extended to 4,000, and later it was adapted for the staging of aquatic shows. The Thermopolium in Via di Diana was once a bar; you can still see the marble counter, washbasins, stove, benches for the customers and wall paintings illustrating the menu. Excavations continue, and in spring 2010 tombs were discovered containing remains from the first century AD.

INFORMATION

www.itnw.roma.it/ostia/scavi
www.ostia-antica.org
468 G10 Via Romanogli 717, 000125 Ostia 5635 8099 Apr–Oct Tue–Sun 8.30–7; Nov–Feb 8.30–5; Mar 8.30–6. Closed 1 May Adult €6.50, under 18s free Ostia Antica

Above *Detail of a Corinthian capital*

Above *The main square of San Severino Marche, founded by refugees who were fleeing raiding Barbarians in the sixth century*

SAN LEO

www.turismo-marche.com

Some 12.5km (8 miles) east of Novafeltria, San Leo sits precariously on top of a tall cliff and is reached by a single-track road cut into the rock. Named after a Dalmatian saint, who was said to have converted the area to Christianity in the fourth century, the town was originally a defensive fortress. The dramatic landscape was the inspiration for Dante's *Purgatorio*.

San Leo is dominated by its castle (summer daily 9–12, 2–6.30; reduced hours in winter), which the statesman and writer Machiavelli (▷ 37) considered to be the greatest fortress in Italy. It also served as a prison, notably to Count Alessandro di Cagliostro, a leading freemason, alchemist and medium who was sentenced to death during the Inquisition. The little village sits in the shadow of the fortress, on the remarkably preserved cobbled square, Piazza Dante. Here—in addition to several good restaurants and cafés—is the 12th-century Romanesque duomo, erected in honour of St. Leo, and La Pieve, the town's oldest church, founded in the eighth century.

467 G6 Piazza Dante 10, 91018 San Leo 0541 916306

SAN MARINO

www.visitsanmarino.com

Marino, a stonemason fleeing religious persecution, supposedly founded this autonomous town in AD301. Between Romagna and the Marche, 14km (9 miles) southwest of Rimini, the town has a commanding position on a hilltop, with impressive battlements on the highest ridges. It covers an area of just 61sq km (24sq miles) and still declares itself an independent republic, with its own mint, postage stamps and international soccer team. This makes it the longest-surviving republic in Europe.

San Marino is something of a tourist trap, so you have to fight your way past numerous souvenir shops to enjoy its main attraction—the views from the fortress on Mount Titan. For philatelists there is an excellent stamp museum (Museo Filatelico e Numismatico).

467 G6 Palazzo del Turismo, Contrada Omagnano 20, 47031 San Marino 0549 882914

SAN SEVERINO MARCHE

A town with a rich artistic heritage, San Severino Marche was the birthplace of the Salimbeni brothers, whose works adorn the local churches and art gallery. The town's past is revealed further in the archaeological museum, which also has remains from the Roman town of Septempeda.

There are two parts to the town: the Borgo, which focuses on the medieval Piazza del Popolo, and the ancient *castello* (castle) on Montenero Hill, the heart of the old town. The Pinacoteca Civica (art gallery), just above the piazza in the lower part of town, has works by Lorenzo and Jacopo Salimbeni, paintings by Alunno, and the great Renaissance artist Pinturicchio's painted wood masterpiece, the *Madonna della Pace*. In the sixth-century Church of San Lorenzo in Doliolo, at the top of Via Salimbini, are the remains of a pagan temple and frescoes by the Salimbeni brothers. The 10th-century Duomo Vecchio is also decorated with frescoes by the brothers. The Duomo Nuovo, with a *Madonna* by Pinturicchio, is also worth visiting.

467 H8 Pro Loco, Piazza del Popolo 43, 62027 San Severino 0733 638414 San Severino

SPERLONGA

www.turislazio.it

Sperlonga is Lazio's most fashionable resort, 98km (61 miles) southeast of Castel Gandolfo. Like the town of Gaeta, Sperlonga juts into the Tyrrhenian Sea, on the region's prettiest stretch of coastline, shaped by little coves and promontories and several attractive beaches. The houses are whitewashed, and the narrow streets make the town an appealing place to explore, although it can get very busy in summer. Combine time on the beach and a leisurely meal in a restaurant with a visit to nearby historical sites—perhaps the Grotta di Tiberio (Cave of Tiberius) and its museum, with works of art and several classical sculptures.

At Gaeta you can also visit the tomb of Cicero, the great Roman orator and writer, killed in 43BC.

469 H11 Piazza Traniello (in Gaeta's bus terminal), 04024 Gaeta 0771 461165; summer only Fondi Sperlonga

SUBIACO

Subiaco is an isolated town on the edge of the Simbruini Mountains, 28km (17 miles) south of Anticoli Corrado. There were once 12 monasteries around the town, but now only two remain, both a short distance from the town. It was here in the fifth century that St. Benedict wrote the famous *Benedictine Rule*, the cornerstone of Western monasticism. He lived in a nearby cave, the Sacro Speco, now part of the Convento di San Benedetto. The cave is in a lower part of the monastery; steps lead down to an early 13th-century fresco of St. Francis. It is this monastery and the Monastery of Santa Scolastica that attract most visitors to the town. Reached by a 25-minute walk from town, the Convento di Santa Scholastica has three painstakingly restored cloisters. The first, from 1580, is decorated with columns from Nero's villa, the second (1052) is one of the oldest in Italy, and the third dates from the 13th century.

✚ 468 H10 ℹ Via Cadorna 59, 00028 Subiaco ☎ 0774 822013

TARQUINIA

The cultural and political capital of Etruscan Italy, Tarquinia, now a UNESCO World Heritage Site, is famous for its necropolis, 6,000 original Etruscan tombs that honeycomb the Monterozzi plateau to the east of the town. There are a handful that can be visited within the ancient town. The Hellenistic-style wall paintings inside span about 500 years, depicting mythical scenes, banquets, games and horse races.

The modern town overlooks the Tyrrhenian Sea, and here are more reminders of the past in a museum that has a wide variety of Etruscan objects. On display are tomb paintings, jewellery, coins and vases, but the highlight is a pair of Etruscan terracotta winged horses from the fourth century BC. There are also some medieval sites worth visiting here, including the 12th-century Church of Santa Maria in Castello.

✚ 468 F9 ℹ Piazza Cavour 1, 01016 Tarquinia ☎ 0766 849282 🚉 Tarquinia

TIVOLI

▷ 330–331.

TOLENTINO

Tolentino is one of Italy's lesser-known towns but it has plenty to attract history-lovers, including frescoes in the Basilica di San Nicola, several Romanesque churches and a fine 18th-century theatre.

Its position in the Chienti River valley, 100km (62 miles) north of Ascoli Piceno, made it an important industrial focus in the Middle Ages, the river water being used to drive mills. Today Tolentino has kept its industrial tradition, and the historic heart is surrounded by a sprawl of uninspiring modern buildings.

An ancient bridge, the Ponte di Diavolo (Devil's Bridge), leads to the 13th-century Basilica di San Nicola da Tolentino, the home of St. Nicholas until he died in 1305. Inside is a fresco cycle by Pietro da Rimini, painted in the 14th century in the style of Giotto.

Tolentino also has some interesting museums: the Museo dell'Opera del Santuario has paintings, frescoes and rich religious objects, while the slightly more unusual Museo della Caricatura e dell'Umorismo nell'Arte, in the Palazzo Sangallo, displays a collection of caricatures by Italian and foreign artists.

✚ 467 H8 ℹ Piazza della Libertà 18, 62029 Tolentino ☎ 0733 972937 🚉 Tolentino

URBINO

▷ 332–333.

VITERBO

www.apt.viterbo.it
www.viterboonline.com

Viterbo is the largest town in northern Lazio, 81km (51 miles) north of Rome. Originally an Etruscan town, it was colonized by the Romans in 310BC. The outskirts are uninspiring, but the walled centre is lively, with plenty of good bars and restaurants, as well as a number of cultural sites.

It is worth visiting simply to soak up the atmosphere of the medieval quarter, San Pellegrino—an intriguing maze of narrow streets lined with romantic-looking houses, enticing archways, balconies and external staircases. The town was home to artists such as Lorenzo da Viterbo (1440–76), and it was the official papal residence for many years.

The heart of town is Piazza del Plebiscito, from where you can walk along Via San Lorenzo to Piazza San Lorenzo, an airy square built on the site of an Etruscan acropolis. The 13th-century Palazzo Papale and the striking Romanesque duomo are both found here. At the Villa Lante at nearby Bagnaia, you can walk in the Renaissance garden and enjoy its open-air thermal pools.

✚ 468 G9 ℹ Piazza San Carluccio 5, 01100 Viterbo ☎ 0761 304795 🚉 Viterbo Porta Romana

Below *The Convento di San Benedetto in Subiaco*

TIVOLI

Tivoli's scenery and cool hilltop location 40km (25 miles) east of Rome made it a popular spot for wealthy Romans to build their country villas—a trend revived during the Renaissance.

VILLA ADRIANA

www.villa-adriana.net

The Villa Adriana's ruins sprawl lazily away from Tivoli through peaceful olive groves. Begun in AD125 and completed 10 years later, the Villa Adriana was so vast that it covered an area as great as the heart of imperial Rome. It was the most expensive palace ever built in the empire, with two bathhouses, libraries, temples and a Greek theatre, as well as apartments. It even had a beach heated by steam pipes buried under the sand, and a series of underground service passages big enough to accommodate horses and carts. The parkland is dotted with pools and buildings connected by covered walkways. The Teatro Marittimo is a small palace built on a private island in an artificial lagoon; it is thought to have been Hadrian's private retreat.

Via di Villa Adriana, 00010 Tivoli 0774 382733 May–Aug daily 9–6; Apr, Sep 9–5.30; Mar–Oct 9–5; Feb 9–4.30; Nov–Jan 9–3.30 Adult €8, under 18s free

VILLA D'ESTE

www.villadestetivoli.info

The Villa d'Este is in Tivoli itself, next to the main square, Largo Garibaldi. Pirro Ligorio adapted the former convent into a country retreat for Cardinal Ippolito d'Este, son of Lucrezia Borgia and the Duke of Ferrara, in 1550. The gardens are both theatrical and elegant, with water spouting from all corners and cascading down every surface. Particularly impressive are the Viale delle Cento Fontane (Avenue of a Hundred Fountains) and the Fontana dei Draghi (Fountain of the Dragons), built in honour of Pope Gregory XIII, whose emblem was a short-tailed dragon. But the most visually striking aquatic display is the Fontana di Biccierone (Fountain of Glass) by Bernini. A curious addition is the Rometta, with scale models of Rome's major buildings.

Piazza Trento, 00010 Tivoli 0445 230310 Tue–Sun 8.30–one hour before sunset (also Jul to mid-Sep Fri–Sat 8.30pm–midnight). Last entry 1 hour before closing Adult €6.50, under 18s €3.25 Audioguides in Italian, English, French, German, Spanish €4

INFORMATION

www.tivoli.it/turismo

468 H10 Largo Garibaldi, 00019 Tivoli 0774 334522 Wed–Fri 9–1, 3–6, Mon–Tue, Sat 9–1 Tivoli Both villas are so popular that many companies run bus tours from Rome.

TIP

» Spring and autumn are the best times to visit to avoid the biggest crowds.

» Villa d'Este's famous Birdsong Fountain and Organ Fountain (Fontana della Civetta) have recently been cleaned; the Fontana della Civetta can be heard daily from 10am every two hours.

» For evening visits to the Villa d'Este, a maximum of 2,000 guests is allowed per night, so reserving ahead is recommended. Last entry 11pm.

Opposite *The fountains at Villa d'Este*
Left *The grounds of Villa Adriana*
Below *Detail of a fountain at Villa d'Este*

INFORMATION
www.urbinoculturaturismo.it
467 H7 Via Puccinotti 35, 61029 Urbino 0722 2613 Mon–Sat 9–1, 3–7, Sun 9–1

URBINO

Urbino lies on two hills above the valleys of the Metauro and the Foglia, still enclosed within walls built in 1507. The Romans built a city here, of which only the ruins of their Teatro survive. The Goths, Byzantines and Lombards followed, but nothing remains of their occupancy. Today's small city, apart from a few churches, was built in the 15th and 16th centuries; since then time seems to have stood still. Urbino is unique in that, after a golden age that lasted little more than 150 years, it slipped off the map and was forgotten.

The good times started when the counts of nearby Montefeltro, a successful mercenary family, became dukes of Urbino. The second duke was Federigo di Montefeltro, the epitome of a Renaissance man—*condottiere* (mercenary), patron and humanist. His military skills brought in the cash as he fought for Florence, Naples and the Pope, and he used his wealth not only to create a far larger dukedom and beautiful city, but to attract the finest artists and scholars to what was one of Europe's most glittering courts. He commissioned Luciano Laurana to rebuild the Palazzo Ducale, employed 40 scribes for 14 years to fill his library, imported tapestry weavers from Flanders and hired Italy's finest painters to decorate his palace. His son married a Gonzaga heiress and carried on the tradition of a rich and cultured court, but in 1508 the Montefeltros ceded to the della Rovere family and by 1626 Urbino had become little more than a backwater of the Papal States.

PALAZZO DUCALE AND GALLERIA NAZIONALE DELLE MARCHE

The Palazzo Ducale (Piazza Duca Federico; Tue–Sun 8.30–7.15, Mon 8.30–2), by far the largest building in Urbino, was rebuilt by Federigo around an older building. The architect, Laurana, was given a more or less free hand and the result is a triumph: an impeccably balanced and rational building on a huge scale that nevertheless retains an atmosphere of intimacy. Its centre is a harmonious courtyard, the Cortile d'Onore, while the main facade overlooks the valley rather than the town, and is flanked by two slender towers. Inside, the proportions and architectural details of the inner courtyard are pure Renaissance—balanced and simple. A magnificent flight of shallow steps, the Scalone d'Onore, leads up to the *piano nobile* (state floor), a succession of beautiful, lofty rooms with marble detailing that now houses the Galleria Nazionale delle Marche.

This is the most important picture collection in the Marche, with works by many of Italy's big names. Most visitors come here to see two paintings by the enigmatic Tuscan Piero della Francesca, the *Flagellation* and the *Madonna di Senegallia*. The iconography of the *Flagellation* has been endlessly discussed by art historians, and this mysterious picture, with its three dominant foreground figures and background flagellation scene, all bathed in shafts of light, is now thought to be *The Dream of St. Jerome*. The Madonna is more straightforward, a statuesque representation of the Virgin and Child, set against a serene grey stone background and flanked by two angels. Elsewhere you'll find the *Città Ideale*, possibly attributed to Piero, and a perfect image of the Renaissance ideal of town architecture. The gallery also has pictures by Signorelli, Raphael *(The Mute)* and Titian *(The Last Supper)* and don't miss Federigo's *studiolo*, a beautiful little study panelled with marvellous inlaid wood carvings. The gallery also has a wonderful collection of majolica from all over Italy.

THE DUOMO

The Duomo (daily 7.30–1, 2–7) dates from the 15th century and was rebuilt by Giuseppe Valadier after it collapsed in an earthquake in 1789. The Museo Diocesano Gianfrancesco Albani (daily 9.30–1, 2.30–6.30), within the cathedral, contains 14th-century frescoes from a local church and paintings by Andrea da Bologna and Iacopo Barocci. The late 14th-century Oratorio di San Giovanni Battista is decorated with a dazzling fresco cycle by Lorenzo and Jacopo Salimbeni.

Opposite *The Palazzo Ducale houses the major museums and galleries of the town*

THE CASTELLI ROMANI HILLS

From the frenetic centre of Rome to the quiet Albani hills, this route takes you past secluded villas, bustling towns and the serene lakes of Albano and Nemi. Wealthy Romans have escaped to the cool hills and lakes for centuries, and they remain a popular weekend retreat.

THE DRIVE
Distance: 76km (47 miles)
Allow: 4 hours (or longer depending on traffic leaving Rome)
Start/end at: Rome

★ Leave Rome on the Via Appia Antica (▷ 98), the ancient road from the city lined with catacombs, where you will find the tomb of Romulus, legendary founder and first king of Rome. About 12km (7.5 miles) from the city centre you will pass the remains of an ancient Roman aqueduct on the right-hand side. After the turn for the airport (Ciampino), the road becomes the SS7. Continue along this road, following the signs for Albano/ Ciampino and you will soon see the town of Castel Gandolfo in the distance.

About 8km (5 miles) after the aqueduct take a left turn and join the SS140 for Castel Gandolfo, after which the route becomes quieter and rural. The road soon starts to climb and shortly you reach the outskirts of Castel Gandolfo (▷ 324).

❶ You won't be able to park in the heart of Castel Gandolfo, but it is worth the walk uphill into the middle to see the Church of San Tommaso di Villanova and the exterior of the Pope's summer residence, and to admire the views over Lago Albano (▷ 324).

Leave the town and continue along the Via Appia, following signs to Albano Laziale, home to a small museum and the tomb of the legendary warriors Horatius and Curiatii. You will also find the remains of a Roman amphitheatre (Anfiteatro Severiano), which once seated 10,000 spectators. From Albano Laziale it is about 2km (1.3 miles) to Ariccia, entered over a high bridge.

❷ Ariccia is a popular destination for Romans, who come here to enjoy alfresco pizza on summer evenings. The town also contains the Palazzo Chigi, in which there is a museum.

Leave Ariccia and follow the SS7. There are large villas on either side of the road and bushy umbrella pines that provide welcome shade in the summer months. After about 2km (1.3 miles) you reach the outskirts of Genzano di Roma, where you will see a large church on the left. Continue past a large sports stadium on the left, where the landscape has a more industrial appearance. Just outside Genzano, take a left turn for Nemi (it is easy to miss) onto Via Sardegna. At the next intersection, turn left in the direction of Nemi, and go right at the intersection, which brings you to Piazzale Cina. Follow the SP76D, and after 1km (0.6 mile) you will approach the outskirts of Nemi, with the lake of the same name down on the left.

❸ The ancient Romans were so inspired by the still azure waters of

Lago di Nemi that they named it Mirror of Diana and built a temple to the goddess on the lake's angled shores, surrounded by a sacred grove.

The road now winds uphill, and is lined with bars and restaurants. You will soon spot Nemi, which overlooks the lake, with its distinctive tower and narrow streets. If you want to explore further, park in the outskirts rather than in the crowded town. The centre is pedestrian only.

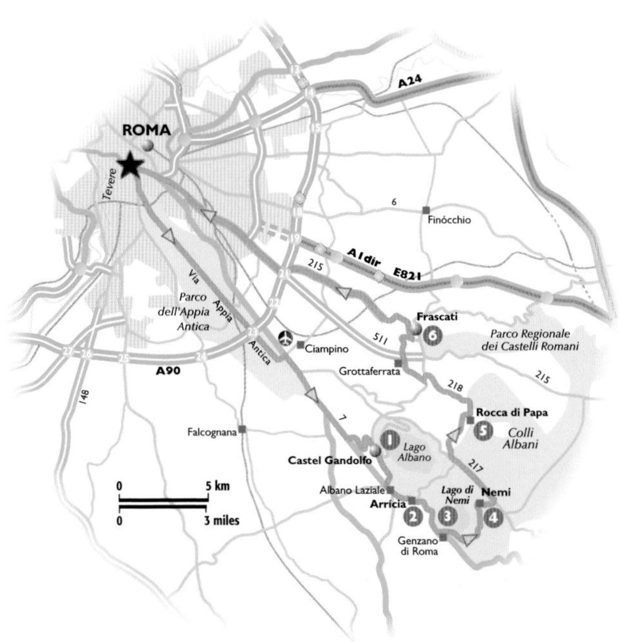

❹ Nemi became famous in 1930 when the remains of a Roman ship were discovered at the bottom of its lake. See them in the Museo delle Navi Romane. Staircases run up and down this village, which is famous for its miniature strawberries *(fragoline di Nemi),* grown along the lake's shores. The tiny fruit, soaked in lemon juice and topped with fresh cream, is a local treat in the bars lining the belvedere overlooking the water.

Leave Nemi, and about 1km (0.6 miles) from the middle of the town turn right. The road winds uphill and passes under a bridge. Follow the signs for Velletri/Roma. Shortly there is an intersection, where you turn left to join the SS217, a fairly busy, winding road. Turn right for Rocca di Papa, joining the SS218, which climbs uphill through rows of mature chestnut trees. After 2km (1.3 miles) you will reach Rocca di Papa, with broad views over Rome on the left. Continue and go left as the road forks and follow the SS218 into the heart of Rocca di Papa. Once again it is best to park in the outskirts if you want to explore the town.

❺ The narrow streets and houses of Rocca di Papa are built up around the hillside. The town's name comes from the days when it was the official papal residence (500 years before Castel Gandolfo). From here you can admire the 360-degree views of Rome, the battlefields where Hannibal met the Romans and, in the distance, the sea.

Now go downhill to leave the town, following the SS218 for about 4km (2.5 miles) to Grottaferrata, famous for its wine and 11th-century abbey. Leave Grottaferrata, following the SS218 until you reach Frascati (▷ 325).

❻ Frascati is the most famous of the Castelli towns, noted for its wine and sumptuous villas. The Villa Aldobrandini is occasionally open to the public and with a large cascade in its grounds is particularly impressive. After exploring the town, follow the signs back to Rome on the SS215.

WHERE TO EAT

Castel Gandolfo, Genzano and Frascati are full of restaurants and pizzerias. In Castel Gandolfo, Ristorante La Gardenia in Via Bruno Buozzi (tel 06 936 0001; closed Mon) and in Albano La Volpe e L'Uva on Via Collegio Nazareno (tel 06 9322251) are worth a try.

WHEN TO GO

Come in spring or autumn to avoid the summer crowds. This drive is popular with locals on weekends, however, at any time of year.

PLACES TO VISIT

MUSEO CIVICO

✉ Via Risorgimento 3, 00041 Albano Laziale ☎ 06 932 3490 🕒 Daily 9–12.30, Wed–Thu 9–12.30, 4–7.30 ✋ €3

PALAZZO CHIGI

✉ Piazza di Corte 14, 00034 Ariccia ☎ 06 933 0053 Tue–Fri 11, 4 and 5.30, Sat and Sun 10.30, 11.30, 12.30, 4, 5, 6, 7 ✋ €10

MUSEO DELLE NAVI ROMANE

✉ Via di Diana 13, 00175 Nemi ☎ 06 939 8040 🕒 Mon–Sat 9–7, Sun 9–1 ✋ Adult €3, child (under 18) free

VILLA ALDOBRANDINI

✉ Via Cardinal Massaia, Frascati, 00019 Tivoli ☎ 06 9420192 🕒 Villa: Mon–Fri 9–1, 3–6 (closes at 5 in winter). Gardens: Mon–Sat 9–1, 3–6 ✋ Free. Permits to visit villa available from visitor centre in Piazza G. Marconi in Frascati

Opposite *A view of Lake Albano from Castel Gandolfo*

THROUGH MONTEFELTRO FROM SAN LEO TO URBINO

This lovely drive winds through an undiscovered area of the Marche known as Montefeltro, with panoramic views all the way. En route, you'll cross over the slopes of Monte Carpegna, before dropping down to drive through fertile agricultural valleys to ancient Urbania—famous for its ceramics—before following a scenic route through the hills to historic Urbino, a perfect Renaissance city.

THE DRIVE
Distance: 65km (41.3 miles)
Allow: 4 hours with time for stops
Start at: San Leo
End at: Urbino

★ Start your drive in San Leo (▷ 328), one of the most dramatically sited towns in the Marche and well worth a visit before you start. Exit the town down the hill and through the tunnel that passes under the Rocca. At the junction turn right and take the road marked Villagrande. After 8.5km (5.3 miles) turn left and drive through the village of Villagrande and continue on the same road for 11km (6.8 miles) until you come to a junction of three roads. At this point follow the signs into the little hillside town of Carpegna.

❶ As you drive towards Carpegna, you'll cross the shoulder of Monte Carpegna (1,415m/4,500ft), a limestone massif with long grassy slopes and beautiful beech woods. In winter it's the base for the local ski industry, with people coming here from the coastal towns for weekend winter sports. Carpegna was the seat of the dukes of Carpegna, who ruled here from the Middle Ages until 1749, and whose descendants became the dukes of Montefeltro and, subsequently, Urbino. Their palace, built in 1675, stands in the centre of this quiet little town.

Leave Carpegna and backtrack to the main junction, then turn right and follow the winding road downhill; you'll be able to see Frontino on its outcrop ahead of you. After 5km (3 miles) turn off this road and follow the signs uphill to Frontino. Park outside the village and walk up the one main street to explore the village.

❷ Frontino is a medieval village in the heart of Montefeltro, the area ruled by the family that became the dukes of Urbino. Built in medieval times as a fortress and garrison town,

Frontino retains its encircling walls, gates and ancient fortress of the Rocca di Malatesta, now a hotel and restaurant. This tiny and untouched settlement is a lovely place to wander, with splendid views back towards Monte Carpegna. You might like to pop into the 15th-century Palazzo Vandini, where travellers from many countries study Italian and attend courses on cooking, painting and ceramics, and explore the surrounding countryside on foot. Visitors are welcome and there's plenty of information about what's on offer.

Go back down the hill and turn right at the bottom, following the signs down the valley to Lunano. After 6.7km (4.2 miles) you'll come to a road junction. Turn left, then right after 200m (220 yards), just before the village, and cross the River Foglia. Continue on this road through the widening valley for another 10km (6 miles) to the village of Peglio, which lies off the main road. Bypass Peglio and continue for 5km (3 miles) to the old town of Urbania, set in fertile agricultural land.

❸ Urbania, surrounded by tobacco fields and laid out on a grid pattern with long straight streets dividing its four quarters, stands in the Metauro valley. It was founded in the Middle Ages and named Casteldurante after its founder, Guglielmo Durante, who built a castle here. Its name was changed in 1636 when it passed from the possession of Urbino to the hands of the Pope Urban VIII, who declared it a city. Since early times, it has been famed for its majolica ceramics industry; many of the world's finest museums have pieces made here, and there are still pottery workshops in the town. You can also see examples of the ceramics in the town's Museo Civico (Mon–Sat 10–12.30, 3–6), housed in the Palazzo Ducale, a huge palace built for the Brancaleone family between the 15th and 16th centuries. Many visitors are fascinated by the mummies and skulls displayed in the Chiesa dei Morto—the Church of the Dead (closed Mon).

Leave Urbania by turning left out of town to take the minor road across country towards Urbino. Ignore the signs to the E78, the fast main road. This lovely route winds along the hillsides, passing through the little villages of San Giovanni in Pozzuolo and San Cipriano. At the junction (16 km/9.9 miles) turn left and follow this wider road towards Urbino. After a kilometre (0.6 mile) or so you'll be able to see the town rising ahead of you (▷ 332–333).

WHEN TO GO

Leave San Leo mid-morning to see the landscape at its best—the spring and autumn months are the ideal time for this drive.

WHERE TO EAT

Have lunch at the Rocca dei Malatesta (Via Giovanni XXIII, 1, tel 0722 71121) in Frontino, a friendly little restaurant-hotel, housed in an old keep with a pretty terrace, which specializes in dishes particular to the Montefeltro area.

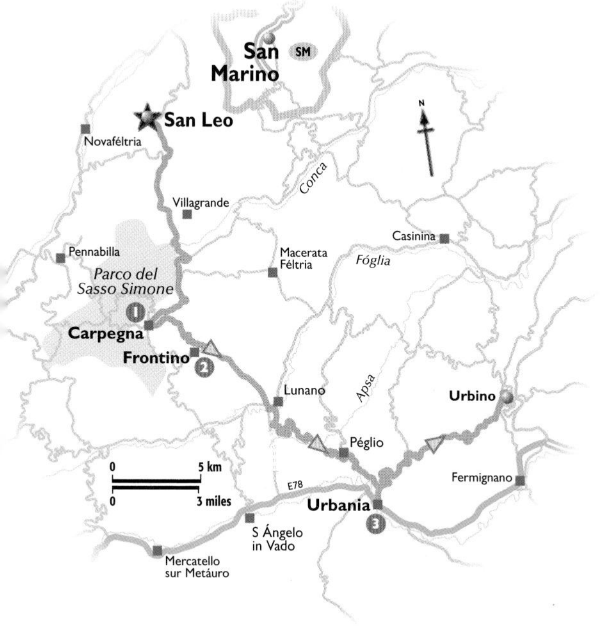

Opposite *Mountains in the Parco del Sasso Simone in the Montefeltro region*

Above *Listen to jazz in Ascoli Piceno*

ASCOLI PICENO

COTTON JAZZ CLUB

www.cottonjazzclub.it

With so many good jazz festivals in the vicinity (Ancona, Urbino, Umbria), it's no surprise that a jazz scene has evolved in Ascoli Piceno. Big-name performers drop by to jam in informal surroundings.

✉ Largo Cattaneo 4, 63100 Ascoli Piceno
☎ 348 605 6390 or 0861 80401
🕐 Tue–Sun 8pm–1.30am

FIERA DELL'ANTIQUARIATO

Every Italian town has its flea market, but few could be described as antiques fairs. However, at Ascoli Piceno's monthly antiques market—against the backdrop of the Chiesa di San Francesco—you can find real treasures. Look out for the glazed ceramics.

✉ Via del Trivio, 63100 Ascoli Piceno
🕐 9–dusk, third weekend of every month

LAUDI SAVINA CERAMICS

In past times Ascoli Piceno's local economy was fuelled by its ceramics industry. Take a walk up Via del Trivio to the oldest and prettiest district of the town and see today's artisans working in dim studios. One of the most talented is Laudi Savina, whose floral and geometric designs are reminiscent of Renaissance pieces.

✉ Via Pisa 4, 63100 Ascoli Piceno
☎ 0736 44024 🕐 Mon–Sat 9–1, 3–8

TEATRO VENTIDIO BASSO

www.teatroventidiobasso.it

Named after a local military hero, this mighty 1846 opera house has wedding-cake layers of balconies and a neoclassical facade. The playbill is eclectic, from Puccini to *The Full Monty*.

✉ Via del Teatro 4, 63100 Ascoli Piceno
☎ 0736 24459. Box office: Palazzo dei Capitani, Piazza del Popolo 0736 244970
🕐 Thu–Sat 8.30, Sun 5.30, 8.30. Box office daily 9–1, 3–8.30 ✋ €10–€25

FRASCATI

ENOTECA SAN MARCO

The bottles of wine are stacked right up to the ceiling in this wine shop, but the friendly assistants will help you choose the right one. There is an ample list of wines from Italy and abroad, including the celebrated local Frascati. Vintage and dated wines are available for the more demanding buyer, plus grappa, champagne and calvados.

✉ Piazza San Pietro 8, 00044 Frascati
☎ 06 941 9519 🕐 Mon–Thu 10–1, 4.30–8, Fri–Sun 9.30–1, 4.30–8

GABICCE MARE

BAIA IMPERIALE

www.baiaimperiale.net

Must be seen to be believed. Baia Imperiale claims to be the biggest nightclub in the world—and the most photographed. Imperial Roman decor, complete with a column-lined amphitheatre and Caesar statues for theme park appeal. Dance to the live bands, DJs and Latin grooves by the outdoor pool.

✉ Via Panoramica, 61011 Gabicce Mare
☎ 0541 950312, 0541 952135 🕐 Mid-Jun to Aug daily 9pm–3.30am ✋ €20 🚌 Bus info line 335 324535 🚗 From Urbino, drive 15km (9 miles) to the Adriatic coast at Gabicce Mare, near Pesaro. Via Panoramica is the coastal road. Look for signs before the town

GUIDONIA MONTECELIO

AQUAPIPER

www.aquapiper.it

This is an aquatic theme park with children's pools, water slides, wave machines and a hydro-massage lagoon—perfect for hot summer days. There is an ice-cream kiosk, a fast-food restaurant and a picnic area.

✉ Via Maremmana Inferiore Km 29.300, 00012 Guidonia Montecelio ☎ 0774 3265 38 ⏲ Mid-Jun to mid-Sep daily 9–7 Adult €16, child €10 Mon–Sat; adult €20, child €15 Sat–Sun; one child free when accompanied by an adult

URBINO

CAPPELLA MUSICALE DEL SS SACRAMENTO

Music students and visiting ensembles perform at this frescoed music venue (in the Sala Vecchiotti), which has existed for centuries. The classical performances include everything from string quartets to church choirs.

✉ Via Valerio 7, 61029 Urbino ☎ 0722 4120 ⏲ Sat–Sun 9pm (usually) Free

MERCATO SETTIMANALE DI URBINO

Arrive early Sunday morning for the best finds at this market, including World War I helmets, 1950s chrome lamps and 16th-century dressers.

✉ Viale B. Buozzi, 61029 Urbino ☎ 0722 2631 (tourist office) ⏲ Sun 7–12.30

SALA MANISCALCO, RAMPA DI GIORGIO MARTINI

Next to the Teatro Sanzio is a curious music and theatre venue built inside what looks like a giant staircase. Events include everything from jazz to experimental theatre.

✉ Corso Garibaldi, 61029 Urbino ☎ 0722 2613 ⏲ 8.30pm (usually) From €12

TEATRO SANZIO

When this theatre was built in 1845, local citizens thought it an eyesore that clashed with Urbino's Renaissance harmony. Today the Sanzio is considered one of the city's most important architectural sights and music venues.

✉ Via Matteotti, 61029 Urbino ☎ 0722 2281 ⏲ Thu–Sun 8.30. Box office daily 9–1, 3–8.30 €10–€70

VITERBO

LAGO DI BOLSENA

www.lagodibolsena.org

www.volere-velare.com

Europe's largest volcanic lake (▷ 325) has clear and limpid waters on which to enjoy sailing, canoeing or windsurfing. Boats can be hired from the Bolsena tourist office in Piazza Matteotti or Volere Velare sailing club.

✉ Volere Velare sailing club, Piazzale Dante Alighieri, 01023 Bolsena, Viterbo ☎ 328 872 1863 Boat excursions from €8 for 1 hour

PARCO DEI MOSTRI

www.parcodeimostri.com

This fantasy Renaissance theme park 21km (13 miles) northeast of Viterbo is full of monsters *(mostri)*—grotesque stone creatures, gruesome beasts and scary sculptures, created by the hunchbacked Duke of Orsini in 1552 in his Sacro Bosco (sacred wood). Now restored, it is one of Lazio's top tourist attractions—especially popular with children, who delight in clambering over the dragons, bloodthirsty stone ogres, animals with three heads, giant warriors and many other examples of 16th-century Mannerism.

✉ Località Giardino, 01020 Bomarzo, Viterbo ☎ 0761 924029 ⏲ Daily 8am–sunset Adult €9, child (4–8) €7 🚍 From Viterbo to Bomaro

TERME DEI PAPI

www.termedeipapi.it

Beautiful grounds and a sumptuous wooden-decked swimming pool greet visitors to the Terme dei Papi in northern Lazio, 75km (47 miles) north of Rome. Mud baths, herbal inhalations, facials and organic treatments are all available.

✉ 12 Strada Bagni, 01100 Viterbo ☎ 0761 3501 ⏲ Wed–Fri, Sun–Mon 9–7, Sat 9.30am–1am €35 spring mud treatment with hydro massage 🚍 Coach from Piazza Mancini in Rome daily at 8.30am, return at 1.15 🚗 Spa is 5km (3 miles) outside town

FESTIVALS AND EVENTS

JUNE–SEPTEMBER

FRASCATI SUMMER FESTIVALS

Throughout the summer, festivals are organized in Frascati's parks and villas, with open-air shows, dance, cinema, fireworks and night markets.

✉ Villa Torlonia, Frascati ☎ 06 941 7195 (Frascati Cultural Office)

AUGUST

INCHINATA

In this religious festival celebrating the Assumption of the Virgin, images of Christ and his mother bow *(inchinare)* to each other in Tivoli's Piazza Trento at the end of the procession. Live music and fireworks follow.

✉ Piazza Trento and nearby streets, Tivoli ☎ 0774 311249, 0774 319051 ⏲ 14–15 August

TORNEO DELLA QUINTANA

One of the Marche's loveliest towns, Ascoli Piceno is the setting for this summer festival of parades and jousting. More than 1,200 people participate in the processions, with bands, drums and flag-waving. It's a totally authentic and passionate spectacle.

✉ Ascoli Piceno ⏲ 1st weekend in August

OCTOBER

SAGRA DELL'UVA

This famous festival celebrates the new wine vintage with a parade in the afternoon. Later, the main fountain, Fontana dei Quattro Mori, bubbles and overflows with wine.

✉ Piazza dei Quattro Mori, 00047 Marino ☎ 06 938 5555 ⏲ 1st Sunday in October 🚗 From Frascati take SS216 following signs for Marino

PRICES AND SYMBOLS

The restaurants are listed alphabetically within each town. The prices given are the average for a two-course lunch (L) and a three-course dinner (D) for one person, without drinks. The wine price given is for the least expensive bottle.

For the key to symbols, ⊳ 2.

ALBANO

LA VOLPE E L'UVA

Beside Albano's duomo, this restaurant-wine bar is a harmonious blend of good food, wine and art. The fixed menu changes weekly, with dishes paired with their complementary wines. This is the best place in the Castelli Romani for food and wine. Reservations are essential. Credit cards are not accepted.

✉ Via Collegio Nazzareno 14, 00042 Albano ☎ 06 932 2251 🕒 Sep–end Jun Tue–Sat 7–11.30 ✋ D €35 including wine, Wine €6

ASCOLI PICENO

GALLO D'ORO

First courses here include fried calamari, while main courses are topped with truffles or wild porcini mushrooms. The house special is *fritto misto* with fried olives, lamb cutlet, veal brain and courgettes (zucchini). A tourist menu is available for €20.

✉ Corso Vittorio Emanuele 54, 63100 Ascoli Piceno ☎ 0736 253520 🕒 Mon–Fri 12–4, 7.30pm–12.30am, Sat 7.30pm–12.30am; closed 31 Dec–4 Jan, 15–20 Aug ✋ L €27, D €35, Wine €10 ❄

GASTRONOMIA ENOTECA MIGLIORI

Ascoli Piceno's most famous foodstuff is *olive ascolane* (meat-stuffed fried olives), and nobody makes them better than the Enoteca Migliori. This is a great place for cocktails or afternoon snacking, and it has a vast wine selection.

✉ Piazza Arringo 2, 63100 Ascoli Piceno ☎ 0736 250042 🕒 Tue–Sat 9–9, Sun 9–3 ✋ L €15, Wine €6 ❄

CASTEL GANDOLFO

ANTICO RISTORANTE PAGNANELLI

www.pagnanelli.it

This elegant restaurant is gloriously situated perched over the lake. The food is typical *cucina romana* (Roman cuisine), and many of the ingredients are sourced from the family farm. There is a labyrinthine wine cellar with plenty of tasting possibilities.

✉ Via Gramsci 4, 00040 Castel Gandolfo ☎ 06 936 0004 🕒 Wed–Mon 12–2.30, 7.30–10; also Tue May–Oct ✋ L €35, D €50, Wine €10 🚌 From Rimini 🚆 From Rome to Castel Gandolfo

FRASCATI

CACCIANI

www.cacciani.it

You can see all the way back to Rome from the lovely terrace of this centrally situated and elegant restaurant—wonderful on a summer evening. The cooking is traditional but executed with a light touch, herbs and spices are discreetly used to great advantage—try the *pappardelle in bianco ed erbe di caccia* (ribbon pasta with white wine and wild herbs). The restaurant has a terrific wine list and serves locally produced oil and house wine.

✉ Via A. Diaz 13–15, 00044 Frascati ☎ 06 940 1991 🕒 Tue–Sat 12.30–2.30, 7.30–10; also Sun evening Jun–Sep; closed 7–14 Jan, 16–23 Aug ✋ L €38, D €52, Wine €12 ❄ Ⓜ From Rome, Metro A: Anagnina, then bus to Frascati 🚆 From Roma Termini station to Frascati

OSTERIA ZARAZÀ

This simple and well-run family restaurant has spectacular views from the terrace, where you can dine in summer. The cooking is authentic Lazio regional, using regional

produce, all served up in extremely generous portions.
Via Regina Margherita 45, 00044 Frascati 06 942 2053 Tue–Sat 12–2.30, 7–11, Sun 12–2.30; also Sun evening Jun–Sep L €25, D €33, Wine €8 From Roma Termini station to Frascati

PESARO

DA ALCEO

www.ristorantealceo.it

Among Le Marche's best dining experiences, this Michelin-starred restaurant enjoys splendid views over the sea at Pesaro. Alceo's wife, Grazia Ravagnan, is the award-winning chef and specializes in creative dishes using fine fresh fish and seafood, sourced daily from the splendid Ancona fish market, Signature dishes include *gran piatto di crudità di pesce, crostacei ed ostriche* (catch of the day with seafood and plump oysters), turbot, sumptuous fish soups and many other delicacies. Alceo's service is impeccable. In summer you can dine on the panoramic terrace. Reservations advised.
Strada Panoramica Ardizio 119/121, 61100 Pesaro 0721 51360 Tue–Sun 12.30–2.30, 7.30–10.30; closed Sun dinner mid-Sep to May, Sun lunch Jun to mid-Sep L €40, D €90, Wine €16 Pesaro

SAN LEO

CASTELLO

www.hotelristorantecastellosanleo.com

This is the town's best hotel and restaurant. Genuine local dishes are served in the dining room.
Piazza Dante Alighieri 11, San Leo, 61018 Pesaro e Urbino 0541 916214 Fri–Wed 12–2.30, 7.30–10; closed Oct–Mar L €19, D €24, Wine €8 From Rimini From Rimini take the SS258 west and turn left at Pietrocuta for San Leo

TIVOLI

ADRIANO

www.hoteladriano.it

Set in a very attractive terracotta-coloured villa among cypresses, next to the entrance to the Villa Adriana, this elegant restaurant has welcomed a long roll-call of celebrity visitors over the years, from Jackie Kennedy to Queen Elizabeth II. Homemade bread and pasta feature alongside well-prepared local and national dishes, and all the tempting desserts are freshly made. Smaller appetites are also catered to with light snacks.
Largo M. Yourcenar 2, 00010 Tivoli 0774 382235 Mon–Sat 12–2.30, 7.30–10, Sun 12–2.30 L €25, D €55, Wine €9

RISTORANTE ANTICHE TERME DI DIANA

www.termedidiana.it

The choice is vast and appetizing at this underground restaurant, but don't miss the fresh egg pasta. There is also a lovely garden for summer dining.
Via dei Sosii 6, 00019 Tivoli 0774 335239 Daily 12.30–2.30, 7.30–10 L €20, D €38, Wine €7 33km (21 miles) from Rome. Follow the Via Tiburtina or the Gran Raccordo Anulare (GRA). Turn off at Tivoli Città and follow signs for Villa d'Este; from the A24 (Rome/L'Aquila) take the exit for Tivoli (3km/2miles)

RISTORANTE SIBILLA

www.ristorantesibilla.com

This elegant 18th-century restaurant serves typical Roman cuisine, homemade pasta and succulent grilled meat. Reservations are recommended at weekends.
Via della Sibilla 50, 00019 Tivoli 0774 335281 Tue–Sun 12.30–3, 7–10.30; also Mon May–Sep L €25, D €40, Wine €8 33km (21 miles) from Rome. From the A24 (Rome/L'Aquila) take the exit for Tivoli (3km/2 miles)

URBINO

L'ANGOLO DIVINO

This *enoteca/osteria* is a paradise for wine- and truffle-lovers, in an atmospheric subterranean setting adorned with wine bottles. Casciotta d'Urbino cheese and spicy salami will whet your appetite, and the lamb in a balsamic vinegar and truffle sauce will satisfy. All meals are served with plenty of Urbino's famous white and black truffles.
Via Sant'Andrea 14, 61029 Urbino 0722 327559 Tue–Sat 12–4, 7–12; also Sun 11.30–4 Jun to mid-Dec L €28, D €50, Wine €8 From Pesaro and Rome Pesaro then frequent local bus service

Opposite *Truffles are popular in Urbino*

TAVERNA LA VECCHIA FORNARINA

This is the place to go to find rustic charm, a local clientele and hearty food smothered in decadent sauces. Two popular dishes are the pasta with a meat sauce and stewed rabbit. Credit cards are not accepted.
Via Mazzini 14, 61029 Urbino 0722 320007 Wed–Mon 12–2.30, 7–10.30 L €20, D €33, Wine €8

LA VECCHIA URBINO

www.vecchiaurbino.it

This is a gastronomic wonderland, and one of the most famous restaurants in the Marche. Dishes to look out for include *delizia del Montefeltro* (ravioli with white truffles). There is a sommelier on call and an encyclopaedic wine list.
Via dei Vasari 3/5, 61029 Urbino 0722 4447 Wed–Mon 12–4, 7–11 L €35, D €54, Wine €15 To Porta Lavagine

VITERBO

RISTORANTE ENOTECA LA TORRE

www.enotecalatorrevt.com

Set in the medieval walled area of Viterbo in the former stables of the 16th-century Palazzo dei Mercanti, this elegant restaurant is suffused with bright colours. Japanese excellence and regional Italian tastes are deliciously and creatively combined under the expertise of chef Noda Kodaro and sommelier Luigi Picca. The very good wine list features more than 1,000 labels, including Italian and international wines with ample opportunity for tastings by the glass. A *menu degustazione* is offered, either meat- or fish-based, from €50; or allow the chef to surprise you.
Via della Torre 5, 01100 Viterbo 0761 226467 Thu–Mon lunch and dinner, Wed dinner L €45, D €62, Wine €12 Viterbo

PRICES AND SYMBOLS

Prices are the lowest and highest for a double room for one night, unless otherwise stated. Breakfast is included, and all the hotels listed accept credit cards unless otherwise stated. Note that rates vary widely throughout the year.

For the key to symbols ▷ 2.

ASCOLI PICENO

AGRITURISMO VILLA CICCHI

www.villacicchi.it

Set 3km (1.2 miles) southwest of Ascoli Piceno in a peaceful, secluded spot, this fine rustic property has been lovingly restored and offers excellent accommodation and food. Each room is tastefully decorated with antique beds and dressers and frescoed ceilings, and there is a good-size swimming pool. Meals are prepared using the owners' fresh produce, olive oil and wine from their farm, and you can even sign up for a cookery course.

Via Salara Superiore, Abbazia di Rosara, Ascoli Piceno 0736 252272 Closed 15 Nov–2 Dec, 10 Jan–10 Feb €80–€300 6 Head south out of Ascoli Piceno onto the SS14 heading west, then take the turn-off for Rosara; after 100m take the right turn for Rosara; Villa Cicchi is about 1km (0.6 miles) down the road on your right

GIOLI

www.hotelgioli.it

This is one of Ascoli Piceno's most highly recommended hotels, although it loses points for sketchy service. It is just steps away from the busy Piazza Arringo and the tower-lined Piazza del Popolo. It even has a small garden, which adds a refreshing touch of green. The interior is light and modern but comforting and classy, with fresh cut flowers and newly plumped pillows. There is 24-hour room service and parking is available.

Viale A. de Gasperi 14, 63100 Ascoli Piceno 0736 255550 €119 56 2, 3 Ascoli Piceno; train to San Benedetto del Tronto and change for Ascoli Piceno From the A14 take the San Benedetto del Tronto exit and follow signs to Ascoli Piceno and then to the *centro storico;* from Rome take Via Salaria

PALAZZO GUIDEROCCHI

www.palazzoguiderocchi.com

This beautiful, fully renovated 16th-century palazzo, once the home of a local tyrant, is grand and stylish and has a very pleasant internal courtyard. The rooms are opulently decorated with frescoes and some have original features. Some rooms have wood-beamed ceilings while others have lofty barrel vaults. Local cuisine is served in the restaurant in the cross-vaulted rooms on the ground floor.

Via Cesrae Battisti 3, 63100 Ascoli Piceno 0736 244011 €70–€200 37 Ascoli Piceno; train to San Benedetto del Tronto and change for Ascoli Piceno

FRASCATI

BELLAVISTA

www.hbellavista.it

In historical Palazzo Senni, this hotel looks out over Frascati's main square. The rooms are comfortable and simply furnished, designed to make the best of the original architecture. They each have television and telephone and a small bathroom with a shower. There is private parking in the courtyard and a reading room.

Piazza Roma 2, 00044 Frascati 06 942 1068 €95–€120 12 5 rooms From Rome take Metro A: Anagnina, then bus Blue bus from Rome to Frascati Train from Roma Termini station to Frascati

FLORA

www.hotel-flora.it

The rooms in this art nouveau hotel are refined and spacious. Some have a terrace with excellent views.

There is a veranda, terrace and roof garden. Airport transfers are available on request.
Viale Vittorio Veneto 8, 00044 Frascati
06 941 6110 €120–€170 37
From Rome take Metro A: Anagnina, then bus Blue bus from Rome to Frascati
Train from Roma Termini station to Frascati

MACERATA

VILLA SIBILLINI

www.villasibillini.com
A country house hotel offering bed and breakfast, Villa Sibillini overlooks the Sibillini mountains. Guest rooms are spacious with good views. There is a full restaurant service. The medieval hilltop town of San Ginesio nearby is a delight to explore.
Contrada Collalto 10, 62026 San Ginesio, Macerata 0733 653081, 338 701 3337
€100 bed and breakfast, or villa rental with staff €4,000–€6,000 per week 5
Outdoor From Ancona take the A14 motorway and exit for Macerata Ancona, Pescara

OSTIA

ARAN BLU HOTEL

www.aranhotels.com
Overlooking the sea at Lido di Ostia, this four-star designer hotel's rooms all have private balconies. Furnishings are sleek and contemporary, blending glass and steel with modern works of art and some interesting sculptures. Rooms are spacious and airy, aided by the use of many mirrors—to decorative and sometimes interesting effect. The treasures of Ostia Antica are about 15 minutes' drive away.
Lungomare Duca degli Abruzzi 72, 00121 Lido di Ostia 06 5634 0225
€130–€180 68 Train to Lido di Ostia station

SAN LEO

CASTELLO

www.hotelristorantecastellosanleo.com
This 16th-century palazzo is the town's only hotel and its best restaurant. The simple and spotless bedrooms are peaceful.
Piazza Dante Alighieri 11, San Leo, 61018 Pesaro e Urbino 0541 916214 Closed 2 weeks in Nov and Jan €55–€76 14
From Rimini From Rimini take the SS258 west and turn left at Pietrocuta for San Leo

SPERLONGA

MAYOR

The essence of the Italian seaside hotel, the Mayor has airy, good-size rooms, some of which have balconies. Set a couple of blocks back from the sea, with access to its own private beach area, the hotel rooms all have internet access; there's a good bar and breakfast room; and a solarium and a cool green outside space to relax. It's excellent value and a real taste of summertime Italy.
Via Romita 4, 04029 Sperlonga 0771 549245 €70–€180 room only, €120–€200 half-board (minimum 3 nights) 20
Fondi Sperlonga on Roma–Napoli line Exit A1 autostrada at Ceprano and take N82 to Sperlonga, then follow signs to hotel

TIVOLI

LA PANORAMICA

Rooms in this 19th-century bed and breakfast establishment, close to the Villa d'Este (▷ 331), are all comfortable, with private bathroom and television. Double rooms with extra bunk-beds are available for families. The terrace has a splendid view of Rome.
Viale Arnaldi 45, 00019 Tivoli
0774 335700 €65–€80 10
Ponte Mammolo or Rebibbia, then bus to Tivoli 33km (21 miles) from Rome. From the A24 (Rome/L'Aquila) take the exit for Tivoli (3km/2 miles)

SIRENE

In this 19th-century villa the rooms are spacious and gracefully decorated. All have private bath and some have a private terrace. There is a restaurant and café with a terrace with panoramic views.
Piazza Massimo 4, 00019 Tivoli
0774 330605 €160–€200 40
Ponte Mammolo or Rebibbia, then bus 33km (21 miles) from Rome. Follow the Via Tiburtina or the Gran Raccordo Anulare (GRA). Turn off at Tivoli Città and follow signs for Villa d'Este; from the A24 (Rome/L'Aquila) take the exit for Tivoli (3km/2 miles)

Opposite *A sign pointing the way to a hotel*

URBINO

BONCONTE

www.viphotels.it
The Bonconte is Urbino's most luxurious hotel. It is embedded in the thick southern walls of the city, with cityscapes to the north, and cypress-lined hills to the south. The restaurant serves good local cuisine.
Via della Mura 28, 61029 Urbino
0722 2463 €86–€190 23
Exit A14 at Pesaro/Urbino and then follow signs to *centro storico*. From here follow signs for hotel

RAFFAELLO

www.albergoraffaello.com
This hotel is in a 14th-century palace on a hill in the old town. The top-floor rooms look out over San Francesco's bell tower and the Palazzo Ducale. The decor is rather dated but most of the bedrooms are a good size.
Via Santa Margherita 40, 61029 Urbino
0722 4896 €115–€120 14
Exit A14 at Pesaro/Urbino and then follow signs to the *centro storico*. From here follow signs for hotel

VITERBO

RELAIS IL MERLANO

www.tenutadiferento.com
Standing in a private country estate dating back to the 1600s, the Merlano is surrounded by ancient olive trees and flower-filled gardens. The rooms are elegantly designed, with antique furnishings, many of which are Parisian. Four-poster beds, statues, antique furniture and mirrors are the opulent trademarks of this very stylish 'country chic' residence, which also has every 21st-century comfort. Cookery courses are also on offer, using the estate's own produce, including Merlano DOP extra virgin olive oil.
Strada Sammartinese 10, 01100 Viterbo
0761 228082 €180–€300 5
Ascoli Piceno, then transfer by private car with driver

THE SOUTH

Italy's deep south, sun-baked, vibrant and economically years behind the north, stretches from the southern border of Lazio down to Reggio di Calabria, perched on the toe of the peninsula, and across dramatic mountains to Puglia, with undiscovered towns and rich olive- and wine-producing farmland. It is a region of both majestic and barren beauty, rich and yet achingly poor, where the exuberance of the people often seems at odds with the poverty and torpor found in some of its towns and villages. The landscape, too, is incredibly diverse, ranging from the high peaks of the Gran Sasso and the Abruzzo to arid plains and some of the most beautiful coastlines in the Mediterranean.

Chaotic, noisy Naples, a treasure house of art, is the big city, but equally dynamic are the little-known cities of Bari, home to St. Nicholas, and Lecce, famed for its golden baroque architecture. There are treasures from ancient times in the shape of some of Italy's most compelling archaeological sites. Pompeii, in the shadow of volcanic Vesuvius, tops the bill, but Paestum, with its Greek temples, and the Greek cities of Calabria and Matera with its cave dwellings, are equally fascinating. The coastline is superb; on the west lie Sorrento, the island of Capri and the impossibly idyllic villages of the Amalfi Coast, while the Puglian coast has the lovely Gargano promontory and unspoilt fishing villages such as Gallipoli. There are wonderful places to explore—Alberobello, with its unique beehive-shaped houses, the *trulli*, and the mysterious Castel del Monte, a vast castle perched in solitary splendour. The inland mountains are among the most dramatic in Italy, with peaks soaring above woods and fields rich in a huge variety of flowers, birds and animals—great walking country. Southern Italians add to the pleasures—warm, excitable and welcoming, they add a new dimension to travelling here, as do the simple, super-fresh food and intensely flavoured wines and oils.

ALBEROBELLO

www.alberobellonline.it
www.prolocoalberobello.it
Trulli are unusual whitewashed limestone houses of a style that may date back to prehistoric times. They have a few tiny windows and cone-shaped roofs formed from spirals of grey limestone slabs. With more than 1,000 of them, Alberobello is the *trullo* capital and looks quite unlike any other town. Built mainly in the 18th century, this unique community is a UNESCO World Heritage Site. Enjoy the other-worldly atmosphere of the streets—ignoring the souvenir shops. Some of these bizarre dwellings have been converted into art galleries, craft shops and cafés with rooftop panoramas. The oldest *trulli* are in the Aia Piccola area, north of Via Indipendenza. Other highlights include Trullo Sovrano, a rare two-storey *trullo* built in the 18th century and now a museum-house (summer daily 10–8; winter daily 10–5), and Rione Monti, where hundreds of *trulli* are home to the best of the galleries and craft shops. Visit too the *trullo*-style parish church, Chiesa di Sant'Antonio (1926).
471 N12 Trullo Sovrano, Piazza Sacramento 10, 70011 Alberobello 080 432 6030 Alberobello

L'AQUILA

www.turismoaq.com
The capital of the sparsely populated region of Abruzzo is L'Aquila (the eagle), gazing out from its eyrie onto the spectacular Gran Sasso massif. It suffered a catastrophic earthquake in April 2009, measuring 6.3 on the Richter Scale, which killed 295 people, drove 50,000 from their homes and destroyed many buildings. However, reconstruction of the historic centre is underway and there is much to appreciate in this cultured town. The 15th-century moated fortress that dominates the old town houses the Museo Nazionale d'Abruzzo (Tue–Sun 9–8). Icons, sculptures and artworks from the 16th to 18th centuries are displayed, along with archaeological finds.

Walk along the steep cobbled path into Piazza San Vito to the extraordinary Fontana delle 99 Cannelle, a fountain with 99 gargoyle heads.
469 H9 Via XX Settembre 8, 67100 L'Aquila 0862 22306, fax 0862 27486 L'Aquila

BARI

www.pugliaturismo.com/aptbari
Puglia's rival to Naples is the biggest town on the long heel of Italy's boot, and most visitors use it as a ferry port for Greece, Croatia and Turkey, or as a gateway to the southeast coast. The modern city is brash and smart, but the old town is a delightfully confusing warren of narrow streets, courtyards and archways—deliberately designed to confuse invading pirates and armies. Fine Romanesque churches can be found before emerging in front of the reassuring fortifications of the massive *castello* (castle). The Basilica di San Nicola (daily 7–1, 4–7) is a beautiful example of 11th-century Romanesque architecture, with relics of the original Santa Claus, Bishop Nicholas. The modern town, south of Corso Vittorio Emanuele II, has luxury boutiques that rival any in Milan, Florence or Rome.
471 N11 Piazza Aldo Moro 33a, 70122 Bari 080 524 2361 Bari

CAPRI

▷ 348.

CASERTA

www.reggiadicaserta,beniculturali.it
The magnificent Reggia di Caserta, to the northeast of Naples, is a compulsory stop for lovers of formal gardens and royal palaces. It is Italy's largest royal palace and a UNESCO World Heritage Site. Built at the foot of Mount Tifitani, this impressive white palace was commissioned by the Bourbon King Carlos VII in 1752, and took almost 100 years to complete. There are 1,000 elaborately decorated rooms in the royal apartments, but they are now almost empty. It is the external grandeur that is so striking, and the extensive gardens, both formal Italian and English in style, are on a par with those of Versailles in France. A cascading waterfall flows through one part of the gardens, flanked by manicured lawns and trees. Discover other water features in the 18th-century English garden, a paradise in spring and early summer; guided tours available.
469 J11 Via Douhet 22, Falciano, 81100 Caserta 082 344 8084 Wed–Mon 8.30–7.30 Royal apartments €7; park and English garden €3

CASTEL DEL MONTE

www.proloco.andria.ba.it
Of Holy Roman Emperor Frederick II's many south Italian fortresses, Castel del Monte is by far the most impressive and handsome. Cresting a peak with views of the low hills of the surrounding Murge, 18km (11 miles) south of Andria, this octagonal, crown-like fortress has an austere Gothic exterior. A slim octagonal tower stands at each of the eight corners, and the eight rooms on each of the castle's two floors are set around an octagonal courtyard. Frederick's refined tastes are reflected in the finely sculpted columns and arches of pink, green and white cipollin marble—inspiration for the monks' monumental library in the 1986 film *The Name of the Rose*, based on Umberto Eco's book.
470 M11 Via Vespucci 114, 70031 Andria 0883 569997 Mar–end Sep daily 10–7.45; rest of year daily 9–6.45 Adult €3, under 18s free

Opposite and below *Reggia di Caserta*

INFORMATION

www.capritourism.com
www.capri.net
469 J12 Piazza Umberto 1, 80070 Capri 081 8370686 Easter–end Oct daily 8.30–8.30; Nov–through Easter daily 9–1, 3.30–6.30 Via G. Orlando 59, 80071 Anacapri 081 8371524 Mon–Sat 9–3 Regular ferry or hydrofoil services from Sorrento and Naples on the mainland

Above *The Faraglioni rocks characterize Capri's coastline*

CAPRI

Capri is at the mouth of the Gulf of Naples, with the Faraglioni, two great jagged rocks, rising sentry-like off its coast. Capri town's heart is the Piazzetta, where the baroque cathedral watches over the café scene. An impressive list of royals, stars, politicians and other VIPs, including Graham Greene and D. H. Lawrence, have lost their hearts to Capri, either acquiring homes here or anchoring their yachts in the bay.

Caesar Augustus fell under Capri's spell in about 29BC, when he traded the bigger and richer island of Ischia to Naples in exchange for Capri. The Villa Jovis, built for Emperor Tiberius in AD1, is an imposing example of the Roman love affair with the island. Tiberius moved his court here and lived on the island until his death in AD37. A 45-minute walk from Capri town, the villa overlooks the Gulf of Naples. Stand and admire the views on the spot where unfortunate enemies of the emperor were flung to their death.

MONTE SOLARO

Mount Solaro, the highest peak on the island at 589m (1,932ft), surveys the streets of terraced houses winding their way uphill, brushing past olive groves and fragrant rosemary bushes. A trip to Capri is worth it just for the chairlift ride to the top of Monte Solaro; it skims the tops of the pine trees and provides fantastic views over the Bay of Naples and the Amalfi coast. Anacapri is the highest settlement, a charming village where you can visit the Villa San Michele, built by the Swedish author Axel Munthe (1857–1949), in a superb panoramic setting. Here small terraced houses sit alongside immaculate white villas immersed in Mediterranean and subtropical vegetation.

GROTTA AZZURRA

If you are staying longer than a day or so, consider a boat trip to the Grotta Azzurra (Blue Grotto). Experience the unique blue glow of the cave, caused by the reflection of natural sunlight passing through its underwater cavity. Small rowing boats carry passengers through the opening of the grotto, so small that you have to lie flat on the bottom of the boat. Boats leave regularly from the Marina Grande, the main harbour.

Above *Mosaics in the House of Neptune Amphitrite at Ercolano (Herculaneum)*

ERCOLANO (HERCULANEUM)

www.pompeiisites.org

This interesting archaeological site is often bypassed for the more glamorous Pompei, but the eruption of Vesuvio in AD79 that buried Pompei also submerged Ercolano, preserving both settlements.

Probably the most famous of the well-preserved houses is the Villa dei Papiri, the home of a rich and powerful Roman statesman, thought to be either Lucius Calpurnius Piso, Julius Caesar's father-in-law, or his son. More than 50 marble and 20 bronze sculptures were found in the villa, together with an amazing collection of 1,700 Greek and Roman papyri. At the time of writing the villa is closed for ongoing restoration.

Other highlights include the Casa del Atrio Mosaico, with its beautifully preserved mosaic flooring, the Casa dei Cervi (House of the Deer) and the new Maritime Pavilion with the faithfully reconstructed remains of a Roman boat. Most excavated objects are in the Archaeological Museum in Naples (▷ 354–357).

469 J12 Ercolano Scavi, Corso Resina, 80056 Ercolano 081 777 7008 Nov–Mar daily 8.30–5; Apr–Oct 8.30–7.30; last entry 1.5 hours before closing Adults €11, under 14s €5.50; 3-day combined ticket valid for Pompei €22 Circumvesuviana railway connects Ercolano to Sorrento and Naples

FORESTA UMBRA

www.parks.it/parco.nazionale.gargano

Take a break from the summer heat in this forest at the heart of the Gargano Peninsula (▷ 350). Signposted trails lead through a nature reserve, with picnic areas along the way.

The Foresta Umbra's 15,000ha (37,065 acres) account for half of Gargano's woodlands. After the Aleppo pines of the coast, the dominant trees are maple, hornbeam, birch and beech. The Valle del Tesoro is where you will find the forest's biggest beech tree *(faggio)*, a giant 40m (131ft) specimen with a 5m (16.5ft) circumference (signposted *Colosso del foresto*). The forest also has 65 species of orchid. Animals to look for include deer, curly-horned moufflon (wild sheep), boar and Italy's largest colony of badgers, while birdwatchers can spot the Dalmatian woodpecker, sparrowhawk and royal or tawny owl.

470 M10 CTA National Forest Service, 71030 Foresta Umbra 0884 560967 Mar–Sep daily 8–2, 4–8; Oct–Feb phone for opening times (0884 991104) Gargano railway runs along forest periphery between San Severo and Peschici

GALLIPOLI

Gallipoli is built on an extended headland, 37km (23 miles) south of Lecce, with the old town standing on an island linked to the modern town by a seven-span bridge. While the new town may seem unprepossessing, the old town has the mysterious charm of a labyrinthine Arab city.

Not to be confused with the World War I battlefield in Turkey, Gallipoli is Greek in origin (the ancient Greek name, *Kalé polis*, means 'beautiful city'). The old town is full of white-painted houses along narrow, winding streets and alleys and has a fine 17th-century baroque cathedral. The handsome carved friezes of the honey-coloured facade are influenced by the cathedral of its sister city, Lecce (▷ 352–353), where Gallipoli-born painter Giovanni Andrea Coppola went on to make his name.

From the waterfront Riviera road, which encircles the old town, there are views of the fishing port and the nearby beaches.

471 P13 Piazza Imbriani 9, 73014 Gallipoli 0833 262529; summer only, plus Tue and Thu, Oct and Mar Gallipoli

GARGANO PENINSULA

▷ 350.

ISCHIA

ww.infoischiaprocida.it

About 10km (6 miles) long and 7km (4 miles) wide, the island of Ischia is surrounded by soft golden sands and enjoys a temperate climate almost all year round. It is famous for its spa facilities, from mud-bath treatments to natural hot springs. Safe family beaches and summer nightlife make this a popular holiday destination.

The gardens of the beautiful villa of La Mortella (Apr–Oct Tue, Thu, Sat–Sun 9–7), created by British composer William Walton and his widow Susana, have more than 1,000 different species of plants. Forio is an attractive town with a sunny beach, backed by the magnificent Poseidon Gardens. The village of Sant'Angelo can be reached only on foot and is connected by a causeway to the Rocca di Sant' Angelo, a green lava rock rising out of the sea.

Near to the port at Ischia Ponte, the 15th-century Castello Aragonese (Apr–Oct daily 9–7, Nov–Mar 10–5) is spectacularly perched on a rocky isle. Within the fortress there is a cathedral, small churches, a rather creepy Nuns' Cemetery and a Weaponry Museum.

469 J12 Via Sogliuzzo 72, Ischia Porto, 80077 Ischia 081 507 4211 Hourly ferries from Naples; 55 mins on the fast service

INFORMATION

www.parks.it/parco.nazionale.gargano
www.pugliaturismo.com
470 L–M10 Via S. Antonio Abate 121, 71037 Monte Sant'Angelo 084 568911 Tue and Thu 9–12.30, 4–6 Peschici

TIPS

» To swim in high summer, avoid the beaches and rent a boat to get to a secluded cove.
» Cool off in the inland forests.

Above *Steep outcrops of limestone form the many promontories of the heavily wooded Gargano Peninsula*

GARGANO PENINSULA

Cave paintings on the peninsula's southeast coast are evidence that there were Stone Age settlements in the Gargano some 20,000 years ago. In the 13th century, Emperor Frederick II and his son Manfred built castles and watch-towers along the coast to fend off pirates and Saracens. The following centuries saw invasions by the Normans, Angevins and Spanish, and in the 17th century the Turks. The area remained relatively neglected until the 20th century. In 1979 a campaign to save the peninsula from the threat of real estate development began, leading to the creation of the Gargano National Park in 1995.

WHAT TO SEE AND DO

Known as the *sperone d'Italia*, the 'spur' of the Italian boot is about 45km (28 miles) wide in the middle and juts out 65km (40 miles) into the Adriatic Sea. Citrus groves and umbrella pines on the coast give way to the national park's densely wooded hills of the cooler interior.

Manfredonia is a good starting point, with a visit to Emperor Manfred's Castello (1256), now an archaeological museum. Southwest of the town is Siponto and the lovely 11th-century Romanesque Church of Santa Maria. The eastern coast, beyond the Baia di Vignanotica, is rugged and lined with rocky coves and grottoes, notably the Grotta Smeralda and Grotta dei Marmi.

At the eastern tip of the peninsula, Vieste (▷ 365) is a popular resort with a castle, cathedral and sandy beaches at Pizzomunno and Castello. On the northern coast the fishing village of Peschici has preserved its picturesque medieval heart (▷ 359). At the green heart of the peninsula you will find the beech and hornbeam woodlands of the Foresta Umbra (▷ 349) and the little town of San Giovanni Rotondo. Its monastery, which was home to the 20th-century miracle-worker Padre Pio da Petralcino, is one of the most revered sites in Italy.

East from here is the pilgrimage town of Monte Sant'Angelo, where a church was built in 1273 over the Santuario di San Michele, a cave where the archangel Michael had appeared in a vision some 800 years earlier. Steps inside the church lead down to the sanctuary past a pair of 11th-century sculpted bronze doors.

ISOLE TREMITI

www.pugliaturismo.com/aptfoggia

The three tiny islands known as the Isole Tremiti lie in the Adriatic 22km (14 miles) north of the Gargano Peninsula. Consisting of limestone rocks and cliffs, with pine-wooded hills in the interior, they have a combined surface area of 3sq km (1.2sq miles).

They are the perfect place for a day trip from the mainland: you can swim in the clear waters of secluded coves, explore grottoes and walk along the rugged cliffs or through the interior's shady pine woods.

San Nicola is the smaller of the two inhabited islands, with a 15th-century monastic fortress and the small, 11th-century Church of Santa Maria a Mare. The island has no beaches, but there are delightful rocky coves to swim in; there is nude bathing on the east coast.

The larger, more spectacular island of San Domino is 10 minutes by shuttle-boat (€1.25 each way). Its beaches are lovely—some accessible only by a climb down steep cliffs—and the caves, Grotta del Bue Marino, Grotta di Sale and Grotta delle Viole, are a major attraction.

470 L10 Via E. Perrone 17, 71100 Foggia 0881 723141/723650 Hydrofoils and ferries operate to the islands from Manfredonia (agents: Galli e Figlio, Corso Manfredi, tel 0884 58220; €48) and Vieste (agents: Gargano Viaggio, Piazza Roma 7, tel 0884 708501; €30); the journey by hydrofoil takes 2 hours, from Vieste 1 hour. Tirrenia (www.tirrenia.com) runs catamarans from Vieste and Manfredonia. You can buy tickets at the port before boarding

Below *The rugged coastline of Maratea*

LECCE

▷ 352–353.

MARATEA

www.costadimaratea.com

Here verdant mountains sweep down to a craggy coast with numerous coves and small, secluded beaches. The little town of Maratea lies in the folds of the hills, connected to the sea by its pretty port. Confusingly Maratea has also given its name both to the port, which has very good fish restaurants, and to the main beach, Marina di Maratea, 5km (3 miles) away. The town itself is divided into Superiore and Inferiore. Superiore, the higher part, is largely in ruins after being deserted during the Middle Ages in favour of Inferiore, site of the present town of steps and narrow alleys. The Church of San Vito is the oldest church, built in the 11th and 12th centuries. There are fine views from the top of Mount Biagio, where you can also get a closer look at the enormous 22m (72ft) marble statue of Christ, 'Il Redentore'.

472 L13 Piazza del Gesù 32, 85040 Maratea 0973 876908 Marina di Maratea, then bus

MATERA

www.materaturismo.it/english/index.htm

This is a startling troglodyte town of dwellings cut into the limestone *sassi* (rockfaces) of a deep ravine, 80km (50 miles) south of Bari. Some were inhabited up to 7,000 years ago. There are many *chiesi rupestri* (cave churches) in the area, carved out by monks and often decorated with Byzantine murals. The poverty and disease that held the town in the early half of the 20th century were eventually cleaned up and the town became a UNESCO World Heritage Site in 1993. Now a few of the houses have been converted into apartments and art galleries. One of the best is the terrific modern sculpture museum (Museo della Scultura Contemporanea; Apr–Oct Tue–Sun 10–2, 4–8; Nov–Mar 10–2).

A *strada panoramica* (scenic route) on the east side of the ravine has views over the two *sassi* districts, Sasso Caveoso to the southeast, and Sasso Barisano to the northwest. Leave time to visit San Pietro Caveoso and the nearby Santa Maria de Idris churches, which have 14th-century Byzantine rock paintings.

471 M12 Via Spine Bianche 22, 75100 Matera 0835 331983 Matera

METAPONTO

Archaeology buffs can combine a visit to the region's most important ancient Greek settlement with some pleasant sunbathing or swimming at the nearby beach resort, Lido di Metaponto. Metaponto is 50km (31 miles) south of Matera.

The ancient site that was home to the mathematician Pythagoras in the seventh century BC is best seen in conjunction with a visit to the town's excellent Museo Archeologico (Mon 2–7, Tue–Sun 9–7). Its collection of ancient Greek jewellery and gold ornaments, ceramics and sculpture are displayed in a handsome modern museum. At the archaeological site, signed 'Zona Archeologica', you can see the remains of a theatre, the marketplace *(agora)* and four temples, notably the Temple of Apollo Licius (sixth century BC).

Better preserved, 3km (2 miles) north of the main site, is the Temple of Hera (or Tempio delle Tavole Palatine), with 15 of its outer columns still standing (daily 8am to half an hour before sunset).

471 N12 Via Spine Bianche 22, 75100 Matera 0835 331817 Bus from Matera (1 hour)

INFORMATION

www.pugliaturismo.com/aptlecce
471 P13 Via Vittorio Emanuele 24, 73100 Lecce 0832 332463 or 0832 248092 Mon–Sat 9-1, 4.30–9; reduced hours in winter Lecce

Above *The ornate stonework of the baroque Basilica di Santa Croce*

INTRODUCTION

For years, Lecce slumbered in the southern sun, a city whose past glories were largely forgotten. It is the principal town of the Salentine peninsula, the product of 17th-century mercantile money and the zeal of the religious orders. Today, it is firmly on the map and visitors flock here to wander its streets and marvel at the architecture, whose style, existing nowhere else, is known as Leccese baroque. It's opulent, extravagant, yet airy, with churches, palaces and houses all a riot of gambolling *putti*, windswept saints and angels, garlands, wreaths and curlicues.

Lecce's history is long: it was first settled by the Greeks in the fifth to fourth centuries BC, becoming an important Roman settlement, named Lupiae, then Licea, during the reign of Augustus. The main piazza occupies the site of a first-century amphitheatre. Lecce's first bishop and patron, Sant'Oronzo, one of Nero's Christian martyrs, is now honoured with a statue set on a Roman pillar. After the Dark Ages, the Normans put Lecce back on the map in the 11th century, and the city expanded under the German emperors, before coming under Spanish rule in the 16th century. It was under the Spaniards that the city acquired its golden Renaissance and baroque heart (Emperor Charles V is celebrated by a triumphal arch), and with money to be made, bankers and merchants from Florence, Milan, Venice and Genoa arrived. Their money funded the construction of the grand palazzi along Via Palmieri and Via Libertini.

To add to its pleasures, Lecce is renowned for its cuisine, and you'll find restaurant menus offering delicious local specialties. Look out for lamb and kid *(capretto)* dishes, oven-baked aubergine (eggplant), *puccia* (black olive bread), and fine regional wines—Alezio, Copertino and Leverano.

WHAT TO SEE

PIAZZA DEL DUOMO AND VIA LIBERTINI

Head first for the Piazza del Duomo, from where stretch two of Lecce's finest streets, Via Palmieri and Via Libertini. The Duomo (cathedral; daily 6.30–12, 4–6.30) was rebuilt between 1659 and 1670 to designs by Giuseppe Zimbalo, the most important of Lecce's baroque architects, who was responsible for many of the city's finest buildings. Its best facade runs along one side, and it is overshadowed by a five-tiered slender campanile (1682); the interior is beautiful, with spiral columns and some good paintings. The Duomo is flanked in a wonderfully theatrical way by the splendid Palazzo Vescovile (1632), fronted by a graceful loggia, and the Palazzo del Seminario, the seminary designed by Giuseppe Cino in 1709; don't miss its interior courtyard. From here, walk down Via Palmieri to admire the ornate and brilliantly decorated Palazzo Palmieri, Palazzo Guarini and the Teatro Paisello, all great examples of the Lecce style. Left of the Duomo, Via Libertini leads to the church of the Rosario, Zimbalo's last and most elaborate design, completed in 1691.

PIAZZA SANT'ORONZO AND SANTA CROCE

From the duomo, Via Vittorio Emanuele leads east to Piazza Sant'Oronzo and the excavations of the Roman amphitheatre (daily 10–12, 4–6), built in the second century AD. Overlooking this is the Palazzo del Seggio (1592), the ancient seat of the town's government, and the column topped by a statue of the saint—it's said it once marked the end of the Roman Via Appia, one of the great consular roads that fanned out from Rome, in Brindisi. You can walk north from here to the Giardini Pubblici and Lecce's greatest baroque masterpiece, the Basilica di Santa Croce (daily 9–12.30, 5–9), built between 1548 and 1646. Zimbalo was mainly responsible for the central part of the facade, with its great rose window surrounded by *putti*, flowering swags and garlands. Left of the church is the Palazzo del Governo, another stunner of a building, again designed by Zimbalo though Giorgio Riccardi, another famous Lecce architect, had a hand in the enormous courtyard. From here, Via Principe di Savoia runs west to Charles V's Arco di Trionfo, built in 1548. Walk past it and through the line of the old walls and you'll come to the Romanesque church of Santi Nicolò e Cataldo, founded by Tancred in 1180. Its interior is a rare combination of Norman austerity and baroque ornament. The adjoining 12th-century monastery has an elegant Renaissance fountain in its first cloister.

TIPS

» Don't even think of driving in Lecce's chaotic traffic; park outside the *centro storico* (old town).

» The yellow-pinkish tinged stone of Lecce is uniquely malleable and carved to perfection by skilled architects and stonemasons. To see the effect at its most dazzling, walk around town at sunset.

» As well as the fine stone, another Lucchese speciality is papier-mâché and especially *pupi* (figures), which you will find in the shops. Mostly they are religious, but there are also a few secular ones.

Below left *Lecce's duomo*
Below *The campanile at night*

INTRODUCTION

Naples is southern Italy's great city, pulsing with life, full of wonderful buildings and museums and flanked by an idyllic bay. Capital of the region of Campania, on Italy's west coast, it is two hours by fast train from Rome. It is as famed for its citizens as its monuments, and there is nowhere else in Italy where you can find such a level of life lived on the streets. With more than a million inhabitants, Naples is a big, sprawling city, so be prepared to walk; the upshot will be some fascinating discoveries and fabulous views.

Greek settlers founded Neapolis in 750BC, and the city prospered under both Greek and Roman rule before declaring itself independent in 763. The Normans took the city in 1139, and were soon followed by the Hohenstaufens, German rulers who held on until the Angevins took over in 1269. The Spanish moved in next in 1422 and remained in control for over 300 years. Bourbon and French rule followed before Naples became part of united Italy.

The city has a long history of foreign rule and neglect by government. Despite money pouring into the south under the Mezzogiorno scheme in the late 20th century, unemployment and social deprivation remain common, but the late 1990s, when Antonio Bassolino was mayor, saw a burgeoning civic pride and a burst of creative activity.

INFORMATION

www.inaples.it

469 J12 Piazza del Gesù Nuovo 7, 80134 Napoli 081 552 3328 Via San Carlo 9 081 402394 Via Santa Lucia 081 240 0911 Mon–Sat 9–2 (but times are notoriously subject to change) Napoli Centrale

WHAT TO SEE

SPACCANAPOLI

The grid plan of streets that makes up the *centro storico* was the core of ancient Neapolis, and its three main streets—the ancient *decumani*—still slice relentlessly through the oldest part of the city. Spaccanapoli is one of these *decumani;* its name means 'split Naples' and it crosses the heart of the old city, a thoroughfare teeming with people and lined with churches, palazzi and idiosyncratic shops selling everything from books and musical instruments to religious objects and woodcarvings.

Spaccanapoli is made up of a string of streets, now mainly pedestrianized, from Piazza del Gesù Nuovo to Via Viccaria Vecchia. The heart of the university district, it has plenty of bars and restaurants, including Scaturchio, one of Naples' oldest and best *pasticcerie* (cake shops). Along its length, highlights include the rococo obelisk, the Guglia dell'Immacolata in Piazza del Gesù, the Church and Convent of Santa Chiara (▷ 356), Piazza San Domenico with its obelisk and 13th-century castellated church, and some fine Renaissance palaces.

357 B1 Via Capitelli, Piazza del Gesù Nuovo, Via Benedetto Croce, Via San Biagio del Librai

MUSEO ARCHEOLOGICO NAZIONALE

The Museo Archeologico Nazionale houses one of the world's most important collections of classical Roman sculpture, mosaics, gems, wall paintings, glass and silver, much of it plundered from the excavations around and to the south of Naples. The museum is badly labelled and confusingly laid out, with whole sections often closed, but it is nevertheless outstanding, and the exhibits do much to enhance visits to Pompei (▷ 360–363) and Ercolano (▷ 349).

The ground floor is devoted to sculpture, much of it from the 17th-century Farnese collections, which were largely discovered in Rome. Highlights are the muscular *Farnese Hercules* and the *Farnese Bull* (200BC), the largest surviving classical sculptural group. There is a wonderfully vivid mosaic collection and the *Gabinetto Segreto* (Secret Chamber), a collection of Roman erotica from Pompei, which ranges from sensual wall paintings to phallic charms. Upstairs, rooms are filled with more finds from Pompei and Ercolano, including a naturalistic wall

Opposite *Boats moored in the Bay of Naples*

TIPS

» Most areas are safe if you remain alert to petty crime—do not wear expensive jewels or carry much cash, and avoid back streets during the siesta or late at night. Look confident—the more 'lost tourist' you look, the more of a target you'll be for thieves who whizz past on their mopeds.

» Traffic is chaotic and moves at a snail's pace, so use public transport and then walk.

» Opening times in general can be erratic, so be prepared to make more than one visit.

» At present the Museo Archaeologico's Egyptian Collection is closed indefinitely for restoration work.

» Try riding the new glossy underground line from Piazza Dante to Vomero; each station displays bold contemporary artworks on the walls.

Below *A view of the buildings of Naples from Castel Sant' Elmo*

painting of a graceful *Flora* scattering spring flowers, and a *cave canem* (Beware of the Dog) mosaic from the entrance to a house in Pompei.

357 B1 Piazza Museo 19, 80135 Napoli 081 440166 Wed–Mon 9–7.30 €6.50, under 18s free

CERTOSA DI SAN MARTINO

The huge hilltop Carthusian complex of the Certosa di San Martino was founded in 1325, but what you see today dates mainly from the 16th to 18th centuries. The baroque church is crammed with the best of Neapolitan painting and sculpture, and there are more riches in the choir, sacristy and treasury. Explore the expertly restored, arcaded 16th-century Chiostro Grande, the lavishly decorated Quarto del Priore and the Pinacoteca in rooms set around the cloister with views over the city and the bay. Don't miss the exhibition of *presepe*—people and animals fashioned for 18th-century Christmas cribs. The Certosa is surrounded by terraced gardens, with sweeping views.

357 A2 Largo San Martino 5, 80129 Napoli 081 558 640 Thu–Tue 8.30–7.30 €6, under 18s free

SANTA CHIARA

Santa Chiara is Naples' great Franciscan church, a simple and austere 14th-century Gothic conventual complex. Founded by King Robert of Anjou for his wife, Sancia, in 1310, it became a focal point for Naples' Angevin rulers, several of whom are buried here. The original church, greatly altered over the centuries, was catastrophically bombed in 1943. Rebuilding started almost at once, using whatever could be salvaged, and the church, restored to its original Gothic appearance, re-opened in 1953. Three Angevin royal tombs survive: that of Robert himself and those of his son, Carlo, and daughter-in-law, Mary of Valois.

Behind the church is the 14th-century cloister, remodelled by Domenico Vaccaro in 1742. He decorated the central garden with 72 octagonal pillars, interspersed with benches, each of which is covered with hand-painted majolica tiles. The church's Museo dell'Opera (Thu–Tue 9–1, 4–6) lies off the cloister, also providing access to a fascinating Christmas crib scene, complete with street life, flying angels and a variety of people and animals.

357 B2 Via Benedetto Croce/Via Santa Chiara 49, 80134 Napoli 081 1957 5915 Mon–Sat 9–1, 4.30–7.30, Sun and holidays 8–1, 5.30–7.30

MUSEO E PARCO DI CAPODIMONTE

Built in 1738 as King Charles III's hunting lodge, and surrounded by a wooded park, the Palace of Capodimonte houses one of Italy's richest museums. The bulk of the collection is made up of works acquired by Charles from his mother, Elizabeth Farnese. You can wander freely through the opulent royal apartments on your way to the majolica and porcelain collection, much of it made by the Neapolitan Capodimonte factory and painted with local scenes. Upstairs is a picture gallery, a collection amassed by the Farnese and Bourbon rulers and spanning the 15th to 17th centuries, with the emphasis on Renaissance painting. Botticelli, Perugino and Pinturicchio are all represented, but it is the High Renaissance works that shine, particularly the portraits by Titian, Raphael and Sebastiano del Piombo. Leave time to wander through the shady avenues of the surrounding park.

357 off B1 Via Miano 2, Parco di Capodimonte, 80132 Napoli 081 749 9111 Thu–Tue 8.30–7.30 €7.50, under 18s free

MORE TO SEE

DUOMO DI NAPOLI

A 13th-century Gothic cathedral dedicated to San Gennaro, patron saint of Naples; the first chapel on the right contains two phials of his blood, said to liquefy three times a year. Also part of the complex are the fourth-century

Basilica Santa Restituta (the oldest church in Naples), a baptistery and a Renaissance crypt.

357 B1 Via Duomo 147, 80138 Napoli 081 449097 Duomo: Mon–Sat 8–12.30, 4.30–7. Museo del Tesoro di San Gennaro: Tue–Sat 9.30–5, Sun 9.30–2.30 Adult €6, under 18s €3.50

PALAZZO REALE

The 17th-century palace of the Spanish viceroys of Naples was extended in the 18th century by the Bourbons and altered in the 19th century by the French. It houses the historic Biblioteca Nazionale (National Library) and a series of grandiose state rooms.

357 B3 Piazza del Plebiscito 1, 80133 Napoli 081 400547 or 081 580 8111 Thu–Tue 9–7 €4

CASTEL NUOVO

A huge castle erected in 1282 by the Angevins, converted into a royal residence by the Aragonese; the Castel Nuovo now accommodates the council offices and the Museo Civico.

357 B2 Piazza Municipio, 80133 Napoli 081 420 1241 Mon–Sat 9–7 €5

MERGELLINA

This is the waterfront area and ferry port, with an attractive harbour and spread of chalets, ramshackle bars and ice-cream parlours; a popular place for seafood.

357 off A3

CASTEL DELL'OVO AND SANTA LUCIA

The oldest castle in Naples (ninth century) attained its present form in 1503. Restored in the 1970s, it is now used for exhibitions and concerts. There are some excellent fish restaurants around the Santa Lucia district, near the harbour.

357 A3 Borgo Marinari, 80132 Napoli 081 240 0055 Mon–Fri 9–6, Sat–Sun 9–1

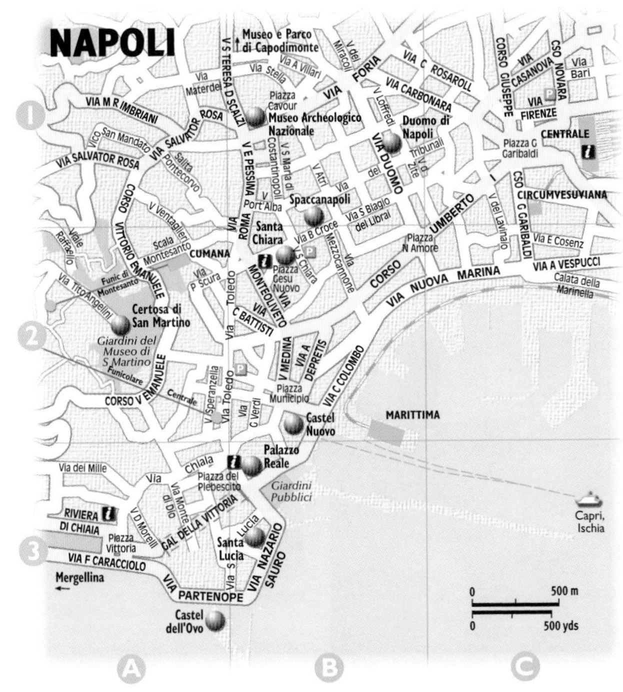

Above *A statue set into a niche on the facade of the Palazzo Reale*

OTRANTO

www.comune.otranto.ie.it

This charming little fishing village has some splendid monuments to its Greek, Byzantine and Norman past—in the 11th century it was an important Crusader and pilgrim port. In the areas just outside the town people still speak a Greek patois rather than Italian even today, and in summer a car ferry runs from the port to Greece.

Many visitors come to Otranto for its convenient sandy beaches, which have good watersports facilities and fishing coves. The Normans' 11th-century Cattedrale di Santa Maria Annunziata (daily 8.30–12, 4–7) has some spectacular Byzantine floor mosaics depicting Adam and Eve, Noah and the Flood, the Queen of Sheba, Alexander the Great and King Arthur. In grim contrast, the Martyrs' Chapel contains the bones of 800 Christians massacred by the Turks in 1480. A hill covered with cypress trees on the southern edge of town marks the spot where the martyrs were beheaded. The massive *castello* (castle) (exhibitions Oct–end Mar Mon–Sat 9.30–12, Sun 10.30–12.30, 3.30–6.30) dominates the south side of the port, built after the Turkish attack. The best beaches, notably Torre dell'Orso, are north of town.

471 Q13 Piazza Castello, 73028 Otranto 0836 801436 Otranto

PAESTUM

www.infopaestum.it

Paestum, about 35km (22 miles) south of Salerno and about 3km (2 miles) from Capaccia Scalo, has some of the best-preserved Greek temples outside Greece, standing with mountains on one side and a marine vista on the other.

The area includes a temple dedicated to Poseidon (the site was known as Poseidonia), the god of the sea, known to the Romans as Neptune (450BC), a temple to Athena, and the basilica, which historians believe to have been built in honour of Heres or Zeus. The site was created by the Greeks in the sixth century BC and was taken over by the Romans 200 years later, who changed the name. The structures are all built of a golden stone that glows richly in the afternoon sun. The site was deserted from the ninth century and rediscovered in the 18th century.

The Museo Archeologico (daily except first and third Mon of month, 9–6.45) illustrates the fascinating history of this exceptional site. Of particular interest is the *Tomba del Tuffatore* (Diver's Tomb), one of the few remaining and best-preserved Greek mural paintings from the fifth century BC.

The area south of Paestum is worth exploring for its emerald-green sea and deserted beaches.

470 K12 Via Magna Grecia 887, 84063 Paestum 0828 811016

Ancient site of Paestum 0828 811023 Summer daily 8.45–7; winter 8.45–4; last entry 1 hour before closing €4, or €6.50 including museum Paestum (1km/0.5 mile from site)

PARCO NAZIONALE D'ABRUZZO

www.abruzzoturismo.it

The Parco Nazionale d'Abruzzo was set up in 1923 by conservationists to protect native species of animals and plantlife threatened with extinction—a small revolution for a predominantly agricultural region with a strong hunting tradition.

Particularly rare animals were the brown *marsicano* bear, the golden eagle and the chamois deer, all of which are now thriving again in their natural habitats. With more than 300 species of birds and 12,000 different species of wildflower, it is reputedly the oldest park of its kind in Europe.

This fertile wilderness covers an area of 44,000ha (108,720 acres) in the south of the Abruzzo region. The park's Visitor Centre in Pescasseroli has a small museum and rehabilitation centre for injured animals.

Steeped in tradition, Pescasseroli has managed to maintain its traditional sheep farming, woodcarving and stonework customs. The village is also the birthplace of Benedetto Croce (1866–1952), the Italian writer, philosopher and politician. Stay to sample the local way of life and benefit from the range of park facilities, including horseback riding, mountain-bicycling and guided tours along some 150 marked walks and trails.

Within driving distance of Pescasseroli, in the terraced white-stone village of Civitella Alfedena, is the Centro Lupo (Wolf Museum), where you can learn all about the wolf packs that live in the park (▷ 15).

469 J10 Via Principe di Napoli, 67032 Pescasseroli 0863 910461 Avezzano, then bus to Pescasseroli

Left *The Doric Temple of Poseidon at Paestum*

PARCO NAZIONALE DEL GRAN SASSO

www.abruzzoturismo.it
www.parconazionalegransasso.it/eng/index.htm

The Parco Nazionale del Gran Sasso, nicknamed 'Little Tibet' because of its 2,912m (9,551ft) Gran Sasso mountain peaks, was set up in 1991 to preserve the animals and plants unique to the area. Three mountain ranges, a fertile, cultivated valley and the nearby Adriatic coastline are all visible. Well-signposted footpaths and trails throughout the park make this an ideal destination for walkers, while winter-sports enthusiasts can choose from the many ski resorts in the area. The Cima Alta, a rocky vista about 1km (0.5 mile) from Prati di Tivo, is easily accessible and a good place to begin any walk. The soft rock characteristic of this section of the Apennines forms caves, gorges and impressive waterfalls, including those at Cento Fonti, Morricana and Volpara. In spring the flowers in the meadows and plains are a riot of different shades and at higher altitudes you can find edelweiss and wild orchids.

The Abruzzo chamois, an agile goat/antelope once threatened with extinction in this region, has recently been reintroduced and about 50 now live in the park. There are also small packs of the Apennine wolf, as well as polecats, beech-martens, badgers and wildcats.

469 H–J9 Via XX Settembre 8, 67100 L'Aquila 0862 22306

PARCO NAZIONALE DEL POLLINO

www.parcopollino.it

The Parco Nazionale del Pollino is the largest national park in Italy and one of the richest in terms of wildlife. Famous for the loricate pines *(Pinus leucodermis),* found only here and in the Balkans, the park is also home to eagles, ravens, pine martens, wildcats, roe deer and the very rare Italian wolf *(Canis lupus italicus).* Here, too, are over 1,700 species of wildflowers, including periwinkle, asphodels, gentians and peonies.

This vast national park covers about 196,000 ha (484,000 acres) of mountainous terrain, equally divided between Basilicata and Calabria, with areas of woodland, rocky outcrops, alpine meadows and unpolluted streams. The highest peaks are Monte Pollino (2,248m/7,344ft) and Serra Dolcedorme (2,267m/7,436ft), in the middle of the park. Along the park's eastern borders, towns such as San Costantino Albanese and San Paolo Albanese are home to Albanian (Arbresh) communities which have largely preserved their own language, traditions and religious festivals since their arrival in the 16th century.

Southwest, the wildest area of the park, the Monti di Orsomarso, is named after the brown bear *(orso)* that once roamed here. There are many interesting towns scattered through the park, including Rotonda, the park's capital, whose visitor centre organizes excellent excursions into the park.

472 M13 Park Centre (Sede Ente Parco), Via delle Frecce Tricolori 6, 85048 Rotonda (Potenza) 0973 669311

PESCHICI

www.peschici.it

At the northern tip of the Gargano Peninsula (▷ 350) and 80km (50 miles) north of Manfredonia, this tiny, walled medieval fishing village makes an ideal base for exploring the Gargano National Park—in particular the nearby grottoes just east along the coast at San Nicola and the Foresta Umbra in the interior (▷ 349). Dependent on an abbey on the Isole Tremiti (▷ 351), built in the 10th century to fend off Saracen raids, its grey-domed houses and the maze of narrow winding streets are reminiscent of an Arab village. The sandy bay at the foot of Peschici's promontory is where some of the Gargano's most attractive and popular beaches are to be found.

470 M10 Via Magenta 3, 71010 Peschici 0884 964139 Calenella, then bus

POMPEI AND VESUVIO

▷ 360–363.

Above *Bronze warrior in Reggio's museum*

REGGIO DI CALABRIA

www.provincia.reggio-calabria.it

Reggio di Calabria is noteworthy mainly for being the gateway to Sicily, but it is also worth visiting if only for the Museo Nazionale (Tue–Sun 9–7.30), which has some priceless treasures from Calabria and Basilicata. In particular, seek out the *Bronzi di Riace* (460–430BC), two magnificent bronze warriors, and two rare painted panels by Antonello da Messina (*c*1460).

A busy modern city and seaport, Reggio was largely rebuilt in an organized grid fashion after the devastating earthquake of 1908. This is the toe of Italy's boot, and the coast of Sicily can clearly be seen from here. The city may not be the brightest star in Calabria's firmament, but the gardens of the Villa Comunale and the tree-lined coastal promenade along Viale Matteotti, with a diversity of palms, trees and shrubs akin to a botanical garden, leaven the traffic pollution and noise. At the northern end of the promenade, almost hidden by a grove of pines, is a small museum of musical instruments.

Nearby are the remains of a Greek defensive wall, and some ruins of baths and mosaics from the later Roman period.

472 L16 Via Roma 3, 89100 Reggio di Calabria 0965 22530 Reggio di Calabria Centrale or Lido (fewer trains) Napoli and Catania (Sicily)

INFORMATION

POMPEI

www.pompeiisites.org
www.pompei.biz
469 K12 Scavi di Pompei, Piazza Esedia/Porta Marina/Piazza Anfiteatro (3 entrances), 80045 Pompei 081 857 5347 Apr–end Oct daily 8.30–7.30 (last entrance 6); rest of year daily 8.30–5 (last entrance 3.30) Adult €11, EU youths (18–25) €5.50, under-18s free. Combined ticket for Pompei, Ercolano, Oplontis, Stabiae and Boscoreale (valid 3 days): adult €20, youth €10 Circumvesuviana train from Naples to Pompei Scavi Villa dei Misteri 2-hour guided tours in Italian, English, French, German and Spanish, €100–€200 (always choose an official guide); audioguides in English, French, German, €6.50 €8–€15 Bar/restaurant with self service—expensive and usually very crowded; numerous restaurants just outside the site

Above *Detail of a fresco in the Casa della Venere (House of Venus) at Pompei*

INTRODUCTION

Mount Vesuvio, half an hour by train and bus from Naples, rises to the south of the city, a peak of 1,281m (4,203ft) that forms the backdrop to the beautiful Bay of Naples. On the lower slopes, 13 communities house over 750,000 inhabitants, all of whom choose to ignore the threat that looms over them. The Roman town of Pompei, on the volcano's southern slopes, was caught unawares by a massive eruption in AD79, which smothered the town, its people and their goods and chattels. Preserved for centuries, the site has been, and continues to be, excavated, so as you walk up and down the streets you can peer into shops and private homes, read advertisements and graffiti—and generally get a unique picture of daily life in Roman times.

Pompei is the world's best-preserved Roman town, frozen in time by the catastrophic eruption of Vesuvio on 24 August AD79. Founded as a Greek colony, the town became part of Rome in about 200BC, thriving as a chic holiday resort for rich Romans and as a trading place exporting wine and fish products. It was severely damaged by an earthquake in AD63, and the volcanic eruption 16 years later was the final nail in the coffin. Of the 20,000 inhabitants it is thought that about 2,000 people died, including Pliny the Elder, the Roman naturalist, at Stabiae (Castellammare) nearby. His nephew, Pliny the Younger, recorded the events of the days in a letter to the historian Tacitus. Excavations began in earnest in 1748, and continue today. Pompei has yielded more information about everyday Roman life than any other site, as well as artistic treasures.

Vesuvio, the cause of the disaster, is the only active volcano in mainland Europe. It last blew in 1944 and it is generally thought to be well overdue for another eruption—the longer the period of quiescence, the greater the risk. The mountain is constantly monitored. Scientists believe that the danger lies not in ash deposits and lava flows, but in a surge of super-heated, poisonous gas that could roll down the slopes at more than 80kmh (50mph)—much like the cloud that was responsible for so many deaths in AD79.

VESUVIO

www.parconazionaledelvesuvio.it

469 K12 Path from car park at the summit to the crater: Jun–Aug daily 9–6.30; Apr–May 9–5.30; Sep–Oct 9–5; Nov–Mar 9–3 €6.50 (includes tour) Bus from Pompei to car park below crater €8.90 return; Vesuviana Mobilità, tel 081 963 4420 Circumvesuviano train from Naples to Ercolano, then bus

WHAT TO SEE

VIA DELL'ABBONDANZA

Via dell'Abbondanza was Pompei's most important thoroughfare, running through the middle of the town from the Porta Marina in the west (the main harbour gate) to the Anfiteatro (amphitheatre) in the east. The Foro, the civic heart of the town, lies off the west end of Abbondanza, an elongated open space with a colonnade running along three sides and the remains of the Tempio di Giove (Temple of Jupiter) on the north side. To the left is the porticoed entrance to the *macellum*, the covered meat and fish market, while across the road from the entrance to the Foro stands the basilica, site of Pompei's law court and stock exchange. Farther along the street are the Terme Stabiane, a large public bath complex with an exercise court in the middle and some well-preserved wall paintings.

Via dell'Abbondanza carries on past shops and houses; look for the shop counters and the symbols outside many of the commercial premises, which were aimed at drawing in the illiterate country people shopping in town.

VILLA DEI MISTERI

The Villa dei Misteri lies outside the main walls of Pompei, and was a working farm for much of its existence. It is probably the best preserved of all Pompei's grand villas, a series of chambers and courtyards first built in the third century BC. Its name comes from the superb series of wall paintings in the *triclinium* (dining room)—a cycle of vibrant scenes showing a young woman's initiation rites into the Dionysiac mysteries, a popular cult in the early imperial era. The paintings, in vivid reds and ochres, are intensely clear and show sacrifice, dancing and flagellation. They are thought to have been copied by a local artist from third-century BC Hellenistic originals. Here you can also see a reconstruction of a wine press, with a decorative ram's head used for crushing grapes.

CASA DEI VETTI (HOUSE OF THE VETTII)

The House of the Vettii is named after its owners, the wealthy merchants Aulus Vettius Conviva and Aulus Vettius Restitutus, who spent their profits decorating their house with mythological paintings. It is one of Pompei's most beautiful houses, and gives an excellent picture of the domestic life of the town's upper-middle-class citizens. The house was altered in the first century AD and the atrium, complete with strongboxes, leads straight through into the peristyle. There are frescoed chambers all around, illustrating such scenes as Hercules struggling with serpents, Ixion tied to a wheel and tortured for daring to set

Above left *The crater of Vesuvius*
Below *A statue amid the ruins of Pompei*

TIPS

» Signposts in Pompei are few and far between, so make sure you have a good map before you start.

» Remember that most of the important artistic finds are now in the Museo Archeologico Nazionale in Naples (▷ 355–356). Visit it either before or after your Pompei trip.

» A new cycle path from the Amphitheatre Square to the Villa of the Mysteries opened in 2010. The route covers 4km (2.5 miles), with suggested stops at specially equipped areas with spellbinding views of Vesuvius and the excavations. Bikes for rent on site.

» Wear comfortable, flat shoes and be prepared for rough walking at both Pompei and Vesuvio.

» Tackle Vesuvio in the early morning and avoid windy days, when conditions near the crater can be difficult.

» Pompei is exposed and it can be very hot, so take plenty of drinking water.

eyes on Zeus's wife, and Dirce being dragged to her death. Even the servants' quarters are decorated with erotic wall paintings, including a more than potent Priapus (phallic symbols were believed to ward off the evil eye).

CASA DEL FAUNO (HOUSE OF THE FAUN)

A block away from the House of the Vettii, the House of the Faun is one of the largest and most sophisticated houses in Pompei. It gets its name from the copy of the charming second-century BC bronze statue in the middle of the *impluvium* (an opening in the roof of the atrium); the original is now in the Museo Nazionale in Naples (▷ 355–356). The house, sprawling over almost 3,000sq m (32,300sq ft), probably belonged to a local dignitary. The floor mosaic at the entrance welcomes visitors with its inscription *'Ave'* ('Hail'). The front of the house is arranged around two atria (halls); behind is a peristyle and graceful portico, which led to a discussion hall for public meetings. This was decorated with a million-piece mosaic floor depicting the 300BC Battle of Issus (now in the Museo Nazionale in Naples). As in many of Pompei's grander houses, the gardens have been lovingly restored.

MOUNT VESUVIO

Mount Vesuvio's fertile volcanic soil has made it attractive to farmers for centuries, and even today the lower slopes are heavily planted with olives, vines and vegetable crops, while wild plants cover the scars of the lava flows left after the last eruption, in 1944, which caused widespread damage to nearby towns.

Vesuvio is now a designated national park and a UNESCO Biosphere Reserve, seen at its best in early summer, when the slopes are covered in wildflowers and bird life is at its liveliest and most interesting. It is only when you climb the slopes above the official parking area that you first appreciate its rocky aridity. The stony zigzag path up to the rim of the crater winds through lava, gravel and cindery rock. At the top, you can peer down into the crater 200m (650ft) below and enjoy good views of steaming fumaroles and stratified pyroclastic deposits across the void.

The Museo dell'Osservatorio Vesuviano has interesting exhibits that outline the volcano's geology and the threat that future eruptions pose.

Below *Detail of bronze faun statue in the Casa del Fauno (House of the Faun)*
Right *The ruins at Pompei*

MORE TO SEE

TERME DEL FORO

These public baths, north of the Forum, still have much of their original stucco decoration. There is a fine fountain in the hot room with a bronze inscription that records the cost of the fountain and the names of those who donated money towards its construction.

CASA DEL POETO TRAGICO (HOUSE OF THE TRAGIC POET)

One of the up-market houses on Via di Mercurio, named after its theatrical mosaics. The entrance mosaic of a fierce but welcoming dog bears the inscription *cave canem* (Beware of the Dog).

TEATRO GRANDE

A well-preserved theatre, built in the second century BC in a horseshoe plan. It accommodates about 5,000 people and is used for summer performances.

ANFITEATRO

This is one of Italy's oldest amphitheatres. Built in 80BC, it had capacity for between 12,000 and 14,000 people and was used for gladiatorial combats. It could hold about half of Pompei's population; much of the seating area is intact. From June to September there is an outdoor festival of plays and concerts.

CASA DEL MENANDRO (HOUSE OF MENEANDER)

One of the largest houses in Pompei, this probably belonged to the family of Nero's wife, Poppaea. It dates from the third century BC and has a central garden and peristyle with an intricate floor mosaic, a domestic shrine *(lararium)* in the atrium and a room painted with scenes from the Trojan War.

CASA DEI CASTI AMANTI (HOUSE OF THE CHASTE LOVERS)

Named after a decorative panel representing the innocent kiss of two lovers, this was once the house of a rich baker, Julius Publius. Discovered only in 1987 on the north side of the Via dell'Abbondanza, it has been on view since 2010, showing the perfectly preserved bakery oven, two stables with animal skeletons, splendid frescoes and mosaics and a faithfully reconstructed garden. All can be viewed from a suspended walkway while archaeologists and restorers continue their work. Visits are by guided tour only and have to be booked in advance, for an additional charge.

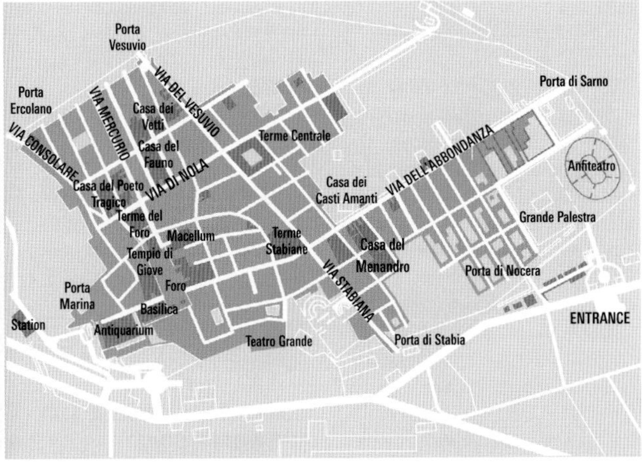

Above *A fresco at Pompei*

REGIONS THE SOUTH • SIGHTS

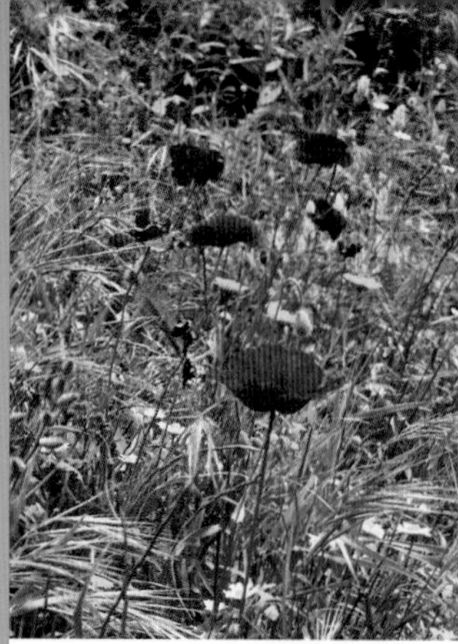

Above *Wild flowers in the Riviera Calabrese*

RIVIERA CALABRESE

www.turismo.regione.calabria.it

The Calabrian Riviera is a term used to describe a succession of beaches and resorts along the Tyrrhenian coast. The more popular resorts, such as Tropea (▷ 365), are busy in the summer, but away from these areas and out of season it should be possible to find a quiet spot to swim and relax.

For most of its length, the Tyrrhenian coast is a comparatively narrow strip of land flanked by the Appennino Lucano and Appennino Calabro mountains, where rocky, tree-lined shores give way to coves and long, sandy beaches. Worth visiting are the beaches of Praia Mare, close to the Basilicata border, and the nearby Isola di Dino. Diamante, an attractive town with narrow streets and good restaurants, also merits a visit. Amantea, another coastal resort, has a recently discovered sixth-century BC Greek sanctuary, while Pizzo is famous for its beach and curious little church, Chiesa di Piedigrotta, decorated with rock carvings of religious icons and famous people.

442 N14 Corso Mazzini 92, 87100 Cosenza 0984 27271 Rail line runs right along the coastline

SCILLA

www.lacostaisola.it

This pretty fishing town lies 20km (12 miles) north of Reggio di Calabria (▷ 359), with fine views across the Straits of Messina to the hills on the island of Sicily. It has an interesting fishermen's quarter, a beautiful bay that is perfect for swimming and sunbathing, and plenty of cafés and restaurants.

The town of Scilla occupies a rocky crag and the shore on either side. To the east is the port and fishermen's quarter and to the west is a suburb built around the beach. The old houses of the Chianalea (fishermen's area) reach right down to the water's edge, with front doors opening directly onto the port.

The crag supporting the castle is allegedly the Scylla of Greek legend, and the swirling waters of the straits are its counterpart, Charybdis—the mythical sea monsters that were the personification of these hazards. There have been fortifications on the rock since the fourth century BC, but the present castle dates mainly from the 17th century and is now used for cultural events. During the Napoleonic Wars the castle was occupied by the French, then the English, and later by Garibaldi, who came here during his reunification campaign (▷ 40).

472 L16 Co/Pro Loco, Piazza San Rocco, 89058 Scilla 0965 754003 Scilla

SIBARI

The Sibari region is blessed with long stretches of beach, especially in Villapiana, 9km (6 miles) to the north, but it is most famous for the ancient site of Sybaris-Copia, founded on the banks of the River Crati almost 3,000 years ago. It grew to become an immensely rich city (the word *sybarite*, someone who enjoys luxury, comes from its name), but it was destroyed in the fourth century BC when Croton (modern Crotone) obliterated the city by diverting the River Crati over the remains. Today nothing is visible above ground, but the excavations can be viewed, and the nearby museum, the Museo Nazionale Archeologico della Sibaritide in Casa Bianca (daily 9–7), has finds excavated from here and other sites.

Sibari is on the Ionian coast 70km (44 miles) southwest of Taranto. Ancient Sybaris gave its name to this fertile coastal plain between Cape Spulico and Cape Trionfo. The mouth of the River Crati is home to one of the few colonies of Mediterranean seals.

472 M13 Via Amendola 1, 87011 Cassano allo Ionio 0981 76352

LA SILA

This extensive, mountainous plateau lies at the heart of Calabria, east of Cosenza and north of Catanzaro, and supports some of southern Italy's most unusual plantlife and animals. It is wonderful walking territory, particularly in spring, and the winter snows provide ample opportunities for downhill and cross-country skiing, mostly around the towns of Camigliatello Silano and Lorica.

Since controls in tree felling and hunting have been introduced, forests of beech, oak and pine clothe much of the mountainsides, and are inhabited by foxes, badgers, black squirrels, otters and even a few specimens of the rare Italian wolf (▷ 15).

A wild and unspoiled region, the plateau, which includes the small Parco Nazionale della Sila, is composed of three separate massifs: La Sila Grande to the north, La Sila Greca, and La Sila Piccola to the south. The average height is 1,000m (3,280ft).

The visitor centre at Cupone, close to Lago Cecita, has a display of the natural history of the park, a botanical garden and an arboretum. Head for Lago Arvo and Cecita for walking, good scenery and a chance to fish for trout in Lago Arvo.

Camigliatello Silano, the area's capital, is a great place to enjoy the local crafts and food. It is also the best place seek out hotels, restaurants and tourist information.

444 N14 Corso Mazzini 92, 87100 Cosenza 0984 27271

SORRENTO PENINSULA AND THE AMALFI COAST

▷ 366–367.

TARANTO

www.comune.taranto.it
www.pugliaturismo.com

An ancient Greek colony, founded by the Spartans in 706BC, Taranto has fine Greek sculpture, gold jewellery and Roman mosaics in its celebrated Museo Nazionale.

Vestiges of the Temple of Poseidon can be seen in the medieval quarter *(città vecchia)*. The commercial and industrial districts of the modern town *(borgo nuovo)*, on the mainland, joined to the old town by bridges, may put off casual visitors, but it is worth staying to see the Museo Nazionale Archaeologico di Taranto (daily 8.30–7.30) in Via Cavour. This important museum has a collection of masterpieces, including a sixth-century BC bronze of Poseidon, two marble sculptures of Eros and Aphrodite (fourth century BC) and a beautiful collection of gold jewellery in the Sala degli Ori.

Taranto is also famous as the ancient home of the hairy tarantula spider that caused a disease traditionally cured by dancing the *tarantella*. The latter is not to be confused with *tarentello*, a local culinary delicacy (tuna fish pie) that is a good enough reason in itself for many gourmets to make the trip here.

471 N12 Corso Umberto I, 74100 Taranto ☎ 0994 532397 Taranto

TRANI

www.traniweb.it

The region's finest Romanesque cathedral, a charming harbour, some first-rate art galleries and good seafood restaurants make Trani one of the most appealing towns on the coast of Puglia.

The town and its people enjoy an uncommon reputation for sophisticated elegance. The beauty of the 12th-century cathedral is enhanced by its isolated position on a promontory overlooking the Adriatic. The handsomely weathered limestone of this three-tiered church, at once graceful and massive, changes from pink to white to gold through the day. Grand bronze doors lead into the Norman interior, built over a crypt in which is housed the Ipogea di San Leucio, a sixth-century Palaeo-Christian tomb.

Around the sheltered harbour, beside the 15th-century Gothic Palazzo Caccetta, several good restaurants serve seafood brought in from the early morning fish market.

Street names in the medieval *centro storico* behind the harbour are evidence of the town's mercantile heyday and Jewish heritage, notably Via Cambio (Street of the Moneychangers) and Via Sinagoga. Today the narrow streets contain attractive art galleries and antiques shops. The view from the Spanish fort, Fortino di San Antonio, is outstanding.

470 M11 Piazza Trieste 10, Palazzo Palmieri, 70059 Trani ☎ 0883 588830 Trani

TROPEA

www.tropeaonline.it

Tropea is Calabria's most beautiful seaside town, and its charms are self-evident. Built on a sandy cliff, the little town of narrow streets and pleasant squares overlooks the sea and its two sandy beaches, from where you can make out the island of Stromboli and the coast of Sicily. There are plenty of cafés, restaurants and pizzerias, as well as two small museums displaying Roman and medieval pottery and a collection of early Christian tombstones.

A short climb takes you to the most eye-catching feature of the town, the Benedictine Monastery of Santa Maria dell'Isola, up on a rock near the sea. Nearby is the town's port, recently enlarged to accommodate visiting yachts as well as fishing vessels.

Each year on 3 May, the Sagra del Cammello (Festival of the Camel) commemorates the defeat of the Saracens, when the vanquished Saracen commander was paraded on a camel before being burned at the stake. Today a symbolic burning of a straw camel and fireworks suffice.

472 L15 Pro Loco, Piazza Ercole, 89861 Tropea ☎ 0963 61475 Tropea

VIESTE

www.vieste.com

Quite simply Puglia's best beach resort, Vieste, 57km (35 miles) northeast of Manfredonia, has convenient sandy beaches, popular with families, secluded rocky coves and picturesque sea caves that can be explored from boat cruises.

The peninsula's easternmost town is also an ideal starting point for day trips by ferry to the Isole Tremiti (▷ 351) and a great base from which to explore the Gargano Peninsula (▷ 350).

The town's whitewashed houses sprawl over two promontories jutting into the Adriatic. At the edge of the *centro storico*, the cathedral is 11th-century Romanesque with 18th-century baroque embellishments. The *castello* (castle), built by Emperor Frederick II in 1240, is closed to the public, but you can enjoy a great view of the Gargano coast from the outside.

South of town are the long sandy beaches of Pizzomunno and Castello, along with Grotta Smeralda (Emerald Cave) and Grotta dei Marmi (Marble Cave).

470 M10 Piazza Kennedy, 71019 Vieste ☎ 0884 708806 Ferries to Isole Tremiti May–Sep

Below *A narrow street in Vieste, with the cathedral beyond*

Antichi Sapori d'Amalfi

SORRENTO PENINSULA AND THE AMALFI COAST

At the southern end of the Bay of Naples, the Sorrento Peninsula juts out towards the idyllic island of Capri. Its southern coastline is known as the Costiera Amalfitana, the Amalfi Coast. Sheltered in a microclimate all its own, the shoreline is protected by towering hills and precipitous cliffs. Tiny, postcard-perfect villages tumble down to the sea, there are beautiful gardens, grand villas and, wherever you look, magnificent views over water and green mountains. A wonderfully scenic corniche road runs along the coast, linking a string of villages—Sorrento, Positano, Praiano, Amalfi and beautiful Ravello, set high above the sea.

It's a tourist coast par excellence, but in the 11th to 12th centuries Amalfi was a power to be reckoned with, an independent trading state with links to north Africa, the Middle East, Constantinople and all over Italy. The advance of the Normans from the south and the Pisans from the north put an end to local mercantile might, but eastern influence remained in local architecture and art, as well as in the narrow alleyways and whitewashed, enclosed vernacular housing—it owes as much to the souks of the east as to the demands of the southern Italian climate.

SORRENTO

Sorrento, on the north of the peninsula, is the largest resort, popular with package tours, though none the worse for that. Its main square, Piazza Tasso, named after the poet Torquato Tasso who was born here in 1544, is the quintessential Italian piazza. Sit at one of the outdoor cafés and drink in the atmosphere around the maze of narrow streets and shops selling bottles of *limoncello*, the local lemon-flavoured liqueur. Above the town, grandiose hotels overlooking the sea are perched along the cliffs, each surrounded by lush gardens rich in subtropical planting.

Take time out from the beaches and cafés to visit the Palazzo Correale and its museum. This 15th-century villa has an impressive collection of porcelain, glass and paintings dating from the 17th to 19th centuries. The duomo (cathedral), rebuilt in the 15th century, is fronted by a whimsical belltower, set on an arch on top of four ancient columns. Inside, you'll find paintings by artists of the Neapolitan School, a marble Archbishop's Throne and, best of all, wonderful wood *intarsia* choir stalls. Take the public ferry or one of the many well-publicized private boat trips from Sorrento along the coast and around the bay to Capri (▷ 348).

THE AMALFI COAST

From the southern side of the Sorrento Peninsula, the beautiful Amalfi Coast runs east to Salerno, with steeply terraced villages of stuccoed houses and seafood restaurants clinging to jagged cliffs. It is best known for its thrilling coastal drive, the 80km (50-mile) stretch of corniche road that leads from Positano to Salerno, with vistas over the shimmering Gulf of Salerno at every turn.

Amalfi's houses are steeply stacked in terraces above the sea. The 10th-century duomo dates from its glory days as a maritime republic; it was rebuilt in the Sicilian Arab-Norman style in 1203. The town itself, so the legend goes, was created by Greek hero Hercules, who fell in love with a nymph called Amalfi. Their love was short-lived as she died young, but Hercules promised to bury her in the most beautiful spot in the world, and built the city of Amalfi in her honour. History books, on the other hand, tell us that it was founded after the death of Emperor Constantine, in AD447.

Drive or take the blue SITA bus to the pretty villages of Praiano, Positano and Cetara. Praiano is 10km (6 miles) west of Amalfi. A further 6km (4 miles) from Praiano is Positano, popular with artists, stars and sophisticates, with an excellent if expensive array of restaurants and hotels. In spite of this, it has kept its fishing-village charm. East from Amalfi, Cetara has two lovely beaches.

INFORMATION

www.sorrentoweb.it
www.turismoregionecampania.it
469 J–K12 Corso delle Repubbliche Marinare 33, 84011 Amalfi
089 871107 Jul–Aug Mon–Fri 8.30–12, 3–7.15, Sat 8.30–12; Sep–Jun Mon–Fri 8.30–1.30, 3–5, Sat 8.30–12
Sorrento; Circumvesuviana–light railway from Naples to Sorrento
Ferries from Sorrento to Capri hourly in summer; at least six times daily in low season

TIP

» Petty theft is rife, particularly in crowded areas, so avoid carrying large amounts of money or valuables and keep a close eye on bags.

Opposite *Duomo di Sant'Andrea, Amalfi*

THE PARCO NAZIONALE DEL GRAN SASSO

This drive takes you through the breathtakingly beautiful Gran Sasso National Park (▷ 359). Its unusual mountain landscape has earned it the name 'Little Tibet'. With so much to explore en route, it would be better to take your time and spread it over two days (▷ Tips).

THE DRIVE
Distance: 444km (276 miles)
Allow: 8 hours
Start/end at: L'Aquila
Roads: Although the route is full of tight mountain bends, the road surface is generally good

★ Take the motorway from L'Aquila (A24) in the direction of Teramo. Pass through the tolls and after 10km (6 miles) you will reach the Assergi Valley, where the area becomes fertile and green. Go through the tunnel, Traforo del Gran Sasso d'Italia, that cuts straight through the mountain. Exit the motorway at San Gabriele Colledara and follow the sign for Prati di Tivo. Drive through the middle of the resort following signs for Cima Alta. After 1km (0.6 miles) there is a parking area. From here walk about 200m (220 yards) up the hill, where you can enjoy an extraordinary view over the mountain range that stretches right down to the sea.

❶ Prati di Tivo is both a ski and summer resort at one of the highest points in the Gran Sasso mountain range. There are several bars and restaurants where you can find refreshments, and places where you can ride horses or rent a bicycle.

From here take the ST43 in the direction of Ponte di Rio Arno Sotto. After 14km (9 miles) turn right onto the SS80 in the direction of Teramo. Ignore signs for the motorway marked Roma/L'Aquila, and continue along the main road following the signs for Castelli–San Gabriele.

❷ Castelli sits 550m (1,805ft) above sea level under the picturesque Monte Camicia. This is a good starting point for trekking as you can cross over and climb the eastern face of the Gran Sasso Mountains from here. Castelli became famous for its majolica ceramics in the 16th century, and there are a number of ceramic shops to visit in the village, where you can see the painters at work.

Drive through the village in the direction of Rigopiano. On the left you will see signs for a steep path that leads 1km (0.6 mile) up to the tiny Church of San Donato in Martire.

❸ The church has a majolica ceiling dating back to 1615. If the church is closed, the caretaker who lives in the house opposite will let you in. A further 500m (1,640ft) up the slope is the Castelli majolica museum, in a former Franciscan convent.

Take the southbound road to Rigopiano, which after 47.5km

(30 miles) of bends brings you to Castel del Monte. This is a tortuous road, but it is worth navigating all the hairpin bends for the scenery.

❹ Castel del Monte (▷ 347) is another quaint stone village with a fortified quarter, Ricetto, and steep streets with flights of stone steps.

From Castel del Monte descend down the same road for 9km (6 miles) in the direction of Calascio/Rocca Calascio.

❺ At 1,450m (4,757ft) above sea level, Calascio was one of the starting points of the migratory shepherds' trail, the Via della Transumanza. The shepherds would accompany their sheep from the Abruzzo to the more temperate region of Puglia, farther south, in the winter, and then bring them back in the spring. They slept in stone huts, some of which are still visible en route.

From Calascio you can visit the 16th-century Church of Santa Maria della Pietà or leave the car and climb up the scenic path that leads to the ruins of the 13th-century fortress of Rocca Calascio, a further 3km (2 miles) from the village. If you want to drive, bear in mind that the last 300m (330 yards) are rough and the road is not surfaced, which can be treacherous in wet conditions. From this vantage point 1,464m (4,800ft) above sea level the eye can roam freely over the mountain peaks and valleys of the Maiella and Mount Sirente. The *rifugio alpino* (mountain refuge) contains a small restaurant and has four charming rooms—an ideal place to stop for lunch or an overnight stay. Several panoramic trails start from here, suitable for all abilities during the warmer months, the longest going as far as Campo Imperatore (13km/8 miles).

Continue driving in the direction of Santo Stefano di Sessanio, the last point on this drive.

❻ This formerly abandoned village has been sensitively restored by a Milanese investor using traditional building methods. Its 120 inhabitants produce some of the country's best lentils, and you can buy them from one of the tiny shops. There are also plenty of artisans' shops selling candles, soaps and herbal remedies. Grey stone houses line the steep cobbled slopes, and at every turn there are views over the barren mountain range visible through the gaps in the narrow alleys.

From Santo Stefano di Sessanio descend to Barisciano and turn onto the SS17, which leads back into L'Aquila.

WHEN TO GO

Fine, dry weather is essential for this drive because of the hairpin bends. Avoid November to late March, when the roads are icy and may be closed in the high reaches. Spring and autumn are the prettiest months, when the flowers are at their best, but high summer is refreshingly cool. Remember that August is the main holiday month for Italians and everywhere will be crowded.

WHERE TO EAT

There are many places to eat in Prati di Tivo and Castelli and plenty of good picnic spots. Rocca Calascio, Agriturismo al Borgo, is a mountain refuge that serves meals and snacks made from local produce (tel 338 8059430; open daily). Hotel Prati di Tivo is a hotel and restaurant that serves good local and Italian food (Località Prati di Tivo, Pietracamela, tel 0861 959636). Ristorante Ostello del Cavaliere in Santo Stefano di Sessanio is a good, inexpensive place to stop to sample traditional food (Via della Giudea, tel 0862 89679, closed Thu).

TIPS

» Some of the mountainous roads and tortuous bends are unmarked and the signs are often hidden.
» Consider an overnight stop or divide the drive into two half-day itineraries: L'Aquila–Prati di Tivo–Castelli on the first day and L'Aquila–Santo Stefano–Calascio–Castel del Monte on the second day.
» It is possible to cut the drive short and return directly to L'Aquila from Castelli.

Opposite *The Gran Sasso range*

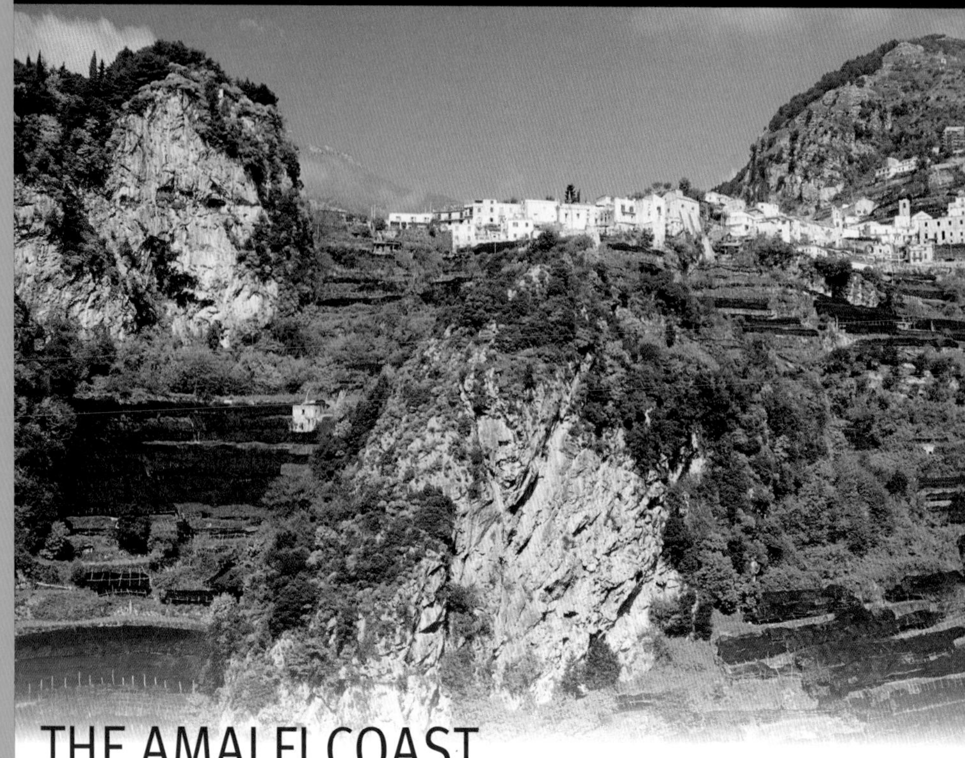

THE AMALFI COAST

This drive from the historic centre of Sorrento to the beautiful gardens and villas of Ravello follows a stretch of coastline in the middle of the protected marine area of Punta Campanella, stopping off at the enchanting Emerald Grotto along the way.

THE DRIVE
Distance: 32km (20 miles)
Allow: 7–8 hours
Start at: Sorrento
End at: Ravello

★ From Sorrento (▷ 366–367) take the road for Massa Lubrense, passing the hotels Bristol and Brittania on your left. After 50m (55 yards) you come to an intersection. Take the left-hand fork marked Sant'Agata–Positano, a fairly wide but winding road. After 6km (4 miles) you reach Sant'Agata sui Due Golfi, with the Hotel Due Golfi on your left. Go straight on along the winding road with hairpin bends and after 4km (2.5 miles) you will come to an intersection at the end of the road with the Ristorante Teresinella facing you. Turn right onto the main Positano–Amalfi road.

❶ After 1km (0.6 miles) there is a good stopping place to view the Galli Islands, three rocky islets in the bay known in mythical times as the haunt of the beautiful sirens who lured sailors to a watery end. Continue along the road to a wide lay-by (rest stop), with a prominent white statue of the Virgin Mary on the right. From here you can look down onto Positano and appreciate the view across the sea.

A bit further on take the right-hand turn down a narrow one-way road with hairpin bends that leads into Positano. Ignore the first parking area you see and continue along this road until you come to the petrol (gas) station and Mandara, which is the largest parking area. If it's full, a few metres farther along on the right is the Di Gennaro parking area. Park, walk past the second parking area, and a few metres along to the right is a pathway that leads to the beach.

❷ The path is fairly steep, but it is lined with a variety of small shops. After 150m (165 yards), steps lead down to a square, to the left of which is the Church of Santa Maria Assunta with its imposing majolica dome. Take time to see the 13th-century Byzantine painting known as *The Black Madonna* and the ceiling covered with frescoes. Opposite the church more steps lead down to another path. Turn left and you will pass through a narrower pathway, lined with shops whose outer walls are adorned with a variety of wares. At the end of the pathway is a terrace with steps leading down to the beach. It is worth walking part of the way down the beach to get a view of the houses above that seem to have tumbled over the edge of the cliff.

Return to your car and follow the one-way road out of Positano. When you reach the intersection, turn right onto the road that passes through the village of Praiano. You will soon come to the entrance to the Grotta di Smeraldo (Emerald Grotto) on your right. There is parking here and two bars. Farther on, a tunnel leads down into the port of Amalfi (▷ 367). There is a small island in the road here where a statue of Flavio Gioia, the inventor of the compass, stands. Turn right here into the parking area.

❸ Walk back to the statue and cross over into Amalfi's main square. At the top of a steep flight of steps is the imposing Cattedrale di Sant'Andrea. The ornate striped facade was rebuilt in the 19th century but the interior is mainly baroque, with fine 12th- and 13th-century mosaics. Alongside, the 13th-century Chiostro del Paradiso (Cloister of Paradise) is a harmonious blend of Romanesque and Arab-influenced style. Continue up this street for 200m (220 yards) and you will pass the papyrus maker next to the bank (Monte dei Paschi di Siena). The tourist information office is next to the post office, close to the statue on the road leading out of Amalfi towards Ravello.

Go back to your car and turn right in front of the statue onto the Ravello road. After 1km (0.6 miles) at the first intersection on your left go left and follow the road to Ravello. The parking area is in front of you, with steps leading up to the main square.

❹ Ravello is famous for providing refuge to the people of Amalfi when the Saracens landed in AD877. The Church of San Pantaleone stands in the square. At the top of the left aisle is a small altar with a phial containing the solidified blood of the saint, which miraculously liquefies twice a year. To the right of the church you will find the entrance to the Villa Rufolo, dating back to the 11th century, with its beautiful gardens. Richard Wagner wrote his opera *Parsifal* here (1879), and during the summer season the villa is the venue for Wagner concerts. Tickets are available from the villa or the tourist information office to the left of the church. Another villa with magnificent gardens is the 11th-century Villa Cimbrone.

WHERE TO EAT

If you walk along the seafront in Amalfi you will pass the Lido Azzurro, which serves good food at a reasonable price. The Compà Cosimo in Ravello also serves delicious food.

PLACES TO VISIT

VILLA RUFOLO

Piazza del Duomo, 84010 Ravello 089 857657 Daily 9–sunset €6

Opposite *The town of Ravello*
Above *Colourful houses in Positano*

VILLA CIMBRONE GARDENS

Via Santa Chiara 26, 84010 Ravello 089 858072 Daily 9 until 1 hour before dusk €6

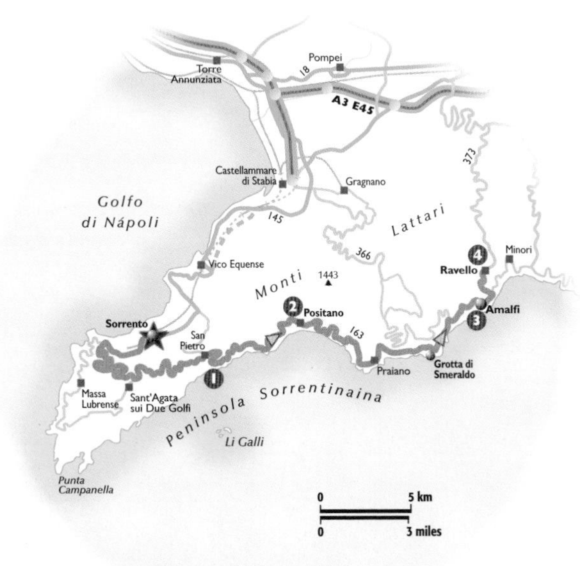

SORRENTO—MASSA LUBRENSE

On this walk, make the most of the rich scenery and memorable views over the Bay of Sorrento and the surrounding hills (▷ 367).

THE WALK
Distance: 3.5km (2 miles)
Time: 1 hour
Start at: Piazza Tasso, Sorrento
End at: Massa Lubrense

★ From Piazza Tasso head down Via Cesareo, a narrow, cobbled shopping street selling wood and leather goods and liqueurs. Towards the end of the road you will see the Church of Sant'Annunziata on the left.

At the end of the road go right, then continue straight ahead and turn left at the parking sign, which leads to the restaurant Zintonio Mare. Here there is a slightly sloping road with a sheer rock face in front. Pass along the high walled path, which narrows and becomes a tight passage between two houses, one yellow and one pink. Walk up the steps, go around the railing, and you will find yourself on the busy main road.

At the International Camping sign, a little farther up on the right, turn left up the steep, cobbled road. Look over your shoulder to admire the view over the bay. Negotiate the bends by taking the three paths that act as a short cut. Continue up on the road that climbs away from Sorrento. The road curves left but goes straight over onto Via Priora, which is little more than a path. This takes you over a main road—beware of scooters. Continue uphill to a shrine of the Madonna and Child and fork left.

You are now on a country trail in the middle of vineyards and lemon groves. It is around 600m (655 yards) to the top of the hill. Continue for another 400m (440 yards) to a crossroads and join Via Bagnulo. Pass under the arch below the white house and take the first right. Go down around two bends to an intersection and turn left, then take the first right heading straight towards Massa Lubrense.

The Church of Santa Maria delle Grazie, on Largo del Vescavado, stands on the foundations of the 16th-century cathedral of Massa Lubrense. The original structure was completely rebuilt in 1760 by Bishop Bellotti when the Episcopio was added. Among the many pieces of art inside are paintings by Cardisco and Negroni. Noteworthy is the sacristy, with oval portraits of the bishops of Massa Lubrense and 18th-century wooden furniture.

Frequent buses run back to Sorrento from Massa Lubrense.

WHEN TO GO
Don't attempt this walk in August, when it is intensely hot. Always take plenty of water with you.

WHERE TO EAT
You can stop for refreshment either in Sorrento or at Massa Lubrense, but there is nothing on the walk itself. The Red Lion (Il Leone Rosso; Via Marziale 25; tel 081 807 3089) in Sorrento, despite its name, has typical local and national dishes on the menu at reasonable prices served in a pub-like atmosphere. Meals begin with a free tomato bruschetta and end with a free *limoncello* liqueur.

Above *The rooftops of Sorrento*
Opposite *Looking over the Bay of Sorrento*

THE GARGANO PENINSULA

Spend a day touring the spur on Italy's boot, along the winding roads of the rugged coast and through the interior's limestone plateaux and forests that make up Gargano National Park. This tour takes you past medieval castles, pilgrimage churches, fishing villages, sandy beaches and the beautiful Foresta Umbra.

THE DRIVE
Distance: 208km (129 miles)
Allow: 1 day
Start at: A14 *autostrada*
End at: San Severo/A14 *autostrada*

★ From the A14 *autostrada*, take the Foggia exit and follow signs for Manfredonia on the SS89. Just before Manfredonia, follow the road as it forks right onto the SS159, past the Church of Santa Maria di Siponto.

❶ Santa Maria di Siponto is a handsome 11th-century Romanesque church built over a fifth-century crypt.

Continue for 3km (2 miles) to Manfredonia.

❷ Manfredonia is a good place to shop for picnic refreshments for lunch. Its *castello* (castle), built by King Manfred (1232–66), now serves as a museum preserving the history of the Gargano Peninsula.

From Manfredonia, continue northeast on the SS89 and follow the road as it forks left towards Monte Sant'Angelo. The road winds north into the hills with several hairpin bends—beware of tour buses.

❸ Monte Sant'Angelo is a popular pilgrimage town, with many souvenir shops. It is celebrated for its Santuario di San Michele Arcangelo, a cave-shrine 90 steps down, where the Archangel Michael appeared in the fifth century to the Bishop of Siponto.

Drive east towards the coast and Mattinata. Continue until you reach Baia delle Zagare.

❹ East of Baia delle Zagare is the Grotta Smeralda (Emerald Cave), one of several caves along this stretch of coast.

From Baia delle Zagare you can bypass some of the corniche's more alarming bends by taking a detour inland to Testa del Gargano, heading back on the coast road towards Vieste.

❺ The peninsula's eastern-most point, Vieste (▷ 365), is a pleasant resort with good sandy beaches, ideal if you feel like a swim.

The coast road from Vieste continues in a northwest direction to Peschici.

❻ Peschici is a pretty fishing village perched on a promontory with good swimming on the sandy beach (▷ 359).

After Peschici, turn south off the coastal highway at the village of

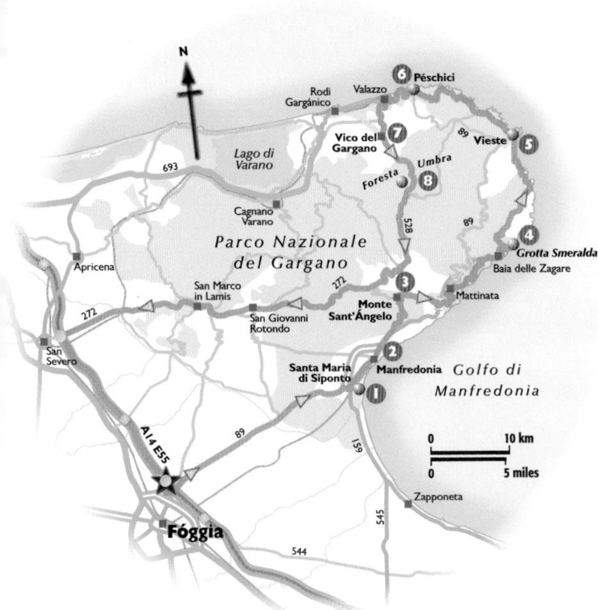

Valazzo and wind your way inland to Vico del Gargano.

❼ Vico del Gargano, with views over the Adriatic, is renowned for its olive oil.

From here, a narrow road winds up to the heart of the Foresta Umbra.

❽ The woodland road passes groves of beech trees, Foresta Umbra's pride (▷ 349), as well as maple, hornbeam and birch. You may glimpse rare orchids, deer or moufflon (wild sheep) on the plateaux.

The SS528 continues south through the forest and meets the SS272 (west of Monte Sant'Angelo). Drive through San Giovanni Rotondo via San Marco in Lamis. This tour ends at the San Severo entrance to the A14 *autostrada* (73km/45 miles).

WHERE TO EAT

The Locanda Dragone in Vieste is a good place to stop for lunch (Via Duomo 8, tel 0884 701212; www.aldragone.it; Closed Nov–Mar and Tue Apr–May). Alternatively, you could wait and eat later at Trabucco Da Mimi in Peschici—a romantic seafood restaurant right by the sea (Punta San Nicola; tel 0884 962556; www.altrabucco.it).

PLACES TO VISIT

PARCO NAZIONALE DEL GARGANO

www.parcogargano.it
ℹ Via S. Antonio Abate 121, 71037 Monte Sant'Angelo ☎ 0884 568911

CASTELLO MANFREDONIA

✉ Castello Svevo-Angioino, 71043 Manfredonia ☎ 0884 587838 🕒 Daily 9.30–6.30; closed first and last Mon of month except Jul and Aug 🖐 €3

SANTUARIO DI SAN MICHELE ARCANGELO

✉ 71037 Monte Sant'Angelo ☎ 0884 561150 🕒 Jul–Sep daily 7.30–7.30; Apr–Jun, Oct 7.30–12.30, 2.30–7; Nov–Mar 7.30–12.30, 2.30–5

Opposite *Vieste, the Gargano Peninsula's easternmost point*
Below *Boats on Peschici's sandy beach*

THE SALENTINE PENINSULA

From the baroque town of Lecce, this drive traces the varied coastline around the rocky Salentine Peninsula. The cliff-top road occasionally descends to sea level, running along sandy shores, across creeks and through small fishing villages. At the tip of the heel of Italy, Capo di Santa Maria di Léuca, the road turns north to Gallipoli, with its medieval *centro storico.*

THE DRIVE
Distance: 150km (93 miles; plus 190km/118 miles back to Lecce)
Allow: 1 day
Start at: Lecce
End at: Gallipoli

★ Start by enjoying Lecce's baroque jewels on the Piazza del Duomo, the Chiesa di Santa Croce and the palazzi on Via Palmieri (▷ 352–353).

On the east side of Lecce's ring-road, the Via della Libertà meets up with the SS543 highway to San Cataldo (7km/4 miles). The highway to the coast passes through olive groves and past farmland and small fields reclaimed from the once malarial marshes on the coast. You will then pass the fine sands and pine woods of San Cataldo with its ancient Roman port, an area now known as the Lido di Lecce. From San Cataldo, turn back west for 1km (0.6 mile) on the SS543, then turn south onto the SS611 through the Riserva Naturale Le Cesine, past the Roca Vecchia towards Otranto.

❶ The World Wide Fund for Nature (WWF) Riserva Naturale Le Cesine covers 620ha (1,532 acres) of pine and holm-oak woodland and shrub (myrtle, mastic, broom and juniper). The wetlands are the migratory home for herons, coots, mallards and moorhens.

The 14th-century castle ruin of Roca Vecchia has a grand cliff-top view of the sea and there is good swimming at Torre dell'Orso's sandy beach. West of the coast road is the fishing lake of Alimini Grande.

❷ The fishing and ferry port of Otranto has a Norman cathedral, famous for its 12th-century mosaic (▷ 358).

From the SS173 outside Otranto, turn east onto the coast road that leads out towards Capo d'Otranto.

❸ Capo d'Otranto is the Italian mainland's easternmost point, close to Albania. On a clear day you can see the island of Sazan and beyond to the Acrocerauni Mountains. Along the dramatic rocky coastline is Porto Badisco, a fishing hamlet where Aeneas, legendary hero of the Trojan Wars, is said to have landed in Italy.

Rejoin the SS173 at Porto Badisco. Continue heading south via Santa Cesarea Terme.

❹ In the spa resort of Santa Cesarea Terme (recommended for respiratory ailments and tired bones), you can admire the art nouveau and Moorish-style Villa Sticchi over the thermal baths.

Continue to Castro.

❺ The ancient Roman cliff-top garrison-town of Castro overlooks a superb bay, where you can explore the subterranean Grotta Zinzulusa.

The SS173 continues south from Castro to Capo Santa Maria di Leuca.

❻ Capo Santa Maria di Leuca is on the heel tip of Italy's boot. Its sanctuary, also known as Santuario de Finibus Terrae (Land's End), marks the point where St. Peter is said to have begun his mission to bring the Gospel to Italy.

Follow the coast road through Marina di Leuca, which winds its way past Punta Ristola northwest to Gallipoli. Punta Ristola is the boot's southernmost point. The coast road is punctuated by a series of Spanish-built watchtowers and modern beach resorts, notably Torre San Giovanni, Posto Racale and Baia Verde. Alternatively take a faster route inland along the SS274 (45km/28 miles).

❼ The medieval *centro storico* (old town) of Gallipoli was originally an island. Now joined to the mainland by a causeway, it has a Byzantine *castello* (castle) and a baroque cathedral (▷ 349).

From Gallipoli, the SS101 returns north to Lecce.

WHERE TO EAT

Try Il Bastione in Gallipoli (tel 0833 263836), which offers creative yet traditional cuisine in a romantic harbour setting.

PLACES TO VISIT

WWF RISERVA NATURALE LE CESINE

www.wwf.it/puglia

✉ Approximately 5km (3 miles) from San Cataldo ☎ 0832 892264 🕐 Daily Oct–end Apr ☞ Sat–Sun 9.30–2.30

GROTTA ZINZULUSA

☞ Organized from Castro Marina ☎ 0836 943812 🕐 Daily 9.30–7 ✋ €3

Opposite *Clear waters at Gallipoli*
Right *The Roman amphitheatre in Lecce*

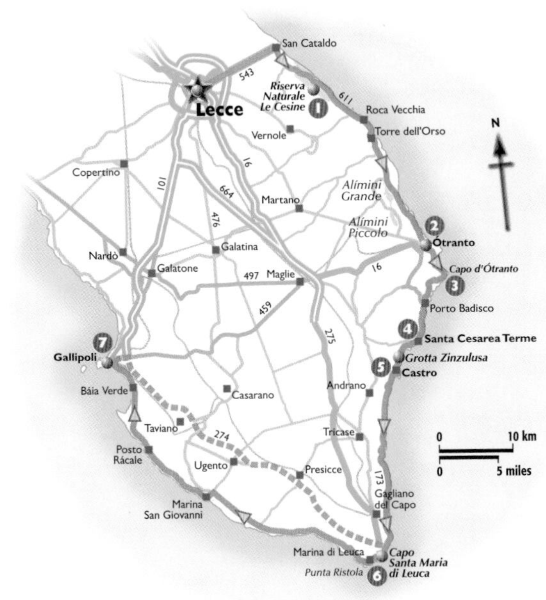

Above *Festival time in Naples*

ARCO FELICE

CIRCOLO GOLF NAPOLI CARNEY PARK

This golf course is right next to Lago d'Averno, an eerie lake that is the entrance to Hell according to the ancient Greeks. The nine-hole Circolo Golf Napoli has equipment hire, putting greens, a bar and restaurant.
✉ Via Campiglione 11, 0078 Arco Felice, Napoli ☎ 081 526 4296 🕑 Wed–Mon 8–dusk, Tue afternoon only 🖐 €25 🚇 Pozzuoli 🚆 Cumana train 🚗 Take the Tangenziale (Naples Circular) and exit at Pozzuoli for Via Campana

BAIA

SEA POINT ITALY

www.seapointitaly.it
A wonderful place to go diving, the Baia is rich in aquatic wildlife and submerged Greek and Roman sites. Sea Point Italy offers a range of diving courses.
✉ Via Molo di Baia 14, 80070 Baia ☎ 081 868 8868 🕑 May–end Sep Tue–Sun 9–7; rest of year Tue–Sun 9–1, 3–7 🖐 Open-water diving course €230, snorkelling course €140 🚆 Cumana train to Baia

CAPRI

CORALLIUM

Four generations of the same family have worked producing coral jewellery at this treasure trove of a shop, where you can buy classic pieces beautifully carved and incised, or opt for chunky necklaces and bracelets of unworked coral where the quality is left to shine without embellishment.
✉ Via G. Orlandi 163–165, 80071 Anacapri ☎ 081 837 2108 🕑 Mon–Sat 10–1, 4–8

LIMONCELLO DI CAPRI

www.limoncello.com
Limoncello liqueur may be abundant in these parts, but there's no denying this shop is one of the best of its kind on the island. The lemon-based spirit is great mixed with champagne or *prosecco* (sparkling white wine from the Veneto), and as an after-dinner *digestivo*.
✉ Via Listrieri 25A, 80073 Capri ☎ 081 837 3059 🕑 Daily 9–7

MARIORITA

www.mariorita.com
This upmarket ladies' fashion store is far and away the best on Capri, stocking designers such as Armani, Missoni, Valentino and shoes by Ferragamo and other famous names. Beautifully laid out, the shop includes an area that sells Capodimonte porcelain from Naples as well as inlaid tables and *objets d'art*.
✉ Piazza Vittoria, 80071 Anacapri ☎ 081 837 3659 🕑 Tue 4–8, Wed–Sat 10–8

LECCE

SUN S.A.S.

Relieve those weary limbs after sightseeing and strolling the Salento sand with a visit to this health and beauty parlour. Facial and body treatments are reasonably priced. They have a team of masseurs, and a great range of beauty products to take home.
✉ Via Orsini del Balzo 70, 73100 Lecce ☎ 0832 349444 🕑 Mon–Sat 9–9 🖐 Massage €30

TEATRO PAISIELLO

www.teatro.org
Expect neo-Renaissance architecture, classical Greek motifs on a handsome 1872 facade and sumptuous interiors at Teatro Paisiello, named after the 18th-century composer Giovanni Paisiello. There is jazz, cabaret, classical and pop, plus Italian and international drama and dance productions.
✉ Via Giuseppe Palmieri 72, 73100 Lecce ☎ 0832 245499 🕑 Box office: Mon–Sat 10.30–1, 4.30–7 🖐 €15–€40

NAPOLI (NAPLES)

ARENILE DI BAGNOLI

www.arenilereload.com

This is the closest beach club to the city and the biggest. Live jazz music alternates with dance and indie and the disco is on the beachside dance floor. Especially popular for sunset and dancing under the stars.

Via Coroglio 10, 80124 Napoli 081 019 9156 Apr–Sep daily 9pm–4am Disco free. Live gigs from €10 Bagnoli

IL CANTUCCIO DELLA CERAMICA

You'll find this ceramics studio down a small street between Piazza del Gesù Nuovo and Piazza San Domenico Maggiore. Ceramics in a multitude of hues are for sale, but you can also take classes here and make your own.

Via Benedetto Croce 38, 80134 Napoli 081 552 5857 Mon–Fri 10–6 Piazza Cavour

CIRCOLO DEL REMO E DELLA VELA 'ITALIA'

www.crvitalia.it

For those interested in sailing, this club has lessons and courses to suit all abilities.

Banchina Santa Lucia, 80132 Napoli 081 764 6393 Daily 8.30am–midnight 102, 140, 150

CLUB ALPINO ITALIANO

www.cai.it

If you fancy exploring the hills in the Campania region, the local branch of the Club Alpino should be your first port of call. They run trekking and climbing excursions to the summits of Vesuvio and Cervati.

Via Trinità degli Spagnoli 41, 80132 Napoli 348 053 6215 Information Tue, Fri 7pm–9pm 102, 140, 150

EDENLANDIA

www.edenlandia.it

This theme park is just a short train ride away from the city. There are lots of attractions for all ages, including a fantasy castle, a 3-D cinema, variety shows, water rides and the exciting Star Wars ride.

Viale Kennedy, Campi Flegrei, 80125 Napoli 081 239 4090 Opening times are complicated. Broadly, Apr–Sep daily; Oct–Mar Sat–Sun only except over Christmas; check before you travel Admission: €2.50. Unlimited use of all rides/facilities €10 152 Cumana train to Campi Flegrei

ENOTECA PARTENOPEA

www.enotecapartenopea.it

Don't leave Naples without tasting some of the region's fine wines. The rich volcanic soil gives the wine a remarkable richness; ask the staff for an introduction to the region's offerings and grab a few bargain bottles to take home.

Viale Augusto 2, 80125 Napoli 081 593 7982 Fri–Wed 9–1.30, 4.30–7.30, Thu 9–1.30 Campi Flegrei

FONDAZIONE NUOVA ORCHESTRA ALESSANDRO SCARLATTI

www.nuovaorchestrascarlatti.it

The Orchestra Scarlatti stages concerts at San Severo al Pendino and other historical sites and theatres around Naples. The performances are well-known classical works and Neapolitan music through the ages.

Salita Betlemme 13, 80132 Napoli (headquarters) 081 410175 From €10 C4, 102, 128

GIUSEPPE FERRIGNO

Naples is famed for its wonderful *presepi* (Christmas cribs), and Ferrigno is the acknowledged master of the myriad figures that go into these scenes—many of them non-religious subjects of great charm, which would make lovely ornaments and good gifts.

Via San Gregorio Armeno 8, Spaccanapoli 80138 Napoli 081 552 3148 Mon–Sat 10–1.30, 4.30–8 Dante

GRAN CAFFÈ GAMBRINUS

www.caffegambrinus.com/ing/home.htm

Sit out in Piazza Trieste e Trento or inside in the beautiful old-fashioned tea room of this Naples institution for a cocktail or to enjoy a pot of tea and exquisite Neapolitan cakes. Then you can buy their fine china cups and saucers, gift-wrapped in a rich blue box. The china is designed by Richard Ginori exclusively for this historic café. They also sell fine chocolates and fragrant fruit pastries *(sfogliate)* to take away. The tea room is decorated with the works of art and priceless sculptures, making it Naples' most prestigious snack bar.

Via Chiaia 1–2, 80132 Napoli 081 417582 Daily 8.30am–9pm 24, C22, C25

MARINELLA

www.marinellanapoli.it

If formal style is what you're after, then Marinella should be right up your street. The shop is famed for made-to-measure ties in silk, wool and other fabrics. Tie guru Don Eugenio Marinella's mantra is 'it's the total of the little particulars that make the man elegant'. Today's clients include Bill Clinton, Prince Albert of Monaco and Silvio Berlusconi.

Riviera di Chiaia 287, 80122 Napoli 081 764 4214 Mon–Sat 9.30–1.30, 3.30–8 Piazza Amedeo 102, 108, 122

MARIO VALENTINO

www.mariovalentino.it

Come to this iconic store for shoes and clothes to fall in love with; a huge range of this season's must-have styles and heels and a collection of classics for everyday and formal wear, all beautifully made by one of Italy's finest designers.

Via Fontanelle 85, 80136 Napoli 081 544 1380 Mon–Sat 10–8 C23

MERCATO DI SANT'ANTONIO

This market is always a feast for the senses and a little bewildering to the uninitiated. It's crammed with local produce, and traders use the local dialect. Try the fantastic tomatoes grown in the foothills of Vesuvio. If you would like a small amount of something, ask for *un etto, per favore* (100g, please).

Via Sant'Antonio Abate, 80139 Napoli Mon–Sat 9–8 14, 135, 254

MURAT LIVE CLUB

This club on Piazza Dante has an adventurous music policy—the

eclectic schedule includes lots of jazz and funk, all imbued with a touch of Neapolitan style. It also has the occasional world music night.
✉ Via Bellini Vincenzo 6, 80135 Napoli ☎ 081 544 5919 Daily 10pm–late Montesanto 137, 160, 161

SOLFATARA

www.solfatara.it
Get closer to the volcanic rumblings of the earth's crust at Solfatara, a dormant volcano. Sulphurous fumes hang over the site, but the bubbling mud, fumaroles and hot waters are the real spectacle to see.
✉ Via Solfatara 161, Pozzuoli, 80078 Napoli ☎ 081 526 2341 Daily 8.30am to 1 hour before sunset Adult €6, child (under 10) €4 Pozzuoli–Solfatara and then bus P9 or 152

TEATRO POLITEAMA

www.teatropoliteamanapoli.com
This theatre often has lavish productions by the Scuola di Ballo del Teatro di San Carlo in conjunction with illustrious international companies, including the Birmingham Royal Ballet and the Conservatorio di San Pietro a Majella.
✉ Via Monte de Dio 80, 80132 Napoli ☎ 081 764 5001 Box office: Tue–Sat 10–1, 4.30–6.30 €12–€50 102, 128

TEATRO SAN CARLO

www.teatrosancarlo.it
The oldest opera house in Italy (opened in 1737) has been described as the most beautiful theatre in the world and stages ballet as well as opera, classical concerts and short comic operas. Some of the first ballet productions were performed here, in the intermission between opera acts. Reserve tickets in advance; you can book online.
✉ Via San Carlo 98F, 80132 Napoli ☎ 081 797 2331 Box office: Tue–Sat 10–7 €20–€100+ C4, 140, 149

VELVET ZONE

www.velvetnapoli.it
This long-established club attracts a discerning crowd with its eclectic, alternative music policy. Live bands and international DJs often play here.
✉ Via Cisterna dell'Olio 11, 80134 Napoli ☎ 339 670 0234 Tue–Sun midnight–dawn €15 membership Montesanto

VIBES ON THE BEACH

A lot of Neapolitan clubs move to the beach in the summer and this, originally a city centre bar, has moved here full time. Expect cool jazz vibes, frozen cocktails and a chilled crowd.
✉ Via Miseno 52, Capo Miseno, 80070 Napoli ☎ 081 523 2828 Jun–Sep daily 9pm–2am; Oct–May Fri–Sat 9pm–2am Free Circumvesuviana

YES BRAZIL

www.yes-brazil.it
Join the fun-loving crowd at this tropical club with Brazilian beats. Dancers in skimpy outfits shake their tassels to the accomplished percussionists and the staff will keep you topped up with Brazilian drinks and fare all night long.
✉ Via Posillipo 405/c, 80123 Napoli ☎ 349 806 2385, 333 299 9332 Daily 8pm–2am Mergellina

POSITANO

MARIA LAMPO

'Lampo' means in a flash and this fashion store got its name after World War II when the owner ran up easy-to-wear, pretty holiday clothes in a flash. There's a huge range of feminine beach and street wear and laid-back, quietly elegant clothes for men: a Positano legend.
✉ Via Pasitea 12–16, 84017 Positano ☎ 089 875021 Apr–Oct daily 9.30–9; Nov–Mar Mon–Sat 9.30–7

MUSIC ON THE ROCKS

www.musicontherocks.it

This is an elegant club hewn out of the rocks and serving fine cocktails. It offers Italian-style piano bar most evenings and frequent appearances by well-known international DJs who spin house music.

Via Grotte dell'Incanto 51, 84017 Positano 089 875874 Apr–end Sep daily 8pm–late €20

PRAIANO

L'AFRICANA

L'Africana is the most celebrated nightclub on this stretch of the Amalfi Coast. A walkway hewn out of the rock leads to a network of caves that sit above the sea. Commercial dance and house music are played.

Vettica Maggiore, 84010 Praiano 089 874042 Thu–Sun 10–5 €15

RAVELLO

GIARDINI DI VILLA RUFOLO

www.ravellofestival.it

This Moorish-style villa and its gardens are a magnet for classical music fans. Wagner lived and composed at the nearby Palazzo Sasso. Ravello is a music capital, especially during the annual Festival Musicale di Ravello held from late June to October.

Piazza Vescovado 1, 84010 Ravello 089 857 657 Apr–Sep daily 9–8; Oct–Mar 9–6 €6

SALERNO

WIND'S AMICI DI GUIDO

www.flysurfsalerno.it

This windy spot is the best place to windsurf and fly power kites on the Amalfi Coast. Equipment rental and lessons are available.

Via Rocco Cocchia 181–185, 84132 Salerno 089 339316 Daily 10–8 Lessons from €40 per day A3 Napoli–Salerno, exit Vietri sul Mare

SORRENTO

ARTIS DOMUS

www.artisdomus.com

This elegant 19th-century villa is the Sorrentine haunt of poets and artists. Live pop/rock/jazz/folk music and club nights are held in an evocative and intimate setting. The food is excellent and there is a fabulous cocktail bar *Ibirreria*.

Via San Nicolà, 80067 Sorrento 081 877 2073 Sat 8pm–late €10–€15

ENOTECA BACCHUS

www.enotecabacchus.com

Sommelier Paolo Schiattarella selects the vintages here. There are more than 1,000 labels to choose from, as well as grappa, cognac, whisky, brandy, rum and various liqueurs.

Piazza San Antonio 20, 80067 Sorrento 081 807 4610 Jun–end Sep daily 9–1, 4.30–10; rest of year 8.30–10pm

MATILDA CLUB

www.tiscali.it/matilda_club

A superb, six-level nightclub, Matilda has live acts and regular club nights with house, Latin and dance music. Style and decor varies from elegant exposed walls to British pub to contemporary chic. Internet access is also available on the fifth floor.

Piazza Tasso 1, 80067 Sorrento 081 877 3236 Daily 7.30pm–4am €12

SINISCALCHI

The Amalfi Coast towns are famous for beautiful handmade sandals and you can have a pair made for you here overnight. There's a multitude of leathers, fabrics, colours and decorations to choose from, all guaranteed to make you feel a real part of the summertime scene.

Via S. Cesareo 101, 80067 Sorrento 081 877 1515 Mon–Sat 10–8

TENNIS SORRENTO

There are two tennis clubs in Sorrento, both very busy in the summer. Each has half a dozen clay and concrete courts. Equipment rental is available.

Viale Montariello 4, 80067 Sorrento 081 807 4181

Tennis Sport Sorrento Via Califano, 80067 Sorrento 081 807 1616 Daily 10–10 €10 per hour daytime, €14 per hour evening

FESTIVALS AND EVENTS

MAY

FESTA DI SAN DOMENICO

This pre-Roman festival was adopted by the early Christian Church. It's dedicated to San Domenico Abbate, who delivered the town of Cocullo from poisonous snakes. On his feast day, his statue is carried through the town, and draped en route with hundreds of live snakes.

Cocullo 1st week in May

SAGRA DI SAN NICOLA

Three festivities honour St. Nicholas, patron saint of Bari. A parade processes to the basilica to symbolically deliver the saint's bones, which sailors brought back to the city in 1807. The next day, the saint's statue is carried to a fishing boat, where it is the focus of another three days of celebration. It's a festival untouched by tourism.

Bari 1st weekend in May

MAY/SEPTEMBER/ DECEMBER

FESTA DI SAN GENNARO

The fourth-century martyr San Gennaro is Naples' patron saint, and his blood has been kept in a vessel in a side chapel of the Duomo since 1497. Three times a year, the blood is exhibited to a seething crowd and it liquefies. The time it takes to do so is said to portend the city's fortunes for the next year.

Napoli Saturday before the 1st Sunday in May, 19 September, 16 December

SEPTEMBER

TROPEA BLUES FESTIVAL

In early September the seaside town of Tropea buzzes with the Tropea Blues Festival. The piazza and streets become a stage for groups, bands and jam sessions, recreating the atmosphere of New Orleans.

Tropea 6 days in early September

PRICES AND SYMBOLS

The restaurants are listed alphabetically within each town. The prices given are the average for a two-course lunch (L) and a three-course dinner (D) for one person, without drinks. The wine price given is for the least expensive bottle.

For the key to symbols, ⊳ 2.

ALBEROBELLO

CANTINA

www.ilristorantelacantina.it

Housed in the old cellars of a palazzo, the friendly, family-run Cantina is proud of presenting Puglia's *cucina povera*, the traditional, simple cuisine of the working people. The pasta therefore lacks eggs but is rich in flavour from tomatoes and herbs, meat is plainly grilled and sausages are a specialty. This type of cooking is rare in restaurants—try it while you can.

✉ Vico Lippolis 9, 70011 Alberobello ☎ 0804 323 473 🕑 Wed–Mon 12.30–3, 7.30–10; closed 2 weeks Feb and Jul ✋ L €20, D €38, Wine €9

AMALFI

LA CARAVELLA

www.ristorantelacaravella.it

The proud bearer of a Michelin star, this acclaimed restaurant has been producing excellent cuisine that marries traditional elements with innovative twists since 1959. There are plenty of seafood dishes to choose from and lightly boiled filleted fish with freshly squeezed lemon. Simplicity is the key, using fresh local ingredients. The service is first class and the choice of wines exemplary.

✉ Via Matteo Camera 12, 84011 Amalfi ☎ 089 871029 🕑 Wed–Mon 12–2.30, 7.30–10.30; closed 3 Nov–15 Dec, 6 Jan–13 Feb ✋ L €60, D €80, Wine €16 ❄

TARI

www.amalfiristorantetari.it

This family-run restaurant is an intimate place to dine on quality traditional cookery. Expect some wonderful pasta and seafood creations using the freshest of produce, or simply opt for a delicious pizza for €6. The wine list has something to suit most tastes and includes lots of good local labels.

✉ Via Capuano 9–11, 84011 Amalfi ☎ 089 871832 🕑 Wed–Mon 11.30–3, 8–11; closed Nov ✋ L €15, D €45, Wine €8 ❄

BARI

AI DUE GHIOTTONI

www.ai2ghiottoni.it

Old stone walls and modern design combine to give this buzzing restaurant a great sense of style. They serve genuine Puglian cooking, so lots of fresh fish, seafood and high-quality vegetables are on offer here. Try the *risotto ai due ghiottoni*, a rich rice dish with spinach, cream, ham and fontina cheese, then move on to simply grilled fish, or *branzino al sale* (sea bass baked in salt). There is an excellent *macedonia* (fruit salad) along with some creamier treats on the dessert menu. The wine list has Italian and foreign wines.

✉ Via Putignani 11, 70121 Bari ☎ 0805 232240 🕑 Mon–Sat 12.30–3.30, 7.30–12; closed 16–24 Aug ✋ L €38, D €65, Wine €12 ❄

Opposite *An authentic Italian pizza*

CAPRI

CAPANNINA

www.capannina-capri.com

The menu at this prestigious restaurant includes *ravioli alla caprese*, aubergines (eggplants) stuffed with ricotta, luscious avocados and prawns and fresh local lobster. The wine list has more than 200 labels, and the desserts are devilishly rich. Reservations are required.

Via le Botteghe 12/14, 80073 Capri 081 837 0732 20 Mar–Oct daily 12–3, 7.30–11.30; closed Wed Apr and Oct L €45, D €70, Wine €12

DA GEMMA

Gemma's has been the hangout of the *bella gente* since the 1930s. Savour the wonderful *pizza napoletana* and soak up the history documented on the walls. Highlights include fisherman's risotto, *ravioli alla caprese* and *maccheroncelli* with potatoes and mussels. There is an *antipasti* buffet and dessert-lovers have a mouth-watering choice. The wine list is excellent.

Via Madre Serafina 6, 80073 Capri 081 837 0461 Daily 12–3.30, 7–12; closed 3 weeks in Jan L €30, D €55, Wine €10

RONDINELLA

This friendly, family-run rustic restaurant has a good range of typical Campanese fish and seafood dishes and also serves crisp, thin and delicious *pizze*. There's an outside terrace for summer eating.

Via Orlandi 295, 80073 Anacapri 0818 371223 Fri–Wed 12.30–2.30, 7.30–10; closed Jan, Feb L €30, D €44, Wine €9

VERGINIELLO

Always busy, this is a very popular choice with both locals and tourists. It's just below the Via Roma and has superb views over the Marina Grande. Choose between the mural-covered walls of the dining room and the pergola-shaded terrace and do try an *insalata caprese*—Capri's own salad of mozzarella, tomatoes and basil. Other specialities include seafood and fish of the day and fine homemade pasta. Service is fast, efficient and friendly.

Via lo Palazzo 25a, 80073 Capri 081 837 0944 Daily 12–3.30, 7.30–12; closed Nov L €20, D €30, Wine €9

GALLIPOLI

LA PURITATE

You can eat on the terrace overlooking the sea at this fish restaurant beside the walls of the old town. Enjoy a succession of fish dishes, ranging from delicate shellfish antipasti, through pasta with black cuttlefish and its ink in a sauce, to a perfectly grilled sole. Try the local house white wine to accompany it all.

Via S. Elia 18, 73014 Gallipoli 0833 264 205 Jun–Sep daily 12.30–3, 7.30–10.30, Apr–May, Nov–Mar Thu–Tue 12.30–3, 7.30–10; closed Oct L €40, D €50, Wine €11

GARGANO PENINSULA

AL BARONE

www.albarone.it

Two elegantly vaulted 16th-century rooms house this pleasant restaurant/ *enoteca* (wine bar), where you can sample local cooking from the Gargano. Try the *orecchiete* (little ear) pasta with a sauce of bitter green turnip tops—better than it sounds—or a rich lasagne, before moving on to a mixed selection of meats from the grill or a slice of succulent roast meat. The best bet for dessert is the ricotta tart.

Via Bartolomeo Gambadoro 3, 71037 Monte Sant'Angelo 0884 562 577 Wed–Mon 12.30–3, 7.30–10, closed mid-Jan to mid-Feb L €28, D € 50, Wine €11

MEDIOEVO

www.ristorantemedioevo.it

Pilgrims often miss this wonderful restaurant in Monte Sant'Angelo. Start with some of the region's best *salumi* and cured meats and order from the small but excellent wine list. You can't leave Puglia without sampling the local *orecchiette* (ear-shaped pasta) with a meaty lamb sauce. The dried figs with almonds bathed in rum must be tasted.

Via Castello 21, 71013 Monte Sant'Angelo 0884 565356 Daily 12.30–2.30, 8–10; closed 15–30 Nov and Mon in winter L €18, D €38, Wine €9

OSTERIA DEGLI ANGELI

www.osteriadegliangeli.info

All summer, tables are scattered on the cobbled *piazzetta* outside this lovely restaurant and pizzeria, whose interior features vaulted ceilings and terracotta tiling. The food is classic, cheap and of exceptional quality. Kick off by selecting a plate of *antipasti* from the huge buffet, then try the *orecchiete* pasta with a *ragù* or vegetable sauce, before tucking into fresh fish or grilled meat.

Via Adige 3, 71019 Vieste 0884 701 112 Apr–Oct daily 12.30–3, 7.30–11 L €20, D €30, Wine €9

LECCE

OSTERIA DEGLI SPIRITI

www.osteriadeglispiriti.it

This very pleasing trattoria, close to the public gardens, specializes in traditional Puglian cuisine. The decor is like that of an old *masseria* (farmhouse) and the service is very attentive. This is a popular spot, so reservations are recommended.

Via Cesare Battista 4, 73100 Lecce 0832 246274 Mon–Sat 12.30–2.30, 8–10.30, Sun 12.30–3; closed 2 weeks Sep L €22, D €50, Wine €10

PICTON

www.acena.it/picton

Deep in the heart of the baroque city is one of Lecce's finest restaurants. You'll find a menu largely filled with traditional Puglian meals and the odd surprise. Seafood dominates the antipasti and pastas. The potato gnocchi with swordfish is outstanding, and steak and other meat choices sit alongside main-course fish dishes. Divine desserts and excellent regional wines complete this great culinary journey.

Via Idomeneo 14, 73100 Lecce 0832 332383 Tue–Sun 12.30–2.30, 8–11.30; closed 2 weeks Jun and Nov L €30, D €55, Wine €10

MARATEA

TAVERNA ROVITA

On one of old Maratea's most picturesque streets is the Rovita, an elegantly laid-back establishment with touches of rustic charm. The cooking is regional, the bread and pasta home-made. Expect dishes like the delicate citron-spiked seafood risotto, plainly grilled fish and fruit-studded *cassata*. Some French wines augment the local and Italian list.

Via Rovita 63, Maratea, 85046 Potenza 0973 876588 Easter–Dec Wed–Mon 12.30–2, 7–11 L €30, D €45, Wine €6

MATERA

BACCANTI

Literally a series of grottos carved out of the tufa, this wonderful restaurant, emphasizes local produce served in imaginative ways, while paying homage to tradition. Wild herbs, local cheeses, fresh pasta and lamb figure strongly, and don't miss the excellent almond *cannolo* stuffed with ricotta on the dessert menu.

Via Sant'Angelo 58–61, 75100 Matera 083 533 704 Tue–Sat 12.30–2.30, 7.30–9.30, Sun 12.30–2.30; closed Jan, Feb L €28, D €50, Wine €11

LE BOTTEGHE

www.lebotteghemt.it

In the heart of the Sassi protected area, this stylish restaurant has a minimalist whitewashed interior that is both cool and welcoming. Fresh, hand-made pasta dressed with typical, seasonal ingredients, such as porcini mushrooms or homemade sausages, is followed by the house special of grilled meats, especially local lamb and *chianina* beef prepared over the restaurant's open fire.

Piazza San Pietro Barisano 22, 75100 Matera 0835 344072 Mon–Sat 12.30–3, 7.30–10.30, Sun 12.30–3; closed 2 weeks in Jan or Feb L €30, D €47, Wine €11

NAPOLI (NAPLES)

EXCELSIOR-LA TERRAZZA

www.excelsior.it

The Hotel Excelsior's restaurant, La Terrazza, is hard to beat, with its stunning views, exquisite food and luxurious touches. The wine list has been compiled by a professional sommelier. There are some inventive pasta creations and a superb mixed grill garnished with mussels.

Via Partenope 48, 80121 Napoli 081 761 0111 Mon–Sat 12.30–3, 8–11 L €68, D €93, Wine €16 C52, E5, 140, 152

GINO SORBILLO

www.accademiadellapizza.it

Gino's website address says it all—truly spectacular and quintessentially Neapolitan *pizze* are on offer here. Founded in 1935, this pizzeria serves the real thing, made with the best ingredients, and will deliver within the city centre—go to the website to order.

Via Tribunali 32, 80138 Napoli 081 446643 Mon–Sat 11–4, 7–midnight L and D €15

MIMÌ ALLA FERROVIA

This splendidly traditional restaurant, with its solid interior and deep leather chairs in the bar, is a real institution, serving totally correct Neapolitan cuisine. The *zuppa di mare* (fish soup) is superb, or try the *torta di alici* (anchovy tart) and follow it with a classic fish grill or roast meat. The dessert menu is excellent and the wine list interesting and large.

Via Alfonso d'Aragona 21, 80139 Napoli 081 553 8525 Mon–Sat 12.30–2.30, 7.30–10; closed 2 weeks in Aug L €28, D €42, Wine €11 Garibaldi

POMPEI

DE VIVO

www.lapasticceriadevivo.it

This superb bar/ice-cream parlour/pastry shop has a good range of beverages and snacks, including small pizzas and filled flat-bread sandwiches and *panini*. There are lots of pastries and cakes, including Neapolitan *pastiera* (Easter orange and ricotta-filled pie), *sfogliatelle* (crunchy pastry wth a custard filling) and *babà al limoncello* (a soft cake with limoncello liqueur). The *gelati*, *sorbetti* and *semifreddi* will delight kids. Credit cards are not accepted.

Via Roma 26, 80045 Pompei 081 863 1163 Aug daily 9am–10pm; rest of year Wed–Mon 9am–10pm; closed 2 weeks Jul Pastries from €3, ice cream from €2.50

PRESIDENT

www.ristorantepresident.it

This is an excellent choice for seafood-lovers. The fish is freshly caught and of the highest quality—the choice catches of the day are cooked in the oven using traditional methods. There is a superior selection of wines. There is also a water and an oil list (24 oils!).

Piazza Schettino 12, 80045 Pompei 081 850 7245 Tue–Sat 12.30–3.30, 8–11, Sun 12.30–3.30; closed 10–25 Aug, 23–25 Dec and Mon Oct–Apr L €40, D €50, Wine €11

RISTORANTE-PIZZERIA CARLO ALBERTO

www.ristopizzacarloalberto.it

This is a small, well-designed eatery not far from the archaeological site. Choose from a wide selection of pastas and pizzas. Delicious creations include seafood served in a tangy, slightly spicy lemon sauce. The wine list is adequate and the desserts top notch. Polish off the meal with a drop of *grappa del Vesuvio*, made from the Lacrima Christi grape that grows on the slopes of the dormant volcano.

Via Carlo Alberto 15, 80045 Pompei 081 863 3231 Daily 12–3, 7–11.30 L €20, D €35, Wine €8

POSITANO

CAPITANO

www.hotelmontemare.it

A feeling of elegant refinement pervades Capitano. Dine under the pergolas on the terrace, which has magical sea views. First courses include a delicious calamari and scampi salad. Seafood dishes dominate. You shouldn't leave this part of the world without trying fried prawns with tangy orange mayonnaise.

Via Pasitea 119, 84017 Positano 089 811351 Daily 12.30–3.30, 7.30–11 L €33, D €50, Wine €14

AL PALAZZO
www.ristorantealpalazzo.it
The terrace of this refined restaurant in the Palazzo Murat hotel is covered in luxuriant foliage. Of particular note is the spaghetti *ai frutti del mare*—a perfect marriage of various types of seafood and pasta. The Neapolitan aubergine (eggplant) *parmigiana* is alive with the fresh essential tastes of this fertile region.
Via dei Mulini 23, 84017 Positano 089 875177 Daily 7.30–11; closed Nov–Easter D €80, Wine €18

LA SPONDA
www.sirenuse.it
Lemon trees and bougainvillaea fill the air with scents in the summer months at this glamorous restaurant belonging to the ultra-chic Sirenuse Hotel. The Sersale family are famed for their classic Neapolitan pasta dishes and produce a very special *spaghetti al pomodoro e basilico* (tomato and basil).
Via Cristoforo Colombo 30, 84017 Positano 089 875066 Mar–end Nov daily 1–3.30, 8–10.30 L €67, D €125, Wine €20 Train from Napoli to Sorrento then local bus

RAVELLO

CUMPÀ COSIMO
This is a magnet for visitors thanks to its great-value dishes and famous matriarch, Netta Bottone. The spicy *penne all'arrabiata* is particularly tastebud-tingling. Main courses include catches of the day from land and sea. There is a limited selection of local wines. The homemade ice cream is excellent.
Via Roma 44/46, 84010 Ravello 089 857156 Apr–Oct daily 12.30–3.30, 8–11; Nov–Mar Tue–Sun 12.30–3.30, 8–11 L €23, D €40, Wine €9

ROSSELLINIS
www.palazzosasso.com
This acclaimed, two Michelin-starred restaurant, part of the beautiful Palazzo Sasso hotel, is perched 300m (984ft) above the sea. Look out for the asparagus *raviolini* with artichoke and carrot sauce, and the classic aubergine (eggplant) cannelloni. There are wonderful fish dishes and an irresistible dessert selection.
Via San Giovanni del Toro 28, 84010 Ravello 089 818181 Daily 7.30–10.30; closed Nov–end Mar D €105, Wine €35

SCILLA

ALLA PESCATORA
You'll find this primarily fish restaurant right beside the sea, with plenty of tables outside. Come here to enjoy true Calabrian fish cookery, with dishes such as *spaghetti al nero di seppie* (spaghetti with black cuttlefish sauce), linguine with mixed fish, fat prawns and skewers of swordfish and tuna. There's a handful of meat choices as well for those who don't fancy fish.
Via Cristoforo Colombo 32, 89058 Scilla 0965 754 147 Feb–Nov Thu–Tue 12.30–3, 7.30–10.30 L€ 27, D €33, Wine €9

SORRENTO

L'ANTICA TRATTORIA
www.lanticatrattoria.com
In summer, you can sit and eat in the flowery garden of this family-run restaurant, where pretty wrought-iron tables are set beneath the pergola. Pasta is served imaginatively—try the ricotta ravioli with a citrus sauce—and fish dishes are either simple, grilled or baked in salt, or interesting modern combinations of types and flavours. There's a tasting menu and a special gluten-free menu.
Via Padre Giuliani 33, 80067 Sorrento 081 8071 082 Daily 12.30–2.30, 7.30–10; closed 15 Jan–15 Feb and Mon Nov–Feb L €40, D €65, Wine €10

IL BUCO
www.ilbucoristroante.it
Creative yet traditional cuisine is on the menu in this atmospheric, Michelin-starred restaurant set in the wine cellars of an ex-monastery in central Sorrento. Specialties include delights from both *terra* (land) and *mare* (sea). Try to leave room for local cheeses and sublime puddings such as *baba scomposto con crema al limone e croccante di sfogliatella* (limoncello cream encased in crispy puff pastry). The wine list is as extensive as it is well chosen. Reservations advised for dinner.
2a Rampa Marina Piccola 5, 80067 Sorrento 081 878 2354 Thu–Tue 12.30–2.30, 8–10.30; closed Jan adn first 2 weeks Feb L €55, D €90, Wine €15

CARUSO
www.ristorantemuseocaruso.com
This restaurant is named after Enrico Caruso, the celebrated tenor and gastronomic genius. The gramophone plays crackling classics by the maestro in the background. The menu has lots of vegetable, fish of the day and seafood dishes.
Via Sant'Antonino 12, 80067 Sorrento 081 807 3156 Daily 12–3.30, 7.30–11.30; closed Mon in Jan L €45, D €70, Wine €15

O' PARRUCCHIANO – LA FAVORITA
www.parruchiano.it
Dining is quite an event in this cavernous greenhouse filled with luxuriant foliage. Highlights include the traditional stuffed peppers and ravioli filled with mozzarella, tomatoes and basil.
Corso Italia 71, 80067 Sorrento 081 878 1321 Apr–Oct daily 12.30–3.30, 8–11; early Nov and late Mar Thu–Tue 12.30–3.30, 8–11; closed mid-Nov to mid-Mar L €37, D €50, Wine €6

TRANI

OSTERIA CACCIANFERNO
www.osteriacaccianinferno.it
The charming interior of this restaurant features the original oven, checked curtains and sparkling table settings. Here you can enjoy straightforward Puglian classics such as baked pasta with *mortadella* and mozzarella, spaghetti with cherry tomatoes and anchovies and roast and grilled meats. Look out for the grape varieties Aglianico, Primitivo and Negroamaro on the purely Puglian wine list.
Vicolo S. Nicola 9, 70059 Trani 0883 585 978 Jul–Aug 12.30–3, 7.30–10, Sep–Jun Tue–Sun 12.30–3, 7.30–10; closed 2 weeks Nov L €20, D €30, Wine €9

Above *La Bussola hotel in Amalfi*

PRICES AND SYMBOLS

Prices are the lowest and highest for a double room for one night, unless otherwise stated. Breakfast is included, and all the hotels listed accept credit cards unless otherwise stated. Note that rates vary widely throughout the year.

For the key to symbols ▷ 2.

ALBEROBELLO

DEI TRULLI

www.hoteldeitrulli.it

Sample the full *trulli* experience in this deluxe hotel converted from a group of Alberobello's distinctive conical stone houses. Totally traditional from the outside, the interior has been skilfully converted to provide the comfort that its numerous foreign guests expect. This hotel is popular with group tours, but the gardens and pines provide a calm setting and the bedrooms' whitewashed walls, simple decoration and well-equipped bathrooms are oases of tranquillity.

✉ Via Cadore 32, Alberobello, 70011 Bari ☎ 080 432 3555 €170–€230 28 Outdoor From Bari Alberobello from Bari Exit the A14 at Bari Nord and follow signs to Alberobello, then follow signs to the hotel

AMALFI

LA BUSSOLA

www.labussolahotel.it

This former mill and pasta factory is on the outskirts of Amalfi. Its attractions include a small private jetty and a terrace with views of the azure waters below. The restaurant serves very good regional dishes. The lobby has a 1970s feel, while the lounge area has some elegant 18th/19th-century furnishings. Guest rooms are simply furnished with amusingly kitsch artworks, and have basic facilities. Private parking is €10 per day.

✉ Lungomare dei Cavalieri 16, 84011 Amalfi ☎ 089 871533 €98–€200 62 12 rooms only (€10 extra)

LIDOMARE

www.lidomare.it

The Lidomare is in a 14th-century building just off the main piazza. It is good value for this part of Italy. Many of the rooms have high ceilings, bright tiled floors, and a mixture of modern and dark wood furniture. Facilities include private bathroom, TV, safe, heating and telephone. There's a pleasant terrace with superb views where breakfast is served.

✉ Largo Piccolomini 9, 84010 Amalfi ☎ 089 871332 €103–€145 15 From Naples or Salerno Salerno then bus to Amalfi Take the A3 from Naples then turn right to Amalfi and follow signs for *centro*

RELAIS VILLA ANNALARA

www.villaannalara.it

This attractive villa is set in gardens with a courtyard and enjoys enchanting views. The (air-conditioned) rooms are newly decorated and are all individually designed in elegant syle with every comfort. As this is such a sought-after, small hotel, advance reservations are recommended.

✉ Via delle Cartiere, 84011 Amalfi ☎ 089 871147 €80–€180 6

CAPRI

DA GELSOMINA MIGLIERA

www.dagelsomina.com

This hotel provides good-value accommodation, near the sublime Migliera cliff-top vantage point. It has excellent facilities and a wonderful restaurant. The rooms are decorated in cool hues and have tiled floors. All have television, telephone, minibar, hairdryer and private bathroom. There are jaw-dropping views from each balcony and a large swimming pool and sundeck.

Via Migliara 72, 80071 igliara 081 837 1499 Closed Nov–Mar €130–€150 5 Outdoor From Capri town From Naples and Sorrento then funicular to town (also from Salerno and Positano in Aug)

GRAND HOTEL QUISISANA

www.quisisana.com

Marble floors, elegant statues, Chesterfield sofas and chandeliers greet you in the lobby of this well-established luxury hotel—quality and service are the watchwords here. The rooms are filled with a blend of cool and warm pastel shades, and a mixture of comfortable modern and elegant Venetian-style furnishings. There are superb views throughout and top-class facilities, including a relaxing spa and a first-rate restaurant.

Via Camerelle 2, 80073 Capri 081 837 0788 Closed Nov–Mar €320–€820 133 rooms, 15 suites Indoor and outdoor

LA TOSCA

www.latoscahotel.com

This is a lovely little hotel with wonderful views of the monastery of San Giacomo and the distinctive Faraglioni rocks. The comfortable rooms are light and airy. Facilities include private bath in most rooms and telephone. Breakfast costs an additional €8 per person.

Via Birago 5, 80073 Capri 081 837 0989 €75–€150 10 From the port take the funicular to Piazzetta di Capri (Piazza Umberto VII and La Tosca is a 5-min walk away)

FASANO

BORGO EGNAZIA

www.borgoegnazia.com

From the same owners as the famous Masseria San Domenico nearby, this beautiful property opened in May 2010. As well as a deluxe five-star hotel, the grounds encompass a typical Apulian village with houses offering luxurious suites clustered around a central piazza with private Arabian-style gardens and roof gardens. There is also an 18-hole championship golf course, private beach club, swimming pools, tennis courts and a state-of-the-art Roman-inspired spa/wellness centre.

Contrada Masciola, 72015 Savelletri di Fasano 080 225 5000 From €210 for hotel rooms 47 rooms, 10 suites Off the SS16 roughly halfway between Bari and Brindisi

GARGANO PENINSULA

ALBA DEL GARGANO

www.albadelgargano.it

For great value on the Gargano coast, this is a sure-fire hit. The guest rooms are simply furnished with modern fittings, and facilities include a television, telephone and compact bathroom with shower. The restaurant serves decent regional cooking. The hotel's wonderfully private sandy beach (2km/1.3 miles away) is well equipped.

Corso Matino 102, 71030 Mattinata 0884 550771 €60–€86 bed and breakfast, except Aug half-board rate only €135; many special offers available online 40 10 rooms Bari to Foggia Foggia then local bus A14 to Foggia exit then SP89 to Mattinata

SEGGIO

www.hotelseggio.it

Set in the heart of the picturesque old town, this cliff-top hotel has its own private beach and waterside pool, both accessed by the private elevator. The rooms are charming, some with balconies looking out to sea, others giving access to the cobbled streets. Family-run and friendly, the Seggio also prides itself on its cooking—half board here is no hardship.

Via Veste 7, 71019 Vieste 0884 708123 €80–€170, Aug half board only €155–€165 30 From Manfredonia take N89 to Vieste; the hotel is in the old town

ISCHIA

MEZZATORRE RESORT & SPA

www.mezzatorre.it

Set around a 16th-century Saracen tower, this characterful hotel overlooks the sea with plenty of terraces from which to drink in the beautiful views. The rooms are elegant and spacious, while the dining room is full of decorative touches, including a collection of antique candelabras—especially atmospheric at night. There is a very well-equipped spa in which to indulge in the therapeutic thermal waters and beautifying mud, among other treatments, for which Ischia is so famous.

Via Mezzatorre 23, Località San Montano Nord, 80075 Ischia 081 986111 €460–€720 47 rooms, 10 suites Outdoor

LECCE

CENTRO STORICO B&B

www.bedandbreakfast.lecce.it

On the second floor of a 16th-century palazzo, this hotel offers excellent value just a short walk from the rail station. The guest rooms are attractively and stylishly furnished and clean. The suite sleeps two to three people, with a kitchen area. Enjoy the cityscape from the terrace. Credit cards are not accepted.

Via Andrea Vignes 2b, 73100 Lecce 0832 242727 €55–€100 6 From Bari, Napoli, Taranto Lecce

PATRIA PALACE

www.patriapalacelecce.com

This 5-star hotel is in the 17th-century Palazzo D'Anna. The guest rooms, decorated in warm hues, are immaculate and refined. Feast on quality *cucina pugliese* served in the evocative restaurant, or enjoy a drink in Danny's Bar.

Piazzetta Riccardi 13, 73100 Lecce 0832 245111 €190–€350 67

MARATEA

VILLA DEL MARE

www.hotelvilladelmare.com

A week or more can be happily spent at this resort hotel. Inside, the style is Mediterranean; cool and white, with shady, flower-filled terraces. Many of the bedrooms are big enough for families. There's also a crèche for kids. An elevator will whisk you down to the private beach. If you want total peace, check when the in-house disco operates. Parking is available.

Acquafredda, Maratea, 85046 Basilicata 0973 878007; fax 0973 878102

Closed Nov–Mar €125–€235 55 rooms, 20 mini suites Outdoor Sapri (Napoli/Reggio di Clabria line) then bus to Acquafredda Exit the Autosole at Lagonegro-Nord and follow the Valle del Noce *superstrada* to the Sapri exit. At Sapri, turn left onto the N18 towards Maratea. The hotel is 6km (9.5 miles) along this road

MATERA

ITALIA

www.albergoitalia.com

Hotels as comfortable as this are thin on the ground in Basilicata. The building is an old palazzo, so there are high ceilings, marble and flagged floors and gracious architecture. Bedrooms are big, and the staff will happily add a couple of beds to your room for the kids.

Via Ridola 5, 75100 Matera 0835 333561; fax 0835 330087 €98–€104 46 From Naples, Bari, Taranto and Potenza Exit the A14 at Taranto Nord and take the N7 west to Matera. From the town outskirts follow yellow signs to the hotel

NAPOLI (NAPLES)

ART RESORT GALLERIA UMBERTO

www.artresortgalleriaumberto.it

There can't be a better location than Naple's iconic Galleria Umberto, where you'll find this elegant hotel. Opened in 2007, this is grand luxe at competitive prices, with levels of service as high as you'd expect in a hotel of this class. Rooms and public areas are furnished with antiques and sumptuous textiles, the bar and dining room are well-stocked and elegant and the helpful staff can arrange just about anything.

Galleria Umberto I 83, 80123 Napoli 081 410 4114 €140–€250 10 Piazza Garibaldi

COSTANTINOPOLI 104

www.costantinopoli104.it

A hidden gem, this elegant, homely hotel is in the historical city centre. An enormous art nouveau stained-glass window dominates the main facade of the building. The interior is bright and airy with all modern comforts. Try to get a room on the roof level, which has a terrace with sunbeds. The hotel has a charming secluded garden with a swimming pool and terrace. There is garage parking as well.

Via Santa Maria di Costantinopoli 104, 80138 Napoli 081 557 1035; fax 081 557 1051 €230 19 Outdoor Naples Piazza Dante, Piazza Cavour

GRAND HOTEL EUROPA

www.sea-hotels.com

A convenient location and decent service make this a good bet for accommodation near the *centro storico*. Most of the soundproofed rooms have cheerful paintings hung on whitewashed walls. Facilities include television, telephone, safe, hairdryer and minibar. Traditional music is often played in the adjoining La Grande Abbuffata restaurant.

Corso Meridionale 14, 80143 Napoli 081 267511 €85–€180 80 Piazza Garibaldi, Napoli Centrale ALIBUS to Piazza Garibaldi

GRAND HOTEL VESUVIO

www.vesuvio.it

Many notable figures, such as Grace Kelly and tenor Enrico Caruso, have passed through the doors of the Grand Hotel Vesuvio since it opened in 1882, built by a Belgian financier. Both public rooms and guest rooms are filled with antiques and exquisite fabrics. Dine in style at Caruso, the rooftop restaurant, or take advantage of the fitness, health and beauty facilities.

Via Partenope 45, 80121 Napoli 081 764 0044 €310–€450 144 rooms, 16 suites C52, E5, 140, 152

HOTEL IL CONVENTO

www.hotelilconvento.com

This handsome 17th-century palace, next to the convent of Santa Maria Francesca, is newly renovated and has subtle lighting and attractive antique furniture. Two junior suites have balcony views, but all the rooms have excellent amenities.

Via Speranzella 137/A, 80132 Napoli 081 403977 €65–€140 10 rooms, 4 suites R2 from the Naples train station

STARHOTEL TERMINUS

www.starhotels.com

Standing right outside Napoli Centrale station, the Terminus resembles a dull concrete block. Inside is a chic, sophisticated hotel with soundproofing to create an oasis of peace in the bustling city. This is largely a business hotel. The result is that July, August and Christmas are considered low season, and the Terminus could be a good choice for a bargain leisure break in the heart of Naples. There is garage parking and a restaurant and roof terrace.

Piazza Garibaldi 91, 80142 Napoli 081 779 3111; fax 081 206689 173 €85–€290 Naples Napoli Centrale Piazza Garibaldi

Below *Antiques and period furniture give character to the top hotels in Naples*

POMPEI

AMLETO

www.hotelamleto.it

The Amleto is a great base from which to explore the ruins of Pompei, Ercolano and the Vesuvio. The marble floors, subtle lighting and fresh, vibrant walls give the hotel an air of spacious tranquillity. The roof garden and solarium have bird's-eye views of Pompei. Free parking is available.

Via Bartolo Longo 10, 80045 Pompei 081 863 1004 €80–€120 26 Circumvesuviana train from Naples

HOTEL FORUM

www.hotelforum.it

A charming hotel in the heart of Pompei town, with some rooms overlooking the ruins and Vesuvio. The rooms are tastefully decorated, and some have been converted into suites. The hotel has secure parking.

Via Roma 99, 80045 Pompei 081 850 1170; fax 081 850 6132 €100–€140 35 From the Naples–Salerno motorway, Via Roma is one of the main roads into the town centre Circumvesuviana from Naples Piazza Garibaldi, Trenitalia main line trains from Napoli Centrale

POSITANO

ALBERGO CASA ALBERTINA

www.casalbertina.it

A flight of 60 steps descending from the road leads to this family-run hotel on the cliffs above Positano. Whitewashed vaulted ceilings and cool, blue-tiled majolica flooring create a relaxing air. There are first-rate facilities in the guest rooms—some have hydromassage baths and all have a private terrace with a sublime panorama. A twisting path leads down to the beach. The restaurant serves excellent seafood and traditional Neapolitan dishes. Parking is available.

Via Tavolozza 3, 84017 Positano 089 875143 €140–€240 20 Hydrofoil from Naples Jun–Sep

HOTEL DI SAN PIETRO

www.ilsanpietro.it

This luxury hotel has stunning views, excellent facilities and sumptuous suites. Each room has a huge marble bathroom and a private terrace. Relax in the tranquil gardens and dine in the Michelin-starred terrace restaurant. There is a private beach, a swimming pool and a tennis court.

Via Laurito 2, 84017 Positano 089 875455 €420–€650 55 rooms, 7 suites Outdoor Take the A3 from Naples and follow signs for Sorrento, then pass Positano and follow signs for the hotel (2km/1.2 miles) on the SS163 towards Amalfi

SAVOIA

www.savoiapositano.it

In a town as expensive as Positano, the Savoia offers good value and a great position in the heart of the old village. Expect terrazzo flooring, marble bathrooms and fair-sized rooms, with a good breakfast buffet served by the friendly family who run the hotel. There's no pool and sea views are limited, but for value for money it's a real find.

Via Cristoforo Colombo 73, 84107 Positano 0898 75003 Closed 2 Nov–29 Dec €140–€200 39

VILLA FRANCA

www.villafrancahotel.it

The cool blue-and-white facade hints at the relaxing qualities of this hotel's interior. Guest rooms vary in size, but all have subtle shades and bright decorative touches. The pool and terrace overlook the beach and the terrace restaurant serves excellent Neapolitan food. Facilities include a health club and gym.

Viale Pasitea 318, 84017 Positano 089 875655 €180–€410 37 Outdoor

RAVELLO

VILLA AMORE

Villa Amore is a peaceful hotel just a short stroll from Piazza Duomo, and is good value in the chic, pricey town of Ravello. There are spellbinding views from the terrace and a very good bar/restaurant serving traditional local dishes. Guest rooms are compact with modern furnishings. Most have views of the gardens and the Thyrrhenian Sea. Reserve well in advance.

Via Santa Chiara, 84010 Ravello 089 857135 €75–€100 14

VILLA SAN MICHELE

www.hotel-villasanmichele.it

This hotel of great charm, 6km (3.5 miles) south of Ravello, is a well-kept secret on this coast, an oasis of laid-back and relaxed comfort in a superb setting above the sea. The colour theme is blue and white, with paved floors, sun terraces perched on the cliff and simple, comfortable rooms. From the terrace, where breakfast is served, gardens run down the cliff. Some of the rooms overlook these and also have little balconies.

Località Castiglione, via Carusiello 2, 84010 Ravello 0898 72237 Mar to mid-Nov €100–€170 12

SORRENTO

GRAND HOTEL EXCELSIOR VITTORIA

www.excelsiorvittoria.com

This magnificent hotel brims with Victorian style. The guest rooms and suites have belle époque decorative touches and top-class facilities. Many have terraces with views of the gardens or sea. Self-catering apartments are also available. At the restaurant you can dine in style under a celestial ceiling or by candlelight on one of the terraces.

Piazza Tasso 34, 80067 Sorrento 081 877 7111 €240–€550 82 rooms, 16 suites Outdoor From Naples and Sorrento

IMPERIAL TRAMONTANO

www.tramontano.com

This 16th-century palazzo, a hotel since 1812, has been the choice of royalty as well as literary icons such as Byron, Shelley and Goethe. Most guest rooms have parquet flooring and elegant furnishings. Many have magnificent views, and there is access to a private beach and swimming pool.

Via Vittorio Veneto 1, 80067 Sorrento 081 878 2588 Closed Jan–Feb €230–€340 108 rooms, 5 suites Outdoor

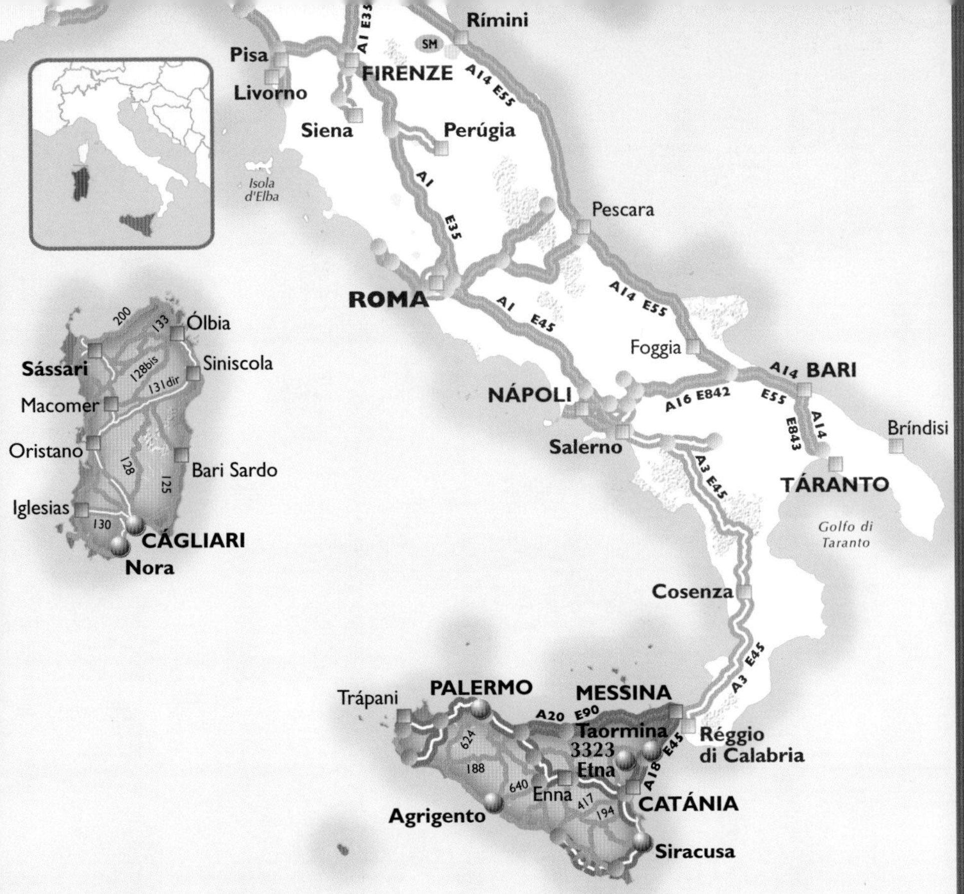

SICILY AND SARDINIA

Sicily and Sardinia are Italy's two largest offshore islands, each a place apart, with its own rich history, traditions and way of life. Both offer astounding diversity—landscape that ranges from a mountainous interior to sublime coastline, cities and towns whose artistic and architectural treasures tell each island's story, and food and wine that adds another dimension. Each island has its problems; poverty and the iron hand of the Mafia still grip much of Sicily, while Sardinia has to balance the wealth brought in by its sophisticated resorts with the traditional ways of the agricultural villages in the interior.

Sicily stands on the edge of Europe; cross the Straits of Messina and you enter a different world whose 2,000-year history has seen just about every Mediterranean power ensconced as rulers, each leaving its mark in the shape of art, architecture, cuisine and attitudes. The capital, Palermo, with its ancient buildings, magnificent churches and intense vibrancy, encapsulates Sicily's history, echoed in the ancient city of Siracusa and coastal and mountain towns such as Cefalù, Trapani, Enna and Erice, perched high above the sea. The classical past is present too, in the shape of some of Europe's finest Greek sites, where, at Agrigento and Segesta, temples finer than those in Greece itself still survive. Factor in Noto, one of Italy's loveliest baroque towns, impossibly picturesque Taormina, with its classical theatre and superb views, and ever-rising standards of accommodation, and it's easy to see why Sicily attracts increasing numbers of visitors.

Sardinia also has a rich past, with prehistoric fortresses in the Gesturi, Phoenician and Roman ruins at Nora, and medieval relics in the main towns of Cagliari and Alghero. The island's greatest magnet, though, is its coastline, where some of Europe's most exquisite beaches attract rich and glamorous visitors, particularly to the white sands and turquoise waters of the Costa Smeralda.

SICILY

AGRIGENTO

Even if ancient Greek ruins are not usually part of your itinerary, make this group an exception. Most of the temples in Akragas, to use the name given to the site by the sixth-century BC Greek colonists, were built in the fifth century BC, a period of prosperity that ended with the Carthaginian invasion of 406BC. The city was successively reconquered—and its name changed—by Corinthians, Romans, Saracens and Normans. It was only in 1927, under Mussolini, that the name Agrigento came into use.

Agrigento lies along a ridge on the southwest coast of Sicily. The medieval heart is west of the ridge, where Arab and Norman influences can still be seen and the steep streets are dominated by the cathedral. East of the medieval quarter, north of Via Atenea, is the beautiful 13th-century Cistercian Monastero di Santo Spirito and its museum (daily 10–1, 4–6).

Along the SS115 towards Porto Empedocle, birthplace of Nobel Prize-winning dramatist Luigi Pirandello (1867–1936), is now a museum dedicated to his life.

THE VALLEY OF THE TEMPLES

The famous archaeological zone, the Valle dei Templi, south of the city, is where the ruined temples rise from a plain dotted with almond, eucalyptus and pine trees. Three huge temples lie in the Eastern Zone, the most spectacular being the Doric Tempio della Concordia (430BC), one of the world's best-preserved Greek temples. The Temple of Hercules (sixth century BC) is the oldest, while the stately Temple of Hera dates to 500BC. The Western Zone contains the ruins of the Temple of Olympian Zeus, which was once the largest Greek temple in the world. The Museo Archeologico (Tue–Sat 9–7, Mon 9–1; €6) has finds from local sites, notably a giant stone telamon (male figure) and a fifth-century BC *krater* (bowl) depicting Perseus and Andromeda.

INFORMATION

www.provincia.agrigento.it
www.agrigento-sicilia.it
473 H17 Piazza Vittorio Emanuele, 92100 Agrigento 800 236 837 Mon–Fri 8–2, 3–7 Via Cesare Battisti 15, 92100 Agrigento 0922 20 454 Mon–Sat 8.30–1 Valle dei Templi (at main site entrance) 0922 45873 Mon–Sat 9–12, 2–6 Agrigento

VALLE DEI TEMPLI

www.parcovalledeitempli.it
0922 621611 Apr–Sep daily 8–7; Oct–Mar 9–4; also open and floodlit at night Jul–Aug €8; joint ticket with museum €10

Opposite *Tempio della Concordia in the Valle dei Templi*
Above *Fallen telamon at the Tempio di Giove Olimpico*

CEFALÙ

www.cefalu-tour.pa.it

As you approach Cefalù the view is unforgettable—the cathedral rising above the medieval streets, all squeezed onto a promontory between the sea and a towering crag, La Rocca. This lively, popular seaside town has it all, from scenery and sandy beaches to museums and historical monuments, shops, cafés and restaurants. Cefalù's most important treasure is the cathedral, founded in 1131 by Sicily's first king, Ruggiero II. Particularly precious are the mosaics of Christ Pantocrator in the apse—the oldest Byzantine-Norman mosaics in Sicily. For a view of the town and the second-century BC Temple of Diana, climb to the top of the 278m (912ft) La Rocca.

473 J16 Corso Ruggiero 77, 90015 Cefalù 0921 421050 Cefalù

Above *Colourful boats at Cefalù*

ENNA

www.apt-enna.com

At 1,000m (3,280ft), Enna is Sicily's highest provincial capital and notable for its views of the mountains, including, on a clear day, Mount Etna. The fortress town, inhabited before the arrival of colonists from Gela in 664BC, has an imposing ruined 13th-century castle, Castello di Lombardia. Don't miss the view from the Torre Pisana (480BC) at the Rocca Cerere, site of the temple to Ceres, Greek goddess of agriculture. The Museo Archeologico (daily 9–6.30) in Via Roma has treasures from the duomo. The Chiesa San Salvatore (1261) is an exquisite little baroque church; get the keys from Signore Armenio, owner of the barber shop in Via Salvatore.

473 J17 Via Roma 413, 94100 Enna 0935 528228 Enna

ERICE

www.apt.tapani.it/erice

This medieval town, at the top of a 755m (2,476ft) mountain, is one of the most beautiful in Sicily, with impressive views of Trapani and the Egadi Islands. It has aged gracefully and from the time of the Elymian settlers, who came here around 1500–1250BC, through to the Roman era, Erice was venerated as a place where deities were honoured. The Museo Civico Antonio Cordici displays a head of Aphrodite and an *Annunciation* by Antonello Gagini.

473 G16 Via Tommaso Guarrisi 1, 91016 Erice 0923 869388 From Trapani Funicular from Trapani (dependent on weather)

ETNA

▷ 395

ISOLE EGADI

These islands provide what many visitors seek: a slower pace of life, idyllic scenery, country walks, the occasional sandy beach, rocky coves and crystal-clear water for diving and snorkelling. All this is only minutes by hydrofoil, or a bit longer by ferry, from Trapani. The islands can get busy, especially during May and June, when the brutal spectacle of *La Mattanza* (slaughter of tuna) takes place in Favignana.

The largest of the three islands is Favignana. The Grotta del Genovese, on Levanzo, has some of the oldest known wall paintings in Sicily, dating from 10,000 to 6000BC. These can be visited overland via a footpath or, more easily, by sea.

473 F16 Piazza Saturno, 91100 Trapani 0923 545511 Trapani

ISOLE EOLIE

www.isole-eolie.com

Each island in this fascinating archipelago has its attractions: Alicudi and Filicudi—remoteness and tranquillity; Panarea—beauty and sophistication; Salina (where the movie *Il Postino* was filmed)—Malvasia wine; Stromboli and Vulcano—volcanoes; and Lipari—encounters with the islands' ancient past. Most of the islands have beaches; all have rocky coves and inlets perfect for sunbathing, swimming and diving.

The islands were originally volcanic but now only Stromboli and, to a lesser extent, Vulcano show signs of activity. Lipari's Museo Archeologico Eoliano, near the Duomo, houses an important collection of Greek theatrical masks, some beautiful fourth-century BC *kraters* (bowls) and carved obsidian, a type of volcanic glass that in the Neolithic period was traded for its sharp cutting edges and was the source of Lipari's wealth.

The islands become very busy in July and August. Lipari is the largest and most developed, while the more remote Alicudi and Filicudi are relatively untouched by tourism.

473 K15 Corso Vittorio Emanuele 202, 98155 Lipari 0909 880095 Milazzo or Naples

ETNA

Europe's largest and most active live volcano, with its lava fields and wooded lower slopes, is one of Sicily's most compelling and awe-inspiring sights.

THE VOLCANO

Mount Etna (*c*3,329m/10,924ft) is the highest volcano in Europe and among the world's most active. The ancients called it Aetna and believed it was the site of Vulcan's forge; the Arabs named it Mongibello, the 'mountain', still its Sicilian name. Throughout the centuries its eruptions have engulfed farmland, towns and Catania itself, with lava flows reaching as far as the sea. Vulcanologists agree that the main crater is becoming increasingly active, and there were complex explosions in July 2001 and an earthquake in 2002. Bulldozers were used to build dykes and divert the flow, which threatened many villages, and the damage was contained, but further eruptions were inevitable. The newest crater, Bocca Nuova (new mouth) came to life in November 2006 when fiery explosions and cascades of lava engulfed the mountain. Further eruptions came in 2008 and continue sporadically, although so far all have been minor in comparison with those of 2001 and 2002. The whole area is a regional park with a unique geology, flora and fauna, and its traditional farming and way of life are protected.

TACKLING ETNA

The Circumetnea, a private railway line, loops the 114km (71 miles) around the lower slopes of the volcano, taking in a string of little villages and giving some spectacular views of the mountain and its slopes. By car, you can follow the Strada dell'Etna, which was constructed in 1934 and runs through the little town of Nicolosi, a ski resort that's home to the Museo Vulcanologico Etneo (Via Cesare Battisti 32, Fri–Wed 9–1, 4–6, though times subject to change; €2), which will fill you in on Etna's history and geology. From here, the road ascends through increasingly impressive lava fields to the Rifugio Sapienza, where you can scramble down the lava slopes to explore extinct craters. From the Rifugio, a cable car runs further up the mountain, or you could take one of the 4-wheel drive minibuses that run between April and October. Accompanied by a guide, the vehicles negotiate the lava slopes up to the Torre del Filósofo, built to celebrate the Roman Emperor Hadrian's climb to the summit. Beyond here, the southeast active crater of the summit is visible, dramatically spewing smoke; explosions and molten lava are common at this height. You'll take in the extraordinary lunar landscape of the upper slopes, a desolate expanse of gritty black, grey and red lava, punctuated by pockets of snow.

INFORMATION

www.prg.it/parcodelletna (Italian only)
473 K17 Via Ethea 107/A, 95030 Nicolosi 959 14588 Nicolosi

TIPS

» Be properly equipped; the wind is always strong and the temperature often below freezing. Wear a warm jacket, strong shoes, a hat and glasses to protect your eyes from flying grit and debris.

» Anoraks and boots are available for rent at the Rifugio Sapienza.

» Visits to the summit are always subject to volcanic activity and visibility is often obscured by cloud and the direction of the smoke.

» A return ticket on the *funivia* (cable car) from Rifugio Sapienza costs €27. From the top of the cable car there are 4x4 vehicles to take you up farther and a guided walk (45 mins) around the Bocca Nuova (€60 including return cable car ride). It is also possible to do the walk (around 4 hours round trip) from the top of the *funivia* to the authorized crater zone at 2,920m (9,578ft).

Below *Rifugio Sapienza tourist station at the crater of Mount Etna*

PALERMO

Sicily's capital, Palermo, lies on a coastal plain in the northwest of the island. Chaotic and noisy, it can be exhausting, but there are some incredible sights: Arabo-Norman and Byzantine architecture jostles with Spanish and baroque. There is excellent shopping on the elegant Viale della Libertà and Via Maqueda, while Via Roma has lively bars, cafés and markets. At the hub of the old city are the Quattro Canti, four 17th-century Spanish baroque facades forming gateways to the ancient quarters of the city. Old Palermo lies south of the Cattedrale, a Norman foundation within a few hundred metres of the other great early monuments. Behind the main streets lie warrens of alleyways, home to lively markets such as the Vucciria, while to the north, the grid-like streets of the 19th-century city stretch towards Monte Pellegrino and the beaches of Mondello. Farther out from the centre, traffic-jammed, teeming streets lead away from the coast and up the hill to Monreale (▷ 398).

Founded by the Phoenicians in the eighth century BC and subsequently occupied by the Romans and Byzantines, Palermo was a major Arab power under Saracen occupation, a major focus of civilization and an intellectual beacon of light during some of Europe's darkest ages. This legacy was adopted by the Normans, who established their kingdom in the 12th century and endowed the city with an extraordinary architectural heritage. This golden age was followed by the rule of the Holy Roman Empire under Frederick II (Frederick I of Sicily), the French Angevins, and then, by the late 14th century, Spanish control. Palermo remained a backwater for the next 400 years, neglected, plundered and by-passed by the advances of the Renaissance. A facelift arrived in the 18th century in the shape of some fine baroque building, but on the whole the city was heading downhill, and unification with the new Italy in 1860 did little to halt the slide into disrepair. It is only in the past 30 years that restoration has repaired, renewed and cleaned up increasing areas of the city.

NORMAN HERITAGE

Visit the Arab-Norman church of San Cataldo (Mon–Sat 9–1, 3.30–7, Sun 8.30–1), with its three squat red domes and wonderfully simple interior. It was built between 1154 and 1160 by the Norman chancellor Maio of Bari, slightly later than the neighbouring church of La Martorana (Mon–Sat 9.30–1, 3.30–7), founded in 1146. In 1233, the church was given to the nuns of a nearby convent founded by Eloise de Marturanu—hence its name. The nuns inherited one of the most beautiful Greek churches in Sicily, a Greek cross structure with a fine campanile (belltower), whose interior was decorated with dazzling mosaics by the same Greek craftsmen who worked on the Cappella Palatina (Mon–Sat 8.30–12, 2–5, Sun 8.30–2) in the Royal Palace. Today, the Palace, much altered over the centuries, houses the Regional Parliament but you can visit the glittering Palatine Chapel, with its mosaic-covered walls, carved Arab ceiling and inlaid marble pavements, perhaps the most accomplished example of all of Arabo-Norman art. Near here, down Corso Vittorio Emanuele, is the Cattedrale (Mon–Sat 8.30–5.30, Sun 7.30–1.30, 4–7; closed during services); the exterior, with its austere Romanesque lines, is a masterpiece of Sicilian-Norman carving, while the baroque interior houses their tombs.

OTHER HIGHLIGHTS

In Via Roma, the Museo Archeologico Regionale (Tue–Sat 8.30–6.15, Sun 9–1), reopened after restoration in 2010, has a rich collection of Greek sculptures, including the fifth-century bronze *Youth of Selinunte* and carved friezes from the same site; the museum is a good preparation for visiting Sicily's classical sites. Don't miss the Museo delle Marionette (Piazzetta Niscemi 5, Mon–Sat 9–1, 3.30–8.30, Sun 9–1) and the bizarre Convento dei Cappuccini (Via Pindemonte, daily 8.30–1, 2.30–6) where over 8,000 bodies dating from the 16th century to the early years of the 20th century are preserved in underground corridors.

INFORMATION

www.palermotourism.com

473 H16 Piazza Castelnuovo 34, 90141 Palermo 091 583847 Mon–Fri 8.30–2, 3–7, Sat, Sun and public holidays 9–1 Palermo Centrale

TIP

» Driving in Palermo is not fun, and parking is worse. If you can, come by train. The station is 15 minutes' walk and buses run regularly. If you have to drive, Sunday is best, when many Sicilians leave the city or lunch with their families.

» Don't take anyone to the Convento dei Cappuccini who is sensitive about dead bodies. Even for the non-squeamish it can be quite gruelling.

Opposite *Palermo's Cattedrale*

MARSALA

www.marsalatuttolanno.it

For wine-lovers, a visit to the heart of Sicily's famous wine-producing region is a must. Authentic Marsala wine can still be sampled in *enoteche* (wine shops). Best-known is the Cantine Florio (established 1833), who offer tours, tastings and opportunities to buy (Lungomare Florio; tel 0923 781111). The town has another claim to fame: it was here, in May 1860, that Garibaldi and the one thousand landed at the start of the campaign to unify Italy (▷ 40).

Marsala, on Cape Lilibeo, is the site of the ancient Carthaginian colony of Lilybaeum; the historic quarter is in the northwest of town, next to the Roman archaeological site. The Museo Archeologico (Fri–Sun, Wed 9–1.30, 4–7, Mon–Tue, Thu 9–1.30) has finds from the site as well as the only Punic battleship ever found, dating from the third century BC.

The Museo degli Arazzi Fiamminghi (Tue–Sun 9–1, 3–6) has 16th-century Flemish tapestries. If you have time, visit the Convento del Carmine, a 12th-century Carmelite monastery (Tue–Sun 10–1, 6–8).

473 G16 · Via XI Maggio 100, 91025 Marsala · 0923 714097 · Marsala

MONREALE

The hillside town of Monreale has treasures to equal those of the capital, Palermo. The city is set on the lower slopes of the hills that surround Palermo, with views to the sea beyond. There are some attractive piazzas and cafés and a massive 12th-century cathedral (tel 091 640 4413; Duomo and Treasury daily 8.30–12.30, 3.30–6; free but take €1 coins to illuminate the mosaics). The greatest Norman building in Sicily, it is an inspiring sight. It was commissioned by William II in an attempt to undermine the influence of his rival, the Archbishop of Palermo, whose power base was the less impressive cathedral of Palermo. Glittering mosaics cover almost every surface of the interior, culminating in the main apse with Christ Pantocrator with angels and saints. Climb the stairs near the right aisle for a view of the Gulf of Palermo, Monreale and the beautiful, mesmerizing cloisters of the former 12th-century Benedictine abbey (tel 091 640 4403; daily 9–6.30; €6). Set around a garden planted with bay and olive trees, framed by 228 slender inlaid columns, this is an exquisite Islamic-style retreat.

473 H16 · Salita Belmonte 1, Villa Igea, 90142 Palermo · 0916 398011 · Bus 389 from Palermo (30 mins)

NOTO

www.comune.noto.sr.it

The golden facades of Noto's handsome buildings are masterpieces of Sicilian baroque architecture. The town is also known for its almond pastries and its wine, notably Moscato di Noto. In May, Via Corrado Nicolaci is carpeted with flowers for the *Primavera Barocca* (Baroque Spring) flower festival.

The catastrophic earthquake of 1693 razed Noto Antica (Ancient Noto), claiming 1,000 lives and leaving the old site to a lonely hilltop. The new town was built in the valley below by the finest architects of the age. Over the years the local white sandstone has mellowed to a honey hue, yet the stone is also fragile. The collapse of the cathedral dome in 1996 was a wake-up call and for many years buildings were shrouded in scaffolding while repairs were carried out. The covers finally came off the cathedral in 2007 and the town has been almost completely renovated to its full baroque glory. The Palazzo Ducezio is wonderfully proportioned and has a beautiful portico; ask to see the Sala degli Specchi (Hall of Mirrors), which displays the text of a telegram from Garibaldi to the patriots of Noto, and a fresco by Antonio Mazza. Other highlights include the balconies of the Palazzo Villadorata, with their carvings and the Church of San Domenico.

473 K18 · Piazzale XVI Maggio, 96117 Noto · 0931 573779 · Mon–Fri 9–2, 3.30–6.30, Sat 9–12, 3.30–6.30 · Noto

PALERMO

▷ 396–397.

PIAZZA ARMERINA (VILLA DEL CASALE)

Piazza Armerina, a small town in the Erei Mountains, is famous for the Roman mosaics in the third-century AD Villa del Casale, at the foot of Monte Mangone. Abandoned in about the year 1000 and engulfed by a landslide in the 12th century, it was not excavated until the early 1900s. Buildings discovered include a central courtyard, baths and gymnasium. The mosaics depict animals and birds, and in the renowned Sala delle Dieci Ragazze (Room of the Ten Girls), lithe 'bikini'-clad gymnasts. The quantity and quality of the mosaics indicate the villa belonged to someone of importance, perhaps Emperor Maximianus Herculius (AD286–305). It is a World Heritage Site.

473 J17 · Via Cavour 15, 94015 Piazza Armerina · 0935 680202 · Villa May–Sep daily 8–6; Oct–Apr 9–4 · €6

Below *Mosaics in the Villa del Casale, Piazza Armerina*

SIRACUSA

Siracusa lies on Sicily's southeast coast, 60km (37 miles) south of Catania, divided between the mainland and the island of Ortygia. The city's historic heart, Ortygia (▷ 408–409), is a maze of small streets, shabby in parts but with much baroque charm, with shops, cafés and restaurants. The sixth-century BC Tempio di Apollo, in Piazza Pancali, is one of the oldest in Sicily, but more impressive is the fifth-century BC Temple of Athena, incorporated into the cathedral (daily 8–12, 4–7) in Piazza del Duomo. Some of its Doric columns can be seen embedded in the walls. The facade was rebuilt in baroque style after a massive earthquake in 1693, along with many of the surrounding buildings, transforming the piazza into a beautiful square. In Via Capodieci, the Galleria Regionale di Palazzo Bellomo (Tue–Sat 9–7, Sun 9–1) exhibits Sicilian and Arabic ceramics, sculpture and paintings.

In 734BC the Corinthians colonized the island of Ortygia, swiftly expanding onto the mainland. The colony flourished under the first of Siracusa's 'tyrants', Gelon (540–478BC), and eventually grew to rival the power of Athens. In 415BC Athens invaded, but her fleet was annihilated and prisoners were confined in the quarries that are now the archaeological park. After falling to the Romans in 213BC, the city began to decline, a process unrelieved by Byzantine and Saracen occupations. Things improved under Norman, then Spanish rule. Extensive rebuilding followed the 1693 earthquake, and Ortygia has many fine examples of baroque style.

CLASSICAL REMAINS

The Parco Archeologico Neapolis (Apr–Oct daily 9–6; Nov–Mar 9–3; €8) lies northwest of Siracusa's high-rise developments. Classical ruins stand in a pleasant, open setting dotted with pines. The great third-century BC Teatro Greco is cut into the white rock of the hillside. Not far away is the second-century AD Roman amphitheatre, while in the southern area is the Ara di Ierone II, an altar on which, at one feast, no fewer than 450 oxen were sacrificed. Other important sites include the Orecchio di Dionisio (Ear of Dionysius), an ear-shaped grotto with extraordinary acoustics, named by the painter Caravaggio after the Syracusan tyrant Dionysus (405–367BC), who supposedly imprisoned his enemies here and overheard their whispered conversations through the small opening at the top.

INFORMATION

www.apt-siracusa.it
473 K18 Via S. Sebastiano 45, 96100 Siracusa ☎ 0931 481232 Daily 8.30–2, 3.30–6 Via della Maestranza 33 (Ortygia), 96100 Siracusa ☎ 0931 464 255 Mon–Sat 8–2, 4.30–7.30 Siracusa

TIP

» Ortygia's prettiest stretch of waterfront is by the Fonte Aretusa—the spring that attracted the first settlers (▷ 408). Nowadays it's a much-photographed spot, full of ducks and clumps of papyrus.

Above *Doric columns from the Temple of Athena are embedded in the walls of the cathedral*

SEGESTA

For the sheer beauty of their setting, the ruins of Segesta are hard to beat. The jewel is the beautiful fifth-century BC Doric temple, one of the finest remaining examples of classical architecture. Segesta was founded in the 12th century BC by the Elymians, but subsequent alliances with the Carthaginians brought the city into conflict with the Greeks. In the third century BC Segesta capitulated to the Romans and the city began to decline. The ruins, largely unexcavated, are spread across a low hill overlooking a wide fertile valley and surrounded by rolling hills. Built into the hillside, the third-century BC theatre could seat some 4,000 spectators.

473 G16 Parco Archeologico, 91013 Segesta 0924 952356 Summer daily 9–7; wnter 9–4 €6, under 18s free Segesta Tempio

SELINUNTE

www.selinunte.net

Selinunte was founded in about 650BC. For a long while the city maintained an alliance with the Carthaginians and most of its temples were built. during this period, between about 550 and 480BC. The death knell sounded in 250BC, when its citizens razed it to the ground before fleeing ahead of the invading Romans. This vast archaeological park occupies about 270ha (667 acres). Highlights include Temple E, built in the fifth century BC and reconstructed in the 1950s, and the Temples of the Acropolis—particularly the mid-sixth-century BC Temple C, the oldest on the site.

473 G17 Parco Archeologico, 91022 Selinunte 0924 46251 Apr–end Sep daily 9–6; Oct–end Mar daily 9–4 €6, under 18s free Castelvetrano

SIRACUSA

▷ 399.

TRAPANI

www.apt.trapani.it

The town of Trapani occupies a sickle-shaped peninsula on the northwest coast of Sicily. At its tip are the historic heart, with a tangle of alleyways, and the port and ferry terminal, while the modern town lies at its base, at the foot of Mount Erice.

Trapani is a perfect base from which to visit Erice, Segesta, Marsala, the Isole Egadi—which can be reached from the ferry terminal of La Stazione Marittima di Trapani—and the salt pans and salt museum at Nubia, 5km (3 miles) south. Nearby, framed by the dazzling white salt pans, is the tiny island of Mozia, site of an important eighth-century BC Phoenician city, with a fascinating museum containing some of Sicily's finest Greek statues (daily 9.30–1.30, 2.30–6.30).

Trapani itself has some unusual works of art in its churches and museums. In the western part of the old town, the Chiesa del Purgatorio houses the *Gruppi dei Misteri*, 20 tableaux of life-size figures that tell the story of Christ's final days. Each is owned by a specific city guild, and on Good Friday they are carried in procession through the town for one of the island's major festivals. The 14th-century convent of Santuario dell'Annunziata in Via Conte Agostino Pepoli, in the eastern part of the city, has a delicate rose window and the venerated *Madonna di Trapani* sculpture, possibly by Nino Pisano. The adjacent Museo Nazionale Pepoli (Tue–Sun 9–1.30, Sun and public holidays 9–12.30) houses historic items, including a guillotine, works of art dating from the 17th century and the flag of the ship that brought Garibaldi to Sicily.

473 G16 Piazza Garibaldi, 91100 Trapani 0923 29000 Trapani

Above *Roman ruins at Segesta*

TAORMINA

The town's prominent position on the slopes of Monte Tauro, 48km (30 miles) south of Messina, provides views of the coast and Mount Etna. Narrow alleyways lead from the main thoroughfare, Corso Umberto I, on which most places of interest are located. In Piazza Vittorio Emanuele, Palazzo Corvaja houses the Museo Siciliano d'Arte e Tradizione Popolari (Tue–Sun 9–1, 4–8), with fascinating collections from religious paintings to domestic utensils. Farther south are Piazza IX Aprile and La Porta di Mezzo, gateway to the oldest part of town.

Taormina became a city of high status after the Roman conquest of 241BC. However, prosperity ended when the city allied itself with Pompey rather than his rival Octavian, who wreaked his revenge by deporting the entire population. When he became emperor, Octavian repopulated the city, but the golden days were over and under Saracen, Norman and Spanish occupations the city sank into obscurity. Civil unrest after the death of Frederick II in 1250 all but destroyed the town, and it was not until the 18th century and the advent of the Grand Tour, when the fashionable toured the Mediterranean visiting ancient ruins, that Taormina's fortunes improved. The Villa Comunale (Taormina's public gardens; free) were laid out in the 19th century by a Scot, Lady Florence Trevelyan, who was forced to leave Britain after an affair with King Edward VII. She came to Taormina and, like so many others, instantly fell in love with it and began the creation of this lovely oasis. This is one of Sicily's most beautiful green spaces, perched on a terrace above the sea, and is packed with exotic year-round interest.

THE GREEK THEATRE

Via Teatro Greco leads to Taormina's most famous monument, the third-century Greek theatre (Apr–Oct daily 9–7; Nov–Mar 9–4.30). With excellent views of Etna, it is thought to have held up to 5,400 spectators. It was rebuilt in the second century BC by the Romans to present gladiatorial shows rather than drama.

INFORMATION

www.gate2taormina.com

473 K16 Palazzo Corvaja, Corso Umberto 1, 98039 Taormina 0942 23243 Mon–Sat 8.30–2, 4–7 Taormina-Giardini, then bus or steep climb up to town

TIPS

» During July and August Taormina is crowded and expensive. Don't drive–parking places will be scarce.

» The Teatro Greco not only has a stunning setting but also excellent acoustics and, in summer, hosts a programme of concerts, theatre and film.

» The little hill village of Castelmola, 5km (3 miles) above Taormina, is a delightful spot to savour the views of Mount Etna.

Below *Isola Bella, just off the coast below Taormina*

ALGHERO

www.comune.alghero.ss.it

The coast around Alghero is known as the Coral Riviera for its production of beautiful coral jewellery in shades from pink to blood red. Bathed in a warm apricot glow, Alghero is Sardinia's most picturesque medieval town. It is both tourist town and fishing port, with a long, proud history. The centre is a tangle of narrow lanes filled with bars, restaurants and shops, and nearby there are beautiful beaches.

Once under Aragonese rule, Alghero has a distinctly Spanish feel to it, and the local dialect is a mixture of Catalan and Sardinian. Enclosed by ramparts *(bastioni)*, the town still retains some 14th-century towers, including the Torre Porta a Terra (tel 079 973 4045; daily), which has a good multimedia museum explaining the history of the town, and a panoramic terrace. The imposing cathedral and its campanile are in the Catalan-Gothic style, while the Church of San Michele is opulent baroque. Its brilliantly coloured majolica dome is echoed in the ornate stucco interior.

About 10km (6 miles) out of Alghero on the road to Porto Torres, the Necropolis of Anghelu Ruju (Apr–Oct daily 9–7; Nov–Mar 9.30–4). has about 40 *ipogei* (funeral monuments), including sepulchres known as the *domus de janas* (fairy houses).

From Alghero there's easy access by boat to the fascinating sea cave, the Grotta di Nettuno—one of Sardinia's top sights (Apr–Sep daily 9–7; reduced hours in winter).

473 B11 Piazza Porta Terra 9, 07041 Alghero 079 979054 Daily 8–8; closed Sun in winter An open tourist train, the Trenino Catalano, tours Jun to early Sep. Departs from the port daily: Apr, Jun, Sep 10, 1, 3.30, 9; Jul, Aug 10, 1, 4.30, 11. Adult €6.50, child €3 Alghero

BARBAGIA

The Barbagia area is on the west side of the Gennargentu Mountains. This isolated region was once a land of bandits, infamous throughout the ages for feuds and vendettas. The largest town, Orgosolo, the 'capital of the Barbagia', has little more than 3,200 inhabitants. It once harboured the region's most notorious bandits but is now most visited for the colourful murals that adorn the streets and corners—often portraying a political message or the struggle to preserve local customs and culture—and its Feast of the Assumption celebrations on 15 August. The hamlets and towns are not geared up for tourists; however, the people have a strong sense of hospitality and it is worth trying to overcome the language barrier to get an insight into local life, folklore and ancient traditions. Several roads wind through the region, and those who brave the tortuous bends are rewarded with views over the steep, harsh slopes and the beech and chestnut forests.

Aritzo has several hotels and restaurants and is famous for its delicious handmade *torrone* (nougat). A chestnut festival is held on the last Sunday of October, when sweet and savoury chestnut concoctions are the attraction. Look for the *tacchi*, stone relics from the Mesozoic era found in several areas, including Belvì and Desulo. The most famous is the mushroom-shaped 'Texile', near Aritzo and visible from miles away.

473 C12 Corso Umberto I, 08301 Aritzo 0333 617 5974

CAGLIARI

▷ 403

CALA GONONE

www.calagonone.com

Cala Gonone is one of the most spectacular coastal areas on Sardinia. The rocky, barren cliffs that tower over the limpid Tyrrhenian Sea on the scenic east coast reach almost 1,000m (3,280ft). The coast of Orosei, where Cala Gonone is located, is now a marine reserve. Swim in the clear, emerald waters, sunbathe on the soft white sand or take a boat trip to the Grotta del Bue Marino (Cave of the Monk Seal, though this endangered species is long gone), a natural limestone formation with wide arches.

Set in the province of Nuoro, Cala Gonone began life as a port for ships transporting wood, coal, wine and cheese, but as early as the 18th century it developed its present role as a tourist port. In the peak season it hums with chic yachts and boats going back and forth to the bays and coves. One of the most secluded but most popular coves, Cala Luna, can be reached only from the sea or by a long, though scenic, walk (▷ 404).

Dorgali, in the hills 9km (6 miles) above Cala Gonone and overlooking Lake Cedrino, is a large agricultural town with a flourishing craft industry. It also produces excellent sheep's and goats' cheeses, and fine wine.

473 D11 Viale Bue Marino a/a 0784 93696

CASTELSARDO

Ancient walls encircle the historic area of this little medieval town, clinging to a spear of rock on a promontory overlooking Asinara Bay. Every year the historic hub is taken over by the Feast of Luni Santi, which begins at dawn on the Monday before Easter. Members of the Confraternità dell'Oratorio di Santa Croce represent the 12 *apostoli* (apostles) and carry sacred objects. Twelve other people form the *cantori* (choir) and sing polyphonic chants, the ancient form of the spiritual Sardinian music. The songs and processions go on for 24 hours and are rounded off with a Pantagruelian dinner.

Castelsardo is famous for its crafts, especially *l'intreccio* (straw weaving). There's a museum devoted to this ancient art in the castle, and many shops around sell good-quality items.

473 B10 Piazza del Popolo, 07031 Castelsardo 079 471506

CAGLIARI

Cagliari is thought to date back to Phoenician days and has been invaded countless times over the centuries by the Carthaginians, the Romans, the Barbarians, the Pisans, the Spanish and, in 1718, the English, before surrendering to the Italian royals, the Savoia. Inevitably, all these civilizations and cultures have left their mark on the city.

The city is at the heart of the Gulf of Cagliari, also known as the Bay of Angels. Its medieval quarter sits on the Colle di Castello hill. The most scenic of the access roads is Viale Regina Elena, from where you can admire the view of the cathedral and the Palazzo Reale. The Belvedere del Bastione di Santa Croce is a tranquil area that looks out over the city to the Sulcis Mountains.

Cagliari is a large modern city, but its *centro storico* (old town), overlooked by the remains of the *rocca* (fortress), is compact, and many hours can fruitfully be spent wandering around. The Castello, the attractive medieval quarter and home to many of the more interesting monuments, is isolated from the rest of the city by the walls and towers built by the Pisans. These culminate at the north end in the Bastione de St. Remy, a wide and beautiful esplanade created in the early 1900s when the Spanish defensive system was opened out. From here, there are spectacular views. Walk back through the Castello along Via la Marmora, lined with antique shops and craft workshops. Outside the walls is the Citadella dei Musei, a modern complex, converted from the old arsenal, which houses the city's most important museums, including the Museo Archeologico Nazionale and Pinacoteca Nazionale.

A short stroll from here, the Roman Amphitheatre (Tue–Sun 10–4; occasionally closed for musical events), carved into the rock on the slopes of Buon Cammino Hill, dates from the second century AD. It is thought to have had a capacity for around 10,000 spectators, and the pits for the lions and other wild beasts are still visible. In the summer, concerts and operatic performances take place here. If you can get a ticket, the atmosphere is magical.

OTHER ATTRACTIONS

Monte Arcosu is an oasis of wildlife where Sardinian deer and other indigenous animals and plants are actively preserved. Typical liquors of the province include Mirto, distilled from native myrtle berries, and Gennargentu and Filu di Ferro (iron wire) grappa, so called because when the farmers produced it in secret during World War II they buried the bottles under the ground and left a wire protruding a few inches to mark the spot.

INFORMATION

www.sardegnaturismo.it
www.marenostrum.it
473 C13 Piazza Matteotti 9, 09124 Cagliari 070 669255 Daily 8–2, 4–8 Alcide de Gasperi 1, 09124 Cagliari 070 677 8470 Daily 8–2, 4–8 Cagliari

TIPS

» In August the area is particularly hot and humid, and the city loses some of its local shine as residents go on holiday.
» You can climb the Torre dell'Elefante, from where you get spectacular views over the city and the Bay of Angels.
» Driving in Cagliari isn't to be recommended as it is congested. The best option is to leave your car at one of the car parks by the waterfront.
» Inland, but within striking distance of Cagliari, is Su Nuraxu—the nuraghic civilization's most complete settlement. For details of excursions contact the tourist office.

Above *View over Cagliari from the Castello district*

COSTA SMERALDA

www.costasmeralda.com

The Costa Smeralda is widely known as a playground for the rich and famous. Celebrity-spotting is best in July and August. No stay would be complete without a boat trip to nearby islands such as Soffi, Bisce or Mortorio, part of the Parco Nazionale della Maddalena. The 55km (34-mile) Costa Smeralda has some lovely beaches, including Poltu di Li Cogghji and Spiaggia del Principe.

Karim Agha Khan, an Islamic prince, fell in love with the Costa Smeralda when he came here in 1962. He settled in the little fishing village of Porto Cervo and transformed it into a sophisticated resort. This part of Sardinia is stunningly beautiful, with pure white beaches and clear turquoise and emerald waters, but for those whose budget will not stretch to this, there are other areas that are just as lovely, with hotels a fraction of the price.

Some of the bends along the coastal roads are hair-raising, but a drive in any direction is rewarded with panoramic vistas. The natural spectacle of Capo d'Orso, a granite sculpture above Palau, has views as far as Punta Sardegna and is not to be missed.

473 C10 Via Nanni 39, 07026 Olbia 078 955 7732

GIARA DI GESTURI

www.regione.sardegna.it

This plateau lies above Gesturi, an attractive village with an interesting history, ancient stone houses and a 15th-century Gothic church. Volcanic in origin, the plateau is about 500m (1,640ft) above sea level, approximately 4km (2.5 miles) wide and 12km (7.5 miles) long. This is the last place in Europe where wild horses—numbering 600 or 700—truly roam free. Other wildlife here includes boar, woodpeckers and foxes.

Not far away, on the main Giara road, the village of Bruncu Màdugui is famous for its prehistoric *nuraghi*. These towers were used as dwellings, fortresses or sacred sites and are thought to date from about 6000BC. They connected up with other Nuraghic settlements, forming a defensive network that covered 45sq km (17sq miles).

473 C12 Via Umberto 4, 09020 Gesturi 070 936 0017

NORA

▷ 405.

PARCO NAZIONALE DEL GENNARGENTU

www.parcogennargentu.it

www.trenino verde.com

This park is one of the last great Mediterranean wildernesses, characterized by cropped, bare valleys and grazing animals. Explore cork, walnut, hazelnut and chestnut woods in the valleys. Wild boar, hares, foxes, moufflons (wild mountain sheep) and wild cats thrive here, and majestic golden eagles soar through the intense blue skies over the highest peak, Punta la Marmona (1,834m/6,017ft).

The inhabitants of the villages and hamlets maintain ancient crafts, such as embroidery and the making of *launeddas* (traditional bamboo instruments), and culinary traditions, such as cheese-making, aniseed, hazelnuts, honey and biscuits made with alcohol.

The Trenino Verde, a tourist train, links Mandax and Arbatax. The journey of 159km (99 miles) takes almost 5 hours and can be broken up with overnight stops.

A delightful 3- to 4-hour walk through woods and past caves and waterfalls leads to Cala Luna, a beautiful beach.

473 C12 Via Trieste 64, 08100 Nuoro 0784 35501 Ferrovie Sardegna trains call at several stations (timetables for the Trenino Verde at FS rail offices or travel agents 070 578163)

Above *A medieval fortified castle built on a promontory of the Costa Smeralda, on the northeastern coast of Sardinia*

NORA

Sardinia's Carthaginian capital and its most compelling archaeological site stands on a promontory beside the sea and preserves relics of its ancient history.

THE SITE AND ITS PAST

Nora occupies a narrow, and strategically important, neck of land at Capo di Pula, some 32km (20 miles) west of Cagliari. The site was probably first occupied by the indigenous Nuraghi people, but they were ousted by the Phoenicians, who took advantage of its coastal position to establish a trading base. The city was expanded under the Carthaginians and soon became the island's most important city. After the Roman invasion, Nora became the capital of the Roman Province in AD238. Once Rome fell, the city suffered repeated Saracen raids and the surrounding productive land became worked out, causing Nora to be abandoned in the early Middle Ages, probably during the eighth century. Its ports silted up and the sea encroached on the low-lying areas of the city. Excavations are still ongoing and many of the archaeological finds are now housed in the Museo Archeologico Nazionale (▷ 403) in Cagliari.

THE EXCAVATIONS

The site sprawls over the headland, dominated by the Spanish Torre del Coltelazzo. Near here are the vestiges of the temple of Tanit, the Carthaginian goddess of fertility, and the vestiges of some Punic walls and houses. Tomb findings attest to the riches of the Carthaginian colony, with trade goods from all over the Mediterranean—copper, gold, lead, silver and gold jewellery and ivory from Africa. Following Roman colonization Nora grew fast and the excavations have revealed the solid walls of the second-century theatre, still sometimes used for summer concerts, the Forum, and the fourth-century Terme di Levante, the baths. These are decorated with white, black and ochre mosaics. As you walk through the site, you can trace the lines of the roads and the city's surprisingly impressive sewage system. Nearby is the 11th-century Romanesque church of Sant'Efisio.

INFORMATION

473 C13 Nora Sito Archeologico, 09010 Capo di Pula 070 920 9138 Summer daily 9am–dusk; winter 9am–dusk Adult €6, under 14s €3 (includes admission to Museo Archeologico in Pula) Guided visits every hour

TIPS

- The site is very exposed, so take drinking water and be mindful of the sun.
- Nora will make more sense if you also visit the Museo Archeologico in Cagliari.
- Pula's small archaelogical museum has finds excavated from Nora, including ceramics from tombs, Roman glassware and jewellery.

Below *Ruins of the Roman amphitheatre*

THROUGH THE MADONIE MOUNTAINS

Take this wonderfully varied, circular route into the heart of one of Sicily's most beautiful mountain areas to discover untouched hill towns and villages set in superb scenery in an area that stretches from the north coast towards the interior.

THE DRIVE
Distance: 135km (84 miles)
Allow: 7 hours (includes stops)
Start/end at: Cefalù

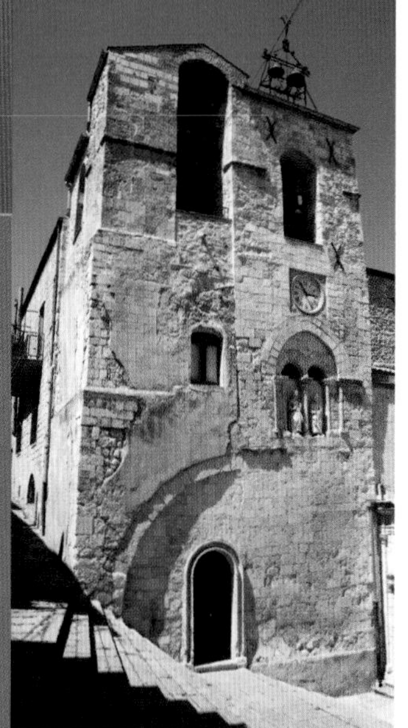

★ Start outside the station in Cefalù (▷ 394) and follow the signs right to the *centro*, picking up the green signs to the *autostrada*. Drive uphill, away from the sea, then swing left to descend to the sea and drive along the coast towards Messina on the N113. After 8km (4.9 miles) turn right following the brown sign to Parco Naturale delle Madonie and the blue sign to Castelbuono, a distance of 13km (8 miles).

❶ Castelbuono, billing itself as the capital of the Madonie, is a handsome town that spreads itself across the lower slopes of the mountains. The 14th-century seat of the powerful Ventimiglia clan, it is dominated by their castle (Tue–Sun 8.30–2, 2.30–8), built in 1438, a sober fortress enlivened by the graceful stucco work of Giacomo Serpotta in its little chapel. Elsewhere, you'll find the 14th-century Matrice Vecchia, a lovely old church with some good frescoes. The Madonie's rich heritage of natural history is well displayed in the Museo di Minà Palumbo (Via Roma 52; daily 9–1, 3–7), which is named after a local 19th-century naturalist. The town hit the international press in 2007 when the fervently green mayor replaced motorized rubbish collection with council-funded donkeys and carts—a move viewed with deep suspicion by the locals, who saw it as a retrograde step to the poverty-ridden past.

Leave town on the N236, following the signs to Geraci Siculo along the road known as the Strada dei Castelli. Continue deeper and higher into the mountains on the same road for 5.5km (3.4 miles) to the *bivío* (junction) Geraci. At the junction turn right on the N120, signposted Petralia, and continue for 4.7km (3 miles) to the outskirts of Petralia Soprana. Leave the main road and head uphill to explore the village, parking your car on the outskirts to

Opposite top *Beautiful countryside in the Madonie Mountains*
Opposite bottom *Petralia Soprana*

avoid the steep and narrow streets of the town.

Rejoin the main road and continue to Petralia Sottana, leaving your car in the car park on the left as you enter the village if you're planning to explore.

❷ The ruling hand of the Ventimiglias of Castelbuono extended as far as this wonderfully stony mountain village, with its steep streets and tall houses. Founded in the 13th century as a defensive outpost for Soprana, it is well endowed with churches—a fine Chiesa Madre near the top of the town and two older ones, facing each other. If you want to know more about the Madonie natural park, created in 1989, this is the place to come—the park's headquarters are on the main street, at Corso Agliata 16 (tel 0921 684011; www.parcodellemadonie.it). They'll fill you in on the park's background, including the conservation programme to preserve the seriously threatened *abies nebrodensis*, the Sicilian fir.

Leave Petralia Sottana and fork right, following the signs to Collesano, Piano Battáglia and Piano Zucchi. This 15km (9.5-mile) stretch of road climbs higher and higher through increasingly mountainous country, with wooded hills planted with mixed deciduous and coniferous trees and spreads of heather on either side of the road. Piano Battáglia is one of the highest settlements in the Madonie and the centre of a tiny ski area, complete with Swiss-chalet-style houses.

❸ The ski facilities here are pretty low key, but nevertheless attract thousands of Palermitani during winter weekends. In spring and summer, these limestone hills are particularly rich in wild flowers such as orchids, gentians and spreads of heavenly blue myosotis and globularia in particular.

Follow the road round to the right at Piano Battáglia, following the brown signs to Piano Zucchi and the blue signs to Isnello. At Piano Zucchi continue straight on towards Isnello. After 7km (4.3 miles) turn right to Isnello, a very typical inland village. If you want to explore, it's a short detour off the main road—follow the signs to the *centro*.

❹ Piano Zucchi is another winter sports centre, though, due to its lower altitude, its season is much shorter. It's a beguiling place, with scattered houses and a couple of hotels; the walking from here is superb. From now onwards you lose altitude rapidly as the road snakes its way north down the wooded slopes. This stretch is a good place to spy wild boar, who sometimes cross the road followed by a procession of tiny striped piglets. Isnello, a short detour off the road, is a quintessentially Sicilian inland mountain village, in some ways barely touched by the 21st century.

About 2.8km (1.8 miles) after Isnello turn left and follow the steeply descending road for 22km (13.6 miles) back to Cefalù. This road rejoins the main coastal road on the upper outskirts of Cefalù.

WHEN TO GO

This drive is best in spring and autumn, though lovely at any time of year; avoid mid-winter, when inland roads can be icy and snow-covered.

WHERE TO EAT

The Pizzeria da Salvatore (Piazza San Michele 3, tel 0921 680169; Jun–Sep daily lunch and dinner; Oct–May Sat–Sun lunch and dinner, Wed–Fri, Mon lunch only) in Petralia Soprana serves *pizze* from its wood-burning oven in the evening and has a good menu of local specialties. In summer you might want to bring a picnic to eat en route.

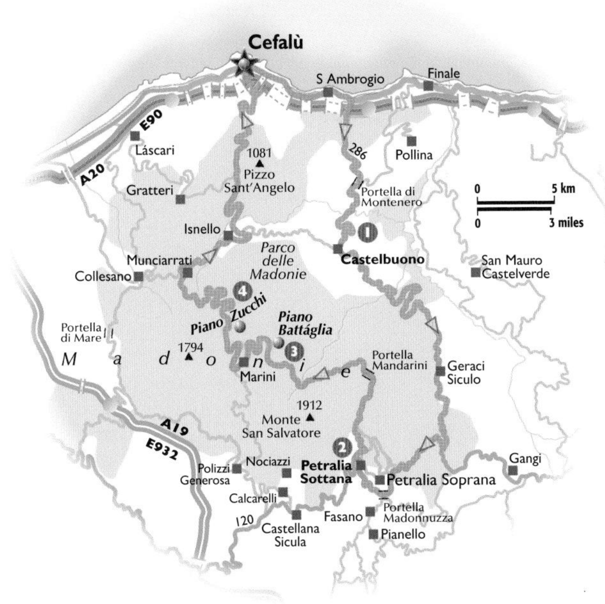

ORTYGIA, SIRACUSA

Follow this route to enjoy the wonderful variety of Siracusa's island centre, where local life hums along in the shadow of classical monuments, medieval palazzi and baroque churches.

THE WALK
Length: 3.5km (2.2 miles)
Allow: 1.5–2 hours
Start at: Ponte Umbertino
End at: Piazza del Duomo

★ Walk across the Ponte Umbertino and up through Piazza Pancali to the sixth-century Tempio di Apollo. Take Via Savoia to the right in front of the temple and walk along to the Porta Marina.

❶ The Porta Marina, built in the 15th century, was conceived as the gateway to the Porto Grande, the Great Harbour, and formed part of the city's medieval walls. In front spreads the vast natural harbour, dotted with fishing boats, tankers, liners and pleasure boats.

Walk through the gateway. Just inside, look to your left and you'll see the little church of Santa Maria dei Miracoli, its doorway resting on the back of two little lions. Walk along Via Ruggero Settimo until you see trees below you on the right. Turn left up Via Collegio. As you walk up Via Collegio, the church of the Collegio, built between 1635 and 1687, is on your left. When you reach the T-junction turn right and continue along Via Landolina to the Piazza del Duomo.

❷ The Piazza del Duomo occupies a space first inhabited by the original Sicilians, the Sikels, whose tombs were found below here when the piazza was being re-paved. The Greeks built a major temple, now the duomo, and later generations added to the square's monuments. The Town Hall (1628) stands on the site of another Greek temple, while next to the duomo you'll see the beautiful facade of the 18th-century Palazzo Arciescovile (Archbishop's Palace). The curved, pink building is the Palazzo Gaetani, and the church at the end of the piazza is dedicated to Santa Lucia.

At the far end of the piazza from the duomo, head straight on down Via Picharale and bear right to emerge at the Fonte Aretusa.

❸ The spring of the Fonte Aretusa was one of the most venerated spots in the classical world. Legend tells of the nymph Arethusa bathing in the River Alpheus, near Mount Olympia, when she was surprised by the Alpheus river god. Fleeing in terror, she plunged into the Ionian Sea, only to re-emerge here. The goddess Artemis transformed her into a spring, and the Greeks believed that the river god mingled his water with that of the spring, and that this Sicilian water source was connected with the river in the Peloponnese. In actuality, it was probably the abundance of the water here that had much to do with colonization of Ortygia; 2,000 years later Lord Nelson used the spring to fill his water barrels before the Battle of the Nile.

From the Fonte Aretusa, detour along the Foro Vittorio Emanuele, known locally as the Marina, a good place for a pause. Shaded with magnificent ficus trees, it is a lovely place to walk beside the harbour, and there are plenty of bars to stop for a drink. Backtrack to the Fonte Aretusa and continue on to the Castello Maniace, at the end of Ortygia.

❹ As you approach the Castello Maniace, today a barracks, you'll get a better idea of the huge bulk of this medieval fortress, built around 1239 and named after the Byzantine admiral George Maniakes, who fought the Arabs here in 1038.

With your back to the Castello, head down Via Salomone, cross the road at the junction and continue along Via San Martino. At the junction with Via Capodieci, you'll see the Galleria Regionale. Turn right, then almost immediately left down Via Roma and continue all the way down the street to Piazza Archimede.

❺ Piazza Archimede is the principal square on Ortygia, known as the *'salotto'* (drawing room), and is linked to the bridges by Corso Matteotti, a wide modern street with plenty of shopping opportunities. The central fountain (1910) shows the nymph Arethusa as she was transformed into the spring, and some of the surrounding buildings still show traces of their medieval origins. For the real thing, pop round the corner into Via Montalto, where the Palazzo Montalto (1397) is a fine example of Siracusan Gothic.

Turn right along Via Maestranza (once the home of the wealthy guilds; it's a lovely and varied street, with some great buildings and tempting shops) and continue to a crossroads and the church of the Immacolata. Turn right here down Via Giudecca, then take the second right on to Via del Crocifisso. At the junction, turn left, then right to follow Via Minerva back to the Piazza del Duomo.

As you turn into Via Minerva, you'll walk along the side of the duomo, giving you a splendid view of how the columns of the Greek temple were incorporated into the cathedral.

WHEN TO GO

Morning, when the streets are lively, is a good time.

WHERE TO EAT

Finish up by sampling the very best of Sicilian pastries or ice cream at Corsino, Le Antiche Siracusa, Via Maestranza 2.

Opposite *Looking down on Fonte Aretusa, a freshwater spring*
Above *Street cafés in Piazza del Duomo*
Below *Carriage in Piazza del Duomo*

Above *Olives for sale at a market in Palermo*

SICILY

CEFALÙ

SAPORI DI SICILIA

Typical flavours and products of Sicily fill this shop. Whether you're after picnic provisions of *salumeria* (delicatessen), cheese and wine or souvenirs of extra virgin olive oil and jams to take home, this is a gourmet's delight.
✉ Via Vittorio Emanuele 93, 90137 Cefalù ☎ 0921 422871 🕐 Mon–Sat 9–1, 4.30–7

PALERMO

CARNEVALISSIMO

This wonderful shop is devoted entirely to costumes for babies, kids and adults, with a range of designs from ancient Rome via Disney to *Rocky Horror*—great fun.
✉ Via Volturno 33, 90139 Palermo ☎ 091 585 787 🚌 102, 103, 104

MANFREDI BARBERA E FIGLI

It would be sacrilege to leave Sicily without some olive oil—and this is the place to come. It's a family-run business founded in 1894, producing some of the island's finest oils. The staff will happily help you choose the style and strength—from light and delicate *extra vergine* (extra virgin) to wonderfully peppery, aromatic and newly pressed.
✉ Via E. Amari, 55/A, 90100 Palermo ☎ 091 582 900 🚌 101

MUSEO INTERNAZIONALE DELLE MARIONETTE

www.museomarionettepalermo.it
Children will love this museum of puppetry. It has a wonderful collection of puppets from all over the world, such as Britain's Punch and Judy and some sinister local characters.
✉ Piazzetta Niscemi 5, 90133 Palermo ✉ 091 328060 🕐 Mon–Sat 9–1, 2.30–6.30, Sun 10–2 ✋ Adult €5, child €3 🚌 103, 105, 139, 824

LA RINASCENTE

www.rinascente.it
Opened in spring 2010, this branch of the venerated and glamourous department store is a welcome addition to the Palermian lifestyle. Five floors are devoted to fashion, accessories, beauty, housewares and gourmet food, with established and cutting-edge designers, both Italian and international, well represented. The food hall, bars and restaurants are open until midnight (evening entrance in Piazza San Domenico).
✉ Via Roma 255, 90133 Palermo ☎ 091 601 7811 🕐 Daily 9–9 🚌 101, 104, 107

SICILY'S FOLK

Sicilian ceramics are among the most collectable in Italy. Caltagirone ceramics use blue, green and yellow glazes, depicting flowers, foliage and birds, and are Arab in style. There are some interesting, detailed figurines here, too.
✉ Corso Vittorio Emanuele 450, 90133 Palermo ☎ 091 651 2787 🕐 Mon–Sat 8.30–1, 3.30–7.30 🚌 101, 122, 212

TEATRO MASSIMO

www.teatromassimo.it
Completed in 1897, this opera house heralded the beginning of Palermo's *belle époque*. The house is certainly one of Europe's finest. The year-round entertainment includes opera, ballet and classical music.
✉ Piazza Verdi 9, 90138 Palermo ☎ 091 589575 or 091 589070 ✋ €60 🚌 101, 102, 104

VUCCIRIA

The Vucciria, near San Domenico, has a host of fresh produce, including shiny swordfish, plump San Marzano

tomatoes and tasty figs. The sights and smells are unforgettable.
✉ Via Meli, 90213 Palermo 🕐 Mon–Sat 8–1 🚌 101, 212, 250

SIRACUSA

LA BOTTEGA DEL PUPARO

Puppet shows are popular in this part of Sicily. These traditional marionettes make great gifts or mementoes.
✉ Via della Giudecca 19, 96100 Siracusa ☎ 0931 465540 🕐 Mon–Sat 10–1, 5–8 🚌 1

GALLERIA BELLOMO

www.bellomogallery.com
Just around the corner from the Fonte Aretusa, this fascinating shop gives an insight into the papyrus industry in Ortygia. Articles for sale range from papyrus notebooks and cards to large water-colours costing hundreds of euros.
✉ Via Capodieci 47, 96100 Siracusa ☎ 0931 61340 🕐 Mon–Sat 10–1, 4.30–8 🚌 1

MUSEO DEL PAPIRO

www.museodelpapiro.it
Syracuse has a long tradition associated with papyrus, which still grows prolifically around the area. The museum has a film in English about its history, together with an interesting display of artefacts.
✉ Via Teocrito 66, 96100 Siracusa ☎ 0931 61616 🕐 Tue–Sun 9–1 🎫 Free

ORTIGIA

www.ortigia-srl.com
Glorious toiletries, candles and more made from traditional and natural ingredients, that are all exquisitely scented and packaged. These beautiful products can be found in glamorous shops internationally, but this is where they are created.
✉ Via Maestranza 12, 96100 Siracusa ☎ 0931 461365 🕐 Mon–Sat 10–1.30, 4.30–7.30 🚌 1

PESCHERIA

The partially walled island of Ortygia is a fabulous setting for Siracusa's fish market. Ask for a tub of seafood salad, which you can eat on the *lungomare* (seafront).
✉ Molo Arezzo della Targia, 96100 Siracusa 🕐 Mon–Sat 8–1 🚌 1

RICCIOLI SALVATORE

This superb jeweller specializes in creating pieces using the rare amber found on the coast near Siracusa, as well as elegant bracelets, necklaces and earrings crafted in gold and silver and inlaid with semi-precious stones. Remarkable work at excellent prices.
✉ Via dei Mille 3, Ortygia, 96100 Siracusa ☎ 0931 65444 🕐 Tue–Sat 10–1.30, 4–7

TAORMINA

LE COLONNE

One of the best places in Sicily for handmade jewellery. Inspired by antique designs and using old stones, coral and unvarnished precious metals, owners Santina Alvaro and Leila Correnti will design and make any piece to your specifications. They learnt their craft from their fathers and have had their work exhibited as far afield as London and New York.
✉ Corso Umberto 164, 98039 Taormina ☎ 094 223680

TEATRO GRECO

Built by the Greeks around 250BC, this is arguably one of the greatest auditoriums in the world. Perched on the cliffs, it has stunning views of Mount Etna and the Bay of Axons. A variety of theatre, opera, cinema and music is shown here in the summer, but it's the views that steal the show.
✉ Via Teatro Greco, 98039 Taormina ☎ 0942 232220 🕐 Jul, Aug 🎫 €60

SARDINIA

CAGLIARI

CINEMA SOTTO LE STELLE

This 'cinema under the stars' shows general releases and cult films on a huge open-air screen at Marina Piccola—a magical way to watch a film on a warm summer's evening.
✉ Marina Piccola, Viale Poetto, 09128 Cagliari 🕐 Jul, Aug 🎫 €10

ISOLA

ISOLA is the Sardinian Institute of Handicrafts, which represents artisan craftspeople from all over the island, selling their rugs, textiles, ceramics, leather, jewellery and wood carvings at various outlets. The quality is high and you're bound to find something special that's unique.
✉ Via Bacaredda 176–8, 01927 Cagliari ☎ 070 492756 ✉ Via Monsignor Bua 10, 08100 Nuoro ☎ 0784 31507 ✉ Via Catalogna 54, 07041 Alghero ☎ 079 952144 🕐 Mon–Sat 10–1.30, 4–7

JENNA E LUA

This little shop is crammed full of Sardinian delicacies, such as cheese, salami, wines and *dolci sardi* (pastries). It is also a good place to pick up ceramic items and other souvenirs, which are all beautifully packaged for you.
✉ Corso Vittorio Emanuele 27, 09124 Cagliari ☎ 070 682161 🚌 30

NOTTE DEI POETI

Evenings of prose and poetry are held in the Roman amphitheatre in the town of Nora, just south of Cagliari. Events are organized by a local theatre company.
✉ Nora, 09010 Cagliari ☎ 070 270577 🕐 Jul, Aug 🚌 Cagliari–Nora A/R

PASTICCERIA PIEMONTESE

www.pasticceria-piemontese.com
Stop off at this shop for traditional Sardinian pastries such as *pistoccheddu prenu* (almond cream-filled pastry). They also make beautifully wrapped confectionary and pralines.
✉ Via Cocco Ortu 39, 09128 Cagliari ☎ 070 41365 🕐 Mon–Sat 9–1, 5–7 🚌 30, 31

SHIPWRECKS OFF SARDINIA AIRSUB

www.airsub.com
This company organizes year-round dives to the Roman and Spanish wrecks off the south coast of Sardinia. All equipment can be rented, and their shop sells a good range of snorkelling and diving gear.
✉ Via Balilla 24–26, 09134 Cagliari–Pirri ☎ 070 506863 🕐 Mon–Sat 8.30–1, 4.15–8.15 🎫 Dives €50–€300, equipment €15–€30

FESTIVALS AND EVENTS

SICILY

FEBRUARY

FESTA DI SANT'AGATA

The celebration of the martyrdom of Catania's patron saint compares with any great fiesta anywhere in the world. Watched by a million, it lasts three days and involves 5,000 men pulling the silver reliquary of the saint through the streets. Agata had her breasts removed before she died, and one of the favourite confections at fiesta time are *minni di Sant'Aita* (St. Agatha's breasts), pastries topped with a glazed cherry or a chocolate raisin and filled with cream or sweet ricotta.
☒ Catania ◷ 3–5 February

ALMOND BLOSSOM FESTIVAL

www.festedisicilia.it/febbraio
Almond trees bloom early in Sicily and this festival, founded in 1937, celebrates both the coming of spring and popular culture from all over the world. Events take place in the impressive Greek temples, and the week culminates with parades and fireworks.
☒ Agrigento ◷ Exact date varies—see website

CARNEVALE

www.carnevaleacireale.com
Carnevale is enthusiastically celebrated with floats, parades, dancing and fireworks all over Sicily, and particularly at Acireale, Taormina and Sciacca, which is famous for its extravagant floats. Acireale festivities take place over 10 days and involve the entire town, with spectacular pyrotechnics on the final Tuesday.
☒ All over Sicily and especially at Taormina, Acireale and Sciacca

MARCH–APRIL

HOLY WEEK CELEBRATIONS

Towns all over Sicily mark Settimana Santa (Holy Week) with religious processions of great intensity. Statues are paraded through the streets and re-enactments of the Passion of Christ take place. Enna's parades are particularly entertaining.
◷ Week before Easter

MAY–JUNE

TEATRO GRECO

www.indafondazione.org
The excellently preserved Greek theatre in the archaeological zone at Siracusa is the main venue for a festival of classical drama, when Greek plays are performed in their original setting.
☒ Siracusa, Sicily

JULY–SEPTEMBER

KALSART FESTIVAL

The vibrant Kalsa area of Palermo is the summer venue for a huge programme, staged both indoors and outside, of dance, music, theatre and cinema.
☒ Palermo ◷ Mid-July to mid-September

AUGUST

FERRAGOSTO

www.festedisicilia.it/agosto
The great feast of the Assumption is celebrated in towns and villages all over Sicily with processions, parades, music and fun. Expect to see sumptuously decorated statues carried shoulder-high and the whole community letting its hair down late into the night.
◷ 15 August

SARDINIA

JANUARY

SAN ANTONIO ABATE FIRES

This pagan festival takes place in Mamoiada, Orisei, Torpè and other villages in the province of Nuoro. Villagers perform religious rites and blessings, and the festivities culminate in the lighting of huge bonfires.
◷ 16/17 January

FEBRUARY

LA SARTIGLIA

Riders test their skills to the limits at this horseback tournament in Oristano—mounted competitors try to pierce a star that hangs above the streets with a sword and a carved wooden stick.
☒ Oristano ◷ Last Sunday in Carnival and the following Thursday

APRIL

SA DIE DE SA SARDIGNA (SARDINIA'S DAY)

This festival commemorates the Sardinian Vespers, which brought about a popular rebellion on 28 April 1794 that led to the expulsion of the Piedmontese and the Viceroy Balbiano from Cagliari and Sardinia.
☒ Cagliari ◷ 28 April

MAY

SAGRA DI SANT'EFISIO

Sardinia's most important religious festival commemorates Sant'Efisio, a fourth-century Roman martyr. The feast dates from 1657, when prayers to the saint were believed to have delivered Cagliari from the plague. Decorated oxcarts and horsemen accompany the statue of the saint through the streets, and there is feasting, dancing and general jollity into the night.
☒ Cagliari ◷ 1 May

AUGUST

SS. REDENTORE

This festival in Nuoro is a wonderful visual display of traditional costumes, horses, *traccas* (decorated carts), handicrafts and folk traditions. A singing competiton gives budding tenors the opportunity to showcase their talents.
☒ Nuoro ◷ 29 August

Opposite *Horsemen take part in the festival commemorating Sant'Efisio in Cagliari*

Above *Sicilian seafood salad*

PRICES AND SYMBOLS

The restaurants are listed alphabetically within each town. The prices given are the average for a two-course lunch (L) and a three-course dinner (D) for one person, without drinks. The wine price given is for the least expensive bottle.

For the key to symbols, ▷ 2.

SICILY

AGRIGENTO

TRATTORIA DEI TEMPLI

www.trattoriadeitempli.com

Terracotta floors and vaulted ceilings add to the charm of this restaurant, situated between the town and the Valley of the Temples. The emphasis is on seafood, with dishes such as *fettucini all'aragosta* (fresh pasta with lobster) and *tagliolini con gamberoni rossi e pistachio* (with prawns and pistachio) setting the tone.

✉ Via Panoramica dei Templi 15, 92100 Agrigento ☎ 0922 403110 🕐 Sat–Thu 12.30–2.30, 7.30–9.30; closed Sun Jul–Aug and Fri Sep–Jun 🖐 L €25, D €35, Wine €8 ❄

CEFALÙ

OSTARIA DEL DUOMO

www.osteriadelduomo.com

The grilled fish, seafood, pasta and *antipasti* are particularly good here. It can be busy at lunchtime, but it is worth waiting to get a table.

✉ Via Seminario 5, Cefalù, 90015 Palermo ☎ 0921 421838 🕐 May–early Nov daily 12.30–3, 7–12; early Nov–Apr Tue–Sun 12.30–3, 7–12 🖐 L €25, D €43, Wine €10 ❄

LO SCOGLIO UBRIACO

Right at the bottom of the Corso Ruggiero with a lovely terrace hanging over the sea, the 'Drunken Rock' gets its name from La Rocca. There's more than a touch of glitz in this big, bustling restaurant, its walls hung with photos of its illustrious patrons, but the food is excellent and there's something for everyone.

✉ Via Corso Bordanaro 2–4, 90015 Cefalù ☎ 0921 423370 🕐 Tue–Sun 12.30–2.30, 7.30–10; closed 2 weeks Jan 🖐 L €25, D €42, Wine €8 ❄

ENNA

CENTRALE

www.ristorantecentrale.net

Run by the same family for over 100 years, this restaurant is part of the Buon Riccordo confederation—hence the ceramic plates on the walls. Here, you can enjoy splendid inland cooking, with everything cooked to order and locally sourced. The Centrale is famed for its *antipasto* buffet—start your meal by helping yourself to a range of more than 20 vegetable dishes from the central table. There is a good wine list,

✉ Piazza VI Dicembre 9, 94100 Enna ☎ 0935 500963 🕐 Daily 12.30–3, 7.30–10; closed Sat Oct–May 🖐 L €18, D €36, Wine €10

MONREALE

TAVERNA DEL PAVONE

www.tavernadelpavone.eu

The Pupellas started their restaurant in 1969 and today's owners are the second generation to follow the

family maxim of genuine, no-frills cooking, excellent service and a warm welcome. Sit inside or out and choose from a range of classic Sicilian specialties, with *primi* such as *caponata*, *sarde a beccafico*, *pasta alla norma* and *secondi* that include meat and fish dishes.
✉ Vicolo Pensato 18, 90046 Monreale ☎ 091 6406209 ⏲ Tue–Sun 12.30–3, 7.30–10; closed 2 weeks Jun and Jan ✋ L €25, D €35, Wine €10

PALERMO

OSTERIA DEI VESPRI

www.osteriadeivespri.it
This is one of Sicily's finest restaurants. Popular on the Palermian dining circuit for some while, this intimate little restaurant serves local, regional cuisine with creative flair. Not a place for a hurried meal. The penne pasta with tuna sauce is recommended.
✉ Piazza Croce dei Vespri 6, 90133 Palermo ☎ 091 6171631 ⏲ Sep–end Jul Mon–Sat 12–3, 8–midnight; rest of year Mon–Sat 8–midnight; closed 1 week in Aug ✋ L €40, D €81, Wine €13 🚌 101, 122, 220

SANT'ANDREA

Set in the raucous, vibrant Vucciria market area, this is a tranquil and excellent dining retreat among the cobblestones and stalls in this rather down-at-heel piazza. Expect traditional, regional cuisine with an emphasis on fish at extremely good prices. Very popular with well-heeled Palermitans and visitors alike, so reservations are recommended.
✉ Piazza Sant'Andrea 4, 90133 Palermo ☎ 091 334999 ⏲ Mon–Sat 7.30pm–11pm; closed mid- to end Jan ✋ D €35, Wine €10

SIRACUSA

JONICO A RUTTA 'E CIAULI

The uniquely Sicilian menu here offers plenty of opportunity to be adventurous; try fresh pasta and marinated octopus. The restaurant has spectacular surroundings with views over the sea.
✉ Riviera Dionisio il Grande 194, 96100 Siracusa ☎ 0931 65540 ⏲ Wed–Mon 12–3, 8–10.30 ✋ L €20, D €35, Wine €11

OINO'S

www.oinosrestaurant.it
Sicilian and Piedmontese specialities are on the menu in this lovely designer restaurant, where the white napery matches the cool, pale colours of the interior. The cuisine is creative and well presented. In summer you can eat out on the terrace—the perfect spot for sampling the homemade ice cream.
✉ Via della Giudecca 69–75, 96100 Siracusa ☎ 0931 464900 ⏲ Mon–Sat 12.30–3, 7.30–11; closed 2 weeks in Feb ✋ L €30, D €45, Wine €11

TAORMINA

CASA GRUGNO

www.casagrugno.it
In a beautiful 16th-century former palazzo, the Michelin award-winning chef, Andreas Zangerl, prepares dishes in both Sicilian and European styles, with the menu changing dramatically with the season. Generally regarded as the best place to eat in Taormina, and accordingly expensive. Reservations essential.
✉ Via Santa Maria de' Greci, Taormina ☎ 094 221208 ⏲ Mon–Sat 7.30pm–11pm; closed 7 Jan–9 Mar ✋ D €85, Wine €20

RISTORANTE LICCHIO'S

www.licchios.it
Licchio's has a buzz that is reflected in an equally exciting menu, using local produce from both land and sea. The garden is available all year round, but it's especially appealing in summer.
✉ Via C. Patricio 10, 98039 Taormina ☎ 0942 625327 ⏲ Fri–Wed lunch and dinner; also open Thu Jun–Aug; closed 10Jan–25 Feb ✋ L €35, D €40, Wine €10

TRAPANI

CANTINA SICILIANA

The food is delicious and excellent value at this family restaurant run by Pino Maggiore. A native of Trapani, he's keen to showcase local produce and it's the fish and produce of the *terra* that inspire him. Homemade *busiate* are served with *pesto all trapanese* (tomato, basil, garlic and almond pesto) and fresh swordfish accompanied by tiny tomatoes and capers from Pantelleria. They also sell local wines and food.
✉ Via Giudecca 36, 91100 Trapani ☎ 0923 28673 ⏲ Daily 12.30–3, 7.30–10 ✋ L €20, D €35, Wine €10

SARDINIA

ALGHERO

AL TUGURI

www.altuguri.it
Al Tuguri is an elegant fish restaurant. Set in an old property in the centre of town, the tables are small and close together, but the excellent food more than compensates.
✉ Via Maiorca 113, Alghero, 07041 Sassari ☎ 0799 76772 ⏲ Mon–Sat 2.30–2, 8–10.30; closed Dec–Feb ✋ 2 courses minimum: L €35, D €48, Wine €13

CAGLIARI

CORSARO

www.dalcorsaro.com
Notable dishes at Corsaro include *saccaia* (lamb with broth) and pasta stuffed with ricotta and vegetables.
✉ Viale Regina Margherita 28, 09125 Cagliari ☎ 070 664318 ⏲ Mon–Fri 12.30–3, 7.30–11, Sat 7.30–11; closed 2 weeks in Aug and 23–27 Dec ✋ L €33, D €50, Wine €17 ❄ 🚌 5, 6

CALA GONONE

AL PORTO

Try the fish soup with lobster or the day's catch *alla griglia* (charcoal-grilled) in this popular waterside spot, known affectionately as Hotel Pop, or Pop's Place (▷ 418).
✉ Piazza del Porto 2, Cala Gonone, 08020 Nuoro ☎ 0784 93185 ⏲ 12.30–3.30, 7.30–11.30; closed first 2 weeks in Dec and last 2 weeks in Jan ✋ L €30, D €40, Wine €11

PORTO ROTONDO

DA GIOVANNINO

This elegant restaurant is renowned for its wines.
✉ Piazza Quadrata, Porto Rotondo, 07020 Sassari ☎ 0789 35280 ⏲ Apr to mid-Nov daily 12.30–2.30, 8–10.30; mid-Nov to Mar Tue–Sat 12.30–2.30, 8–10.30, Sun 12.30–2.30 ✋ L €75, D €90, Wine €18 ❄

PRICES AND SYMBOLS

Prices are the lowest and highest for a double room for one night, unless otherwise stated. Breakfast is included, and all the hotels listed accept credit cards unless otherwise stated. Note that rates vary widely throughout the year.

For the key to symbols ▷ 2.

SICILY

AGRIGENTO

KAOS

www.athenahotels.com

This 18th-century villa has been sensitively converted into one of the area's nicest hotels, belonging to the Best Western consortium. The rooms are big and cool, and facilities include tennis courts, spacious grounds and a private beach.

✉ Villagio Pirandello, 92100 Agrigento ☎ 0922 598622; fax 0922 598770 €140–€180 105 Outdoor From Catania and Palermo Agrigento from Catania and Palermo Take the A20 from Messina to Palermo and the Caltanisseta exit. Follow the signs to Agrigento on the SS640, then take the SS189 to Agrigento and follow signs to the hotel

CEFALÙ

KALURA

www.kalura.it

Nearly all the big, airy rooms here have balconies overlooking the sea. One of the most beautifully positioned hotels in Sicily, with lovely gardens, tennis courts and a children's playground; steep steps lead down to the beach.

✉ Via V. Cavallaro 13, Cefalù, 90015 Palermo ☎ 0921 421354; fax 0921 423122 €120–€210 68 Outdoor and private beach From Palermo Cefalù then bus From Palermo or Messina take the A20 and exit at Cefalù Ovest. Follow the yellow hotel signs to the hotel; approx 1.5 km (0.9 mile) east of the old town on the coast

ENNA

SICILIA

www.hotelsiciliaenna.it

A charming hotel in the heart of this little town. The facilities are modern, and it has large rooms, some with a spectacular view of Etna. Garage parking is available.

✉ Piazza Coloianni 7, 94100 Enna ☎ 0935 500850 €70–€120 60 Palermo, Catania Palermo, Catania Take the A19 between Catania (84km/52 miles) and Palermo (119km/75 miles)

ERICE

ELIMO

www.hotelelimo.it

This pleasant hotel, right on Erice's picturesque main street, has wonderful views down to Trapani. All the rooms have beamed ceilings, old tiles and marble bathrooms. You can relax in the snug bar, or sit out on the terrace or in the courtyard. There's an excellent breakfast buffet and the restaurant, with more great views, has a good range of delicious options, all tastefully presented. There is private parking, or leave the car just outside the town gates.

✉ Via Vittorio Emanuele 73, 91016 Erice ☎ 0923 869377; fax 0923 869252 €100–€150 21

MODERNO

www.hotelmodernoerice.it

You're in for a treat at this hotel. There is a lovely courtyard for breakfast and an excellent restaurant serving Sicilian cuisine.

✉ Via Vittorio Emanuele 63, Erice, 91016 Trapani ☎ 0923 869300; fax 0923 869139 €95–€120 40 From Trapani (10km/16 miles) Take the A29 from Palermo and exit at Trapani, then follow signs to Erice and yellow signs to the hotel

ISOLE EOLIE

GATTOPARDO PARK

www.gattopardoparkhotel.it

The rooms to go for here are in the private dwellings that nestle in the flowery garden. The hotel is close to some of the island's best beaches.

Viale Diana, 98055 Lipari, Isole Eolie 0909 811035; fax 0909 880207 Closed Nov–end Feb €100–€256 53 From Messina, Naples and Palermo May–end Oct Take a taxi from the port

PALERMO

GRAND HOTEL PIAZZA BORSA

www.piazzaborsa.com

Very well-placed hotel in the heart of Palermo, with decor, style and quality that belie its 4-star rating and reasonable price range. It came into being in 2010 with the merger of three ancient palazzi in the city centre. The central part of the structure was a 16th-century convent and the church of Mercedarian Fathers. The hotel lobby is bordered by the original cloisters with a delightful winter garden conservatory. There's a wellness centre and elegant art nouveau restaurant.

Via dei Cartari 18, 90133 Palermo 091 320075 €145–€182 127

PRINCIPE DI VILLA FRANCA

www.principedivillafranca.it

Villa Franca is near the Teatro Politeama. This elegant, opulent hotel showcases Sicilian craftsmanship, from the bedspreads to the furniture. The restaurant is worth a visit for its traditional cooking.

Via Giuseppina Turrisi Colonna 4, 90140 Palermo 091 611 8523 €230–€280 34 101, 107, 614

RAGUSA

LOCANDA DON SERAFINO

www.locandadonserafino.it

Set in the baroque heart of Ragusa's World Heritage Site, this was once a crumbling eighth-century town house. Now it has been beautifully and diligently restored as an intimate, chic and charming boutique hotel with old-world charm and modern fittings. The Rosa family who run it also keep a superb wine cellar.

Via XI Febbraio 15, Ragusa Ibla 0932 222 0065 €99–€205 10

SCIACCIA

ROCCO FORTE VERDURA GOLF & SPA RESORT

www.roccofortecollection.com

Located near the fishing village of Sciaccia and within reach of Agrigento's Valley of the Temples, this stunning addition to the prestigious Rocco Forte portfolio opened in 2009. All the rooms and suites have sea views and private terraces, and in addition to the private beach, there is a state-of-the-art spa and every imaginable amenity and luxury in this designer property.

Contrada Verdura, 92019 Sciaccia 0925 998180 From €430 203

SIRACUSA

GRAND HOTEL VILLA POLITI

www.villapoliti.com

This hotel's 18th-century Liberty-style elegance and level of service set it apart from other hotels.

Via Politi 2, 96100 Siracusa 0931 412121 €125–€210 100 Outdoor Circolari 1, 3

GUTKOWSKI

www.guthotel.it

Take your breakfast on the terrace at this simple, airy hotel and soak up the dazzling Mediterranean views.

Lungomare Vittorini 26, 96100 Siracusa 0931 465861 €85–€110 26 Circolare 20 Take the Catania–Siracusa motorway and exit at Siracusa Sud. Follow this to the *centro storico*. The hotel is on the east coast of the island of Ortygia

HOTEL RELAX

www.hotelrelax.it

It may verge on the modern and bland, but there's no denying the comfort of this good-sized hotel near the Neapolis. Bedrooms are well equipped and comfortable with plenty of storage, the breakfast buffet will keep most people going all day and the restaurant is a good choice at the end of a day's sight-seeing. The distance from Ortygia is compensated for by the fact that the hotel is surrounded by lovely grounds and has a wonderful pool.

Viale Epipoli 159, 96100 Siracusa 0931 740 122 €89–€108 55 rooms, 2 suites

TENUTA DI ROCCADIA

www.roccadia.com

This *agriturismo* hostel (pictured opposite) provides guests with the opportunity to experience rustic Sicily. It arranges outdoor activities such as horseback riding. The rooms sleep two to four and have private bathrooms. A car is essential for getting around.

Contrada Roccadia, Carlentini, 96013 Siracusa 0959 90362 €38–€55 per person 20 2 Outdoor Train to Lentini Take the Catania–Siracusa motorway and exit at Brucoli–Carlentini, 30km (19 miles) from Siracusa

TAORMINA

VILLA BELVEDERE

www.villabelvedere.it

This is one of the area's best places to stay. The rooms have small balconies, many with beautiful views.

Via Bagnoli Croce 79, 98039 Taormina 0942 23791 Closed Nov to mid-ar €110–€230 49 Outdoor

VILLA CARLOTTA

www.villacarlotta.net

A very smart and welcoming boutique hotel just set back from the San Domenico Palace, but enjoying the same spectacular sea views. The rooms are elegantly furnished, and breakfast is served on the delightful rooftop terrace. There's a shuttle to the beach.

Via Pirandello 8, 98039 Taormina 0942 626058 Closed mid-Jan to mid-Feb €129–€329 23 rooms, 1 suite

VILLA DUCALE

www.villaducale.com

This hotel's terrace offers spectacular views of Naxos Bay and Mount Etna.

Opposite *Tenuta di Roccadia, Siracusa*

It is outside the centre of Taormina and away from the bustle. The hotel has a free bus shuttle or you can walk into the town in 10–15 minutes.
Via Leonardo da Vinci 60, 98039 Taormina
0942 28153; fax 0942 28710
€130–€290 17 Taormina-Giardini Naxos station 5km (3 miles)
Off the A18 motorway; from Taormina centre take the road in the direction of Castelmola

VILLA PARADISO
www.hotelvillaparadisotaormina.com
With the deep sofas, antique pieces and old prints and pictures, there's more than a touch of the country-house style about the public rooms of this lovely hotel, with its stunning views south over the coast towards Etna. You'll have to pay more for a room with a view, but all 37 have balconies and are nicely furnished; many overlook the garden. Breakfast is served on the covered terrace looking towards the mountain; it acts as the restaurant in the evenings after which you can stroll into town—the hotel is right on the edge of the historic centre.
Via Roma 2, 98039 Taormina 0942 23921 Mar–Oct €120–€220 37

SARDINIA

ALGHERO
AGRITURISMO VESSUS
www.vessus.it
This family-run countryside hotel is an oasis set in olive groves and attractive gardens, where the traditional-style rooms encircle the swimming pool. The very good restaurant specializes in traditional, homemade Sardinian food that includes home-grown fruit, vegetables and, of course, olives and olive oil. The restaurant is only open from June to September for dinner.
SS292 km1.85 per Villanova Monteleone, 07041 Alghero 079 973 5018
€86–€114; €70 per person B&B 11
3km (1.8 miles) south of Alghero on the SS292 heading towards Villanova Monteleone

HOTEL VILLA LAS TRONAS
www.hotelvillalastronas.it
Spectacularly located on a private promontory overlooking the sea, this former Italian Royal Family holiday home is Alghero's most luxurious hotel. Antiques, marbled halls, chandeliers and rich brocades ooze opulence in this 19th-century pleasure palace. There is a saltwater swimming pool, beauty centre and gym, as well as a wellness centre. Private parking is an added boon.
Lungomare Valencia 1, 07041 ALghero
079 981818 €182–€427 22 rooms, 5 suites

CAGLIARI
FORTE VILLAGE
www.fortevillageresort.com
This sprawling, 5-star resort is the ideal place to be pampered. An extensive range of accommodation, bars and restaurants is available, set in lush gardens with a beautiful beach. The resort has plenty of sport and recreation facilities such as golf, go-carting and outdoor ice-skating, as well as a luxury spa and wellness centre.
Santa Margherita di Pula, 09010 Cagliari 070 92171 Mar–Oct
€400–€920. Half board only 771 rooms, suites and bungalows
Outdoor From Piazza Matteotti rail station and Elmas bus from the airport on request Follow road SS195

T HOTEL
www.thotel.it
Cagliari's first designer hotel, the inspiration of Milanese architect Marco Piva, is a symphony of design and technology set in a steel and glass round tower with splashes of southern colour. The very stylish rooms are themed on four different colours—vibrant orange, fiery red, relaxing green and tranquil blue—and all have spacious, airy bathrooms, glistening mosaic tiles and huge mirrors. The T Bistrot has become a popular meeting point, especially for Sunday lunch.
Via dei Giudicati, 09010 Cagliari
070 47400 €120–€270. 200 rooms, 7 suites Indoor 1, M

CALA GONONE
HOTEL POP
www.hotelpop.com
Just opposite the port, this friendly and welcoming three-star hotel, run by the charismatic anglophile Simone Spanu and his family, is a meeting point for locals, The service is excellent, the rooms are modern and clean and every kind of excursion can be arranged. There is a lovely terrace outside overlooking the boats. The hotel also has one of Cala Gonone's best restaurants (▷ 415).
Piazza del Porto 2, 08020 Cala Gonone, Nuoro 0784 93185 €65–€100
16

CASTELSARDO
RIVIERA DA FOFÒ
www.hotelriviera.net
Set in a lovely position between the castle walls and the beach, the Riviera offers good, simple rooms, some with balconies overlooking the sea, all with satellite TV. The hotel restaurant has a good reputation, making half board an option worth considering, and there's access to a section of beach with waiter service.
Lungomare Anglona 1, 07031 Castelsardo 0794 70143; fax 0794 71312
€78–€195 34

OLBIA
OLLASTU
www.ollastu.it
In a village 8km (5 miles) south of Olbia, the Ollastu Hotel is great for getting away from it all. The complex is set on a promontory with magnificent sea views, and each room is actually a separate mini-villa with its own entrance. A beach is nearby and there is also a swimming pool and tennis court in the hotel grounds.
Località Costa Corallina, 07026 Olbia
0789 36744; fax 0789 36760
Mar–end Oct €130–€80 54
Outdoor Take the main coast road south from Olbia towards Nuoro/San Teodoro Olbia Ferry from Genoa to Porto Torres/Olbia, Livorno, Piombino or Cittavecchia to Olbia

PRACTICALITIES

Practicalities gives you all the important practical information you will need during your visit, from money matters to emergency phone numbers.

WEATHER

Contrary to the picture-postcard image of perpetual sunshine and blue skies, Italy has variable weather. Apart from the summer months, when temperatures soar and the sun shines all day, this mountainous country has the full range of conditions. The climate is predominantly Mediterranean, with the far north experiencing Alpine trends and the far south arid and hot. Spring is pleasant everywhere, but there's frequent rain right through into May, and temperatures north of Rome only start to climb in June. Farther south, April and May see the start of summer. Italy's hot months are from July to late September, when average temperatures are around 30°C (86°F) and the sirocco, a hot wind from Africa, pushes humidity up. In summer, the area around the Alps experiences numerous thunderstorms, which regularly help clear the air, but inland parts of southern Italy suffer extremely hot nights, often making sleeping difficult. As in the spring, the sirocco may well bring very high temperatures to parts of Italy during the autumn, accompanied by high humidity. Temperatures start to drop everywhere towards the end of September, with increasingly frequent bouts of rain and the first frosts in the Alps. Winter in the north is cold, with snow in the mountains, heavy frosts and thick fog on the plains. These conditions are also found to an extent in central Italy, with Tuscany and Umbria both experiencing bitter spells during the winter months. Winter is the wettest season in the south, and average daytime temperatures range from 7°C to 13°C (45°F to 55°F). November is dank and wet everywhere. Around Christmas you

ROME

TEMPERATURE

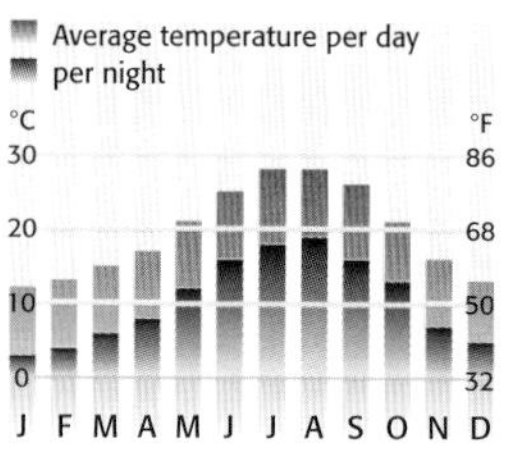

RAINFALL

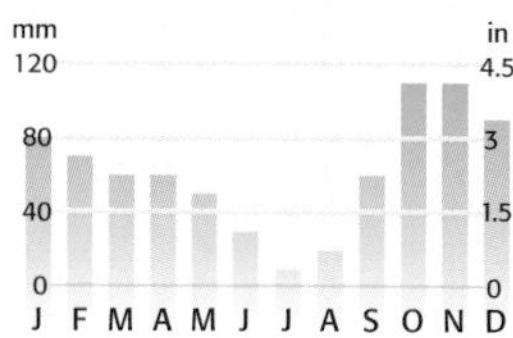

can hope for some crystal-clear, cold, sunny days. Mountain regions are colder, with heavy winter snowfalls (▷ below).

WEATHER REPORTS

BBC World News and CNN News have websites and broadcast regular global weather updates in English, and The Weather Channel and the Met Office in the UK have global weather websites too (www.bbc.co.uk, www.CNN.com, Weather Channel—www.weather.com, www.metoffice.gov.uk).

MOUNTAINOUS AREAS

The weather can change very quickly in the mountains throughout the year, so prepare for all eventualities. Always carry raincoats and extra clothing, as sudden drops in temperature and changes in conditions are common even in summer. Remember to carry enough water when you are in remote areas. At high altitudes the sun can be fierce and it is magnified in winter when it reflects off the snow, so cover up and wear plenty of sunblock. Most ski resorts monitor avalanche reports and close runs that are at risk, but if you intend to go off-piste or climb in remote areas without a guide, you should check the weather and avalanche reports beforehand (www.eurometeo.com, www.csac.org).

NATURAL HAZARDS

These include landslides, avalanches, mudflows and flooding, mainly in the winter months. Earthquakes are occasionally felt in many parts of the country, and caused havoc in Abruzzo in 2009. Northern and central Italy may experience bad flooding in winter and shorter periods of localized flooding during dramatic summer thunderstorms, particularly around the northern lakes. Flooding and land subsidence are an ongoing problem in Venice. In autumn, especially in October and November, tides flood houses, churches and shops, causing damage to businesses and affecting visitors and residents alike.

Parts of southern Italy lie on a major seismic fault line and minor tremors and earthquakes are almost a daily occurrence. There has

TIME ZONES

CITY	TIME DIFFERENCE	TIME AT 12 NOON IN ITALY
Amsterdam	0	noon
Auckland	+11	11pm
Berlin	0	noon
Brussels	0	noon
Cairo	+1	1pm
Chicago	-7	5am
Dublin	-1	11am
Johannesburg	+1	1pm
London	-1	11am
Madrid	0	noon
Montreal	-6	6am
New York	-6	6am
Paris	0	noon
Perth, Australia	+7	7pm
San Francisco	-9	3am
Sydney	+9	9pm
Tokyo	+8	8pm

Italy is one hour ahead of GMT/UTC. The clocks are moved forward an hour for daylight saving time on the last Sunday in March. The clocks go back an hour on the last Sunday in October. The chart shows time differences from Italy.

Opposite *The Rialto Bridge in Venice is lined with interesting shops*

MILAN

TEMPERATURE

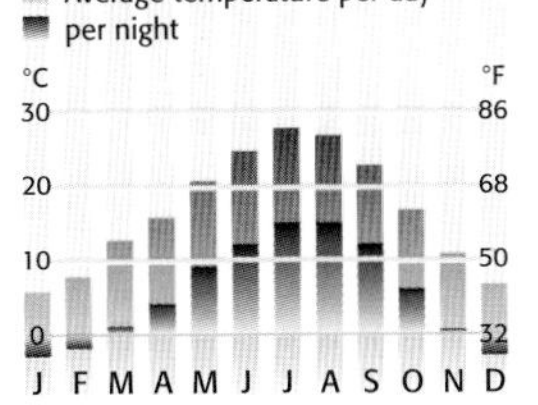

RAINFALL

VENICE

TEMPERATURE

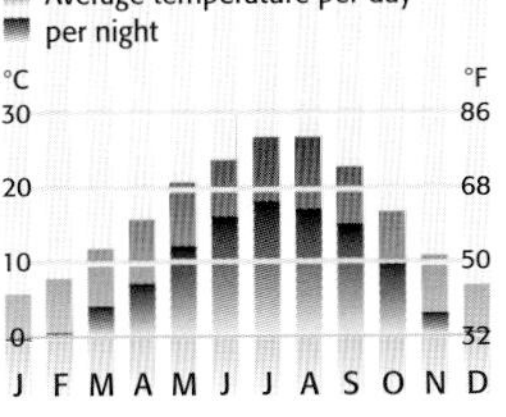

RAINFALL

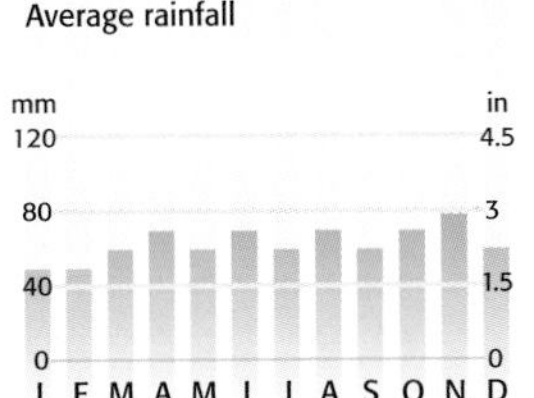

PALERMO

TEMPERATURE

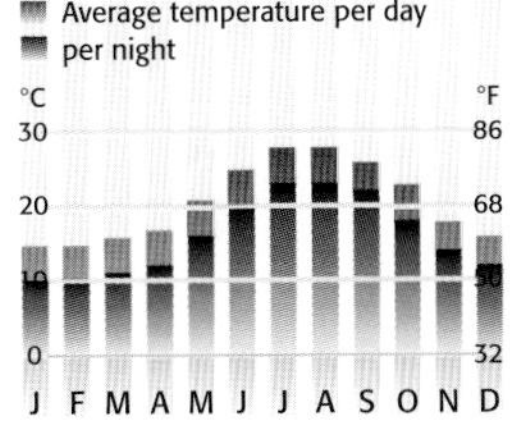

RAINFALL

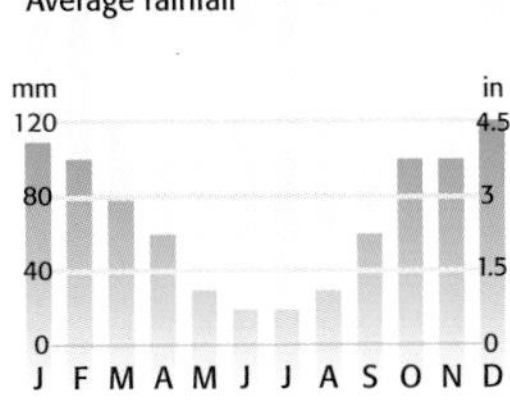

been renewed volcanic activity on Mount Etna in Sicily. The eruptions themselves appear to have subsided for the time being, but if you plan to climb Etna you should always follow the advice of guides near the summit and keep to the designated routes at all times. There is ongoing volcanic activity on the island of Stromboli.

WHAT TO TAKE

You will need mainly lightweight cottons and linens to wear during the summer, except in the mountains, where sudden drops in temperature and changes in weather conditions are common. Natural fabrics are more comfortable than synthetics in humid conditions. Light- to medium-weight clothing is worn in the south during winter, while warmer clothes are worn elsewhere. Alpine wear is needed during winter in the mountain resorts. In fashion-conscious cities such as Rome, Milan and Venice, people tend to dress smartly at all times. Bring clothes that cover your shoulders and knees if you plan to visit churches or other religious buildings.

DUTY-FREE AND DUTY-PAID GUIDELINES

There are few restrictions on the personal items you may bring into Italy—illegal drugs and firearms are not permitted, of course—but you should carry receipts for valuable items to prove you owned them before visiting Italy.

Duty-paid guidelines for UK citizens

You cannot buy goods duty-free if you are travelling within the EU. If you bring back goods on which you have paid tax in Italy, you will not normally have to pay any tax or duty on them in the UK. However, any alcohol or tobacco you bring from Italy must be for your own use and not for sale back home. HM Revenue and Customs considers anything over the following limits to be commercial quantities and may demand payment of some UK tax and duty unless you can prove the quantities are for your personal use, such as a wedding reception or a big party.

You cannot bring back goods for payment (including payment in kind) or for resale. These are considered to be commercial items and you could be made to pay UK taxes and duties, or have the goods seized by Customs officers.

- 3,200 cigarettes
- 400 cigarillos
- 110 litres of beer
- 90 litres of wine
- 3kg of tobacco
- 200 cigars
- 10 litres of spirits
- 20 litres of fortified wine (such as port or sherry)

For up-to-date information see the website of HM Revenue and Customs: http://customs.hmrc.gov.uk where there is a section on advice for travellers. There is also a telephone advice line: 0845 010 9000.

Duty-paid allowances for US citizens

US citizens can bring home up to $800 of duty-paid goods, provided they have been out of the country for at least 48 hours and haven't made another international trip in the past 30 days. This limit applies to each member of the family, regardless of age, and allowances may be pooled. For the most up-to-date information, see the US Department of Homeland Security's website: www.customs.treas.gov

- 1 litre of alcohol
- 200 cigarettes (if trademarked in the US)
- 100 cigars (non-Cuban)
- 1 bottle of perfume

REMEMBER TO PACK...

- Rainwear, particularly if you are visiting the north in winter, or mountainous areas at any time
- A folding umbrella (as above)
- A small bag for daily use, such as a shoulder bag that can be worn across the body, or a money belt
- Your driver's licence and passport
- Comfortable shoes
- A compass
- Your address book, for emergency contacts or postcards
- Photocopies of all important documents: passport, insurance details, credit card, debit card and passport numbers and registration numbers for mobile phones, cameras and other expensive items
- A torch (flashlight) and binoculars
- A first aid kit, including plasters (Band-Aids), antiseptic cream, painkillers and any prescribed medication
- An Italian phrasebook—any attempt at Italian is appreciated (▷ 456–459), especially off the beaten track
- Toiletries and sunscreen in screw-top containers inside plastic bags to guard against leakage caused by variable pressure in aircraft luggage holds

LUGGAGE ALLOWANCES

On international flights within Europe, IATA allowances are 20kg (44lb) per person for economy class and 30kg (66lb) for first class, but ask your airline before you fly as there may be restrictions (particularly with budget airlines) and you may have to pay excess baggage charges. You can usually take more luggage on transatlantic flights as you are only restricted to two pieces of luggage no larger than 170cm (67in) across.

Opposite *Tourists in Piazza di San Marco, Venice prepared for all weathers*

DOCUMENTS

PASSPORTS

» You will need a passport to enter Italy, which should be valid for at least another six months from the date of entry.

» If you lose your passport, you should contact your embassy (▷ below and 431).

» Keep a note of your passport number or carry a photocopy of the information page separately from your passport. Alternatively, scan the information pages of your passport and any other important documentation and email them as attachments to a secure email account that can be accessed from anywhere in the world.

» If you intend to work or study in Italy, make sure your passport is stamped with your date of entry. You will need it to apply for a *permesso di soggiorno* (permit to stay; ▷ below).

VISAS

» If you are an EU national, or from Australia, Canada, New Zealand or the United States, you do not need a visa for stays of up to 90 days. To extend your visit you can, one time only, apply to any police station for an extension of a further 90 days. This extension cannot be used for studying or employment, and you will have to prove that you can support yourself financially.

» Regulations can change at short notice so check before making your travel arrangements.

» If you are a citizen of a country other than those mentioned above, you should contact the Italian embassy in your home country to check visa requirements.

WORKING IN ITALY

EU citizens do not need permits or visas to work in Italy but you must register at the police station and apply for a *permesso di soggiorno* (permit to stay), essential if you intend to live, work or study in Italy. This will necessarily involve an experience of Italian bureaucracy—it can be a lengthy process. The documentation you need changes every year, but will usually include your passport (with your date of entry into the country stamped inside), four passport-sized photographs, and proof that you will be able to support yourself financially while in the country. You can apply for a *permesso di soggiorno* at the foreigners' bureau *(ufficio stranieri)* at any police station.

Non-EU citizens must apply for a *permesso di lavoro* (work permit). If you are working for an Italian company, it will organize the permit and forward the documents to your home country's Italian consulate, which will then issue you with a visa. If you are going to work for a non-Italian company (or if you are self-employed or paid in a foreign currency), you will have to organize the permit yourself through the Italian consulate in your own country. Allow plenty of time—the process can take several months.

STUDYING IN ITALY

EU citizens will need a *permesso di soggiorno* (▷ above).

Non-EU citizens will need a visa. You should apply to the Italian consulate in your home country, who will need proof of your enrolment, proof of payment of fees and evidence of your financial support. The visa will only cover you for the length of your course.

TRAVEL INSURANCE

Check your insurance policy and buy a supplementary policy if necessary. Most policies cover cancellation, medical expenses, accidents, personal liability, and loss of personal belongings (including money). It should cover the cost of getting you home in case of medical emergency. If you have private medical insurance, check your policy, as you may be covered while you are away.

HEALTH DOCUMENTS

European citizens should carry a European Health Insurance Card (EHIC), which provides access to state-provided medical treatment (▷ 425–426). However, travel insurance is still recommended for all visitors to Italy, and is essential for non-EU visitors.

ITALIAN EMBASSIES AND CONSULATES ABROAD

COUNTRY	ADDRESS	WEBSITE
Australia	12 Grey Street, Canberra ACT 2600, tel 612 6273 3333	www.ambitalia.org.au
Canada	275 Slater Street, 21st Floor, Ottawa (ON), KIP 5HP, tel 1 613 2322401	www.italyincanada.com
Ireland	63/65 Northumberland Road, Dublin 4, tel 1 6601744	www.italianembassy.ie
New Zealand	34 Grant Road, PO Box 463, Thorndon, Wellington, tel 644 4735339	www.italy-embassy.org.nz
South Africa	796 George Avenue, Arcadia 0083 Pretoria, tel 2712430 5541	www.ambital.org.za
UK	No. 14 Three Kings Yard, London W1Y 2EH, tel 020 7312 2200	www.embitaly.org.uk
US	3000 Whitehaven Street NW, Washington DC 20008, tel 202/612-4400	www.italyemb.org

MONEY

CREDIT AND DEBIT CARDS

MasterCard, Diners Club and Visa are widely accepted, as well as Eurocheque cards. Credit cards *(carta di credito)* are becoming more widely accepted, but some smaller establishments still do not take them. Look for the credit card symbols in the shop window or check with the staff.

ATMs

Cash machines, called *bancomats* in Italy, are plentiful and many are accessible 24 hours a day. You will need a four-digit PIN number; call your bank if yours is longer. Most have instructions in English and other languages. You avoid commission and the exchange rates are better when you withdraw cash with a debit card (Cirrus/Visa/ Maestro/Delta) from ATMs rather than using a bureau de change, although you may incur bank charges.

TRAVELLER'S CHEQUES

With the growth in the use of plastic cards for payments and cash withdrawals, there has been a decline in the acceptance of traveller's cheques and few places now accept them for payment. Personal cheques drawn on a bank outside Italy cannot easily be changed for cash.

CURRENCY EXCHANGE

Traveller's cheques, cheques and foreign currency can be changed at banks, railway stations and airports, and very often at major hotels (generally at a poorer rate). Shop around before you buy.

BANKS AND POST OFFICES

The largest banks in Italy are Unicredito and Monte dei Paschi di Siena. Most major banks have cash machines (ATMs) and exchange facilities, although they are often very busy. Banks are usually open from 8.30 until 1 or 1.30, and again for a short time in the afternoon. Some open on Saturday morning. Central post offices usually have a currency exchange that is open throughout the day until 6.30.

BUREAUX DE CHANGE

There are bureaux de change *(cambio)* in all the main cities, usually open throughout the day until around 7.30. They often change money commission-free, but the exchange rates are not as good as those from banks.

CURRENCY RESTRICTIONS

Import and export of local and foreign currency is limited to €10,330, but check with your embassy before

TIPPING

Italians do not tip heavily. Service is often included in your hotel or restaurant bill, although a little extra is appreciated if the service has been good. The following is a general guide:

Pizzerias/trattorias: round up to the nearest euro

Smart restaurant: 10%

Bar service: up to €0.25

Taxis: round up to nearest €0.50

Porters: €0.50 to €1 per bag

Chambermaids: €0.50 to €1 per day

Cloakroom attendants: €0.50

Toilets: €0.20–€0.50

LOST/STOLEN CREDIT CARDS

American Express	06 7228 0371
Diners Club	800 864064
Maestro	+44 870 6000 459
MasterCard/Eurocard	800 870866
Visa/Connect	800 877232

CONVERSION CHART

FROM	TO	MULTIPLY BY
Inches	Centimetres	2.54
Centimetres	Inches	0.3937
Feet	Metres	0.3048
Metres	Feet	3.2810
Yards	Metres	0.9144
Metres	Yards	1.0940
Miles	Kilometres	1.6090
Kilometres	Miles	0.6214
Acres	Hectares	0.4047
Hectares	Acres	2.4710
Gallons	Litres	4.5460
Litres	Gallons	0.2200
Ounces	Grams	28.35
Grams	Ounces	0.0353
Pounds	Grams	453.6
Grams	Pounds	0.0022
Pounds	Kilograms	0.4536
Kilograms	Pounds	2.205
Tons	Tonnes	1.0160
Tonnes	Tons	0.9842

departure if you need to bring large sums into the country. Amounts greater than this should be declared and validated in Italy.

WIRING MONEY

Wiring money is quite a lengthy process and the bureaucracy involved means that it is probably not worthwhile unless you are planning to spend quite a long time in Italy. Ask your bank at home for a list of affiliated banks. You can get money wired out to any bank from home, but if your bank is already in contact with certain banks in Italy it will make the process a lot easier. Always ask for a separate letter, telex or fax confirming that the money has been sent and ask that it be sent to Swift. It can take up to a week for the money to transfer. If you have a bank account in Italy and at home, you can transfer money directly if both the banks are part of the Swift system of international transfers. Again it takes about 5 to 7 days, if not longer. American Express Moneygram and Western Union Money Tranfers are faster from the US, but more expensive.

TAX REFUNDS

All non-EU shoppers are entitled to an IVA (sales tax) refund on expensive purchases. Ask for a *fattura* (invoice) when shopping, then present this at customs for stamping when leaving the EU. Return the stamped invoice to the store within four months of the date of purchase and the shop will refund the IVA direct.

10 EVERYDAY ITEMS AND HOW MUCH THEY COST	
Sandwich	€3
Bottle of water	€0.65
Cup of tea or coffee	€1.50–€4
0.5 litres of beer	€3.20–€6.50
Glass of wine	€0.85–€4.50
Daily newspaper	€0.90–€3
Roll of camera film	€5
20 cigarettes	€4.70
An ice cream cone	€2
A litre of petrol (gas)	€1.40

HEALTH

BEFORE YOU GO

No vaccinations are necessary for a trip to Italy, unless you are coming into the country from an infected area. If you have any doubts, contact your doctor before you leave.

You should always take out health insurance, and most people do so as part of their travel insurance (▷ 423). Ensure that it covers the cost of getting you home in an emergency. If you already have health insurance to cover treatment at home, check with your insurer before you leave that you will be covered while abroad.

In addition to health insurance, which is normally included in travel insurance, European nationals should carry a European Health Insurance Card (EHIC). This gives you access to state-provided medical treatment, and you'll be treated on the same basis as an 'insured' person living in the country you're visiting. In Italy this could include free medicines on a doctor's prescription, but it might not cover all the things you'd expect to get free of charge from the NHS in the UK. You may have to make a contribution to the cost of your care.

The EHIC also covers any treatment you need for a chronic disease or pre-existing illness. You need to make arrangements in advance for kidney dialysis and oxygen therapy. To arrange for kidney dialysis while you're away, contact your NHS renal unit in the UK before you travel. For information on oxygen supply services in the countries covered by the EHIC arrangements, including Italy, call the Department of Health's Customer Service Centre on 020 7210 4850. The EHIC won't cover you if the main purpose of your trip is to get medical treatment.

You can apply for an EHIC through the Department of Health website (www.dh.gov.uk or www.ehic.aq.uk) or by calling 0845 606 2030, or by collecting an application form from a post office.

MEDICAL ASSISTANCE
Ambulance (emergencies) 118

For up-to-date information on travel health issues, see the Department of Health's website on www.dh.gov.uk (in the UK), or the website of the National Center for Infectious Diseases on www.cdc.gov/travel (in the US).

WHAT TO TAKE WITH YOU

It is a good idea to take photocopies of all important documentation and keep them separate from the originals. You could scan the photocopies and send them to an email address that can be accessed anywhere in the world.

If you are on regular medication, you should ensure that you have adequate supplies for your trip. Make a note of the chemical name (rather than the brand name) in case you need replacement supplies.

HOW TO GET A DOCTOR (UN MEDICO)

» To get in touch with a doctor, ask at your hotel or consult the Yellow Pages *(Pagine Gialle)* under *Unità Sanitaria Locale*.
» For an ambulance, call 118.
» If you need emergency treatment, go directly to the Pronto Soccorso (casualty department/emergency room) of the nearest hospital.

HOW TO GET TREATMENT WITH YOUR EHIC

» If you need medical treatment while you are away, take your EHIC to the USL *(Unità Sanitaria Locale)* office, which will provide you with a certificate of entitlement.

SELECTED HOSPITALS WITH EMERGENCY DEPARTMENTS		
CITY	ADDRESS	TELEPHONE
Rome	Policlinico Gemelli, Largo Agostino Gemelli 8	06 30151
Florence	Santa Maria Novella, 17 Piazza Santa Maria Novella	055 215555
Venice	San Giovanni e Paolo, Campo San Giovanni e Paolo	041 529 4111

» Take this to any doctor or dentist on the USL list to receive free treatment. If they need to refer you to a hospital, they will give you a certificate that entitles you to free treatment.

» If you go to a hospital without being referred by a doctor, make sure you show your EHIC to the member of staff who attends to you.

» If you do not have a USL certificate, you will have to pay for treatment. It may be difficult to get the money back afterwards, and you will probably only receive a partial refund.

» It is advisable to carry a photocopy of your EHIC.

HOW TO GET TREATMENT WITH INSURANCE

» You are strongly advised to take out comprehensive health insurance before you travel. This can be for a single trip or an annual policy. Check that it covers all activities you intend to pursue; an extra premium must be paid for winter sports or hazardous activities such as scuba-diving.

» Take a copy of your insurance documents to the doctor or hospital—they may be able to bill your insurance company directly.

» If you have to pay for treatment, keep all of your receipts for your insurance claim.

PHARMACIES (FARMACIA)

Most pharmacies are open during normal shop hours, but they take turns staying open overnight so that there is at least one open at all times. The name of the nearest on-duty pharmacy is displayed in the window.

DENTAL TREATMENT (UN DENTISTA)

If you have an EHIC, contact the USL, as above. If you do not have an EHIC, contact a private dentist (in the Yellow Pages under *Dentista*). Again, take a copy of your insurance details and keep your receipts.

OPTICIANS

Opticians can usually carry out minor repairs to your glasses, such as replacing screws, on the spot, for little or no charge. Lenses can often be replaced overnight. If you really cannot survive without your glasses or contact lenses, bring a copy of your prescription with you so that you can have replacements made up if necessary.

FOOD AND DRINK

Italy's tap water is generally safe to drink, but you should watch for signs that say *acqua non potabile*, which means the water is not drinkable. Bottled mineral water is widely available. Local meat, dairy products, poultry, seafood, fruit and vegetables are all safe to eat.

SUMMER HAZARDS

From April to the end of September the sun is extremely strong and you will need to wear sun cream.

Insect bites are not usually dangerous. There is no malaria in Italy, but there is an ongoing mosquito problem, even inland—Milan is particularly bad. Use insect repellent or a mosquito net at night in the summer months and be vigilant near water and woodland areas.

Below *Pharmacies display a green cross*

HEALTHY FLYING

» People visiting Italy from as far as the US, Australia or New Zealand may be concerned about the effect of long-haul flights on their health. The most widely publicized concern is deep vein thrombosis, or DVT. Misleadingly known as economy class syndrome, DVT is the formation of a blood clot in the body's deep veins, particularly in the legs. The clot can move around the bloodstream and could be fatal.

» Those most at risk include the elderly, pregnant women and those using the contraceptive pill, smokers and the overweight. If you are at increased risk of DVT, see your doctor before departing. Flying increases the likelihood of DVT because passengers are often seated in a cramped position for long periods of time and may become dehydrated.

To minimize risk of DVT:

drink water (not alcohol);
don't stay immobile for hours at a time;
stretch and exercise your legs periodically;
do wear elastic flight socks, which support veins and reduce the chances of a clot forming.

Other hazards

Other health hazards for flyers are airborne diseases and microbes spread by the plane's air-conditioning system. These are largely unavoidable but seek advice from a doctor before you leave if you have a serious medical condition.

ALTERNATIVE MEDICAL TREATMENTS

You can buy homeopathic remedies in most pharmacies. For more detailed advice, contact one of the following associations for practitioners in your area:

Italian Medical Association of Acupuncture (AMIA)
Piazza Navona 49, 00186 Roma, tel 06 6868 556

Associazione Terapie Naturale (A.Te.Na)
Piazza Wagner 8, 20145 Milano, tel 02 468798

Research Institute in Clinical Homeopathy, Acupuncture and Psychotherapy (CSOCAP)
Via Sabotino 2, 00195 Roma, tel 06 3751 6391

BASICS

ELECTRICITY

Electricity in Italy is 240 volts, and electrical appliances are fitted with sockets that have two round pins. If your appliances are manufactured for 240 volts, you just need a plug adaptor. If your voltage is different (e.g. in the US), you need an adaptor and transformer.

LAUNDRY

Most visitors trust their cleaning to their hotel, where your clothes are returned to your room and the (often high) charge added to your bill. Self-service launderettes *(la lavandaria automatica)* are few and far between, but they are emerging in the larger cities.

MEASUREMENTS

Italy uses the metric system, with all foodstuffs sold by the kilogram or litre. They also use the *ettogrammo* (100g), usually abbreviated to *etto*.

PUBLIC TOILETS

There are public toilets at railway stations and in larger museums, but otherwise they are rare. You will probably end up using the facilities in a bar or café. Facilities can be basic, to say the least. Toilet paper may or may not be provided, and sometimes there is only one toilet for both men and women. In some places there is a dish for gratuities—you should leave around €0.25.

SMOKING

» Smoking is not permitted on public transport, inside airport buildings and in public offices and buildings.
» Cigarettes and other tobacco products can only legally be sold in *tabacchi* (tobacconists) to those over 16. The stand-alone *tabacchi* are only open during normal shop hours (⊳ 434). Those attached to bars stay open longer.

VISITING ITALY WITH CHILDREN

Children are welcomed at most hotels and in almost all restaurants. Disposable nappies (diapers) and baby foods are available in many food shops *(il negozio di alimentari* or *il supermercato)*. On the down side, the lack of public toilets and changing facilities, most of which may not be as clean as you are used to, can make things difficult for people with very young children.
» Italian children stay up late—if parents are eating out, the kids go too. This means that most hotels do not offer a baby-sitting or listening service.
» Put on a high-factor sunblock and keep children covered up. If they're swimming, persuade them to cover up and swim in a T-shirt.
» Children are susceptible to heat stroke, so seek shade in the middle of the day and keep their heads and necks protected.
» Most hotels will put up to three or four beds in a room so families can stay together; the add-on cost is around 30 per cent of the room price.
» Italian hotels are unheated until the end of October, and, in the south, some remain so.
» If you are bottle-feeding your baby, you might want to bring the formula with you.
» Children between 4 and 12 qualify for a 50 per cent discount on trains; those under 4 go free.
» Books with ideas on how to keep children occupied are available in Rome, Florence and Venice bookshops, and local tourist information offices are also able to help.
» Strollers and pushchairs can be hard work on cobbled streets in hill towns.

VISITORS WITH DISABILITIES

Wheelchair access is improving in the larger cities, but it is virtually non-existent in the rest of the country. It is always worth asking individual establishments what access is like. The narrow, cobbled streets and lack of pavements (sidewalks) in many of the old towns can prove difficult and places like Venice present their own unique set of problems for people with mobility issues (⊳ 62).
» Holiday Care in the UK publishes information on accessibility on holiday in Italy (Tourism for All, The Hawkins Suite Enham Place, Enham Alamein, Andover SP11 6JS,tel 0845 124 9971, fax 0845 124 9972, www.holidaycare.org.uk).
» In the US, SATH (Society for Accessible Travel and Hospitality) has lots of tips for visitors with visual impairment or reduced mobility (www.sath.org).

PLACES OF WORSHIP

You will find Catholic churches in even the smallest towns and villages in Italy and there are plenty of famous pilgrimage sites to track down. Saints' days and religious festivals are celebrated enthusiastically throughout the year (⊳ 434, 449). Every Wednesday at 11am the Pope celebrates Mass in St. Peter's or the Aula Paolo VI in Vatican City (see www.vatican.va for details).

In Rome, members of other Christian denominations are well catered for. The church of All Saints (Ogni Santi) in Via del Babuino is an Anglican church, and St. Paul's within the Wall (San Paolo entro le Mura) in Via Napoli is an American Episcopalian church. The Presbyterian Church of Scotland is at 7 Via XX Settembre. There are several Methodist and Baptist churches in the city and a Lutheran church in Via Sicilia. Seventh Day Adventists meet at Lungotevere Michelangelo 7.

There is a large Jewish community in Italy too. Rome has a Jewish quarter and the religion is widely practised in Venice, Florence, Ferrara and the north. To find synagogues and Jewish community centres in Italy, try visiting www.kosherdelight.com or www.mavensearch.com.

There are few mosques in Italy, but the main centre for Islam is in Milan. For information contact the Unione delle Comunite ed Organizzazione Islamiche in Italia (UCOII) (Via Padova 38, 20127 Milano, tel 01 83660253).

COMMUNICATION

CALL CHARGES

Free phone numbers *(numeri verdi)* usually begin with 800 and national call rate numbers begin with 848 or 199. Hotels tend to charge a very high rate for long-distance and international calls, so it is best to make calls from public phones, using telephone cards. Rates are lowest all day Sunday and between 10pm and 8am on weekdays and Saturday.

REVERSE-CHARGE (COLLECT) CALLS

From major Italian cities, you can place a direct call abroad by reversing the charges or by using a phone credit card number. To reverse the charges, call the International Operator on 170 or, for a cheaper alternative, dial the country's operator direct on one of the following free numbers:

Australia (Optus): 800 172 611
Australia (Telstra): 800 172 601
Canada: 800 172 213
France: 800 172 226
New Zealand: 800 172 641
UK: 800 172 440
US (AT&T): 800 172 444
US (MCI): 800 905 825
US (Sprint): 800 172 405

AREA CODES FOR MAJOR CITIES	
Bologna	051
Brindisi	0831
Florence	055
Genoa	010
Milan	02
Naples	081
Palermo	091
Perugia	075
Pisa	050
Rome	06
Siena	0577
Turin	011
Venice	041
Verona	045

CALLING ABROAD
A call from outside Italy would be dialled as 0039 (011 39 from the US) + 06 (code for Rome) + phone number.
A call from Rome to the UK would be dialled as 0044 + the area code missing off the first 0 (e.g. 01780 becomes 1780) + the number.
A call from Rome to the US would be dialled as 001 + the area code + the number.
For all calls within Italy, local and long distance, you must dial the regional area code (*prefisso*), which begins with a 0, as 06 for Rome, 041 for Venice.

PUBLIC TELEPHONES

If you are calling from a public phone you must deposit a coin or use a phone card to get a dial tone. Note that some pay phones will only accept coins and others only a *scheda telefonica* (phone card). Phones that only take coins tend to be less reliable than phone card phones. Call-centre telephones are a better bet than the often poorly maintained public telephones. Here you are assigned a booth to make your call and you pay for the call when you have finished.

PHONE CARDS

Prepaid *schede telefoniche* (phone cards) are used widely. You can buy them from post offices, tobacconists, newsstands and bars. Tear off the corner of the card and insert it in the slot of the public phone. When you dial, the number of units that it holds appears in the window. After you hang up, the card is returned so you can use it until it runs out. The Time phone card is good value, allowing you to call Europe and the United States at 28c per minute during peak time, but if you are calling between 10pm and 8am, or on Sunday, conventional phone cards are cheaper. You can also make cheap international calls from the call centres in all major cities.

MOBILE PHONES

It can be very expensive to use your mobile phone abroad and you will often be charged to receive calls as well as make them. If you travel abroad frequently and intend to use your phone, consider swapping your SIM card for a card from an alternative provider—either a foreign network or a dedicated provider of international mobile phone services.

Text messages are often a cheaper alternative to voice calls, but check the charges for making calls and text messages with your service provider. Italian mobile numbers begin with 330, 335, 347, 368, etc.

INTERNET CAFÉS

Internet points, as the Italians prefer to call them, are relatively widespread—expect to pay around €5 per hour, except in hotels when it can be up to €10 per hour. There is an online directory of internet points in Italy listed by region at http://cafe.ecs.net.

After using a public-access computer, make sure you log off fully. Make sure that no one using the computer after you can gain access to your credit card number, password, etc. At the start, select the options instructing the computer not to retain your details. It is also a wise precaution to delete the history of any web-browsing before logging off.

Many hotels are now equipped with WiFi or HotSpot facilities that enable you to use your own laptop computer to access the internet. You will need a wireless notebook network card compatible with 802.11g slotted into your computer.

LAPTOPS

If you intend to use your own laptop in Italy, remember to bring a power converter to recharge it and a plug socket adaptor. A surge protector is also a good idea. To connect to the internet you need an adaptor for the phone socket. If you use an

POSTAGE RATES			
Posta Prioritaria	Letter (20g)	Letter (21–100g)	Delivery time
Europe	€0.65	€1.70	3 days
US, Africa, Asia	€0.85	€1.85	4–8 days
New Zealand and Australia	€1.00	€2.10	4–8 days

INTERNET CAFÉS

REGION/TOWN	POPULAR INTERNET CAFÉS
ROME	Netgate Internet, Piazza Firenze 25 (Pantheon), tel 06 6893 445
	Mondadori MultiCenter, Via San Vicenzo (Trevi Fountain), tel 06 697 6501
	Stargate I-Café, Via Marrucini 12, tel 06 445 4953
THE NORTHWEST	
Milan	Gr@zianet, Piazza Duca d'Aosta 14, Stazione Centrale, tel 02 670 0543
	Phone@Point, Viale Sabotino 5, tel 02 5830 7274
Turin	BU.NET, Internet Wine Café, Via San Quintino 13f, tel 011 440 7517
Venice	TheNetgate, Crosera San Pantalon, Dorsoduro 3812a, tel 041 244 0213
THE NORTHEAST AND EMILIA-ROMAGNA	
Bologna	Net Arena, Via de' Giudei 3/b, tel 051 220850
Padua	Bowling Padua, Via Venezia 124, tel 049 776465
Ravenna	Bowling, Via Romea Nord 231, tel 0544 697863
Verona	Eurospazi Internet Point, Banco Lavori 30, tel 045 621 1422
Florence	Internet Point, Via Ricusoli 19/5, tel 055 280 119
TUSCANY AND UMBRIA	
Perugia	The NetGate, Via Cesare Battista 19, tel 075 572 0771
Pisa	Internet Planet, Piazza Cavallotti, tel 050 830702
Siena	Netgate Internet, Via del Porrione 88, tel 057 723 6412
THE SOUTH	
Capri	I-Point, Piazza Vittoria 13, Anacapri, tel 081 837 3283
Naples	I-cafe Piazza Garibaldi 73, Stazione Centrale, tel 081 563 4836
	InternetNapoli, Piazza Cavour 146, tel 081 298877
SICILY AND SARDINIA	
Cagliari	Intermedia Point, Via Eleonora d'Arborea 4, Sardinia, tel 070 652201
Palermo	Everalways, Corso Tukory 198, Sicily, tel 091 217652
Siracusa	Punto Rete, Via Cristoforo Colombo 38, Sicily, tel 0931 976906

USEFUL TELEPHONE NUMBERS

International operator-assisted service and Italian operator: **170**

Italian directory enquiries: **12**

Information in foreign languages: **176**

Information on addresses from phone numbers: **1412**

COURIERS

DHL	800 345345
Federal Express	800 833040
UPS	199 199 345
EMS–International Express Courier (Italian postal service)	800 009966

COUNTRY CODES FROM ITALY

Australia	00 61
Belgium	00 32
Canada	00 1
France	00 33
Germany	00 49
Greece	00 30
Ireland	00 353
Netherlands	00 31
New Zealand	00 64
Spain	00 34
Sweden	00 46
UK	00 44
USA	00 1

international internet service provider, it's cheaper to dial up a local node rather than the number in your home country. Dial-tone frequencies vary between countries, so set your modem to ignore dial tones.

POSTAL SERVICES

Poste Italiane, the Italian postal service, has 14,000 post offices *(posta, ufficio postale* or *PT)* across Italy. You can buy stamps and send letters and packages from here and send faxes and telegrams from larger post offices. The introduction of the priority mail *(posta prioritaria)* service for all post has transformed the Italian system, which is now more or less on a par with other EU countries.

Vatican City has its own postal service, which is more efficient than the Italian State system. There is a Vatican City post office in the square in front of the Basilica di San Pietro. Stamps *(francobolli)* are also available from tobacconists. The value of the stamps they sell you for a letter will be an approximation of the delivery cost. If you need to send a heavy letter or a package, take it to a post office where it can be weighed.

For information on all Italy's postal services, contact Poste Italiane (tel 800 222666, www.poste.it). In general, post offices are open Monday to Saturday from 8 to 1.45.

POSTCARDS

If you want them to arrive at their destination within a couple of weeks, put them in an envelope.

SENDING ITEMS OF VALUE

You can use the registered post *(raccomandato)* to send valuable items; add €2.60 to the price of normal postage. The cost of insured mail *(assicurato)* depends on the value of the items (€5.75 for packages up to €55.65 in value). Insured mail services are not available to the US.

RECEIVING POST IN ITALY

Poste restante, or general delivery, is known as *fermo posta*. These letters are held at the *fermo posta* counter in the main post office of the town to which the letter is addressed. To pick them up you must present your passport as identification and there is a small charge. *Fermo posta* letters should be addressed in the following way: Rebecca Brown, Fermo Posta, 00185 Roma, Italy. If you are receiving items via courier, you may have to pay IVA of up to 20 per cent to pick up the package.

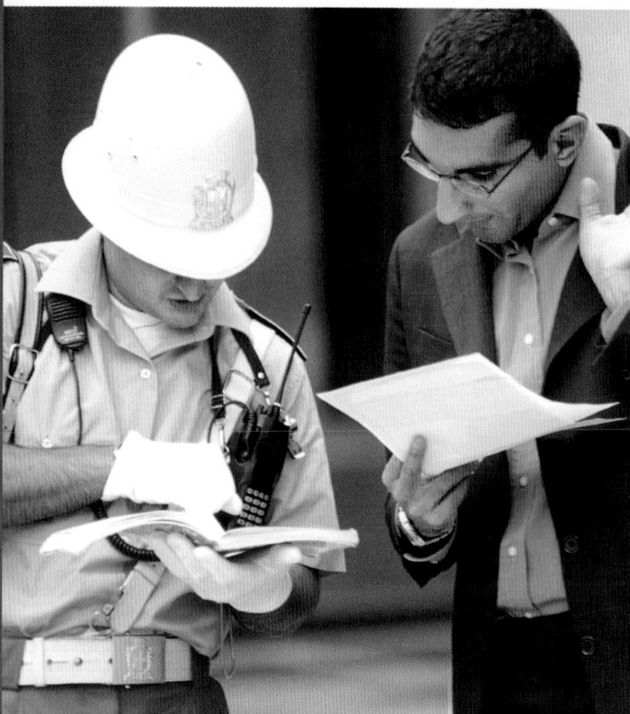

FINDING HELP

PERSONAL SECURITY

» Though levels of crime are low, you should take care around railway stations, on public transport and in crowded areas in the larger cities where pickpockets and bag snatchers may be operating. Be particularly wary of groups of children, who may try to distract your attention while stealing your valuables.

» Passports, credit cards, travel tickets and cash should not be carried together in bags or pockets. Only carry with you what you actually need for the day and consider making use of safe deposit facilities in hotels.

» An increasing number of robberies are taking place from cars at rest stops/petrol (gas) stations on motorways. You should treat with caution offers of help if you find yourself with a flat tyre, particularly on the motorway from Naples to Salerno, as sometimes the tyre will have been punctured deliberately.

» Lock your vehicle and never leave valuables in the vehicle even if you will only be away for a short time or are nearby. Cars containing luggage have been the targets of car thieves, so avoid leaving luggage in cars overnight or for any length of time.

» Be vigilant when on sleepers/night trains as thieves sometimes operate on the trains and may take the opportunity during the night to rob sleeping passengers. Theft on trains doesn't just happen at night, so do not leave bags containing valuables unattended at any time.

» Never carry money or valuables in your back pocket. Always keep them secure in a money belt or similar.

» Do not flaunt your valuables. Leave valuable jewellery in hotel safes and, if you are a woman walking around on your own, consider turning any rings with stone settings or similar around so that only the band is visible and not the jewels.

» Never put your camera or bag down on a café table or on the back of a chair, from where it could be snatched.

» Carry bags or cameras on the side of you that is farthest away from the road, to minimize the risk from bag snatchers.

» Keep a close eye on your bags and possessions in crowded areas.

» Wear bags across your body, rather than just over your shoulder, from where they can be easily snatched.

» If you have a programmable safe in your hotel room, do not use your date of birth as the code. It is on your passport and your hotel registration.

EMERGENCY NUMBERS	
FROM ANYWHERE IN ITALY	
Ambulance (Ambulanza)	118
Automobile Club d'Italia (ACI)	803 116
Fire Brigade (Vigili del Fuoco)	115
Police (Carabinieri, ▷ 431)	112
Police (Polizia, ▷ 431)	113
Roadside Rescue (Soccorso Stradale)	803 116
Roadside Rescue (Europ Assistance Vai)	803 803
Samaritans (English-speaking volunteers available 1–10pm)	06 7045 4444

CREDIT CARD EMERGENCY NUMBERS	
CREDIT CARD/TRAVELLER'S CHEQUES	TELEPHONE
American Express	06 7228 0371
American Express traveller's cheques	800 914912
Diners Club	800 864064
Eurocard/CartaSi	800 018548
MasterCard	06 4925 9200
Visa	800 819014

LOST PROPERTY

In Rome, ATAC has lost property offices for articles left on buses or trams, as do FS trains for anything left on their trains.

» To claim on your insurance, you need to report the loss to the police to get a statement *(denuncia)*.

» If your passport is lost or stolen, report it to the police and your consulate. The whole process of getting a replacement is easier if you have kept a copy of your passport number or a photocopy of the information page safe (▷ 423).

» If your credit card or bank card is stolen, report it to the police and phone the appropriate bank card/credit card emergency number to cancel your card. All are open 24 hours a day and have English-speaking staff.

» If your traveller's cheques are stolen, notify the police, then follow the instructions given with the cheques.

EMBASSIES AND CONSULATES IN ITALY		
AUSTRALIA		
Embassy	Via Antonio Bosio 5, 00161 Roma	tel 06 852721
Consulate	Via Borgogna 2, 20122 Milano www.italy.embassy.gov.au/	tel 02 7770 4217
CANADA		
Embassy	Via Salaria 243, 00199 Roma www.canadainternational.gc.ca/italy-italie	tel 06 8544 43937
Consulate	Via Zara 30, 00198 Roma	tel 06 8544 43937
IRELAND		
Embassy	Piazza di Campitelli 3, 00186 Roma	tel 06 697 9121
Consulate	Piazza F. Pietro in Gessate 2, 20122 Milano www.ambasciata-irlanda.it	tel 02 5518 7569
NEW ZEALAND		
Embassy	Via Clitunno 44, 00198 Roma	tel 064 417171
Consulate	Via Guido d'Arezzo 6, 20145 Milano www.nzembassy.com	tel 02 4801 2544, fax 02 4801 2577
UK		
Embassy	Via XX Settembre 80a, 00187 Roma http://ukinitaly.fco.gov.uk	tel 06 4220 0001
Consulate	Lungarno Corsini 2, 50123 Firenze	tel 055 284133, fax 055 219112
Consulate	Via S. Paolo 7, 20121 Milano	tel 02 723001, fax 02 864 65081
Consulate	Via dei Mille 40, 80121 Napoli	tel 081 423 8911, fax 081 422434
Consulate	Piazzale Donatori di Sangue 2/5, 30171 Venezia Mestre; www.ukve.it	tel 041 505 5990, fax 041 950254
US		
Embassy	Via Vittorio Veneto 119a–121, 00187 Roma www.italy.usembassy.gov	tel 06 46741
Consulate	Lungarno Amerigo Vespucci 38, 50123 Firenze	tel 055 266951
Consulate	Via Principe Amadeo 2/10, 20121 Milano	tel 02 290351, fax 02 28035273
Consulate	Piazza della Repubblica, 80122 Napoli	tel 081 583 8111
Consulate	Via Vaccarini 1, 90141 Palermo	tel 091 305857
Consulate	Via Dante 2/43, 16121 Genova	tel 010 584492

REPORTING THEFT

Report thefts to a police station, where you will need to make a statement. It is unlikely that you will get your belongings back, but you need the statement *(denuncia)* to make a claim on your insurance. You can find the address and contact details of your nearest police station in the Yellow Pages *(Pagine Gialle)* under *Commissariato, commando di polizia* or *stazione dei carabinieri*.

POLICE

There are three branches of the police in Italy, any of whom should be able to help you if you are in difficulty. The *carabinieri* are military police, easily recognizable by the white sash they wear across their bodies. They deal with general crime, including drug control. The *polizia* is the state police force, whose officers wear blue uniforms. They too deal with general crime, and if you are unfortunate enough to be robbed (or worse) they are the ones you will need to see. The *vigili urbani*, the traffic police, wear dark blue uniforms and white hats.

WHAT TO DO IF YOU ARE ARRESTED

If you are taken into custody by the police, you could be held for up to 48 hours without appearing before a magistrate. You can also be interviewed without a lawyer present. You do, however, have the right to contact your consul, who is based at your country's consulate, but you are still bound by Italian law. Your consul will not be able to get you out of jail, but will visit you and put you in touch with English-speaking lawyers and interpreters, offer advice and support and contact your family on your behalf. Try to keep hold of your passport and contact your travel insurance company, as you may be covered for legal costs.

EMBASSIES AND CONSULATES

Lists of embassies and consulates are available from tourist offices. You can also look under *Ambasciate* or *Consolati* in the phone book or visit embassyworld.com.

MEDIA

MAGAZINES

Many Italian magazines are adorned with pictures of scantily clad women, but this isn't necessarily a reflection of their content. If you read a little Italian, magazines such as *Panorama* and *L'espresso* are good for news, while *Oggi* is a more light-hearted alternative with the focus on celebrity gossip and lifestyle. *L'espresso* is renowned for its restaurant reviews and is highly respected in Italy.

English-language magazines can be hard to track down in Italy. *Roma C'è* and *Time Out Roma* (monthly) both have English-language sections. *Wanted in Rome* is aimed at resident English-speakers, but also has listings for what's going on in the city. *Italy* is a monthly magazine with an associated website at www.italymag.co.uk, which has informative and stimulating articles on all things Italian.

ENGLISH-LANGUAGE NEWSPAPERS

Newsstands in airports and central train stations of major Italian cities carry English-language newspapers such as *The Times, Financial Times,* The *Guardian, The Daily Telegraph, The New York Times* and *International Herald Tribune*. Some British papers are available only in their shorter international editions, and you will not get all the supplements in the Sunday papers. Expect to pay about €4 for a foreign newspaper. Some hotels can order a British or US newspaper for you, but it may be a day late. In Milan and Rome it's usually possible to get newspapers on the day of publication after about 2pm.

ITALIAN-LANGUAGE NEWSPAPERS

La Repubblica has a good listings on Thursdays and a glossy magazine supplement on Saturdays called *La Repubblica delle Donne,* with excellent articles reflecting all aspects of Italian life and society. There are two daily sports papers published in Italy—*La Gazzetta dello Sport* (pink paper) and the *Corriere dello Sport*; these are mainly dominated by football and motorsports news. *La Gazetta dello Sport* also publishes a supplement on Saturday called *Sport Week,* which tends to cover a wider range of sports and contains excellent full-colour photos and features on the week's events. *Il Messaggero* is a local paper, popular with Romans. *La Repubblica, Corriere della Sera, La Stampa* and *Il Sole/24 Ore* are the main national newspapers. *La Repubblica* and *Corriere della Sera* both publish special editions in Rome.

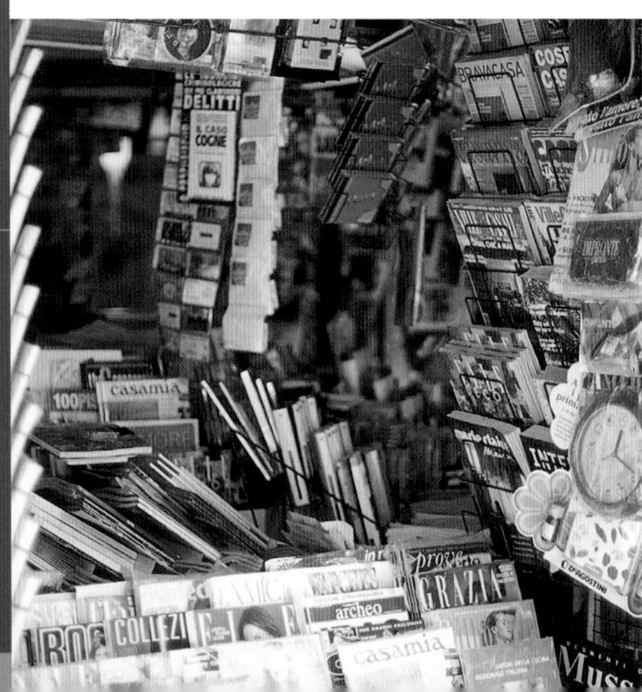

TELEVISION

Italy has three state-run television stations (RAI-1, -2 and -3), which broadcast some worthy entertainment, three stations run by Silvio Berlusconi's Mediaset group (Italia Uno, Rete Quattro and Canale Cinque), and a number of local channels. RAI-3 has international news broadcasts, which include an English-language section. It starts at 1.15am. Italian television is generally pretty frivolous, usually comprising a mixture of soaps, chat shows and American imports dubbed into Italian. Quiz shows also remain popular.

Most hotels, from mid-range upwards, have satellite television, so you can keep up to date with the news and sport on BBC World, CNN and Eurosport.

RADIO

RAI Radio 1, 2 and 3 (89.7FM, 91.7FM and 93.7FM), the state-run stations, have a mixture of light music, chat shows and news—all in Italian. If you are in Rome, Radio Vaticano (93.3FM) broadcasts news in a number of languages, including broadcasts in English at 5.10pm and 9.50pm daily. Radio Italia Network (90–108FM) is the best national radio station for dance music and Radio Deejay (99.7–107FM) plays a variety of popular music and also broadcasts chat shows.

If you have your computer with you while travelling, you can get BBC radio stations including Radio 1, Radio 2, Radio 3, Radio 4, 5 Live and 6 Music on the internet via www.bbc.co.uk/radio. The BBC World Service frequencies in Italy are MHz 12.095, 9.410, 6.195 and 0.648. Visit www.radio-locator.com to track down information on US radio stations online.

FILMS AND BOOKS

FILMS

Italy has been making films from the earliest days of cinema art. Mussolini recognized the cultural value of cinema and in 1937 established Cinecittà outside Rome, a huge campus of studios and technical facilities that is still in operation today. Italy has produced some world-class filmmakers, including Federico Fellini, Pier Paolo Pasolini, Dino De Laurentii, Michelangelo Antonioni and Roberto Rossellini, to name but a few.

» The so-called 'Spaghetti Westerns' were the creation of Sergio Leone, who counted Clint Eastwood among his favourite leading men, in films such as *Per Un Pugno di Dollari* (*A Fistful of Dollars*, 1964) and *Il Buono, Il Brutto e Il Cattivo* (*The Good, The Bad and the Ugly,* 1967).

» The golden age of Roman filmmaking was in the 1950s and 1960s. The much-acclaimed *Roman Holiday* (1953) thrust Audrey Hepburn into the limelight. You'll recognize many of the landmarks the stars visit, including the Bocca della Verità (▷ 95).

» *Three Coins in a Fountain* (1954) is still a great travelogue for Rome.

» Probably the most famous movie image of Rome is Anita Ekberg's dip in the Trevi Fountain in *La Dolce Vita* (1960), which was also filmed in Tivoli (▷ 330–331) and Viterbo (▷ 329).

» *The Italian Job* (1969), an action-packed comedy with Michael Caine, is famous for its car chases around the streets of Turin. In *Death in Venice* (1971) the city is as big a star as the leading man, Dirk Bogarde; and views of Florence feature highly in *A Room with a View* (1985).

» Travelling around Italy you may recognize other locations made famous in movies. Scenes in Kenneth Branagh's adaptation of Shakespeare's *Much Ado About Nothing* (1993) were shot in the rolling countryside of Tuscany, and the hilltop Villa Vignamaggio, with its knot gardens and vineyards.

» Terni in Umbria and Arezzo in Tuscany feature in *La Vita è Bella* (*Life is Beautiful,* 1997), a movie set in 1940s Italy telling the dark but heartwarming story of a Jewish bookkeeper who struggles to hold his family together during WWII.

» The streets of Ancona are the setting for Nanni Moretti's drama *La Stanza del Figlio (The Son's Room)*, which won the coveted Palme D'Or at the 2001 Cannes Film Festival.

» The village of Follina, near Treviso, and the mountainous landscape of the Veneto Alpine foothills provided the backdrop for Richard Attenborough's film *In Love and War* (1997).

» *The Talented Mr Ripley* (1999) was filmed all over Italy, including Rome, Isola d'Ischia and Isola di Procida near Naples, Palermo, Positano and Venice. The sequel, *Ripley's Game* (2002), was shot mainly in the north of Italy and captures the classical architecture of Asolo and Vicenza in the Veneto region. The late Heath Ledger, and Venice itself, both starred in *Casanova* (2005).

BOOKS

There are many good books covering Italy's long and eventful history and social life in the present day.

» For history in novel form, try *I, Claudius* (1934), by Robert Graves, or Irvine Stone's *The Agony and the Ecstasy* (1965).

» Research is going on all the time at Italy's archaeological sites, and new books still emerge offering fresh insights into how people lived in past ages. *Pompeii: History, Life and Afterlife* is a major modern work by Roger Ling, of Manchester University, while in *Pompeii: The Living City* a historian and dramatist have collaborated to describe what life was like in the 25 years before the city was engulfed in AD79.

» For younger readers, Caroline Lawrence's *Roman Mysteries* series is set in the Roman Empire, and *The Rotten Romans*—part of the *Horrible Histories* series—takes a light-hearted look at ancient times.

» Anyone interested in Italian politics and society should read *The Dark Heart of Italy* (2003) by Tobias Jones, which describes Italian life under Silvio Berlusconi's administration. The theme is also taken up by Geoff Andrews in *Not a Normal Country*, which explores the rise of Berlusconi at a time of widespread cynicism about politics.

Above *Anita Ekberg in* La Dolce Vita

» The Teach Yourself series now includes an introduction to Italian life. *Teach Yourself World Cultures—Italy* by Derek Aust and Mike Zollo (2004) gives you a basic overview that will enrich your time in Italy.

» *Venice—Tales of the City* (2003) is a collection of essays on Venice, edited by Michele Lovric.

» Marlena de Blasi is an American who made a name for herself as a food writer and for her book *A Thousand Days in Venice,* which describes her life and recipes in the city married to a Venetian. When the couple relocated to Tuscany, she wrote *A Thousand Days in Tuscany*, exploring the culinary traditions of the region.

» In *We Etruscans* Anna Rist observes life in a Tuscan hill town over 30 years, and charts changes in local lifestyle, landscape and aspirations.

» *The Humorists' Guide to Italy* is an anthology to keep you amused on a long train journey or on a quiet afternoon by the pool. It includes pieces by D. H. Lawrence, Charles Dickens, Edward Lear, E. M. Forster, Henry James and Mark Twain.

OPENING TIMES

BANKS

Usual opening times are 8.30 to 1.30, and 3 to 4.30, Monday to Friday. Some larger branches also open on Saturdays to 1.30.

POST OFFICES

These are generally open 8 to 1.45, Monday to Saturday.

PHARMACIES

Pharmacies are usually open the same hours as shops, but they take turns staying open overnight (▷ 426). Look for the list displayed in the shop window providing details of other pharmacies in the area, their opening times and the nearest on-duty pharmacy.

MUSEUMS AND GALLERIES

The opening times for museums and galleries vary greatly, according to the season and the location. Some are open all day, while others close at lunchtimes. Many close one day a week, usually Mondays. Check the individual sight in this guide, or contact the museum or gallery concerned for the most up-to-date information.

CHURCHES

Most churches open early in the morning for Mass, often around 7. They close at lunchtime, opening again around 4 and closing at 7. Some of the larger churches are open all day, and some may be closed to visitors during services. Check the individual sight in this guide for specific opening times or contact the church directly.

CAFÉS AND BARS

The hours kept by Italy's cafés and bars vary considerably from place to place and according to the season. Some are open for breakfast, others open in time for lunch, and some are only open in the evenings. Wine bars usually close at midnight or later. See the listings in the What to Do sections of the Regions for specific opening times.

RESTAURANTS

Restaurants that serve lunch open from noon and usually close during the afternoon. They reopen, along with those that only serve dinner, sometime after 7pm, and stay open late. Pizzerias are usually only open in the evening. Some restaurants close in August—look for the sign *Chiuso per ferie.* See the Eating and Staying sections of the Regions for specific opening times.

SHOPS

Traditionally, shops open in the morning between 8 and 9 and close for lunch at around 1. They reopen in the afternoon at 3.30 or 4 and close at 8. Most are closed Sundays and Monday mornings, but shops in the larger cities are beginning to stay open all day—look out for the sign *Orario continuato.* See pages 438–439 and the What to Do sections for specific opening times.

NATIONAL HOLIDAYS

Shops and banks generally close on public holidays. The road and rail networks are usually very busy at this time. There is a limited public transport service on Labour Day and the afternoon of Christmas Day. However, with the exception of Labour Day, Assumption and Christmas Day, most bars and restaurants remain open.

ENTRANCE FEES

Admission to churches tends to be free, but you may be asked to make a small donation or pay to see inside a church, or part of a church, that is of particular artistic or historic interest. Museums and archaeological sights charge for admission.

If you are intending to do a lot of sightseeing in a particular area, enquire about combined tickets. Further details of these are available from tourist offices (▷ 435).

NATIONAL HOLIDAYS

If a public holiday falls on a weekend, it is not celebrated on the Monday, as it is in the UK. If the holiday falls on a Tuesday or Thursday, many people take the Monday or Friday off to make a *ponte* (bridge) to the weekend.

1 Jan	New Year's Day
6 Jan	Epiphany
Mar/Apr	Easter Monday
25 Apr	Liberation Day
1 May	Labour Day
2 Jun	Republic Day
15 Aug	Assumption of the Virgin (Ferragosto)
1 Nov	All Saints' Day
8 Dec	Feast of the Immaculate Conception
25 Dec	Christmas Day
26 Dec	St. Stephen's Day

LOCAL HOLIDAYS

Banks, offices and shops in cities are also closed on local feast days honouring their patron saints. These are usually also the days for a traditional festival and city-wide celebrations, which can be very colourful and entertaining.

25 Apr	St. Mark	(Venice)
24 Jun	St. John the Baptist	(Florence, Genoa, Turin)
29 Jun	SS Peter and Paul	(Rome)
15 Jul	Santa Rosalia	(Palermo)
19 Sep	St. Gennario	(Naples)
4 Oct	St. Petronio	(Bologna)
30 Oct	St. Saturnio	(Cagliari)
3 Nov	St. Giusto	(Trieste)
6 Dec	St. Nicola	(Bari)
7 Dec	St. Ambrose	(Milan)

TOURIST OFFICES

Broadly there are three types of tourist office in Italy—regional, provincial and local. The main office is the APT (Azienda di Promozione Turistica), which should have information on the surrounding province in addition to the town in question. IAT (Informazione e Assistenza ai Turisti) has local tourist offices, mostly in the north, while in the south AAST (Azienda Autonoma di Soggiorno e Turismo) are more widespread and should be able to give advice on opening times for sights and local transport. Pro Loco is the local office in villages and small towns that again should be able to advise on museum openings and the like.

The efficiency and quality of tourist information offices is extremely variable throughout the country, as are the hours. Generally, however, offices in the larger destinations remain open throughout the summer, including at weekends, and there is usually an information point at airports and main rail stations.

OVERSEAS TOURIST OFFICES	
Italian State Tourist Offices Overseas (ENIT)	www.enit.it or www.italiantourism.com
Australia	Level 4, 46 Market Street, Sydney 2000, NSW; tel 02 9262 1666
Canada	175 Bloor Street E, Suite 907, South Tower, Toronto, Ontario M4W 3R8; tel 416 9254 882
UK	1 Princes Street, London W1B 2AY; tel 020 7399 3562
US	630 Fifth Avenue, Suite 1565, New York, NY 10111; tel 212-245-5618 12400 Wilshire Blvd, Suite 550, Los Angeles, CA 90025; tel 310-820-1898 500 North Michigan Ave, Suite 2240, Chicago, Illinois 60611, tel 312-644-0996

TOURIST OFFICES IN ITALY

ROME

Via Parigi 5, tel 06 488991 or 06 3600 4399, fax 06 481 9316, www.romaturismo.com

THE NORTHWEST

Genoa

Via Acqua Verde—Stazione Piazza Principe, tel 010 576791, fax 010 581408, www.apt.genova.it

Turin

Atrium Torino, Piazza Solferino, tel 011 535181, fax 011 530070, www.turismotorino.org

Como

Via Cavour 17, tel 031 269712, fax 031 240 111, www.lakecomo.org

Mantova (Mantua)

Piazza Mantegna 6, tel 0376 432432, fax 0376 432433, www.turismo.mantova.it

Milan

Via Marconi 1, tel 02 7252 4301, fax 02 7252 4350, www.milanoinfo.eu

VENICE

Piazza San Marco 71F, tel 041 529 8711, fax 041 523 0399, www.turismovenezia.it

THE NORTHEAST AND EMILIA-ROMAGNA

Padua

Riviera dei Mugnai 8, tel 049 876 7911, 049 650794, www.turismopadovat.it

Verona

Piazza Brà, Via degli Alpini 9, tel 045 806 8680, fax 045 800 3638, www.tourism.verona.it

Vicenza

Piazza Duomo 5, tel 0444 544122, fax 0444 325001, www.turismo. provinicia.vicenza.it

Bologna

Palazzo della Podestà, Piazza Maggiore 1, tel 051 246541, fax 051 639 3171, www.iat.bologna.it

Ravenna

Via Salara 8–12, tel 0544 35755, fax 0544 35094, www.turismo.ravenna.it

FLORENCE

Via Manzoni 16, tel 055 23320, fax 055 234 6286, www.firenzeturismo.it

TUSCANY AND UMBRIA

Lucca

Piazza S. Maria, tel 0583 919931, fax 0583 91663, www.luccaturismo.it

Pisa

Via Pietro Nenni 24, tel 050 929777, fax 050 929764, www.pisaturismo.it

Siena

Piazza del Campo 56, tel 0577 280 551, fax 0577 281041, www.terresiena.it

Assisi

Piazza del Comune, tel 075 812450, fax 075 813727, www.umbriaonline.com

Perugia

Piazza IV Novembre 3, tel 075 573 6458, fax 075 572 0988, www.umbriaturismo.it www.perugiaonline.com

LAZIO AND THE MARCHE

Ascoli Piceno

Piazza Arringo 7, tel 0736 298204, fax 0736 298232, www.comune.ascoli-piceno.it

Tivoli

Largo Garibaldi, tel 0774 334 522, fax 0774 331294, www.tivoli.it

THE SOUTH

Capri

Piazza Umberto I 19, tel 081 837 0686, fax 081 837 0918, www.capritourism.com

Naples

Palazzo Reale, Piazza del Plebiscito, tel 081 252 5720, fax 081 418619, www.inaples.it

Pompei

Via Sacra 1, tel 081 850 7255, fax 081 863 2401, www.pompeiicast.it

Sorrento

Via T. Maio 35, tel 081 807 4033, fax 081 877 3397, www.sorrentotourism.com

SICILY AND SARDINIA

Palermo

Piazza Castelnuovo 34, tel 091 583847, fax 091 605 8366, www.aapit.pa.it

Siracusa

Via Maestranza 33, tel 0931 464 255, fax 0931 60204, www.siracusaturismo.it

Taormina

Palazzo Corvaja, Piazza Santa Catarina, tel 0942 23243, fax 0942 24941, www.gate2taormina.com

Cagliari

Piazza Matteotti 9, tel 070 669255, fax 070 664923, www.cagliaridascoprire.it

WEBSITES

TOURISM

Abruzzo and Molise
www.abruzzoturismo.it
www.turismomolise.net

Basilicata
www.aptbasilicata.it

Calabria
www.turismo.regione.calabria.it

Campania
www.in-campania.com

Emilia-Romagna
www.apt.emilia-romagna.it

Florence
www.firenze.net
www.firenzeturismo.it

Friuli-Venezia Giulia
www.turismofvg.it

Lazio
www.turislazio.it

Liguria
www.regione.liguria.it

Lombardy
www.turismo.regione.lombardia.it

Marche
www.turismo.marche.it

Piemonte
www.regione.piemonte.it

Puglia
www.puglia.org
www.pugliaturismo.it

Rome
www.enit.it
www.enjoyrome.com
www.romaturismo.it

Sicily
www.regione.sicilia.it/turismo

Sardinia
www.sardegnaturismo.it

Trentino-Alto-Adige
www.trentino.to
www.provinzia.bz.it (Alto Adige)
www.suedtirol.info (South Tyrol)

Tuscany
www.turismo.toscana.it

Umbria
www.umbriaonline.com
www.umbria.org

Val d'Aosta
www.regione.vda.it/turismo

The Vatican
www.vatican.va

Veneto
www.regione.veneto.it

Venice
www.comune.venezia.it
www.turismovenezia.it

GENERAL

www.enit.it
The Italian national tourist board ENIT gives general information
www.estateolie.it
www.firenzemusei.it
www.fodors.com
www.italiansrus.com
www.italiantourism.com
www.itwg.com
www.museionline.it
www.parks.it
www.theaa.com
www.travel-guide.com
www.whc.unesco.org
Details of world Heritage Sites in Italy
www.virtualtourist.com

HOTELS

www.1stvenicehotels.com
www.allitalianhotels.com
www.florencehotelsnetwork.com
www.italyhotels.it

WEATHER

www.bbc.co.uk/weatherr
www.weather.com
www.weatheronline.co.uk/ Italy.htm

TICKETS AND ADVICE

www.cheapflights.com
www.flynow.com
www.lastminute.com
www.skyscanner.net
www.tripadvisor.com

TELEPHONE NUMBERS

www.paginegialle.it
Italian Yellow Pages.

TRANSPORTATION

www.atac.roma.it
www.trenitalia.it

AIRPORTS

www.adr.it
www.ancona-airport.com
www.pisa-airport.com
www.sea-aeroportimilano.it
www.veniceairport.it

NEWS

www.corriere.it
www.ilmessaggero.it
www.repubblica.it

MAJOR SIGHTS QUICK WEBSITE FINDER

SIGHT	WEBSITE	PAGE
Basilica di San Pietro (Rome)	www.vatican.va	74–75
Dolomites	www.dolomiti.com	207
Duomo (Florence)	www.operaduomo.firenze.it	236–239
Duomo (Pisa)	www.opapisa.it	283
Etna	www.prg.it/parcodelletna	395
Foro Romano (Rome)	www.capitolium.org	78–79
Galleria dell'Accademia (Florence)	www.firenzemusei.it	242
Galleria Borghese (Rome)	www.galleriaborghese.it	80–81
Gargano Peninsula	www.parks.it/parco.nazionale.gargano	350
Lago di Como	www.lakecomo.com	123
Musei Capitolini (Rome)	www.museicapitolini.org	83
Musei Vaticani (Rome)	www.vatican.va	84–87
Ostia Antica	www.itnw.roma.it/ostia/scavi	327
Palazzo Doria Pamphilj (Rome)	www.doriapamphilj.it	88
Palazzo Vecchio (Florence)	wwww.comune.fi.it	249
Parco del Conero	www.parcoconero.it	326
Parco Nazionale del Gran Paradiso	www.parks.it/parco.nazionale.gran.paradiso	132
Parco Nazionale dei Monti Sibillini	www.sibillini.net	280
Parco Nazionale dello Stelvio	www.stelviopark.it	209
Pompei	www.pompeiisites.org	360–363
Santa Maria Gloriosa dei Frari (Venice)	www.basilicadeifrari.it	184
Santa Maria della Concezione (Rome)	www.cappucciniviaveneto.it	95
Santa Maria sopra Minerva (Rome)	www.basilicaminerva.it	95
Vesuvio	www.vesuviopark.it	360–363

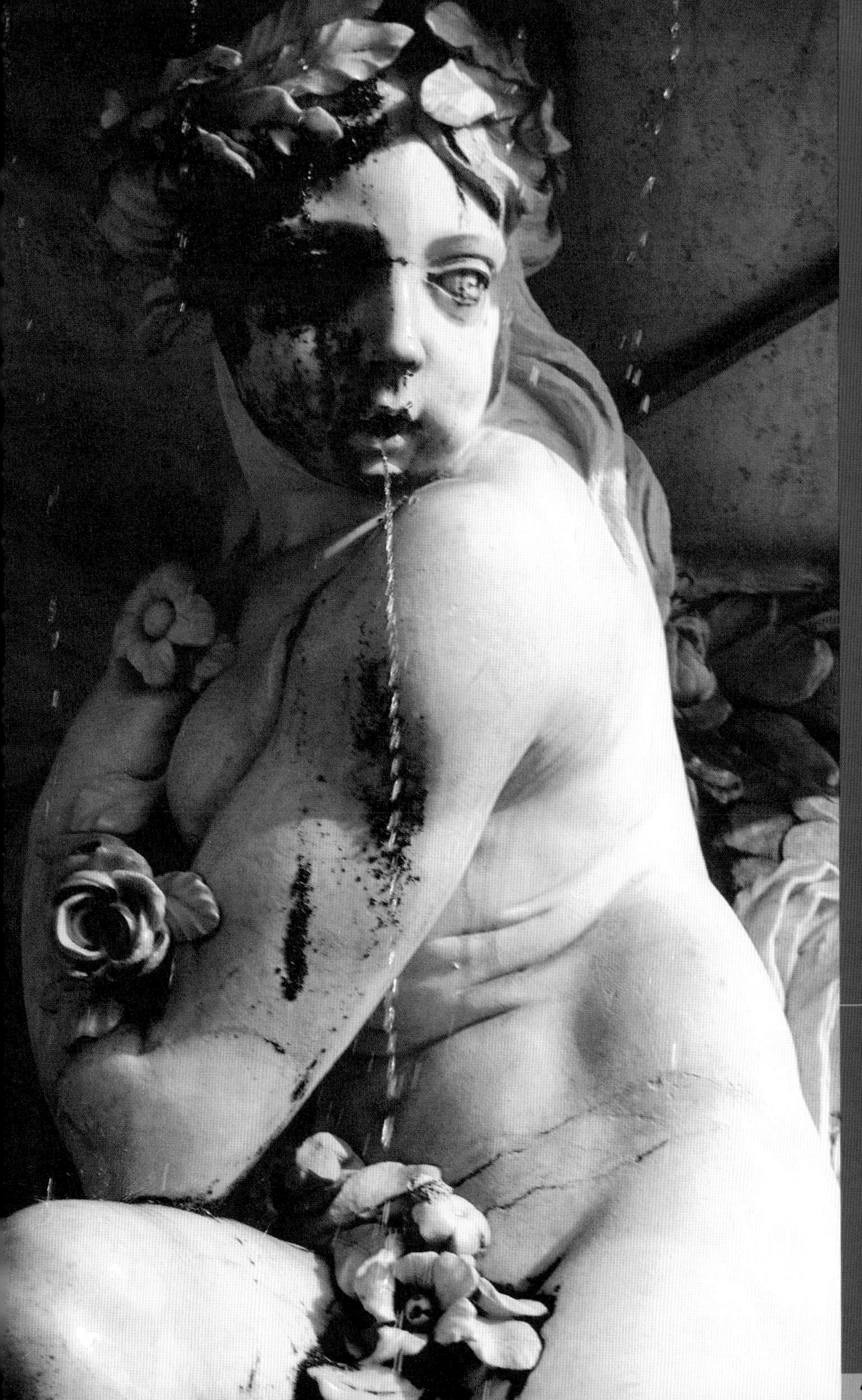

SHOPPING

Shopping is an essential part of *la bella figura* (▷ 19). It is taken seriously by both men and women in Italy, where quality is the focus, and personal service reigns supreme. It's seen at its best in the affluent north, particularly in Milan, Florence, Turin, Rome and Bologna, but every provincial capital has its fair share of stylish shops, and you'll find some nice surprises in even the smallest towns. In design and fashion, the big names have conquered the world, but there's more to retail therapy than *haute couture* and designer labels. Craftsmanship is highly valued and everything from furniture to underwear can still be made to order. The back streets are the place to go to find tiny stores and workshops selling souvenirs and unusal items.

MARKETS

There are daily food markets in provincial and regional capitals and other large towns throughout the country. They generally take place in a specially built market hall or in a specific piazza or street, selling meat, groceries, fish, dairy products, fruit and vegetables. Where there's a daily food market, the weekly market will be devoted to clothes, shoes, household goods, plants, flowers, toys, toiletries and fabrics. Rome's major markets are held around Piazza Vittorio, Piazza Testaccio, Porta Portese and Via Sannio. In Florence the most prominent are Mercato Centrale, Mercato di Sant'Ambrogio and Mercato Nuovo. In Venice, head for the Rialto, a famous focal point for trade since the 10th century, and still the best place in the city for stocking up on fresh produce, especially fish.

OUTLET SHOPPING

You can pick up bargains in big-name fashion and luxury goods at outlet shopping malls, usually located outside big cities. Fidenza Village, for example, is halfway between Milan and Bologna off the A1 motorway, and has Versace, Elena Miro, Phard, Nike, Bodum and Lindt, among many other top brands.

KEEP YOUR RECEIPT

Till receipts may seem a minor nuisance unless you've bought a major item and they are part of the guarantee or warranty. It's different in Italy. Keep a receipt for every last thing you buy in Italy, and ask for one—*scontrino* (not to be confused with *scontino,* meaning discount) or *ricevuta*—if it is not volunteered by the shopkeeper. The authorities have tightened up on cash trading to cut down on tax abuse, and the Guardia di Finanza patrols cities and towns like a police force. You could be asked by an officer, sometimes in plain clothes but carrying ID, to show a receipt as you leave a shop, to prove that the shop has declared the sale. Failure to produce a receipt can result in a fine of up to €155.

OPENING HOURS

These are fairly standard and apply for most of the year, but be prepared for erratic changes.

» Supermarkets, larger stores and tourist-oriented shops generally stay open all day *(orario continuato)*.
» Shops are open from 8.30–1 and 5.30–7 Monday–Saturday.
» Clothes shops may not open until 10am.
» Hours may change from mid-June until the end of August; some shops close completely when their owners go on holiday, while others stay open later for visitors.
» Small shops may close for anything from a week to a month during July and August.
» A chemist/pharmacy *(farmacia)* somewhere around the area you are staying in will be open for prescriptions 24 hours a day; this is done on a rotation system and chemists post addresses and opening times in their windows.

WHAT TO BUY

Handicrafts

There is a huge range of regional handicrafts to seek out, such as olive-wood bowls and plates in Tuscany and Murano glass in Venice, with many products only available in the area where they are made. Florence has an abundance of artisan workshops specializing in picture frames, soft furnishings, accessories and antique furniture.

Handmade Paper

Beautiful hand-made paper, often marbled or block-printed, is one of the top buys in Florence, Tuscany and Venice.

Ceramics

Ceramics and pottery are produced all over Italy with designs and glazes varying from region to region. The town of Deruta in Umbria is overflowing with workshops. Other top places for ceramics are Santo Stefano di Camastra in Sicily, the northern lakes, and Puglia. You can buy ceramics all over the country, but there's more choice and items are cheaper in their home town.

Fashion

You will find big names and chain stores in every major city and large town. Stores selling popular Italian exports generally carry a larger range than you'd find at home, and at more competitive prices. Smaller stores sell individual items with a distinct Italian twist.

Jewellery

Italy is one of the world's biggest jewellery manufacturers. Production is most prolific in Arezzo in Tuscany. Naples is famous for its coral and cameos, but there's a well-established tradition of in-house design across the country, and many jewellers will make pieces to order.

Shoes and Leather

You'll find shoes, belts, bags and accessories in Italy at both ends of the price range—don't neglect the markets, which are great trawling grounds for bargains.

Linens and Underwear

Italian women see luxurious underwear as their birthright, and you'll find plenty to choose from among the wisps of silk, satin and lace. Como is a major silk-producing town.

Food and Wine

Every region has its own unique food and wine, available in shops, markets and delicatessens. Buy such items when you see them—move on and you may find that you have unwittingly moved out of the production area.

DESIGNER LABELS

DESIGNER	LINES	MAJOR STORES	WEBSITE
Giorgio Armani	Fashion, shoes, leather goods	Rome, Venice, Florence, Milan	www.armani.it
Benetton	Fashion	Venice, Florence, Milan	www.benetton.com
Bottega Veneta	Shoes, leather goods	Rome, Venice, Milan	www.bottegaveneta.com
Bulgari	Jewellery	Rome, Florence, Milan	www.bulgari.com
Dolce & Gabbana	Women's fashion	Rome, Milan	www.dolcegabbana.it
Emporio Armani	Fashion, shoes, leather goods	Rome, Venice, Florence, Milan	www.emporioarmani.com
Fendi	Shoes, leather goods	Rome, Venice, Florence, Milan	www.fendi.it
Ferrè	Women's fashion	Milan	www.gianfrancoferre.it
Gucci	Fashion, shoes, leather goods, jewellery	Rome, Venice, Florence, Milan.	www.gucci.com
Krizia	Women's fashion	Rome, Milan	www.krizia.net
Laura Biagiotti	Women's fashion	Rome, Venice, Florence, Milan	www.laurabiagiotti.it
La Perla	Fashion, children's fashion, shoes	Rome, Venice, Florence, Milan	www.laperla.com
Max Mara	Women's fashion	Rome, Venice, Florence, Milan	No website
Missoni	Women's fashion	Rome, Venice, Florence, Milan	www.missoni.com
Prada	Fashion, shoes, leather goods	Rome, Venice, Florence, Milan	www.prada.com
Pucci	Women's fashion	Florence, Milan	www.emiliopucci.com
Roberto Cavalli	Women's fashion	Rome, Milan	www.robertocavalli.net
Salvatore Ferragamo	Men's fashion, shoes, leather goods	Rome, Florence, Venice, Milan	www.salvatoreferragamo.it
Trussardi	Fashion, shoes, leather goods	Rome, Florence, Milan	www.trussardi.it
Valentino	Women's fashion	Rome, Florence, Milan	www.valentino.it
Versace	Fashion, shoes, leather goods, jewellery, linens, tableware	Rome, Milan	www.versace.it

ENTERTAINMENT AND NIGHTLIFE

There is plenty to keep you entertained in Italy, from cinema and theatre to classical music and opera. This is the home of opera, and you should be able to catch something from the year-long schedule in a romantic or historic venue. The main concert and theatre seasons run throughout the winter, while festivals and outdoor spectacles take over in the summer. Rome and Milan are the big party cities, closely followed by university towns like Bologna, Florence and Perugia, and major provincial centres such as Turin, Genoa and Naples. Night-time activity moves to the coastal resorts during the summer, when the open-air bars and clubs attract huge crowds.

BARS

Bars are open from early until late and serve everything from breakfast, coffee and snacks to beer, wine and aperitifs, with no licensing hours to curtail your drinking. Evening-only bars often have live music nights and guest DJs. The main objective for most Italians is to be seen, so there's plenty of posing and little hard-core drinking going on.

CLASSICAL MUSIC, BALLET AND DANCE

The huge number of summer classical music festivals testifies to the Italian passion for the great composers. During the winter months, most cities and towns of any size will have a regular schedule of classical and orchestral music, though you're unlikely to hear anything avant-garde or contemporary.

As in so much else, when it comes to musical taste, Italians are staunchly conservative, happy with a diet of popular classics. Conscious of their funding, organizers, with the odd exception, stick to the tried and tested.

Ballet and dance are in much the same position. Unlike theatre, ballet gets no official subsidies and little corporate sponsorship, and consequently standards, even in Rome, are low. Most major opera houses have a ballet season, but the best time to see ballet is during the summer festivals, the most famous being the International Ballet Festival held in Nevi, near Genoa, in July. Contemporary dance has little support and even less funding; the best time to see something memorable is during the summer festivals.

CLUBS

» There is not much difference between music bars and small clubs in Italy.

» Many clubs charge an entrance fee, which usually includes a free drink.

» Some clubs make you take out membership *(tessera)*. Prices vary and it may be free.

» If there is no entrance fee, you may receive a card, which is stamped when you buy drinks or go to the toilet, and totalled up when you leave.

CINEMA

Italy makes around 100 films a year, and the Cinecittà cinematic powerhouse near Rome is constantly busy producing foreign and Hollywood films and nurturing native talent. Given this, it's not surprising that cinema is thriving in Italy, and you can catch anything from the latest blockbuster to the most obscure art-house movie.

The main problem will be the language. It's acknowledged that Italian dubbing is the best in the world, so films are automatically dubbed rather than subtitled. In Rome, Milan, Florence and Naples, you should be able to find a cinema showing VO *(versione originale)* movies, however; elsewhere, outside film festivals, films are likely to be in Italian. In summer films may be screened outdoors, in piazzas and parks.

» City cinemas generally have four showings in the afternoon and evening; 4.30, 6.30, 8.30 and 10.30. Smaller cinemas show films at 8.30 and 10.30.

» Box offices usually open half an hour before the first showing.

» Arrive early on Fridays and Saturdays, when cinemas can be very busy.

» Tickets normally cost around €8, with reductions for the early shows on Monday, Tuesday, Thursday and Friday and all day Wednesday.

» Very few cinemas accept payment by credit card.

» At busy times, some cinemas sell *posto in piedi* (standing only) tickets; there is no discount for these.

FOLK AND REGIONAL MUSIC

If you're looking for the sounds of traditional Italy, head for the *festas* when local bands and groups will be out in force. In more remote areas, you may catch a glimpse of some national costumes and dances. Sardinia, Sicily, the Abruzzo, Puglia and the German-speaking northern regions are good places to hear folk music.

The festivals organized by the political parties are also good for folk music, often accompanied by dancing. The *Festa dell'Unità*, child of the *Democratici di sinistra,* is the biggest of these, taking place in towns and villages all over the country. There's more folk and regional music at some of the city summer festivals, where lively Latin-American and Cuban music sets the tone.

MUSIC IN CHURCHES

Concerts are often staged in some of Italy's most beautiful churches, providing a chance to hear organ, orchestral and choral recitals in superb surroundings, often with the acoustics to match. Look for posters or ask at local tourist offices.

OPERA

There are hundreds of opera houses in Italy, mainly dating from the late 18th and 19th centuries. Many are still home to their own opera companies, or are at least in regular use throughout the season. Permanent companies pay their way by putting on classical music concerts and ballet for part of the season.

If you are an opera fan, don't miss the opportunity to see Italian opera performed on home soil—popular entertainment with a great deal of audience participation. Shows can be held up after arias for minutes at a time while the audience show their appreciation (or disapproval), and many houses still have unofficial cliques that attend every performance and control the crowd. It makes a refreshing change from the reverent hush that accompanies opera in other countries.

» The season runs from October to the end of March, with minor differences from city to city.

» Top names tend to sing for the first few nights of a production only, so keep an eye on cast lists.

» Italian opera houses generally have stalls, three to four tiers of boxes around the house, and a gallery. Stall seats and middle- and lower-tier boxes are the most expensive. Prices range from €20 to €70 upwards depending on the venue and company.

» Top places for summer opera outdoors are the Roman sites of the Terme di Caracalla in Rome (www.opera.roma.it) and the Arena in Verona (www.arena.it).

ROCK AND JAZZ

International bands and stars tend to concentrate on Milan, Rome and other major cities, performing in the larger stadiums. Concerts are well advertised with posters. Local rock is performed all over the country—it's at its best and most innovative in central and northern Italy and in the university towns.

Jazz takes centre stage at a number of summer festivals, notably Umbria Jazz, held in July and August. Visit www.allaboutjazz.com/italy for the latest listings and jazz news.

THEATRE

Many of the most beautiful and historic provincial theatres are primarily opera houses, doubling up as venues for drama, music and dance, so it's worth checking the press to see what's on (▷ 432).

Apart from Rome and Milan, other cities with a thriving theatre scene include Turin, Bologna, Venice, Florence, Naples and Palermo.

In summer, there are open-air festivals throughout the country celebrating theatre, music and dance. These often take place in classical theatres and arenas, or in the grounds of historic buildings.

OPENING HOURS

Things start to heat up around midnight, but many bars have a prolonged happy hour from 7 to 9. In smaller towns and rural areas, the opposite is the case, and you may struggle to find a bar open after 11.

HOT SPOTS

Rome

The *centri sociali* have catapulted Rome's night scene into the 21st century. Emerging 20 years ago, the *centri* were originally squats, where young people occupied abandoned public buildings, turning them into art spaces and music venues.

Rome's main clubs and bars are in Testaccio, the *centro storico* (around Piazza Navona and Campo dei Fiori), Trastevere and San Lorenzo.

Florence

Many central bars and clubs are underground and have no air-conditioning. Some close in summer, when the action moves to the coast. As in Rome, there's a clutch of *centri sociali*, organizing live music and dance nights. Opening times are erratic and, as with everywhere, things can change without warning.

Venice

There's not much nightlife in Venice at first glance. For the pick of the live venues and clubs head for Mestre and Marghera, or take a boat to Jesolo or Cavallino in summer. The liveliest areas are Campo Santa Margherita in Dorsoduro and Fondamenta della Misericordia in Cannaregio.

Rimini

Italy's answer to Ibiza, Rimini has a frenetic summer club scene that stretches along the coast from Bellariva to Cattolica. The whole area is served by public transport that runs through the night. There are more than 1,600 hotels, plus amusement parks, bars and restaurants: find current listings in *Chiamami Città* or *Guida d'Estate*, or visit www.riminifiera.it or www.riminiturismo.it

GAY AND LESBIAN SCENE

Over the last 10 years Italians have become far more tolerant towards gay and lesbian relationships, but there's still a long way to go in rural areas, and the gay scene remains low profile in the south. If you're looking for gay bars and clubs, head for the larger cities; Florence is particularly gay-friendly, and there's plenty going on in Rome and Milan.

» *Babilonia* is a monthly publication that includes gay listings for the whole of Italy (€5.20 at newsstands).

» Log on to www.arcigay.it, the official site of Italy's foremost gay and lesbian network, or www.mariomieli.org, a prominent Rome-based gay and lesbian group.

LISTINGS

Rome

Trovaroma—free on Thursdays with *La Repubblica*.
Roma C'è—Fridays from newsstands.
Zero6—free in shops and bars.

Milan

Hello Milano (hellomilano.it)—available from tourist offices.
ViviMilano—free on Wednesdays with *Corriere della Serra*.

Venice

Leo Bussola—free from tourist offices.
Venezia News—from newsstands.

Florence

Firenze Oggi (Florence Today)— free in hotels and bars.
Firenze Spettacolo—Fridays from newsstands.

TICKETS

Major venues throughout Italy generally have online booking facilities.

Rome

Available direct from venues or agencies, who charge a *diritti di pervendita* (supplement):
Orbis ✉ Piazza Esquilino, Roma ☎ 06 482 7403
Ricordi ✉ Via Cesare Battista, Roma ☎ 06 679 8022

Florence

Available direct from venues or from:
Box Office ✉ Via Alamanni 39, Firenze ☎ 055 210804

Venice

Available direct from venues or from ticket booths:
Vela ✉ Piazzale Roma, Venezia ☎ 041 2424
www.hellovenezia.it

SPORTS AND ACTIVITIES

Italy's best-loved spectator sport is football (soccer), passionately followed by millions of fans. Hot on its heels is basketball, introduced after World War II and now hugely popular, with the national team ranked among the best in the world. Baseball and American football have also crept in from across the Atlantic, while the Italian passion for bicycling is totally homegrown. A bit of exercise is often just the antidote to sightseeing or lazy days on the beach, and you'll find sports facilities all over Italy. During the long, hot summers, swimming and watersports are popular, and there are plenty of pools and beaches. Classy resort hotels have pools and tennis courts, and some will fix you up with a round of golf. Many *agriturismo* enterprises organize activities such as horseback riding, mountain bicycling and walking—all great ways to explore the countryside.

ATHLETICS

International athletics meetings are held in both Rome and Milan.

BASKETBALL

Find more information on Italy's seven major basketball leagues at www.basketball.it.

BICYCLING

Bicycling is a way of life in Italy, and a hugely popular spectator sport. You can easily rent a bicycle to get around cities or venture out of town onto marked bicycle routes—tourist offices provide maps of the trails. Join the locals and rent a bicycle to get around the prosperous towns of Italy's flatlands. There are excellent bicycle routes throughout the Po Valley, with well-thought-out itineraries and general information provided by local tourist boards. If you're in hilly country, think twice before embarking on what could be a tough day in high temperatures. Renting a bicycle is straightforward; ask at local tourist offices for further information, or consider an organized cycling trip.

Hundreds of local clubs take to the roads each weekend, so large groups of cyclists with spectators lining the streets are a common sight all over the country. The main event is the *Giro d'Italia,* an annual around-Italy race, which takes place in the second half of May, attracting competitors from all over the world.

FOOTBALL (SOCCER)

» The season runs from the end of August until late June, with a two-week break from the end of December into January.

» The Italian League is divided into four main divisions: Serie A, Serie B, Serie C1 and C2. There are 18 teams in Serie A.

» Matches take place on Sunday afternoons. Home games are played virtually every Sunday from September to late June in cities with two major teams, such as Milan and Rome.

» Ticket prices range from €15 to €85. The cheapest seats are in the *curva* at each end of the pitch and the most expensive are along the side of the pitch, in the *tribuna.*

» Tickets can be purchased online, from venues, merchandise outlets or agencies.

» General information: www.lega-calcio.it

» Team websites:
www.acfiorentina.it
www.acmilan.it
www.asromacalcio.it
www.inter.it
www.juventus.it
www.sslazio.it
www.veneziacalcio.it

GOLF

Golf is still a prestigious game in Italy and fairly exclusive. The main Italian cities all have upscale clubs on their outskirts and you'll find courses attached to some resort hotels in the northern regions.

Most clubs will want to see proof of membership of your home club and may also ask for handicap details before allowing you to play. Green fees normally cover the whole day, so there's always the chance to squeeze in a couple of rounds to get your money's worth. Expect to pay upwards of €75 and extra for club, trolley and electric cart rental. If you want to play a lot of golf while you are in the country you can opt for an all-inclusive golf package such as those organized by The Holiday Group (www.golfingtrips.co.uk) in Britain, or USA Golf Holidays (www.usagolfholidays.com) or Jerry Quinlan's Celtic Golf (www.celticgolf.com) in the US.

GRAND PRIX

Italy hosts two Formula 1 Grand Prix motor races annually: the San Marino Grand Prix at Imola in April (www.formula1.sm) and the Italian Grand Prix at Monza near Milan in September (www.monzanet.it).

GYMS

Italian gyms are mainly private, so you'll need to take out a temporary membership. Larger city gyms charge a daily rate ranging from €10 to €25.

Expect to find weights and machine rooms and a good choice of classes; the entrance fee sometimes includes a class—Tai chi, yoga or Pilates. Bigger gyms may have a sauna, Turkish bath and solarium, and you can reserve a massage or some hydrotherapy; big city gyms may have squash or tennis courts.

HORSEBACK RIDING

This is becoming an increasingly popular holiday activity in Italy, and you'll find horseback riding establishments all over the country, with specialized tour operators offering guided riding trips through some of the most beautiful areas. Trips are better organized in central and northern Italy and information is available at APT offices. Many *agriturismo* enterprises offer riding as an activity.

If you intend to ride on holiday, bring your own riding hat and any safety equipment with you, as it may be of a low standard or not provided.

JOGGING

Italians are gradually coming around to the idea of running, though it's still largely a middle-class occupation and only popular in the more prosperous parts of the country. Rome, Milan, Florence and Venice all organize annual marathons, and running clubs are beginning to make their mark. If you just want to get out early and jog, avoiding ankle-twisting cobbled streets, try the suggestions below.

ROME

Villa Borghese: Rome's most prestigious park is home to the Galleria Borghese and is only a few minutes from the Spanish Steps. It has wide paths lined with cool pines, but it can be crowded on weekends.
Villa Pamphilj: A lovely park on the slopes of the Gianicolo behind Trastevere, it serves one of Rome's wealthier suburbs and has good paths and some workout stations.
Circo Massimo: Run around the pine-fringed expanse of the city's biggest chariot-racing venue near the Forum and Colosseum for a workout and a taste of ancient Rome.
Villa Ada: Out in the suburbs, this leafy park is near the Catacombe di Priscilla. Its lakes are lined with running paths, a green retreat at the heart of the modern Salaria residential area.

FLORENCE

Giardino dei Semplici: Once a Medici physic garden, this oasis of greenery near the church of San Lorenzo has some good shady paths.
Giardino di Boboli: On a hill across the Arno, central Florence's only park has some testing wide paths.
Forte Belvedere: This area at the top of the Boboli Gardens is a great place to get away from the busy, crowded streets and run while enjoying the superb views over the city.

VENICE

Zattere: Head for this wide waterfront area in Dorsoduro with views across Giudecca.
Giardini: Head east along the Fondamenta to Venice's public gardens, with great views over the lagoon, towards the residential area of Sant'Elena.

NATIONAL PARKS

Abruzzo, Lazio e Molise

www.parks.it
This is Italy's third-largest national park. The wild Apennine country is ideal for brown bears, wolves and chamois. There are information offices in Pescasseroli (tel 0863 910097), Opi (tel 0863 910622) and Villetta Barrea (tel 0864 89333).

Cinque Terre

www.parks.it/parco.nazionale.cinque.terre
A coastal park in Liguria that preserves agricultural and natural landscapes (tel 0187 920633).

Gargano Peninsula

www.parcogargano.it
An extensive limestone promontory—the spur of the boot of Italy (tel 0884 586972).

Gran Paradiso

www.parks.it
Italy's oldest national park covers three valleys, Cogne, Valsavarenche and Val de Rhêmes, in Val d'Aosta around the Gran Paradiso mountain range. Noted for chamois, ibex and mountain flora. Information offices at Noasca (tel 0124 901070) and Ceresole Reale (tel 0124 953186).

Gran Sasso e Monti Della Laga
www.parks.it
www.gransassolagapark.it
In the Abruzzo this park has the highest Apennine peaks flanking the Campo Imperatore. Information office at Amatrice (tel 0746 826344/9336609).

Monti Sibillini
www.parks.it
www.sibillini.net
Spread over eastern Umbria and the Marche, this park is famous for its wolves, excellent birdwatching and superb alpine flora. Information office at Norcia (tel 0743 817090).

Stelvio
www.parks.it
www.stelviopark.it
A spectacular Dolomite park stretching from Lombardy to Trentino-Alto Adige. Superb summer high-level walking, flora and fauna. Information offices at Bormio (tel 0342 910100), Fraches (tel 0473 830510), Cogolo di Peio (tel 0463 754186) and Rabbi Fonti (tel 0463 985190).

RUGBY

Rugby is beginning to make its mark, and interest has grown since Italy's inclusion in the Six Nations Championship in 2000. Home games are played at the Flaminio Stadium in Rome (www.web.tiscali.it/rugbytoitaly).

SHOW JUMPING

The Concorso Ippico Internazionale di Piazza di Siena, a prestigious show-jumping event, takes place in Rome from the end of April to the first week in May (www.fise.it).

SWIMMING

During the searing heat of summer it's a relief to take to the water. In the main cities, where swimming pools, like gyms, are usually privately run, you may need to take out temporary membership to enjoy the facilities. Some pools offer day-tickets as well as weekly and monthly subscriptions.

Above *On Monte Baldo, above Lake Garda*

Italian resort beaches are divided into sections, each run as a *stabilimento balnearo* (bathing establishment). These are private, and you'll have to pay a fee to cover the use of a changing cabin, sun lounger and umbrella. Each *stabilimento* normally has eating and drinking facilities, which can be quite grand.

Beach standards are high, with sand cleaned and raked overnight, but water cleanliness can vary. The Blue Flag award is given to beaches that offer cleanliness and safe bathing areas (www.blueflag.org). In 2010 225 beaches and 60 marinas were awarded Blue Flag status in Italy. Overall, Sardinia has the highest number of Blue Flag beaches, while on the mainland the winner is Puglia. Avoid swimming near major cities, ports or industrial coastal areas.

All Italian resorts have a legal obligation to allow free access to a section of the beach, so it is possible to avoid payment if you want a quick dip.

Lakes and rivers, particularly in mountain regions, are cool and refreshing choices for a swim on a hot day. Alternatively, splurge on a visit to the mineral-rich waters of one of Italy's many natural hot springs (▷ 447).

TENNIS

Most towns and cities have clubs where you can rent a court throughout the day, and some hotels have their own facilities—reserve in advance during the summer.

The Italian Open tournament takes place in May in Rome (www.tennistours.com).

WALKING AND HIKING

Italy's mountainous north is the obvious place to go if you're looking for the best hiking and walking. From Val d'Aosta in the west across to Trentino-Alto Adige in the eastern Dolomites, there's superb walking to cater for all abilities.

Serious hikers and climbers can make for the hills and enjoy long-distance, high-altitude routes, sleeping at refuges and not seeing a valley floor for days on end. If you fancy something gentler, gondola cable cars provide easy access to well-marked paths and trails, or you could simply stroll through the quiet lanes that link the villages. The mountain regions are all keen to promote their walking opportunities, and tourist offices provide a variety of brochures and itineraries.

HIKING TIPS

» You'll find detailed maps of the more popular areas in bookshops and tourist shops; Kompass is a good series.

» If you are planning to go into the mountains or off the beaten track, take a map with a scale of no less than 1:50,000.

» Always wear suitable clothes and footwear, take plenty of water, something to eat, and leave word of where you're going and what time you expect to be back.

WATERSPORTS

With their country's long Mediterranean coastline, it's hardly surprising that Italians have embraced watersports. There's the choice of lake or sea if you're planning on joining in.

You can sail and windsurf on the northern lakes and all around the coastline, while river canoeing and kayaking are extremely popular, particularly in Val d'Aosta, Piedmont, Lombardy and Trentino-AltoAdige. Waterskiing is banned on many northern lakes, especially the northern reaches of Lake Garda. Increasingly, jetskiing is also becoming more restricted; in 2010 Ischia announced it was banning jetskiing in its waters all summer.

Italians are keen scuba-divers and Campania, Calabria and Sicily have the best underwater gardens to explore, but the less experienced can enjoy snorkelling along the rocky parts of the west coast. At many resorts you can sign up for a day's introductory course, or rent equipment if you're already experienced. Unfortunately few instructors for beginners speak fluent English. Local tourist offices have details of schools and there are plenty of advertisements around in seaside resorts.

WINTER SPORTS

The Italian Alps are a major European skiing destination, with many specialized tour operators offering all-in skiing packages to the main resorts. The Alps are accessible from Milan, Turin, Bologna and Venice (for the Dolomites), while the Abruzzi Mountains are easily reached from Rome and Naples.

There are weekend, low-key resorts with a handful of lifts and a few runs virtually all over the country. Good options for a couple of days on the slopes include the Tuscan and Umbrian Apennines, the Abruzzo, the Sila in Calabria and inland Sicily.

If you want to arrange your own ski package, *Settimane Bianche* (White Weeks) are excellent value. They offer an all-inclusive accommodation package and hefty reductions on ski rental and lift passes—all you have to arrange is your transport to the resort. The regional tourist boards in Val d'Aosta and Trentino-Alto Adige have brochures, which give details of participating hotels, prices and contact details.

A.I.A.T AOSTA

www.regione.vda.it/turismo
✉ Piazza Chanoux 42, 11100 Aosta
☎ 0165 236627; fax 0165 40532

APT ALTO ADIGE

www.bolzano-bozen.it
✉ Piazza Walther (Waltherplatz) 8, 39100 Bolzano ☎ 0471 307000; fax 0471 980128

LISTINGS

Events are advertised in listings magazines, Italy's two daily sports newspapers, *La Gazzetta dello Sport* (the pink paper) and the *Corriere dello Sport*, and in Friday newspapers. Local tourist offices may be able to help you find out where you can buy tickets.

HEALTH AND BEAUTY

Italy is blessed with mineral-rich, naturally heated springs, and there are *terme* (spas) all over the country. There is a long, well-established tradition of using mineral waters to encourage better health, and to treat everything from allergies and skin problems to liver complaints, arthritis and rheumatism. Many spas still function purely as therapeutic clinics, where doctors will work out a regime for different medical conditions, but an increasing number of *centri benessere* (wellness centres) are catering for those who want to be pampered in style. Spa hotels now provide much more than the odd massage or dip in a pool, and you can check in for a few days of total relaxation and indulgence in a resort hotel. To find out more visit www.hotelbenessere.it, with links to spas all over Italy.

ABANO TERME AND MONTEGROTTO TERME, VENETO

www.abanoterme.net
www.abanomontegrotto.it
Two spas in the Euganean hills of the Veneto. Both specialize in water and mud treatments, considered beneficial in the treatment of rheumatic and arthritic conditions and skin disorders.

Consorzio Terme Euganee Abano–Montegrotto
✉ Largo Marconi 8, Abano Terme, 35031 Padova ☎ 049 866 6609; fax 049 866 6613

MERANO, TRENTINO-ALTO-ADIGE

www.emmeti.it/Salute/TAA/Merano
A large spa resort in the eastern Dolomites, surrounded by mountains. The radioactive waters are used to treat a range of medical disorders.

Terme di Merano
✉ Piazza Terme, Merano, 39012 Bolzano
☎ 0473 252000; fax 0473 252022

MONSUMMANO TERME, TUSCANY

Historic thermal resort with restorative canyons deep underground where you descend through three areas named Paradiso, Purgatorio and Inferno—each getting progressively hotter.

Grotta Giusti Spa Resort
✉ Via Grottagiusti 1411, 51015 Monsummano Terme ☎ 0572 90771

CHIANCIANO TERME, TUSCANY

www.chiancianoterme.com
www.termechianciano.it
This southern Tuscan spa specializes in treating liver and bladder complaints.

Terme di Chianciano Spa
✉ Via delle Rose 12, Chianciano Terme, 53042 Siena ☎ 0578 68292/3 or 848 800243 (freephone in Italy); fax 0578 60622

MONTECATINI TERME, TUSCANY

www.montecatini-terme.com
www.termemontecatiniweb.it
A huge spa, with nine springs and beautiful *fin-de-siècle* buildings. The emphasis is on health and rehabilitation rather than pampering. They focus on the treatment of gastric disorders, heart conditions and circulatory and respiratory problems.

Montecatini Terme
✉ Viale Verdi 41, Montecatini Terme, 51506 Pistoia ☎ 0572 7781/0572 778487; fax 0572 778444

SATURNIA, TUSCANY

www.termedisaturnia.com
Saturnia is popular with those seeking rest and relaxation. This long-established luxury spa resort hotel is more dedicated to pampering and beauty than to medical treatments, though the highly sulphurous waters have many beneficial qualities.

Hotel Terme di Saturnia
✉ Saturnia, 5805 Grosseto ☎ 0564 600111; fax 0564 600863

LUIGIANE, COSENZA, CALABRIA

www.termeluigiane.it
The Luigiane thermal baths, in Cosenza province, Calabria, have a long history—the health benefits of their sulphur-rich waters were known to the Romans 2,000 years ago. The water gushes from a spring at a pleasant 37°C (99°F), and the baths offer a wide range of therapies.

Terme Luigiane
✉ Uffici Terme Luigiane, Località Terme Luigiane, 87020 Acquappesa
☎ 0982 94052

FOR CHILDREN

Children are considered part of mainstream society in Italy, so you'll find few child-specific facilities and amusements. There is still plenty for children to do, though, with the bonus that they are respected and integrated into whatever's going on.

BEACHES

The seaside holiday is a major part of Italian family life. Resorts all over the country are busy during the holiday period from July to late August. Small children will be happier at resorts along the Adriatic coast and in the flatter areas of the west coast (Tuscany, Lazio and Calabria), where there are plenty of sandy beaches with shallow bathing, beach games and playgrounds. Older children will probably prefer the more scenic areas such as the Cinque Terre or the Amalfi Coast—underwater gardens that are great for snorkelling and spotting fish. Bear in mind that few *stabilimenti balneari* (▷ 445) have lifeguards, so children should not be left unattended.

CITIES

Tourist information offices will be able to recommend attractions that are likely to appeal to children. In Rome, Florence and Venice you can buy guidebooks aimed at children. Cities that older children may enjoy include Rome (lots of ruins and bloodthirsty tales), Milan (some excellent child-oriented museums) and Florence (Museo dei Ragazzi di Firenze in the Palazzo Vecchio, Museo Stibbert and the Museo di Storia della Scienza).

DISCOUNTS

In Italy, charges for museums, galleries and other attractions are nearly always reduced for children and some are free.

FAMILY-FRIENDLY AREAS

The northern lakes are great for watersports and boat trips, as well as walking and horseback riding. Tuscany and Umbria have plenty to keep most outdoor families occupied, from exploring tiny towns to bicycling, hiking and horseback riding. The mountain regions of the Veneto, Lombardy and the Alto Adige have hotels specializing in family activities.

PARKS

Although all the major cities have parks, only the biggest have grassy areas large enough for children to play games and run around on. However, many have playgrounds, with a selection of swings, slides and roundabouts, and they are good places for a picnic. Ask at tourist offices if there is a travelling funfair coming to town; fairs tend to visit on or around the community's major feast day.

THEME PARKS

There are several theme parks in Italy, so you should be able to find some amusements near your base. Some are very large, with exciting rides and rollercoasters for all ages and new attractions added every year. Gardaland (▷ 143) is Italy's biggest theme park, a Disney-style complex with an Italian twist. The park's mascot is Prezzemolo (Parsley), a kindly green dinosaur. The park has everything from stomach-churning rollercoasters to scary space rides and water rapids. Italians flock to *The Flying Island,* an orbiting space station, and *The World of Barbie*, dedicated to Italy's most popular doll. Most parks are open all year and have long summer opening hours—many are open until midnight.

FESTIVALS AND EVENTS

There's no shortage of festivals in Italy celebrating religious holidays, the arts and gastronomic delights—a great excuse for a local community to party. Celebrations are organized by Italians for Italians, but they are open to anyone who's willing to participate in the right spirit. That spirit differs enormously according to each festival's focus, so be prepared for everything from intense religious feeling to exuberant high spirits. Major festivals, such as Venice's Carnevale and Siena's Palio, attract visitors from all over the world, so if you're planning on attending, reserve your accommodation well in advance. You'll find low-key local events everywhere during the summer. Keep an eye open for posters and ask at tourist offices for information.

ARTS FESTIVALS

Italy has a lively arts festival scene, most active during the summer, when amphitheatres, arenas, churches and piazzas are transformed into venues for many of the cultural events. These festivals cover everything from Greek theatre to opera, dance, rock and jazz, and many run for well over a month. Some, such as Spoleto's Festival dei Due Mondi, Venice's Biennale and the Verona Opera Festival, are world-class events, for which tickets need to be reserved well in advance.

Central Italy is particularly prolific, and if you're in Tuscany or Umbria during the summer an evening dose of culture is easy to find. The main ones to look out for are Florence's Maggio Musicale Fiorentino, Umbria's Sagra Musicale Umbra and Umbria Jazz, all ranking high on the international circuit. (See individual listings.)

FOOD FESTIVALS

For a true taste of Italy seek out the *sagre* (food festivals), where you can sample many local products. Everything from truffles to trout is celebrated, with stands and long tables laid out with the local fare and handicrafts in all their guises. These are truly small-town festivities, providing a unique insight into rural Italian life. The eating and drinking is often accompanied by brass bands and dancing, all rounded off with a noisy fireworks display.

RELIGIOUS FESTIVALS

These festivals are closely linked to the church calendar. Holy Week, Christmas, which is celebrated by elaborate *presepi* (cribs) set up in churches, Corpus Domini, commemorating the cult of the Blessed Sacrament, and the August Feast of the Assumption of the Virgin are celebrated across the country. The Day of the Dead (1 November) is when Italians return to their native towns and villages to tend their relatives' graves and reunite with the whole family.

At local levels, every town and village has its own patron saint, whose feast day is celebrated with processions and solemn church services, culminating in late-night partying. You'll find religious festivals everywhere, and the farther south you travel, the more fervent they become.

TRADITIONAL FESTIVALS

The Venetian festivals, celebrating the city's past grandeur, are superb, but for an adrenaline rush head for Siena and the passion and spectacle of the Palio, a hair-raising bareback horse race. Inhabitants of many small towns around the country celebrate their history by dressing up in traditional costumes and processing through the streets, drumming and waving flags.

FRESH REGIONAL PRODUCE

Italian cooking is straightforward, its quality dictated by the superlative standard of ingredients. Italian cooks are obsessed with freshness and food shopping is a daily social event in smaller places. This is beginning to change in cities though, as huge supermarkets start to take over. Outside the big cities, you're also unlikely to find restaurants serving anything other than local food, so don't expect to eat Venetian dishes in Tuscany, let alone exotic cuisine. If you're desperate for international cooking, head for Milan, Rome or Turin; cities this size are also the places to find regional restaurants offering food from all over Italy.

MEALS AND MEALTIMES

Many working Italians eat breakfast *(prima colazione)* in a bar—a *cappuccino*, strong coffee with plenty of hot milk, and a sweet pastry, a *brioche* or *cornetto*, a jam- or custard-filled croissant. Hotels catering to foreigners usually serve a buffet-style breakfast with fruit juice, cereal, cold meat and cheeses. If you are having breakfast in a bar, most open for business around 7–7.30; hotel breakfast normally starts at 8, or earlier in business hotels.

Lunch *(pranzo)* and dinner *(cena)* both follow the same pattern—though it's unlikely that you will want to tackle the full menu twice in one day. The first course is the *antipasto* (starter, but literally 'before the meal'), generally a selection of *crostini* (bread with a savoury topping), cold meats and salami, seafood or vegetable dishes. The next course, *il primo* (first course) is designed to fill you up and consists of pasta, soup or risotto. This is followed by the *secondo* (second course), a portion of a meat or a fish dish, served on its own—if you want vegetables *(contorni)* or a salad *(insalata)* order them separately. You finish with dessert *(dolci)* or cheese *(formaggio)*. The former is often a bowl of fruit, fruit salad *(macedonia)* or an ice cream *(gelato)*, though fancier places will have desserts such as *tiramisù, zuppa inglese* (trifle) or something rich made with ricotta cheese or chocolate. There's no pressure to wade through the whole menu, and it's quite acceptable to order a *primo* and salad, or an *antipasto* and *secondo*.

Italians drink mineral water *(acqua minerale)* with every meal, either sparkling *(frizzante* or *con gas)* or still *(senza gas)*, accompanied by a relatively modest amount of wine or a beer. Excessive drinking is frowned upon in Italy, where it is rare to see anyone inebriated in public. Bread is automatically included with every meal.

Restaurants normally open for lunch around 12.30 or 1 and stop serving at 3; they close for the afternoon and reopen for dinner around 7.30–8. All restaurants have one official closing day a week, usually indicated on the door or front window, but many places open daily during the summer.

Smoking is not allowed in restaurants and bars, except at tables in the open air such as on a terrace or in a garden.

WHERE TO EAT AND WHAT TO EXPECT

» ***Trattorie*** are usually family-run, serving home-style cooking *(casalinga)*. They are generally simpler than restaurants. Sometimes there is no written menu and the waiter will reel off the list of the day's specials. They are open during lunchtime and in the evening.

» ***Ristoranti*** are more up-market and are not always open for lunch. The food and surroundings are usually more sophisticated than those of a *trattoria*. Both *trattorie* and *ristoranti* add a cover charge *(coperto)*, which includes bread, and a service charge to the bill.

» ***Pizzerie*** specialize in pizzas, but often serve simple pasta dishes as well. Look out for the sign *forno al legno* (wood-fired pizza oven).

» ***Osterie*** can either be old-fashioned places specializing in home-cooked food or extremely smart, long-established restaurants.

PAYING THE BILL (IL CONTO)

Pay by requesting the bill *('il conto, per favore')*, and check to see whether service is included *('il servizio è incluso?')*. Scribbled bills on scraps of paper are illegal; if you don't get one, say that you need a receipt *('Ho bisogno di una ricevuta, per favore')*, which all restaurants, bars and shops are legally obliged to issue. Both they and you can be fined if you do not take this with you.

» Smaller establishments will normally expect to be paid in cash; you'll be able to use a credit card in more expensive establishments. If service isn't included, it's customary to leave a small tip—some loose change will do.

SNACKS AND ICE CREAM

» Bars serve hot and cold drinks, alcohol and snacks throughout the day. It's customary to eat or drink standing up; you will pay a surcharge if you sit down either inside or at a table outside. In busier city bars make your request and pay at the cash desk, then take the receipt *(scontrino)* and go to the bar where you will be served. Snacks include *panini* (filled rolls), *tramezzini* (sandwiches made on soft white bread), *mini-pizze*, toasted sandwiches *(toast)* and sometimes vol-au-vents. Smarter bars willl bring olives, crisps or nuts with your drink if you're sitting down. All bars have toilets *(bagni/gabinetti)*; you may have to ask for the key *(chiave)*.

» ***Alimentari*** (general grocers) sell breads and will often make you up a *pannino* (filled roll).

» **Pizza**, Italy's own contribution to fast food, is available all over the country and served by the slice from tiny *pizzerie* to take away–look for the sign *pizza al taglio*. There are also a few international chains.

» ***Tavole calde*** are stand-up snack bars that serve freshly prepared hot food; some have seating as well.

» ***Forni*** (bakers) sell *foccace*, flat oil and herb bread.

» ***Rosticcerie*** serve spit-roasted and ready-cooked food, particularly chicken, pasta and vegetable dishes to eat in or take away.

» ***Gelaterie*** sell a range of varieties of ice cream, served in a cone *(cono)* or a tub *(coppa)* of varying sizes. The best ice cream is homemade on the premises—*produzione propria*. Many bars sell commercial ice cream.

» **Fast food** Larger towns and cities have branches of McDonalds and Burger King.

» **International cuisine** is very limited in Italy. Chinese restaurants are becoming increasingly popular in medium- to large-size towns, but you'll have to go to places such as Rome or Milan if you want a wider choice.

WHAT TO DRINK

» **Coffee** *(caffè)* is served in bars and cafés. Choose from either a small black coffee *(caffè* or *espresso)*, a *cappuccino* (with frothy milk), *caffè latte* (very milky coffee), *caffè macchiato* (an espresso with a drop of milk) or a *caffè corretto* with a slug of spirits. If you want weaker coffee, ask for a *caffè lungo* or an *Americano*. Decaffeinated coffee goes by the generic name Hag.

» **Tea** *(tè)* is generally served black; ask for *latte freddo* (cold milk) if you want milk. In summer *tè freddo* (ice tea), with lemon or peach, is popular.

» **Hot chocolate** *(cioccalata calda)*, often served with whipped cream *(panna)*, is available during the winter months.

» **Beer** *(birra)* is widely available, either bottled or draught *(alla spina)*. Preferred Italian brands include Nastro Azzurro, Peroni and Moretti, and imported beers are also available.

» **Wine** is served in bars as well as in restaurants. Ask for white *(bianco)*, red *(rosso)* or the less common rosé *(rosato)*. House wine is either *vino de la casa* or *vino sfuso*, and can be very good. Bottled wines are locally produced, except in better restaurants; the best are DOCG wines *(Denominazione d'Origine Controllata e Garantita)*; the label guarantees its origin. Many producers are marketing some superb wines as *vino da tavola*, which are well worth sampling.

» **Spirits** are usually known by their generic names, and you will find all the usual ones on sale. Italians are also fond of *aperitivi* such as Martini, Campari, Cinzano and the artichoke-based Cynar, and firmly believe in settling the stomach after eating with a *digestivo*. Fiery *grappa* is the most common, but herb-based liqueurs *(amari)*, such as Averna and Montenegro, are drunk everywhere and there are dozens of local varieties—Amaretto, based on almonds, Strega, made from herbs and saffron, and limoncello, a lemon liqueur. Stock and Vecchia Romagna are Italy's preferred brandies.

» **Cocktails** are popular in Venice. Why not try a *bellini*, peach juice and sparkling wine, a *rossini*, strawberry juice and sparkling wine, or a *puccini*, mandarin juice and sparkling wine.

» **Soft drinks** such as cola and lemonade compete with native refreshments—*spremuta di arancia* (freshly pressed orange juice), *granita* (fruity crushed ice), *sugo di albicocca* (bottled apricot juice) and *frullata*, a type of milkshake.

To fully appreciate Italian cuisine you will need to venture away from the beaten track and the sanctuary of tourist resorts and sample the local dishes. If you don't speak Italian this can be a daunting prospect, but knowledge of a few key words will help you to work out what's on the menu and order what you want. Below is a menu reader, to help you translate common words and familiarize yourself with dishes and ingredients.

PIATTI—COURSES
antipasti .... starter
stuzzichini .... appetizers
primi piatti .... first courses
secondi piatti .... main courses
contorni .... vegetables/side dishes
dolci .... desserts
spuntini .... snacks

CARNE—MEAT
agnello .... lamb
cacciagione .... game
coniglio .... rabbit
fegato .... liver
maiale .... pork
manzo .... beef
pancetta .... bacon
pollame .... poultry
pollo .... chicken
prosciutto .... Parma ham
prosciutto cotto .... cooked ham
salsiccia .... sausage
tacchino .... turkey
vitello .... veal

PESCE—FISH
alici .... anchovy
baccalà .... dried salt cod
branzino .... sea bass
dorate .... bream
fritto misto .... mixed fried fish
merluzzo .... cod
pesce spada .... swordfish
sarde .... sardines
sogliola .... sole
tonno .... tuna
triglia .... mullet
trota .... trout

FRUTTI DI MARE—SEAFOOD
aragoste .... lobster
calamari .... squid
canestrelli .... scallops
cozze .... mussels
gamberetti .... prawns (shrimp)
granceola .... spiny spider crab
molluschi .... shellfish
ostriche .... oysters
seppia .... cuttlefish
vongole .... clams

VERDURE—VEGETABLES
asparagi .... asparagus
broccolo .... broccoli
carciofo .... artichoke
carote .... carrots
cavolfiore .... cauliflower
cavolo .... cabbage
cetriolino .... gherkin
cetriolo .... cucumber
cicoria .... chicory
cipolla .... onion
fagioli .... beans
fagiolini .... green beans
finocchio .... fennel
latuga .... lettuce
melanzane .... aubergines (eggplant)
patate .... potatoes
peperone .... red/green pepper (capiscum)
piselli .... peas
pomodori .... tomatoes
spinaci .... spinach
verdure cotte .... cooked greens
zucchini .... courgettes (zucchini)

METODI DI CUCINA—COOKING METHODS
affumicato .... smoked
al forno .... baked
alla griglia .... grilled
arrosto .... roast
bollito .... boiled
casalinga .... homemade
crudo .... raw
fritto .... fried
frulatto .... whisked
ripieno .... stuffed
stufato .... stewed

LA PASTA—PASTA
cannelloni .... meat- or cheese-filled tubes
conchiglie .... shell shapes
farfalle .... butterfly shapes
fettucine .... wide strips

fusilli .... spiral shapes
lasagne .... layers of pasta, meat sauce and béchamel
linguine .... very thin strips
pappardelle .... rippled strips
penne .... quill shapes
ravioli .... pasta cushions filled with meat, cheese or spinach
tagliatelle .... thin ribbons or strips
tortellini .... little 'hats' with meat or cheese filling
trenette .... long narrow strips

SALSI/SUGI–SAUCES

amatriciana .... bacon, tomato and onion
arrabbiata .... tomato and hot chilli
brodo .... broth
cacciatore .... sauce for meat: tomato, onion, garlic, wine
carbonara .... smoked bacon, egg, cream and black pepper
passata .... sieved tomatoes
pesto .... basil, garlic, pine nuts, olive oil and pecorino cheese
puttanesca .... tomato, garlic, hot chilli, anchovies, capers
ragù .... minced meat, tomato and garlic
salsa di pomodoro .... tomato sauce
salsa verde .... piquant/vinaigrette
sugo di carne .... gravy

SPECIALITÀ–SPECIAL DISHES

carpaccio .... thinly sliced raw beef served with a cold vinaigrette. (Invented in 1961 at Harry's Bar in Venice and named after the painter Vittore Carpaccio)
pastiera .... Neapolitan Easter grain pie, filled with ricotta and seasoned with orange
peperonata .... sweet pepper and tomato stew
polpetti .... meatballs
saltimbocca .... veal escalopes with ham and sage cooked in white wine
scaloppini .... thinly sliced veal cooked in white wine
stracotto .... beef stew
timballo .... meat and vegetable pie

CONTORNI–SIDE DISHES

insalata mista .... mixed salad
insalata tricolore mozzarella, tomato and fresh basil
insalata verde .... green salad
pane .... bread
patate fritte .... chips (french fries)
polenta .... maize meal dish

ALTRI PIATTI–OTHER DISHES

antipasto misto .... mixed cold meats: salami, ham, etc.
frittata .... omelette
gnocchi .... small dumplings made from potato and flour or semolina
minestra .... soup
minestrone .... thick vegetable soup with pasta
risotto .... rice cooked in stock with meat, seafood or vegetables
risotto alla Milanese ...... risotto with saffron
zuppa .... soup

DOLCI–DESSERTS

cassata .... Sicilian fruit ice cream
cioccolata .... chocolate
crema .... custard
gelato .... ice cream
macedonia .... fruit salad
panettone.. Milanese Christmas cake with candied peel and sultanas
panna .... cream
panna cotta ...set dessert made with cream and sugar
una pasta .... a cake/pastry
semifreddo .... chilled dessert made with ice cream
tiramisù .... chocolate/coffee sponge dessert
torta .... tart
zabaglione .... egg, sugar and Marsala dessert
zabaione di Verduzzo .... custard pudding with Friuli wine
zuccotto .... ice-cream sponge
zuppa inglese .... trifle

FRUTTI–FRUIT

ananas .... pineapple
arancia .... orange
fragola .... strawberry
lampone .... raspberry
limone .... lemon
mela .... apple
melone .... melon
mirtillo .... blueberry
pere .... pear
pesca .... peach
pesca noci .... nectarine
uve .... grapes

FORMAGGI–CHEESES

fontina .... smooth, rich cheese
formaggio di capra ... goat's cheese
formaggio nostrano.... local cheese
parmigiano .... parmesan
pecorino .... sheep's cheese

BEVANDE–DRINKS

acqua minerale .... mineral water
birra .... beer
caffè corretto .... coffee with liqueur/spirit
caffè freddo .... iced coffee
caffelatte .... milky coffee
caffè lungo .... weak coffee
caffè macchiato .... coffee with a drop of milk
caffè ristretto .... strong coffee
digestivo .... after-dinner liqueur
dolce .... sweet
frizzante .... fizzy
ghiaccio .... ice
liquore .... liqueur
rinfreschi .... refreshments
secco .... dry
spumante .... sparkling wine
succo di arancia .... orange juice
tè .... tea
tè al latte .... tea with milk
tè freddo .... ice tea
vini da tavola .... table wines
vini pregiati .... quality wines
vino bianco .... white wine
vino rosato .... rosé wine
vino rosso .... red wine

CONDIMENTI–SEASONINGS

aglio .... garlic
aromatiche .... herbs
basilico .... basil
capperi .... capers
pepe .... pepper
peperoncino .... chilli
prezzemolo .... parsley
sale .... salt
salvia .... sage
senape .... mustard
zucchero .... sugar

IL CONTO–THE BILL

IVA .... VAT (sales tax)
paghi alla cassa .... pay at the till
servizio compreso..... service charge included
servizio non compreso .... service charge not included
coperto .... cover charge

HOTELS

Italian hotels *(alberghi)* are graded by regional authorities on a star rating of 1 to 5. These refer to the facilities provided—air-conditioning, telephone and television, lift (elevator), swimming pool—rather than character or comfort. You can expect 5-star hotels to be grand, with superb facilities and a high level of service; they will sometimes be in converted historic buildings, combining antique furnishings with 21st-century luxury. Four-star establishments will be almost as good and the accommodation usually first class. Three-star hotels are more idiosyncratic. Prices can vary enormously between them, as can the public areas, and staffing levels will be considerably lower. All 3-star rooms will have television, telephone, and sometimes air-conditioning.

One- and 2-star hotels are relatively inexpensive, but are clean and comfortable, and rooms in 2-star places almost always have private bathrooms. Breakfast is usually included. During high season at seaside resorts half- or full-board is often compulsory, and single people may have to pay full price for a double if all singles are taken.

Smoking is not allowed in Italian hotels, except in the open air such as on a terrace or in a garden.

PRICING

» Italian hotels are legally required to post rates for high and low season on the back of every bedroom door. Note that some hotels have only one price all year.

» Rates vary according to the season, sometimes by as much as 25 per cent. Some hotels have high season *(alta stagione)* and low season *(bassa stagione)* rates; others charge the same rate year round *(tutto l'anno)*.

» During high season, hotels in seaside resorts may insist visitors eat their meals at the hotel.

» Hotels often quote their most expensive rates; ask if they have cheaper rooms.

» City-centre hotels sometimes have reduced weekend rates.

» Smaller hotels can be open to gentle bargaining, particularly during quieter times.

» Hotels are often willing to put another bed in a room for an extra 35 per cent, ideal for families with young children.

AGRITURISMI

The *agriturismo* scheme encourages farmers and landowners to convert redundant farm buildings into holiday accommodation. This can take the form of a small and luxurious hotel, a self-catering apartment, or a handful of rooms in a converted barn. Accommodation can be on a weekly basis, but many owners have rooms to rent by the night, and meals are often provided. *Agriturismi* are often in beautiful surroundings and frequently provide activities such as riding, escorted walking and mountain bicycling. Many have swimming pools and serve home-grown produce at meal times. The movement is particularly strong in Tuscany and Umbria. You'll need a car as *agriturismi* can be well off the beaten track. Most require advance reservations, but a couple of days ahead will often be fine.

CAMPSITES

There are plenty of campsites, especially along the Adriatic coast, which are normally open between April and September. The better sites will have swimming pools, bars, children's play areas, restaurants and shops; these look more favourably on caravans (trailer houses) and camper vans (RVs), so if you're in a tent, stick to the smaller sites.

SELF-CATERING

There are many old farmhouses and villas to choose from, particularly in the affluent north and in Tuscany and Umbria. You can also rent apartments or houses in many of the coastal resorts, but Italian families tend to snap these up for the whole summer season. Tour operators sell villa packages, which include flights and car rental, but if you want to be independent, contact the local visitor offices well in advance. There are also websites devoted to private house rentals: check out www.holidayrentals.com.

RIFUGI

If you're hiking or climbing in the mountains, you can stay in a network of *rifugi alpini*, mountain huts, owned by the Club Alpino Italiano. Most are fairly basic, and you'll probably find yourself in a dormitory bunk bed and washing in cold water. However, they are all very reasonably priced and surrounded by wonderful countryside with spectacular views. For more information contact Club Alpino Italiano (www.cai.it).

ROOMS TO RENT

In popular areas you may see signs saying 'rooms', *'camere'* or *'zimmer'*. These are rooms to rent in private houses and are a good option if money is tight or you can't find a hotel. Local visitor offices keep a list of what's available.

RESERVATIONS

Reserve in advance in the main cities and popular resorts during the high season. In Rome, Florence and Venice you will need to reserve in advance all year round. Italians are on holiday during August, when you'll be competing with them for beds. If you're reserving in advance from home, make certain you get written confirmation by fax or email and take it with you. Without this, you may turn up and find all knowledge of your reservation denied.

FINDING A ROOM

» If you haven't reserved in advance, start looking around the main piazza or in the *centro storico*. In hilltop villages and towns it is also worth looking outside the *centro storico* or town walls. The tourist information office will have lists of accommodation and may be willing to make a reservation for you.
» Yellow signs direct you to hotels on the outskirts of towns and villages.
» In big cities, there is often a cluster of hotels near the railway station. Check them before you reserve as some are more respectable than others.
» It's perfectly acceptable to ask to see the room before you decide to stay there.
» You will be asked to leave your passport at reception. Don't forget to ask for it back when you leave.
» Check-out time is normally noon, but hotels will usually store your luggage till the end of the day.

FURTHER SOURCES OF INFORMATION

Hotels

» *Perfect Places to Stay in Italy*, published by the AA in conjunction with Touring Club Italiano, lists 500 recommended bed and breakfasts, farmhouses and town houses across Italy (£14.99, www.theaa.com).
» The Touring Club Italiano (TCI), the Italian equivalent of the AA in Britain or AAA in the US, publishes *Alberghi e Ristoranti d'Italia*, which lists hotels in all price ranges. It comes out in early spring every year and is €22 (www.touringclub.it).

Agriturismi

www.agriturist.com
Agriturist publishes *Vacanze in Fattoria*, a guide to farm holidays in English. The TCI publishes *Agriturismo e vacanze in campagna* annually at €43.
Agriturist ✉ Corso V Emanuele 101, 00168 Roma ☎ 06 852 1342

Camping

The TCI publishes an annual guide to campsites, *Campeggo e Villaggi Turistici* (€22).

Villas

CV Travel
www.cvtravel.net
Good villas, palazzi and farmhouses.
☎ 020 7591 2800

Guest in Italy
www.guestinitaly.com
Online rental agency.

Interhome
www.interhome.co.uk
Villa and apartment rentals by the week throughout Italy.

Magic of Italy
www.thomson.co.uk/villas
Villa rental packages.
☎ 0870 888 0228

Vacanze in Italia
www.britishtravel.com/vacanze.htm
Farmhouses, villas and apartments, mainly in Tuscany and Umbria and the Lakes.

Once you have mastered a few basic rules, Italian is an easy language to speak: it is phonetic and, unlike English, particular combinations of letters are always pronounced the same way. The stress is usually on the penultimate syllable, but if the word has an accent, this is where the stress falls.

Vowels are pronounced as follows:

a c**a**sa as in m**a**t short 'a'
e v**e**ro closed as in b**a**se
e s**e**tte open as in v**e**t short 'e'
i v**i**no as in m**ea**n
o d**o**ve closed as in b**ow**l
o **o**tto open as in n**o**t
u **u**va as in b**oo**k

Consonants as in English except:
c before **i** or **e** becomes **ch** as in **ch**urch
ch before **i** or **e** becomes **c** as in **c**at
g before **i** or **e** becomes **j** as in **J**ulia
gh before **i** or **e** becomes **g** as in **g**ood
gn as in o**ni**on
gli as in mi**lli**on
h is rare in Italian words, and is always silent
r is usually rolled
z is pronounced **tz** when it falls in the middle of a word

All Italian nouns are either masculine (usually ending in **o** when singular or **i** when plural) or feminine (usually ending in **a** when singular or **e** when plural). Some nouns, which may be masculine or feminine, end in **e** (which changes to **i** when plural). An adjective's ending changes to match the ending of the noun.

MONEY

Is there a bank/currency exchange office nearby?
C'è una banca/un ufficio di cambio qui vicino?

Can I cash this here?
Posso incassare questo?

I'd like to change sterling/dollars into euros
Vorrei cambiare sterline/dollari in euro

Can I use my credit card to withdraw cash?
Posso usare la mia carta di credito per prelevare contanti?

CONVERSATION

What is the time?
Che ore sono?

I don't speak Italian
Non parlo italiano

I only speak a little Italian
Parlo solo un poco italiano

Do you speak English?
Parla inglese?

I don't understand
Non capisco

Please repeat that
Può ripetere?

Please speak more slowly
Può parlare più lentamente?

Write that down for me, please
Lo scriva, per piacere

Please spell that
Come si scrive?

My name is
Mi chiamo

What's your name?
Come si chiama?

Hello, pleased to meet you
Piacere

This is my friend
Le presento il mio amico/la mia amica

This is my wife/husband
Le presento mia moglie/mio marito

This is my daughter/son
Le presento mia figlia/mio figlio

Where do you live?
Dove abiti?

I live in ...
Vivo in ...

I'm here on holiday/vacation
Sono qui in vacanza

Good morning
Buon giorno

Good afternoon/evening
Buona sera

Goodbye
Arrivederci

How are you?
Come sta?

Fine, thank you
Bene, grazie

I'm sorry
Mi dispiace

That's all right
Si figuri

USEFUL WORDS

yes .... sì
no .... no
please .... per favore
thank you .... grazie
you're welcome .... prego
excuse me! .... scusi!
what .... che
where .... dove
here .... qui
there .... la
when .... quando
now .... adesso
later .... più tardi
why .... perchè
who .... chi
may I/can I .... posso
open .... aperto
closed .... chiuso

SHOPPING

Could you help me, please?
Può aiutarmi, per favore?

How much is this?
Quanto costa questo?

I'm looking for ...
Cerco ...

Where can I buy ...?
Dove posso comprare ...?

How much is this/that?
Quanto costa questo/quello?

When does the shop open/close?
Quando apre/chiude il negozio?

I'm just looking, thank you
Sto solo dando un'occhiata, grazie

This isn't what I want
Non è quel che cerco

I'll take this
Prendo questo

Do you have anything less expensive/smaller/larger?
Ha qualcosa di meno caro/più piccolo/più grande?

Are the instructions included?
Ci sono anche le istruzioni?

Do you have a bag for this?
Può darmi una busta?

I'm looking for a present
Cerco un regalo

Can you gift wrap this please?
Può farmi un pacco regalo?

Do you accept credit cards?
Accettate carte di credito?

I'd like a kilo of ...
Vorrei un chilo di ...

Do you have shoes to match this?
Ha delle scarpe che vadano con questo?

Can you measure me please?
Può prendermi la misura, per favore?

This is the right size
Questa è la taglia (misura—*for shoes*) giusta

This doesn't suit me
Questo non mi sta bene

Do you have this in ...?
Avete questo in ...?

Should this be dry cleaned?
Questo è da lavare a secco?

Is there a market?
C'è un mercato?

NUMBERS

0 .... zero
1 .... uno
2 .... due
3 .... tre
4 .... quattro
5 .... cinque
6 .... sei
7 .... sette
8 .... otto
9 .... nove
10 .... dieci
11 .... undici
12 .... dodici
13 .... tredici
14 .... quattordici
15 .... quindici
16 .... sedici
17 .... diciassette
18 .... diciotto
19 .... diciannove
20 .... venti
21 .... ventuno
22 .... ventidue
30 .... trenta
40 .... quaranta
50 .... cinquanta
60 .... sessanta
70 .... settanta
80 .... ottanta
90 .... novanta
100 .... cento
1,000 .... mille
million .... milione
quarter .... quarto
half .... mezza
three quarters .... tre quarti
first .... primo/prima
second .... secondo/seconda
third .... terzo/terza

IN TROUBLE

Help!
Aiuto!

Stop, thief!
Al ladro!

Can you help me, please?
Può aiutarmi, per favore?

Call the fire brigade/police/an ambulance
Chiami i pompieri/la polizia/un'ambulanza

I have lost my passport/wallet/purse/handbag
Ho perso il passaporto/il portafogllio/il borsellino/la borsa

Where is the police station?
Dov'è il commissariato?

I have been robbed
Sono stato/a derubato/a

I have had an accident
Ho avuto un incidente

Did you see the accident?
Ha vista l'incidente?

I need information for my indurance company
Ho bisogno d'informazioni per la mia compagnia d'assicurazione

I need to see a doctor/dentist
Ho bisogno di un medico/dentista

When is the doctor's open?
Quando apre l'ambulatorio?

Do I need an appointment?
Ho bisogno di un appuntamento?

Where is the hospital?
Dov'è l'ospedale?

I feel sick (nauseous)
Mi sento male

I am allergic to ...
Sono allergico/a a...

I have a heart condition
Ho disturbi cardiaci

GETTING AROUND

Where is the train/bus station?
Dov'è la stazione ferroviaria/degli autobus (dei pullman–*long distance*)?

Does this train/bus go to ...?
È questo il treno/l'autobus (il pullman—*long distance*) per ...?

Where are we?
Dove siamo?

Do I have to get off here?
Devo scendere qui?

When is the first/last bus to ...?
Quando c'è il primo/l'ultimo autobus per ...?

Can I have a single/return ticket to ... please?
Un biglietto di andata/andata e ritorno per ... per favore

I would like a standard/first-class ticket to ...
Un biglietto di seconda/prima classe per ...

Where is the timetable?
Dov'è l'orario?

Do you have a subway/bus map?
Ha una piantina della metropolitana/degli autobus?

Where can I find a taxi?
Dove posso trovare un tassì?

Please take me to ...
Per favore, mi porti a ...

How much is the journey?
Quanto costerà il viaggio?

Please turn on the meter
Accenda il tassametro, per favore

I'd like to get out here, please
Vorrei scendere qui, per favore

Is this the way to ...?
È questa la strada per ...?

Excuse me, I think I am lost
Mi scusi, penso di essermi perduto/perduta

COLOURS

black .... nero
brown .... marrone
pink .... rosa
red .... rosso
orange .... arancia
yellow .... giallo
green .... verde
light blue .... celeste
sky blue .... azzuro
purple .... viola
white .... bianco
grey .... grigio

AROUND THE TOWN

on/to the right .... a destra
on/to the left .... a sinistra
around the corner .... all'angolo
opposite ... . di fronte a ...
at the bottom (of) .... in fondo (a)
straight on .... sempre dritto
near .... vicino a
cross over .... attraversi
in front of .... davanti
behind .... dietro
north .... nord
south .... sud
east .... est
west .... ovest
free .... gratis
donation .... donazione
open .... aperto
closed .... chiuso
cathedral .... cattedrale/duomo
church .... chiesa
castle .... castello
museum .... museo
monument .... monumento
palace .... palazzo
gallery .... galleria
town .... città
old town .... centro storico
town hall .... municipio
boulevard .... corso
square .... piazza
street .... via
avenue .... viale
island .... isola
river .... fiume
lake .... lago
bridge .... ponte
no entry .... vietato l'accesso
push .... spingere
pull .... tirare
entrance .... ingresso
exit .... uscita

TOURIST INFORMATION

Where is the tourist information office/tourist information desk, please?
Dov'è l'ufficio turistico/il banco informazioni turistiche, per favore?

Do you have a city map?
Avete una cartina della città?

Can you give me some information about ...?
Puo darmi delle informazioni su ...?

What sights/hotels/restaurants can you recommend?
Quali monumenti/alberghi/ristoranti mi consiglia?

Can you point them out on the map?
Me li può indicare sulla cartina?

What is the admission price?
Quant'è il biglietto d'ingresso?

Is there a discount for senior citizens/students?
Ci sono riduzioni per anziani/studenti?

Is there an English-speaking guide?
C'è una guida di lingue inglese?

Are there organized excursions?
Ci sono escursioni organizzate?

Do you have a brochure in English?
Avete un opuscolo in inglese?

Could you reserve tickets for me?
Mi può prenotare dei biglietti?

Can we make reservations here?
Possiamo prenotare qui?

TIMES/DAYS/MONTHS

Monday .... lunedì
Tuesday .... martedì
Wednesday .... mercoledì
Thursday .... giovedì
Friday .... venerdì
Saturday .... sabato
Sunday .... domenica
day .... giorno

week .... settimana
month .... mese
year .... anno
today .... oggi
yesterday .... ieri
tomorrow .... domani
January .... gennaio
February .... febbraio
March .... marzo
April .... aprile
May .... maggio
June .... giugno
July .... luglio
August .... agosto
September .... settembre
October .... ottobre
November .... novembre
December .... dicembre
Easter .... Pasqua
Assumption .... Ferragosto
Christmas .... Natale
26 December .... Santo Stefano
New Year's Eve .... San Silvestro
New Year .... Capodanno
spring .... primavera
summer .... estate
autumn .... autunno
winter .... inverno

RESTAURANTS

Waiter/waitress
Cameriere/cameriera

I'd like to reserve a table for ... people at ...
Vorrei prenotare un tavolo per ... persone a ...

A table for ..., please
Una tavola per ..., per favore

Can we sit there?
Possiamo sederci qui?

Is this table taken?
Questa tavola è occupata?

Are there tables outside?
Ci sono tavole all'aperto?

We would like to wait for a table
Aspettiamo che si liberi una tavola

Could we see the menu/wine list?
Possiamo vedere il menù/la lista dei vini?

Do you have a menu/wine list in English?
Avete un menù/una lista dei vini in inglese?

Where are the toilets (bathrooms)
Dove sono i gabinetti?

What do you recommend?
Cosa consiglia?

What is the house special?
Qual è la specialità della casa?

I can't eat wheat/sugar/salt/ pork/ beef/dairy
Non posso mangiare grano/ zucchero/sale/maiale/manzo/latticini

I am a vegetarian
Sono vegetariano/a

I'd like ...
Vorrei ...

I ordered ...
Ho ordinato ...

Could we have the salt and pepper?
Può portare del sale e del pepe?

The food is cold
Il cibo è freddo

The meat is overcooked/ too rare
La carne è troppo cotta/non è abbastanza cotta

This is not what I ordered
Non ho ordinato questo

Can I have the bill, please?
Il conto, per favore?

Is service included?
Il servizio è compreso?

The bill is not right
Il conto è sbagliato

We didn't have this
Non abbiamo avuto questo

The food was excellent
Abbiamo mangiato benissimo

HOTELS

I have a reservation for ... nights
Ho prenotato per ... notti

Do you have a room?
Avete camere libere?

How much per night?
Quanto costa una notte?

Double/single room
Camera doppia/singola

Twin room
Camera a due letti

With bath/shower
Con bagno/doccia

May I see the room?
Posso vedere la camera?

I'll take this room
Prendo questa camera

Could I have another room?
Vorrei cambiare camera

Is there a lift in the hotel?
C'è un ascensore nell'albergo?

Is the room air-conditioned/ heated?
C'è aria condizionata/riscaldamento nella camera?

Is breakfast included in the price?
La colazione è compreso?

When is breakfast served?
A che ora è servita la colazione?

The room is too hot/too cold/dirty
La camera è troppo calda/troppo fredda/sporca

I am leaving this morning
Parto stamattina

I need an alarm call at ...
Potete svegliarmi alle ...

Can I pay my bill?
Posso pagare il conto?

Please order a taxi for me
Mi chiama un tassi, per favore

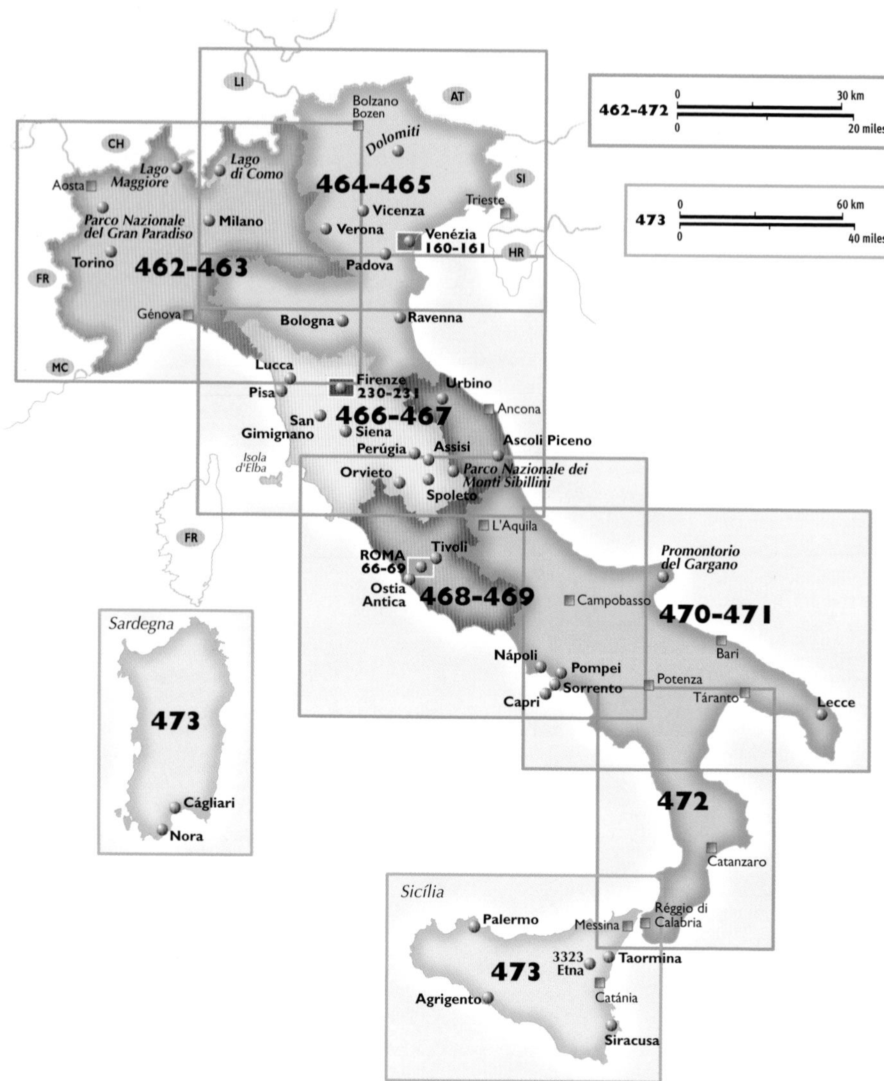

Toll motorway (Turnpike)

Motorway (Expressway)

Motorway junction with and without number

Motorway service area

National road

Regional road

Local road

Minor road

Featured place of interest

City / Town

National / Natural park

Railway

International boundary

Regional boundary

Airport

621 Height in metres

Port / Ferry route

MAPS

Map references for the sights refer to the atlas pages within this section or to the individual town plans within the regions. For example, Siena has the reference ✚ 466 F7, indicating the page on which the map is found (466) and the grid square in which Siena sits (F7).

CH
Rhône
Martigny
Domodóssola
Santa Maria
Maggiore
Monte Bianco
4810
Entrèves
Courmayeur
Morgex
La Thuile
Aosta
Breuil-
Cervinia
Valtournenche
Champoluc
Gressoney-
la-Trinité
Macugnaga
Cánnero Ri
Maggio
Baveno
Omegna
Stresa
Varallo
Lago d'Orta
Lesa
Arona
Scopello
Châtillon
VALLE
D'AOSTA
Cogne
Verrès
Borgosèsia
Borgomanero
Gattinara
Parco Nazionale del
Gran Paradiso
Ceresole Reale
Biella
Cossato
Olèggio
Cuorgnè
Castellamonte
Cavaglià
Ala di Stura
Balme
Rivarolo
Canavese
Santhià
Nova
Lanzo
Torinese
Caluso
Ciriè
Vercelli
Bardonècchia
Susa
Sacra di
San Michele
Caselle
Torinese
Crescentino
Trino
Chivasso
Mortara
Oulx
Sauze
d'Oulx
Fenestrelle
Rivoli
Orbassano
TORINO
Casale Monferrato
Cesana
Torinese
Sestriere
Chieri
PIEMONTE
Lomello
Pinerolo
Carignano
Poirino
Valenza
Torre
Pèllice
Carmagnola
Asti
Castelnu
Cavour
Alessándria
FR
Paesana
Racconigi
Nizza
Monferrato
Castellazzo
Bòrmida
Bra
Canelli
Saluzzo
Alba
Verzuolo
Savigliano
Novi
Ligure
Ácqui Terme
Busca
Fossano
Ovada
Gavi
Accèglio
Molare
Dronero
Dogliani
Cortemília
Cúneo
Piana Crixia
Borgo San
Dalmazzo
Mondovì
Ceva
Cáiro Montenotte
Pontedècimo
Vinàdio
LIGURIA
Voltri
Arenzano
Chiusa
di Pèsio
Frabosa
Soprana
Varazze
Celle Lìgure
GÉNOVA
Savona
Limone Piemonte
Vado Lìgure
Spotorno
Noli
Ormea
Garèssio
Finale Lìgure
Pietra Lìgure
Loano
Pieve di Teco
Albenga
Alàssio
Laiguèglia
Dolceacqua
Diano Marina
Imperia
Ventimiglia
Bordighera
San Remo
Ospedaletti
A40
E25
E9
A5
A43
A4/A5
A4
A26/A4
E64
A26
A32
E70
E612
A21
A26 E25
A26/A7
A6
E717
A10
E80
A8
E62
A
B
C
2
3
4
5
6

D
E
F
Madèsimo
St Moritz
Silandro
Parco Nazionale
dello Stelvio
Bòrmio
Santa Caterina
Valfurva
A2 E35
Chiavenna
Locarno
Bellinzona
Sondalo
Gròsio
Malé
Cles
Dimaro
Ponte di Legno
Pizzano
Tirano
Madonna
di Campiglio
Gravedona
Cólico
Sondrio
Morbegno
Aprica
Edolo
Mezzolombardo
Lago di
Lugano
Oria
Lugano
Menàggio
Bellano
Lago di Como
Varenna
Bellàgio
Argegno
Lago di
Lecco
Fòppolo
Capo di Ponte
Lavis
Vezzano
Tione
di Trento
Cernòbbio
Varese
Como
Erba
Lecco
Breno
San Pellegrino
Terme
Clusone
Darfo
Riva del
Garda
Arco
Cantù
LOMBARDIA
Selvino
Gandino
Lòvere
Pisogne
Bagolino
Storo
Còllio
Limone
sul Garda
Nago-
Tòrbole
Busto
Arsizio
Saronno
Seregno
Bérgamo
Lago d'Iseo
Lago d'Idro
Malcesine
Lemprato
Lago di Garda
Monza
E64
Sàrnico
Gardone Val
Trompia
Gargnano
Iseo
Ala
Rho
Gorgonzola
A4
Concésio
Toscolano-
Maderno
Torri del
Benaco
MILANO
Magenta
Treviglio
Caravàggio
Rovato
Chiari
Gavardo
Salò
Garda
Bosco
Chiesanuova
Valdagno
Antegnate
Torbole-
Casàglia
BRESCIA
Bardolino
Pandino
Sirmione
Lazise
Grezzana
Arzignano
Soncino
Orzinuovi
Lonato
del Garda
Peschiera
del Garda
VERONA
Melegnano
Crema
Bagnolo Mella
Ghedi
Soave
A7 E62
Manèrbio
Leno
Càstiglione
delle Stiviere
Carpenedolo
Castelleone
Pellegra
A1 E35
Villafranca
di Verona
San Bonifácio
Pavia
Casalpusterlengo
Asola
Gòito
Ìsola della
Scala
Po
Codogno
A21
E70
E45
Broni
Cremona
Mantova
Nogara
Cerea
Castèggio
Castel
San Giovanni
Voghera
Piacenza
Piadena
San Giovanni
in Croce
A22
Ostíglia
Carpaneto
Piacentino
Casalmaggiore
Sabbioneta
Suzzara
Varzi
Fiorenzuola
d'Arda
Viadana
Colorno
Luzzara
Pòggio Rusco
Sèrmide
Lugagnano
Val d'Arda
San Sebastiano
Curone
Fidenza
Guastalla
Mòglia
Bòbbio
Bèttola
Salsomaggiore
Terme
Noceto
Novellara
Mirándola
Pellegrino
Parmense
Parma
Finale Emília
Collecchio
Corréggio
Carpi
Ottone
Ferriere
Réggio
nell'Emília
Camposanto
Bardi
Fornovo di Taro
Cento
Torriglia
Langhirano
Crevalcore
E33
Módena
San Polo
d'Enza
Rubiera
San Giovanni
in Persiceto
Bedònia
Borgo Val
di Taro
A15
Berceto
Castelfranco
Emília
Sassuolo
Casina
Corniglio
Maranello
12 E80
Rapallo
Santa Margherita
Lìgure
Chiávari
Varese
Lìgure
EMÌLIA-ROMAGNA
Pontrémoli
Vignola
Bazzano
BOLOGNA
Lavagna
Sestri Levante
Montefiorino
Pavullo nel
Frignano
Sasso Marconi
Pianoro
Riviera di Levante
A12
E80
Monèglia
Bonassola
Aulla
Fivizzano
Vergato
Cinque Terre
Garfagnana
Pievepelago
Sèstola
Piazza
al Serchio
La Spézia
Lerici
Sarzana
Porretta
Terme
Castiglione
dei Pèpoli
Castel del Rio
Portovénere
Carrara
Castelnuovo
di Garfagnana
Marina di Carrara
Massa
Barga
San Marcello
Ponte della
Venturina
2
3
4
5
6
464
466

D
E
F
I
CH
A13
E25
Colle Isarco
Vipiteno
San Valentino alla Muta
Màlles Venosta
Tubre
Sluderno
Silandro
Naturno
Merano
Meran
Madèsimo
St Moritz
Parco Nazionale dello Stelvio
Bòrmio
Santa Caterina Valfurva
Bolzano
Bozen
2
Chiavenna
Fondo
Sondalo
Gròsio
Malé
Cles
Nova Levante
Bellinzona
Tirano
Ponte di Legno
Pizzano
Dimaro
Ora
Gravedona
Còlico
Sondrio
Madonna di Campiglio
Morbegno
Aprica
Edolo
Mezzolombardo
Lago di Lugano
Bellano
Menàggio
Lago di Como
Varenna
Bellàgio
San Michele all'Adige
Lavis
TRENTINO ALTO ADIGE
Argegno
Lago di Lecco
Fòppolo
Capo di Ponte
Vezzano
Trento
Pèrgine Valsugana
Cernóbbio
Como
Erba
Lecco
463
Breno
Tione di Trento
San Pellegrino Terme
Clusone
Lèvico Terme
Darfo
Riva del Garda
Arco
Cantù
Selvino
Gandino
Lòvere
Storo
Bagolino
3
LOMBARDIA
Pisogne
Cóllio
Limone sul Garda
Nago-Tòrbole
Rovereto
Folgaria
Seregno
Bérgamo
Lago d'Iseo
Lago d'Idro
Sàrnico
Lemprato
Malcesine
Arsiero
Monza
E64
Iseo
Gardone Val Trompia
Gargnano
Lago di Garda
Ala
Gorgonzola
Concésio
Toscolano-Maderno
Torri del Benaco
Recoaro Terme
Schio
Thiene
MILANO
Treviglio
Caravàggio
Rovato
Chiari
A4
Gavardo
Salò
Valdagno
Garda
A22
E45
Bosco Chiesanuova
A31
Antegnate
Torbole-Casàglia
BRESCIA
Bardolino
Pandino
Sirmione
Lazise
Vicenza
Grezzana
Arzignano
Melegnano
Crema
Soncino
Orzinuovi
Bagnolo Mella
Ghedi
Lonato del Garda
Peschiera del Garda
VERONA
Montécchio Maggiore
Manèrbio
Leno
Càstiglione delle Stiviere
Soave
Castelleone Pellegra
Carpenedolo
Grisignano di Zocco
A1
E35
Villafranca di Verona
San Bonifàcio
Lonigo
Casalpusterlengo
Gòito
Ìsola della Scala
Cologna Veneta
Noventa Vicentina
Po
4
Codogno
Asola
E70
Bovolone
Cremona
Broni
Castel San Giovanni
A21
Piadena
Mantova
Nogara
Cerea
Montagnana
Piacenza
San Giovanni in Croce
Legnago
Carpaneto Piacentino
Casalmaggiore
Ostíglia
Badia Polèsine
Lendinara
Sabbioneta
Fiorenzuola d'Arda
Suzzara
Viadana
Lugagnano Val d'Arda
Luzzara
Pòggio Rusco
Sèrmide
Colorno
Fidenza
Guastalla
Mòglia
Bòbbio
Bèttola
Salsomaggiore Terme
Noceto
Mirándola
Novellara
Bondeno
Pellegrino Parmense
Parma
Corréggio
Finale Emília
Ferrara
Collecchio
5
Ferriere
Carpi
Fornovo di Taro
Réggio nell'Emília
Camposanto
Bardi
Cento
Langhirano
466
Crevalcore
San Pietro in Casale
E33
Bedonia
San Polo d'Enza
Rubiera
Módena
San Giovanni in Persiceto
San Nicolò
Borgo Val di Taro
A15
Berceto
Castelfranco Emília
Altedo
Sassuolo
Molinella

G
H
J
I
2
3
4
5
AT
SI
HR
FRIULI-VENÉZIA GIULIA
VENETO
San Pietro
Campo Tures
Brunico
Bressanone Brixen
Monguelfo-Tésido
San Càndido
Dobbiaco
Sesto
Lienz
Spittal an der Drau
Villach
Ortisei
Corvara in Badia
Arabba
Cortina d'Ampezzo
Auronzo di Cadore
Sappada
San Vito di Cadore
Pieve di Cadore
Alleghe
Falcade
Forno di Zoldo
Agordo
Longarone
Paluzza
Pontebba
Tarvisio
Ampezzo
Forni di Sopra
Tolmezzo
Chiusaforte
Càrnia P
Venzone
Gemona del Friuli
Tarcento
Tricèsimo
Cividale del Friuli
Parco Nazionale delle Dolomiti Bellunesi
Ponte nelle Alpi
Belluno
Sèdico
Trichiana
Feltre
Bàrcis
Maniago
San Daniele del Friuli
Spilimbergo
Dignano
Aviano
Údine
Vittorio Véneto
Sacile
Pordenone
Codròipo
Valdobbiàdene
Conegliano
Azzano Decimo
San Vito al Tagliamento
Palmanova
Gorìzia
Gradisca d'Isonzo
Asolo
Bassano del Grappa
Montebelluna
Oderzo
Motta di Livenza
Cervignano del Friuli
Aquiléia
Monfalcone
Castelfranco Veneto
Ponte di Piave
Portogruaro
Treviso
Cittadella
Santo Stino di Livenza
Grado
TRIESTE
Golfo di Trieste
Mùggia
Scorzè
Eraclea
Càorle
Mestre
VENÉZIA
Lido di Jésolo
Lido
Mira
Dolo
Strà
Piove di Sacco
Conselve
Chióggia
Cavàrzere
Rosolina Mare
Loreo
Ádria
Ancona
Porto Viro
Ariano nel Polesine
Taglio di Po
Porto Tolle
Parco Delta del Po
Pila
Mésola
Codigoro
Migliarino
Lido di Pomposa
Comacchio
Porto Garibaldi
A4 E70 E55
A23 E55
A27
A28
A10 E55
A11
A2
A3
A4 E70
467

Bòbbio
Bèttola
Salsomaggiore Terme
Noceto
Novellara
Mirándola
Bondeno
Pellegrino Parmense
Finale Emília
464
Carpi
Ottone
Ferriere
Collecchio
Camposanto
Bardi
Fornovo di Taro
Réggio nell'Emília
Crevalcore
Cento
San Pietro in Casale
Langhirano
Rubiera
Módena
San Giovanni in Persiceto
Bedònia
San Polo d'Enza
Borgo Val di Taro
Berceto
Sassuolo
Castelfranco Emília
Altedo
Molinella
Corniglio
Casina
Maranello
Varese Ligure
EMÌLIA-ROMAGNA
Vignola
Bazzano
Pontrémoli
BOLOGNA
463
Montefiorino
Pavullo nel Frignano
Sasso Marconi
Villa Minozzo
Pianoro
Monèglia
Castel San Pietro Terme
Bonassola
Aulla
Fivizzano
Imola
Cinque Terre
Sèstola
Vergato
Garfagnana
Pievepelago
Loiano
La Spézia
Piazza al Serchio
Lerici
Sarzana
Porretta Terme
Castiglione dei Pèpoli
Castel del Rio
Portovénere
Carrara
Castelnuovo di Garfagnana
Barga
San Marcello Pistoiese
Ponte della Venturina
Marina di Carrara
Massa
Firenzuola
Marina di Massa
Forte dei Marmi
Pietrasanta
Marradi
Marina di Pietrasanta
Camaiore
Bagni di Lucca
Lido di Camaiore
Pistoia
San Benedetto in Alpe
Viareggio
Pescia
Lucca
Prato
Borgo San Lorenzo
Monsummano Terme
Sesto Fiorentino
Dicomano
Migliarino
Vecchiano
Pisa
Vinci
Signa
Fiesole
Lastra
Fucécchio
Empoli
Stia
Marina di Pisa
Cascina
FIRENZE
Pontassieve
Consuma
Tirrenia
Pontedera
San Miniato
San Casciano in Val di Pesa
Poppi
Ponsacco
Incisa in Val d'Arno
Reggello
Bibbiena
Livorno
Collesalvetti
Castelfiorentino
TOSCANA
Greve in Chianti
Casciana Terme
Certaldo
Terranuova Bracciolini
San Giovanni Valdarno
Subbia
Montevarchi
Rosignano Marittimo
San Gimignano
Chianti
Poggibonsi
Castellina in Chianti
Bucine
Rosignano Solvay
Volterra
Colle di Val d'Elsa
Monteriggioni
Cécina
Siena
Monte San Savino
Pomarance
Larderello
Asciano
Monteverdi Marittimo
Sinalunga
San Vincenzo
Abbazia di Monte Oliveto Maggiore
Isola di Capràia
Monticiano
Torrita di Siena
Buonconvento
Massa Marittima
San Quirico d'Orcia
Populònia
Montalcino
Pienza
Roccastrada
Piombino
Chianciano Terme
Bagno Vignoni
Cavo
Golfo di Follònica
Isola d'Elba
Follònica
Marciana Marina
Portoferràio
Città della
Punta Ala
Porto Azzurro
Castiglione della Pescàia
Marina di Campo
Arcidosso
Capoliveri
Grosseto
Roccalbegna
Marina di Grosseto
Acquapendente
Isola Pianosa
Maremma
Magliano in Toscana
Sovana
San Lorenzo Nuovo
Manciano
468
Talamone
Valentano
Farnese
Porto Santo Stèfano
Orbetello
Marta
Canino
Monte Argentàrio
Porto Ercole
Ansedònia
Tuscània
Isola del Giglio
Montalto di Castro
Sardegna
D
E
F
5
6
7
8
9

465
469
Ravenna
Rímini
San Marino
SM
Pésaro
Fano
Urbino
Ancona
MARCHE
UMBRIA
Perúgia
Assisi
Gúbbio
Foligno
Spoleto
Terni
Ascoli Piceno
Parco Delta del Po
Parco del Conero
Parco Regionale Monte Subasio
Parco Nazionale dei Monti Sibillini
Parco Nazionale del Gran Sasso e Monti della Laga
Monti della Laga
Gran Sasso d'Italia
Venézia
Comacchio
Porto Garibaldi
Lido di Pompose
Lido di Spina
Marina Romea
Marina di Ravenna
Cesena
Cesenàtico
Cèrvia
Milano Marittima
Riccione
Cattòlica
Gabicce Mare
Senigállia
Falconara Marittima
Loreto
Macerata
Civitanova Marche
Porto San Giórgio
San Benedetto del Tronto
Giulianova
Roseto degli Abruzzi
Téramo
Norcia
Città di Castello
Sansepolcro
Fabriano
Jesi
Camerino
Tolentino
Todi
Narni
467

Punta Ala
Castiglione della Pescàia
Grosseto
Marina di Grosseto
Arcidosso
Roccalbegna
Città della Pieve
Tavernelle
Deruta
Spello
Bevagna
Foligno
Montefalco
Trevi
Ficulle
Marsciano
Acquapendente
Orvieto
Todi
Valnerina
Maremma
466
Magliano in Toscana
Sovana
San Lorenzo Nuovo
Bolsena
Spoleto
Talamone
Manciano
Pitigliano
Montecchio
Acquasparta
Monteluco
Valentano
Lago di Bolsena
Abbazia di San Pietro in Valle
Porto Santo Stèfano
Farnese
Marta
Amèlia
Terni
Orbetello
Canino
Monte Argentàrio
Porto Ercole
Ansedònia
Narni
Isola del Giglio
Tuscània
Soriano nel Cimino
Montalto di Castro
Viterbo
Terminillo
Contigliano
Vignanello
Isola di Giannutri
Vetralla
Lago di Vico
Rieti
Magliano Sabina
Cittàducale
Civita Castellana
Tarquinia
Sutri
Lago del Salto
Vejano
Nepi
Tolfa
Trevignano Romano
Fiamignano
Lago di Bracciano
Lago del Turano
Civitavécchia
Bracciano
Orvinio
Palombara Sabina
Santa Marinella
Monterotondo
Santa Severa
Cerveteri
LAZIO
Vicovaro
Arsoli
Tívoli
Città del Vaticano
ROMA
Subiaco
Fregene
Palestrina
Fiumicino
Óstia Antica
Ciampino
Frascati
Valmontone
Lido di Óstia
Castel Gandolfo
Lago Albano
Albano Laziale
Colleferro
Pomézia
Velletri
Ardea
Aprília
Cisterna di Latina
Carpineto Romano
Nettuno
Sezze
Anzio
Latina
Pontinia
Sabáudia
Parco Nazionale del Circeo
San Felice Circeo
Isole Ponziane
Isola Zannone
Isola di Ponza
Palermo
F
G
H
8
9
10
11
12
A1
E35
E45
E80
A12
A24
E80

J
K
L
8
9
10
11
12
467
470
Sarnano
Servigliano
Montalto delle Marche
Offida
Áscoli Piceno
Arquata del Tronto
Acquasanta Terme
Grottammare
San Benedetto del Tronto
Martinsicuro
Alba Adriatica
Giulianova
Roseto degli Abruzzi
Pineto
Silvi Marina
Pescara
Francavilla al Mare
Ortona
Chieti
Bucchianico
Orsogna
Lanciano
Guardiagrele
Palombaro
Càsoli
Vasto
Cupello
Atessa
San Salvo
Térmoli
Campomarino
Montenero di Bisàccia
Guglionesi
Isole Trèmiti
Lago di Lesina
Lèsina
Apricena
Monti della Laga
2455
Téramo
Montòrio al Vomano
Parco Nazionale del Gran Sasso e Monti della Laga
Gran Sasso d'Italia
2912
Corno Grande
Penne
Loreto Aprutino
L'Aquila
Barisciano
Rocca di Mezzo
Navelli
Pópoli
Parco Nazionale della Maiella
ABRUZZO
Avezzano
Pescina
Civitella Roveto
Palena
Lago del Sangro
Lago di Scanno
Scanno
Pescocostanzo
Parco Nazionale d'Abruzzo
2242
Marsicano
Roccaraso
Capracotta
Agnone
Castiglione Messer Marino
Castelmàuro
Castel di Sangro
Alfedena
2247
Petroso
Sora
Isola del Liri
Alatri
Guarcino
Frosinone
Ceprano
Arce
Atina
Forlì del Sànnio
Isérnia
Carpinone
MOLISE
Larino
Serracapriola
Casacalenda
Santa Croce di Magliano
Bonefro
Petrella Tifernina
Torremaggiore
San Severo
Campobasso
Castelnuovo della Daunia
Abbazia di Montecassino
Cassino
Venafro
Capriati a Volturno
Bojano
Vinchiaturo
Jelsi
Riccia
Lucera
Fóggia
Pico
Pratella
Piedimonte Matese
Lago del Matese
San Bartolomeo in Galdo
1533
Petrella
Minturno
Formia
Gaeta
Roccamonfina
Sessa Aurunca
Teano
Morcone
San Marco dei Cavoti
Troia
Pontelandolfo
Castelluccio dei Sauri
Baia Domizia
Caiazzo
Telese Terme
Guardia Sanframondi
Buonalbergo
Savignano Irpino
Mondragone
Grazzanise
Capua
Caserta
Benevento
Ariano Irpino
Grottaminarda
Candela
Santa Maria Capua Vetere
Maddaloni
Castèl Volturno
Casal di Principe
Montesarchio
Villa Literno
Aversa
CAMPANIA
Vallata
Lacedonia
Casoria
Paternopoli
NÁPOLI
Nola
Avellino
Andretta
Calitri
1281
Vesuvio
Lioni
Pozzuoli
Bacoli
Ercolano
Sarno
Monti Picentini
Montella
Isola Ventotene
Casamicciola Terme
Procida
Forio
Ischia
Isola di Procida
Isola d'Ischia
Pompei
Pescopagano
Castellammare di Stabia
Muro Lucano
Vico Equense
Sorrento
Positano
Salerno
Montecorvino Rovella
Contursi Terme
Eboli
Amalfi
Praiano
Battipaglia
Isola di Capri
Capri
Sicilia, Sardegna
Golfo di Salerno
A14 E55
A24
A25 E80
A1 E45
A16
A30
A3 E45
A16 E842
E55
E847

Lanciano
Guardiagrele
Palombaro
Càsoli
Vasto
Cupello
Atessa
San Salvo
Lago del Sangro
Tèrmoli
Campomarino
Montenero di Bisàccia
Castiglione Messer Marino
Guglionesi
Capracotta
Agnone
Castelmàuro
Serracapriola
Larino
Casacalenda
MOLISE
Petrella Tifernina
Bonefro
Santa Croce di Magliano
Torremaggiore
San Severo
Carpinone
Campobasso
Vinchiaturo
Bojano
Jelsi
Riccia
Lago del Matese
Piedimonte Matese
Morcone
San Marco dei Cavoti
Pontelandolfo
Guardia Sanframondi
Telese Terme
Buonalbergo
Savignano Irpino
Ariano Irpino
Caserta
Benevento
Grottaminarda
Maddaloni
Montesarchio
CAMPANIA
Nola
Avellino
1281 Vesuvio
Sarno
Pompei
Castellammare di Stabia
Salerno
Positano
Amalfi
Praiano
Golfo di Salerno
Monti Picentini
Montecorvino Rovella
Battipaglia
Eboli
Paestum
Capaccio
Roccadaspide
Agropoli
Ogliastro Cilento
Castellabate San Marco
Parco Nazionale del Cilento e Vallo di Diano
Sanza
Torre Orsaia
Pisciotta
Palinuro
Scario
Sapri
Lagonegro
Isola Pianosa
Isole Trèmiti
Lago di Lesina
Lèsina
Rodi Gargànico
Pèschici
Vico del Gargano
Vieste
Lago di Varano
Parco Nazionale
Cagnano Varano
Promontorio del Gargano
Foresta Umbra
del Gargano
Apricena
Pugnochiuso
San Marco in Lamis
San Giovanni Rotondo
Monte Sant'Angelo
Manfredonia
Golfo di Manfredonia
Castelnuovo della Daunia
Lucera
Fóggia
San Bartolomeo in Galdo
Troia
Castelluccio dei Sauri
Zapponeta
Trinitapoli
Margherita di Savoia
Barletta
Orta Nova
Ascoli Satriano
Cerignola
San Ferdinando di Puglia
Canosa di Puglia
Ándria
Corato
Castèl del Monte
Ruvo di Puglia
Minervino Murge
Candela
Ofanto
Vallata
Lacedonia
Paternopoli
Melfi
Lavello
Rapolla
Venosa
Spinazzola
PUGLIA
Andretta
Calitri
Lioni
Rionero in Vulture
Palazzo San Gervasio
Montella
Pescopagano
Muro Lucano
Genzano di Lucania
Gravina in Puglia
Altamura
Oppido Lucano
Irsina
Contursi Terme
Potenza
Tolve
Tricarico
Grassano
Vietri di Potenza
Auletta
Miglionico
Brienza
Laurenzana
BASILICATA
Accettura
Marsico Nuovo
Stigliano
Corleto Perticara
Craco
Pisticci
Montesano sulla Marcellana
Missanello
Casalbuono
Moliterno
Senise
Rotondella
Latronico
Noepoli
Lauria
Maratea
Episcopia
Parco Nazionale del Pollino
Oriolo
Terranova di Pollino
Praia a Mare
Mormanno
Cerchiara di Calabria
Papasidero
Morano Calabro
Trebisacce
Scalea
Castrovillari
Lungro
Sibari
Diamante
469
472
K
L
M
10
11
12
13
A14
E55
A16
E842
A1
A30
A3
E45
E847
16
652
650
647
17
89
90
545
159
655
230
7
93
407
19
18
653
534

N
P
Q
10
11
12
13
BARI
Mola di Bari
Rutigliano
Polignano a Mare
Conversano
Casamassima
Monópoli
Turi
Castellana
Grotte
Savelletri
Torre Canne
Putignano
Noci
Fasano
Alberobello
Gioia
del Colle
Locorotondo
Ostuni
Martina Franca
San Vito
dei Normanni
Bríndisi
Mottola
Ceglie
Messapica
Castellaneta
Massafra
Palagiano
Grottaglie
Mesagne
Latiano
Francavilla
Fontana
Oria
TÁRANTO
Marina di Ginosa
Metaponto
San Pancrazio
Salentino
Squinzano
San Cataldo
Manduria
Campi
Salentina
Lecce
Campomarino
Porto Cesareo
Scanzano Jonico
Policoro
Nardò
Martano
Galatina
Galatone
Ótranto
Maglie
Parabita
Gallipoli
Casarano
Golfo di
Taranto
Tricase
Ugento
Gagliano del Capo
Marina di Leuca
A14
E843
E55
E90
16
7
7ter
100
106
172
379
613
101
274
275

BASILICATA
Laurenzana
Marsico Nuovo
Stigliano
Bernalda
TARANTO
Parco Nazionale del Cilento e Vallo di Diano
Corleto Perticara
Craco
Pisticci
Marina di Ginosa
Metaponto
Montesano sulla Marcellana
Missanello
Sanza
Casalbuono
Moliterno
Scanzano Jonico
Torre Orsaia
Senise
Rotondella
Policoro
Lagonegro
Sapri
Latronico
470
471
Palinuro
Scario
Lauria
653
Noepoli
Episcopia
Oriolo
Maratea
Parco Nazionale del Pollino
Golfo di Taranto
Terranova di Pollino
Praia a Mare
Mormanno
Cerchiara di Calabria
Trebisacce
Papasidero
Morano Calabro
Scalea
Castrovillari
Lungro
Sibari
Diamante
534
San Sosti
Spezzano Albanese
Belvedere Marittimo
Tarsia
Corigliano Calabro
Rossano
A3 E45
Bisignano
Acri
Cetraro
Cariati
Luzzi
Longobucco
Fuscaldo
279
CALABRIA
Campana
Páola
San Lucido
107
E846
Cirò Marina
Savelli
Cosenza
San Giovanni in Fiore
Strongoli
Riviera Calabrese
Rogliano
La Sila
Grimaldi
Amantea
Coraci
Petilia Policastro
Soveria Mannelli
Taverna
Cutro
Crotone
Sersale
Lamezia Terme
Catanzaro
280
Isola di Capo Rizzuto
Isola Strómboli
Golfo di Santa Eufemia
Maida
Girifalco
Catanzaro Marina
Golfo di Squillace
Pizzo
Tropea
Vibo Valéntia
Chiaravalle Centrale
Soverato
Mileto
Serra San Bruno
Rosarno
Stilo
Gioia Tauro
Polistena
Palmi
Taurianova
Grotteria
473
Bagnara Calabra
Oppido Mamertina
Cittanova
Torre Faro
Roccella Jonica
Marina di Gioiosa Jonica
Scilla
Delianuova
Gerace
Siderno
MESSINA
Platì
Locri
Villa San Giovanni
Parco Nazionale dell' Aspromonte
Bovalino Marina
Réggio di Calabria
Bianco
A18 E45
Alì Terme
Lazzaro
Melito di Porto Salvo
Bova Marina
Brancaleone Marina
Taormina
L
M
N
13
14
15
16
18
19
92
106
E90
110

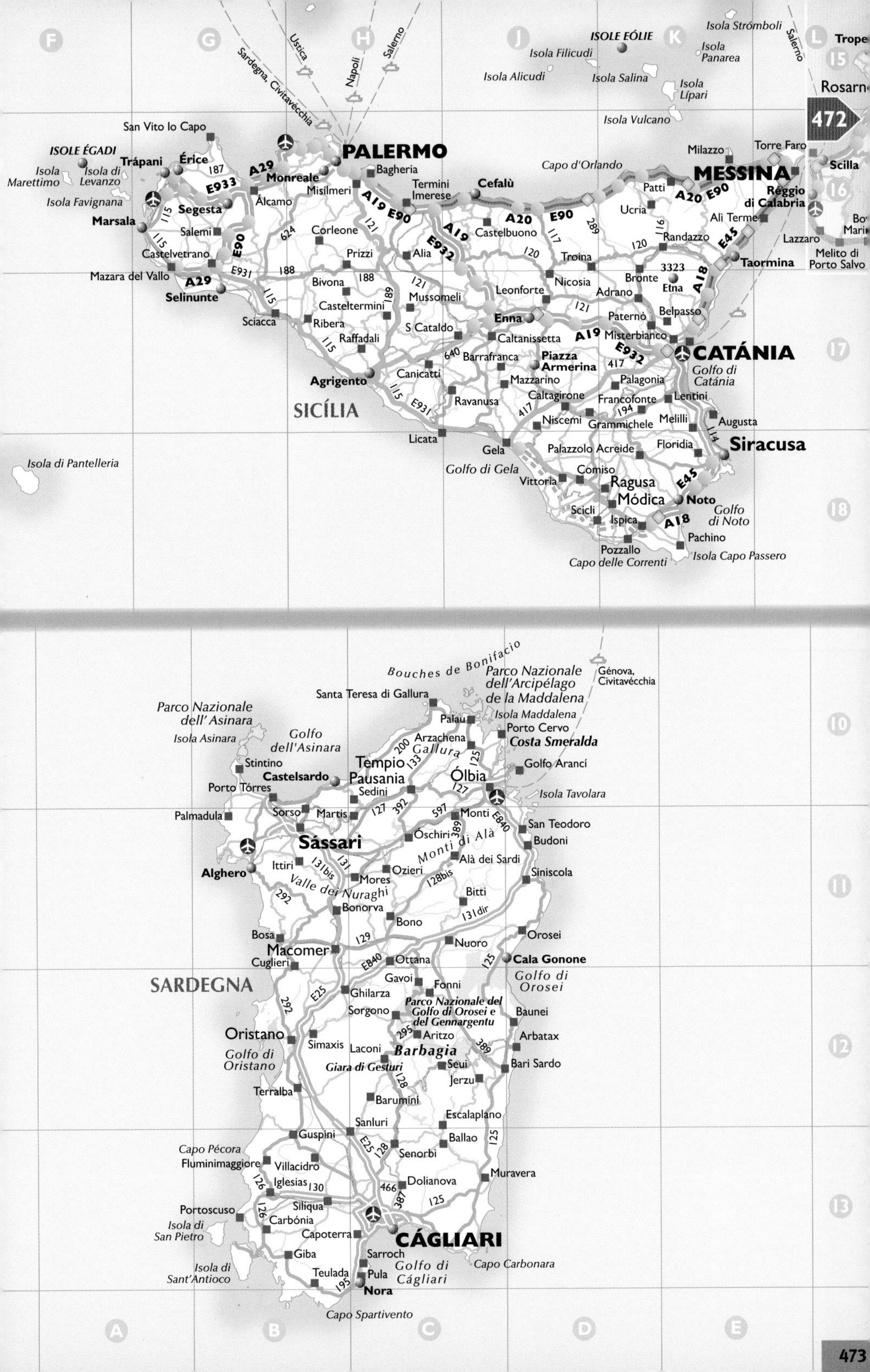

F
G
H
J
K
L
Ustica
Sardegna, Civitavécchia
Napoli
Salerno
ISOLE EÓLIE
Isola Strómboli
Isola Filicudi
Isola Panarea
Isola Alicudi
Isola Salina
Isola Lípari
Isola Vulcano
Tropea
15
Rosarno
472
San Vito lo Capo
ISOLE ÉGADI
Isola Marettimo
Isola di Levanzo
Isola Favignana
Trápani
Érice
Marsala
Segesta
Salemi
Castelvetrano
Mazara del Vallo
Selinunte
Sciacca
PALERMO
Monreale
Bagheria
Misilmeri
Álcamo
Corleone
Prizzi
Bivona
Casteltermini
Ribera
Raffadali
Agrigento
Termini Imerese
Cefalù
Castelbuono
Alia
Mussomeli
S Cataldo
Caltanissetta
Canicattì
Barrafranca
Ravanusa
Licata
Capo d'Orlando
Milazzo
Torre Faro
MESSINA
Scilla
Réggio di Calabria
16
Patti
Ucria
Randazzo
Alì Terme
Lazzaro
Bova Marina
Melito di Porto Salvo
Taormina
Troina
Nicosia
Leonforte
Enna
Bronte
3323
Etna
Adrano
Paternò
Belpasso
Misterbianco
CATÁNIA
Golfo di Catánia
17
Piazza Armerina
Mazzarino
Caltagirone
Palagonia
Francofonte
Lentini
Augusta
Niscemi
Grammichele
Melilli
Gela
Golfo di Gela
Palazzolo Acreide
Floridia
Siracusa
Vittoria
Comiso
Ragusa
Módica
Noto
Golfo di Noto
18
Scicli
Ispica
Pachino
Pozzallo
Capo delle Correnti
Isola Capo Passero
SICÍLIA
Isola di Pantelleria
A29
E933
A19
E90
A20
E932
E931
E45
A18
187
115
624
188
121
189
120
117
289
116
640
417
194
114
Bouches de Bonifacio
Génova, Civitavécchia
Parco Nazionale dell'Arcipélago de la Maddalena
Santa Teresa di Gallura
Palau
Isola Maddalena
Porto Cervo
Costa Smeralda
Parco Nazionale dell' Asinara
Isola Asinara
Golfo dell'Asinara
Arzachena
Gallura
10
Stintino
Tempio Pausania
Golfo Arancí
Castelsardo
Ólbia
Porto Tórres
Sedini
Isola Tavolara
Palmadula
Sorso
Martis
Monti
San Teodoro
Óschiri
Budoni
Sássari
Monti di Alà
Alà dei Sardi
Alghero
Ittiri
Mores
Ozieri
Siniscola
Valle dei Nuraghi
Bitti
11
Bonorva
Bono
Bosa
Orosei
Nuoro
Macomer
Cala Gonone
Cuglieri
Ottana
Golfo di Orosei
SARDEGNA
Gavoi
Fonni
Ghilarza
Parco Nazionale del Golfo di Orosei e del Gennargentu
Sorgono
Baunei
Oristano
Aritzo
Arbatax
Simaxis
Laconi
Barbagia
12
Golfo di Oristano
Giara di Gesturi
Seui
Bari Sardo
Jerzu
Terralba
Barumini
Escalaplano
Sanluri
Guspini
Ballao
Capo Pécora
Fluminimaggiore
Villacidro
Senorbi
Muravera
Iglesias
Dolianova
Portoscuso
Siliqua
13
Isola di San Pietro
Carbónia
Capoterra
CÁGLIARI
Giba
Sarroch
Isola di Sant'Antioco
Teulada
Pula
Golfo di Cágliari
Capo Carbonara
Nora
Capo Spartivento
A
B
C
D
E
200
133
125
127
392
597
389
E840
131
131bis
128bis
292
131dir
129
E25
295
128
466
387
130
126
195

D

M

N

Q

R

S

T

U

V

W

PICTURES

The Automobile Association would like to thank the following photographers, companies and picture libraries for their assistance in the preparation of this book.

Abbreviations for the picture credits are as follows: (t) top;
(b) bottom;
(l) left;
(r) right;
(c) centre;
(AA) AA World Travel Library.

2 AA/S McBride;
3t AA/A Kouprianoff
3ct AA/A Mockford & N Bonetti
3cb AA/T Harris
3b AA/C Sawyer
4 AA/C Sawyer;
5 AA/M Jourdan;
6 AA/T Harris;
7r AA/C Sawyer;
7l AA/A Mockford & N Bonetti;
10 AA/K Paterson;
11 AA/C Sawyer;
12 AA/A Mockford & N Bonetti;
13 AA/A Kouprianoff;
14 AA/A Mockford & N Bonetti;
15l Ingo Arndt/Nature Picture Library;
15r Photodisc;
16 Franco Origlia/Getty Images;
17l LaMalfaFoto/Team/Grazia Neri;
17r Photolibrary Group;
18 AA/T Souter;
19t AA/J Holmes;
19b AA/M Jourdan;
20 Photolibrary Group;
21bl AA/C Sawyer;
21tr AA/C Sawyer;
21cr AA/C Sawyer;
22 Sipa Press/Rex Features;
23bl AA/J Holmes;
23br AA/A Kouprianoff;
24 Luca Lozzi/Getty Images;
25b AA/T Harris;
25tr AA/M Jourdan;
25tc AA/C Sawyer;
26l Allstar/Cinetext Collection;
26r AA/C Sawyer;
27 AA/A Kouprianoff;
28 AA;
29bl AA;
29cr AA/J Holmes;
29br AA/C Sawyer;
30 Musée des Beaux-Arts André Malraux, Le Havre, France, Giraudon/The Bridgeman Art Library;
31l AA;
31r AA/A Kouprianoff;
32 San Vitale, Ravenna, Italy /The Bridgeman Art Library;
33l Mary Evans Picture Library;
33r AA/A Mockford & N Bonetti;
34 British Library, London /The Bridgeman Art Library;
35bl AA/S McBride;
35cr AA/M Jourdan;
35br A/C Sawyer;
36 AA/S McBride;
37cl Galleria degli Uffizi, Florence, Italy, Giraudon/The Bridgeman Art Library;
37bl AA;
37tl AA;
37tr Biblioteca Marucelliana, Florence, Italy/Bridgeman Art Library/Alinari;
37cl AA;
37cr AA;
38 AA;
39cl AA/C Sawyer;
39bl AA/P Wilson;
39r AA;
40 Illustrated London News;
41l Mary Evans Picture Library;
41r Mary Evans Picture Library;
41cr Illustrated London News;
42l Sipa Press/Rex Features;
42r AA/T Souter;
43 AA/N Setchfield;
45 Aeroporto di Venezia Marco Polo;
48 AA/N Setchfield;
52 AA/C Sawyer;
53 AA/A Mockford & N Bonetti;
62 AA/A Mockford & N Bonetti;
63 AA/C Sawyer;
64 AA/D Miterdiri;
72 AA/S McBride;
73 AA/S McBride;
74 AA/A Kouprianoff;
75tr AA/C Sawyer;
75b AA/P Wilson;
76 AA/S McBride;
77 AA/S McBride;
78 AA/S McBride;
79bl AA/S McBride;
79br AA/S McBride;
80 AA/P Wilson;
81 AA/D Miterdiri;
82 AA/J Holmes;
83 Photolibrary Group;
84 AA/S McBride;
85 AA/J Holmes
86 AA/J Holmes
87 AA/S McBride;
88 AA/P Wilson;
89 AA/S McBride;
90 AA/A Kouprianoff;
91 AA/J Holmes;
92 AA/J Holmes;
93 AA/J Holmes;
94 AA/S McBride;
95 AA/C Sawyer;
96 AA/D Miterdiri;
97l AA;
97r AA/A Kouprianoff;
98l AA/D Miterdiri;
98r AA/C Sawyer;
99 AA/D Miterdiri;
100 AA/S McBride;
102 Contarelli Chapel, S. Luigi dei Francesi, Rome, Italy/The Bridgeman Art Library;
104 AA/C Sawyer;
106 AA/J Holmes;
108 AA/A Mockford & N Bonetti;
110 AA/C Sawyer;
113 AA/C Sawyer;
114 AA/A Mockford & N Bonetti;
117 AA/A Mockford & N Bonetti;
118 Photolibrary Group;
120 AA/A Mockford & N Bonetti;
121 AA/M Jourdan;
122 AA/T Souter;
123 AA/A Mockford & N Bonetti;
124 AA/A Mockford & N Bonetti;
125 AA/M Jourdan;
126 AA/C Sawyer;
128 AA/C Sawyer;
129 AA/M Jourdan;
130 AA/C Sawyer;

131 AA/T Souter;
132 Robert Harding Picture Library Ltd / Alamy;
133 AA/C Sawyer;
134 Turismo Turino;
135 Photolibrary Group;
136 AA/T Souter;
137 Pictures Colour Library;
138 AA/T Souter;
139 AA/T Souter;
140 AA/M Jourdan;
141t AA/A Mockford & N Bonetti;
141b AA/A Mockford & N Bonetti;
142 AA/M Jourdan;
144 AA/M Jourdan;
145l AA/M Jourdan;
145r AA/P Bennett;
146 AA/M Jourdan;
148 AA/M Lynch;
150 AA/A Mockford & N Bonetti;
153 AA/C Sawyer;
154 AA/M Jourdan;
157 AA/M Jourdan;
158 AA/A Mockford & N Bonetti;
164 AA/A Mockford & N Bonetti;
165 AA/S McBride;
166 AA/A Mockford & N Bonetti;
167 AA/S McBride;
168 AA/A Mockford & N Bonetti;
169 AA/A Mockford & N Bonetti;
170 AA/A Mockford & N Bonetti;
171 AA/A Mockford & N Bonetti;
172 AA/A Mockford & N Bonetti;
173 AA/D Miterdiri;
174 AA/C Sawyer;
175 AA/C Sawyer;
176 AA/S McBride;
177 AA/A Mockford & N Bonetti;
178 AA/A Mockford & N Bonetti;
179t AA/A Mockford & N Bonetti;
179b AA/A Mockford & N Bonetti;
180 AA/S McBride;
181 AA/D Miterdiri;
182 AA/S McBride;
183 AA/A Mockford & N Bonetti;
184 AA/S McBride;
185 AA/A Mockford & N Bonetti;
186 Scuola Grande di San Rocco, Venice, Italy / The Bridgeman Art Library;
187 AA/C Sawyer;
188 AA/A Mockford & N Bonetti;
189 AA/A Mockford & N Bonetti;
190 AA/S McBride;
192 AA/C Sawyer;
196 AA/A Mockford & N Bonetti;
198 AA/A Mockford & N Bonetti;
200 Photolibrary Group;
202 © Eye Ubiquitous/Gerd Wagner;
204 Ian Dagnall / Alamy;
205 Jon Arnold Images Ltd / Alamy;
206 World Pictures/Photoshot;
207 World Pictures/Photoshot;
208 Italian Tourist Board;
209 Photolibrary Group;
210 AA/T Souter;
211 AA/C Sawyer;
212 AA/A Mockford & N Bonetti;
213 AA/A Mockford & N Bonetti;
214 AA/A Mockford & N Bonetti;
215 AA/C Sawyer;
216 Sally Roy;
217 World Pictures/Photoshot;
218 Fototeca ENIT;
219 Sally Roy;
220 Cantina Bentivoglio;
221 AA/A Mockford & N Bonetti;
222 AA/A Mockford & N Bonetti;
225 AA/S McBride;
226 AA/A Mockford & N Bonetti;
228 AA/K Paterson;
234 AA/T Harris;
235 AA/C Sawyer;
236 AA/S McBride;
237t AA/S McBride;
237b AA/C Sawyer;
239 AA/T Harris;
240 AA/T Harris;
241 AA;
242 AA/S McBride;
243 AA/S McBride;
244 AA/C Sawyer;
245 AA/C Sawyer;
246 AA/S McBride;
248 AA/S McBride;
249 AA/J Edmanson;
250 AA/J A Tims;
251 AA/S McBride;
252 AA/S McBride;
253 AA/T Harris;
254 AA/J Edmanson;
256 AA/J A Tims;
259 AA/S McBride;
260 AA/S McBride;
264 AA/S McBride;
266 AA/J A Tims;
268 AA/T Harris;
269 AA/C Sawyer;
270 AA/P Davies;
271 AA/K Paterson;
272 AA/J Edmanson;
273 AA/T Harris;
274 AA/C Sawyer;
275 AA/T Harris;
276 AA/K Paterson;
277 AA/T Harris;
278 AA/S McBride;
279 AA/ K Paterson;
280 World Pictures/Photoshot;
281 AA/T Harris;
282 AA/T Harris;
283 AA/T Harris;
284 AA/C Sawyer;
285 AA/K Paterson;
286 AA/T Harris;
287bl AA/T Harris;
287br AA/S McBride;
288 AA/C Sawyer;
289 AA/T Harris;
290 AA/K Paterson;
291bl AA/K Paterson;
291br AA/K Paterson;
292 AA/K Paterson;
293 AA/S McBride;
294 AA/S McBride;
296 AA/T Harris;
297 AA/J A Tims;
298 AA/K Paterson;
300 AA/T Harris;
302 AA/T Souter;
303 Photolibrary Group;
304 AA/T Harris;
306 Rafting Umbria;
312 Photodisc;
314 AA/M Jourdan;
316 AA/T Souter;
318 AA/T Harris;
320 Pete Turner/The Image Bank/ Getty Images;
322 AA/C Sawyer;
323 AA/C Sawyer;
324 Peter Adams/The Image Bank/ Getty Images;
325 AA/S McBride;
326 AA/T Souter;
327 AA/C Sawyer;
328 AA/T Souter;
329 AA/C Sawyer;
330 AA/S McBride;
331bl AA/S McBride;
331br AA/S McBride;
333 AA/T Souter;
334 AA/C Sawyer;
336 Photolibrary Group;
338 Digitalvision;
339 AA/P Kenward;
340 AA/K Paterson;
342 AA/A Mockford & N Bonetti;
344 AA/M Jourdan;
346 AA/M Jourdan;
347 AA/M Jourdan;

348 World Pictures/Photoshot;
349 AA/M Jourdan;
350 AA/C Sawyer;
351 AA/T Souter;
352 AA/C Sawyer;
353l Fototeca ENIT;
353r Fototeca ENIT;
354 AA/M Jourdan;
356 AA/M Jourdan;
357 AA/M Jourdan;
358 AA/T Souter;
359 AA/C Sawyer;
360 AA/M Jourdan;
361t AA/T Souter;
361b AA/C Sawyer;
362l AA/M Jourdan;
362r AA/M Jourdan;
363 AA/M Jourdan;
364 AA/T Souter;
365 AA/T Souter;
366 AA/C Sawyer;
368 AA/C Sawyer;
370 AA/M Jourdan;
371 AA/M Jourdan;
372 Travelshots.com/Alamy;
373 Photolibrary Group;
374 Photolibrary Group;
375 AA/C Sawyer;
376 APT Puglia;
377 AA/T Souter;
378 AA/M Jourdan;
380 AA/A Mockford & N Bonetti;
382 AA/C Sawyer;
385 AA/M Jourdan;
386 La Bussola;
388 AA/A Mockford & N Bonetti;
390 AA/N Setchfield;
392 AA/N Setchfield;
393 AA/N Setchfield;
394 AA/C Sawyer;
395 AA/C Sawyer;
396 AA/C Sawyer;
398 AA/C Sawyer;
399 AA/N Setchfield;
400 AA/C Sawyer;
401 AA/N Setchfield;
402 AA/N Setchfield;
403 AA/N Setchfield;
404 AA/C Sawyer;
405 AA/N Setchfield;
406t AA/N Setchfield;
406b AA/N Setchfield;
408 AA/N Setchfield;
409t AA/C Sawyer;
409b AA/N Setchfield;
410 AA/C Sawyer;
412 AA/N Setchfield;
414 AA/N Setchfield;
416 Tenuta di Roccadia;
418 AA/A Mockford & N Bonetti;
419 AA/M Jourdan;
420 AA/A Mockford & N Bonetti;
423 AA/A Mockford & N Bonetti;
424 AA/A Mockford & N Bonetti;
426 AA/J A Tims;
430 AA/M Jourdan;
432 AA/C Sawyer;
433 © J Tavin/Everett/Rex Features;
437 AA/M Jourdan;
438 AA/C Sawyer;
440 AA/C Sawyer;
442 AA/D Miterdiri;
443 AA/A Mockford & N Bonetti;
445 AA/A Mockford & N Bonetti;
446bl AA/N Setchfield;
446br AA/N Setchfield;
447 De Agostini Picture Library;
448 AA/N Setchfield;
449 AA/D Miterdiri;
450 AA/M Jourdan;
452 AA/C Sawyer;
454 AA/A Mockford & N Bonetti;
461 Fototeca ENIT

Every effort has been made to trace the copyright holders, and we apologize in advance for any accidental errors. We would be happy to apply the corrections in the following edition of this publication.

CREDITS

Series editor
Sheila Hawkins

Project editor
Stephanie Smith

Design
Tracey Butler

Cover design
Chie Ushio

Picture research
Carol Walker

Image retouching and repro
Jackie Street

Mapping
Maps produced by the Mapping Services Department of AA Publishing

Main contributors
Jack Altman, Anna Maria d'Angelo, The Content Works, Charlotte Eager, Rebecca Ford, Alex Johnson, Simona Marchetta, Lee Marshall, Sally Roy, Jenny Squillaci, Vittorio Squillaci, Nicky Swallow

Updater
Adele Evans

Indexer
Marie Lorimer

Production
Lorraine Taylor

See It Italy
ISBN 978-1-4000-0554-3
Fourth Edition

Published in the United States by Fodor's Travel and simultaneously in Canada by Random House of Canada Limited, Toronto.
Published in the United Kingdom by AA Publishing.
Fodor's is a registered trademark of Random House, Inc., and Fodor's See It is a trademark of Random House, Inc.
Fodor's Travel is a division of Random House, Inc.

Color separation by AA Digital Department
Printed and bound by Leo Paper Products, China
10 9 8 7 6 5 4 3 2

Special Sales: This book is available for special discounts for bulk purchases for sales promotions or premiums. Special editions, including personalized covers, excerpts of existing books, and corporate imprints, can be created in large quantities for special needs.
For more information, write to Special Markets/Premium Sales, 1745 Broadway, New York, NY 10019
or e-mail specialmarkets@randomhouse.com
Important Note: Time inevitably brings changes, so always confirm prices, travel facts, and other perishable information when it matters. Although Fodor's cannot accept responsibility for errors, you can use this guide in the confidence that we have taken every care to ensure its accuracy.